Personality Theories

McGraw-Hill Series in Psychology
CONSULTING EDITOR

Norman Garmezy

Adams: Human Memory
Berlyne: Conflict, Arousal, and Curiosity
Bernstein and Nietzel: Introduction to Clinical Psychology
Blum: Psychoanalytic Theories of Personality
Bock: Multivariate Statistical Methods in Behavioral Research
Brown: The Motivation of Behavior
Campbell, Dunette, Lawler, and Weick: Managerial Behavior, Performance, and Effectiveness
Crites: Vocational Psychology
D'Amato: Experimental Psychology: Methodology, Psychophysics, and Learning
Dollard and Miller: Personality and Psychotherapy
Ferguson: Statistical Analysis in Psychology and Education
Fodor, Bever, Garrett: The Psychology of Language: An Introduction to Psycholinguistics and Generative Grammar
Forgus and Melamed: Perception: A Cognitive-Stage Approach
Franks: Behavior Therapy: Appraisal and Status
Gilmer and Deci: Industrial and Organizational Psychology
Guilford: Psychometric Methods
Guilford: The Nature of Human Intelligence
Guilford and Fruchter: Fundamental Statistics in Psychology and Education
Guion: Personnel Testing
Hetherington and Parke: Child Psychology: A Contemporary Viewpoint
Hirsh: The Measurement of Hearing
Hjelle and Ziegler: Personality Theories: Basic Assumptions, Research, and Applications
Horowitz: Elements of Statistics for Psychology and Education
Hulse, Egeth, and Deese: The Psychology of Learning
Hurlock: Adolescent Development

Hurlock: Child Development
Hurlock: Developmental Psychology
Krech, Crutchfield, and Ballachey: Individual in Society
Lakin: Interpersonal Encounter: Theory and Practice in Sensitivity Training
Lawler: Pay and Organizational Effectiveness: A Psychological View
Lazarus, A.: Behavior Therapy and Beyond
Lazarus, R.: Patterns of Adjustment
Lewin: A Dynamic Theory of Personality
Maher: Principles of Psychopathology
Marascuilo: Statistical Methods for Behavioral Science Research
Marx and Hillix: Systems and Theories in Psychology
Miller: Language and Communication
Morgan: Physiological Psychology
Novick and Jackson: Statistical Methods for Educational and Psychological Research
Nunnally: Introduction to Statistics for Psychology and Education
Nunnally: Psychometric Theory
Overall and Klett: Applied Multivariate Analysis
Porter, Lawler, and Hackman: Behavior in Organizations
Robinson and Robinson: The Mentally Retarded Child
Rosenthal: Genetic Theory and Abnormal Behavior
Ross: Psychological Disorders of Children: A Behavioral Approach to Theory, Research, and Therapy
Shaw: Group Dynamics: The Psychology of Small Group Behavior
Shaw and Costanzo: Theories of Social Psychology
Shaw and Wright: Scales for the Measurement of Attitudes
Sidowski: Experimental Methods and Instrumentation in Psychology
Siegel: Nonparametric Statistics for the Behavioral Sciences
Steers and Porter: Motivation and Work Behavior
Vinacke: The Psychology of Thinking
Winer: Statistical Principles in Experimental Design

Personality Theories

Basic Assumptions, Research, and Applications

Second Edition

Larry A. Hjelle
Associate Professor of Psychology
State University of New York
College at Brockport

Daniel J. Ziegler
Professor and Chairman
Department of Psychology
Villanova University

McGraw-Hill Book Company

New York   St. Louis   San Francisco   Auckland   Bogotá   Hamburg
Johannesburg   London   Madrid   Mexico   Montreal   New Delhi
Panama   Paris   São Paulo   Singapore   Sydney   Tokyo   Toronto

ENCY OF PSYCHO

This book was set in Times Roman by Automated Composition Service, Inc.
The editors were Rhona Robbin and Barry Benjamin;
the production supervisor was Diane Renda.
New drawings were done by Fine Line Illustrations, Inc.
The cover was designed by Nicholas Krenitsky.
R. R. Donnelley & Sons Company was printer and binder.

PERSONALITY THEORIES
Basic Assumptions, Research, and Applications

4 5 6 7 8 9 0   DODO   8 9 8 7 6 5

See acknowledgments on pages 471–474. Copyrights included on this page by reference.

Library of Congress Cataloging in Publication Data

Hjelle, Larry A
    Personality theories.

    (McGraw-Hill series in psychology)
    Includes bibliographies and index.
    1. Personality. I. Ziegler, Daniel J., joint author. II. Title.
BF698.H49 1981   155.2′092′2   80-15615
ISBN 0-07-029063-6

To our wives,
Jean and Elizabeth

To our children,
Anjanette, Christian, Daniel, and Mark

Contents

Preface

As was the case in our first edition, the central theme of this book is that all personality theories rest upon basic assumptions concerning human nature and that no personality theory can be fully or properly appreciated without reference to these assumptions. This theme, explicitly stated in Chapter 1 in terms of nine basic assumptions underlying personality theories, is carried through the book by means of a discussion in each theory chapter of the theorist's position on each of these dimensions.

In developing this approach to the study of personality, our objectives have been to provide the undergraduate student with a means of comparing and contrasting the different theories presented within a common framework and with a way to use this framework to understand other theories of personality or human behavior that may be encountered in the future. Perhaps more important, we attempt with this approach to stimulate students to see beyond the immediate details of a particular theory toward the basic philosophic and profoundly relevant implications of each theory for understanding themselves, those around them, and human behavior in general. Feedback from the numerous students who read our first edition strongly suggests that these objectives have largely been met.

What is new in this second edition? First of all, two new theory chapters have been added, one centering on the work of Alfred Adler and the other on

Albert Bandura. Throughout the Adler chapter, the truly contemporary nature of his ideas are stressed; we treat Adler not so much as a neo-Freudian but as his own theoretical man—and a precursor of modern humanistic psychology. Social-learning theory is an increasingly dominant force in contemporary personology, and Bandura's work remains in the forefront of this movement; our book would not be complete without adequate coverage of this rapidly developing area of psychology. In the first edition, we put forward eight basic assumptions concerning human nature; in the present volume, a ninth has been added, *changeability-unchangeability*, to address the issue of the degree to which personality is seen as capable of fundamental change throughout life. Like the other basic assumptions, this one too is traced through each theory chapter. We also introduce several criteria for evaluating personality theories in Chapter 1 and evaluate the various theories in terms of these criteria in the concluding chapter. In this fashion, students are furnished with an additional perspective from which to compare and contrast theories of personality aside from that provided by our basic assumptions approach.

Throughout the book, there has also been selected rewriting to provide greater clarity and further practical illustrations of theoretical concepts, an updating of research and references, and new coverage of important topics in contemporary personology. As but two examples of the latter, we discuss cognitive processes as a new frontier in personality research in Chapter 12 (a "must" for today's psychology student) and touch upon Daniel Levinson's exciting work on adult development in the Erikson chapter. Finally, each chapter now concludes with discussion questions and a glossary. The former are deliberately designed to stimulate student thinking about the direct relevance of personality theories to their lives, whereas the latter was developed to serve as a much-needed learning aid for students involved in the sometimes arduous struggle to master the abstract theoretical concepts of personality.

Except for the above changes, we have remained close to the format of our very favorably received first edition. (We have been very gratified by this reception and we thank all students and professors who have contacted either of us over the past five years about it.) As in the former edition, each theory chapter follows a specific format. First, a biographical sketch of the theorist is provided, reflecting our belief that a personality theory is better appreciated after catching a glimpse of the nature of the individual who constructed it. Next comes the most lengthy section of each chapter, the detailed presentation of the personality theory itself. Various examples and illustrations are provided in this chapter section so that the student can more readily grasp the theoretical concepts described and their practical significance in everyday life. Immediately following is a graphical representation and analysis of the theorist's basic assumptions concerning human nature, which links the position of the theorist on our nine assumption dimensions with the theoretical concepts presented in the preceding chapter section. In this fashion, students are able to see the intimate relationship between concepts of personality and the basic assumptions upon which they were founded. Then comes a discussion of empirical validation of the theory in question. In this section, our aims are to (1) show the student how different personality concepts can and have been empirically tested, (2) provide a brief overview of the amount and kind of research generated by a particular theory, and (3) present a few illustrative studies which at once reflect these aims. These should be of interest to many readers. Following this is an application section in each chapter, which directly applies the theory, or an aspect of it, to some relevant dimension of human behavior. Our goal here is to indicate that, far from being meaningless academic abstractions, personality theory concepts are vital and relevant and can illuminate a wide range of human behavior and experience. Next comes a summary of the chapter highlights followed by a bibliography and brief list of suggested readings for the student who wishes to pursue the theory further. Last are the discussion questions and glossary.

Unless one is to write an unusually lengthy volume, it is better, we believe, to focus in depth upon a few theorists than to give scant attention to many. Consistent with this central theme, we selected for inclusion in this text ten theorists who hold divergent basic assumptions about human nature, who are clearly recognizable figures in the field, who seem to represent or epitomize a particular tradition in personality theory, and whose positions are likely to be relevant and significant to today's undergraduate student. We believe that potential advantages accrue to students of personality who trace the positions of such diverse figures as Sigmund Freud, Alfred Adler, Erik Erikson, Henry Murray, B. F. Skinner, Albert Bandura, Gordon Allport, George Kelly, Abraham Maslow, and Carl Rogers through the basic assumptions underlying the theories of each, the theories themselves, illustrative attempts to empirically test their concepts, and direct application of their theories to aspects of human behavior. Specifically, we hope that such students will achieve a more meaningful and enduring understanding of personality theory than could otherwise be gained by a more cursory examination of more theorists, the distinctions between whom tend to become blurred rather quickly and whose relevance to actual human behavior might remain somewhat obscure in the students' minds. After examining the theorists mentioned above, we attempt, in the concluding chapter, to place our basic assumptions model in some perspective, evaluate the ten theories previously discussed, and then go out on what we hope is a sturdy limb to make some predictions about the future of personality theory and research.

In developing this book, we wish once again to acknowledge the invaluable assistance of Norman Garmezy, who, as he did for our first edition, read the first drafts of all chapters, provided us with numerous constructive suggestions and criticisms, and remained a significant source of encouragement from beginning to end. Secondly, we thank Rich Wright and Rhona Robbin, our McGraw-Hill editors. Rich Wright competently guided us through our revision plan to the initial reviews; Rhona Robbin then took responsibility and very capably piloted our book to its final manuscript form—both editors continued to make it a pleasure to work with McGraw-Hill people. We also express gratitude to our reviewers—Richard Allgeier, State University College at Fredonia, New York; Nancy Wagner Gillett, Syracuse University; Donald Megenity, University of Southern Colorado; Paul Melchert, Eastern Washington State

College; and George Parks, University of Washington. Each individual offered a number of constructive suggestions to help shape this second edition. Next we thank David Bush, a developmental psychologist and faithful user of our first edition, for giving us the idea for what eventually became the changeability-unchangeability basic assumption in this edition. Finally, we once again express deep appreciation to our wives, Jean and Elizabeth, for their warm encouragement, helpful suggestions, constant emotional support, and sheer capacity to put up with their husbands' theoretical preoccupations throughout the writing of this book. Gratitude is again due to Jean Hjelle for spending countless hours improving the writing style and reading the galley proofs. And very special thanks are due in this edition to Elizabeth Ziegler who typed the entire manuscript, helped prepare all graphic illustrations, and was solely responsible for the physical preparation of every aspect of this manuscript—all accomplished with incredible promptness, efficiency, and not a trace of complaint.

Larry A. Hjelle
Daniel J. Ziegler

The Nature of
Personality Theory

Of all the problems that have confronted human beings since the beginning of recorded history, perhaps the most significant has been the riddle of their own nature. Countless attempts have been made to answer the question "What sort of creatures are we?" A great many avenues have been explored, with an enormous variety of concepts employed along the way, yet a satisfactory answer still eludes us. One important reason for the difficulty in getting a clear answer is that there are so many differences to be accounted for. Human beings come in many shapes and sizes and behave in exceedingly complex ways. Of the several billion people who presently inhabit the earth, no two are exactly alike. The vast differences among them have made it difficult, if not impossible, to identify what they share in common as members of the human race. Consider, for example, the convicted murderer, the dedicated scientist, the hermit, the corrupt politician, the rapist, the priest, the skid-row alcoholic, the civic-minded executive. It is hard to imagine what "human nature" these fellow human beings have in common, and when we expand our horizons to include people of other cultures, we find ever greater diversity in values, aspirations, and styles of life.

Astrology, theology, philosophy, and the life sciences are but a few of the many directions that the quest to understand human nature has taken. Some of these avenues have proved to be dead ends, while others are just beginning to flourish. Today the problem is more pressing than ever, since most of the world's ills—zooming population, global unrest, ecological pollution, racial prejudice, poverty—are brought about by the behavior of people. It may not be overstating the case, therefore, to say that the quality of human life in the future, indeed our very survival, may depend upon an increased understanding of human nature. Psychology is deeply committed to this undertaking.

Objectives of Personality Psychology

Since 1879 there has been a recognizable science of psychology, and one important part of it is directly concerned with the problem of understanding human personality. In fact, *the fundamental objective of the study of personality is to contribute significantly to our understanding of human beings from within the framework of the science of psychology.* Scientific psychology prefers to work with relatively simple, straightforward concepts that are open to empirical test and to use research methods that are as sound and precise as possible. This orientation necessarily limits the kinds of concepts and methods that can legitimately be used in studying personality. However, most psychologists are convinced that these scientifically based concepts and methods will ultimately prove to be of most value in unraveling the complex nature of human behavior.

What characterizes modern personality study as a science is the process of converting speculations about human nature into concepts that can be studied empirically, as opposed to simply offering opinions or beliefs. It is a process beset by many hazards; indeed, efforts to establish a "science of persons" are often viewed with ambivalence. While it may seem fascinating to try to gain insight into the causes of our behavior and development, we may actually resist such efforts to see ourselves objectively. There is even a certain amount of resistance to "objectifying" personality within the field of psychology, and some psychologists argue that going too far in this direction undermines human uniqueness and complexity. Instead, they urge us to concentrate on the intangible qualities of human beings—their struggles for personal and spiritual enlightenment—as evoked in literary and artistic creations such as a Tolstoy novel or a Bergman film. Yet, while literature, art, history, and religion may each provide valuable insights into human behavior, it is necessary to distinguish such information from that obtained by scientific endeavor. Moreover, while science currently does not provide all the answers (and perhaps never will), we must make the most effective use of the scientific information we presently do have while maintaining a clear perspective on the limitations inherent in the scientific method.

A second objective of personality psychology is to help people live their lives more fully and satisfyingly. While still pursuing theory and research, many personality psychologists today are concerned with finding ways to promote more healthy patterns of growth. These efforts include new forms of psychotherapy, various special learning programs, and changes in the psychological environment intended to permit people to develop their full potential. Research on these topics provides one of the sharpest testing grounds for ideas about constructive personality change and is discussed throughout the text.

Theories of Personality

Little agreement presently exists concerning the type or content of personality concepts that psychology should employ. There is currently no one best way to understand human behavior in psychology. In fact, individuals in this field strive continually to develop different systems of internally consistent constellations of concepts called *theories of personality.* This book will describe some of these theories, examine their underlying assumptions, report illustrative research related to each theory, and provide concrete applications of each to relevant aspects of human behavior. There is much to be gained from the study of personality theories.

Our subject is human nature; our goal is the understanding of the diversity and complexity of the whole person functioning in the real world.

If human behavior were fully understood, there would be no need for personality theories. Such theories actually represent elaborate speculations or hypotheses about why people behave as they do. They have both *descriptive* and *predictive* functions in psychology. A personality theory is *descriptive* in that it serves to organize human behavior systematically so as to render it intelligible. In other words, a theory provides a meaningful framework (i.e., a kind of map) for simplifying and integrating all that is known about a related set of events. For example, without the benefit of a theory, it would be very difficult to explain why 5-year-old Raymond has a strong romantic attraction to his mother along with undue resentment toward his father. The problem would be compounded were we to discover that other young boys experience similar feelings. Armed with a theory that posits the universality of these emotions at a certain stage of personality development (along with a rationale for their emergence), we would find it much easier to understand Raymond. We might not be correct, but at least we would be consistent in making sense of these feelings in children. A good personality theory, then, provides a meaningful context within which human behavior can be consistently described and interpreted.

A theory should not only describe past and present events but also predict future ones. The second function of a personality theory is therefore to provide a basis for the *prediction* of events and outcomes that have not yet occurred. This purpose clearly implies that a theory's concepts must be *testable* and capable of being confirmed or disconfirmed. To continue with the example, a theory should furnish a basis for predicting specific changes in Raymond's behavior as a function of parental treatment. What will happen if his mother actively encourages Raymond's romantic overtures? What will happen if his father threatens him about these feelings? Not only should such general predictions be possible but, ideally, the concepts of a theory should be formulated to permit rigorous and precise empirical testing. A good personality theory directly stimulates psychological research. Conversely, the scientific value of theories that are untestable is still unknown.

Personality theories, then, have distinct scientific functions in psychology. A crucially important point, however, is that all theories of human behavior are constructed by human beings. Personality theorists are people, and, like the rest of us, they hold divergent views about human nature. Some theorists, for example, believe that human actions have their roots in unconscious motives whose true nature is outside the individual's awareness and whose sources lie deeply buried in the distant past. Others believe that people are reasonably aware of their real motives and that their behavior is primarily a result of present conditions. Whatever each theorist's specific beliefs may be, we contend that personality theorists have different basic assumptions about human nature, and that their theories can be distinguished from one another on this basis. A theorist may recognize and make explicit these basic assumptions, fail to make them explicit, or simply incorporate them so fully that it becomes difficult to recognize that they are assumptions. In any case, one's basic assumptions profoundly affect one's ideas about the nature of personality. Suppose, for example, that a theorist basically believes that most of our actions result from reason and free choice. The personality conceptions derived from this premise are bound to be different from those set forth by a theorist who believes that human behavior is largely determined by irrational, unconscious factors. To illustrate, Abraham Maslow (Chapter 10) took the former position. Believing in the strength of rationality and freedom in human behavior, Maslow focused on what he felt were the "higher" aspects of human nature, on what we *could* become, and he developed his personality theory accordingly. On the other hand, Sigmund Freud (Chapter 2), assuming the dominance of irrationality and determinism in human actions, evolved a theory full of concepts reflecting the unconscious control of all behavior. Our point is simply that the foundations of a personality theory are rooted in the basic assumptions of the theorist; a theory's implications about human nature, i.e., about what humans are, inevitably extend far beyond the present scope of psychology as a science. Indeed, the personality theories discussed in this text deal with questions that go to the very core of what it means to be a human being.

Evaluation of Personality Theories

Given the sheer number of alternative personality theories, how do we evaluate the relative merits of each? That is, above and beyond the descriptive and predictive functions a theory should serve, what criteria can be used to evaluate a theory? We believe that six major criteria can be employed to evaluate personality theories in a systematic fashion; a personality theory should satisfy each of these criteria to some extent in order to receive a favorable evaluation. We will describe these criteria here, and, in the concluding chapter, we'll compare and contrast the theories discussed in this book in terms of these six criteria.

   1 Verifiability A theory is positively evaluated to the degree that its concepts lend themselves to verification by independent investigators. This means that a theory must be stated in such a way that its concepts are clearly and explicitly defined and logically related to one another. In this fashion, the empirical consequences of the theory can be logically deduced, and the hypotheses generated by the theory can be empirically tested.

   Although this requirement has been easy to specify, it has proved exceedingly difficult for personologists to demonstrate even a moderate amount of empirical validation for their preferred theoretical positions. Theories of personality are not necessarily incapable of generating testable predictions, but there has been a paucity of crucial research with respect to most theoretical conceptions. Nonetheless, a good theory should be empirically testable, leading to modification of the theory if necessary.

   2 Heuristic Value This criterion is of paramount significance to the empirically oriented personologist. The issue is the degree to which a theory directly stimulates research, and personality theories differ immensely in their capacity to fulfill this goal. Some of the most provocative theoretical formulations of personality (e.g., Maslow's self-actualizing theory) are practically devoid of empirical support. This state of affairs usually results from the theorist's failure to define his or her concepts operationally, i.e., in a manner whereby they can readily be subjected to empirical test. Of course, competent followers of a theorist may enhance the heuristic value of a theory by translating the core concepts into a form which allows for relevant research activity.

3   Internal Consistency   This criterion stipulates that a theory should not contradict itself. That is, a good theory accounts for things in an internally consistent way. On the whole, theories of personality fare reasonably well in satisfying this standard, and whenever inconsistent predictions do occur, they can usually be traced to a misunderstanding of the theory's concepts by the investigator. Given a set of assumptions about human nature, it is quite possible to construct an internally consistent personality theory.

4   Parsimony   A theory may also be judged on the basis of the number of concepts it requires to explain events within its domain. The law of parsimony (also known as Occum's razor) states that the preferred explanation is the one which demands the fewest number of concepts, i.e., is most economical. Thus, a theory that makes use of a different concept for every aspect of behavior is a poor theory. Unfortunately, there are no hard-and-fast rules by which the parsimoniousness of a theory may be assessed, and yet parsimony does occupy a pivotal role in the overall evaluation of a theory.

5   Comprehensiveness   This criterion refers to the range and diversity of phenomena encompassed by a theory. The more comprehensive a personality theory is, the more behavioral ground it covers. Thus, a comprehensive theory tends to be favored over a narrow, more circumscribed theory. While some personologists have managed to erect grand-scale theories, other theorists fall short on this score. Relying on a set of assumptions about human nature helps to ensure internal consistency, but it also tends to restrict the theorist's attention to a limited range of behavioral events. In varying degrees, theorists of personality included in this text emphasize biological, emotional, cognitive, social, and cultural factors in human behavior. Each of these approaches to personality inevitably restricts the comprehensive nature of the resulting theory. At the same time, it must be recognized that no present theory can account for all human functioning. Thus, one must decide whether the phenomena accounted for by one theory are as important or central to human behavior as the phenomena encompassed by another theory. Unfortunately, there is no clear-cut way of determining the relative importance of each, since it is often unclear just how critical any given phenomenon really is to our understanding of human behavior.

6   Functional Significance   Finally, a theory may be evaluated on the basis of how useful it is in helping people to understand everyday human behavior. This is hardly surprising, given the fact that virtually all of us are interested in knowing more about ourselves and other people. Indeed, the value of a personality theory for the layperson rests in its ability to illumine both the self and interpersonal relationships. A knowledge of the personal and social insights provided by personality theorists can greatly enrich one's understanding and appreciation of the subtleties of human affairs. Hopefully, the reader will find something of functional significance in each theory presented in this text.

THE MEANING OF "PERSONALITY"

Personality has many meanings. It is a reasonably distinct subfield of psychology that comprises theory, research, and assessment. However, even within psychology there is disagreement about the meaning of the term. In fact, there may be as many different meanings of the term "personality" as there are psychologists who have tried to define it.

What Is Personality? Alternative Answers

The word "personality" in English is derived from the Latin *persona*. Originally, it denoted the masks worn by theatrical players in ancient Greek dramas; eventually, the term came to encompass the actor's role as well. Thus, the initial conception of personality was that of a superficial social image that an individual adopts in playing life roles, a "public personality" that people display to those around them. This view is consonant with that of the contemporary layperson who equates personality with charm, social poise, popularity, physical attractiveness, and a host of other socially desirable characteristics. For example, in our daily language we often hear such comments as "Randy has a lot of personality" and "Susan has a great personality." It is in this sense too that schools advertising glamour courses promise to give those who enroll "more personality." Such a conception is generally outside the realm of scientific psychology because it limits the number and kinds of behavior deemed worthy of incorporation into the study of personality.

Personality has also been viewed as the individual's most striking or dominant characteristics. In this sense, a person may be said to have an "aggressive personality" or a "shy personality," meaning that his or her most distinctive attribute appears to be aggressiveness or shyness. So conceived, personality refers to the overall impression that an individual makes on others, that is, a sum total or constellation of characteristics that are typical of the individual and thus observable in various social settings. Unfortunately, such usage of the term neglects the possibility that the individual may be either aggressive *or* shy, depending on situational circumstances. Furthermore, the term "personality" as it is used by all personality psychologists does not imply an *evaluation* of a person's character or social skills. When one describes Tim as having a "terrific personality," one may be referring to his pleasant disposition, his sincerity, or his willingness to help others. However, this evaluative use of the word (i.e., personalities as good or bad) is not employed by personality theorists.

A quick overview of the meaning of personality in psychology can be gained by briefly considering the views offered by a few recognized theorists in the field. For instance, Carl Rogers (Chapter 11) views personality in terms of self, an organized, permanent, subjectively perceived entity which is at the very heart of all our experiences. Gordon Allport (Chapter 8) defines personality as that which an individual really is, an internal "something" that guides and directs all human activity. For Erik Erikson (Chapter 4), life proceeds in terms of a series of psychosocial crises, and personality is a function of their outcome. George Kelly (Chapter 9) regards personality as the individual's unique way of "making sense" out of life experiences. Still another conception is that of Sigmund Freud (Chapter 2), who described the structure of personality as composed of three elements—the id, ego, and superego.

These different conceptions clearly indicate that the meaning of personality in psychology extends far beyond the original "superficial social image" concept. It refers to something much more essential and enduring about a person. Beyond this basic point of agreement, theoretical definitions of personality have other features in common.

1 Most definitions depict personality as some kind of hypothetical structure or organization. Behavior, at least in part, is seen as being organized and integrated by personality. In other words, personality is an abstraction based on inferences derived from behavioral observation.

2 Most definitions stress the need to understand the meaning of individual differences. With the word "personality," the palpable uniqueness in all individuals is indicated. Further, it is only through the study of personality that the special properties or combination of properties that distinguish one person from another can be made clear.

3 Most definitions emphasize the importance of viewing personality in terms of a life history, or developmental, perspective. Personality represents an evolving process subject to a variety of internal and external influences, including genetic and biological propensities, social experiences, and changing environmental circumstances.

Aside from these common themes, personality definitions differ substantially. In fact, within psychology *one's definition of personality depends on one's theory of personality*. To understand what a particular theorist means by the term "personality," his or her theory must be examined in considerable detail. We shall consider ten such major theories in the ensuing chapters of this text.

Personality as a Field of Study

As any observant psychology student will note when flipping through a departmental catalog of course offerings, academic psychologists teach a wide variety of subjects, including the nature of exceptional children, biopsychology, perception, human development and change, and animal learning. These areas represent subfields of psychology; personality is one of these. What distinguishes personality from the other psychological domains is its attempt to *synthesize* and *integrate* the principles of these other areas. For example, in the psychology of perception, the basic structures and processes underlying how people perceive and interpret the world around them are examined. As a field of study, research into perception has uncovered important basic principles; the same is true for the other content areas of psychology, such as learning, motivation, and cognitive psychology. But it is personality as a field of study that combines these principles in an effort to understand all of human behavior.

To be comprehensive, a personality theory must incorporate all the principles of general psychology. Further, the dynamic interrelationships among these principles must be taken into account. We need to know how perception relates to learning, how learning relates to motivation, how motivation relates to development, and so on. Students of personality attempt to formulate theoretical concepts that describe and explain these kinds of relationships. All the factors that influence or determine an individual's behavior and experience fall within the domain of the *personologist*, a term that has been used to designate both personality theorists and researchers (Murray, 1938).

In light of all this, it is evident that no other area of psychology attempts to cover as much territory as the field of personality. Indeed, the study of personality is at the crossroads of most other areas of psychology: it is the converging point of the study of social and intellectual development, of psychopathology and self-actualization, of learning and interpersonal relations, and a host of other important threads that constitute the fabric of modern psychology. The breadth of the discipline is not surprising because, for many psychologists, the focus of study has been nothing less than the "total individual." Given such an ambitious goal, the reader can rightfully expect the study of personality to be an exciting and challenging undertaking, one in which the questions are still more readily forthcoming than the answers.

SOURCES OF INFLUENCE UPON MODERN PERSONALITY THEORY

Current conceptions of personality have been shaped by many events. To see personality theory in a meaningful perspective, it is necessary to examine some of the more important historical and contemporary influences upon it.

Historical Factors: The Past

As an integral part of the science of psychology, personality theory has been touched in some way by all the factors that have influenced psychology. Of the many historical forces that have coalesced to produce contemporary psychology, four appear to have been direct and major influences upon current personality theory—*European clinical medicine, psychometrics, behaviorism,* and *gestalt psychology.* After examining these historical factors, more contemporary sources of influence upon personality will be discussed.

European Clinical Medicine   Throughout history, medicine has always been intimately associated with concepts of the human personality. However, the clinical medicine of eighteenth- and nineteenth-century Europe (particularly France) had the most direct influence upon the structure of twentieth-century personality theory. The European clinical medicine of that time primarily dealt with the understanding, classification, and treatment of mental disorders. Based upon the then current mechanistic, physiological conceptions of mental activities, the noted French physician Philippe Pinel (1745–1826) was able to conceive of psychotic personality disorders in terms of brain dysfunction. This physicalistic conception of psychoses set in motion a scientifically based attempt to classify psychotic disorders, as illustrated in the work of the German physician Emil Kraepelin (1856–1926), as well as a widespread series of humanitarian reforms in the treatment of psychotics. The consistent important thread in these events for personality theory was that serious personality disorders could be conceptualized and classified in scientific terms. Yet, as Murphy notes: "Remarkably enough, there was throughout the nineteenth century very little recognition among physicians that normal psychology had anything to offer, and very little recognition among psychologists that mental disorder could teach them anything" (1949, p. 128). It is precisely within twentieth-century personality theory, particularly as it was initiated by Sigmund Freud, that such recognition came into being. Contemporary personality theory, rooted in today's clinical psychology and psychiatry, effectively unites the tradition of European clinical medicine with the history of psychology.

Another relevant aspect of the European clinical medicine of this period was the attempt to understand and treat neurotic disorders. Throughout the eighteenth and nineteenth centuries, these disorders were treated largely by various techniques of suggestion (some skeptical psychologists believe that they are still treated in this way). The term "suggestion" refers to the fact that a person's behavior can be altered by his or her uncritical acceptance of some notion or belief. Physicians, sometimes unknowingly, were able to alleviate neurotic symptoms simply by convincing the patient that their particular method would do so. Eventually, suggestion was recognized as the basis of *hypnosis,* and hypnotic suggestion became a means of treating certain kinds of neurotic disorders. The prominent French physician Jean-Martin Charcot (1825–1893), in theoretical disagreement with others in the field, developed his own unique interpretation of hypnosis as a phenomenon. Charcot attracted many outstanding students from all over Europe to pursue the scientific and therapeutic study of hypnosis. One of these students was Sigmund Freud.

European clinical medicine, then, furnished the intellectual climate in which Freud was to develop his unique psychoanalytic techniques and, ultimately, the first personality theory of major significance in the history of psychology. All of contemporary personality theory, in some way, has been affected by his views. European clinical medicine, because of its profound influence upon Freud, its scientific attempts to understand and classify personality disorders, and its therapeutic approaches to the treatment of disturbed persons, has left an indelible imprint upon modern personality theory.

Psychometrics　Psychometrics, or psychological measurement, has significantly helped to make a *science* of psychology. Before the advent of psychometrics, it was not possible, or even conceivable, to measure aspects of human psychological functioning, e.g., intelligence, aptitudes, interests, motives, personality traits. Now, within certain limitations, such measurements can be obtained.

Contemporary psychometrics can be traced to the work of the German scientist and philosopher Gustav Fechner (1801–1887). Fechner conceived of the idea that there might be an observable and measurable relationship between an external stimulus and an internal sensation or, stated in broader terms, quantifiable relationships between the physical and mental worlds. On this historical foundation others subsequently developed various psychometric approaches to measure these relationships. Moreover, statistical techniques were developed to analyze these relations mathematically. When psychological testing was introduced, the field of personality acquired the potential for quantification and measurement of its concepts. In brief, psychometrics made possible meaningful research in personality.

Consider a personologist who wishes to study the relationship between need for affiliation or friendship and a person's vocational interests. Without psychometric tools, he or she would have to be content with simply speculating that people with a high affiliation need are probably interested in occupations that permit close interpersonal contact. But this could never be known for sure. With current psychological measurement techniques, a personality researcher can quantify both need for affiliation and vocational interest as well as determine the mathematical degree of their relationship in the group studied. As will be seen in the research sections of succeeding chapters, concepts of personality can now be empirically tested.

Behaviorism Behaviorism as a school of psychology was founded in 1913 by the American psychologist John B. Watson (1878–1958). It became an extraordinarily influential movement in American psychology and, although the days of psychology "schools" are distinctly over, its pervasive influences are still quite evident today. The historical roots of behaviorism are deep. A venerable procession of philosophers and scientists before Watson in one way or another proclaimed the virtues of an objective approach to the study of human beings based upon a mechanistic, materialistic view of their nature. However, it was the Russian physiologist Ivan Petrovich Pavlov (1849–1936) who was most influential in setting the stage for the focus of contemporary behavioristic approaches to personality.

Every student of psychology is familiar with Pavlov and his salivating dogs. His immensely important experimental work on conditioning progressively influenced Watson as the latter developed his views. In Watson's hands, Pavlovian conditioning became the key to an objective, scientific approach to the study of behavior. Watson's emphasis upon conditioning, within the behaviorist framework, was instrumental in stimulating enormous interest among American psychologists in the scientific study of *learning*. Learning became the central focus of interest for those of behaviorist persuasion and, in large part, it remains so today. Stimulated by such giants as Edwin Guthrie (1896–1959), Clark Hull (1884–1952), and Edward Tolman (1886–1959), all of whom developed their own elaborate theories of learning, behavioristically inclined psychologists of today continue to fill the psychological journals with studies designed to clarify, refine, and further enhance our understanding of the learning process (Hilgard and Bower, 1975). And more—this wealth of scientific investigation has furnished the basis for a group of innovative therapeutic techniques collectively known as *behavior therapy*.

Contemporary behaviorists view the study of *personality* as a branch of the general field of learning (Lundin, 1974). As will be seen subsequently, their imprint upon personality theory, therapy, and research has been great. Behaviorism has profoundly influenced personality because of its emphasis upon the centrality of learning in personality development, the necessity of rigorous scientific research in the personality field, and the relevance of animal investigations for understanding aspects of the human personality. Social learning theories such as that of Albert Bandura (Chapter 7) also reflect the influence of behaviorism.

Gestalt Psychology   The German noun *gestalt* cannot precisely be translated into English. The closest approximations of its meanings are the words "form," "figure," "shape," "configuration," "structure." Gestalt psychology as a distinct school was founded in 1912 by the German psychologist Max Wertheimer (1880–1943). His ingenious and varied experiments upon the *holistic* nature of perception stimulated Kurt Koffka (1886–1941) and Wolfgang Kohler (1887–1967), two of his experimental subjects and colleagues, to develop and extend the principles of gestalt psychology to psychological spheres other than perception. For example, where the behaviorists discussed learning in terms of conditioning, the gestaltists conceived of learning in terms of insight; where the behaviorists investigated learned specific responses to simple stimuli, the gestaltists studied learned patterned responses to complex stimulus fields; where the behaviorists emphasized elements, the gestaltists stressed wholes.

Gestalt psychology, then, stresses the impossibility of understanding complex psychological processes by attempting to break them down into their component parts. The whole is greater than, and different from, the sum of its parts. While this general idea is found in the writings of many philosophers and psychologists before Wertheimer's time, it was the gestalt psychologists who crystallized this notion and applied it to twentieth-century psychology. The gestalt influence in contemporary personality theory can best be seen in the various attempts to conceptualize and assess personality in a holistic manner. Whether or not they formally identify themselves as gestaltists, many psychologists view personality as an organized dynamic whole that cannot be reduced to the sum of its parts. Holistic conceptions of this type are an integral part of the theories of Alfred Adler (Chapter 3), Gordon Allport (Chapter 8), Abraham Maslow (Chapter 10), and Carl Rogers (Chapter 11).

Contemporary Factors: What's Happening Now

While the shape of today's personality field has been determined by historical factors, new directions in personality will result from events occurring now. Any discipline that studies the behavior of people must, to remain viable, be responsive to emerging factors that have direct implications for understanding human nature. In a world of constant change, these factors are numerous indeed.

Within psychology, expanding knowledge in such diverse areas as *cross-cultural psychology, cognitive processes, life-span developmental psychology,* and *motivation* appears to be influencing both the present and foreseeable future of personality theory. Cross-cultural research has forced a reevaluation of the generalizability of psychological findings from one culture and/or subculture to another; what holds true for American college students may not apply to young people in the Trobriand Islands. Because of recent increased interest in the study of cognitive, or thinking, processes, human conceptual abilities are becoming a more salient aspect of personality theory (Lindsay and Norman, 1977). George Kelly's personal construct theory (Chapter 9) presently reflects this cognitive emphasis. Interest in adult psychology has greatly accelerated during recent years, partly as a result of Erik Erikson's efforts (Chapter 4) to construct a life-cycle conception of human development. In fact, a whole new area of psychological inquiry focused on personality change during adulthood and old age has come into being (Newman and Newman, 1975). In the area of motivation, attention to the study of growth, fulfillment, and self-actualization has stimulated followers of theorists such as Maslow and Rogers to develop an emphasis on human motivation as a legitimate part of personality.

Outside the field of psychology, contemporary influences upon personality are even more varied. For example, traces of *existential philosophy,* with its emphasis upon the individual as a free, self-determined, and changing organism, are unmistakably found in the thinking of major humanistic personality theorists (Buhler and Allen, 1972; Frick, 1971). The factor of *constant social change* is forging new directions for personality theory and research, while *computer technology* (Loehlin, 1968) continues to open up new and exciting research possibilities. On a broader scale, the *person revolution* of the 1970s has brought about a deeper awareness of the relativity of values, life-styles, and the meaning of life itself. These are but a few of the diverse contemporary influences upon the personality field; many forces, both within and outside the boundaries of psychology, will continue to shape its development. This must be so because the subject is fundamentally concerned with *what human nature is.* There have been and will continue to be important developments in many areas and disciplines that are highly relevant to an understanding of the nature of human beings.

The different *basic assumptions* that personality theorists make concerning human nature will now be discussed. These basic assumptions are of paramount significance in understanding and evaluating all personality theories; they will play an important part in the presentation of each theory included in this book.

BASIC ASSUMPTIONS CONCERNING HUMAN NATURE

All thinking people entertain certain basic assumptions about human nature. Personality theorists are no exception to this principle. The suppositions that people make about the nature of human beings are, in all likelihood, rooted in their personal experiences. Such basic assumptions profoundly influence the way that individuals perceive one another, treat one another, and, in the case of personality theorists, construct theories about one another. The basic assumptions themselves may or may not be fully recognized by the individual, whether a personologist or not.

In this section each of the basic assumptions that one could hold about human nature will be made explicit. We are convinced that *all major theories of personality are built upon different positions on these basic assumptions and that no major personality theory can be fully or properly understood without reference to them.* The differences among theories of personality, to some extent, reflect more fundamental differences among theorists on these assumptions.

The basic assumptions concerning human nature fall within these polarities:

1 Freedom . . . . Determinism
2 Rationality . . . . Irrationality
3 Holism . . . . Elementalism
4 Constitutionalism . . . . Environmentalism
5 Changeability . . . . Unchangeability
6 Subjectivity . . . . Objectivity
7 Proactivity . . . . Reactivity
8 Homeostasis . . . . Heterostasis
9 Knowability . . . . Unknowability

The assumptions are portrayed here as relatively continuous, bipolar dimensions along which any personality theorist can place herself or himself or be placed in terms of his or her basic position regarding that assumption. In other words, each assumption is depicted as a continuum with a pole, or extreme position, at its opposite end, e.g., freedom is at one pole of the first continuous dimension above, while determinism is at the opposite pole or end. From a philosophic viewpoint, the issues inherent in these assumptions might be considered to be dichotomous rather than continuous, e.g., people are either free *or* determined. However, among personologists, there are various differences in the extent to which a basic assumption is perceived as characteristic of humanity. For example, theorist A may see persons as less determined than does theorist B. Thus, it is desirable to conceptualize these assumptions as continuous so that important differences among theorists may be more readily apparent. A brief consideration of each basic assumption follows.

Freedom–Determinism

One of the most basic questions that individuals can ask about themselves is what degree of internal freedom, if any, they actually possess in directing and controlling their everyday behavior. To what extent is the subjective sense of freedom experienced by people in decision making valid? To what extent is their behavior actually determined by factors that are partially or totally outside the sphere of their conscious recognition? Philosophers and other thinking people have debated this issue for centuries. It is therefore not surprising to find that it is by no means a dead issue in modern psychology (Immergluck, 1964; Phares, 1976).

That major contemporary personality theorists differ sharply from one another on this basic assumption about human nature is quite clear. For example, Carl Rogers states that "man does not simply have the characteristics of a machine, he is not simply in the grip of unconscious motives, he is a person in the process of creating himself, a person who creates meaning in life, a person who embodies a dimension of subjective freedom (Shlien, 1963, p. 307)." By way of direct contrast, B. F. Skinner asserts that "autonomous man is a device used to explain what we cannot explain in any other way. He has been constructed from our ignorance, and as our understanding increases, the very stuff of which he is composed vanishes (1971, p. 200)." At this point neither of these positions is established as fact. Rather, they are *basic assumptions* made about the nature of man.

If a given personality theorist, based on personal experience and a host of other influences upon her intellectual development, assumes that human beings are genuinely capable of free choice, her theory will thereby be profoundly affected. She will tend to formulate a personality theory in which people are seen as primarily responsible for their own actions and, at least to some extent, capable of transcending various environmental influences upon their behavior. In brief, she will see free choice as a quintessential part of what it means to be a human being. On the other hand, if a personologist is inclined toward determinism, his theory will depict human behavior as being controlled by definable factors. It then becomes incumbent upon the personologist to specify these factors, and much of his theory will involve this task. In point of fact, deterministically based personality theories differ markedly on the nature of these factors. For example, human behavior could be determined by unconscious motives, external reinforcements, early experiences, physiological processes, cultural influences—each one open to various interpretations. The major source of agreement among these types of personality theories, in this context, is that human behavior is determined.

The position, then, that a personality theorist assumes in the freedom-determinism dimension greatly influences the nature of his or her theory and the implications of the theory as to what humans are. This is also true for the other basic assumption dimensions as well. *A personality theory reflects the configuration of positions that a theorist takes on the basic assumptions about human nature.*

Rationality–Irrationality

The basic issue underlying the rationality–irrationality dimension is the degree to which our reasoning powers are capable of influencing our everyday behavior. Are humans primarily rational beings who direct their behavior through reason, or are we principally directed by irrational forces? While no major personality theorist holds that people are "purely" rational or "purely" irrational, there are clear-cut differences among personologists on this basic assumption. For instance, George Kelly (1963) has employed the rational processes that people engage in as a model in constructing his entire theory of personality. Kelly sees man as "man the scientist," whose intellectual processes are of paramount significance in his overall behavior.

In direct contrast to this view is Freud's psychoanalytic theory, a basic tenet of which is the essential unconsciousness of mental activities. Freud held that "it is our inflated self-esteem which refuses to acknowledge the possibility that we might not be undisputed master in the household of our own minds (Kohut and Seitz, 1963, p. 118)." Are we then the rational masters of our fate, the captains of our behavioral ships, or are we controlled by deep irrational forces whose very existence may not be fully known to us?

A personologist's position on this issue powerfully influences the nature and focus of his or her theory. As an example, if a theorist assumes that rationality is a particularly potent force in people, her personality theory would depict behavior as being largely governed by cognitive processes. Furthermore, it is quite likely that, at least to some degree, her theory would be concerned with the nature, variety, and development of cognitive processes in personality. If a personologist gravitated toward the opposite position, his theory would tend to portray behavior as motivated primarily by irrational forces of which the person is partially or totally unaware. Depending on the theory's content, the relationship between conscious, rational processes and unconscious, irrational processes might be depicted as analogous to an iceberg, with the conscious, rational processes above the ever slightly fluctuating waterline that separates them from the vast unrecognized depths below. The major focus of this theory would be the content of the "submerged" forces as well as their operation in human behavior. While both "rational-oriented" and "irrational-oriented" theorists may disagree among themselves regarding the nature of "rational" or "irrational" factors in personality, the differences between them on the basic assumption of rationality–irrationality are their most fundamental differences in this regard.

Holism–Elementalism

The *holistic* assumption is that human nature is such that behavior can be explained only by studying persons as totalities. Conversely, the *elementalistic* position assumes that human nature is such that behavior can be explained only by investigating each specific, fundamental aspect of it independently of the rest. The fundamental scientific issue here is the level and unit of analysis to be employed in studying individuals. Are persons best studied as totalities or can they be better understood by examining each of their characteristics separately? Disagreements about this research issue among personologists reflect their more fundamental differences on this basic assumption.

The holistic view assumes that persons can only be understood as total entities. To explain the elements, it is argued, does not account for the total configuration they form (the influence of gestalt psychology is evident here). Holists maintain that the more one fragments the organism, the more one is dealing with abstractions and not the living human being. As Shlien put it: "Half a piece of chalk is still a piece of chalk, only smaller; half a planarian worm is half of one worm, but still a worm in itself; half a man is not a man at all (1963, p. 305)." Those of the holist persuasion, then, attempt to describe and study personality as a totality.

By way of contrast, advocates of elementalism argue that a systematic understanding of human behavior can only be reached by means of a detailed analysis of its constituent parts. Elementalists believe that just as one does not question the underlying reality of cellular structures in the study of gross anatomy, one should not deny the critical importance of studying the specific factors underlying the overall behavior of people. In fact, elementalists have long asserted that propositions which are vague and untestable at a general behavioral level are testable at a more elemental one. In brief, it is argued that a true scientific approach to personality can only be founded upon specific, precise, and elementalistic concepts that are clearly open to empirical test. Elementalists in personality attempt to devise and research these types of concepts.

Constitutionalism–Environmentalism

Students in personality courses often raise a question such as this: "How much of what is called personality is inherited and how much is an effect of the environment?" This issue in one form or another has long plagued philosophers as well as psychologists. How much of the basic nature of individuals is fixed by bodily or constitutional factors and how much is a product of environmental influences? The issue is still with us today; it has a surreptitious way of creeping into the thinking of contemporary personality theorists so as to influence their concepts of human nature and, hence, their conceptions of personality structure.

Constitutionalism has a long history in psychology. As an illustration, the ancient Greek physician Hippocrates believed that an individual's temperament resulted from his or her unique balance of four fundamental bodily humors— blood, black bile, yellow bile, and phlegm. His twentieth-century counterparts (Kretschmer, 1936; Sheldon, 1944) have developed systematic theories relating constitution to temperament. An individual's physical makeup is also an important factor in certain of the major personality theories discussed in this text. For example, it is evident in Sigmund Freud's centrally important concept of the id, the inherited basic component of personality that is fixed in the constitution of the individual.

Environmentalism is also no newcomer to the thinking of psychologists. Watson's behavioristic emphasis upon the centrality of learning in personality is based upon the underlying assumption that environment is of paramount importance in shaping human behavior. In fact, the study of learning is seen as so important precisely because it is the psychological process through which the environment molds behavior. A long and distinguished list of contributors to psychology preceded that point of view; an equally distinguished group of psychologists followed and, in various ways, developed its implications. These implications for personality are most clearly seen in contemporary behavioristic learning theory (Chapter 6), although behaviorism has no monopoly on environmentalism in personality theory. Traces of environmentalism can be found in practically all personality theories.

What are some of the consequences of a personologist leaning toward one or the other side of the constitutionalism–environmentalism dimension? A theorist who is inclined toward constitutionalism will tend to see human nature more as a product of internal physical forces than external environmental agents, e.g., Jane and John are highly aggressive because they have strong ids or because aggression is fundamentally inherited. While the theorist may acknowledge some environmental influences upon behavior, the concepts she or he constructs to describe personality will reflect a constitutional presupposition. In contradistinction, the theorist who leans toward environmentalism will view human nature as much more subject to environmental whim, e.g., Jane and John are highly aggressive because of their past conditioning histories—in essence, their environments made them that way. An environmentally inclined theorist's concepts will reflect this perspective and, in addition, will be much concerned with the processes, e.g., learning, through which the environment presumably affects personality development.

Finally, it must be recognized that almost all psychologists today adopt an *interactionist* position on this assumption (Craighead, Kazdin, and Mahoney, 1976). From this vantage point, human behavior is viewed as always resulting from the interaction of constitution with environment, e.g., a given constitutional factor operates differently under different environmental circumstances; an environmental influence differs in effect depending upon the constitution of the person on whom it is operating. However, for our purposes, constitution will be conceptually separated from environment so that the precise role of each in a theorist's thinking can be more clearly understood.

Changeability–Unchangeability

The basic issue involved in this assumption is the degree to which the individual is seen as capable of fundamental change throughout life. That is, can an individual's basic personality makeup really change to a large degree over time? Going a step further, is basic change a necessary component in the evolution or development of personality? Or are the surface changes that we observe in people merely that— superficial changes in behavior that occur while the basic underlying personality structure remains unalterable and intact? Like the other basic assumptions, differences among personality theorists on this issue are also reflected in the different emphases of their respective theories.

Earlier in this chapter, we noted that most definitions of personality stress a life-history, or developmental, perspective. The changeability–unchangeability assumption addresses the question of how much fundamental change in personality can actually take place throughout a lifetime, i.e., the degree to which basic personality change is possible. Even theorists within the same broad tradition in personology can be found to be at odds with one another on this issue. To wit, both Sigmund Freud and Erik Erikson clearly represent the psychoanalytic tradition within personality theory, yet they profoundly disagree on this basic assumption.

Erikson (1963) assumes a much greater degree of changeability in personality than does Freud. Emphasizing that life is constant change, he depicts persons as necessarily moving through developmental stages, each of which is characterized by a particular psychosocial crisis. Depending on the manner in which people resolve these crises, their personality development will proceed in one direction or another. In sharp contrast, Freud (1925) portrays the basic character structures of individuals as being fixed by the experiences of early childhood. While superficial behavior changes take place throughout life, the underlying character structure remains largely unaltered. For Freud, substantive change in personality can only be achieved with great difficulty at best, and then only through the lengthy and often painful medium of psychoanalytic therapy.

Personologists who are committed to changeability may reveal this predilection in a number of ways. For example, their theories could include (1) the concept of developmental stages characterizing the life span, (2) a focus on the forces that produce behavior change, (3) concepts that explain how people may be discontinuous with their past, or (4) an emphasis upon ongoing personal growth. Regardless of which direction a particular theory takes, it reflects the basic assumption that significant personality changes can and do take place, and that they therefore must be accounted for in theoretical terms. By contrast, personologists inclined toward the unchangeability assumption are likely to reveal it by positing the existence of enduring core personality structures which underlie the individual's behavior throughout life. Such theorists will focus on the nature of these structures, the constitutional or early environmental factors responsible for their formation, and how these structures essentially characterize the individual's behavior throughout life.

Subjectivity–Objectivity

Do human beings live in a highly personal, subjective world of experience that is the major influence upon their behavior? Or is their behavior influenced primarily, if not exclusively, by external, objective factors? This is the essence of the subjectivity–objectivity issue. Personologists differ markedly on this assumption; the differences are clearly reflected in their theories. In fact, a major difference on this assumption, perhaps above all others, seems to be at the philosophic root of the sharp cleavage between behaviorism and phenomenology in contemporary psychology. Some illustrations follow.

Carl Rogers, whose theory will represent the American phenomenological position in this book, has stated: "The inner world of the individual appears to have more significant influence upon his behavior than does the external environmental stimulus (1964, p. 124)." For Rogers (and for phenomenology), the individual's subjective world of experience is of paramount importance, and his observable behavior is forever unintelligible without reference to it. As is so often the case, B. F. Skinner is in direct opposition to Rogers. Skinner (1971), whose position will represent contemporary behaviorism in this text, has asserted: "The task of a scientific analysis is to explain how the behavior of a person as a physical system is related to the conditions under which the human species evolved and the conditions under which the individual lives (p 14)"; "We can follow the path taken by physics and biology by turning directly to the relation between behavior and the environment and neglecting supposed mediating states of mind (p. 15)." For Skinner (and for part of contemporary behaviorism), human behavior is largely the result of external, objective factors acting upon us—it is the lawful relationships between these factors and the organism's behavior with which the science of psychology should be exclusively concerned.

Consequently, a theory constructed by a personologist inclined toward subjectivity would tend to be mainly concerned with the nature of the individual's subjective experience. In fact, this kind of theorist might consider the scientific study of *human experience* as the most important part of psychology. Conversely, a personologist who tended toward objectivity would be likely to construct a theory primarily concerned with objective behavioral events and their lawful relationships to measurable factors in the external world. For such a theorist, psychology would truly be the science of *behavior,* and very little emphasis would be placed upon the individual's subjective experience as such.

Proactivity–Reactivity

The proactivity–reactivity issue is essentially concerned with locus of causality in explaining human behavior, i.e., where are the real causes of human actions to be found? Do people generate their own behavior internally or is their behavior simply a series of responses to external stimuli? At the heart of the proactive view of human beings is the belief that the sources of all behavior reside within the person. Man *acts* rather than *reacts.* Personality theorists adopting a proactive view of human nature firmly believe that the causes of behavior are to be found within; persons beget their behavior internally. Abraham Maslow succinctly portrayed a proactive view of humanity when he stated that "man has his future within him, dynamically active at this present moment (1961, p. 59)." Personologists inclined toward proactivity formulate theoretical concepts that serve to explain how people generate their own behavior.

A reactive position, on the other hand, views behavior as fundamentally a reaction to stimuli from the outside world. Persons do not internally cause their actions; they simply react to outside factors. The real causes of behavior are seen as completely external to the person. The reactive position is vividly described by Kimble as follows: "For all practical purposes, it is possible to construct a science of psychology in which the organism is considered as empty. For my own part, I can conceive of a psychology based on stimulus and response events entirely, one in which the existence of the organism is a completely unimportant fact (1953, p. 158)." Reactive-oriented personologists, in their theories, tend to emphasize concepts concerning stimulus-response and/or behavior-environment relationships.

Homeostasis–Heterostasis

The homeostasis–heterostasis dimension is fundamentally concerned with human motivation. Are individuals motivated primarily or exclusively to reduce tensions and maintain an internal state of equilibrium (*homeostasis*)? Or is their basic motivation directed toward growth, stimulus seeking, and self-actualization (*heterostasis*)? Personologists who take different stands on this issue have diametrically opposed views on the motivational bases of human behavior. As

Charlotte Buhler states: "One cannot simultaneously believe in the end goal of homeostasis and the end goal of a fulfilling self-realization (1971, p. 373)."

In the middle of this century, John Dollard and Neil Miller (1950) eloquently spoke for the homeostatic position. In their view, personality characteristics are acquired through learning, which always involves a relationship between the factors of drive (e.g., hunger) and reinforcement (e.g., food). Reinforcement, in Dollard and Miller's theory, always reduces the strength of the initial drive stimulus. Thus, people are what they are largely because they have acquired stable characteristics that reduce their various drives and maintain their internal states of equilibrium. Without a homeostatic motivational basis, personality development would be impossible.

At about the same time that Dollard and Miller were championing homeostasis, Abraham Maslow (1954) and Carl Rogers (1951) were developing a far different conception of human motivation. Such heterostatic theorists portray individuals as basically motivated by a continuing quest for growth and self-actualization. Man does not live by drive reduction alone. Instead of directing their behavior toward tension reduction, human beings, by nature, constantly seek new stimuli and challenging opportunities for self-fulfillment. Personality development occurs because of this basic motivational tendency.

A few logical derivatives of different positions on this basic assumption follow. Personality theories constructed by those of a homeostatic persuasion would be concerned with the nature and variety of man's basic drives or instincts, the various personality mechanisms individuals develop to reduce the tensions generated by same, and the processes by which these tension-reducing mechanisms are acquired. Conversely, personality theories developed by those of a heterostatic orientation would emphasize the integration of human motives under self-actualization, future-oriented strivings, and the various means by which persons seek growth and self-fulfillment.

Knowability–Unknowability

William James, the great psychologist and philosopher, has written: "Our science is a drop, our ignorance a sea (1956, p. 54)." Herein lies the essence of the knowability–unknowability issue regarding human nature. Ultimately, is human nature fully knowable *in scientific terms* or is there something in it that transcends the potential of scientific understanding? It is clear that we do not now know all there is to know about human beings in psychology—the question posed here is whether we ever will.

Personality theorists differ sharply on this question. To some extent, their differences are related to their positions on the other basic assumptions. For example, a personologist inclined toward *determinism* and *objectivity* would view people as scientifically knowable; these two assumptions, in effect, place human behavior potentially within the traditional realm of scientific knowledge.

John B. Watson is a historical personification of the knowability side of this assumption dimension. According to Lundin (1963), Watson was absolutely

convinced that, through systematic observation and experimentation, the principles underlying human behavior eventually could be discovered. Behavioristic
psychologists since Watson's time have engaged in these processes of careful
observation and experimentation and have thereby developed concepts applicable
to personality. B. F. Skinner's contemporary behavioristic approach to personality,
for example, clearly regards people as ultimately knowable in scientific terms. On
the opposite pole of this dimension is the phenomenological theory of Carl Rogers.
In his book *Client-centered Therapy,* Rogers (1951) argues that each individual
lives in a continually changing world of subjective experience of which she or he is
the center. He develops this notion by asserting that this personal world of
experience is private and can only be known in any genuine or complete sense by the
individual alone. In terms of the present issue, this view necessarily implies that
persons are unknowable in scientific terms (given a science of psychology that is
concerned with all people).

If a personologist believes that individuals are ultimately knowable in scientific
terms, he will proceed to develop and test his theory with methodological rigor,
convinced that human nature will finally be comprehended through this approach.
That this may not come to pass in his lifetime does not deter his efforts, since he
believes that his work will significantly hasten the progress of psychology toward
this ultimate objective. Conversely, should a theorist assume that individuals are
unknowable in scientific terms, she would be more inclined to look beyond the ken
of science in her quest to understand human beings. In fact, she may be tempted to
incorporate traditionally "unscientific" concepts into her theory and/or to argue
strongly for a redefinition of the science of psychology so that such concepts might
be more acceptable to psychologists. In either case, her theory and methodology
reflect the assumption that human nature is unknowable in terms of contemporary
psychology.

Thoughtful examination of the nine basic assumptions discussed above
indicates that there is some conceptual overlap among them. As one example, it is
difficult to imagine a theorist who assumes *reactivity* without a corresponding
commitment to *objectivity.* Part of the belief that human behavior is a reaction to
external factors is the conviction that such external, objective factors are important
in the first place. However, there is sufficient distinction among the nine
assumptions to justify their conceptual separation. The opposite poles of the two
overlapping assumptions we have used as examples, *proactivity* and *subjectivity,*
serve to bear this out. Proactivity relates to a motivation question—do people
generate their own behavior? Subjectivity refers to an experiential issue—what is
the importance of one's subjective world of experience to one's actions?

A major reason for treating these nine assumptions separately is that they
permit relevant distinctions to be made among personality theorists. Certain
assumptions are more salient than others in a given personality theory; the part that
each assumption plays varies from theory to theory. If, for example, a personologist
does not adopt a strong commitment to either pole of the subjectivity–objectivity
dimension, this assumption would play a relatively unimportant part in her theory
construction. Another theorist might lean markedly toward one of these two

extremes—his thinking would then be dominated by his position on the subjectivity –objectivity issue. In succeeding chapters, the position of each theorist on each basic assumption will be made explicit so that the intimate relationship between assumptions and theory can be fully appreciated.

Finally, it seems worthwhile to consider the source of these basic assumptions—where do they originate? They certainly do not descend upon the theorist from the sky (at least, we *assume* that they do not). Instead, basic assumptions about human nature are part and parcel of the way that a theorist *is;* they reflect *his or her own personality structure*. Like other deeply held beliefs, values, and attitudes, a theorist's basic assumptions about human nature contribute to the theorist's complexity as a total person. Thus, these assumptions are acquired and evolve in the same way as the theorist's other basic beliefs about the nature of the world.

The implications of this argument are profound. Specifically, personologists' conceptions of human behavior necessarily reflect to a large extent *what they basically think of themselves* and those around them. For some theorists, the conclusion is inescapable—by studying their theories, we may learn more about *them* than about their viewpoints on personality. Considered in this light, the biographical sketches presented at the beginning of each chapter take on added significance; by studying theorists' lives, we stand to gain additional insight into the personal roots of their theoretical positions.

SUMMARY

Theories of personality represent organized attempts to contribute significantly to our understanding of human nature from within the province of psychology.

There is presently no general agreement within the field on a substantive definition of the term "personality." One's definition of personality depends upon one's theory of personality, and personality theories can be evaluated in terms of six criteria: verifiability, heuristic value, internal consistency, parsimony, comprehensiveness, and functional significance. The field of personality is distinguished within psychology by its attempt to synthesize and integrate important principles from all areas of psychology.

The emergence and development of the personality field is firmly rooted in the historical factors that have shaped modern psychology. Four major historical factors—European clinical medicine, psychometrics, behaviorism, and gestalt psychology—appear to have been particularly important influences upon personality theory as it exists today. Significant contemporary sources of influence upon this field can be found both within and outside of psychology.

Personality theories are founded upon certain basic assumptions about the nature of human beings. Differences among personality theorists on these assumptions constitute the principal basis for the differences among their respective personality theories. In this chapter, nine basic assumptions concerning human nature were specified and discussed: *freedom–determinism, rationality–irrationality, holism–elementalism, constitutionalism–environmentalism, changeability–*

unchangeability, subjectivity–objectivity, proactivity–reactivity, homeostasis–heterostasis, and *knowability–unknowability.*

BIBLIOGRAPHY

Buhler, C. Basic theoretical concepts of humanistic psychology. *American Psychologist,* 1971, **26,** 378–386.

Buhler, C., & Allen, M. *Introduction to humanistic psychology.* Monterey, Calif.: Brooks/ Cole, 1972.

Craighead, E. Kazdin, A., & Mahoney, M. *Behavior modification.* Boston: Houghton Mifflin, 1976.

Dollard, J., & Miller, N. *Personality and psychotherapy.* New York: McGraw-Hill, 1950.

Erikson, E. *Childhood and society* (2d ed.). New York: Norton, 1963.

Freud, S. Some character types met with in psychoanalysis work. In S. Freud, *Collected papers.* London: Institute for Psychoanalysis and Hogarth Press, 1925, Vol. 4.

Frick, W. *Humanistic psychology: Interviews with Maslow, Murphy, and Rogers.* Columbus, Ohio: Merrill, 1971.

Hilgard, E., & Bower, G. *Theories of learning.* Englewood Cliffs, N.J.: Prentice-Hall, 1975.

Immergluck, L. Determinism-freedom in contemporary psychology: An ancient problem revisited. *American Psychologist,* 1964, **19,** 270–281.

James, W. *The will to believe and other essays on popular philosophy.* New York: Dover, 1956 (Orig. Publ. 1896).

Kelly, G. *A theory of personality.* New York: Norton, 1963.

Kimble, G. Psychology as a science. *Scientific Monthly,* 1953, **77,** 156–160.

Kohut, H., & Seitz, P. Psychoanalytic theory of personality. In J. Wepman & R. Heine (Eds.), *Concepts of personality.* Chicago: Aldine, 1963, 113–141.

Kretschmer, E. *Physique and character: An investigation of the nature of constitution and the theory of temperament* (Trans. W. Spratt). New York: Harcourt, Brace & World, 1936.

Lindsay, P., & Norman, D. *Human information processing: An introduction to psychology.* New York: Academic Press, 1977.

Loehlin, J. *Computer models of personality.* New York: Random House, 1968.

Lundin, R. Personality theory in behavioristic psychology. In J. Wepman & R. Heine (Eds.), *Concepts of personality.* Chicago: Aldine, 1963, 257–290.

Lundin, R. *Personality: A behavioral analysis* (2d ed.). New York: Macmillan, 1974.

Maslow, A. *Motivation and personality.* New York: Harper, 1954.

Maslow, A. Existential psychology—What's in it for us? In R. May (Ed.), *Existential psychology.* New York: Random House, 1961, 52–60.

Murphy, G. *Historical introduction to modern psychology.* New York: Harcourt, Brace, & Co., 1949.

Murray, H. (and collaborators). *Explorations in personality.* New York: Oxford, 1938.

Newman, B., & Newman, P. *Development through life.* Homewood, Ill.: Dorsey Press, 1975.

Phares, E. *Locus of control in personality.* Morristown, N.J.: General Learning Press, 1976.

Rogers, C. *Client-centered therapy; its current practice, implications, and theory.* Boston: Houghton, 1951.

Rogers, C. Toward a science of the person. In T. Wann (Ed.), *Behaviorism and phenomenology: Contrasting bases for modern psychology.* Chicago: University of Chicago Press, 1964, 109–140.

Sheldon, W. Constitutional factors in personality. In J. McV. Hunt (Ed.), *Personality and the behavior disorders.* New York: Ronald, 1944, 526–549.

Shlien, J. Phenomenology and personality. In J. Wepman & R. Heine (Eds.), *Concepts of personality.* Chicago: Aldine, 1963, 291–330.

Skinner, B. F. *Beyond freedom and dignity.* New York: Knopf, 1971.

SUGGESTED READINGS

Bronowski, J. *Science and human values.* New York: Harper & Row, 1965.

Hitt, W. Two models of man. *American Psychologist,* 1969, **24,** 651–658.

Nye, R. *Three views of man: Perspectives from Sigmund Freud, B. F. Skinner, and Carl Rogers.* Monterey, Calif.: Brooks/Cole, 1975.

Rosenthal, B. *Images of man.* New York: Basic Books, 1971.

Rychlak, J. *A philosophy of science for personality theory.* Boston: Houghton Mifflin, 1968.

Wolman, B. Does psychology need its own philosophy of science? *American Psychologist,* 1971, **26,** 877–886.

DISCUSSION QUESTIONS

1   Each of us has a working definition of what we mean by the term "personality." What is *your* definition of personality? Does your definition in any way imply a particular theory of personality underlying it?

2   What are some of the advantages of studying personality strictly from within the framework of scientific psychology? What are some of the disadvantages or limitations?

3   Now that you have studied the nine basic assumptions about human nature, what are your own basic assumptions in this regard? Where do you stand on each of these issues? Can you see any factors in your own life that might have contributed to your stance on these assumptions?

4   Defend your position on the freedom–determinism assumption. Why do you believe that people are basically free? Or determined? Is there any way to resolve this issue within the present scope of science?

5   Is human behavior fully knowable through science? If not, why not? Do you think that psychology ever will discover all there is to know about the nature of human beings? If not, what is the value of studying the psychology of personality?

GLOSSARY

Basic Assumptions   Philosophical suppositions that people, including personality theorists, make concerning the nature of human beings.

Behaviorism   School of psychology founded in 1913 by John B. Watson and formerly restricted to direct observation and measurement of overt behavior. It is also a psychology that emphasizes the importance of learning processes in relation to understanding personality.

Behavior Therapy   A group of therapeutic techniques aimed at modification of maladaptive behavior via application of learning principles.

Changeability   Basic assumption that personality is subject to continuous change throughout the individual's life cycle.

Comprehensiveness   Criterion used to evaluate the worth of a theory. An adequate theory must encompass and account for a wide range and diversity of behavioral phenomena.

Constitutionalism   Basic assumption that personality is shaped by genetic and biological factors.

Determinism   Basic assumption that all behavior is caused by the operation of other events and does not occur freely.

Elementalism   Basic assumption that an understanding of human behavior can only be achieved by investigating each specific, fundamental aspect of it independently of the rest.

Environmentalism   Basic assumption that personality is shaped by social forces.

Existential Philosophy   A view of human beings that emphasizes the individual as a free, self-determined, and constantly changing organism.

Freedom   Basic assumption that people are primarily responsible for their own actions and are capable of transcending environmental influences upon their behavior.

Functional Significance   Criterion used to evaluate the worth of a theory. An adequate theory should provide new approaches to the solution of people's problems.

Gestalt Psychology   A school of psychology founded in 1912 by Max Wertheimer and focused on the study of perception. It is also a psychology that emphasizes the notion that personality is an organized, dynamic whole that cannot be reduced to the sum of its parts.

Heterostasis   Basic assumption that individuals are motivated primarily toward growth, stimulus seeking, and self-actualization.

Heuristic Value   Criterion used to evaluate the worth of a theory. An adequate theory should stimulate new ideas for research.

Holism   Basic assumption that behavior can be explained only by studying persons as totalities.

Homeostasis   Basic assumption that individuals are motivated primarily to reduce tensions and maintain an internal state of equilibrium.

Internal Consistency   Criterion used to evaluate the worth of a theory. An adequate theory should account for varied phenomena in an internally consistent way.

Irrationality   Basic assumption that human behavior is governed by irrational forces of which the person is partially or totally unaware.

Knowability   Basic assumption that principles governing human behavior will eventually be discovered through scientific inquiry.

Objectivity   Basic assumption that human behavior is largely the result of external and definable factors acting upon the person.

Parsimony   Criterion used to evaluate the worth of a theory. An adequate theory should contain only those concepts and assumptions necessary to account for the phenomena within its domain.

Persona   Term used to denote the mask worn by theatrical players in ancient Greek dramas.

Personality Psychology   A distinct subfield of psychology that comprises theory, research, and assessment.

Personality Theories   Different systems of internally consistent concepts that are created by investigators to account for the diversity and complexity of the whole person functioning in the real world.

Personologist   Term used to designate personality theorist and/or researcher.

Proactivity   Basic assumption that the sources of all behavior reside within the person.

Psychometrics   The measurement of psychological variables and concepts.

Rationality   Basic assumption that human beings are rational organisms capable of directing their behavior through reasoning.

Reactivity   Basic assumption that the real causes of human behavior are completely external to the person; that behavior is simply a series of responses to external stimuli.

Subjectivity   Basic assumption that each person inhabits a highly personal, subjective world of experience that is the major influence upon his or her behavior.

Unchangeability   Basic assumption that one's personality structure is established in early life and remains intact thereafter.

Unknowability   Basic assumption that human behavior transcends the potential of scientific understanding.

Verifiability   Criterion used to evaluate the worth of a theory. An adequate theory must contain concepts that are clearly defined, logically related to one another, and amenable to empirical validation.

Sigmund Freud *(Courtesy of The Bettman Archive)*.

Sigmund Freud: A Psychoanalytic Theory of Personality

When psychology gained its independence from philosophy and became a science in the second half of the nineteenth century, its goal was to use a laboratory-based introspection to discover the basic elements of mental life in the human adult. Known as the *structural school* and developed primarily by Wilhelm Wundt (who founded the first psychological laboratory in Leipzig, Germany, in 1879), this approach emphasized the analysis of conscious processes into their fundamental elements, together with the discovery of the laws that govern connections among these elements. Thus, even psychologists of that era were taken aback by the thoroughly different and radical approach to the study of human beings which was developed almost single-handedly by Sigmund Freud, then a young Viennese physician. Rather than treating consciousness as the center of mental life, Freud likened the mind to an iceberg, only a small segment of which protruded above the surface of the water. In contrast to the then prevailing view of humans as rational beings, he theorized that individuals are in a perpetual state of conflict motivated by a second, more comprehensive realm of mental functioning—*unconscious* sexual and aggressive urges.

It would be impossible to provide an adequate account of contemporary personality theory without referring to Freud's system. Whether one accepts or rejects any or all of his ideas, no one can reasonably deny that Freud has had an enormous intellectual impact on Western civilization in the twentieth century. Indeed, it can be argued that few ideas in the entire history of civilization have had such a broad and profound influence. This is a sweeping statement, but it is difficult to think of many close competitors for such a distinction. His view of the human condition, striking violently against the prevailing opinions of his day, offers a complex and compelling way to understand those aspects of mental life that are obscure and apparently unreachable.

It is a shattering experience for anyone seriously committed to the Western tradition of morality and rationality to take a steadfast, unflinching look at what Freud has to say. It is humiliating to be compelled to admit the grossly seamy side of so many grand ideals. . . . To experience Freud is to partake a second time of the forbidden fruit (N. Brown, 1959, p. xi).

In forty years of active writing and clinical practice Freud developed (1) the first comprehensive personality theory; (2) an extensive body of clinical observations based on his therapeutic experience and self-analysis; (3) a compelling method for treating mental or behavioral disorders; and (4) a procedure for the investigation of mental processes which are almost inaccessible in any other way. In this chapter, Freud's personality theory and its underlying assumptions will be examined. Selected research stimulated by the theory as well as illustrative applications to everyday human behavior will also be discussed.

BIOGRAPHICAL SKETCH

Sigmund Freud was born May 6, 1856, at Freiberg, Moravia, a small Austrian town now part of Czechoslovakia. When he was four years old, his family suffered financial setbacks and moved to Vienna. He remained a resident of that city until he emigrated to England in 1938. He was the oldest of seven children, although his father had two sons by a former marriage and was a grandfather when Sigmund was born.

From a very early age, Freud excelled as a student. Despite the limited financial position of his family which forced all members to live in a crowded apartment, Freud had his own room and even an oil lamp to study by. The rest of the family made do with candles. Like other young people of his time, he had a classical education, studying Greek and Latin and reading the classics of various countries. He had a superb command of the German language and at one time earned a prize for his literary skills, but he also had considerable fluency in French, English, Spanish, and Italian.

Freud recalled that he often had childhood dreams of becoming a great Austrian general or minister of state. However, since he was Jewish, all professional careers except medicine and law were closed to him—such was the prevailing anti-Semitic climate of the times. He reluctantly decided upon a medical career and entered the Faculty of Medicine of the University of Vienna in 1873. He received his M.D. degree in 1881. Shortly thereafter he accepted a position at the Institute of Cerebral Anatomy and did research comparing adult and fetal brains; he never intended to practice medicine. However, he soon resigned his post and entered private practice as a neurologist primarily because scientific work offered small monetary gain and anti-Semitism within academe curtailed promotions. In addition, Freud had fallen in love and realized that if he ever were to marry, he would need a better-paying position.

The year 1885 marked an important turning point in Freud's career, for it was then that he went to Paris to study for several months with Jean Charcot, one of the most prominent neurologists of the time. Charcot demonstrated that it was possible to induce or eliminate hysterical neurotic symptoms by means of hypnotic suggestion. Although Freud later rejected hypnosis as a therapeutic technique, he was excited by Charcot's lectures and clinical demonstrations. During his brief stay at the famed Salpêtrière hospital in Paris, Freud was transformed from a neurologist to a psychopathologist.

In 1886, Freud married Martha Bernays, a union that produced three daughters and three sons. One daughter, Anna Freud, later became a renowned child analyst. About this time, Freud also began to collaborate with Josef Breuer, a distinguished Viennese physician who had chanced upon *catharsis,* a procedure whereby the patient alleviates anxieties and symptoms by talking about them. Together, Freud and Breuer explored the beneficial effects of catharsis and in 1895 coauthored a book entitled *Studies in Hysteria.* Their friendship was short-lived, however, due to Breuer's strong disagreement with Freud about the role of sex in hysteria, a neurotic disorder. Freud's own convictions led to his resignation from the Vienna Medical Society in 1896.

The years between 1890 and 1900 were lonely yet productive ones for Freud. He worked alone to develop the bedrock of psychoanalytic theory. These efforts culminated in what many experts consider to be his most outstanding work, *The Interpretation of Dreams* (1900). At first, this masterpiece was all but ignored by the psychiatric community and Freud received only $209 in royalties for his labors. From 1901 onward, however, his prestige grew to include the general populace as well as medical practitioners throughout the world. The following year the Vienna Psychoanalytical Society was formed, open to only a select group of his dedicated followers. Many of Freud's colleagues subsequently became famous psychoanalysts (including Ernest Jones, A. A. Brill, Sandor Ferenzci, Carl Jung, Alfred Adler, Hans Sachs, and Otto Rank). Later Adler, Jung, and Rank were to defect from Freud's ranks and develop their own rival schools of thought.

In 1909 a single incident propelled the psychoanalytic movement from relative isolation to international recognition. G. Stanley Hall invited Freud and Jung to deliver a series of lectures at Clark University, Worcester, Massachusetts. Freud later wrote:

> As I stepped on to the platform at Worcester to deliver my "Five Lectures on Psycho-Analysis" it seemed like the realization of some incredible day-dream: Psycho-analysis was no longer a product of delusion, it had become a valuable part of reality. It has not lost ground in America since our visit; it is extremely popular among the lay public and is recognized by a number of official psychiatrists as an important element in medical training (1935, p. 52).

World War I had a profound impact on Freud's life and theory. For one, his clinical work with German soldiers broadened his understanding of the variety and subtlety of psychopathology. The loss of practically all his life savings in 1919, the participation of two sons in the war, and soon thereafter the rise of anti-Semitism strongly affected Freud's conception of the social nature of man. Despite his pessimism about the future of humankind, however, he continued to articulate his ideas in a long series of books. The more important ones include *Introductory Lectures on Psycho-Analysis* (1920), *The Ego and the Id* (1923), *Future of an*

Illusion (1927), *Civilization and Its Discontents* (1930), *New Introductory Lectures on Psychoanalysis* (1933), and *An Outline of Psycho-Analysis* published posthumously in 1940. In 1932 he was a persistent target of Hitler's terror policies (the Nazis in Berlin held numerous book burnings of his publications). Freud commented on the event: "What progress we are making. In the Middle Ages they would have burnt me, nowadays they are content with burning my books (Jones, 1957)." It was only through the diplomatic efforts of influential citizens that he and certain members of his family were allowed to escape from the Nazis.

Freud's final years were difficult ones. From 1923 on he suffered from an advancing cancer of the throat and jaw (he smoked twenty Cuban cigars every day), but he obstinately refused all forms of drug therapy with the exception of a few aspirin. He persisted in his work, despite a total of thirty-three operations to halt the spreading cancer. Freud died September 23, 1939, in London, England, a displaced Jewish expatriate. A three-volume biography written by his friend and colleague Ernest Jones, entitled *The Life and Work of Sigmund Freud* (1953, 1955, 1957), is recommended as a perceptive analysis of Freud's life. Subsequently, a twenty-four-volume edition has been published in England and sold to a worldwide audience.

LEVELS OF CONSCIOUSNESS: HOW PERSONALITY IS ORGANIZED

For a long time in the theoretical development of psychoanalysis, Freud employed a topographical model of personality organization. According to this model, psychic life can be represented by three levels of consciousness—the conscious, the preconscious, and the unconscious. Freud used this mental "map" of the mind to describe the degree to which mental events such as thoughts and fantasies vary in accessibility to awareness.

The *conscious* level includes all the sensations and experiences of which we are aware at any given moment. Freud insisted that only a small part of mental life (thoughts, perceptions, feelings, memories) is contained in the realm of consciousness. Whatever the content of conscious experience may be for a given person at a given time, it is the result of a selective screening process largely regulated by external cues. Moreover, it is actually conscious only for a brief time and can be quickly submerged into preconscious or unconscious levels as the person's attention shifts to different cues. In short, the conscious represents a small and limited aspect of personality.

The *preconscious* domain, sometimes called "available memory," encompasses all experiences that are not conscious at the moment but which can readily be summoned into awareness either spontaneously or with a minimum of effort. This might include memories of everything you did last week, your Social Security number, all the towns you ever lived in, your favorite foods, and a host of other past experiences. In Freud's view, the preconscious bridges the unconscious and conscious regions of the mind. For example, under the influence of certain therapeutic techniques, unconscious material may emerge into the preconscious and from there become conscious.

The deepest and major stratum of the human mind is the *unconscious*. Freud was not the first to focus attention on the importance of unconscious processes in understanding human actions; several eighteenth- and nineteenth-century philosophers had suggested the influence of unconscious experience on behavior. Unlike his philosophical predecessors, however, Freud gave the concept of an unconscious life an empirical status. Specifically, he contended that the unconscious must not be conceived as a hypothetical abstraction but rather as a reality which can be demonstrated and thus proved. Freud firmly believed that the really significant aspects of human behavior are shaped and directed by impulses and drives totally outside the realm of awareness. Not only are these forces unconscious, but there is great resistance within the individual to their ever becoming conscious. In contrast to preconscious modes of thought, unconscious ones are completely inadmissible to awareness, yet they largely determine the actions of people. However, unconscious material may be expressed in disguised or symbolized form, an insight that Freud utilized in his work with disturbed persons. Psychoanalysis thus emphasizes the interpretation of fantasies and dreams as avenues for deeper understanding of the unconscious processes underlying behavior.

THE ANATOMY OF PERSONALITY

The concept of unconscious mental processes was central to Freud's early description of personality organization. However, during the early 1920s he revised his conceptual model of mental life and introduced three basic structures in the anatomy of personality: id, ego, and superego. This tripartite division of personality is known as the *structural model* of mental life, although Freud felt the divisions should be understood as hypothetical processes rather than as specific "structures" of personality. Freud insisted that these structures be considered hypothetical constructs because the field of neuroanatomy was not sufficiently advanced to locate them within the central nervous system. The interrelationships between these personality structures and the levels of consciousness are diagrammed in Figure 2-1. The figure shows that all of the id is unconscious, while both the ego and superego are composites of unconscious, preconscious, and conscious states of experience. The unconscious encompasses all three personality structures, although the major portion of it is made up of id impulses.

The Id

The word "id" comes from the Latin word for "it" and refers exclusively to the biological component of personality. The id is the mental agency containing everything inherited, present at birth, and fixed in the individual's constitution—especially sexual and aggressive instincts. It is raw, animalistic, and unorganized, knows no laws, obeys no rules, and remains basic to the individual throughout life. Operating on a primitive basis, it is free from all inhibitions. The id, as the original or oldest personality system, expresses the primary principle of all human life—the immediate discharge of psychic energy produced by biologically rooted drives (especially sex and aggression) which, when pent up, create tension throughout the

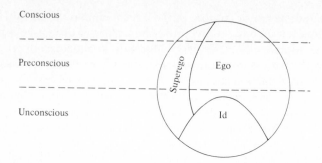

Conscious

Preconscious

Superego   Ego

Unconscious

Id

Figure 2-1 The relationship of the structural model of personality to levels of awareness. (*Adapted from Wolman, 1968.*)

personality system. Immediate tension reduction is called the *pleasure principle,* and the id obeys it, manifesting itself in an impulsive, irrational, and narcissistic (exaggeratedly self-loving) manner, regardless of the consequences of its actions for others or its own self-preservation. Furthermore, since the id does not recognize fear or anxiety, it takes no precautions in expressing its purpose—a fact which Freud felt may result in danger for the individual and/or society. Expressed differently, the id may be likened to a blind king whose brute power and authority are compelling but who must rely on others to properly distribute and use his power.

Freud considered the id as a mediator between the organism's somatic and mental processes. He described it as being "somewhere in direct contact with somatic processes, and takes over from them instinctual needs and gives them mental expression, but we cannot say in what substratum this contact is made (1915–1917, p. 104)." As such, it acts as a reservoir for all the instincts and derives its energy directly from bodily processes.

Freud identified two mechanisms the id employs to rid the personality of tension: *reflex actions* and *primary process.* In the former, the id responds automatically to sources of irritation, thereby promptly removing the tension which the irritant elicits. Examples of such inborn reflex mechanisms are sneezing, coughing, and blinking. On the other hand, primary process is a psychological phenomenon whereby the individual reduces tension by forming a mental image of an object previously associated with satisfaction of a basic drive. It is a prelogical, infantile form of human thought characterized by the inability to inhibit impulses and to discriminate between the real and the unreal, between the me and the non-me. For example, a hungry person experiences partial gratification of the hunger drive by forming a perceptual image of a savory steak or lobster tail. Freud held that the id does not distinguish between such a subjective mental image and the real object—the steak or lobster tail itself. Other examples of primary process thinking are found in dreams, the mental functioning of newborn infants, and the hallucinations of psychotics.

The tragedy of behaving in accord with primary process is that the individual cannot differentiate between the actual object that will gratify a need and a mental image of the object (e.g., between water and a mirage of water for a person stranded in the desert). Confusion of the two would eventually lead to death unless some external source of satisfaction were present. Thus, Freud believed that the most compelling task confronting the infant is to learn to delay gratification of primary needs. The capacity to postpone such gratification first emerges when infants learn that there is an external world apart from their own needs and desires. As this realization develops, the second structure of personality, the ego, appears.

The Ego

The ego is that portion of the psychic apparatus that seeks to express and gratify the desires of the id in accordance with the restrictions of both outer reality and the superego. The ego acquires its structure and functions from the id, having evolved from it, and proceeds to borrow some of the id's energy for its own use in response to the demands of the environment. Ego thus assures the safety and self-preservation of the organism. In its battle for survival against both the external world and the instinctual demands of the id, ego must continuously differentiate between things in the mind and things in the outer world of reality. The hungry man in search of food, for example, must distinguish between a mental image of food and an actual perception of food if tension reduction is to occur. That is, he must learn to acquire and consume food before the tension can be reduced. This task is accomplished through adaptive strategies and enable the id to express its instinctual needs in accordance with the norms and ethics of the social world, a feat not always achieved. Such strategies require one to learn, think, reason, perceive, decide, memorize, and so on, which explains why ego functions are usually regarded as *cognitive capacities.*

In contrast to the id's pleasure-seeking nature, the ego obeys the *reality principle,* the aim of which is to preserve the organism's integrity by suspending instinctual gratification until either an appropriate object and/or environmental condition that will satisfy the need has been found. The reality principle enables the individual to inhibit, divert, or gradually release the id's energy within the bounds of social restrictions and the individual's conscience. For instance, expression of the sexual drive is delayed until an appropriate "object" and environmental circumstances are available. Thus, when the object and conditions are ideal, the pleasure principle is satisfied. Unlike the id, the ego distinguishes between fact and fiction, tolerates moderate amounts of tension, changes as a function of new experience, and develops cognitive-perceptual skills. The purpose of the cognitive-perceptual skills, or what Freud termed *secondary process,* is to establish suitable courses of action to satisfy instinctual needs without endangering the safety of the individual and/or others. The ego, then, is the "executive" of personality and the seat of intellect. One of the main goals of psychoanalytic therapy is to free some of the ego's energy so that it can generate higher levels of problem solving.

The Superego

In order for a person to function constructively in society, he or she must acquire a system of values, norms, ethics, and attitudes which are reasonably compatible with that society. These are acquired through the process of "socialization," and in terms of the structural model of psychoanalysis are developed through the formation of a superego. The superego is the last major system of personality to be developed and represents an internalized version of society's norms and standards of behavior. In Freud's view, the human organism is not born with a superego; rather, children must incorporate it through interactions with parents, teachers, and other "formative" figures. As the moral-ethical arm of personality, the superego results from the child's prolonged dependence upon parents. It makes its formal appearance when the child is said to know right from wrong, good from bad, moral from immoral. Initially, the superego reflects only parental expectations of what is good and right. The child's every effort is expended to match these expectations so as to avoid conflict and punishment. However, as the child's social world begins to broaden (via school, church, peer groups), his or her superego expands to incorporate whatever behavior these groups also deem appropriate. The superego may be considered an individualized reflection of society's "collective conscience," although the child's perceptions of the real values of society may be distorted.

Freud divided the superego into two subsystems—the *conscience* and the *ego-ideal*. Conscience is acquired through the use of punishment by the parents. It is concerned with things that parents say are "naughty" behavior and for which the child is reprimanded. It includes the capacity for punitive self-evaluation, moral prohibitions, and guilt feelings when one fails to live up to what is believed to be ideal. The ego-ideal is derived from whatever the parents approve and reward. It leads the individual to set up goals and aspirations which, if achieved, generate a sense of self-esteem and pride. For example, the child who is rewarded for scholarly efforts will feel proud whenever he or she shows academic accomplishment.

The superego is said to be fully developed when self-control replaces parental control. However, this principle of self-control is not served by the reality principle. The superego, while attempting to control id impulses, also tries to persuade the ego that perfectionistic goals are better than realistic ones.

INSTINCT: WHAT MOTIVATES HUMAN BEHAVIOR?

Psychoanalytic theory is based on the notion that human beings are complex energy systems. Limited by nineteenth-century conceptions of physics and physiology, Freud was taught that human behavior is activated by a unitary kind of energy in accordance with the *law of conservation of energy* (i.e., energy may be converted from one state to another, but it is all the same energy). Freud accepted this principle of nature, translated it into psychological terms, and theorized that the source of psychic energy derives from neurophysiological states of excitation. He further postulated that each individual has a limited amount of such energy available for mental activity, and that the goal of all human behavior was the reduction of tension created by the unpleasant accumulation of energy over time. For example, if most of your energy is presently being expended to recognize the words on this page, then little is left for other types of mental activity like daydreaming or viewing a TV program. Similarly, the reason you are reading these words may be to reduce tension associated with an exam scheduled for next week.

Freud thus depicted human motivation as based entirely upon energy aroused by the body's tissue needs. He believed that the total amount of psychic energy deriving from tissue needs is invested in mental activities designed to reduce the excitation created by the need. In Freudian theory, mental representations of these bodily excitations reflected in the form of wishes are termed *instincts.* An instinct, then, refers to an innate bodily state of excitation that seeks expression and tension release. Freud maintained that all human activity is determined by the instincts; their influence on behavior can be devious and disguised as well as direct. People behave because instinctual tension impels them to behave, their actions serving to reduce this tension. As such, instincts are "the ultimate cause of all activity (Freud, 1940, p. 5)."

A Matter of Life and Death

Although there may be an indeterminate number of instincts, Freud recognized the existence of two basic groups of them—*life* and *death* instincts. The former group includes all the forces which serve to maintain vital life processes and assure propagation of the species. Because of the significance attributed to them in the psychic organization of individuals, the *sex instincts* were singled out by Freud as the most salient of the life instincts for the development of personality. The energy force underlying the sexual instincts is called *libido* (from the Latin word for "wish" or "desire") or *libidinal energy,* a term which came to refer to the energy of the life instincts in general. Libido is that portion of psychic energy which seeks its gratification from purely sexual activities.

A second category, the death instincts (also known as Thanatos), underlies all the manifestations of cruelty, aggression, suicide, and murder. Unlike the libidinal energy of the life instincts, no name was assigned to the energy system of the death instincts. However, Freud considered them to be biologically rooted and equally as important as the life instincts in determining the individual's behavior. Furthermore, he saw an empirical basis for the death instinct in the principle of *entropy,* i.e., a thermodynamic law which states that any energy system seeks a state of balance or equilibrium. Quoting Schopenhauer, Freud dramatically claimed that "The goal of all life is death (1920, p. 38)." What he intended to convey is that there exists in all living organisms a compulsion to reestablish the inanimate state out of which they were formed. That is, Freud believed that every person has an unconscious wish to die.

What Are Instincts Really Like?

All instincts have four components: a source, an aim, an object, and an impetus. The *source* of the instinct is the bodily condition or need from which it arises. The sources of life instincts are clearly embedded in neurophysiology (e.g., hunger or thirst). In the case of death instincts, the sources were not as clearly defined by Freud in physiological terms. The *aim* of an instinct is always to abolish or reduce the excitation deriving from its need. If the aim is achieved, the person then experiences a momentary state of blissfulness. Although there are numerous ways of attaining the aim of an instinct, there is a consistent tendency to maintain the state of excitation at minimal level.

The *object* refers to any person or thing in the environment or within the individual's own body that provides for the satisfaction (i.e., the aim) of an instinct. The activities leading to instinctual pleasure are not necessarily fixed. In fact, the object may be susceptible to change throughout the course of the individual's life. In addition to flexibility in the choice of objects, individuals are capable of delaying expression of instinctual energy for prolonged periods of time. Practically every behavioral process in psychoanalytic theory can be described in terms of (1) the attachment or investment of energy in an object (*cathexis*) or (2) an obstacle preventing gratification of an instinct (*anticathexis*). Object cathexis is exemplified by emotional attachments (i.e., energy being invested) to other people, one's work, and one's ideals, whereas anticathexis is represented by external or internal barriers preventing immediate reduction of instinctual drives. Thus, the interplay between instinct expression and its inhibition, between cathexis and anticathexis, forms the bulwark of the psychoanalytic motivational system.

Finally, the *impetus* refers to the amount of energy, force, or pressure that is used to satisfy or gratify the instinct. It may be estimated indirectly by observing the number and kinds of obstacles the individual will overcome in seeking a specific goal.

The key to understanding the dynamics of instinctual energy and its expression via object-choices is the concept of *displacement*. This concept represents the shift in behavioral activity by which energy is discharged and tension reduction attained. Displacement occurs when, for some reason, the original object-choice of an instinct cannot be reached. In such instances, the instinct can displace and thus express its energy by focusing upon some object-choice other than the original one. Freud claimed that a wide range of social-psychological phenomena could be understood in terms of displacement of the two primary instincts, sex and aggression. For instance, the socialization of the child may be explained, in part, as a result of the sequential displacement of the sexual drive from one object to another in relation to the demands imposed by parents and society. Similarly, racial prejudice and wars can be attributed to the displacement of the aggression drive. Freud even suggested that the entire fabric of modern civilization is a product of displaced sources of libidinal and aggressive energy. Unable to obtain direct and immediate gratification, human beings have learned to displace their instinctual energy onto persons, things, and activities other than those permitting direct tension release. Thus, elaborate religious, political, economic, and other institutional structures result.

HUMAN DEVELOPMENT VIEWED PSYCHOSEXUALLY

The psychoanalytic theory of development is based on two premises. The first, the *genetic* approach, emphasizes that adult personality is shaped by various types of early childhood experiences. The second is that a certain amount of sexual energy (libido) is present at birth and thereafter progresses through a series of *psychosexual* stages that are rooted in the instinctual processes of the organism.

Freud theorized that there are four universal stages of psychosexual development which are decisive for the formation of personality—*oral, anal, phallic,* and *genital.* A period of *latency,* normally occurring between the ages of 6 or 7 and the onset of puberty, was included by Freud in the overall scheme of development, but, technically speaking, it is not a stage. The first three stages of development extend from birth to 5 years of age and are called *pregenital* stages, since the genital zones of the body have not yet attained a dominant role in personality formation. The fourth stage coincides with the onset of puberty. The names of these stages are based on the region of the body whose stimulation allows for the discharge of libidinal energy.

Each stage is earmarked by a *primary erogenous* zone, a region of the body surface where the inner and outer skin join, that is a focus of sexual excitement. For instance, the lips are more sensitive to stimulation than is the calf of the leg or the back of the hand. Freud suggested that the more protruding the mucous membranes, the more susceptible they are to sensual gratification. The following are considered to be erogenous zones: the ears, eyes, mouth (lips), the male and female sex organs, the breasts, and the anal aperture.

The term "psychosexual" emphasizes that the major factor underlying human development is the sexual instinct as it progresses through the erogenous zones during the early developmental years. According to the theory, at any particular point in the developmental sequence some region of the body seeks objects or activities to produce pleasurable tension. Psychosexual development is a biologically determined sequence, invariant in its order of unfolding and characteristic of all persons regardless of their cultural heritage. The individual's social experiences at each stage supposedly leave some permanent residue in the form of attitudes, traits, and values acquired at that stage.

The logic of this formulation was explained by Freud in terms of two factors— *frustration* and *overindulgence.* In the case of frustration, the child's psychosexual needs (e.g., sucking, biting, or chewing) are thwarted by the mothering one and thus fail to be optimally gratified. In overindulgence, the parents provide little or no challenge for the child to master internal functions (e.g., control over elimination activity) and thus instigate feelings of dependence and incompetence. In either the frustrated or overindulged child, Freud felt that the outcome would be an overinvestment of libido which, depending upon its intensity, would then become manifest in adulthood in the form of residual behaviors (traits, values, attitudes) associated with the psychosexual stage at which these experiences occurred.

A related concept in psychoanalytic theory is that of *regression* (reverting to an earlier stage of psychosexual development and displaying the childish behavior appropriate to that period). For example, an adult faced with a highly stressful situation may regress and deal with it by bursting into tears, sucking the thumb, or wanting a good "stiff" drink. Regression is actually a special case of what Freud called *fixation* (remaining at an early psychosexual stage). Regression and fixation are seen as complementary by Freudians; the probability of regression depends mainly upon the strength of fixation (Fenichel, 1945). Fixations reveal inadequately resolved problems in the developmental stage during which they occur. For example, an 8-year-old boy who persists in sucking his thumb is exhibiting an oral fixation; energy is invested in an activity appropriate to an earlier stage of development. The weaker the resolution of psychosexual conflicts, the more vulnerable the individual is to the forces of regression under conditions of emotional or physical stress later in life. Each individual's personality structure is thus characterized in terms of the stage of psychosexuality he has reached or at which he has become fixated. A variety of adult *character types,* soon to be discussed, are correlated with each of the psychosexual stages of development.

The Oral Stage

The *oral* stage of psychosexual development extends throughout the first year of life. Infants are totally reliant upon others for survival; dependence is their only way of obtaining instinctual gratification. The mouth is obviously the body structure most frequently associated at this time with both reduction of biological drives and pleasurable sensations. Infants are nourished—satisfy their hunger drive—through sucking; at the same time, manipulation of the mouth is pleasurable. Therefore, the oral cavity—including the lips, tongue, and associated structures—becomes their basic focus of activity and interest. It is their prime contact with the social and physical environment, capturing most of their sexual energy. In fact, Freud believed that the mouth remains an important erogenous zone through life. Even in adulthood there are vestiges of oral behavior in the forms of gum chewing, nail biting, smoking, kissing, and overeating—all of which Freudians cite as evidence of the attachment of libido to the oral zone.

Pleasure and sexuality are intertwined in Freud's theory of development. In this context, sexuality refers to a state of excitation which, for the infant, is connected with the intake of food. Accordingly, the first pleasure-producing objects are the mother's breast or the bottle, and the first region of the body that experiences the pleasure of tension reduction is the mouth. Sucking and swallowing thus becomes the prototype of every later sexual gratification. A central task of the infant during this oral-dependent period is to establish general attitudes (rudimentary ones, to be sure) of dependence, independence, trust, and reliance in regard to other people. Since the infant is initially unable to distinguish between its own body and the mother's breast (source of nourishment), the gratification of hunger and the expression of affection are confused during sucking. This confusion accounts for the infant's *egocentrism.* In time, the mother's breast loses value as a love object and is replaced by a part of the infant's own body. The infant sucks its thumb or tongue in order to lessen the tension created by a lack of continuous maternal care.

The oral stage ends when the infant is weaned. It is a central premise of psychoanalytic theory that all infants experience some difficulty in giving up the mother's breast (or the bottle) and its accompanying pleasure. The greater such difficulty becomes, that is, the greater the amount of libido concentrated at the oral stage, the less will be available for dealing with conflicts at subsequent stages.

Freud postulated that the infant who is given either excessive or insufficient amounts of stimulation is likely to become an *oral-passive* personality type in adulthood. This is the person who has an optimistic view of the world, who has established trusting dependent relationships with others, who has come to expect that others will "mother" him or her, and who continually seeks approval at the expense of everything else. His or her psychological adjustment is characterized by gullibility, passivity, immaturity, and excessive dependence.

During the latter half of the first year of life, a second phase of orality commences—the *oral-aggressive* or *oral-sadistic* phase. When the infant acquires teeth, biting and chewing become important means of expressing frustration caused by the mother's absence or by delay of gratification. The infant comes to seek oral satisfaction in aggressive acts such as spitting. Fixation at the oral-sadistic stage is reflected in adults who are argumentative, pessimistic, "bitingly" sarcastic, and often cynical about everything around them. People of this personality type also tend to exploit and dominate others as long as their own needs exist.

The Anal Stage

During the second and third years of life, the focus of libidinal energy shifts from the mouth to the anal region. Young children derive considerable pleasure from both the retention and expulsion of feces and gradually learn to enhance this pleasure by delaying bowel movements (i.e., allowing minor pressure to be exerted against the lower intestine and anal sphincter). Although bowel and bladder control are fundamentally the consequence of neuromuscular maturation, Freud was convinced that the way in which parents carry out toilet training has specific effects on later personality development. With the onset of toilet training the child must learn to distinguish between the demands of the id (pleasure from immediate defecation) and the social restraints imposed by parents (self-control over excretory needs). In fact, Freud claimed that all later forms of self-control and mastery have their origin in the anal stage.

Freud identified two types of parental strategies for dealing with the inevitable frustrations of toilet training. If the parent is harsh and repressive, children may withhold their feces and become constipated. If this tendency to "hold back" becomes excessive and generalizes to other modes of behavior, the child will become an *anal-retentive* personality. Adults presumably manifest strong anal-retentive fixations in character traits of obstinancy, stinginess, orderliness, punctuality, and extreme cleanliness or extreme messiness. This is also the prototype for a variety of "expulsive" traits such as the inability to make fine distinctions or to tolerate confusion and ambiguity.

Alternatively, if the parent pleads with the child to have regular bowel movements and showers the child with praise for so doing, the child will develop an *anal-aggressive* character structure. A person fixated at this level would show traits of cruelty, destructiveness, disorderliness, and hostility. With respect to adult love relationships, such a person would tend to perceive others primarily as objects to be possessed.

The Phallic Stage

During the fourth and fifth years, the child's libidinal interests once again shift to a new erogenous zone of the body, the genitals. During this phallic stage of psychosexual development, children can be observed examining their sex organs, masturbating, and expressing interest in matters pertaining to birth and sex. Although their notions of adult sexuality are usually inaccurate, vague, and poorly formulated, Freud believed that most children understand sexual relations more clearly than parents may suspect. They might have witnessed their parents having intercourse, or perhaps they have fantasized the "primal scene" based on parental remarks or the comments of other children. Freud also felt that most children view sexual intercourse as the father's aggressive act against the mother. It should be emphasized that Freud's description of this stage has proved to be the basis for considerable controversy and misunderstanding of his work. Furthermore, many parents cannot accept the idea that their 4-year-old is a sexual being.

The dominant conflict of the phallic stage is what Freud termed the *Oedipus complex* (called the *Electra complex* in girls). Freud modeled his description of this complex after *Oedipus Rex,* the Greek tragedy by Sophocles, in which Oedipus, king of Thebes, unwittingly murdered his father and committed incest with his mother. When Oedipus realized his sin, he punished himself by tearing out his eyes. Although Freud recognized that the story of *Oedipus Rex* was a Greek myth, he also saw this tragedy as a symbolic description of one of man's greatest psychological conflicts. In effect, the myth represents every child's unconscious desire to possess the opposite-sexed parent and simultaneously dispose of the same-sexed parent. The typical male child does not, of course, actually kill his father nor does he have sexual intercourse with his mother, but Freudians believe that he does have the unconscious wish to do both. Moreover, Freud saw support for the Oedipal conflict in the kinship ties and practices within clans in various primitive societies.

The development and resolution of the Oedipus conflict is somewhat different for boys and girls. The boy's initial love object is the mother or surrogate mother. She has been a prominent source of gratification for him since birth. He wants to possess his mother—to express his feelings toward her as older people that he has observed express sexual feelings. He may, for example, try to seduce his mother by proudly showing her his penis. This act shows the little boy aspiring to his father's role, since the father is perceived as a competitor who prevents him from fulfilling his wish for genital gratification. Hence, the father becomes the chief rival or enemy of his son. The boy is dimly aware of his inferiority in comparison to his father (whose penis is larger); he realizes that the father is not likely to tolerate or accept his son's romantic affections for the mother. The ensuing rivalry results in the boy's fear that his father will hurt him—more specifically, he may earnestly believe that his father will cut off his penis! The boy's fear of retaliation from his father, called *castration anxiety,* forces the boy to renounce his wish to have incestuous relations with his mother.

Somewhere between 5 and 7 years of age, the Oedipus conflict is normally resolved as the boy *represses* (puts out of awareness) his sexual desire for the mother and begins to *identify* with his father (incorporate his father's characteristics). The process of father identification, called *identification with the aggressor,* provides the boy with a conglomerate set of values, morals, attitudes, and sex-related behaviors, all of which delineate for him what it means to be a male. Freud further believed that by identifying with the father, the boy can vicariously keep the mother as a love object, since he now possesses the attributes valued by the mother vis-à-vis the father. But even more important than these aspects of Oedipal resolution, at least in terms of societal norms, is the fact that the boy internalizes his parents' prohibitions and standards of good conduct. It is this specific quality of identification that Freud felt led to the child's development of a superego, i.e., the superego is heir to the resolution of the Oedipus conflict.

The feminine version of the boy's Oedipus complex in Freudian theory is the *Electra complex*. Like the boy, the girl's first object of love is the mother. However, as she moves into the phallic stage she discovers that, unlike her father or brother, she lacks a penis. As soon as the girl makes this anatomical discovery, she wishes she had one. In the language of Freud, the girl develops *penis envy* which, in a certain sense, is the psychological counterpart of castration anxiety in the boy. (Little wonder why Freud is anathema to advocates of the feminist movement!) Thereafter, the girl becomes openly hostile toward her mother, blaming the mother for depriving her of a penis, or holding the mother responsible for taking the penis away from her as punishment for some misdeed. In some instances, Freud suggested that the girl may also devalue her own femininity because of her "defective" condition. Simultaneously, the girl wishes to possess her father, since he has the enviable organ. Believing that she is unable to acquire a penis, the girl seeks other sources of sexual pleasure as penis substitutes. Sexual gratification is focused in the clitoris and, for girls aged five to seven, clitoral masturbation is sometimes accompanied by masculine fantasies in which the girl's clitoris becomes a penis.

Most experts agree that Freud's explanation of the Electra conflict resolution is obscure. One reason suggested is that mothers do not have the same apparent power in the family as fathers and therefore are not as threatening. Another is that since she originally does not have a penis, the girl cannot develop the same intensity of fear as the boy regarding mutilation as retribution for an incestuous desire. For the latter reason, Freud theorized that girls develop a less compulsive sense of morality in adulthood. However one wishes to interpret this matter, Freud suggested that both the girl's resentment toward the mother and attraction toward the father slowly undergo modification and the process of identifying with her mother increasingly dominates the girl's activity. Later, some women desire to have as their firstborn a baby boy, a phenomenon which Freudians interpret as an expression of penis substitution—women's liberation to the contrary.

Much criticism has been leveled against Freud's theory that the Oedipal conflict is biologically rooted and occurs in all human beings. In fact, there is some cross-cultural evidence to support the claim that the Oedipus complex is not universal in the species and that, in some cultures, the rivalry between the boy and his father is based upon the latter's powerful position in the family and not upon sexual jealousy. Moreover, advocates of the feminist movement maintain that the Freudian outlook toward women is not only chauvinistic but absurd. Karen Horney (1937), a leading neo-Freudian analyst, argues that the Freudian interpretation of penis envy (that "anatomy is destiny") does not allow for the social and cultural factors that affect the psychology of women. For Horney and others, what most women really envy is the status which is conferred upon men in our achievement-oriented and competitive society. This argument was also emphasized by Alfred Adler (see Chapter 3) in his later writings.

Adult males fixated at the phallic stage are usually brash, vain, boastful, and ambitious. Phallic types strive to be successful (success symbolizes winning out over the opposite-sexed parent) and attempt at all times to assert their masculinity and virility. Such males have to convince others that they are "real men." In the case of women, Freud noted that phallic fixation results in traits of flirtatiousness, seductiveness, and promiscuity, although the individual may appear naive and innocent in sexual relationships. Alternatively, some women may strive to be superior to men by becoming, to the Freudian view, markedly assertive. Unresolved Oedipal problems were also considered by Freud as the primary source of subsequent neurotic patterns, especially those pertaining to impotence and frigidity.

The Latency Period

Between the ages of 6 or 7 and the onset of adolescence, the child passes through a period of comparative sexual quiescence. During the *latency* period, the libido is *sublimated,* i.e., channeled into nonsexual activities such as intellectual interests, athletics, and peer relationships. Latency can be viewed as a period of preparation for the important growth that will take place in the final psychosexual stage. The decline in sexual interest was regarded by Freud as a purely physiological phenomenon. Latency thus does not qualify as a stage of psychosexual develop-ment since no new erogenous zones emerge and the sexual instincts are presumed dormant. Freud devoted only minor attention to the developmental processes occurring during latency, a strange fact when one considers that it occupies a chronological span of the child's life equally as long as that of the combined preceding stages. It seems to be an intermission for the theorist as much as it is for the child.

The Genital Stage

With the advent of puberty comes a resurgence of sexual and aggressive impulses coupled with an increased awareness of and interest in the opposite sex. The initial phase of the *genital* stage (a period extending from adolescence until death) is brought about by biochemical and physiological changes in the organism. The reproductive organs mature, and the endocrine system secretes hormones that result in secondary sex characteristics (e.g., beards in males, breast development in females). These changes have the combined effect of increasing the adolescent's state of excitability and sexual activity. In other words, the genital stage marks the most complete satisfaction of the sexual instinct.

From a Freudian perspective, all individuals go through a "homosexual" period in early adolescence. The new outburst of sexual energy is directed toward a person of the same sex (e.g., teachers, neighbors, peers) in much the same way that characterized the resolution of the Oedipal conflict. Although overt homosexual behavior is by no means a universal experience of this period, Freud believed that young adolescents prefer the company of their same-sex peers. Gradually, however, the object of libidinal energy shifts to a member of the opposite sex, and courting begins. The "crushes" of early adolescence normally lead to the selection of a marriage partner and the raising of a family.

The genital character epitomizes the ideal type of personality in psychoanalytic theory. This is the person who, having developed mature and responsible social-sexual relationships, experiences satisfaction through heterosexual love. While Freud opposed sexual license, he did condone greater sexual freedom than Viennese bourgeois society permitted. To discharge libido through sexual intercourse makes the physiological control of genital impulses possible; it stems the damming up of instinctual energies and thus culminates in a genuine concern for one's fellow man, free from any residue of guilt or conflict.

Freud believed that in order for people to attain the ideal genital character, they must relinquish the passivity of early childhood days when love, security, physical comfort—indeed all gratifications—were freely given and nothing was expected in return. They must learn to work, postpone gratification, become responsible, and above all, assume a more active role in dealing with life's problems. By contrast, if there have been severe traumatic experiences in early childhood with corresponding libido fixations, adequate adjustment during this stage becomes difficult if not impossible.

THE NATURE OF ANXIETY

Freud's initial interest in the phenomenon of anxiety was motivated by his interest in explaining neurotic symptoms and treating people suffering from them. This interest at first led him to propose that anxiety is a consequence of inadequately discharged libidinal energy. He further theorized that the state of increased tension resulting from blocked libido and undischarged excitation was converted into and manifested by anxiety neuroses. However, as he acquired additional insight while treating neurotics, Freud discovered the inadequacy of this interpretation of anxiety. Accordingly, he eventually proposed that anxiety is an ego function which alerts individuals to sources of impending danger that must be counteracted or avoided (Freud, 1926). As such, anxiety enables the individual to react to threatening situations in an adaptive way.

Where Anxiety Originates

According to this later conception, the first source of human anxiety lies in the neonate's inability to master internal and external excitations. Since infants cannot control their new world, a diffuse sense of impending peril overwhelms them. This situation creates a traumatic condition known as *primary anxiety,* the essence of which is exemplified by the birth process.

Other psychoanalytic theorists have suggested that the "birth trauma" is the source of all subsequent feelings of anxiety. Otto Rank (1929) believed that the trauma of birth forms a reservoir of anxiety, portions of which are expended throughout life. Biological separation from the mother's womb was seen by Rank as the most critical aspect of this trauma. Freud, in contrast, accepted the psychic shock attributed to mother-infant separation as only one source of anxiety. He modified Rank's theory by asserting that the birth process is the prototype rather than the original source of human anxiety. He felt that the birth process leaves no indelible imprint upon the infant's psyche. Thus, in Freud's view, the experience of biological separation from the mother acquires a traumatic quality so that later separations (e.g., being left alone, being left in the dark, or discovering a stranger in the place of one's mother) produce strong anxiety reactions. Such a feeling of distress and helplessness is apparent in the birth trauma, in weaning, and later on in castration anxiety; all of these experiences lead to increased tension and apprehension.

Types of Anxiety: In What Ways Do People Feel Anxious?

Based on the sources of threat to the ego (the outside environment, the id, and the superego), psychoanalytic theory identifies three types of anxiety.

Realistic Anxiety   The emotional response to threat and/or perception of real dangers in the external environment (e.g., poisonous snakes, wild animals, earthquakes, final examinations) is called *realistic*, or *objective*, anxiety. It is essentially synonymous with fear and may have a debilitating effect on the individual's ability to cope effectively with the source of danger. Realistic anxiety abates as the source of threat subsides. In general, it helps to ensure self-preservation.

Neurotic Anxiety   An emotional response to the threat that id impulses will become conscious is called *neurotic* anxiety. It is caused by the fear that the ego will be unable to control the id instincts, particularly those of a sexual or aggressive nature. The small child quickly learns that active discharge of his or her libidinal or destructive urges will be met by threats of retaliation from parents or other social agents. For this reason, neurotic anxiety is initially experienced as realistic anxiety, since punishment did originally derive from an external force. *Ego defenses* (to be explained shortly) are thus deployed to hold down the child's id impulses, and they surface only in the form of general apprehension. It is only when the instinctual impulses of the id threaten to break through the ego controls that neurotic anxiety occurs.

Moral Anxiety   When the ego is threatened by punishment from the superego, the ensuing emotional response is called *moral* anxiety. It occurs whenever the id strives toward active expression of immoral thoughts or acts and the superego responds with feelings of shame, guilt, and self-condemnation. Moral anxiety derives from an objective fear of parental punishment for doing or thinking something that violates the perfectionistic dictates of the superego. Hence, it directs behavior into activities that are acceptable to the individual's conscience. The subsequent development of the superego leads to *social anxiety,* which is evident in concerns over exclusion from peer-group membership because of unacceptable attitudes or actions. Freud further believed that anxiety originating from within the superego ultimately extended to fear of death and the anticipation of an afterlife of punishment for one's transgressions.

Ego Defense Mechanisms

The major psychodynamic functions of anxiety are to help the individual avoid conscious recognition of unacceptable instinctual impulses and to allow impulse gratification only indirectly. *Ego defense mechanisms* help to carry out these functions as well as to protect the person from overwhelming anxiety. Freud defined an ego defense mechanism as a strategy used by the individual to defend against open expression of id impulses and opposing superego pressures. He suggested that the ego reacts to the threatened breakthrough of id impulses in either of two ways: (1) by blocking the impulse from expression in conscious behavior, or (2) by distorting it to such a degree that the original intensity is markedly reduced or deflected.

All defense mechanisms share two common features: (1) they operate at an unconscious level and are therefore self-deceptive and (2) they distort one's perception of reality, so as to make anxiety less threatening to the individual. Freud believed that persons rarely rely upon a single defense to protect themselves from anxiety; it is more common for people to use several mechanisms of this type. Some examples of ego defense mechanisms follow.

Sublimation   According to Freud, *sublimation* is an ego defense that enables the individual adaptively to divert impulses so that they may be expressed via socially approved thoughts or actions. Sublimation is considered to be the only healthy, constructive strategy against objectionable impulses because it allows the ego to change the aim or object (or both) of impulses without inhibiting their expression. The instinctual energy is diverted into other channels of expression— ones that society considers acceptable. For example, if during development, masturbation becomes too anxiety-provoking to a young boy, he may sublimate his impulses into a socially approved substitute activity, such as football, swimming, or other sporting endeavor. Or a person with a great deal of unrecognized hostility may become a butcher, able to spend an unconscious lifetime symbolically cutting up the people he hates.

Freud claimed that the sublimation of sexual instincts served as the prime instigator for great advances in Western culture and knowledge. As he said: "The sublimation of the sexual motive is an especially conspicuous feature of cultural evolution; sublimation alone makes it possible for the zealous scientific, artistic, and ideological activities which play so important a part in our civilized lives (Cohen, 1969, p. 34)."

Repression   Freud regarded *repression* as the primary ego defense, not only because it serves as a basis for more elaborate mechanisms of defense but also because it involves the most direct approach in avoiding anxiety. Sometimes described as selective forgetting, repression completely obstructs the expression of unconscious sexual and aggressive impulses so that they cannot be admitted to awareness, at least as long as they remain objectionable to the person. Hence, no tension reduction is permitted. As a result of repression, individuals are neither aware of their own anxiety-provoking conflicts nor do they remember emotionally traumatic past events. For example, a person who has suffered a terrifying personal failure may through repression become unable to recount the experience.

The relief from anxiety provided by repression is not without cost. Freud theorized that repressed impulses remain active in the unconscious and require continuous psychic energy to prevent their emergence into consciousness. This persistent drain on the ego's resources may seriously limit the amount of energy available for more constructive, self-enhancing, and creative behavior. However, the constant striving of repressed impulses for overt expression may find momentary gratification through dreams, jokes, slips of the tongue, and other manifestations of what Freud called the "psychopathology of everyday life." Moreover, from the Freudian perspective, repression is centrally involved in all neurotic behavior, psychosomatic ailments (e.g., ulcers), and psychosexual disorders (e.g., impotence, frigidity). Whether in the realm of normal or abnormal behavior, the importance of repression in psychoanalytic theory is undeniable.

Projection As a defense mechanism, *projection* ranks next to repression in terms of theoretical importance. It refers to the process of unconsciously attributing one's own unacceptable impulses, attitudes, and behaviors to other people or to the environment. Projection thus enables us to blame someone or something else for our own shortcomings. The golf player who muffs a shot and looks critically at his club is engaging in a primitive projection. On a different level, the young woman who is unaware of her own sexual strivings but sees everyone she dates as attempting to seduce her is also projecting. Finally, there is the classic example of the student who inadequately prepares for an examination and then attributes his or her failing grade to an unfair test, the cheating of others, or a professor who failed to explain the points at issue. Projection has also been used as an explanation of social prejudice and scapegoating, since ethnic and racial stereotypes provide a convenient target for the attribution of one's own negative personal characteristics (Adorno, Frenkel-Brunswick, Levinson, and Sanford, 1950).

Displacement In *displacement,* when viewed specifically as a defense mechanism (as opposed to the more general meaning of the term described earlier in this chapter), the expression of an instinctual impulse is redirected from a more threatening person or object to a less threatening one. For example, the student angered by his professor instead swears at his roommate. Or the child scolded by her parents proceeds to hit her little sister, kick her dog, or smash her toys. Displacement is also observed in an adult's hypersensitivity to minor annoyances, e.g., the wife who is criticized by an overdemanding employer reacts with violent rage to the slightest provocation by her husband or children. She fails to recognize that, as objects of her hostility, they are simply substitutes for the boss. In each of these instances, the original object of the impulse has been replaced by one that is far less threatening to the individual. A less common form of displacement is *turning against the self,* whereby hostile impulses toward others are redirected to oneself, producing feelings of depression and self-depreciation.

Rationalization   Another important way in which the ego attempts to cope with frustration and anxiety is to distort reality and thus protect self-esteem. *Rationalization* refers to "fallacious reasoning" in that it misrepresents irrational behavior in order to make it appear rational and thus justifiable to oneself and others. One's mistakes, poor judgments, and failures can be explained away through the magic of rationalization. One frequently employed type, known as "sour grapes," is based on one of Aesop's fables about a fox who couldn't reach the grapes he desired and thus concluded that they were sour anyway. People rationalize in the same way, as in the example of the student who is refused a date by a female classmate and consoles himself by concluding that she wasn't very attractive anyway.

Reaction Formation   Sometimes the ego can control or defend against the expression of a forbidden impulse by consciously expressing its opposite. This is known as *reaction formation.* As a defensive process it operates in two steps: first, the unacceptable impulse is repressed; next, the opposite is expressed on a conscious level. Reaction formation is especially evident in socially acceptable behavior that is compulsive, exaggerated, and rigid. For instance, a woman threatened by her own conscious sexual desires becomes a crusader to disallow pornographic movies in her town. She may also actively picket particular movie houses or write to production companies about the degrading state of films today.

Regression   Still another common defense mechanism that we use to defend ourselves against anxiety, *regression* involves a reversion to an earlier stage of psychosexual development or to a mode of expression that is simpler and more childlike. It is a way of alleviating anxiety by retreating to an earlier period of life that was more secure and pleasant. Readily observed forms of regression displayed by adults include losing their temper, pouting, sulking, giving people "the silent treatment," talking baby talk, destroying property, rebelling against authority, driving fast and recklessly, and similar childish behaviors. Needless to say, while it temporarily reduces anxiety, regression often leaves unresolved the cause of the initial anxiety.

Regression and the other ego defenses described here represent ways in which the psyche protects itself from internal and external tension. In every case psychological energy is expended to maintain the defense, thereby limiting the flexibility and strength of the ego. Moreover, to the extent they are working effectively, defenses create a distorted picture of our needs, fears, and aspirations. It logically follows that while defense mechanisms may be found in healthy individuals, their excessive use is usually an indication of serious underlying psychological problems.

Having concluded our discussion of Freud's central theoretical concepts, let us consider the basic assumptions about human nature that underlie psychoanalytic theory.

FREUD'S BASIC ASSUMPTIONS CONCERNING HUMAN NATURE

The unifying theme of this book is that all personality theorists hold certain basic assumptions about human nature. Furthermore, such assumptions, while neither directly provable or unprovable, help delineate the essential differences and similarities among the various theories. Now that the core concepts of psycho-analytic theory have been discussed, Freud's position on the nine assumptions presented in Chapter 1 can be examined. His position on the respective dimensions (depicted in Figure 2-2) is as follows.

Freedom–Determinism   Freud was a strict biological determinist. He as-sumed that all human events (actions, thoughts, feelings, aspirations) are governed by laws and determined by powerful instinctual forces, notably sex and aggression. Thus, human beings are seen as essentially mechanistic; they are governed by the same natural laws that apply to the behavior of other organisms. If this were not so, a rigorous psychological science could not exist.

In such a theoretical system, there is no room for concepts such as free will, choice, personal responsibility, volition, spontaneity, and self-determination (i.e., people do not have free choice). Freud clearly recognized the individual's overpowering illusion of freedom, yet he insisted that persons are incapable of actually "choosing" between alternative courses of action, and that their behavior is determined by unconscious forces of which they can never be fully aware. The clearest examples of determinism noted by Freud include misplacing personal possessions, forgetting familiar names and addresses, and so-called "slips" of the

	Strong	Moderate	Slight	Midrange	Slight	Moderate	Strong	
Freedom							■	Determinism
Rationality							■	Irrationality
Holism		■						Elementalism
Constitutionalism		■						Environmentalism
Changeability							■	Unchangeability
Subjectivity			■					Objectivity
Proactivity		■						Reactivity
Homeostasis	■							Heterostasis
Knowability		■						Unknowability

Figure 2-2   Freud's position on the nine basic assumptions concerning human nature. (The shaded areas indicate the degree to which the theorist favors one of the two bipolar extremes.)

tongue and pen. He interpreted such occurrences as revealing something of the person's unconscious mental processes.

Rationality–Irrationality   In Freud's view, people are basically irrational. They are motivated by irrational, almost uncontrollable, instincts which are largely outside the sphere of conscious awareness. While a degree of rationality exists within the ego, this part of personality is ultimately subservient to the demands of the id. The only real glimmer of rationality that Freud detected in humanity resided in his conception of psychoanalytic therapy as a vehicle for systematic personality growth. Insight into unconscious motivation via psychoanalysis would pave the road for mastery and control over oneself. His credo—*where id was, there ego shall be*—reflects his optimism that the forces of reason can bring primitive and irrational drives somewhat under conscious control. In spite of his conviction that a higher degree of rationality could be attained through psychoanalysis, Freud's theory of personality is firmly anchored to the importance of irrational elements in human behavior. The idea of a rational person in control of his or her destiny is nothing but a myth in this view.

Holism–Elementalism   Freud leaned toward a holistic view of persons, believing that they must be studied as totalities in order to be understood. Central to his theory is the portrayal of the individual in terms of id-ego-superego interactions and interdependencies. The person's behavior cannot be fully grasped without reference to the dynamic interplay of these three basic structures of mental life. Furthermore, while Freud believed that these structures might ultimately be reduced to a more elementalistic level of analysis (probably biological or neurological), he never attempted this task himself. Finally, Freud relied almost exclusively upon the clinical method in developing his theory, a method which stresses the unity of personality.

Constitutionalism–Environmentalism   Several of Freud's early concepts (e.g., psychic energy, instincts, pleasure principle) were derived from neuroanatomy and neurophysiology (Weinstein, 1968). Psychoanalytic theory never substantially altered its course from this beginning and, on the whole, Freud must be regarded as having adopted a constitutional position concerning human nature. As has been seen, the all-powerful id is the inherited, constitutional basis of personality structure and development. In addition, he conceived of psychosexual development as an invariable, biologically determined sequence characteristic of all persons regardless of their cultural heritage. What human beings are, then, is very much a result of innate biological hereditary factors.

Conversely, Freud emphasized the importance of the person's early environmental history for understanding behavior. He stressed that parental influence during early childhood years had profound, irreversible effects upon subsequent personality growth. Moreover, the ego evolves only to meet environmental demands with which the id cannot deal, while the superego is exclusively a product of the social world. The net importance of environmental factors, however, is secondary to biologically rooted instincts in psychoanalytic theory.

Changeability–Unchangeability   Perhaps more than any other personologist presented in this text, Freud was strongly committed to the unchangeability assumption. Indeed, his entire theory of human development is based upon the genetic approach, which emphasizes that adult personality is shaped by various types of early childhood experiences. As you will recall, Freud depicted the individual as progressing through distinct psychosexual stages; adult personality structure can be described in terms of the psychosexual stage that the person has reached or became fixated upon. Thus, each individual's basic character structure is formed early in life and persists unaltered into the adult years.

Although Freud believed that a person's unique character type is formed in early childhood, he did consider psychoanalytic therapy to be beneficial for those persons seeking to gain insight into the sources of their current problems. By "getting in touch" and learning something new about past experiences in their lives, such persons can learn to cope more adaptively with present and future problems. However, Freud also recognized that psychoanalytic therapists are dealing with personality and behavior patterns that have been repeated and reinforced throughout their patients' lives. Not only must such patients unlearn faulty styles of behavior, they must also acquire new ones, which may be likened to the acquisition of a new skill such as tennis or a foreign language. These goals, while not impossible, are extremely difficult and painful to attain, particularly if the patients, for reasons they only dimly recognize, fight every step of the way. The weapons they use are the same ones they used in childhood to fight their parents' efforts to socialize them, e.g., negativism, domination, helplessness, hostility, and despair. Accordingly, even in psychoanalytic therapy, there is very little optimism about the possibility of real and sustained personality change in adulthood. For Freud, *observed* changes in people's behavior are more often than not merely that—superficial modifications which leave the core structure untouched.

Subjectivity–Objectivity   Freud saw persons as living in a subjective world of feelings, emotions, perceptions, and meanings. While he recognized the "private world" of an individual as an important part of personality, Freud also considered it to be a guide to something else—objective conditions like traumas and repressions, and universal human drives. Thus, psychoanalytic theory claims that a person's uniqueness is partly determined by external realities, e.g., parental attitudes and behavior, sibling relationships, social norms. Once the individual is exposed to these objective conditions, however, they persist experientially to form the permanent world of unique, subjective meanings within which he or she resides. Thus, while Freud leans somewhat toward subjectivity, this assumption does not play an important role in his theory.

Proactivity–Reactivity   Concerning the question of the locus of causality in explaining human behavior, B. F. Skinner (1954) pointed out that Freud's theoretical account of human actions followed a traditional pattern of looking *inside* the person for the causes of behavior. Consequently, in this sense only, Freud must be construed as assuming a proactive view of human nature. As will become evident in subsequent chapters, however, Freud's proactivity takes a form markedly different from that adopted by humanistic or phenomenological theorists.

The essence of Freud's proactive position is clearly reflected in his concept of motivation: the locus of casuality for all human behavior is found in the energy flowing from the id and its instincts. People do not consciously generate their own behavior; rather, the sexual and aggressive instincts generate the psychic energy which underlies the variety and multiplicity of human actions. Freudian man, then, is not proactive in the full sense of the term. He is reactive to the extent that all instincts have external objects that operate as environmental stimuli to elicit behavior. For example, sex "objects" in the environment call forth the activity of the sexual instinct, thus suggesting shades of reactivity within the theory. Weighing all factors, Freud's position on this assumption seems best described as a moderate inclination toward proactivity.

Homeostasis–Heterostasis   Freud believed that all human behavior was regulated by the tendency to reduce excitations created by unpleasant bodily tensions. The id instincts constantly clamor for expression, and people behave to reduce the tensions generated by this instinctual energy source. Thus, instead of seeking growth and self-actualization, individuals are actually driven to seek a tensionless state of nirvana, a view of motivation clearly reflecting a homeostatic position. In psychoanalytic theory, a person is basically an id-driven "instinct satisfier" who never quests for conditions that would upset homeostatic balance.

Knowability–Unknowability   There are many indications that Freud was committed to the belief that human nature is ultimately knowable in scientific terms. For example, he insisted that people obey the same laws of nature as any other living organisms. Likewise, he viewed human beings as biologically determined organisms whose deepest motivations can be uncovered by the scientifically based techniques of psychoanalysis. To be sure, Freud never considered psychoanalysis as a complete theory of personality (Nuttin, 1956). However, he was convinced that psychoanalysis definitely had shed and would continue to shed substantial light upon the true nature of humans. It is likely that Freud's training in natural science, coupled with his personal rejection of the validity of mysticism, religion, and other nonscientific belief systems, fostered his conviction that science holds the key to the enigma of human nature.

Thus we conclude our assessment of Freud's position on the nine basic assumptions regarding human nature. Let us now consider some illustrative empirical studies stimulated by the theory.

EMPIRICAL VALIDATION OF
PSYCHOANALYTIC CONCEPTS

Having studied Freud, students inevitably ask "What scientific evidence is there to support psychoanalytic theory?" Insofar as a theory is regarded as an empirically valid conceptualization of the phenomenon it presumes to explain, it is only natural to expect the scientific testing of hypotheses derived from that theory. In the years that followed his death, personologists all but totally ignored the objective and systematic verification of Freud's central concepts. A quick overview of the history of psychoanalysis as a method of therapy explains in good part why this was so. In Freud's time psychoanalysts generally were not interested in the use of research methods for investigating the theory. In fact, Freud himself did not stress empirical validation as do most psychologists today. When Saul Rosenzweig (1941), an American psychologist, wrote to Freud to tell him of his laboratory studies of the psychoanalytic concept of repression, Freud wrote back that psychoanalytic concepts were based on a wealth of clinical observations and thus were not in need of independent experimental verification. This entire antiresearch attitude was further fostered by the fact that experimental psychology, still in its infancy, had little to offer. Even today, despite their formal training in the biological sciences, some practicing analysts oppose the use of research techniques (Hilgard, 1968). Many believe that the only method appropriate to verify psychoanalytic hypotheses is the clinical interview, that is, the verbalizations of patients undergoing intensive, long-term therapy. Thus, the primary source of evidence for determining the "truthfulness" of psychoanalytic theory until recently has been the systematic accumulation of patients' reconstructed life histories. Most analysts consider the patient's reported experiences as highly relevant confirmations of the theory.

Although clinical observations and case histories have served as the main methods for developing and testing psychoanalytic formulations (indeed, the approach relied upon most by Freud himself), there are several deficiencies associated with their use. Foremost is the fact that despite all efforts to remain objective in the therapeutic setting, the analyst is not a truly impartial observer. Nor does clinical observation adequately meet the experimentalist's demands for objectivity. Silverman has aptly summarized the main difficulties in accepting clinical data as the basis for empirically supporting psychoanalytic theory:

> (a) psychoanalytic reports do not usually provide detailed verbatim clinical material that would allow others to examine the bases for the inferences that are drawn; (b) such material is rarely subjected to a structured replicable assessment procedure; (c) care is not usually exercised in the collection and evaluation of the data to minimize the effects of bias. But even if these steps were regularly taken, clinical data could be viewed only as "soft" support for psychoanalytic theory. . . . the clinical situation is severely limited in its being able to exercise proper investigatory controls—that is, in holding constant all variables but the particular one(s) the clinician wants to study and in using control interventions. Thus, such data must be supplemented and complemented by data from more formal research procedures that are capable of exercising these controls (Silverman, 1976, p. 622).

Another methodological shortcoming derives from the professional training of most analysts. Such training, which necessarily includes a self-analysis plus intensive supervision by a seasoned training analyst during the initial stages of practice, commonly results in an unusually strong philosophical and personal commitment to the assumptions of Freudian theory. This commitment predisposes analysts to bias their interpretations of the patient's disturbance and its causation. Complicating the validity of clinical observations even further is the patient's own bias. Patients often know what is proper and improper to report during therapy sessions—hence, they may subtly seek approval by presenting experiential material which conforms to the analyst's expectations. Collectively, these deficiencies are potent sources for the "self-fulfilling prophecy" concerning the validity of Freud's observations. Given such limitations, it is understandable why most psychologists refuse to consider individual case reports of therapeutic effectiveness as sufficient evidence for Freud's conceptions of personality

The major pitfall confronting the personologist interested in testing Freudian theory is that there is no known way of replicating clinical observations and findings in a controlled experiment. A second major stumbling block in determining the validity of psychoanalysis is the lack of operational definitions of theoretical concepts, i.e., the concepts are often defined in a way that prevents the clear derivation and testing of hypotheses. This does not mean that psychoanalysis is an invalid theory. Rather, it means that, at present, there are no commonly agreed upon methods and procedures by which the theory can be objectively evaluated. Finally, psychoanalytic theory has a "postdictive" character. In other words, it more adequately explains past events than predicts future ones.

Conversely, under certain conditions psychoanalytic concepts can be empirically tested. Sarnoff explains how this might be achieved:

> Since Freudian theory contains a multitude of concepts, the first step in any contribution toward its experimental evaluation requires a researcher to choose a particular concept for focal study. Then, the chosen concept must be clarified in linguistic terms that define its particular psychological properties explicitly and precisely. Finally, the semantically defined concept must be theoretically related to a behavioral or experiential phenomenon by stating how and under what conditions the postulated relationship may be observed to obtain (1971, p. 29).

Where, then, can one look for valid evidence pertaining to psychoanalytic theory? With some justification, personologists debunk most animal studies on the grounds of artificiality and oversimplification of conceptually complicated processes. Basically, the search for adequate evidence has taken the direction of developing experimental analogs (i.e., simulating theoretical concepts in a laboratory context) of psychoanalytic constructs. No attempt is made here to cover exhaustively the literally thousands of studies pertaining to Freudian theory. Instead, the focus is on illustrative and representative research currently being done. Accordingly, four studies characteristic of the kinds of ongoing investigations of major psychoanalytic concepts will be examined: studies of (1) repression, (2) dreams, (3) humor, and (4) first-born preference.

Repression in a Laboratory   Repression is a key concept for most psychoanalysts and there has been more experimental research on it than perhaps any other single concept in Freudian theory (Mischel, 1976; Sarason, 1972). One aspect of repression has to do with the notion that forgetting occurs as a function of unpleasant associations. Glucksberg and King (1967) demonstrated by way of a laboratory analog of repression that ideas connected with unpleasant events are especially likely to be forgotten. These investigators hypothesized that if a given word is associated with an unpleasant event (e.g., electric shock), the saying or thinking of an associated word will evoke fear. Translating this hypothesis into testable terms, Glucksberg and King predicted that the pairing of electric shocks with specific words would cause differential forgetting of previously learned words.

The stimulus materials used in this experiment consisted of a paired-associate list, the first word (A) being a nonsense syllable and the second (B) being an English word. A chained word (C) was assumed to form a link between the English word in the paired-associate list and a second list of English words (D). For example, if the A-B pair were DAX-memory, then the B-C association was memory-mind, and the C-D association, mind-brain. The association between A and D was thus made by way of B-C and C-D verbal links.

Initially, sixteen male undergraduates learned the A-B paired-associate list (ten paired associates) by the method of anticipation. Learning of this list continued until each subject correctly anticipated all pairs for one perfect trial. Then, electrodes were placed on the subject's fingers. Words in the second list (D) were then projected on a screen, with three of the words being accompanied by an electric shock. Subjects were instructed to press a key-operated buzzer whenever one of the shock words appeared. The presentation of words in the second list continued until each subject had correctly anticipated shock for three consecutive trials. Thereafter, subjects were given a single relearning trial of the A-B list of words. The chained words (C) were never presented since they were assumed to occur as implicit associative responses linking the B words with the D words. The measure of "motivated forgetting" was based on the percentage of shock-associated B words forgotten relative to the percentage of control B words (nonassociated shock words) forgotten during relearning. The results were in accordance with Freud's model of motivated forgetting. Specifically, Glucksberg and King found that significantly more of the shock-associated B words were forgotten than were control B words (29.2 percent of the shock-associated A-B pairs as compared with 6.3 percent of the A-B control words). It was found that no subject was better able to recall the shocked words (D) of the second list than he was able to recall the control, nonshocked words. This experiment demonstrates that the pairing of electric shocks with associates of memory items significantly interferes with the subsequent recall of such memory items, i.e., memory items which are associated with an unpleasant event are more readily forgotten (repressed) than are affectively neutral memory items.

Finally, as intriguing as this study is from an experimental perspective, it is only fair to note that Freud himself would have probably regarded it as "typically American" and a long way from his clinical concept of repression. Nonetheless, such empirical investigations of Freudian concepts must continue to be undertaken if psychoanalysis is to gain genuine scientific respectability (e.g., Silverman, 1976).

Castration Anxiety and Penis Envy in Dreams Hall and Van de Castle (1965) have reported a study based on Freud's dream theory. Since dreams are characterized as "the royal road to the unconscious," they reasoned that manifestations of the castration complex would be detectable in dreams. Specifically, it was hypothesized that "Male dreamers will report more dreams expressive of castration anxiety than they will dreams involving castration wishes and penis envy while the pattern will be reversed for females, i.e., they will report more dreams containing expressions of castration anxiety (p. 21)."

This hypothesis was tested by instructing male and female undergraduates to maintain a record of their nocturnal dreams as part of a class project. A scoring manual was developed by the investigators in which specific criteria for castration anxiety, castration wish, and penis envy were set forth. The criteria for scoring castration anxiety dreams involved such themes as actual or threatened loss, removal, or injury to a specific part of the body, inability or difficulty in using the penis, the changing of a man into a woman, and actual or threatened injury to or loss of an object or animal belonging to the dreamer. The criteria for castration wish were the same, except that they do not occur to the dreamer but to another person in the dream. Finally, the system for scoring penis envy included the changing of a woman into a man, envy or admiration for a man's physical characteristics, and the acquisition of objects that have male characteristics. Insofar as scoring dream content for such themes is partly based on subjective interpretation, the researchers had to demonstrate adequate agreement among scorers. Hall and Van de Castle reported interjudge agreement scores higher than 87 percent on each of the three variables considerd here. Consistent with Freudian theory, their results indicated that men evidenced significantly more dreams about castration anxiety than did women, and women reported significantly more dreams expressive of castration wish and penis envy than did men. These findings were interpreted as supporting the theoretical validity of the castration complex.

Why We Laugh   Laughter and humor have always been recognized as a salient feature of human experience. Perhaps the most influential theory of humor to date is that proposed by Freud in *Jokes and Their Relation to the Unconscious* (1905). Briefly stated, Freud theorized that normally inhibited sexual or aggressive impulses are vicariously released through socially sanctioned jokes. Pent-up instinctual energies find expression in the form of laughter. He also believed that pleasure gained from humor depends upon a sudden reduction of inner tension or anxiety. The anxiety arises from intrapsychic conflict concerning the direct expression of an unacceptable wish or impulse activated by the content of most sexual and aggressive types of humor.

If, as Freud postulated, humor depends on relief from a state of anticipated discomfort due to heightened emotional arousal, then the following hypothesis should hold: "the greater the subject's arousal prior to relief, the greater should be the judged humor (Shurcliff, 1968, p. 360)." In a cleverly designed experiment, Shurcliff tested the validity of this hypothesis. Procedurally, he established three levels of anxiety (the index of arousal) by giving separate groups of male students different instructions and directions concerning a laboratory task. The groups were designated as low, moderate, and high anxiety, respectively. Subjects in each group were brought to the laboratory individually and informed that they were to take part in an experiment concerned with their reaction to small animals. During the first phase of the experiment three carrying cages, the first two containing white rats, were made clearly visible to the subject. The third cage was deliberately placed behind the other two in such a way that the subject could not see into it prior to opening the cage door. At this point, the description of and instructions for the experimental task were systematically varied for the different groups. Subjects in the *low anxiety* condition were told that their task was simply to pick up the rat in the third cage and hold him for five seconds. The experimenter then said, "These rats are bred to be docile and easy to handle, and I don't think you will have any trouble with this task (p. 361)." Subjects in the *moderate anxiety* condition were shown two slides which ostensibly contained blood samples from the rats in the two visible cages and were told that their task was to obtain a blood sample from the rat in the third cage and place it on a fresh slide. Specific directions for this procedure were then given, including the use of a hypodermic needle, and it was explained to the subject that the task was easier than it looked. Finally, subjects in the *high anxiety* condition were told that their task was to obtain a blood sample from the third rat, but they were also shown plastic bottles which supposedly contained blood from the first two rats and warned that the procedure of extracting blood was extremely dangerous because the rat might bite them.

Following the task instructions, subjects in each condition reached into the third cage and, with considerable astonishment and relief, discovered a toy rat! They were then given a questionnaire in which they rated the humor of the event that had just occurred as well as the amount of anxiety they had felt prior to discovering the toy rat (a check on the fact that the three groups did represent different levels of experimentally induced anxiety). Shurcliff's results are in strong agreement with the relief theory of humor appreciation. Specifically, it was found that the greater the subjects' anxiety prior to holding the third "rat," the more humorous they judged the event to be.

Preference for a Male versus a Female Child   Freud, as you will recall, theorized that women of all cultures desire to have a boy as their first-born child. The logic underlying this contention is that having a male child symbolizes the possession of a penis and, as such, represents the woman's final resolution of the Electra complex. A study conducted by Hammer (1970) attempts to address this aspect of psychosexual theory. This investigator simply asked single and married college students, and married noncollege adults, the question: "If you knew for sure that you could have only one child, would you prefer that child to be a male or a female? (Hammer, 1970, p. 54)." The results are presented in Table 2-1. It is evident that the data for the noncollege women (admittedly a small sample) do not support the Freudian hypothesis, since 70 percent of the subjects said they would prefer a girl. On the other hand, results for the unmarried and married college students (the former of which is a relatively large sample) may lend some support to Freud's contention. Seventy-eight percent of the former and 73 percent of the latter expressed a preference for a boy.

But how are we to interpret these data in theoretical terms? Like many other

Table 2-1   Preference for Gender of Child as a Function of Sex of Adult Respondents

Preference	Unmarried college students		Married college students		Married noncollege adults	
	Men	Women	Men	Women	Men	Women
Boy	90%	78%	83%	73%	90%	30%
	(156)	(184)	(24)	(15)	(16)	(8)
Girl	10%	22%	17%	27%	10%	70%
	(18)	(52)	(5)	(6)	(2)	(18)
Total number =	174	236	29	21	18	26

Source: Adapted from Hammer, 1970, p. 55.

empirical attempts to tackle psychoanalytic concepts, Hammer's study highlights the difficulties inherent in drawing clear-cut conclusions from such empirical efforts. For example, a hard-nosed Freudian would regard this type of study as irrelevant to the theory since it is based upon individual self-reports. In fact, a Freudian might easily argue that the woman who said she preferred a girl was actually repressing her real desires! Even if one replicated this finding many times with different groups of women, the Freudian might still contend that the women participating in these studies were repressing their true desires. And in any event, aren't there other plausible reasons why some women would prefer a male child, aside from resolving the Electra complex, e.g., family pressures, cultural role expectations, etc.? Thus, while the data from such investigations may be clearly presented, the theoretically relevant conclusions to be drawn from them are far from clear.

Taken collectively, the four investigations described here illustrate how psychoanalytic concepts might be subjected to empirical test. They also reveal something of the breadth of research interest in Freud's concepts. However, careful analysis of these kinds of investigations indicates that many do not serve as direct, unequivocal tests of the particular theoretical concept in question. Freud's theory is extremely difficult to verify. As we see it, the major scientific question for psychoanalytic theory is whether its concepts can be translated into operational procedures which allow for unequivocal test or whether it will eventually yield to another theory that is equally comprehensive and functionally significant but more amenable to systematic investigation and verification. Put differently, psychoanalytic theory, like any complex theory that claims to be scientific, must constantly seek new data, using a variety of research methods, and then evolve accordingly.

APPLICATION: PSYCHOANALYTIC THERAPY— PROBING THE UNCONSCIOUS

Psychoanalytic theory has been applied to the understanding of virtually every area of human behavior. Such diverse fields as anthropology, art, criminology, history, economics, education, philosophy, sociology, and religion have felt its impact.

Without exaggeration, there is no other theory in modern-day psychology that is as manifold in its range of concrete applications as psychoanalysis. To be sure, psychoanalysis has not escaped bitter criticism from contemporary personologists. For example, many believe that in Freud's theory there is an overemphasis upon the negative, pathological side of human life accompanied by a deemphasis upon the positive, healthy, self-actualizing aspects of human existence. However, even those who reject Freud's theory acknowledge his many seminal contributions to the solution of human problems. It is to one of these, perhaps the most significant and far-reaching application of psychoanalytic theory to date, that we now turn.

Freudian Techniques: What Happens in Psychoanalysis

Consideration of psychotherapy seems appropriate since Freud's clinical experience with neurotic patients was the basis for his theoretical system. In fact, Freud adamantly insisted that his concepts could only be properly evaluated by psychoanalytic patients or psychoanalytic therapists: "The teachings of psychoanalysis are based on an incalculable number of observations and experiences, and no one who has not repeated those observations upon himself and upon others is in a position to arrive at an independent judgment of it (1964, p. ix)." Today there are a substantial number of psychoanalysts who practice therapy strictly in accordance with Freud's theoretical views and methods of treatment. In addition, there are many other mental health workers who are distinctly psychoanalytically oriented in their professional activities. To see what a Freudian therapist actually does, consider the following brief case history:

> A young man, 18 years of age, is referred to the psychoanalyst by his family physician. It seems that, for the past year, the young man has experienced a variety of symptoms such as headaches, dizziness, heart palpitations, waking up in the middle of the night with extreme anxiety—all of these pervaded by a constant, periodically overwhelming fear of death. Basically, he thinks that he has a brain tumor and is going to die. Yet, in spite of numerous medical tests and examinations, no physical basis for his symptoms can be found. The physician finally concludes that the "symptoms" of the young man (let's call him Albert) are probably psychologically based.
>
> Albert arrives at the analyst's office, located two blocks away from his home, accompanied by his parents. He describes his problems and depicts his relationships with his parents as "rosy," although he feels that his father is "a little on the strict side" (He doesn't let Albert go out on week nights, makes him come in by 11 P.M. on Saturday nights, and successfully broke off Albert's relationship with a girl one year ago because he thought Albert was getting "too close" to her). But Albert displays no conscious resentment about any of this, instead describing the events in an unemotional, matter-of-fact fashion.

In the eyes of a Freudian psychotherapist, Albert's symptoms are seen as determined, rooted in early childhood experience, and motivated by unconscious factors. Collectively, these facts prevent Albert from using his own resources to change his feelings and behavior. However, Dr. F. (as we shall call our therapist) believes that through psychoanalysis Albert can be led to understand the causes of his intense fear of death and related symptoms, thereby making it possible for him to overcome them. Essentially, Dr. F.'s task in psychoanalysis is to get Albert to face his problems, master them, and then conduct his life with greater conscious awareness of his real motives (i.e., strengthen his ego). Freud believed that psychoanalysis was unrivaled as the vehicle for constructive personality change. Toward this end, Albert would be expected to see Dr. F. almost daily for a period of several years. Successful analysis requires a great deal of time, effort, and expense. Briefly, in Freudian theory, it takes a long time for the patient to become the way that he is; consequently, it will take a long time for him to change. Discussed below are illustrative techniques used in psychoanalysis, applicable to Albert's problem or any other problem area faced by orthodox practicing analysts.

Free Association   The therapeutic situation is arranged in order to maximize free association. In this procedure, Albert would be instructed to relax, either in a chair or on the classic couch, and report everything that comes into his consciousness, regardless of how irrelevant, absurd, or obscene it may seem. Dr. F. would urge Albert to relinquish all conscious reflection, follow his spontaneous thoughts and feelings, and impart *everything,* no matter how trivial, illogical, painful, embarrassing, or seemingly off the point it may appear. As the basic rule agreed upon by those undergoing psychoanalysis, free association is predicated on the assumption that one association leads to another that is deeper in the unconscious. Associations verbalized by the patient are interpreted as disguised expressions of repressed thoughts and feelings.

In line with Freud's deterministic position, then, the patient's "free associations" are not really free at all. Like his other behavior, Albert's cognitive and affective associations are determined by unconscious processes. Because of repression and unconscious motivation, Albert is unaware of the underlying meaning of what he is saying. By employing free association, Dr. F. believes that Albert's relaxed state will permit repressed material to emerge gradually, thus releasing more psychic energy for adaptive use. Dr. F. should also be in a better position to understand the nature of Albert's unconscious conflicts and their presumed causes. Perhaps, for example, Albert's free associations will lead him to recollect his earlier feelings of intense resentment toward his father (the Oedipal theme) and corresponding childhood wishes that his father would die.

Interpretation of Resistance   During the initial stage of psychoanalysis Freud discovered that the patient is usually unable or quite reluctant to recall repressed feelings and ideas. The patient *resists.* Thus, despite the fact that Albert consciously desires to change his feelings and end his suffering, he unconsciously resists Dr. F.'s efforts to help him eliminate his old, unsatisfactory behavior patterns. It is Dr. F.'s task to make Albert aware of his resistance maneuvers; it is necessary to deal with them successfully if therapeutic progress is to occur.

Resistance is a means of keeping the unconscious conflict intact, thereby impeding any attempts to probe into the real sources of personality problems. Resistance reveals itself in many ways. It may cause the patient to be late for therapy sessions, "forget" them, or simply find excuses for not coming. It is also evidenced when the patient is temporarily unable to free-associate, e.g., "I remember one day when I was a little kid and my mother and I were planning to go out shopping together. My father came home and, instead, the two of them went out leaving me behind with a neighbor. I felt . . . (pause) . . . For some reason, my mind is suddenly a complete blank right now." The ultimate form of resistance, of course, is for the patient to discontinue therapy prematurely. Skillful interpretation of the reasons for resistance is one method Dr. F. would employ to help Albert bring repressed conflicts into the open and rid himself of unconscious defenses.

Dream Analysis Another prominent technique for uncovering repressed material from the unconscious is that of dream analysis. Freud considered dreams as a direct avenue to the unconscious, since he viewed their contents as determined by repressed wishes. Dreams are thus understood and interpreted as essentially symbolic wish fulfillments whose contents partially reflect early childhood experiences (Freud, 1953). By means of rather elaborate techniques of dream interpretation involving analysis of the disguised meaning of dream symbols, psychoanalysts believe that they can enhance the patient's understanding of the causes of both symptoms and motivational conflicts.

For example, Albert may report a dream in which his father is departing (death symbol) on a train while Albert remains on the platform holding hands with his mother and former girlfriend, while feeling at once glad and intensely guilty. If the psychotherapeutic moment is right, Dr. F. might help Albert to see that this dream reflects his long repressed Oedipal-related wish for his father's death, reactivated last year by the father's severing of Albert's love relationship with his girlfriend. Thus, through dream analysis and interpretation, Albert may begin to gain greater insight into the real conflict underlying his present symptoms.

Analysis of Transference Earlier in the chapter, displacement was identified as a defense mechanism in which an unconscious impulse is discharged upon some person or object other than the one toward which it was initially directed. When it occurs in psychotherapy, this phenomenon is termed *transference*. More precisely, transference occurs whenever patients displace to the analyst feelings of love or hate which they had previously attached to a significant person (often a parent). Freud believed that transference reflected the patient's need to find a love object in order that repressed love feelings might be expressed. The analyst serves as a substitute love object in such a setting. Transference may reveal itself in direct verbal communication, free association, or the content of dreams. As an example, Albert might be showing signs of transference if he said something like the following: "Dr. F., why the hell did you decide to take a two-week vacation with your damned beloved wife just when we were starting to get somewhere in analysis?" On a deeper level, Albert is emotionally reacting to Dr. F. as he formerly felt toward his father in childhood (the Oedipal theme again).

Insofar as the phenomenon of transference operates unconsciously, the patient is totally unaware of its functional importance. Not interpreting the transference immediately, the therapist encourages its development until the patient has established what Freud called a *transference neurosis*. In essence, this is a "miniature neurosis" that enhances insight into the patient's deep, characteristic ways of perceiving, feeling, and reacting to significant figures from early life. According to Freud, as patients become gradually aware of the true meaning of their transference relationship with the analyst, they gain insight into their past experiences and feelings, relating these more fully to their ongoing difficulties. Orthodox psychoanalysts regard analysis of transference as absolutely vital to the therapeutic process—successful outcomes depend utterly upon it.

In Albert's case, Dr. F.'s interpretation of the transference relationship may reveal that he both loved and hated his father a great deal. Deeply resenting his father's relationship with his mother, Albert strongly wished his father dead. But also loving his father, Albert felt extremely guilty and thus deeply repressed this wish. However, revitalized by his father's severing of the relationship between Albert and his new "love object" (former girlfriend), this old feeling charged into consciousness in the distorted form of a fear of his own death. Thus, Albert's own overwhelming death fear—his central symptom—may be interpreted psychoanalytically as a symbolic wish for his father's death (perhaps an unconscious dread that he will kill his father) accompanied by an overriding guilt resulting in turn, in unconscious self-punishment for this wish. Albert's intense death fear and accompanying symptoms nicely accomplish this self-punishment objective. Other elements, such as a possible relationship between castration anxiety and fear of death, could probably be worked into this kind of interpretation of Albert's symptoms also. And the therapist, of course, employs all the previous techniques (not only analysis of transference) in arriving at the final interpretation.

Emotional Reeducation   Encouraging patients to convert their newly discovered insights into everyday living is called *emotional reeducation*. In different ways, each of the previous therapeutic techniques is designed to help patients achieve greater insight into the causes of their behavior. However, this insight alone, while necessary in psychoanalytic therapy, is not a sufficient condition for behavioral change. Urged by the analyst, patients must eventually apply their self-understanding to their day-to-day existence; they must learn to think, perceive, feel, and behave differently. Otherwise, psychoanalysis is nothing more than an emotionally draining exercise of excessive duration and expense.

Emotional reeducation is primarily employed during the final phases of therapy since the insights upon which it depends must necessarily be acquired first. Thus, Dr. F., having led Albert progressively toward a deeper understanding of the origins of his fear of death and accompanying symptoms, would help him to explore concrete ways of restructuring his feelings and behavior. Based on his newly acquired self-understanding, Albert would be encouraged to get rid of his childhood "hangups," begin to relate to his father as he is now, function more autonomously in relation to his parents, and develop more mature love relationships. In time, Albert should be able to accomplish these objectives with Dr. F.'s help. A good deal of this emotional reeducation would stem from therapeutic discussions of Albert's present life situation in light of his now well-understood past emotional history. When Albert makes substantial progress in these realms on his own, therapy is terminated by mutual agreement.

Each of the procedures discussed above is illustrative of "classical" psychoanalysis as it is practiced today, variations of which are dealt with in detail elsewhere (King, 1965; Kutash, 1976). Albert's case exemplifies the emphasis on the Oedipus complex and the importance Freud placed upon early experience in subsequent neurotic behavior.

Psychoanalysts and other contemporary therapists have introduced many treatment variations and innovations, not the least of which is the practical matter of how long therapy should continue (Harper, 1975). Psychoanalytic therapy can be an extremely lengthy ordeal, often involving one hour per day, five days per week, and extending over a period of one to five years or even longer! Thus, it is a very expensive form of therapy, often limited to the affluent. However, the major goal of analysis is nothing less than to produce basic changes in an individual's personality structure. Increased insight, personal integration, social effectiveness, and psychological maturity are the objectives. Obviously, such goals cannot be accomplished quickly or easily. Regardless of the ultimate judgment that history will pass on its actual therapeutic benefits, psychoanalysis stands as a significant pioneering effort in the continuing attempt to alleviate human misery.

SUMMARY

The psychoanalytic theory of personality was discussed in terms of theory, basic assumptions, research, and applications. Sigmund Freud, the founder of psychoanalysis, based his theory almost entirely on extensive clinical observation of neurotic patients as well as self-analysis.

Freud proposed three levels of consciousness—the conscious, preconscious, and unconscious—to describe the degree to which mental events vary in accessibility to awareness. The most significant mental events take place in the unconscious.

In Freudian theory, human psychological makeup comprises three structural components—id, ego, and superego. The id, representing the instinctual core of the person, is irrational, impulsive, and obedient to the pleasure principle. Reflex actions and primary process thinking are used by the id in obtaining gratification of instinctual urges. The ego represents the rational component of personality and is governed by the reality principle. Its task, through secondary process thinking, is to provide the individual with a suitable plan of action in order to satisfy the demands of the id within the restrictions of the social world and the individual's conscience. The superego, the final structure developed, represents the moral branch of personality. It has two subsystems, the conscious and the ego-ideal.

Freud's motivational theory is based on the concept of instinct, defined as an innate state of excitation which seeks tension release. An instinct has four essential properties: (1) source, (2) aim, (3) object, and (4) impetus.

Freud's account of psychosexual development is based on the premise that sexuality begins at birth and progresses thereafter through a biologically defined set of erogenous zones until adulthood is reached. Freud conceived of personality development as proceeding through the following stages: oral, anal, phallic, and genital.

Freud recognized three types of anxiety: reality, neurotic, and moral. He proposed that anxiety serves as a warning signal to the ego of impending danger from instinctual impulses. In response, the ego employs a number of defense mechanisms, including sublimation, repression, projection, displacement, rationalization, reaction formation, and regression.

Freud's theory is founded upon certain basic assumptions concerning human nature. Psychoanalytic theory reflects (1) a strong commitment to the assumptions of determinism, irrationality, unchangeability, homeostasis, and knowability; (2) a moderate commitment to the assumptions of holism, constitutionalism, and proactivity; and (3) a slight commitment to the assumption of subjectivity.

A number of Freudian concepts have yet to be submitted to rigorous empirical assessment by psychologists. However, illustrative studies related to repression, castration complex in dreams, humor, and first-born preference suggest that certain psychoanalytic constructs are amenable to scientific inquiry.

Applications of psychoanalytic concepts to everyday life are numerous. One of the most significant of these, psychoanalytic therapy, uses well-developed methods such as free association, interpretation of resistance, dream analysis, and analysis of transference to probe the unconscious with the aim of making possible a deeper understanding of the self. These newly acquired self-insights are then converted into a person's everyday life through the method of emotional reeducation.

BIBLIOGRAPHY

Adorno, I., Frenkel-Brunswick, E., Levinson, D., & Sanford, R. *The authoritarian personality.* New York: Harper & Row, 1950.

Breuer, J., & Freud, S. (1895). *Studies in hysteria* (Trans. A. Brill). New York: Nervous and Mental Diseases Publishing Company, 1936.

Brown, N. *Life against death.* New York: Random House, 1959.

Cohen, J. *Personality dynamics: Eyewitness series in psychology.* Chicago: Rand McNally, 1969.

Fenichel, O. *The psychoanalytic theory of neurosis.* New York: Norton, 1945.

Freud, S. (1900). The interpretation of dreams. In J. Strachey (Trans. and Ed.), *The standard edition of the complete psychological works of Sigmund Freud,* Vols. 4 and 5. London: Hogarth Press, 1953.

Freud, S. (1905). Jokes and their relation to the unconscious. *Standard edition.* Vol. 8, 1960.

Freud, S. (1915–1917). *A general introduction to psychoanalysis.* New York: Doubleday, 1943.

Freud, S. (1926). Inhibitions, symptoms, and anxiety. *Standard edition,* Vol. 20, 1959.

Freud, S. (1935). An autobiographical study. *Standard edition,* Vol. 20, 1959.

Freud, S. (1940). An outline of psychoanalysis. *Standard edition,* Vol. 23, 1964.

Glucksberg, S., & King, L. Motivated forgetting mediated by implicit verbal chaining: A laboratory analog of repression. *Science,* Oct. 27, 1967, 517–519.

Hall, C., & Van de Castle, R. An empirical investigation of the castration complex in dreams. *Journal of Personality,* 1965, **33**, 20–29.

Hammer, J. Preference for gender of child as a function of sex of adult respondents. *Journal of Individual Psychology,* 1970, **31**, 54–56.

Harper, R. *The new psychotherapies.* Englewood Cliffs, N.J.: Prentice-Hall, 1975.

Hilgard, E. Psychoanalysis: Experimental studies. In D. Sills (Ed.), *International encyclopedia of the social sciences*. Vol. 13. New York: Macmillan and the Free Press, 1968, pp. 37–45.

Horney, K. *The neurotic personality of our time*. New York: Norton, 1937.

Jones, E. *The life and work of Sigmund Freud:* Vol. I (1856–1900): *The formative years and the great discoveries*, 1953; Vol. II (1901–1919): *Years of maturity*, 1955; Vol. III (1919–1939): *The last phase*, 1957. New York: Basic Books.

King, P. Psychoanalytic adaptations. In B. Stefflre (Ed.), *Theories of counseling*. New York: McGraw-Hill, 1965.

Kutash, S. Modified psychoanalytic therapies. In B. Wolman (Ed.), *The therapist's handbook: Treatment methods of mental disorders*. New York: Van Nostrand Reinhold, 1976.

Mischel, W. *Introduction to personality* (2d ed.). New York: Holt, Rinehart and Winston, 1976.

Nuttin, J. Human motivation and Freud's theory of energy discharge. *Canadian Journal of Psychology*, 1956, **10**, 167–178.

Rank, O. *The trauma of birth*. New York: Harcourt, Brace and Co., 1929.

Rosenzweig, S. Need-persistive and ego-defensive reactions to frustration as demonstrated by an experiment on repression. *Psychological Review*, 1941, **48**, 347–349.

Sarason, I. *Personality: An objective approach* (2d ed.). New York: Wiley, 1972.

Sarnoff, I. *Testing Freudian concepts: An experimental social approach*. New York: Springer, 1971.

Shurcliff, A. Judged humor, arousal, and the relief theory. *Journal of Personality and Social Psychology*, 1968, **8**, 360–363.

Silverman, L. Psychoanalytic theory: "The reports of my death are greatly exaggerated." *American Psychologist*, 1976, **31**, 621–637.

Skinner, B. F. Critique of psychoanalytic concepts and theories. *The Scientific Monthly*, 1954, **79**, 300–305.

Weinstein, E. Symbolic neurology and psychoanalysis. In J. Marmor (Ed.), *Modern psychoanalysis: New directions and perspectives*. New York: Basic Books, 1968, pp. 225–250.

Wolman, B. *The unconscious mind: The meaning of Freudian psychology*. Englewood Cliffs, N.J.: Prentice-Hall, 1968.

SUGGESTED READINGS

Brenner, C. *An elementary textbook of psychoanalysis* (Rev. ed.). New York: Anchor Press —Doubleday, 1974.

Fisher, S., & Greenberg, R. *The scientific credibility of Freud's theories and therapy*. New York: Basic Books, 1977.

Freud, S. Psychopathology of everyday life. *Standard edition*, Vol. 6, 1960.

Kline, P. *Fact and fantasy in Freudian theory*. London: Methuen, 1972.

McGuire, W. (Ed.). *The Freud/Jung letters*. Princeton, N.J.: Princeton University Press, 1974.

Mitchell, J. *Psychoanalysis and feminism: Freud, Reich, Laing, and women*. New York: Pantheon, 1974.

Roazen, P. *Freud and his followers*. New York: Knopf, 1975.

Van de Castle, R. *The psychology of dreaming*. New York: General Learning Corporation, 1971.

DISCUSSION QUESTIONS

1 Do you agree with Freud that the two major motives underlying human behavior are sex and aggression? State your reasons.
2 Which of the defense mechanisms described in this chapter do you think you rely upon? How do they help you feel better?
3 Do you agree with Freud that it is impossible to live a normal, healthy existence without direct gratification of the sex instinct?
4 What are some of the problems encountered in testing the validity of Freudian concepts? What steps might be taken to make such concepts more amenable to empirical study?
5 Imagine yourself lying on a couch talking to a psychoanalyst. Which areas of your life would you be most willing to discuss? Most reluctant? Do you think that you could understand yourself better as a result of this process? What would you expect to gain? How do you think such insight might come about?

GLOSSARY

Anal Stage   The second stage of psychosexual development during which bowel control is achieved and pleasure is focused on the retention or expulsion of feces.
Catharsis   Therapeutic procedure whereby patient alleviates anxiety and symptoms by talking about them.
Cathexis   The attachment of energy in an object.
Conscience   A psychoanalytic term that refers to the individual's capacity for punitive self-evaluation, moral prohibitions, and guilt feelings when he or she fails to live up to internalized standards of perfection.
Conscious   Those thoughts and feelings a person is aware of at any given moment.
Defense Mechanism   The process whereby the individual distorts reality so as to reduce or eliminate anxiety and other unpleasant feelings.
Displacement   Defense mechanism that involves redirection of feelings or impulses to someone to whom they do not apply because of possible retaliation from the appropriate object. For example, a student who is criticized by an instructor and becomes irritated with his or her roommate.
Dream Analysis   Psychoanalytic technique in which the symbolism of dreams is interpreted in order to help patients understand the causes of their symptoms and motivational conflicts.
Ego   The reality-oriented aspect of personality structure in psychoanalytic theory; it involves perception, reasoning, learning, and all other mental activities necessary to interact effectively with the social world.
Ego-Ideal   That aspect of the superego involving standards of perfection taught to the child by the parents. It leads the individual to establish goals which, if achieved, generate a sense of self-esteem and pride.
Electra Complex   The feminine version of the boy's Oedipus complex in Freudian theory.
Emotional Reeducation   A psychoanalytic technique employed during the final phase of treatment whereby the patient is encouraged to convert insights into changes in everyday living.
Entropy   A thermodynamic law which states that any energy system seeks a state of balance. In psychoanalytic theory, entropy means that there exists in all living organisms a compulsion to reestablish the inanimate state out of which they were formed.
Fixation   The arrested development of an individual at one of the early psychosexual stages, caused by an excess of frustration or overindulgence.

Free Association Psychoanalytic procedure for probing the unconscious whereby the individual speaks freely about everything that comes to mind, regardless of how trivial, absurd, or obscene it may seem.

Frustration Thwarting of a need or desire by a mothering one. Also, being blocked in the achievement of personal goals.

Genital Stage Fourth and final stage of psychosexual development in which mature heterosexual relationships are developed (extending from adolescence until death).

Id The aspect of personality structure which contains everything inherited, present at birth, and fixed in the individual's constitution. It is animalistic, irrational, and free from all inhibitions.

Identification The process whereby a child takes on the characteristics of another, usually a parent, in order to relieve his or her own anxieties and reduce internal conflicts.

Instinct An innate bodily state of excitation that seeks expression and tension release. For Freud, mental representations of innate bodily excitations are reflected in the form of wishes.

Latency Period Period during which libidinal energy lies dormant and attention is focused on the development of interests and skills through contact with same-sexed peers.

Libido That portion of psychic energy which seeks its gratification from purely sexual activities.

Moral Anxiety Feelings of shame and guilt experienced by the person when the ego is threatened by punishment from the superego.

Neurotic Anxiety An emotional response of fear experienced when the ego is threatened by uncontrollable instinctual desires.

Oedipus or Electra Complex The process during the phallic stage in which the child desires sexual contact with the opposite-sexed parent, feels threatened by the same-sexed parent, and eventually resolves the conflict by identifying with the same-sexed parent. The child experiences erotic feelings toward the parent of the opposite sex and has feelings of hatred and jealousy toward the parent of the same sex.

Oral Stage The first stage of psychosexual development in which the mouth is the primary source of interest and pleasure.

Penis Envy In psychoanalytic theory, the young girl's desire to possess a penis and her anatomical discovery that she lacks one.

Phallic Stage The third stage of psychosexual development in which the sex organs become the primary focus of pleasure.

Pleasure Principle An orientation that calls for the immediate gratification of all wants and needs, regardless of reality demands or constraints.

Preconscious Those thoughts and feelings of which a person is not aware at any given moment, but which can be summoned to awareness with little or no difficulty (e.g., what is your birthdate?).

Primary Process Gratification of an instinctual need by fantasy. Psychological phenomenon whereby the individual reduces tension by forming a mental image of an object previously associated with satisfaction of a basic drive.

Projection Defense mechanism in which a person attributes his or her own unacceptable desires to others.

Psychoanalysis Theory of personality structure, development, dynamics, and change created by Freud. It places heavy emphasis on the role of biological and unconscious factors in the determination of behavior. It also maintains that human behavior is basically irrational and results from the interaction of the id, ego, and superego.

Psychosexual Development Theory formulated by Freud to account for personality development in terms of changes in the biological functioning of the individual. Social experiences at each stage presumedly leave some permanent residue in the form of attitudes, traits, and values acquired at that stage.

Rationalization   Defense mechanism in which the individual provides plausible but inaccurate justifications for his or her failures.

Reaction-Formation   Defense mechanism in which anxiety is reduced by repressing one set of impulses or feelings and overemphasizing an opposite set of impulses or feelings.

Realistic Anxiety   An emotional response triggered by threat or perception of real dangers in the external environment.

Reality Principle   An orientation that calls for the postponement of instinctual gratification until either an appropriate object and/or condition that will satisfy the urge has been found.

Reflex Action   Process by which the id rids itself of tension by automatically responding to sources of irritation.

Regression   Defense mechanism in which the individual retreats to an earlier developmental stage that was more secure and pleasant and/or to the use of less mature reponses in attempting to cope with stress.

Repression   Defense mechanism in which unwanted thoughts or impulses are barred from entering one's conscious awareness.

Resistance   Tendency to resist uncovering of repressed material in therapy; also tendency to maintain self-defeating behavior patterns by discontinuing therapy prematurely.

Secondary Process   In psychoanalytic theory, cognitive-perceptual skills which enable the individual to satisfy instinctual needs without endangering his or her own safety or that of others.

Structural Model   The tripartite division of personality structure postulated by Freud, consisting of id, ego, and superego.

Superego   The ethical or moral dimension of personality structure in psychoanalytic theory; it represents the individual's internalized version of society's norms and standards of behavior as learned from the parents via reward and punishment.

Transference   An important phenomenon in psychoanalytic therapy whereby the patient transfers feelings toward significant figures from the past (usually one of the parents) onto the therapist.

Unconscious   That aspect of the psyche that contains one's unacceptable conflicts and desires. These can be brought to the conscious mind through techniques such as free association and dream interpretation.

Alfred Adler

Alfred Adler: An Individual Psychology Theory of Personality

That we humans are inherently social beings motivated primarily by social needs is one pervasive theme of contemporary personality theory. Other less recognizable but nonetheless significant themes focus on the ability of individuals to (1) shape their destinies, (2) overcome primitive drives and an uncontrollable environment in striving for more fulfilling lives, and (3) improve themselves and the world around them through self-awareness. Such themes reflect some of the enduring humanistic contributions of the great Viennese psychiatrist, Alfred Adler.

Adler named his theory "individual psychology" to express his holistic conception of the human being as a single, indivisible, self-consistent, and unified entity. He believed that no person can be viewed in isolation, but must always be seen as embedded in a larger context, the social-ecological system of which she or he is an integral part. Adler further insisted that no person can be adequately understood without reference to his or her goals, much as a drama can be understood only in the light of its finale. The goals people envision for themselves and the characteristic ways they struggle to reach them provide the key to an understanding of the meaning they give to their lives. Finally, unlike Freud, Adler depicted the individual neither as victimized by instincts nor doomed by cultural forces and childhood experiences. Adler postulated that, far from being governed by forces we cannot see or control, we are each the creative agents of our own personalities, actively directing and creating our own growth and future:

> Every individual represents both a unity of personality and the individual fashioning of that unity. The individual is thus both the picture and the artist. He is the artist of his own personality, but as an artist he is neither an infallible worker nor a person with a complete understanding of mind and body; he is rather a weak, extremely fallible, and imperfect human being (Adler, 1956, p. 177).

BIOGRAPHICAL SKETCH

Alfred Adler, the second of six children, was born in the Viennese suburb of Penzig on February 7, 1870. Like Freud, he was the son of a lower-middle-class Jewish merchant; but, while Freud was raised in a ghettolike district and remained forever conscious of his membership in a persecuted minority, Adler took his ethnic background lightly. There were few other Jewish children in the locale where he matured so that his accent and general outlook remained more Viennese than Jewish. Unlike Freud who referred to the topic frequently, Adler made no pronouncements on the subject of anti-Semitism. In fact, Adler converted to Protestantism in his adult years.

Embittered by the jealousy of his older brother, despite the fact that four younger children were born to the family, Adler recalled his childhood as an unhappy time. He enjoyed a warm relationship with his mother during his first two years of life, but he lost that pampered position when his younger brother was born. He then acquired a preference for his father, whose favorite he remained throughout his childhood.

Death and illness were Adler's constant companions throughout childhood. When he was 3 years old his younger brother died in a bed next to him. In addition, he twice narrowly escaped being killed in street accidents. At the age of 5 Adler contracted a severe case of pneumonia and came very close to death. He recounted the lasting emotional significance of his brush with death as follows:

> In the joy over my recovery, there was talk for a long time about the mortal danger in which I was supposed to have been. From that time on I recall always thinking of myself in the future as a physician. This means that I had set a goal from which I could expect an end to my childlike distress, my fear of death. . . . So I came to choose the occupation of physician in order to overcome death and the fear of death (Adler, in Ansbacher and Ansbacher, 1956, p. 199).

In addition to repeated encounters with death throughout his youth, Adler was a chronically sick and weak child. He suffered from rickets, a deficiency disease that results in a softening of the bones, which left him awkward and slow. He was thus unable to compete with his older brother or with peers in the physical games of childhood. As he grew up, Adler's physical health improved a bit, but not his place in the family.

Moreover, he was a mediocre student during his early school years. In fact, in secondary school Adler was so poor in mathematics that he had to repeat the course. His teacher advised his father to take him out of school and apprentice him to a shoemaker because he was unfit for anything else. However, his father encouraged him to continue in school and, through persistence and hard work, he subsequently became the best student in the class.

During the period of Adler's emergence into adulthood, Vienna was an affluent, enlightened city, at the pinnacle of Hapsburg power. When at 18 Adler entered the University of Vienna, it was one of the leading European medical centers. Around it surged the life of the theater, music, and the yeasty socialist philosophy which earned the city her nickname, Red Vienna. Throughout his student years, Adler exuberantly joined in. He became particularly intrigued by socialism and attended a number of political meetings. It was at one of these meetings that he met his future wife, Raissa Epstein, a Russian student who was also attending the University of Vienna. Adler courted his bride-to-be fervently, twice following her to her home in Russia. He told his family nothing of his romance. Their introduction to the love affair was a telegram from Russia: AM MARRIED, RETURNING HOME WITH BRIDE, FIND HOME FOR ME. They were married in 1897.

Adler received his medical degree in 1895. For a time after receiving his degree Adler specialized in ophthalmology (eye diseases) in a run-down part of the city. Then after a period of practice in general medicine, he became a psychiatrist. From 1902 to 1911, Adler was an active member of the inner circle that evolved around Sigmund Freud. But Adler soon began to develop ideas which were at odds with those of Freud and others sympathetic to psychoanalytic theory, ideas which became increasingly irreconcilable with those of Freud. Thus Adler eventually resigned as president of the Vienna Psychoanalytic Society in 1911, left the society along with nine of the other twenty-three members, and formed the Society for Free Psychoanalysis—much to the annoyance of Freud and some of his loyal associates. The following year, 1912, the name was changed to the Society for Individual Psychology.

At the close of World War I, the new Austrian government asked Adler to organize a program of child guidance centers in the public schools where disturbed children and their parents could receive counseling. Adler's clinics, staffed largely by volunteer paraprofessionals of his own training, were a pioneer effort in the direction of what is now called community psychiatry.

From the mid-1920s onward, Adler devoted increasing portions of his time to giving lecture tours throughout Europe and the United States. He first visited the United States in 1926 and, after that, sojourned for longer and longer periods of lecturing, teaching, and practice. Soon he was spending only his summers in Vienna. With the rise of Hitler and the totalitarian wave that was sweeping Europe, Adler foresaw a catastrophe and believed that if his psychology were to survive anywhere it would be in America. Accordingly, in 1934, he and his wife took up residence in New York City, shortly thereafter accepting a visiting professorship in medical psychology at the Long Island College of Medicine (now Downstate Medical Center, State University of New York) and continuing his private psychiatric practice.

Adler was an indefatigable lecturer of great spontaneity and popularity. He was on a lecture tour when he suddenly died in Aberdeen, Scotland, on May 28, 1937. When Freud learned of Adler's death, he wrote to a friend who had indicated that he was very much moved by the news: "I don't understand your sympathy for Adler. For a Jew boy out of a Viennese suburb a death in Aberdeen is an unheard-of career in itself and a proof of how far he had got on. The world really rewarded him richly for his service in having contradicted psychoanalysis (Jones, 1957, p. 208)." There can be no stronger indication of Freud's uncompromising anger toward those he viewed as dissidents against psychoanalytic doctrines, and Adler (along with Carl Jung) was a special recipient of this wrath.

Two of Adler's children, Alexandra and Kurt, have continued their father's work. Both are practicing Adlerian psychiatrists in New York City. Also a prolific writer, he published some 300 books and articles during his lifetime. *The Practice and Theory of Individual Psychology* (1927a) is perhaps the best introduction to Adler's theory of personality. Among his many other important books now available in English translation are *The Neurotic Constitution* (1917a); *A Study of Organ Inferiority and Its Psychical Compensation* (1917b); *Understanding Human Nature* (1927b); *The Science of Living* (1929); *The Pattern of Life* (1930a); *What Life Should Mean to You* (1931); and *Social Interest: A Challenge to Mankind* (1939). Several professional journals have also been founded by Adler's followers. Devoted primarily to disseminating theoretical and research papers on individual psychology, they include: *Journal of Individual Psychology; American Journal of Individual Psychology;* and *International Journal of Individual Psychology.*

Adler's ideas have had a profound impact on contemporary developments in clinical and personality psychology. In particular, his emphasis on social interest as a major criterion of mental health has inspired a value orientation to psychotherapy. In addition, Adler's concern with conscious, rational processes encouraged the beginnings of ego psychology (Ansbacher, 1977). His stress on social forces in personality development is evident in the later work of Erich Fromm, Karen Horney, and Harry Stack Sullivan, all of whom are as much neo-Adlerian as neo-Freudian. Relatedly, his focus on the volitional and creative aspects of personality has also influenced either directly or indirectly such prominent psychologists and psychiatrists as Gordon Allport (Chapter 8), Abraham Maslow (Chapter 10), Rollo May, Viktor Frankl, and Albert Ellis. Indeed, this chapter is replete with indicators of the contemporary nature of Adler's concepts: the need for a theory of relevance; the sense of inferiority and compensatory strivings; organ inferiority and psychosomatics; the "inferiority complex" (so much a lay term now)—the forerunner of a psychology of physical handicap; the role of neglect in the development of the antisocial personality; competence as the signpost of maturity; self-esteem and lust for power; the concept of life-style; stress and adaptation; birth order; self-actualization and service to others; psychological health; and creativity—to mention but a handful. Careful study of Adler's ideas should help the reader to see how much a theorist of an earlier decade can speak to the concerns of today.

Today the Adlerian movement numbers several thousand members scattered throughout the globe. It comprises persons representing a variety of disciplines, including psychiatry, psychology, social work, education, as well as lay people who are concerned with the application of Adlerian concepts to family life and personal development. In the United States the central organization is the American Society of Adlerian Psychology. There are Adlerian training institutes in New York City, Chicago, Minneapolis, Los Angeles, and other cities. And there is no doubt that individual psychology still has much insight to offer the student of personality psychology. As Abraham Maslow, a pioneer of the humanistic movement in psychology, noted some time ago: "For me, Alfred Adler becomes more and more correct year by year. As the facts come in, they give stronger and stronger support to his image of man. I should say in one respect especially the times have not yet caught up with him. I refer to his holistic emphasis (1970, p. 13)."

BASIC TENETS OF INDIVIDUAL PSYCHOLOGY

Adler is often portrayed as a disciple of Freud who eventually rebelled against the teachings of his master and then proceeded to develop his own ideas. However, close scrutiny of Adler's life and work reveals that he was actually a colleague of Freud and should in no way be considered a "neo-Freudian." The seeds of Adler's later theories are, in fact, evident in the writings that predate the period of his association with Freud (Ellenberger, 1970). To be sure, Freud claimed that Adler was a disciple who subsequently defected. But Adler strongly denied this, conceding, however, that he had learned a great deal from Freud, although in a negative sense: "I profited by his mistakes (Adler, 1956, p. 358)." Moreover, Adler never considered himself to be a psychoanalyst. He never underwent psychoanalysis himself and could not accept the heavy sexual emphasis that Freud placed on neurosis. Unfortunately, the two never reconciled after their break in 1911, and Freud remained hostile and bitter toward Adler for the rest of his life. He called the physically diminutive Adler a pigmy, saying "I made a pigmy great." Adler retorted that a "pigmy standing on the shoulders of a giant can see farther than the giant can." That may be true of a pigmy, Freud shot back, "but not of a louse in the giant's hair (Scarf, 1971)." As the theory section of this chapter will reveal, much of Adler's individual psychology developed as an antithesis to Freudian theory.

Like all personological systems, individual psychology is predicated upon certain basic tenets. In this section we shall briefly examine the most fundamental tenets of individual psychology, tenets from which Adler proceeded to construct theories of personality and psychopathology and an approach to psychotherapy.

1   The Individual as a Unified and Self-Consistent Entity   The notion that a human being is a unified and self-consistent organism constitutes the foremost assumption of Adlerian psychology (Adler, 1927a). In fact, when Adler chose for his theory the name individual psychology, it was because the term "individual" in its original Latin sense meant indivisible, that which cannot be divided. More specifically, Adler held that no life expression can be viewed in isolation, but must always be regarded in relation to the total personality. The person is an indivisible unity both in regard to the mind-body relationship and to the various activities and functions of the mind. Adler believed that the foremost challenge confronting individual psychology is to prove this unity in each individual: in the thinking, feeling, acting, the so-called conscious and unconscious, in every expression of personality. This self-consistent and unified personality structure Adler designated as the *style of life* of the individual, a concept which more than any other epitomizes Adler's effort to deal with the human being as a totality.

2   Human Life as a Dynamic Striving for Perfection   To regard the human being as an organic unity requires a unitary psychodynamic principle. This Adler derived directly from life itself, namely that life cannot be conceived without ongoing movement, movement in the direction of growth and expansion. Indeed, only in the movement toward identifiable goals can the individual be perceived as a unified and self-consistent entity:

> The most important characteristic of life is motion. . . . The chief characteristic of a
> movement is . . . direction and, therefore in a psychic movement, a goal. . . . Striving
> towards a goal . . . we find everywhere in life. Everything grows "as if" it were striving
> to overcome all imperfections and achieve perfection. This urge toward perfection we
> call the goal of overcoming, that is, the striving to overcome (Adler, 1964, pp. 85–86).

In proposing this striving for perfection, Adler reasoned that people are not
just pushed from behind by internal or external causes but rather are pulled from
the front: they are always moving toward personally significant life goals. In Adler's
system these life goals are largely self-selected, strongly suggesting that people have
the capacity to determine their own actions and their own destinies in the constant
quest for perfection. With the attainment of these goals, individuals will not only
enhance their personal self-esteem but will also provide themselves with niches in
the world.

3 The Individual as a Creative and Self-Determined Entity While acknowledging the importance of heredity and environment in forming personality,
Adler (1964) insisted that the individual was distinctly more than a mere product of
these two forces. Thus, in Adlerian theory people are depicted as possessing a
creative power which places them in control of their lives; free, conscious activity is
the defining character of human beings. This creative power affects virtually every
facet of the person's existence—perception, memory, imagination, fantasy, and
dreaming. It makes each person a self-determined individual, the architect of his or
her own life:

> The important thing is not what one is born with, but what use one makes of that
> equipment. . . . As to the influence of the environment, who would claim that the same
> influences are . . . responded to by any two individuals in the same way? Thus we find
> it necessary to assume the existence of still another force; the creative power of the
> individual (Adler, 1964, pp. 86–87).

It is this belief in human creativity and freedom, more than any other, which
prompts many psychologists to recognize Adler as a forerunner of modern humanistic psychology.

4 The Social Embeddedness of the Individual Adler's holistic vision of
human nature was comprehensive; he saw the individual not only as a unified
relational system, but also as an integral part of larger systems—the family,
community, indeed humanity itself: "Individual Psychology regards and examines
the individual as socially embedded. We refuse to recognize and examine an isolated
human being (Adler, 1956, p. 2)." Paramount to Adlerian theory, then, is the
conviction that all behavior, without exception, occurs in a social context and that
the essence of human nature can only be grasped through the understanding of
social relationships. Thus, every individual has a natural aptitude for *community
feeling* or *social interest,* the innate ability to engage in cooperative reciprocal social
relations. Individual psychology thus assumes an essential cooperative harmony

between individual and society, with conflict as an unnatural condition. The emphasis on the social determinants of behavior is, in fact, so central to Adler's conception of man that it has earned him the reputation of being the first social psychologist in the modern history of personology.

   5   Individual Subjectivity   Firmly anchored in the phenomenological tradition, Adler theorized that behavior is always dependent on people's opinions of themselves and the environments with which they must cope. Individuals live in a world of their own construction, in accordance with their own "schema of apperception." Moreover, Adler argued that people are motivated by *fictional goals*—privately held beliefs about present and future events—that regulate behavior. For example, an individual might live by the credo "honesty is the best policy," "every man for himself," or a belief in an afterlife that will reward the virtuous and punish the wicked. Persons are portrayed as behaving in accordance with these private beliefs, whether they are objectively real or not: "It has the same effect on me whether a poisonous snake is actually approaching my foot or whether I merely believe that it is a poisonous snake (quoted in Ansbacher, 1971, p. 58)." In Adler's scheme of things, then, behavior is clearly a reflection of the individual's subjective perception of reality. Following are the central theoretical concepts grounded in these basic tenets of individual psychology.

CENTRAL CONCEPTS OF INDIVIDUAL PSYCHOLOGY

In constructing the theoretical concepts of individual psychology, Adler (1964) was guided by the notion that the major purpose of a personality theory should be to serve as an economical and fruitful guide for psychotherapists, and ultimately for everyone, in effecting change toward more psychologically healthy behavior. Adler's theory of personality is an extremely parsimonious one in the sense that a limited number of core concepts support the entire theoretical system. It can be presented under seven general headings: (1) inferiority feelings and compensation, (2) striving for superiority, (3) style of life, (4) social interest, (5) creative self, (6) birth order, and (7) fictional finalism.

Inferiority Feelings and Compensation

Very early in his career, while he was still associated with Freud, Adler (1907) published a monograph entitled "Study of Organ Inferiority and Its Psychical Compensation." In this work he developed a theory as to why illness affects people in different ways. He proposed that in each individual, certain organs are somewhat weaker than others, making the person more susceptible to illnesses and diseases involving these organs. More to the point, Adler theorized that every person succumbs to disease in that region of the body which has been less well-developed, less successfully functioning, and generally "inferior" from birth. Thus, for example, some people are born with severe allergies which may affect the lungs in particular. These people would often suffer from bronchitis or upper respiratory infections. Adler then observed that people with severe organic weaknesses or defects will often try to *compensate* for them by training and exercise, which often results in the development of the individual's greatest skill or strength: "In almost all outstanding people we find some organ imperfection; and we gather the impression that they were sorely confronted at the beginning of life but struggled and overcame their difficulties (Adler, 1931, p. 248)."

History records many examples of such compensation for organ inferiority. Demosthenes, a childhood stutterer, became one of the world's greatest orators. Wilma Rudolph, physically handicapped as a child, went on to win three Olympic gold medals in track. Theodore Roosevelt, a weak and sickly child, became a specimen of physical fitness as an adult as well as President. Thus, *organ inferiority*—that is, congenitally weak or poorly functioning organs—can lead to striking accomplishments in a person's life. But it can also lead to an inferiority complex if the individual's attempts at compensation are unsuccessful.

There was, of course, nothing novel in the idea that the organism tries to repair its own weaknesses; physicians had long been aware that where one kidney functioned poorly, for example, the other would become overdeveloped and attempt to do the work of two. But Adler suggested that this process of compensation could also proceed in the *psychological* sphere: that individuals are often driven to compensate not only for organ inferiorities but also for *subjective feelings of inferiority*, those that arise from uniquely felt psychological or social disabilities as well as those that stem from actual bodily weakness or impairment.

Adler (1956) viewed inferiority feelings as the motivational basis for essentially all human striving. All individual progress, growth, and development results from the attempt to overcome one's inferiorities, be they imagined or real. In fact, Adler believed that inferiority feelings and the resultant efforts at compensation are the cause of all improvement in humanity's lot. Thus, it is a condition common to all people and, as such, not a sign of weakness or abnormality.

Organ inferiorities in Adler's scheme have no meaning or importance by themselves. Their importance stems from the fact that they stimulate subjective feelings of inferiority. The feelings, in turn, serve as an impetus toward perfection or completion, motivating the individual toward even-higher levels of self-development. People like Demosthenes, Rudolph, and Roosevelt compensated for their inferiority feelings by striving to overcome specific organ deficiencies. The feeling of inferiority, not the defective organ per se, motivated them. Thus, inferiority, by itself, can never produce greatness. It must be combined with talent, courage, and social concern.

Inferiority Complexes and Their Origins   Adler believed that feelings of inferiority or inadequacy begin in infancy. Specifically, he reasoned that the human infant experiences a prolonged period of dependency during which it is quite helpless and must rely upon adults to survive. This experience causes the infant to develop feelings of inferiority relative to the larger, stronger, and more powerful people in the family. Unavoidable and common to everyone, these feelings are necessary if one is to grow, succeed, and realize one's potential. Indeed, for Adler, all forward and upward movement results from the attempt to compensate for one's inferiority feelings. On the other hand, an inability to overcome inferiority feelings, for whatever reason, frequently reinforces the feelings and leads to the development of what Adler called an "inferiority complex." He described three childhood situations that tend to lead to an inferiority complex: *organ inferiority, spoiling* or *pampering,* and *neglect.*

In the first of these situations, organ inferiority, the physically impaired or chronically ill child is unable to compete successfully with other children; the child thus withdraws into a shell of inferiority. Spoiled or pampered children, on the other hand, grow up lacking confidence in their abilities because others have always done things for them; they are plagued by deep-seated inferiority feelings for they believe it impossible to tackle life's obstacles on their own. Finally, neglect can lead to an inferiority complex because such children basically feel unwanted; they go through life lacking confidence in their ability to be useful and to gain affection and esteem from others. As will be seen later in this chapter, each of these three childhood situations can play a crucial role in the emergence of neurosis in adulthood.

Regardless of the circumstances that give rise to inferiority feelings, however, a person may react by overcompensating and thus develop what Adler called a *superiority complex.* This involves, as you might suspect, a tendency to exaggerate one's physical, intellectual, or social skills. A person, for instance, may believe she is smarter than others but not feel she must show her intelligence by reciting what she knows about cars. Another person may feel he must demonstrate all he knows about cars on every occasion to everyone who will listen to him. The person may even neglect everything else just to prove he knows more than anyone else about cars. In any event, the technique of overcompensation is an exaggeration of a healthy striving to overcome one's inferiorities. Accordingly, the person possessing a superiority complex tends to be boastful, arrogant, vain, egocentric, and sarcastic. One gets the impression that this individual has so little self-acceptance (i.e., such a low opinion of himself or herself) that only by "putting down" others can he or she feel important.

Striving for Superiority

As just noted, Adler held that inferiority feelings are the source of all human striving toward self-expansion, growth, and competence. But what is the ultimate goal for which we strive and which gives a measure of consistency and unity to our lives? Are we simply urged on by the need to be rid of our inferiority feelings? Or are we motivated by the drive to ruthlessly dominate others? In seeking answers to these questions, Adler's thinking changed markedly over the years. As early as 1908 he believed that the great dynamic force governing human behavior was aggression, i.e., a strong initiative to overcome obstacles. Soon after, however, he abandoned the idea of an aggressive impulse in favor of the "will to power." In this concept, weakness was equated with femininity and power with masculinity. It was at this stage that Adler proposed the idea of "masculine protest," a form of overcompensation that both genders employ in an effort to supplant feelings of inadequacy and inferiority. However, by 1912, Adler rejected the concept of masculine protest as a satisfactory explanation for the motivation of normal people. Instead, he developed a much broader viewpoint in which people are seen to be striving for superiority, a condition quite different from the superiority complex. Thus, there were three distinct stages in his theorizing on the ultimate goal of human life: to be aggressive, to be powerful, and to be superior.

In his later years, Adler came to the conclusion that the *striving for superiority* is the fundamental fact of human life, "a something without which life would be unthinkable (Adler, 1956, p. 104)." All people share this "great upward drive" from minus to plus, from below to above, from incompletion to perfection, and from inability to capability in facing the problems of life. Adler writes:

> I began to see clearly in every psychological phenomenon the striving for superiority. It runs parallel to physical growth and is an intrinsic necessity of life itself. It lies at the root of all solutions of life's problems and is manifested in the way in which we meet these problems. . . . The impetus from minus to plus never ends. The urge from below to above never ceases. Whatever premises all our philosophies and psychologists dream of—self-preservation, pleasure principle, equalization—all these are but vague representations, attempts to express the great upward drive (1930a, p. 398).

But from where does the striving for superiority or perfection come? Is it innate or learned? Adler argued that it is innate—that, in fact, we are never free of it because it is life itself: "If this striving were not innate to the organism, no form of life could preserve itself (Adler, 1964, p. 39)."

But while the striving for superiority is innate and governs our adaptation to the environment throughout life, it must nevertheless be properly developed. At birth it exists as potentiality, not actuality. It remains for each individual to actualize this potential in his or her own way. Adler suggested that this process begins during the fifth year when the child develops a life goal that serves as a focus for his or her strivings. Although somewhat obscure and generally unconscious when first formed in childhood, the life goal eventually provides guidelines for motivation, shaping psychological movement and giving it an aim.

Adler offered several additional ideas about the nature and operation of the striving for superiority. First, he saw it as one fundamental motive, rather than a combination of separate urges, with its roots in the infant's realization that it is impotent and inferior to those in its surroundings. Second, this great upward drive is universal in nature: it is common to all, the normal and the neurotic alike. Third, the goal of superiority can take either a negative (destructive) or positive (constructive) direction. As will be evident later, for example, a negative direction is seen in neurotics who strive for *personal* superiority, e.g., self-esteem, power, personal aggrandizement—goals which Adler saw as selfish. In contrast, psychologically healthy people are seen to be striving in a positive direction; their efforts for a superior way of life are intimately bound up with social concern and the welfare of others, i.e., unselfish goals. Fourth, Adler argued that the striving for perfection calls for a considerable expenditure of energy and effort; a person's level of tension is increased rather than decreased as a consequence of this struggle. And fifth, the striving for superiority occurs at both the individual and societal levels: we strive for perfection not only as individuals; as members of society, we strive to perfect our culture. Unlike Freud, then, Adler viewed the individual and society as essentially in harmony with one another.

In summary, Adlerian theory portrays human beings as living in concert with their social world but perpetually striving to construct a better world. Nonetheless, to theorize that humankind has only one ultimate goal—to improve its culture—tells us nothing about how we, as individuals, try to attain this goal. This issue Adler dealt with in his concept of style of life.

Style of Life

Style of life, an extension and refinement of Adler's conception of striving for a goal, represents the most distinctive feature of his dynamic theory of personality. It is this concept, idiographic in nature, which explains the unique configuration of characteristics identifying a particular person—the flavor of a person's life, including not only his or her goal, but also self-concept, feelings toward others, and attitude toward the world. In short, *style of life* refers to the unique pattern of traits, behaviors, and habits which, when taken together, define the particular route we have charted for ourselves in order to reach our life goal.

How does the individual's life-style come into being? To answer this we must briefly return to the concepts of inferiority and compensation, for they determine the basis of our life-style. Adler theorized that in infancy we all experience inferiorities, either imaginary or real, that motivate us to compensate in some way. To illustrate, a child who is poorly coordinated might concentrate his compensatory strivings on developing superior athletic ability. His behavior, shaped by the awareness of his physical limitations, in turn becomes his style of life—a set of behaviors designed to compensate for an inferiority. Our life-style, then, is based on our efforts to overcome our unique sense of inferiority:

> Perhaps I can illustrate this by an anecdote of three children who were taken to the zoo for the first time. As they stood before the lion's cage, one of them shrank behind his mother's skirts and said, "I want to go home." The second child stood where he was, very pale and trembling, and said, "I'm not a bit frightened." The third glared at the lion fiercely and asked his mother, "Shall I spit at it?" The three children really felt inferior, but each expressed his feelings in his own way, consonant with his style of life (Adler, 1931, p. 50).

In Adler's view, the life-style is so firmly implanted by the age of four or five that it is almost totally resistant to change thereafter. Of course, people continue to learn new ways of expressing their unique life-style, but these are merely elaborations and extensions of the basic structure that was laid down at an early age. The life-style so formed persists and becomes the guiding framework for later behavior. In other words, everything we do is shaped and directed by our unique life-style; it determines which aspects of our environment we will attend to and which aspects we will ignore. All of our psychological processes (e.g., perceiving, thinking, feeling) are organized into a unified whole and gain their meaning from the context of our life-style. Consider, for example, the individual who strives to become superior through developing her intellectual competence. From an Adlerian perspective, her life-style would predictably involve sedentary activities—reading, studying, thinking—anything that serves to increase the level of her intellectual competence. She would arrange even the minute details of her daily routine—recreations and hobbies, relations to family, friends, and acquaintances, and social activities—in accordance with the goal of intellectual superiority. By contrast, another individual working toward physical perfection would structure his life in such a way that this goal might be attained. Everything he does is done with an eye to athletic superiority. Clearly, then, all aspects of a person's behavior issue from his or her style of life, in Adlerian theory. The intellectual remembers, reasons, judges, feels, and acts quite differently from the athlete, since the two are psychological poles apart in terms of their respective styles of life.

Personality Types: Life-Style Attitudes As we have seen, the individual's unique life-style lies behind everything she or he thinks, feels, and does. Once created, it is what accounts for the consistency of our basic character structure throughout life as well as our general orientation to the outside world. In this regard, Adler frequently noted that the true form of our life-style can only be discerned from the manner in which we approach and solve certain life problems. Occupational, friendship, and love-and-marriage problems are three "life tasks" that all people embedded in a social system must master. He also stressed that none of these life tasks stands alone—they are always interrelated—and that their solution depends on our life-style: "A solution of one helps toward the solution of the others, and indeed we can say that they are all aspects of the same situation and the same problem—the necessity for a human being to preserve life and to further life in the environment in which he finds himself (Adler, 1956, p. 133)."

Because every life-style is unique to the individual who created it, only gross generalizations about personality types are possible. With this understanding in mind, however, Adler (Dreikurs, 1950) proposed a typology of life-style attitudes which classified individuals according to their attitude and behavior toward the three major life tasks—work, friendship, and love and marriage. The classification itself is generated by a two-dimensional scheme, with "social interest" constituting one dimension and "degree of activity" the other. *Social interest* represents a feeling of empathy for each member of the human race and manifests itself as cooperation with others for social advancement rather than personal gain. It constitutes the major criterion of psychological maturity in Adlerian theory and is the opposite of selfish interest. *Degree of activity* refers to the individual's movement toward the solution of life's problems and would coincide with what today might be called arousal or energy level. All persons, as Adler viewed it, have their own level of energy by which they attack the problems of life. This level of energy or activity, usually established during childhood, may vary from the very lethargic, hesitant person to the one who is constantly in a frenzy of activity. It is only when combined with social interest, however, that degree of activity becomes constructive or destructive.

Adler's first three types of life-style attitudes—the ruling, the getting, and the avoiding—all lack social interest but differ in their degree of activity. The fourth type, the socially useful person, has both high social interest and a high degree of activity.

1   The ruling type   Individuals who are assertive, aggressive, and active with little, if any, social awareness or interest are of the ruling type. Such individuals are active but in an unsocial way, and hence behave without concern for others' welfare. They possess a dominating attitude toward the outside world and confront the major life tasks in an aggressive, antisocial manner.

2   The getting type   As the name suggests, individuals with this life-style attitude relate to the outside world in a parasitic manner, "leaning" on others to satisfy most of their needs. Their main concern in life is getting as much as possible from others. Because they possess a low degree of activity, however, they are not especially dangerous.

3   The avoiding type   People with this predisposition have neither sufficient social interest nor activity to participate in any way in life. Fearing failure more than desiring success, their lives are marked by the socially useless behavior of running away from the tasks of life. In other words, their goal is to sidestep all problems in life, thereby avoiding any possibility of failure.

4   The socially useful type   This type of individual is the epitome of psychological health in Adler's system. Such a person embodies both a high degree of social interest and a high level of activity. Socially oriented, these individuals are willing to cooperate with others to master the tasks of life while simultaneously ministering to their own needs and those of others; they see the three major tasks of occupation, friendship, and love as social problems. They also realize that solution to social problems requires cooperation, personal courage, and a willingness to make a contribution to the welfare of others.

Adler's two-dimensional theory of life-style attitudes is missing one possible combination: high social interest–low activity. It is not possible to have high social interest without also possessing a high degree of activity. In other words, people with social interest are compelled to do something which will benefit other people.

Adler reminds us that no one person can be said to fit any of these four types exclusively and that any typology, no matter how sophisticated it may seem, can never be used as an accurate description of any one person's life-style. In the end, it is the individual and his or her unique way of living that matters. At the same time, however, an understanding of these life-style attitudes can, to some extent, facilitate the understanding of human behavior from Adler's perspective.

Understanding Your Life-Style   Adler repeatedly emphasized that infancy and early childhood are the formative years, the period when our basic style of living is established. He also maintained that the nature of our life-style depends on our interactions with our parents as we struggle to compensate for our sense of inferiority. Thus, our early experiences are paramount in the formation of our life-style and, as Adler viewed it, become enduring influences as we approach all life's later problems. In this vein, Adler proposed that one key to understanding a person's life-style might be found by asking the person to relate his or her *earliest memory*. The veracity of the recollection is of no importance. What is important is the perception of the remembered event. The earliest memory recalled is always consistent with the individual's style of life. Therefore, a subjective account of this experience is a clue to one's goal and one's life-style.

Adler found that if a person's earliest memory is unpleasant, his or her life-style is likely to be marked by the pervasive and fatalistic attitude. "Everything bad happens to me." If, on the other hand, a person's first recollection is pleasant, his or her life-style is likely to be marked by a constructive and optimistic attitude toward the world. In brief, then, Adler believed that early recollections offer a most productive approach to understanding the individual's style of living.

A second way of understanding a person's life-style is to observe him or her in a personal crisis. During stressful times the true life-style emerges, and a person is seen for what she or he is. Thus, for instance, a person who possesses inner strength and courage will likely use these qualities effectively to solve stress-related problems. By contrast, a person with a pampered style of life will act in socially ineffective ways during periods of stress, no matter how socially-oriented she or he appears to be at other times. The behavior can then be seen for what it is: self-centered and self-seeking.

Social Interest

Still another core concept in Adler's system is that of social interest. In fact, it occupies a position equal to, but not competitive with, the concepts of striving for superiority and style of life. The concept of social interest reflects Adler's fervent belief that human beings are social beings—that we must consider our relationship to others and to the larger sociocultural context in which we live if we are to fully understand ourselves. But more than this, it reflects the decisive although gradual change that occurred in Adler's thinking as to what constitutes the great driving force underlying all human striving. Very early in his career while he was still associated with Freud, Adler theorized that people are driven by an insatiable lust for personal power and need to dominate. In particular, he held that individuals are pushed by the need to overcome their deep-seated feelings of inferiority and pulled by their desire to be superior. These views met widespread protest. Indeed, Adler was severely criticized for emphasizing selfish motives while ignoring social ones. Many critics considered Adler's view of motivation as nothing more than a dressed-up version of Darwin's doctrine of the survival of the fittest. In later years, however, as Adler's system matured, he came to feel that persons are strongly motivated by benign social urges. Specifically, he saw human beings as motivated by an innate social instinct which causes them to relinquish selfish gain for community gain. The essence of this view, captured in the social interest concept, is that as individuals we must cooperate with and contribute to society's goals.

Social interest derives from the German neologism *Gemeinschaftsgefuhl,* a term which is not fully expressed by any English word or phrase. It means something on the order of "social feeling," "community feeling," or "sense of solidarity." It implies membership in the human community, i.e., a feeling of identification with humankind and an empathy for each member of the human race:

> Social interest means . . . feeling with the whole, *sub specie aeternitatis,* under the aspect of eternity. It means a striving for a form of community . . . as it could be thought of if mankind had reached the goal of perfection. It is never a present-day community or society, nor a political or religious form. Rather the goal . . . would have to be a goal which signifies the ideal community of all humanity, the ultimate fulfillment of evolution (Adler, 1964, pp. 34–35).

As this passage reveals, *social interest* in its own overriding sense consists of the individual helping society to attain the goal of an ideal community. Stated differently, it is an attitude toward life of giving and of serving, which is expressed in the Bible as "It is more blessed to give than to receive."

Adler considered the potential for social interest to be innate. Since every human being has some amount of it, every person is a social creature by nature, not by habit. However, like any other innate predisposition, social interest does not emerge automatically but needs to be consciously developed. It has to be nourished to fruition through proper guidance and training.

The development of social interest takes place in a social environment. Other people, initially the mother, then other family members, and finally those beyond the home, contribute to this developmental process. However, it is the mother, the child's first and most influential contact with another person, who exerts the greatest impact on the development of social interest. Essentially, Adler viewed her job as twofold: to develop and encourage mature social interest and to help direct it beyond her scope. Both functions are difficult to perform and are always influenced to some extent by how the child interprets the mother's behavior.

Since social interest arises in the mother-child relationship, the mother's task is to foster in her child a sense of cooperation, relatedness, and comradeship, concepts Adler considered to be closely intertwined. Ideally, the mother should display a genuine deep-rooted love for her child—a love centered on the well-being of the child, not the vanity of the mother. This healthy love relationship develops from a true caring about people and enables the mother to foster her child's social interest. Her affection for her husband, her other children, and for people in general, provides a model for the child, who learns from this demonstration of broad social interest that there are other important people in the world. Adler observed that the ability to engender social interest in the child can be realized only by a person who feels comfortable with the three major tasks of life—occupation, friendship, and love and marriage.

Many life-style attitudes associated with mothering may also stifle the child's sense of social interest. If, for instance, the mother concentrates solely on her children, she will not be able to teach them to transfer social interest to other people. Likewise, if she favors her husband and shuns her children and society, her children will feel unwanted and cheated, and their potential for social interest will remain dormant. Any behavior which intensifies the children's feelings of being neglected and unloved brings about a lack of autonomy and an inability to cooperate in the children.

Adler viewed the father as the second most important source of influence in fostering a child's social interest. First, he must have a positive attitude toward his wife, his occupation, and society. In addition, his developed social interest must manifest itself in his relationship with his children. For Adler, the ideal father is one who treats his children as fellow human beings and who cooperates on an equal footing with his wife in caring for them. The father must also avoid the dual errors of emotional detachment and paternal authoritarianism, which, surprisingly, have similar effects. Paternal detachment leads to thwarted social interest in the children, i.e., children who experience paternal detachment tend to pursue a goal of personal superiority rather than one based on social interest. Similarly, paternal authoritarianism also leads to a faulty style of life. Children whose father is tyrannical learn to strive for power and personal, rather than social, superiority.

Finally, Adler considered the relationship between wife and husband to have an enormous impact on the children's development of social interest. If, for instance, the marriage is unhappy, children have little chance of developing social interest. If the wife turns her emotional support away from her husband and toward the children, the children are harmed since overprotection smothers social interest. If the husband openly criticizes his wife, the children lose respect for both parents. If there is dissension between husband and wife, the children learn to play one parent against the other. The eventual losers in this game are the children; they inevitably lose when their parents demonstrate no love for one another.

Social Interest as a Barometer of Psychological Health   According to Adler, the degree of social interest represents a useful yardstick for measuring the individual's psychological health. He referred to it as the "barometer of normality," the criterion to be used in judging the worth of a person's life. Thus, in Adler's view our own lives have value only to the extent that we add value to the lives of others. Normal or healthy persons are genuinely concerned about other individuals and their goal of superiority is social, encompassing the well-being of all people. Although they realize that all is not right with the world, they are committed to the task of improving the lot of humankind. In short, they know that their own lives have no value unless they contribute to the lives of their fellow human beings and even to the lives of those in the future.

Maladjusted people, by contrast, are those who lack social interest. As we will see later, they are self-centered, strive for personal superiority and superiority over others, and lack social goals; each lives a life that has only private meaning (preoccupied with self-interest and self-protection).

Creative Self

Earlier we noted that the foundations of the life-style are laid down and settled in the early years of life. Indeed, Adler believed that the life-style becomes so firmly crystallized by the time children are five years old that they proceed in the same direction for the rest of their days. Viewed one way, this account of how the life-style is formed would seem to indicate that Adler is just as deterministic in his thinking as Freud. Both theorists, in fact, stressed the importance of early experiences in the development of the adult personality. But, unlike Freud, Adler held that behavior in later years is not simply a *reliving* of early experiences, but rather a characteristic expression of the individual's personality that was formed during the first few years of life. More to the point, the notion of the life-style is not as deterministic as it may seem, especially when we consider the particular concept in Adler's system called the *creative self*.

The creative self is the superordinate construct in Adler's theory, his ultimate achievement as a personologist. Once he discovered and incorporated it into his system, all other concepts were subordinated to it. Here at last was the active principle of human life—that which imparts meaning to life—that Adler had been seeking. Succinctly stated, Adler maintained that the *style of life is developed by the individual's creative power*. In other words, each person is empowered with the freedom to create his or her own life-style. Ultimately, people are solely responsible for who they are and how they behave. This creative power is responsible for the person's life goal, determines the method of striving for the goal, and contributes to the development of social interest. This same creative force also influences perception, memory, imagination, fantasy, and dreams. It makes each person a free (self-determined) individual.

Adler actually never used the term "creative self." It was introduced by Hall and Lindzey (1957) in their presentation of Adler. Heinz Ansbacher (1971), a leading Adlerian scholar in this country, writes: "It is in a sense regrettable that their term has caught on so well, because Adler's original term, 'creative power of the self,' is much more dynamic and less conducive to static and elementaristic reification (p. 55)." Be that as it may, Adler firmly believed that the life-style is the creative act of the individual; it is her or his unique interpretation of the environment. Thus, *people are in control of their fate, not the victims of it.*

In essence, the doctrine of a creative self states that people are what they make themselves. Their creative power endows them, within certain limits, with the freedom to be whatever they will. For Adler, human creative power is not something mysterious or unscientific, as it may at first appear. After all, the cultural and technological world in which we find ourselves is a human creation; on this basis alone it is reasonable to assume creative power in human beings. In Adler's sense, such creative power means the ability to envisage goals and make decisions, choices, and all sorts of arrangements consistent with the individual's purposes and values.

In assuming the existence of a creative force, Adler did not deny heredity and environment as determining forces in shaping human behavior. Every child is born with a unique genetic endowment, and he or she soon comes to have social experiences different from those of any other individual. People, however, are much more than products of heredity and environment. They are creative beings who not only react to their environment, but act on it and make it react to them. A person uses heredity and environment as the bricks and mortar of personality, but the architectural design reflects the person's own style. Adler writes:

> Heredity only endows him with certain abilities. Environment only gives him certain impressions. These abilities and impressions, and the manner in which he "experiences" them—that is to say, the interpretation he makes of these experiences—are the bricks which he uses in his own "creative" way in building up his attitude toward life. It is his individual way of using these bricks, or in other words his attitude toward life, which determines this relationship to the outside world (1956, p. 206).

Thus, people mold their personalities out of the raw materials of heredity and experience. Of primary importance is not what people bring with them, but how they put it to use. The building materials of personality are secondary. Persons are their own architects. They are who they are because of the use they have made of their bricks and mortar.

What is the origin of human creative power? What causes it to develop? These questions were not completely answered by Adler. The best answer to the first question seems to be that human creative power is the outcome of a long evolutionary history. Humans possess a creative force because they are human. We know that the creative force blossoms forth during early childhood and that it accompanies the development of social interest, but exactly why and how it develops remains unexplained. Nonetheless, its presence enables each of us to create our own most appropriate life-style out of the abilities and opportunities given us by hereditary and environment.

Order of Birth

In accordance with his emphasis on the social influences upon personality, Adler (1931) suggested that certain life-styles frequently develop as a function of one's ordinal position within the family. Specifically, he reasoned that even though children have the same parents and grow up in nearly the same family setting, they do not have identical social environments. The experiences of being older or younger than one's brothers and sisters and of being exposed to parental attitudes and values that vary as a result of the arrival of more children, additional education, or specific circumstances create unique conditions of childhood that profoundly influence the formation of one's life-style.

For Adler, the child's numerical rank in the family constellation is of considerable importance. Particularly important are the perceptions of the situation that are likely to accompany the position occupied. Thus, it is the meaning that children attach to the situation that actually determines in what way their particular ordinal positions will influence their life-style. Moreover, because perceptions are inevitably subjective, children born in any position may create for themselves any life-style. In general, though, certain characteristics are commonly found in children born at a specific position. Adler focused on four such birth-order positions: the first-born, the second-born, the youngest, and the only child.

The First-Born (Oldest) Child   Because she or he is first-born, the oldest child is in the enviable position for a time of being an "only child." Usually the parents are thrilled if not somewhat anxious about the arrival of their first-born and are thus totally devoted to doing all the "right things" for their new baby. The first-born thus receives the parents' undivided love and care. In turn, she or he often enjoys a secure and serene existence—until another child is born to remove the favored status. This event dramatically changes the child's situation and view of the world.

Adler often referred to the first-born as the "king dethroned," and noted that this might be a very traumatic experience. Seeing that a younger sibling is winning the contest for parental attention and affection, the oldest child's natural inclination is to fight back in order to regain his or her former supremacy in the family. However, the battle to recapture the original position is doomed from the beginning; things will never be quite the same as they were, no matter how hard the first-born tries. Eventually the child learns that the parents are too busy, too harassed, or too unconcerned to tolerate infantile demands. Then, too, the parents exercise far more power than the child and are likely to counter troublesome (attention-getting) behavior with punishment. The final outcome of this family struggle is that the first-born child "trains himself for isolation" and masters the strategy of surviving alone and independently of the need for anyone's affection or approval.

The Second-Born (Middle) Child   The second child has, from the very beginning, a pacesetter in the form of an older brother or sister and is thus stimulated, or perhaps challenged, to outdo the older child's exploits. This spurs the second-born, often generating a faster rate of development than the first-born exhibited. For example, the second child may begin talking and walking at an earlier age than the first child did. "He behaves as if he were in a race, as if someone were a step or two in front and he had to hurry to get ahead of him. He is under full steam all the time (Adler, 1931, p. 148)."

As a result of all this, the second-born is characterized by being highly competitive and ambitious. Her life-style is one of constantly trying to prove that she is better than her older sibling. Thus, the middle child is characterized by being achievement-oriented, using both direct and devious means to surpass the older sibling. It is of some interest to note that Adler was a second-born.

The Youngest Child   The situation of the youngest or last-born child is unique in several ways. First, he never experiences the shock of dethronement by another child and may, as the "baby" or "pet" of the family, be pampered not only by the parents but, particularly in large families, by older siblings as well. Second, if the parents are economically strapped, he may be relegated to the position of "tag-along kid" who has nothing of his own and must get by on hand-me-downs from other family members. Third, with several older models that set the pace, all of whom are bigger, stronger, and more privileged than he is, he is likely to experience strong feelings of inferiority coupled with a lack of independence.

Nevertheless, the last-born possesses one advantage: a high motivation to surpass older siblings. As a result, this child often becomes the fastest swimmer, the best musician, the most talented artist, or the most ambitious student in the family constellation. Adler sometimes spoke of the "fighting youngest child" as the child most likely to become a revolutionary.

The Only Child   According to Adler, the only child is in the unique position of not having other siblings with whom to compete. This fact, coupled with a vulnerability to being pampered by the mother, often leads an only child into an intense rivalry with the father. She or he thus becomes "tied to the mother's apron strings" and expects pampering and protection from all others too. Dependency and self-centeredness are the leading qualities of this life-style.

Such a child continues to be the focus of family attention throughout childhood. In later life, however, occurs a rude awakening—the discovery that he or she is no longer the center of attention. The only child had never had to share the center stage nor to compete with other siblings for it.

Each of the above examples represents a stereotypic description of the "typical" oldest, middle, youngest, and only child. And, as previously noted, not every child in each of these categories will fit the general life-style descriptions proposed by Adler. What he was suggesting is that each child's original position in the family is likely to present certain kinds of problems, e.g., having to give up being the center of attention after having held the limelight for some time, having to compete with others who have more expertise, and so on. Thus, Adler's interest in birth order relationships was nothing more than an effort to discover the kinds of problems faced by children and the kinds of solutions children might develop in trying to cope with these problems.

Fictional Finalism

As already noted, Adler believed that everything we do in life is marked by our striving for superiority, for perfection. More to the point, he felt that the striving for superiority is a general motivation that takes concrete form as a striving toward a subjectively experienced superordinate goal. To appreciate his reasoning here, we need to examine Adler's concept of *fictional finalism,* the idea that fictional goals guide our present behavior.

Soon after Adler broke away from the group that surrounded Freud, he came under the influence of Hans Vaihinger, a prominent European philosopher. Vaihinger, in a book entitled *The Philosophy of "As If"* (1911), proposed the thought-provoking notion that people are more affected by their expectations of the future than by their actual past experience. He further argued that many people proceed through life behaving "as if" certain ideas are true when, in fact, such ideas have no basis in reality. For Vaihinger, then, people are motivated not by what is true, but by what they *believe* to be true. Vaihinger's book so impressed Adler that he modified and adopted several of its concepts for his theory.

Adler theorized that our ultimate goals (those goals which exert the most influence over the course of our lives) are *fictional* goals that can neither be tested nor confirmed against reality. Some persons may, for instance, conduct their lives in terms of the belief that with hard work and a little luck, they can accomplish almost anything. To Adler, this belief constitutes a *fiction* simply because there are many people who work hard and yet never accomplish anything. Another example of a fiction which exerts a powerful influence on the lives of countless individuals is the belief that God will reward them in heaven for living a virtuous life on earth. Belief in God and heaven can be considered fictional in nature because there is no scientific way of proving their existence. Nevertheless, such beliefs are real to persons who embrace a religious system of faith. Other examples of fictional beliefs which affect the course of our lives include "honesty is the best policy," "all people are created equal," "all people are basically selfish," and "men are superior to women."

According to Adler, each individual's quest for superiority is defined by the fictional goal that he or she has adopted. He also believed that the individual's fictional goal of superiority is self-determined; it is formed by the person's own creative power, therefore making it individually unique. Thus, as a subjectively held ideal, the fictional goal of superiority has great significance. When an individual's fictional goal is known, all subsequent actions make sense and his or her life-style takes on added meaning.

Although fictional goals have no counterpart in reality, they often help us to deal with reality more effectively. In fact, Adler insisted that if such goals do not serve us well in coping with daily life, they should be modified or discarded. It may seem strange to say that a fiction may be useful, but an example will clear up this point. A college professor may strive to be excellent in her field of specialization. But excellence has no final limits. She can always learn more about her subject. Certainly, she could devote more time to reading journals and textbooks than she presently does. She might also enhance her knowledge by attending professional conventions, workshops, and seminars. Yet the professor's ultimate goal, by its very nature, will never be completely attained. Her striving to attain excellence is, however, a useful and healthy striving. Both she and her students are likely to benefit from her fictional goal.

Fictional goals may also be dangerous and harmful to the person. Consider, for instance, the hypochondriac who acts as if she were sick. Or the paranoid who acts as if he were being persecuted. Perhaps the most devastating instance of a destructive fiction was the Nazi-induced belief that Aryans constitute a superrace. The belief obviously has no basis in reality, yet Adolf Hitler convinced many Germans to act *as if* Aryans were a superrace.

In summary, Adler's concept of fictional finalism reveals the extent to which he emphasized a teleological, or goal-directed, view of human motivation. Personality, as he saw it, is influenced more by fictions, or expectations of the future, than by experiences of the past. Our behavior is guided by our perception of our fictional goal in life. This goal does not exist in the future but in our present perception of the future. Although our fictional goals have no objective existence, they nonetheless exert an enormous influence on the direction of our lives.

Following are the basic assumptions about human nature which underlie Adler's theoretical concepts and system.

ADLER'S BASIC ASSUMPTIONS CONCERNING HUMAN NATURE

Adler is considered by many a "neo-Freudian," and he undoubtedly did much to develop the psychoanalytic movement as a whole. But while he was admittedly an early associate of Freud's in the Vienna circle, many of Adler's ideas depart more radically from classical psychoanalytic theory than may generally be recognized. Indeed, careful consideration of Adler's theoretical concepts strongly suggests that, far from being a "neo-Freudian," he may actually be more accurately understood as a precursor of contemporary humanistic and phenomenological psychology. Nowhere is this interpretation of Adlerian psychology more compelling than in his basic assumptions concerning human nature (see Figure 3-1).

Freedom–Determinism   Adler's strong commitment to the freedom assumption is clearly revealed in the following quotation: "We regard man as if nothing in his life were causally determined and as if every phenomenon could have been different . . . in psychology we cannot speak of causality or determinism (Adler, 1956, p. 91)." Rejecting the concept of objective determinants in psychology, Adler (1927a) instead argued that each individual's personality is largely his or her own creation. And the embodiment of the freedom assumption in Adler's system is the concept of creative self. Ultimately, the individual's creative powers play a vital part in the construction of a superordinate fictional goal and consequent style of life.

However, there is some limitation on the idea of total freedom in individual psychology in that life-style is at least influenced by the fictional life goal that originates in early childhood experience (e.g., birth order). Even this fictional goal, however, is not a product of objective factors; it stems instead from the budding person's creative powers (e.g., the subjective meaning that an individual attaches to his or her ordinal position within the family). It seems that, as Adler worked toward his crowning theoretical achievement of the creative self, a strong underlying assumption of freedom became more and more evident.

Rationality–Irrationality   Adlerian theory represents a nice blend of the rationality assumption encountered in contemporary ego psychology within the psychoanalytic tradition (e.g., Erikson, Chapter 4) and the irrationality assumption so central to classical Freudian psychology. On balance, Adler definitely

	Strong	Moderate	Slight	Midrange	Slight	Moderate	Strong	
Freedom	■							Determinism
Rationality		■						Irrationality
Holism	■							Elementalism
Constitutionalism				■				Environmentalism
Changeability							■	Unchangeability
Subjectivity	■							Objectivity
Proactivity	■							Reactivity
Homeostasis							■	Heterostasis
Knowability							■	Unknowability

Figure 3-1   Adler's position on the nine basic assumptions concerning human nature.

inclines toward rationality, an inclination most evident in his concept of the creative self. Recall that in individual psychology the creative power of human beings enables them to envisage goals, make decisions, and select various life arrangements consistent with their purposes and values. The notion of such creative power requires a commitment to rationality for its base.

But strains of irrationality can be detected in Adler's theory, most particularly in his concept of the overriding fictional goal which guides one's life. Blurred by an overlay of childhood experiences, this goal is largely unconscious, i.e., people are largely unaware of the fictional goal or at least its true significance in their lives (Adler, 1956). Thus, a significant part of what people strive for in life, however rationally they may do it, remains largely unknown to them. Nevertheless, the sheer weight that Adler assigns the creative self in his theory clearly tilts this parameter in the direction of rationality.

Holism–Elementalism   Adler's complete commitment to the holism assumption is evident in almost every facet of his work. As already indicated, Adler even named his position "Individual Psychology" in order to express his holistic conception of the human being as a single, indivisible, self-consistent, and unified entity. And, as discussed earlier, the foremost tenet of individual psychology is that of "the individual as a unified and self-consistent entity."

On a more specific level, Adler depicts the creative self in childhood as fashioning a fictional final goal toward which people strive all their lives; indeed, one's entire style of life is largely predicated on this final goal. Adler (1956) argued that the ultimate unity of the personality is found in this individually unique final goal, the governing principle of one's life-style and direction. In Adlerian theory, the person's behavior can *only* be understood in the context of this finalistic or teleological conception of human striving: "we can never regard a person other than as a self-consistent being and thus as a goal-directed and purposeful whole (Adler, 1956, p. 177)." Adler's commitment to the holism assumption could not be more explicit or complete.

Constitutionalism–Environmentalism   "Do not forget the most important fact that not heredity and not environment are determining factors. Both are giving only the frame and the influences which are answered by the individual in regard to his styled creative power (Adler, 1956, p. xxiv)." In this assertion Adler clearly establishes his position on the constitutionalism–environmentalism dimension: while both constitution and environment must be acknowledged as factors in personality makeup, each is utterly dwarfed by the significance of the creative self. In individual psychology, it's not what you have (constitution) or what you experience in life (environment) but what *you do* with each that counts.

To be sure, Adler recognized hereditary and constitutional factors in human nature, e.g., social interest and striving for superiority or perfection are innate, and organ inferiority influences personality development. But by the same token, recall that social interest develops in a social environment, striving for superiority or perfection is actualized by each individual in his or her own way, and the effects of organ inferiorities (positive or negative) upon personality development depend on how people react to these constitutional shortcomings. Likewise, while Adler recognized the importance of environmental influences (e.g., order of birth) on personality makeup, the crucial thing again is how the person chooses to perceive and react to such influences. So Adler's position on this assumption might best be understood as "middle of the road"; because of the overriding power of the creative self in fashioning personality, neither constitution nor environment seems invested with very much force in Adlerian theory.

Changeability–Unchangeability   While Freud and Adler differ dramatically on many of the basic assumptions about human nature, they appear to see eye-to-eye on the issue of unchangeability. Like Freud, Adler was convinced that the first five years of life are absolutely formative in personality makeup and that personality *fundamentally* changes little or nought after those formative years. But the unchangeability assumption manifests itself differently in Adler's theory than it does in Freud's.

Specifically, in individual psychology the key reflection of unchangeability is found in Adler's concept of style of life. Rooted in early inferiority feelings and compensation, style of life crystallizes at around age five and thereafter influences all aspects of an individual's behavior. Indeed, via life-style, people live out the rest of their days striving for superiority and forever seeking to attain the fictional final goals created during their early childhood years. And while style of life may manifest itself in different ways at different periods, it basically does not change throughout life. Adler's commitment to the unchangeability assumption seems quite strong indeed.

Subjectivity–Objectivity   Antedating contemporary phenomenological psychology (e.g., Rogers, Chapter 11), Adler was totally committed to the subjectivity assumption. From the very first, with the basic tenet of "individual subjectivity" underlying Adlerian theory as discussed earlier, subjectivity is evident in virtually every major concept of individual psychology. For example, the child's objective order of birth is not as important in personality formation as the subjective *meaning* that the child attaches to the position and its accompanying situation. And again, social interest initially develops as a function of how the child *interprets* the mother's behavior, rather than in response to the objective content of that behavior. Subjectivity is preeminently manifest in Adler's concept of fictional finalism, however, which must ultimately be understood as the individual's pursuit of a fictional goal which, in actuality, is a *subjective* fictional goal *experienced in the present* (Adler, 1930). In Adlerian psychology, one's entire style of life is built around this individually unique, subjective goal.

Adler's (1956, p. 192) term for one's subjective world, *schema of apperception,* refers to a person's opinions of herself or himself and of the surrounding world. In individual psychology, all objective events must first be processed through and transformed by the intermediary psychological metabolism of this subjective schema before they have any impact on personality or behavior: "The conceptual world, is, as we both assumed and found to be the case, subjective in its forms. . . . The whole framework in which we place what is perceived is only subjective (Adler, 1956, p. 83)." Adler's commitment to the subjectivity assumption could not be stronger or more explicitly stated.

Proactivity–Reactivity   As noted earlier, a basic tenet of individual psychology regards "human life as a dynamic striving for perfection." Herein is found the clearest reflection of Adler's total commitment to the proactivity assumption. In Adlerian theory, the locus of behavioral causality is always found *within* the individual—specifically in the persistent, future-oriented, and all-consuming striving for superiority or perfection. Indeed, Adler postulates only one proactive and dynamic force underlying all human activity: the quest for superiority or perfection. Rooted in the subjectively experienced inferiority feelings of infancy and childhood, this ever-present desire is aimed at the individual's self-created fictional final goal; all life activity is organized around this goal. Far from merely reacting to external environmental stimuli, then, the person in Adlerian psychology is depicted solely in terms of self-generated, future-oriented striving.

Homeostasis–Heterostasis   To appreciate Adler's position on this salient assumption, it is worth repeating a brief quote from his writings: "The impetus from minus to plus never ends. The urge from below to above never ceases (Adler, 1930, p. 398)." This is most definitely not the language of a homeostatically inclined theorist who sees people as motivated to reduce tensions and maintain an internal state of equilibrium. Indeed, such language clearly implies tension *increase* in the constant impulse from "minus to plus," from "below to above."

Adler's strong commitment to the heterostasis assumption is evident in his concept of life's fundamental motive—the striving for superiority or perfection. People do not reduce tensions in this lifelong striving; they generate tensions in the ongoing struggle to achieve their fictional goals. But, as will be evident later (e.g., Maslow and Rogers, Chapters 10 and 11), Adler's heterostasis is of a somewhat different nature than that commonly encountered in the humanistic and phenomenological psychologies of today. In the latter versions of heterostasis, individuals are portrayed as self-actualizing, i.e., constantly moving in the direction of actualizing their full potentialities as persons. Typically, these potentialities are seen as innate, and the individual simply follows the natural growth inclination to fulfill them. In the Adlerian version of heterostasis, people are portrayed as constantly striving for superiority or perfection and the overriding fictional final goal, conveying a sense of completing one's subjective life mission rather than fulfilling all of one's potentialities as a person. And the fictional final goal is not innate, since it is ultimately rooted in the inferiority feelings of infancy and childhood. So in Adlerian psychology one could argue that people are actually growing in directions *against* their original inclinations and potentialities, insofar as the striving for superiority, life-style, and fictional goals are rooted in earlier inferiority feelings. Nonetheless, in individual psychology people *are* growing, moving forward, and generating tension increase—all of which reveals Adler's strong commitment to the heterostasis assumption.

Knowability–Unknowability As noted previously, Adler was heavily influenced by Vaihinger's (1911) *The Philosophy of "As If."* This philosophy, which quickly became Adler's, is called *idealistic positivism,* a term which, for our purposes, might best be understood to mean that ideational constructs (e.g., "fictions"), even when they may contradict reality, have great practical value and are indispensable for human life (Adler, 1956). Phrased differently, what is important in life is *not* what is or may be absolutely true (for who can know this?) but what *we believe* to be absolutely true. As regards the knowability-unknowability issue in personology, this philosophical doctrine would seem to apply to psychological science as much as it does to people, viz., rather than fruitlessly searching for the "absolute truth" of human nature, psychological science is better off developing theoretical concepts (personological "fictions"?) that are practical and useful for people attempting to understand themselves and their everyday lives.

This is precisely what Adler did in constructing his personality theory. Viewed in this light, it may be no accident that the first book in which Adler fully addressed the general issue of human nature, *Understanding Human Nature* (1927b), was also his first written for the general public. Thus, the apparent simplicity and pragmatic nature of many of Adler's theoretical concepts, far from suggesting an essential lack of mystery in human nature, may actually reflect Adler's philosophical conviction that this is the best that psychological science can do in depicting human nature. And Adler realized that his science did not, could not, have all the answers: "I must admit that those who find a piece of metaphysics in Individual Psychology are right. . . . Whether you call it speculation or transcendentalism, there is no science which does not have to enter the realm of metaphysics (Adler, 1956, p. 142)." Given his underlying philosophical position, then, Adler clearly must be placed on the unknowability side of this particular assumption dimension.

Let us now turn to the important question of how the concepts of individual psychology have been empirically tested.

EMPIRICAL VALIDATION OF INDIVIDUAL PSYCHOLOGY CONCEPTS

Despite the consistent and enduring influence exerted by Adler's theoretical system noted earlier, we must not overlook the issue of empirical validation, namely, the question of whether or not Adlerian psychology has generated research in support of its core concepts and assertions. Indeed, empirical verification of the principles of individual psychology is essential if Adler's insights are to contribute significantly to the scientific understanding of human behavior. Unfortunately, however, most of the constructs in Adler's theory have not been studied by means of modern experimental research methods. Rotter (1962) has identified three specific problems encountered in trying to establish the validity of Adlerian concepts, problems which at least partially explain why research-minded personologists have neglected to test Adler's views in a systematic way. First, many of Adler's constructs are global in nature, lacking the kind of clear-cut operational definitions that are necessary for rendering a theory testable. This is especially true for a term like "social interest." To illustrate, does concern for other people refer to social attitudes, to observable behavior, to good intentions toward others, or to all three? How does one judge whether or not a given type of behavior reflects social interest? People whose stated goal is to improve the quality of life for everyone might take hostages and make bombs to radically alter governmental policies; their destructive behavior may be motivated by good intentions and commendable goals, but their means are highly questionable. Other people might donate generously to worthwhile causes, but do so primarily in order to enhance their public image or to lower their taxes. Here, the behavior is admirable but the motivation underlying the behavior is selfish. Clearly, then, the concept of social interest is open to several conflicting interpretations and is very dependent upon the values held by the observer. As a consequence, it is often unclear to the experimentalist what logical operations should be used in order to measure such a construct.

A second problem in validating individual psychology as a system lies in the lack of specific lower-order constructs. For example, while "style of life" is an important and often-used construct in the theory, Adler provided no real classification system for characteristics of different life-styles. As a result, prediction and description of individual differences is quite limited. This is not to suggest that a typology of life-styles should be made, but rather that a logical basis for categorizing or grouping should be devised. It goes without saying that individuals within a group will differ and that differences between groups are probably continuous rather than discrete.

Third, Adler's theory is not fully systematized, particularly with regard to overlapping terms (e.g., "neurotic style of life," "mistaken style of life," "pampered style of life"). As a result, the relationship of one concept to another in the system is rather vague. For example, are the struggle for personal superiority and masculine protest the same, or merely overlapping constructs? If different, are they totally separate entities, or related to one another? These problems should be regarded not as criticisms, but as challenges to those who are interested in expanding Adlerian theory in the direction of increased possibilities for rigorous experimental or objective verification (Rotter, 1962). Regrettably, few personologists have heeded Rotter's challenge.

Thus, while individual psychology may be of high practical relevance, direct empirical tests of its concepts are sparse in number. Consequently, it is impossible to offer a definitive statement about the theory's current empirical validity. In fact, much of the evidence for the theory is based on clinical observations in therapy sessions, and is largely unsystematic and retrospective. However, Adlerian psychology has played a significant role in drawing attention to birth order, or ordinal position, and its effect on the development of various kinds of life-style characteristics. An example of birth-order research, partially inspired by Adler's theoretical insights, follows. Additionally, we shall consider a study which employs a recently developed measure of social interest to evaluate the validity of Adler's view of psychological health.

Birth Order, Fear, and Affiliation

Adler, as you will recall, devoted special attention to the individual's ordinal position within the family constellation as an important influence upon life-style development. This emphasis paved the way for a large research literature dealing with the effects of ordinal position on the development of a host of behavioral characteristics. In fact, research in this area has taken on voluminous dimensions, comprising some 400 publications between 1963 and 1971 alone (Vockell, Felker, and Miley, 1973). While potentially relevant to Adler's theory, much of this research does not offer explicit tests of theory-derived hypotheses, and little of it has been used to extend and refine the theory. Moreover, all of the findings by no means support Adlerian theory.

It is not our purpose here to review the vast literature on birth order. Sampson (1965) and Schooler (1972) provide excellent summaries for the interested reader. But it might be instructive to consider in detail one investigator's study which has not only received considerable attention but has also generated widespread interest among research-oriented personologists. We refer to Stanley Schachter (1959), whose study on the relationship of birth order, fear, and affiliative behavior is seminal in the area.

Noting that people who are involved in shipwrecks, blackouts, and natural disasters often become fearful during the event, Schachter (1959) reasoned that affiliation with others might reduce the isolated person's fear; and that being in a fear-arousing situation might cause some people to wish to affiliate with others. Specifically, Schachter hypothesized that highly fearful persons would show affiliative tendencies significantly more than less fearful persons. This hypothesis was examined in a laboratory experiment using the following procedure.

Female college students were ostensibly told that they were about to participate in an experiment concerned with the effects of electric shock on pulse rates and blood pressures. The laboratory setting contained several kinds of electrical equipment and the experimenter, who wore a white lab coat, introduced himself as a member of the department of medicine. Each subject was given a description of the experiment, and the instructions were designed to arouse either a considerable degree of fear (high-fear condition) or a lesser degree of fear (low-fear condition).

In the *high-fear* condition, subjects were told that the electrical shocks would be quite painful, but would produce no permanent tissue damage. In the *low-fear* condition, the experimenter told the subjects that they would receive shocks, but they would be very mild and would only cause a tingling sensation. Manipulation checks demonstrated that subjects in the high-fear condition were much more frightened than those in the low-fear condition, indicating that the two sets of instructions were effective in eliciting different degrees of fear.

Following this arousal of fear, all subjects were informed that there would be a ten-minute delay while the experimenter set up the equipment. The subject was told that she had the option of waiting alone and reading a magazine or waiting in another room with other participants. Subjects were then asked to choose whether they preferred waiting alone, with others, or had no preference. They were also

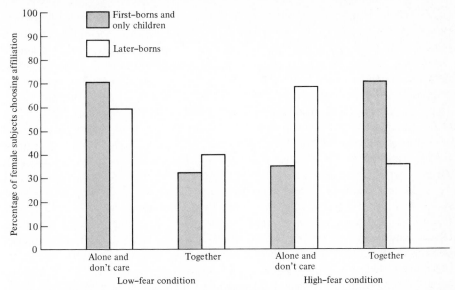

Figure 3-2 Percentage of first-borns (including only children) and later-borns choosing to affiliate under nonstress and stress conditions. (*Adapted from Schachter, 1959, pp. 44–45.*)

asked to rate the strength of their preference. This self-report measure of choice of waiting together (affiliation) or alone (nonaffiliation) was the dependent measure. Incidentally, none of the subjects ever received any shock.

As predicted, subjects in the high-fear condition were significantly more likely to want to affiliate with others than were subjects in the low-fear condition. More intriguing, however, for our purposes, was Schachter's finding that ordinal position of subjects was related to affiliative tendency. Specifically, it was found that first-borns and only children not only reported being more anxious than later-borns, but a larger percentage of them chose to wait together with other women (i.e., their affiliative tendency was stronger). Indeed, Schachter observed that regardless of family size in which they had been reared, first-borns and only children showed greater affiliation than second-borns, second-borns greater affiliation than third-borns and so on. Figure 3-2 presents the data in graphic form.

Schachter interpreted his results as a reflection of differences in the ways in which parents typically interact with first-borns as compared with later-born children. Specifically, he argued that parents are particularly solicitous and perhaps somewhat anxious about their first child. Uncertain and worried about the proper ways to treat their first-borns, these parents are especially likely to pick up the child whenever it shows signs of fear or distress. They also give the child inordinate amounts of attention in order to reduce their own anxiety and the anxiety they have generated in the child. This concern on the part of the parents tends to have a tranquilizing effect, and the child comes to expect that the presence of other people is likely to reduce fear. Presumably, then, first-born children learn to depend upon others as a means of reducing their own anxiety. While there are no doubt exceptions, most parents are probably less anxious and less overprotective in their interactions with later-born children. For example, when their second-born starts to cry, they may not feel compelled to run to its aid immediately, as they did with their first-born. Thus, as Schachter sees it, the association between the presence of others and fear-reduction tends not to become as strong for later-born children as it does for first-borns. Adler, on the other hand, observed that first-born children are often the center of attention and are made anxious not by unpracticed parenting, but by loss of their central position to younger siblings. In turn, they begin efforts to regain their original status by behaving in accordance with parental expectations, thus seeking out others with whom they can affiliate. That first-borns indeed do tend to affiliate more than later-borns under stressful conditions is explained quite differently by Schachter than by Adler. The point is that Schachter's results are not to be construed in the strictest sense as supportive of Adler's theory. In fact, it is all too easy to assume that because Adler emphasized birth order effects, any research outcome in this area must be taken as evidence in support or nonsupport of his theory. Such is not the case. Rather, a major asset of his theory is its heuristic value—its ability to stimulate future thinking and research —and not the amount of scientific evidence which has been accumulated in its support to date.

Measuring Social Interest

Earlier we noted that Adler's concept of social interest has been given various interpretations by different individuals. Indeed, the concept is highly global, with so many ramifications that it does not yield easily to operational definition. Recently, however, efforts to construct a reliable and valid measure of social interest have appeared in the psychological literature (Crandall, 1975; Greever, Tseng, and Friedland, 1973). Here we shall consider one such attempt to develop a standardized measure of the concept as well as a study which examines the validity of Adler's claim that high social interest is associated with optimal mental health.

Greever, Tseng, and Friedland (1973) developed a brief self-report test called the Social Interest Index (SII) for determining an individual's degree of social interest. Items for the test, selected on the basis of Adler's writings and consensus among three prominent Adlerians, reflect a varying relationship to democratic cooperation in the broad sense, acceptance of self and others, having a place in the world, and feeling that one is part of the continuity of that world. Sample items are presented below:

1 I don't mind helping out friends.
2 I feel jobs are important because they make you take an active part in the community.
3 I feel I have a place in the world.
4 As far as I am concerned, marriage is for life.

Instructions require the subject to indicate, using a five-point scale of personal relevance, the extent to which each item applies to him or her ("not at all like me" or "very much like me"). The items are scored to measure the level of social interest the subject has attained in each of four areas: work, friendship, love, and self-significance. The scoring system is such that high SII scores are indicative of high social interest while low SII scores reflect low social interest.

While the SII appears to represent a means of studying social interest, additional research is needed to judge its empirical adequacy or its theoretical relevance to Adler's position. A study conducted by one of the authors (Hjelle, 1975) provides evidence for the validity of the SII as well as support for Adler's assertion that developed social interest is a key attribute of psychological well-being.

Hjelle (1975) reasoned that the concepts of social interest and self-actualization, although formulated in different theoretical contexts, do represent overlapping conceptions of psychological maturity. The rationale for this line of reasoning derived from an examination of Adler's and Maslow's respective views on optimal mental health. Specifically, Adler considered social interest as the sine qua non for the psychological soundness of any individual or group. Similarly, Maslow's portrayal of the self-actualizing person (see Chapter 10) placed considerable emphasis on effective transaction and cooperative effort within the social milieu. Accordingly, it seemed plausible to expect that high social interest persons would manifest greater self-actualization than low social interest persons.

Seventy-two female undergraduates were administered the SII and Shostrom's (1966) Personal Orientation Inventory (POI). The latter instrument was used to measure self-actualization and will be more thoroughly described in Chapter 10. As predicted, women who evidenced high social interest were significantly more self-actualized on the POI than those who evidenced low social interest. These findings support the validity of Adler's criterion for psychological maturity, that is, a cooperative empathic attitude toward others. It should be stressed, however, that these results are restricted to college-age women and that any generalizations to men and/or other segments of the population must await further research. Nonetheless, an important contribution of Hjelle's study is the cross-validation of the SII as an empirical measure of social interest as conceived by Adler. Future research of this type may further open the door to the possibility of measuring Adler's elusive construct of social interest.

We turn now to an examination of how Adler's ideas can be applied to an understanding of neurotic behavior and its therapeutic treatment.

APPLICATION: NEUROSIS AND ITS TREATMENT

Adler wanted above all else to create a practical and useful psychology that would be relevant to the everyday world of human affairs. In particular, he sought to develop a theoretical system that would enable him to account for the causes and development of neuroses as well as furnish him a coherent basis for the psychological treatment of such disorders. In this section, then, Adler's theoretical concepts will be applied to the understanding of neuroses and their mitigation via Adlerian psychotherapy.

The Nature of Neurosis

From Adler's perspective, neurosis was a broad-based diagnostic term designed to encompass a variety of behavioral disorders for which persons often sought treatment from the psychiatrists of the day. These disorders manifested themselves in an equally rich variety of symptoms, e.g., anxiety, morbid doubts or fears, obsessions, compulsions. Each symptom, according to Adler (1956), provided a safeguard for the individual's self-esteem which was always bound up with the person's hidden goal of superiority. Like Freud, then, Adler was intent on explaining neurosis in terms of his own personological constructs.

What Is Neurosis?   While Adler wrote volumes on neurotic behavior (e.g., Adler, 1917a), perhaps his best definition of *neurosis* for our purposes is the following: "Neurosis is the natural, logical development of an individual who is comparatively inactive, filled with a personal, egocentric striving for superiority, and is therefore retarded in the development of his social interest, as we find regularly among the more passive pampered styles of life (Adler, 1956, p. 241)."

Once this definition is separated into its component parts, a number of Adler's theoretical concepts become evident. "Comparatively inactive" refers to the "degree of activity" dimension in Adler's typology of life-style attitudes, i.e., the individual's movement toward the solution of life's problems, his or her arousal or energy level. In Adler's system, then, neurotics are people characterized by a lack of activity required and desirable for the correct solutions to their life problems. Perhaps this is just as well, since Adler believed that if they did have a higher degree of activity, people of this ilk would tend to become criminals!

A second key phrase in Adler's definition, "a personal, egocentric striving for superiority," suggests that neurotics typically strive toward personal, egocentric, and selfish life goals, the antithesis of the Adlerian concept of social interest. In other words, neurotic persons strive unduly hard toward exaggerated goals of self-enhancement at the expense of serious concern for their fellow human beings—the essential meaning of the "retarded in the development of his social interest" phrase in the foregoing definition. Moreover, Adler (1956) believed that neurotic individuals set their superiority goals higher than normal people and then proceed to strive for these goals with more rigidity. Adler saw both tendencies as compensations for the increased inferiority feelings of neurotics.

A final essential phrase in the Adlerian definition of neurosis, "passive pampered styles of life," reflects Adler's (1917a) conviction that neurotics are people who fundamentally *want to be* pampered by others (rather than necessarily those who actually *have been* pampered in the past). Lacking social interest and the degree of activity required to meet life tasks, neurotics want to depend exclusively on others in coping with life's daily problems.

To better appreciate the nature of neurosis from an Adlerian perspective, consider the following brief case illustration:

> Gwen, an 18-year-old mathematics major completing her freshman year, came to the
> college counseling center with complaints of anxiety, bodily signs of stress (e.g., mus-

cular tension in the shoulders and neck region before exams), occasional depression, and great dissatisfaction with her academic performance. She could give no clear reasons for the anxiety and also felt that her somatic tensions were much greater than normal. Further, while her grades ranged from average to above-average (i.e., "C" to "B"), Gwen was intensely dissatisfied and occasionally depressed about this performance, feeling instead that she should be earning "As," particularly in her math courses. As counseling progressed, it also became evident that Gwen had always experienced extreme difficulty making friends and relating to people. She tended to be haughty and aloof in interpersonal relationships, believing most people to be frivolous and intellectually inferior to her. This interpersonal difficulty was most evident in the recitation groups associated with her math courses (a source of great worry and discomfort to her) in which students were expected to work together with the recitation instructor in unraveling the complexities of the math lectures and textbooks.

Gwen was an only child whose father was a successful physician and whose mother was a high school mathematics teacher. She grew up with material things in abundance and parents who catered to her every whim. She was sent to small private schools, given a great deal of tutorial attention, and excelled academically in these circumstances. Matriculating at a large university away from home represented a dramatic change in Gwen's life, and constituted much more of an adjustment problem than it does for most college students. Gwen's neurotic difficulties came to the fore during this period.

From Adler's perspective, then, Gwen fundamentally lacks the degree of activity required to solve her present life problems, is striving toward a personal egocentric goal of superiority, and, lacking in social interest, wants to go through life being pampered by others. Her neurotic symptoms are the result.

What Causes Neurosis? Gwen's unfortunate psychological condition, like that of other neurotics, is by no means exclusively her own doing. While Adler did believe that people are fundamentally responsible for their own behavior and life direction (i.e., the freedom assumption), he also argued that the neurotic life-style tended to result from the person being "overburdened" during childhood (Adler, 1956). Specifically, the same three situations described earlier in this chapter as leading to inferiority complexes were also seen by Adler as likely to overburden the child: (1) organ inferiorities, (2) pampering, and (3) neglect. According to Adler, each of these overburdening childhood situations can result in the self-centered, noncooperative, and unrealistic personal goal-oriented life-style characteristic of neurotics.

Of the three overburdening childhood situations, pampering appears best to fit Gwen's case, since it encompasses all those family environments in which children are raised to receive without giving. Having been pampered and given excessive attention throughout her childhood years, Gwen lacked social interest and failed to learn the give-and-take inherent in adult cooperative relationships, e.g., she could not function in the math recitation classes since total attention could not be focused on her.

In summary, then, neurotics are people who have acquired faulty life-styles, usually because they experienced either physical afflictions, pampering, or rejection during early childhood. Under such conditions, Adler believed, these children became highly anxious, felt insecure, and began to develop protective devices to cope with feelings of inferiority. Underneath her other behavior, then, Adler would argue that Gwen always felt anxious and insecure, and probably developed at least some protective devices to cope with her inferiority feelings, e.g., her haughty and aloof approach to interpersonal relationships and her view of others as intellectually inferior.

The Onset of Neurosis   Born into an overburdening childhood situation, the creative self fashions what Adler termed a "mistaken" or neurotic style of life. Essentially, the neurotically predisposed individual, lacking in social interest, creates a selfish fictional goal, thereby missing out on the fundamental value which Adler (1939) attributed to human life. Such persons necessarily go through life with great underlying insecurity, constantly threatened self-esteem, and oversensitivity (Adler believed that neurotics behave as if they were living in a land of enemies). Almost inevitably, then, this mistaken style of life will clash with human interrelatedness; plainly, as is illustrated in Gwen's case, the neurotic life-style is incompatible with the demands of cooperative social living.

In Adlerian theory, this fundamental conflict occurs in relation to any one or all of the three major life tasks described earlier in this chapter—work, friendship, and love and marriage. Facing these tasks, which demand fellowship and cooperation, the neurotic's entire life-style and unconscious fictional goals are under siege. Thus, what Adler termed an *exogenous factor* always precipitates the outbreak of actual symptoms in a neurotically predisposed individual: "We must remember that it is the exogenous situation which sets the match to the fire (Adler, 1944, p. 4)." Under such circumstances, the creative self reaches frantically for means to protect threatened self-esteem as well as for behavioral excuses for one's life situation. One may begin to believe in an arrogant way that one is superior to others and act in ways consistent with this belief. Similarly, one may strive to be perfect and belittle others.

In Gwen's case, the exogenous factor seemed to be her matriculation at a university away from home and the accompanying demands to function autonomously (in an unpampered fashion) in pursuing her occupational goals. Uprooted from her pampered circumstances, Gwen's entire self-centered life-style was severely threatened; she was being forced to give of herself by the social demands of the educational situation. This was particularly evident in the math recitation class, a situation that caused her considerable worry and discomfort.

The Treatment of Neurosis

The overall approach to treating neurosis in individual psychology logically follows from Adler's theoretical conception of the nature of neurosis. If neurotic symptoms are actually outgrowths of the patient's mistaken style of life and underdeveloped social interest, then the goal of therapy should be to correct such mistakes while encouraging the development of social interest. Succinctly stated, the goals of therapy for Adler are threefold: (1) to reorganize our mistaken beliefs about ourselves and others; (2) to eliminate faulty goals; and (3) to implement new life goals that will enable us to realize our full human potential. In turn, Adler maintained that the realization of these therapeutic goals could best be accomplished through understanding the patient, enhancing patient self-understanding, and strengthening social interest (Adler, 1956).

Understanding the Patient   "The most important element in therapeutics is the disclosure of the neurotic system or life-plan (Adler, 1927a, p. 14)." That is, in order for the therapist to help the patient to achieve greater self-understanding, she or he must first attain a workable understanding of the patient's fictional goals and life-style. For example, what is it that Gwen is unconsciously striving for? What are her egocentric fictional goals and how do these relate to her neurotic life-style? For Adler, such global understanding can best be realized by focusing therapeutic attention upon such patient factors as earliest childhood recollections, birth order position, childhood disorders, dreams, and the exogenous factor precipitating the onset of the neurosis. In the case of earliest childhood recollections, for example, Adler would instruct Gwen to report the earliest experiences that she could recall. Adler would then compare these recollections with related facts that Gwen had already given him about her more recent life experiences to understand the common themes or goals that, often unconsciously, guide her behavior. To illustrate, suppose Gwen's earliest recollection was as follows:

> At one of my birthday parties, I remember that my mother gave me a kind of jigsaw puzzle for a present. Try as I could during the party, I couldn't put it together, even though some of the other children at the party could. When my mother left the room, the other children laughed at me and made fun of me because I couldn't do it. When my mother came back, she did it for me. My mother could always do things like that—she is a mathematics teacher. . . .

Such a reported recollection, irrespective of its accuracy, would provide the Adlerian therapist with a valuable clue to the nature of Gwen's life-style and associated goals of personal superiority.

In attempting to understand the patient's essential life-style, Adler (1956) also employed such procedures as empathy, intuition, and guessing (recall his position on the unknowability assumption). Through empathy, or putting himself in the place of the patient, Adler believed that he could achieve a workable intuition about the patient's mistaken life plan. When uncertain, Adler resorted to guessing, generating hypotheses about the causes of patient behavior that would constantly be tested and revised against the background of subsequent patient behavior. Intimately associated with these procedures was Adler's careful attention to patient expressive behavior (e.g., body language, facial expressions, gait, posture, gestures) and symptoms. Like Freud, Adler observed every facet of patient behavior, leaving little unnoticed.

Through such means an Adlerian therapist should be able to achieve a workable understanding of Gwen's neurotic system or life plan. It may be, for example, that Gwen is unconsciously striving for the fictional goal of total intellectual superiority over all others in a given field (e.g., mathematics). She will symbolically solve those jigsaw puzzles and nobody will ever laugh at her again! She may even wind up superior to her mother in this respect. A "mistaken" life-style such as Gwen's could easily be unconsciously constructed around such fictional goals.

Enhancing Patient Self-Understanding   For treatment to progress successfully, it is not enough that the therapist understand the neurotic person's system or life-plan. The neurotic patient must also come to understand it, and to accept such understanding. In other words, the patient must gain *insight* into the nature of his or her fictional goals, style of life, and consequent neurotic symptoms. Thus, Gwen herself needs to understand her fictional goal of total intellectual superiority, the neurotic life-style that she has constructed around it, and the high symptomatic price that she is currently paying for it. Eventually, she must come to realize that psychological health is contingent upon the development of a cooperative attitude toward others and upon her efforts to contribute to the improvement of society.

Adler was quite clear about what he actually did to enhance such patient self-understanding: "I have found it best merely to search for the patient's neurotic line of operation in all his expressions and thoughts and to unmask it, and at the same time train the patient unobtrusively to do the same (Adler, 1956, p. 334)." Without ever pushing or offending patients, Adlerian therapists carefully bring them to the point where they really want to listen and to understand their basic "mistaken" or faulty life-styles. As the prominent Adlerian therapist Rudolf Dreikurs notes, tact and the avoidance of dogmatic assertions are critical throughout this process, e.g., interpretations are offered by the therapist with phrases such as "Would you like me to tell you . . . ?" or "Could it be . . . ?" (Dreikurs, 1973). Next the therapist provides explanations so clear that "the patient knows and feels his own experience instantly (Adler, 1956, p. 335)." Once she is stripped of her mistaken goals of egocentric superiority and possessed of a clear understanding of the symptomatic consequences of her neurotic life-style, Gwen will presumably reorient herself to life in a nonneurotic, socially constructive fashion. In turn, she should slowly but surely move toward reorganization of her perceptions and begin to behave differently toward others, e.g., perceive others in terms other than intellectual inferiority and begin to discard her haughty and aloof interpersonal style. It should be noted that throughout this process Adler constantly stressed that the patient, not the therapist, bears primary responsibility for a successful outcome (recall Adler's position on the freedom assumption).

Strengthening Social Interest   The centrality of social interest as a therapeutic objective is paramount for Adler: "All my efforts are devoted towards increasing the social interest of the patient. I know that the real reason for his malady is his lack of cooperation, and I want him to see it too. As soon as he can connect himself with his fellow men on an equal and cooperative footing, he is cured (Adler, 1956, p. 347)." Believing that neurotic people are retarded in the development of social interest, then, Adlerian therapy becomes an exercise in cooperation. The task of the therapist becomes one of giving the patient the kind of interpersonal contact with a fellow human being that can enable the patient to transfer this awakened social interest to others. This the therapist does by unconditionally encouraging social interest in the patient, decreasing his or her feelings of inferiority while simultaneously activating the seeds of social interest. In a sense, then, the Adlerian therapist belatedly assumes the functional role of mother in developing social feeling. And as social interest gradually develops in the psychotherapeutic context, the patient substitutes social, useful life goals for selfish ones, gains courage (activity plus social feeling), and learns to live without defensive excuses (neurotic symptoms) for a mistaken life-style.

Essentially, strengthening social interest represents a kind of reorientation and reeducation of the patient, processes viewed by Adlerians as the most important phase in psychotherapy (e.g., Ansbacher, 1977). It is not enough that Gwen simply understand her neurotic life-style: she must take action to change it. From the viewpoint of individual psychology, Gwen must come to see that there is more in life than attaining total intellectual superiority for herself. She must appreciate her place in society, recognize and adopt socially useful goals, and learn to pursue these goals with vigor. A more healthy life-style and a lack of neurotic symptoms should result.

Thus, Adler's individual psychology ends as it began—a personological system devoted to the practical understanding of human beings as they are confronted by the daily problems of living. And Adler's approach to psychotherapy, while alive and well today in its own right, encompasses views that have been incorporated into the mainstream of many other contemporary therapeutic systems. To name but a few, his humanistic emphasis upon holism and subjectivity is reflected in Carl Rogers' *person-centered therapy* (a system in which the total person and his or her subjective experience is of central importance—see Chapter 11), his emphasis on freedom and responsibility in Viktor Frankl's (1967) *existential therapy* (a system highlighting the role of responsible free choice in fashioning the direction of one's life), his ideas about cognitive change (i.e., reorientation and reeducation) in Albert Ellis's (1973) *rational-emotive therapy* (a system focusing on cognitive as well as emotional restructuring to foster adaptive behavior), and his commonsense notions in William Glasser's (1965) *reality therapy* (a system known for its overall pragmatic thrust). Thus clinicians of today, be they formally designated as Adlerians or not, can still find much of relevance in the pioneering work of Alfred Adler. Regardless of the empirical validation difficulties and the actual efficacy of Adlerian therapy (which is still being investigated today), Adler has made a significant contribution to personology through his creation of a system that helps people to understand themselves and others while simultaneously serving as a basis for the therapeutic treatment of disordered behavior.

SUMMARY

Alfred Adler's individual psychology holistically depicts the human being as single, indivisible, self-consistent, and unified. As a personological system, individual psychology has as its basic tenets the individual as a unified and self-consistent entity, human life as a dynamic striving for perfection, the individual as a creative and self-determined entity, the social embeddedness of the individual, and individual subjectivity.

Adler developed a parsimonious and pragmatic theory designed to be helpful to people in understanding themselves and others. In this personality theory, individuals are depicted as experiencing inferiority feelings during childhood for which they attempt to compensate. Rooted in these inferiority feelings of childhood, people spend their lives striving for superiority. Indeed, each person develops a unique style of life in which he or she strives for fictional final goals involving superiority or perfection. Furthermore, Adler believed that a person's style of life is most evident in his or her attitude and behavior toward the three major life tasks—work, friendship, and love and marriage; based upon the dimensions of social interest and the degree of activity in relation to these three life tasks, Adler distinguished four basic types of life-style attitudes: the ruling, getting, avoiding, and socially useful types.

Of paramount importance in developing one's style of life is Adler's superordinate personological construct, the creative self. Essentially, Adler theorized that style of life is developed by the individual's creative power. Also of some influence on personality development is one's ordinal position within the family; Adler focused theoretical attention upon four such birth-order positions: the first-born, second-born, youngest, and only child. A final important construct in individual psychology is social interest, a person's innate tendency and striving to help society attain the goals of an ideal community. In Adlerian theory, degree of social interest is viewed as a barometer of psychological health.

Adler's basic assumptions about human nature strongly suggest that, far from being the "neo-Freudian" that he is often considered, he may actually be more accurately understood as a precursor of contemporary humanistic and phenomenological psychology. Individual psychology reflects (1) a strong commitment to the assumptions of freedom, holism, unchangeability, subjectivity, proactivity, heterostasis, and unknowability; (2) a moderate commitment to the rationality assumption; and (3) a "middle of the road" position on the constitutionalism–environmentalism dimension.

While Adler's theoretical concepts are acknowledged to have high practical relevance, empirical tests of these concepts have been sparse in number. Difficulties in empirically validating the constructs of individual psychology stem mainly from their global nature, the lack of specific lower-order constructs in the system, and the less than fully systematized status of this theoretical position. Nonetheless, in this chapter empirical studies concerned with birth order as well as the measurement of social interest were highlighted.

In the concluding chapter section, Adler's concepts were applied to the understanding of neurosis and its treatment. Adler's ideas about the nature, causes, and onset of neurosis were described, along with his therapeutic treatment approach emphasizing the processes of understanding the patient, enhancing patient self-understanding, and strengthening social interest.

BIBLIOGRAPHY

Adler, A. *The neurotic constitution.* New York: Moffat, 1917a.

Adler, A. *A study of organ inferiority and its psychical compensation: A contribution to clinical medicine* (1907). (Trans. S. Jeliffe.) New York: Nervous and Mental Disease Publishing Co., 1917b.

Adler, A. *The practice and theory of individual psychology.* New York: Harcourt, Brace & World, 1927a.

Adler, A. *Understanding human nature.* Garden City, New York: Garden City Publishing Co., 1927b.

Adler, A. *The science of living.* New York: Greenberg, 1929.

Adler, A. *The pattern of life.* New York: Holt, Rinehart and Winston, 1930a.

Adler, A. *The education of children.* New York: Greenberg, 1930b.

Adler, A. *What life should mean to you.* Boston: Little, Brown, 1931.

Adler, A. *Social interest: A challenge to mankind.* New York: Putnam, 1939.

Adler, A. Physical manifestations of psychic disturbances. *Individual Psychology Bulletin,* 1944, **4,** 3–8.

Adler, A. *The individual psychology of Alfred Adler: A systematic presentation in selections from his writings.* Edited by H. and R. Ansbacher. New York: Basic Books, 1956.

Adler, A. *Superiority and social interest: A collection of later writings.* Edited by H. and R. Ansbacher. Evanston, Ill.: Northwestern University Press, 1964.

Ansbacher, H. The structure of individual psychology. In B. Wolman (Ed.), *Scientific Psychology.* New York: Basic Books, 1965, pp. 340–364.

Ansbacher, H. Alfred Adler and humanistic psychology. *Journal of Humanistic Psychology,* 1971, **11,** 23–63.

Ansbacher, H. Individual psychology. In R. Corsini (Ed.), *Current Personality Theories.* Itasca, Ill.: Peacock, 1977, pp. 45–82.

Crandall, J. A scale for social interest. *Journal of Individual Psychology,* 1975, **31,** 187–195.

Dreikurs, R. *Fundamentals of Adlerian psychology.* New York: Greenberg, 1950.

Dreikurs, R. *Psychodynamics, psychotherapy, and counseling.* Chicago: Alfred Adler Institute, 1973.

Ellenberger, H. Alfred Adler and individual psychology. In *The discovery of the unconscious: The history and evolution of dynamic psychiatry.* New York: Basic Books, 1970.

Ellis, A. Rational-emotive therapy. In R. Corsini (Ed.), *Current psychotherapies.* Itasca, Ill.: Peacock, 1973.

Frankl, V. *Psychotherapy and existentialism.* New York: Washington Square Press, 1967.

Glasser, W. *Reality therapy.* New York: Harper & Row, 1965.

Greever, K., Tseng, M., & Friedland, B. Development of the social interest index. *Journal of Consulting and Clinical Psychology,* 1973, **41,** 454–458.

Hall, C., & Lindzey, G. *Theories of personality.* New York: Wiley, 1957.

Hjelle, L. Relationship of social interest to internal-external control and self-actualization in young women. *Journal of Individual Psychology,* 1975, **31,** 171–174.

Jones, E. *The life and work of Sigmund Freud.* New York: Basic Books, 1957.

Maslow, A. Tribute to Alfred Adler. *Journal of Individual Psychology,* 1970, **26,** 13.

Rotter, J. An analysis of Adlerian psychology from a research orientation. *Journal of Individual Psychology,* 1962, **18,** 3–11.

Sampson, E. The study of ordinal position: Antecedents and outcomes. In B. Maher (Ed.),

Progress in experimental personality research. Vol. 2. New York: Academic Press, 1965, pp. 175–228.

Scarf, M. Psychoanalyst Adler: His ideas are everywhere. *The New York Times Magazine,* Feb. 28, 1971, pp. 10–11, 44–47.

Schachter, S. *The psychology of affiliation.* Stanford, Calif.: Stanford University Press, 1959.

Schooler, C. Birth order effects: Not here, not now! *Psychological Bulletin,* 1972, **78,** 161–175.

Shostrom, E. *Manual: Personal Orientation Inventory.* San Diego: Educational and Industrial Testing Service, 1966.

Vaihinger, H. *The philosophy of "as if"* (1911). New York: Harcourt, Brace & Co., 1925.

Vockell, E., Felker, D., & Miley, C. Birth order literature 1967–1972. *Journal of Individual Psychology,* 1973, **29,** 39–53.

SUGGESTED READINGS

Mosak, H. (Ed.). *Alfred Adler: His influence on psychology today.* Park Ridge, N.H.: Noyes, 1973.

Orgler, H. *Alfred Adler: The man and his work.* New York: New American Library, 1972.

Sperber, M. *Masks of loneliness: Alfred Adler in perspective.* New York: Macmillan, 1974.

Zucker, R., Manosevitz, M., & Lanyon, R. Birth order, anxiety, and affiliation during a crisis. *Journal of Personality and Social Psychology,* 1968, **8,** 354–359.

DISCUSSION QUESTIONS

1 Compare Adler's basic assumptions about human nature to those of Freud. On this basis, can you see why the authors do not regard Adler as truly a neo-Freudian? Do you agree?

2 Do you agree with Adler that childhood feelings of inferiority play an important part in people's lives? To illustrate, can you see any present areas of strength or accomplishment in your own life that seem to have their roots in earlier inferiority feelings?

3 What do you think of Adler's concept of striving for superiority? How do you strive for superiority in your life? Can you see how your own direction and goals in this regard differ from those of your friends?

4 Do you agree with Adler that social interest is the barometer of psychological health? If so, why? If not, why not?

5 Now that you have studied Adler's theory, think about your ordinal position in your family. Can you see how being the first-born, second-born, youngest, or only child has affected your overall personality development?

GLOSSARY

Birth Order   The individual's ordinal position (e.g., first-born) within the family which, in turn, plays an important role in shaping his or her life-style.

Compensation   Attempt by an individual to replace feelings of inadequacy with feelings of adequacy through development of physical or mental skills. A physically weak person who becomes an outstanding athlete serves as an example of compensation.

Creative Self   Concept used by Adler to reflect his belief that each person is empowered with the freedom to actively create his or her own personality.

Fictional Finalism   Term used by Adler to convey the notion that human behavior is guided by imagined or fictional goals that can be neither tested nor confirmed against reality.

Individual Psychology   Name used by Adler to designate his personality theory. The theory emphasizes the uniqueness of each individual and the processes by which people overcome their limitations and struggle to reach their life goals.

Inferiority Complex   Deep pervasive feeling that one is inferior to other people. It is often associated with faulty attitudes and behaviors.

Inferiority Feelings   Feelings of inadequacy, ineptness, and incompetence which emerge during infancy and thus serve as the basis for strivings for superiority.

Organ Inferiority   Congenitally weak or poorly functioning organ in the body (e.g., a visual defect) that gives rise to feelings of inferiority on the part of the individual. For Adler, an organ inferiority often leads an individual to striking accomplishments in life.

Overcompensation   A form of compensation that does more than rid the person of feelings of inadequacy—it leads to superiority or outstanding achievement. A person who overcompensates may act as though he or she feels superior to others (i.e., evidence a superiority complex).

Social Interest   The feeling of empathy for the rest of humanity which manifests itself as cooperation with others for social advancement rather than personal gain. For Adler, social interest is a useful yardstick of psychological health.

Striving for Superiority   The striving to achieve mastery over one's limitations and to develop to one's fullest potential. Adler viewed this striving as the great dynamic force underlying human behavior.

Style of Life   The unique configuration of traits, motives, cognitive styles, and coping techniques that characterizes the behavior of an individual and gives it consistency.

Erik H. Erikson

Erik Erikson: A Psychosocial Theory of Personality

Erik Erikson is one of a number of psychoanalysts who are commonly identified as *ego psychologists.* Like others to whom this label has been applied, he has focused major attention on the development and functions of the ego and has been less concerned with what Freud called the id and superego. For Erikson, it is the ego that merits the greatest attention in relation to individual development. It does not follow, however, that he neglects either biological or social factors in his theory. In fact, he stresses the idea that any psychological phenomenon must be understood in terms of the reciprocal interplay of biological, behavioral, experiential, and social factors. Other features that distinguish Erikson's theoretical orientation include: (1) an emphasis on developmental change throughout the entire human life cycle; (2) a focus on the "normal" or "healthy" rather than the pathological; (3 a special emphasis on the importance of achieving a sense of identity; and (4) an effort to combine clinical insight with cultural and historical forces in explaining personality organization. However, Erikson's discussion of the "Eight Ages of Man" represents his most original and important contribution to personality theory. His attempt to show how culture can influence personality development has provided the student of human behavior with fresh and genuine advances in understanding the major psychological problems that confront humanity today.

BIOGRAPHICAL SKETCH

Erik Erikson was born in 1902 near Frankfurt in Germany. His parents were Danish, and both of them had grown up in Copenhagen. Before his birth, however, his parents separated, and his mother left Denmark. When he was 3 years old, his mother remarried Dr. Theodor Homburger, a Jewish pediatrician who had cured her son of a childhood disease. Young Erik was not told for some years that Dr. Homburger was, in fact, his stepfather. Later, in signing his first psychoanalytic articles, Erikson used his stepfather's surname as his own, although he chose to be known by his original name when he became a naturalized American citizen in 1939.

Unlike any other personologist discussed in this text, Erikson did not pursue formal education beyond high school. He attended a "humanistic gymnasium" in Karlsruhe, Germany, and, although he was a mediocre student, he did excel in the subjects of ancient history and art. Shortly after graduation, spurning his stepfather's urgings that he become a physician, Erikson left home to travel across central Europe. A year later, he enrolled in an art school in Karlsruhe and for a brief period accepted the fact that even an aspiring artist could learn something in an educational setting. However, he soon became restless again and set out for Munich to study at the famous art school there, the Dunst-Akademie. Two years later, Erikson moved to Florence, Italy, although for a period he wandered aimlessly throughout Italy, soaking up sun and visiting art galleries. Fortunately, however, he came to realize that "such narcissism obviously could be a young person's downfall unless he found an overweening idea and the stamina to work for it (Erikson, 1970b, pp. 743–744)."

In 1927, at the age of 25, Erikson ended his occupational "moratorium" when he accepted an unexpected invitation from Peter Blos, a high school classmate, to join him and Dorothy Burlingham as teachers at a small American day nursery in Vienna. The school, known as the Kinderseminar, had been established by Anna Freud for children whose parents were learning to become psychoanalysts. Some of Erikson's young students were in analysis themselves, and eventually their teacher—Herr Erik, as he was affectionately called—joined them.

Erikson's introduction to the study of psychoanalysis began at a mountain spa near Vienna. There, as a tutor, he first came to know the Freud family and was subsequently selected as an acceptable candidate for training at the Vienna Psychoanalytic Institute. From 1927 to 1933, Erikson continued his training in psychoanalysis under the guidance of Anna Freud and August Aichhorn. This constituted his only formal academic training aside from a certificate he acquired from the Maria Montessori Teachers Association in Vienna. Today, requirements are far more stringent for students wishing to prepare for professional careers in the field of mental health.

In 1929, Erikson married Joan Serson, a Canadian teacher and dancer who was then also a member of the experimental school led by Anna Freud. In 1933, the Erikson family (including two sons) went to Copenhagen, where Erikson attempted to regain his Danish citizenship and to help establish a psychoanalytic training center in that country. When this proved impractical, the family emigrated to the United States and settled in Boston where a psychoanalytic society had been founded the year before. Erikson's timely arrival in this country afforded him the distinction of being the first child-analyst in the New England area. For the next two years he practiced in Boston, and for one year, held a clinical and academic appointment as Research Fellow in Psychology in the Department of Neuropsychiatry of the Harvard Medical School. He also enrolled at Harvard as a candidate for the Ph.D. in psychology, although he withdrew from the program a few months later.

While in Boston Erikson also did a bit of work with Henry Murray at the Harvard Psychological Clinic.

During the years 1936 to 1939, Erikson had an appointment with the Department of Psychiatry in the Institute of Human Relations and the Yale University School of Medicine, which allowed him complete freedom to pursue whatever research he desired. During this period he also became interested in cultural anthropology and, in 1938, undertook a field trip to the Pine Ridge Reservation in South Dakota to observe how members of the Sioux Indians raised their children.

In 1939, Erikson moved to San Francisco, where he resumed his analytic work with children and furthered his interest in anthropology and history. By 1942, he was a professor of psychology at the University of California at Berkeley. At the same institution, he participated in the famous longitudinal *Child Guidance Study* under the direction of Jean MacFarlane. What followed was an intense period of close clinical observation and reflection as Erikson prepared to establish—through books—his professional identity as a psychoanalyst. His professorship at Berkeley tragically ended, however, when he refused to sign a loyalty oath. He was later reinstated as politically reliable but chose to resign because others were fired for the same "crime." He published his first book, *Childhood and Society,* in 1950 (revised and reissued in 1963), and this work soon won him recognition as a leading spokesman of ego psychology in this country.

In 1951, Erikson joined a group of mental health professionals at the Austen Riggs Center in Stockbridge, Massachusetts, a private residential treatment center for disturbed young people. He also maintained part-time teaching appointments at the Western Psychiatric Institute in Pittsburgh, the University of Pittsburgh, and the Massachusetts Institute of Technology. For the next decade, his writings and research extended the theory of psychosocial development originally proposed in *Childhood and Society.*

In the summer of 1960, following a year at the Center for Advanced Studies of the Behavioral Sciences at Palo Alto, California, Erikson rejoined Harvard University as lecturer and professor of human development. Erikson says he reentered academia "in order to learn how to teach my whole conception of the life cycle—including identity crisis—to people normatively very much in it (1970b, p. 749)." Although he is now retired, he continues to devote much time and energy to the application of his scheme of the human life cycle to the study of historical persons and American children, predominantly minority groups. His brilliant psychobiographical study of the origins of militant nonviolence, *Gandhi's Truth* (1969), won him a Pulitzer Prize and the National Book Award in philosophy and religion. Moreover, he has published three other important books: *Young Man Luther, A Study in Psychoanalysis and History* (1958), *Insight and Responsibility* (1964a) and *Identity: Youth and Crisis* (1968a), as well as editing another, *Youth: Change and Challenge* (1963b). Robert Coles, a Harvard psychiatrist and student of Erikson, acknowledged his mentor's accomplishments as a theoretician and practitioner of psychoanalysis in a volume entitled *Erik H. Erikson: The Growth of*

His Work (1970). Despite advancing age, Erikson continues to be productive; as of this writing, his most recent publications are *Toys and Reasons* (1977) and *Adulthood* (1978).

EGO PSYCHOLOGY: PSYCHOANALYSIS COMES OF AGE

Erikson's major theoretical formulations are exclusively concerned with growth of the ego. Although he has persistently maintained that his own contributions to the understanding of human development are nothing more than a systematic extension of Freud's conceptions of psychosexual development in light of current social, anthropological, and biological data, Erikson does represent a decisive departure from Freudian theory in four essential ways (Maier, 1965). To begin with, Erikson's work completes a shift in emphasis from the id to the ego, one which Freud only partially acknowledged during the final years of his work. That is to say, Erikson emphasizes the ego rather than the id as the basis of human behavior and functioning. He regards the ego as an autonomous structure of personality (i.e., some portion of ego functioning is not simply determined by the attempt to avoid conflict between the id and the demands of society) which follows a course of social-adaptive development that parallels the development of the id and the instincts. This conception of human nature, called *ego psychology,* constitutes a radical change from earlier psychoanalytic thought in that it depicts persons as much more rational and logical in making decisions and solving problems.

Second, Erikson introduced a new perspective concerning the individual's relationship to parents and the historical matrix in which the family is located. Whereas Freud concerned himself with the influence of parents on the child's emerging personality, Erikson stresses the psychohistorical setting in which the child's ego is molded. He relies on case studies of people living in different cultures to show how the ego's development is inextricably bound up with the changing nature of social institutions and value systems.

Third, Erikson's theory of ego development encompasses the entire life span of the individual (i.e., from infancy to adolescence and eventually maturity and old age). In contrast, Freud limited himself to the effects of early childhood experiences and devoted no attention to development beyond the genital stage. Closer inspection makes it evident, however, that some degree of correspondence does exist between the two theorists with respect to the first five stages of life.

Finally, Freud and Erikson differ on the nature and resolution of psychosexual conflicts. Freud's ambition was to unravel the existence and operation of unconscious mental life and explain how early trauma may bring about psychopathology in adulthood. Conversely, Erikson's mission is to draw attention to the human capacity to triumph over the psychosocial hazards of living. Thus, his theory focuses on *ego qualities* (i.e., virtues) that emerge at various developmental periods. Perhaps this distinction is the key to understanding Erikson's own conception of personality organization and development. Freud's fatalistic warning that man is doomed to social extinction if left to his instinctual strivings is countered by

Erikson's optimistic premise that every personal and social crisis furnishes challenges that are conducive to growth and mastery over the world. To know how a person has mastered each of a series of significant life problems and how the inadequate mastery of early problems incapacitates him or her in dealing with later problems is, for Erikson, the only avenue to understanding a person's life.

Erikson regards himself as squarely in the mainstream of psychoanalytic thought. Robert Coles remarks that "Erikson can be called a strict Freudian because he is loyal to the essential principles that Freud declared to be the core of psychoanalytic work, and because he is very much like Freud—a writer, a man at home in history and philosophy, a clinician who won't let go of the world outside of the office (1970, pp. 267–268)." His own protestations (and those of his interpreters) nothwithstanding, many personologists see Erikson's theoretical efforts as constituting a totally different perspective vis-à-vis the human life cycle. Erikson emphasizes the creative and adaptive powers of the individual and, in agreement with humanists, views persons as potentially good.

Insofar as major theoretical differences between Erikson and Freud have been stressed, it would be only reasonable to note that there are also substantive areas of similarity. For example, both theorists consider the stages of personality as being predetermined and invariant in order of appearance. Erikson also acknowledges the biological and sexual foundations of all later motivational and personal dispositions and is committed to Freud's structural model (id, ego, superego) of personality. Despite these overlapping areas of agreement, many personologists see Erikson's theoretical efforts as fundamentally different from Freud's.

THE EPIGENETIC PRINCIPLE AND MAN'S EIGHT AGES

Central to Erikson's theory of ego development is the assumption that the development of the person is marked by a series of stages that is universal to humanity. The process whereby these stages evolve is governed by the *epigenetic principle* of maturation. By this Erikson means:

> (1) that the human personality in principle develops according to steps predetermined in the growing person's readiness to be driven toward, to be aware of, and to interact with, a widening social radius; and (2) that society, in principle, tends to be so constituted as to meet and invite this succession of potentialities for interaction and attempts to safeguard and to encourage the proper rate and the proper sequence of their enfolding (1963a, p. 270).

In *Childhood and Society* (1963a), Erikson outlined a sequence of eight separate stages of psychosocial ego development, colloquially "the eight stages of man." He postulates that these stages are the result of the epigenetic unfolding of a "ground plan" of personality that is genetically transmitted. An epigenetic conception of development (*epi* means "upon" and *genetic* means "emergence") reflects the notion that each stage in the life cycle has an optimal time (i.e., critical period) in which it is dominant and hence emerges, and that when all of the stages have unfolded according to plan, a fully functioning personality comes into existence.

Furthermore, Erikson hypothesizes that each psychosocial stage is accompanied by a *crisis*, that is, a turning point in the individual's life that arises from physiological maturation and social demands made upon the person at that stage. In other words, each of the eight phases in the human life cycle is characterized by a "phase specific" developmental task, a problem in social development that must be dealt with at that particular time. The different components of personality are determined by the manner in which each of these tasks or crises is resolved. Conflict is a vital and integral part of Erikson's theory, because growth and an expanding interpersonal radius are associated with increased vulnerability of the ego functions at each stage. At the same time, he notes that crisis connotes "not a threat of catastrophe but a turning point and, therefore, the ontogenetic source of generational strength and maladjustment (1968b, p. 286)."

Each psychosocial crisis, when viewed as a dimensional attribute, includes both a positive and a negative component. If the conflict is handled in a primarily satisfactory manner (i.e., the person has a history of ego achievements), the positive component (e.g., basic trust, autonomy) is to a large degree absorbed into the emerging ego and further healthy development is assured. Conversely, if the conflict persists or is primarily resolved in an unsatisfactory fashion, the developing ego is damaged and the negative component (e.g., mistrust, shame, and doubt) is to a large degree incorporated into the ego. While the various theoretically defined conflicts emerge in developmental sequence, this does not mean that earlier achievements and failures are necessarily permanent. Ego qualities attained at each stage are not impervious to new inner conflicts or to changing conditions (Erikson, 1964a). The major point, however, is that the person must adequately resolve each crisis in order to progress to the next stage of development in an adaptive and healthy fashion.

Erikson's reliance on the epigenetic principle of maturation may be clearly seen from his chart of the psychosocial crises of the life cycle (see Figure 4-1). This chart presents the eight developmental stages in terms of a staircase hierarchy arranged in chronological order. The diagonal boxes include both the positive and the negative components of each successive stage, as well as the *psychosocial strength* or *virtue* associated with the successful resolution of each crisis. Consistent with the principle of epigenesis, each stage builds upon the resolution and integration of previous psychosocial conflicts. Erikson proposes, however, that all the conflicts are present in some form from the beginning of postnatal life. For each crisis period, Erikson has delineated the conditions under which relative psychosocial health and corresponding ill health are likely to occur.

Although Erikson assumes that the eight stages are a universal feature of human development, he also believes that there is some cultural variation in the way that an individual deals with the problems of each stage and in the possible solutions to these problems. For example, puberty rites exist in all cultures yet vary widely from one culture to another in their form of expression and their impact on the individual. Moreover, Erikson feels that in every culture there is a "crucial coordination" between the developing individual and the social environment. This coordination is evidenced by what he calls "a cogwheeling of the life cycles," a law of reciprocal development that ensures that society's caretakers are most fit to provide

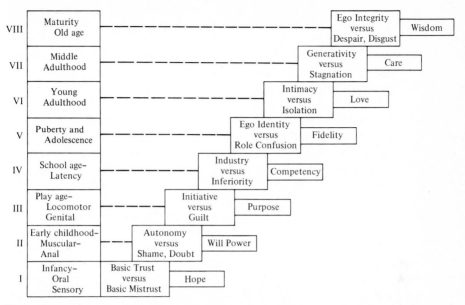

Figure 4-1 Erikson's epigenetic chart of the eight stages of psychosocial development. (*Adapted from* Childhood and Society, by *Erik H. Erikson, 1963a, p. 273.*)

care and support at the time when developing individuals need it most. Thus, in Erikson's view, the needs and capacities of the generations intertwine. This complex pattern of interdependence between the generations is reflected in Erikson's concept of *mutuality.*

Erikson's analysis of socialization can best be presented by describing the distinctive features of the eight stages of psychosocial development.

I Infancy: Basic Trust versus Mistrust—Hope

The first psychosocial stage corresponds to Freud's oral stage and extends through approximately the first year of life. For Erikson, a general sense of trust is the cornerstone of a healthy personality, while others regard this same characteristic as "confidence." A child with a basic sense of "inner certainty" sees the social world as a safe, stable place and people as nurturant and reliable. This sense of certainty is only partially conscious during infancy.

Erikson suggests that the degree to which infants are able to acquire a sense of trust in other people and in the world depends upon the quality of maternal care that they receive. It is the mother who controls both gratification and security:

> Mothers, I think, create a sense of trust in their children by that kind of administration which in its quality combines sensitive care of the baby's individual needs and a firm sense of personal trustworthiness within the trusted framework of their culture's life style. This forms the basis in the child for a sense of being "all right," of being oneself, and of becoming what other people trust one will become. . . . Parents must not only have certain ways of guiding by prohibition and permission; they must also be able to

represent to the child a deep, an almost somatic conviction that there is a meaning to what they are doing (Erikson, 1963a, p. 249).

Thus, a sense of trust does not depend on the amount of food or the expressions of affection the infant receives; rather, it is related to the mother's ability to give her child a sense of familiarity, consistency, continuity, and sameness of experience. In addition, Erikson stresses the fact that infants must trust not only the external world but the internal world as well; they must learn to trust themselves and, in particular, the capacity of their organs to cope effectively with biological urges. Such behavior is shown when the infant can tolerate the mother's absence without suffering undue "separation" anxiety.

The question of what evokes life's first major psychological crisis for the child has been carefully considered by Erikson. He attributes the crisis to a quality of maternal care which is unreliable, inadequate, and rejecting, thus fostering in the infant a psychosocial attitude of fear, suspicion, and apprehension toward the world in general and people in particular that will manifest its ill effects in later stages of personality development. Furthermore, Erikson feels that a sense of mistrust may be augmented when the mother turns from the baby as the primary focus of her attention to other pursuits that she had given up during pregnancy and the early postnatal life of the child (e.g., resuming a career or becoming pregnant again). Finally, parents who display divergent patterns of child care, who lack self-confidence in their role as parents, and who have value systems conflicting with the dominant life-style of the culture may create an atmosphere of ambiguity for the child, resulting in feelings of distrust. The behavioral consequences of a seriously defective development of basic trust, according to Erikson, are acute depression in infants and paranoia in adults. He observes that such individuals, when they enter into a psychotherapeutic relationship, must first be reassured that they can trust the therapist and then trust themselves and finally come to trust the world.

A basic premise of psychosocial theory is that the crisis of trust versus mistrust (or any other subsequent crisis) is not permanently resolved during the first year or two of life. Consistent with the epigenetic principle, trust versus mistrust will reappear at each successive stage of development, although it is focal during infancy. However, adequate resolution of the crisis of trust does have major consequences for the future development of the infant's personality. The establishment of self-trust and trust in mother enables infants to tolerate the frustrations that they will inevitably experience during subsequent stages of development.

Erikson notes that the emergence of healthy growth in the infant does not result exclusively from a sense of trust but rather from a favorable ratio of trust over mistrust. It is as important to learn what not to trust as to learn what to trust. The ability to anticipate danger and discomfort are also essential for mastery of the environment and effective living; thus, basic trust should not be viewed in terms of an achievement scale. In animals, Erikson contends, there is almost an instinctive readiness to acquire this psychosocial ability, but in humans it must be learned. Moreover, he suggests that mothers in different cultures and classes will teach trust and mistrust in different ways, thus reflecting the impact of cultural variation. Yet the attainment of a sense of trust is universal in substance, namely, that one can trust the social world in the form of one's mother, that she will come back and feed one the right thing at the right time.

The psychosocial strength, or virtue, gained from successful resolution of the trust-versus-mistrust conflict is termed *hope* by Erikson. Trust, in other words, becomes the infant's capacity for hope, which, in turn, is the foundation of the adult's faith in some form of institutionalized religion. Hope as the first psychosocial strength also serves to maintain the individual's belief in the meaning and trustworthiness of a common cultural world. Conversely, Erikson emphasizes that when religious institutions fail to provide tangible significance for the individual, these institutions may become irrelevant, outmoded, and possibly even be replaced by other more significant sources of faith and conviction in the future (e.g., commitment to scientific and artistic endeavors, and social action programs).

II Early Childhood: Autonomy versus Shame and Doubt—Will Power

Acquisition of a sense of basic trust sets the stage for the attainment of a sense of autonomy and self-control. This period coincides with Freud's anal stage and roughly spans the second and third years of life. According to Erikson, the child has during this period a choice of social modes—to keep or let go.

Muscular maturation sets the stage for an ambivalent set of social modalities— holding on and letting go. To hold on can become *either* a destructive retaining or restraining *or* a pattern of care—to have and to hold. To let go, too, can turn into either an inimical letting loose or a relaxed "letting be." This stage, therefore, becomes decisive for the ratio of goodwill and willfulness. A sense of self-control without loss of self-esteem is the ontogenetic source of confidence in free will; a sense of overcontrol and loss of self-control can give rise to a lasting propensity for doubt and shame (Erikson, 1968b).

Prior to this stage, children are almost totally dependent on the adults who care for them; their behavior is largely governed by external forces. However, as they rapidly gain neuromuscular maturation, verbalization, and social discrimination, they begin to explore and interact with their environment more independently. In particular, they feel pride in their newly discovered locomotor skills and want to do everything themselves (e.g., dressing and feeding themselves). There is a tremendous desire to explore, choose, and manipulate coupled with an attitude toward parents of "let me do it" and "I am what I will."

In Erikson's view, satisfactorily meeting the psychosocial crisis of this stage depends primarily on the parents' willingness to gradually allow children freedom to control those activities that affect their lives. At the same time, Erikson stresses that parents must maintain reasonable but firm limits in those areas of children's lives that are either potentially or actually harmful to themselves or destructive to others. Autonomy does not mean giving the child unrestricted freedom; rather, it means that parents must maintain "degrees of freedom" over the child's growing ability to exercise choice.

Erikson perceives the child's experience of shame as something akin to rage turned inward because the child has not been allowed to exercise autonomy. Shame may come about if the parents are impatient and insist on doing for children what they are capable of doing themselves or, conversely, if parents expect of children what they are not capable of doing themselves. To be sure, every parent has occasionally pushed his or her child beyond the limits of appropriate expectation. It is only when parents are persistently overprotective or insensitive that children acquire a dominant sense of shame with respect to others and a dominant sense of doubt about their own effectiveness in controlling the world and themselves. Rather than feeling self-confident about their ability to cope effectively with the environment, such children are conscious of being scrutinized (disapprovingly) or of being considered essentially helpless. They are uncertain of their "will power" and of those who would dominate or exploit it. The result is a psychosocial attitude of self-doubt, ineptitude, and powerlessness.

Since each psychosocial stage builds upon the ones preceding it, the attainment of a stable sense of autonomy adds substantially to the child's sense of trust. This interdependence of trust and autonomy may sometimes have the effect of impairing future psychosocial growth. For example, children who have acquired a "shaky" sense of trust may, during the stage of autonomy, become hesitant, fearful, and insecure about asserting themselves; hence, they continue to seek help and encourage others to do things for them. As adults, Erikson finds that such individuals are likely to manifest obsessive-compulsive behavior (to ensure control) or paranoid apprehension of secret persecutors.

The societal counterpart of autonomy is the institution of "law and order." Despite the possibly emotional connotation of this term, Erikson believes that parents must convey a deep and abiding commitment to justice and a respect for the rights and privileges of others if their children are to be prepared to accept a limited autonomy in adulthood. In Erikson's words:

> Willpower is the unbroken determination to exercise free choice as well as self-restraint in spite of the unavoidable experience of shame, doubt, and a certain rage over being controlled by others. Good will is rooted in the judiciousness of parents guided by their respect for the spirit of the law (1968b, p. 288).

III Play Age: Initiative versus Guilt—Purpose

Initiative versus guilt is the final psychosocial conflict experienced by the preschool child during what Erikson calls the "play age." It corresponds to the developmental period Freud designated as the phallic stage and extends from about age 4 to entry into formal school. This is when the child's social world challenges him or her to be active, to master new tasks and skills, and to win approval by being productive. Children also begin to assume additional responsibility for themselves and for that which constitutes their world (bodies, toys, pets, and, occasionally, younger siblings). They become interested in the work of others, in trying out new things, and in assuming the responsibilities available in the society around them. The facility for language and locomotor skills makes possible associations with peers and older children beyond their immediate home environments, thus allowing participation in a variety of social games. This is the age when children begin to feel that they are counted as persons and that life has a purpose for them. "I am what I will be" becomes the child's dominant sense of identity during the play age. To quote Erikson: "Initiative adds to autonomy the quality of undertaking, planning, and "attacking" a task for the sake of being on the move, where before self-will, more often than not, inspired acts of defiance or, at any rate, protested independence (1963a, p. 155)."

Whether children will leave this stage with their sense of initiative favorably outbalancing their sense of guilt depends largely upon how parents react to their self-initiated activities. Children who are encouraged to undertake their own activities have their sense of initiative reinforced. The development of initiative is further facilitated when parents acknowledge their children's curiosity and do not ridicule or inhibit fantasy activity. As Erikson notes, successful development in this stage leads to a "goal-directedness" in the child's behavior:

> The child begins to envisage goals for which his locomotion and cognition have prepared him. The child also begins to think of being big and to identify with people whose work or whose personality he can understand and appreciate. "Purpose" involves this whole complex of elements. For example, when the child plays, it's not just a matter of practicing his will or practicing his ability to manipulate. He begins to have projects, as it were (Evans, 1967, p. 25).

In psychosocial theory, the sense of guilt in children is caused by parents who are unwilling to allow them the opportunity of completing tasks on their own. A sense of guilt is also fostered by parents who employ excessive amounts of punishment (verbal or physical) in response to the child's urge to love and be loved by the opposite-sexed parent. Erikson endorses the Freudian conception of the sexual nature of the developmental crisis involved (i.e., sex-role identification and the Oedipus or Electra complex), although his own conception is decidedly more social in scope. In any event, the child who is immobilized by guilt experiences feelings of resignation and unworthiness. Such children are fearful of asserting themselves, hang on the fringes of groups, and rely unduly on adults. They lack the purpose or courage to establish and pursue tangible goals. Erikson also suggests that a persistent sense of guilt may evolve into a variety of adult forms of psychopathology including generalized passivity, sexual impotence or frigidity, and psychopathic acting out.

Finally, the degree of initiative acquired in this phase of the child's life is related by Erikson to the economic system of the community. He states that the child's future potential to work productively and achieve self-sufficiency within the context of his or her society's economic system depends markedly upon the ability to master this psychosocial crisis.

IV School Age: Industry versus Inferiority—Competency

The fourth psychosocial period occurs from about 6 to 11 years of age ("school age"), and corresponds to the latency period in Freudian theory. Here for the first time the child is expected to learn the rudimentary skills of the culture via formal education (i.e., reading, writing, cooperating with others in structured activities). This period of life is associated with the child's increased powers of deductive reasoning and self-discipline, as well as the ability to relate to peers according to prescribed rules. For example, it is not until this age that children can participate in "take-turn" games that demand compliance with elaborately structured rules. The child's love for the parent of the opposite sex and rivalry with the same-sexed parent are typically sublimated and expressed by an intense desire to learn and to be productive.

In primitive cultures, Erikson notes, the education of children is uncomplicated and socially pragmatic. Facility with utensils, tools, weapons, and other objects is directly related to the child's future role as an adult. Conversely, in cultures where there is a written language, children are first educated in the tools of literacy which, in time, enable them to master the complex skills demanded by various occupations and activities. In effect, although the kind of instruction offered children will vary with the culture, children do become sensitized to the *technological ethos* of their culture and their identity with it.

According to Erikson, children develop a sense of industry when they begin to comprehend the technology of their culture through attending school. The term "industry" characterizes the major developmental theme of this period because children are now preoccupied with the manner in which things are made and operate. Such interest is reinforced and facilitated by people in their neighborhoods and schools who introduce them to the "technological elements" of the social world by teaching and working with them. The child's ego identity is now "I am what I learn."

The danger of this stage lies in the potential development of a sense of inferiority or incompetence. For example, if children doubt their skill or status among their peers, they may be discouraged from pursuing further learning (attitudes toward teachers and learning are established during this period). A sense of inferiority may also develop if children discover that their sex, race, religion, or socioeconomic status—rather than their own skill and motivation—is what determines their worth as persons. The result is that children may lose confidence in their ability to take part in the working world.

As noted above, the child's feeling of competence and industry is, at least in literate cultures, largely affected by her or his educational achievement. Erikson perceives a possible negative effect from this limited definition of success. To be specific, if children accept scholastic accomplishment or work as the only standard by which to judge their self-worth, they may become mere slaves to their culture's work force and its established role hierarchy (Karl Marx described such persons as submitting to "craft-idiocy"). Therefore, a genuine sense of industry involves more than simply one's educational achievements and occupational aspirations. For Erikson, industry includes a feeling of being interpersonally competent—the confidence that one can exert positive influence on the social world in quest of meaningful individual and social goals. The psychosocial strength of competency thus underlies the basis for participation in the social-economic-political order.

V Adolescence: Ego Identity versus Role Confusion—Fidelity

Adolescence, the focus of the fifth stage in Erikson's chart of the life cycle, is regarded as highly significant in the individual's psychosocial development. No longer a child but not yet an adult (roughly from the age of 12 or 13 to about 20 in our society), the adolescent is confronted with various social demands and role changes that are essential for meeting the challenges of adulthood. In fact, Erikson's theoretical interest in adolescence and the problems accompanying it have led him to present a more elaborate analysis of this phase than of any other stage of development.

Erikson theorizes that the new psychosocial dimension which appears during adolescence has a sense of ego identity at the positive end and a sense of role confusion at the negative end. The task confronting adolescents is to consolidate all the knowledge they have gained about themselves (as sons or daughters, students, athletes, musicians, Girl Scouts, choirboys, etc.) and integrate these various self-images into a personal identity that shows awareness of both a past and a future that follows logically from it. Erikson stresses the psychosocial nature of ego identity, with the focus not on conflicts between psychic structures but rather on a conflict within the ego itself, namely, of identity versus role confusion. Emphasis is placed on the ego and the way it is affected by society, particularly peer groups. Ego identity can therefore be defined as follows:

> The growing and developing youths, faced with this physiological revolution within them, are now primarily concerned with attempts at consolidating their social roles. They are sometimes morbidly, often curiously, preoccupied with what they appear to be in the eyes of others as compared with what they feel they are and with the question of how to connect the earlier cultivated roles and skills with the ideal prototypes of the day. . . . The integration now taking place in the form of ego identity is more than the sum of the childhood identifications. It is the inner capital accrued from all those experiences of each successive stage, when successful identifications led to a successful alignment of the individual's basic drives with his endowment and his opportunities. The sense of ego identity, then, is the accrued confidence that one's ability to maintain inner sameness and continuity (one's ego in the psychological sense) is matched by the sameness and continuity of one's meaning for others (Erikson, 1963, p. 261).

Erikson's definition reveals three elements involved in the formation of an identity. First, individuals must perceive themselves as having "inner sameness and continuity," i.e., they must, over time, experience themselves as essentially the same persons they have been. Second, the persons in one's social milieu must also perceive a "sameness and continuity" in the individual. This means that adolescents need confidence that the inner unity that they have developed earlier will be recognized in others' perceptions of them. Insofar as adolescents may be uncertain about both their self-concepts and their social images, then feelings of doubt, confusion, and apathy may counteract their emerging sense of identity. Finally, individuals must have "accrued confidence" in the correspondence between the internal and external lines of continuity. Their self-perceptions must be validated by appropriate feedback from their interpersonal experiences.

Socially and emotionally, the maturation of the adolescent encompasses new ways of appraising and evaluating the world and their relationship to it. They can conceive of ideal families, religions, philosophies, and societies which, in turn, they can compare and contrast with the imperfect persons and institutions of their own limited experience. To quote Erikson: "The adolescent mind becomes an ideological mind in search of an inspiring unification of ideas (1968b, p. 290)." Thus, a "diffusion of ideals" results from the failure to find enduring values in one's culture, religion, or ideology. The person who suffers from identity diffusion has neither reevaluated past beliefs nor achieved a resolution that leaves her or him free to act.

Finally, an appropriate adult sex role is essential for the development of a sense of personal identity. Erikson indicates that where adequate feminine and masculine identifications take place, the personality develops a healthy and harmonious blend of sexually defined qualities. Failure to achieve an appropriate sexual identity frequently results in "bisexual diffusion," thus weakening the identity structure. Where sex identity is unclear, overall ego identity will inevitably be adversely affected.

Erikson claims that the foundation for a successful adolescence and the attainment of an integrated identity originate in early childhood. Above and beyond what adolescents bring with them from childhood, however, the development of a sense of personal identity is significantly affected by the social groups with which they identify. Erikson has stressed, for example, how overidentification with popular heroes (movie stars, superathletes, rock musicians) or counterculture groups (revolutionary leaders, "acidheads," delinquents) cuts off a "budding identity" from its milieu, thus stifling the ego and restricting emergent identity. Likewise, ego identity may be harder for certain groups of people to attain than for others. For instance, it may be difficult for a young woman to achieve a firm sense of identity in a society where she is accorded second-class status. In Erikson's view, the feminist movement has attracted many supporters for the very reason that society, until recently, has frustrated women's effort to attain a positive identity (i.e., society has been unwilling to assimilate women into new social and occupational roles). Minority group members are also beset by difficulties in establishing a firm and coherent sense of identity (Erikson, 1964b).

Erikson also considers the adolescent's vulnerability to the stresses of rapid, social, political, and technological change to be a factor which may jeopardize the development of identity. Such change, exacerbated by the information explosion, contributes to a nebulous sense of uncertainty, anxiety, and discontinuity. It also threatens to break down many traditional and cherished values which young people have learned and experienced as children. The gap between generations reflects at least some of this generalized dissatisfaction with the values of society, perhaps best illustrated by the turmoil on college campuses throughout the United States during the sixties. The truths of one generation become the myths of the next. Accordingly, Erikson interprets much of the social action movement of youth as an attempt to establish some continuity between past, present, and future—a search for identity.

The failure of the young person to develop a personal identity, because of unfortunate childhood experiences or present social circumstances, results in what Erikson has called the "identity crisis." The crisis of identity, or role confusion, is most often characterized by an inability to select a career or pursue further education. Many adolescents in the throes of this age-specific conflict experience a profound sense of futility, personal disorganization, and aimlessness. They feel inadequate, depersonalized, alienated, and sometimes even seek "negative identity," an identity which is opposite to the one prescribed for them by their parents and peers. Some delinquent behavior is interpreted by Erikson in this way. However, the failure to establish adequate personal identity does not necessarily doom the adolescent to a life of perpetual defeat. Perhaps more than any other personologist discussed in this text, Erikson has emphasized that life is constant change. Resolving problems at one stage of life is no guarantee against their reappearance at later stages—or against the discovery of new solutions to them. Ego identity is a lifelong struggle.

In most and perhaps all societies, special delays in the assumption of adult roles and commitments are granted to certain segments of the adolescent population. Erikson coined the term *psychosocial moratorium* to denote these intervals between adolescence and adulthood. In the United States, the psychosocial moratorium has been institutionalized in the form of a system of higher education that enables young people to explore a number of different social and occupational roles before deciding what to do with their lives. In other instances, young people in large numbers have taken to wandering, joining cults, or exploring alternatives to traditional marriage and family life before settling down in a community.

Fidelity emerges from adequate resolution of the ego-identity—role-confusion crisis. As used by Erikson, it refers to the adolescent's "ability to sustain loyalties freely pledged in spite of the inevitable contradictions of value systems (1968b, p. 290)." As the cornerstone of identity, fidelity represents the young person's capacity to perceive and abide by the social mores, ethics, and ideologies of society. The meaning of the term "ideology" as used in this context should be clarified. According to Erikson, an *ideology* is an unconscious set of values and assumptions reflecting the religious, scientific, and political thought of a culture; the purpose of an ideology is "to create a world image convincing enough to support the collective and the individual sense of identity (1958, p. 22)." Ideologies provide young people with oversimplified but definite answers to the basic questions associated with identity conflict, i.e., "Who am I?" "Where am I going?" Inspired by ideology, young people also become drawn to activities that challenge the established ways of a culture—rebellions, riots, and revolutions. On a broader scale, Erikson contends, lack of a faith in an ideological system may result in widespread confusion and disrespect for those who govern the systems of social rule.

VI Young Adulthood: Intimacy versus Isolation—Love

Stage six in the life cycle marks the formal beginning of adult life. This is generally the period when a person becomes involved in courtship, marriage, and early family life; it extends from late adolescence until early adulthood (age 20 to 24). During this time, young adults usually orient themselves toward enriching vocations and "settling down." Erikson maintains, as did Freud, that it is only now that a person is genuinely ready for social as well as sexual intimacy with another person. Prior to this time, much of the person's sexual behavior was motivated by the search for ego identity. In contrast, the earlier attainment of a sense of personal identity and the involvement in productive work that mark this period give rise to a new inter-personal dimension with intimacy at one extreme and isolation at the other.

Erikson's use of the term "intimacy" is multidimensional in meaning and scope. He has in mind the sense of intimacy most of us share with a spouse, friends, brothers and sisters, and parents or other relatives. However, he also speaks of intimacy with oneself, that is, the ability to "fuse your identity with somebody else's without fear that you're going to lose something yourself (Evans, 1967, p. 48)." It is this aspect of intimacy (i.e., merging one's own identity with that of another person) that Erikson sees as essential for the establishment of a meaningful marriage. Likewise, he contends that a true sense of intimacy cannot be attained unless the person has already achieved a consolidated personal identity. In other words, to be really intimate with another person or oneself, a person must have already developed a firm sense of who and what she or he is. By contrast, adolescent "falling in love" may be nothing more than an attempt to explore one's own identity through the use of another person. This is corroborated by the fact that marriages of the young (aged 16 to 19) are not as stable (in terms of divorce statistics) as marriages of those in their twenties. Erikson sees this as a result of the fact that many people, especially women, marry someone in order to find their own identity in and through that person. In Erikson's view, it is not possible to attain intimacy by seeking for one's identity in this fashion.

Erikson's description of one who is capable of intimacy closely resembles Freud's definition of the healthy person, namely one who has the ability to love and to work. Although Erikson does not feel that this formula can be improved, it is intriguing to consider the question of whether (in Erikson's scheme) a celibate (e.g., priest) is capable of developing a sense of intimacy. The answer is yes, since Erikson believes that intimacy involves more than just sexuality; it may also include the deep relationship between friends or, in the broader sense, a commitment to one's fellow human beings.

The chief danger of this psychosocial stage is self-absorption or the avoidance of interpersonal relationships which commit one to intimacy and social involve-ment. The inability to enter into comfortable and intimate personal relationships leads to feelings of social emptiness and isolation. Self-absorbed people may seek interpersonal encounters which are purely formal (employer-employee) and superficial (bridge clubs). They insulate themselves against any type of real involvement because they are threatened by the demands of intimacy. Self-absorbed people are also likely to have attitudes of futility and alienation about their vocations. Finally, Erikson believes that social conditions (e.g., the difficulty of achieving intimacy in an urbanized, mobile, impersonal, technological society) may hinder the establishment of a sense of intimacy. In cases of extreme isolation, he cites examples of antisocial or psychopathic personality types (i.e., people who lack an ethical sense) who manipulate and exploit others without feeling remorse. These are the young adults whose inability to share their identities with others makes it impossible for them to enter into intense and long-term relationships.

Healthy resolution of the intimacy-versus-isolation crisis produces the psychosocial strength of *love*. In addition to its romantic and erotic qualities, Erikson regards love as the ability to commit oneself to others and abide by such commitments, even though they may require self-denial and compromise. This type of love is expressed when a person shows an attitude of care, respect, and responsibility toward another.

The social institution that is the counterpart of this stage of the life cycle is *ethics*. For Erikson, an ethical sense evolves as one recognizes the value of committing oneself to lasting friendships and social obligations—as well as the importance of honoring such commitments even if they require personal sacrifice. People who lack such an ethical sense are hardly prepared to face the next stage in psychosocial development.

VII Middle Adulthood: Generativity versus Stagnation—Care

Stage seven in the Eriksonian scheme corresponds to the middle years of life (25 to 65) and encompasses what Erikson describes as either generativity or stagnation. Generativity occurs when a person begins to show concern not only for the welfare of the next generation but also for the nature of the society in which that generation will live and work. He contends that each adult must either accept or reject the challenge of assuming responsibility for the continuation and betterment of whatever is instrumental to the maintenance and enhancement of the culture. This conviction is based on Erikson's belief that evolutionary development has "made man the teaching and instituting as well as the learning animal (1968b, p. 291)." Generativity, then, represents the older generation's concern to establish and guide those who will replace them. It is best exemplified by the sense of personal fulfillment associated with the production, rearing, and subsequent achievement of one's offspring. However, generativity resides not only in parents but also in those who contribute to the betterment of young people. The creative and productive elements of generativity are personified in everything that is passed from one generation to the next, e.g., technological products, ideas, books, and works of art. An ultimate concern for the welfare of humanity embodies the developmental theme of this second phase of adulthood. As Erikson puts it, the new generation depends on the adults and the adults depend on the young (1968b).

From the psychosocial crisis of generativity emerges the strength of *care*. Care stems from the feeling that something or someone matters; it is the psychological opposite of apathy. Those who fail to establish a sense of generativity slip into a state of self-absorption in which their personal needs and comforts are of dominant concern. These are persons who care for no one and nothing except that which nourishes their self-indulgence. Lacking generativity, such persons cease to function as productive members of society, live only to satisfy their needs, and are interpersonally impoverished. This is commonly known as the "crisis of middle age"—a sense of hopelessness and feeling that life is meaningless.

VIII Maturity: Ego Integrity versus Despair—Wisdom

The final stage in the epigenetic chart marks the period when individuals reflect upon their nearly complete efforts and achievements. In practically all cultures this period signals the onset of old age, a time often beset with numerous demands: adjustments to deterioration of physical strength and health, to retirement and reduced income, to the death of spouse and close friends, and the need to establish new affiliations with one's age group. During this period, there is also a definite shift in a person's attention from future to past life.

According to Erikson, this final phase of adulthood is not so much marked by the appearance of a new psychosocial crisis but rather by the summation, integration, and evaluation of all the preceding stages of ego development:

> Only in him who in some way has taken care of things and people and who has adapted himself to the triumphs and disappointments adherent to being, the originator of others or the generator of products and ideas—only in him may gradually ripen the fruit of these seven stages—I know no better word for it than ego integrity (Erikson, 1963a, p. 268).

The sense of ego integrity thus arises from the individual's ability to glance back on his or her life in full perspective (including marriage, children or grand-children, job, accomplishments, hobbies, social relationships) and humbly but as-suredly affirm "I am satisfied." Death is no longer feared, since such persons see their own existence continuing through either their offspring or creative ac-complishments. Erikson also believes that only in old age does true maturity and a practical sense of the "wisdom of the ages" come into being, provided that the person is so "gifted." At the same time, he notes that "the wisdom of old age remains aware of the relativity of all knowledge acquired in one lifetime in one historical period. Wisdom is a detached and yet active concern with life in the face of death (1968b, pp. 291–292)."

At the other extreme are the individuals who regard their lives as a series of unfulfilled opportunities and missed directions. Now, in the sunset years, they realize that it is far too late to start over again. The lack or loss of ego integration in such a person is marked by a hidden dread of death, a feeling of irrevocable failure, and an incessant preoccupation with what "might have been." Alternately, Erikson observes that there are two prevailing moods in the embittered and disgusted old person—regret that life cannot be lived over again and rejection of one's shortcomings and deficiencies by projecting them onto the outside world. At times, Erikson is poetic in his description of despair in the old person:

> "fate is not accepted as the frame of life, death not as its finite boundary. Despair indi-cates that time is too short for alternate roads to integrity: this is why the old try to "doctor" their memories (1968b, p. 291)."

In cases of severe psychopathology, Erikson suggests that bitterness and remorse may lead the old person to become senile, depressed, hypochondriacal, and intensely spiteful and paranoid. Fear of being placed in an institution is common among such individuals.

Now that we have concluded a description of the eight stages of ego development, reflection upon what they offer in the way of new perspectives is in order. First, Erikson has formulated a theory in which the roles of society and of persons themselves are accorded equal emphasis with respect to the development and organization of personality. This perspective, in turn, has enabled those in the helping professions to look upon the problems of adults as—at least to some extent—failures to resolve genuine adult personality crises, rather than see them merely as residual effects of early childhood frustrations and conflicts. Second, Erikson has been sensitive to the age of adolescence, a period largely ignored by Freud, regarding this period as pivotal in the formation of a person's psychological and social well-being. Finally, Erikson has stimulated a sense of optimism by demonstrating that each stage of psychosocial growth has the potential for both strength and weakness, so that failure at one stage of development does not necessarily indicate doom at a later stage. Let us now consider Erikson's position on the nine basic assumptions about man's nature.

ERIKSON'S BASIC ASSUMPTIONS CONCERNING HUMAN NATURE

Robert Coles, in a biographical account of Erikson's work, observed that "When a man builds on another man's work, as Erikson has on Freud's, he does not always have to repeat his predecessor's every single tenet or assumption (1970, p. xx)." Erikson's assumptions about man do in fact differ from those of Freud. His positions on the basic assumptions about human nature, discussed below, are depicted in Figure 4-2.

Freedom–Determinism In Erikson's view, human behavior is primarily determined. Biological maturation interacting with the individual's expanding social radius produces a rich complexity of behavioral determinants. Parental treatment, school experiences, peer groups, and differential cultural opportunities all play a powerful role in charting the course of one's life. In fact, the outcomes of the first four stages of psychosocial development are practically fixed by these types

	Strong	Moderate	Slight	Midrange	Slight	Moderate	Strong	
Freedom						■		Determinism
Rationality		■						Irrationality
Holism	■							Elementalism
Constitutionalism						■		Environmentalism
Changeability	■							Unchangeability
Subjectivity						■		Objectivity
Proactivity		■						Reactivity
Homeostasis						■		Heterostasis
Knowability		■						Unknowability

Figure 4-2 Erikson's position on the nine basic assumptions concerning human nature.

of environmental forces, whereas resolutions of the crises associated with the remaining four stages are less dependent upon such external factors. Erikson believes that each person, especially during the latter four developmental stages, has some capacity to resolve earlier and present crises. Thus, there is some acknowledgment of freedom in Erikson's theory; individuals, to this extent, are responsible for their successes and failures.

Although Erikson accepts the id as the biological foundation of personality, he is less than completely committed to determinism, as is reflected in his theoretical preoccupation with ego development. Erikson regards the ego as an autonomous personality structure that is particularly prone to alteration from adolescence onward. Unlike Freud, he does not believe that personality is utterly fixed by experiences in childhood. The choices of adults, however, are always restricted by the ever-present effects of childhood experiences. For example, it is difficult to achieve intimacy in young adulthood without a previously developed sense of basic trust. When Erikson's total theory is placed on the freedom–determinism scale, determinism is accorded more weight.

Rationality–Irrationality   The mixture of rationality and irrationality in Eriksonian man appears to contain considerably more of the former. Erikson's primary theoretical concern, the psychosocial development of the autonomous ego, reveals his abiding commitment to the importance of rationality, since reasoning processes are such an integral part of ego functioning. Such processes are most evident in the individual's attempts to resolve the last four psychosocial crises in Erikson's theory.

Along with other ego psychologists in the psychoanalytic movement, Erikson feels that an emphasis on rationality was lacking in Freud's account of human behavior. His theory thus represents an important effort to extend the Freudian view of man. However, as Erikson has often noted, he is clearly within the orthodox psychoanalytic tradition and, as such, accepts Freud's basic theoretical concepts, e.g., the biological and sexual foundations of personality, and the structural model (id, ego, superego). Within the psychoanalytic framework, Erikson helped to move the emphasis toward ego and rationality. Erikson invests people with a much larger measure of rationality than did Freud.

Holism–Elementalism   Erikson's strong commitment to a holistic conception of persons is clearly evident in the essence of his theory, the eight stages of man. To be understood, human beings must be viewed as developing totalities. Individuals are depicted as moving through eight broad stages of psychosocial development; while doing so, they are attempting to resolve crises of the most profound nature— e.g., ego identity, ego integrity—and always within the matrix of highly complex individual, cultural, and historical forces.

Consider, for example, the holistic theme underlying the two concepts of ego identity (adolescence) and ego integrity (maturity and old age). In the former, persons are seen as expending many years discovering who they are and developing a stable sense of continuity between past and future. Specific elements of adolescent behavior can only be fully understood when interpreted within the total gestalt of the ego-identity versus role-confusion crisis. During the period of maturity and old age, the person attempts to grasp his or her life as a totality, to see meaning in it, and to view it in perspective. Old-age-related behaviors are understood within the holistic framework of the ego-integrity versus despair crisis. In Erikson's epigenetic conception, then, an individual's personality can be understood only with reference to her or his entire life cycle as it is lived within the context of complex and interacting environmental forces.

Constitutionalism–Environmentalism   Erikson's tendency toward environmentalism is revealed in his strong emphasis upon parental, cultural, and historical factors in personality development. The individual must be understood in the context of these environmental influences. The degree to which persons resolve their early psychosocial crises is largely determined by parental treatment; child-rearing practices, in turn, are significantly influenced by cultural and historical factors. Resolution of subsequent psychosocial crises is a function of the individual's interaction with cultural opportunities. Erikson's environmentalism, then, is broad in scope. However, his environmentalist commitment, while strong, is somewhat less than entire, since he accepts Freud's emphasis upon the biological, instinctual basis of personality.

Changeability–Unchangeability   Erikson's theory reflects an undeniably strong commitment to the changeability assumption. He has carefully delineated the way in which the ego progresses through a series of psychosocial stages, beginning at birth and continuing until old age and death. Each psychosocial stage, as you will recall, is characterized by a "phase-specific" developmental crisis; depending on how each crisis is resolved, the individual's personality development progresses in one direction or another. In other words, Erikson depicts people as constantly evolving and attempting to meet the challenges posed by each developmental stage that they encounter.

For Erikson, then, human life is marked by inevitable change. Viewed in a rich psychohistorical context, persons are forever grappling with new developmental tasks, facing turning points in their lives, acquiring new ego qualities, and changing. Perhaps more than any other point of divergence between Erikson and Freud, their disagreement on the changeability–unchangeability assumption captures the essential difference in their respective theoretical positions. For Freud, adult personality is fully determined by interactions that take place during the first years of life. Erikson, by contrast, maintains that there is no end to human development—that it continues throughout the life cycle.

Subjectivity–Objectivity   The major theoretical concepts employed by Erikson in describing psychosocial growth—e.g., trust, mistrust, hope—refer to significant subjective experiential states. Furthermore, each individual's capacity to deal with a given psychosocial crisis depends upon his or her unique resolutions of former crises. However, the crises themselves are evoked by biological maturation interacting with an expanding social world. Biological maturation is not unique to an individual, and such maturation is seen by Erikson as constantly interacting with objective, external factors (e.g., parental treatment). In this sense, psychosocial stages and crises are objectively determined, strongly suggesting that Erikson leans somewhat toward the assumption of objectivity.

Proactivity–Reactivity   From largely reactive developmental beginnings, Eriksonian man becomes progressively more proactive over time, with the unfolding of each successive psychosocial stage. In fact, successful resolution of the first four crises (hope, will power, purpose, competence) is a prelude to proactive functioning in subsequent life stages. During these earlier periods, however, the biological maturation level of persons limits the part that they can play in generating their own behavior.

By way of contrast, Erikson's descriptions of the stages from adolescence to old age clearly convey the idea that people are capable of internally generating their behavior. Concepts such as the search for an adequate sense of ego identity, intimacy, generativity, and ego integrity are best understood from a proactive frame of reference. In Erikson's scheme, then, individuals are primarily proactive for most of their lives. Throughout the life stages, however, the course of human development is seen largely in terms of reactions to biological, social, and historical realities; in this broad sense, there is some acknowledgment of reactivity in Erikson's view of human nature.

Homeostasis–Heterostasis   In Erikson's theory, human beings are depicted as constantly challenged by psychosocial crises, each of which is potentially conducive to growth and mastery over the world. As persons successfully resolve one crisis, they move on to the next. There is an unmistakable sense of forward movement in Erikson's portrayal of human development that clearly suggests a heterostatic view of motivation at its base. It is man's nature to grow and attempt to meet the different challenges of each developmental stage.

A further suggestion of Erikson's heterostatic commitment is the fact that successful resolution of each psychosocial crisis allows a person more opportunity for growth and self-fulfillment. Consider, for example, that the entire adult stage (approximately forty years of life) is described in terms of generativity versus stagnation. The use of such concepts reflects the intimate relationship between personal growth and healthy development in Erikson's system. However, Erikson's tendency toward heterostasis is tempered by his acceptance of the biological-instinctual basis of personality proposed by Freud. Eriksonian man seeks to grow— but only within the constraints imposed by the instinctual roots of his development. Thus, his commitment to the heterostasis assumption is best construed as moderate.

Knowability–Unknowability   While Erikson has adopted several traditional psychoanalytic concepts of personality, he has also developed new ones by resorting to various clinical, anthropological, and psychohistorical research strategies. Some commitment to the ultimate knowability of human nature is suggested by his development of a comprehensive account of the human life cycle. However, Erikson's reliance upon multidisciplinary approaches outside "hard-core" science coupled with his lack of a single, rigorous scientific means of researching personality suggests a less-than-complete commitment to man's knowability through science. When compared with Freud, Erikson seems less convinced of the indispensability of science for understanding human nature.

Erikson, then, has not repeated his predecessor's every single assumption. It is again worth noting that the uniqueness of Erikson's theory, like that of each major personality theorist, depends markedly upon his assumptions about the nature of human beings. Let us now turn to some illustrative research that has been engendered by Erikson's theory.

EMPIRICAL VALIDATION OF PSYCHOSOCIAL CONCEPTS

Erikson's theory has had a major impact on general developmental psychology as well as upon psychoanalytic ego psychology (Newman and Newman, 1975). His ideas have also found widespread use and application in the fields of early childhood education and social work. It should further be noted that Erikson has paved the way for a new subdiscipline within psychology, namely *psychohistory,* a form of inquiry which attempts to relate the major themes of a person's life to historical events and circumstances (Lifton, 1974).

Despite its popularity, Erikson's theory has generated only a minimal amount of empirical research. In part, the scarcity of systematic research bearing on Erikson's position may reflect the fact that he has yet to outline his conception of how psychosocial constructs should be examined within an empirical framework. More to the point, he has not sufficiently specified or detailed the theoretical concepts he uses. Concepts such as mutuality, fidelity, and psychosocial moratorium are not defined with the precision needed to establish their empirical adequacy. In fairness to Erikson, however, he does admit that his own conceptions of personality development may not be directly amenable to experimental verification: "Maybe my formulations of a series of interlocking stages, based as it is on clinical and developmental observations, does not lend itself easily to . . . empirical validation (1972, personal communication)." Moreover, he does not believe that a theorist has the exclusive responsibility of showing the experimental personologist how to study theoretical concepts.

Occasionally, one will come across a study which attempts to explain a set of findings by reference to the conceptual perspective of psychosocial theory. Such post hoc interpretation, however, adds little to the goal of ascertaining the empirical adequacy of Erikson's descriptions of the eight ages of man. Another difficulty stems from the fact that psychosocial theory represents a strong developmental orientation (Ciaccio, 1971). This has tended to minimize the personologist's interest in evaluating several of the psychosocial stages, since a developmental perspective is considered inadequate by some investigators with respect to the goal of understanding adult behavior.

In a more positive vein, certain concepts of psychosocial theory are quite amenable to rigorous investigation. For instance, Erikson has established the criteria for psychosocial health and ill health for each crisis period in terms of well-defined behavioral characteristics. Such well-formulated descriptions constitute a definite advantage over psychoanalytic theories which attempt to reconstruct the individual's previous life history, since the descriptions allow for the direct study of the resolution of earlier crises in currently manifested behaviors and attitudes. The theory also seems to lend itself to empirical test inasmuch as it deals with the social dimensions of development as opposed to theories which focus on the intrapsychic nature of personality. Hypothetical internal factors are often more difficult to study than observable social behavior. Finally, Erikson has achieved an orderly sequential account of the relevant psychosocial phenomena of personal development, whereas other theorists often lack this longitudinal synthesis of developmental problems. Until carefully planned studies are brought to fruition, however, the empirical status and developmental implications of Erikson's theory remain obscure.

Let us now examine some of the studies bearing upon Erikson's theory.

Sex Differences in Children's Play: Toys and Anatomy

As a first example of pertinent research, let us briefly consider Erikson's own classic study of sex differences in the play constructions of children. This study, although admittedly unrelated to the empirical validation of psychosocial concepts, has provided the observational basis for Erikson's controversial views on the psychology of women.

As a child-analyst, Erikson observed that children would often reveal their problems better when playing with toys than they would with words. This observation led him to investigate the play constructions of 150 girls and boys between the ages of 10 and 12 who were subjects in a longitudinal study of child development at the University of California (Erikson, 1963a). His method of inquiry was quite simple: the children were invited, one at a time, to construct on a play table an exciting scene from an imaginary motion picture, using a random selection of small toys and doll figures. The children were then asked to tell a story about the scenes they had constructed.

The results of the study demonstrated the existence of clear-cut differences between girls and boys in the use of play space in the scene constructions. Specifically, Erikson found that girls tended to build serene and peaceful interior scenes, with furniture groupings that employed people and animals either in static positions or doing sedentary things such as playing the piano. Enclosures consisted of low walls with gates or vestibules. In a number of cases, an intruder would cause an uproar, forcing the women in the scene to hide or become fearful. This intruder was always an animal, man, or boy, never a woman or girl. Interestingly, however, girls did not attempt to block these intruders by erecting walls or closing doors. Erikson comments that "the majority of these intrusions have an element of humor and of pleasurable excitement (1963a, p. 105)." In contrast, boys tended to erect structures, buildings, and towers, introducing the exciting element of downfall and either causing it to occur or making it plain that catastrophe was imminent. In several cases, elaborate walls and facades were ornamented with protrusions, such as cones and cylinders. The boys' scenes also included a lot of implied action, e.g., traffic moving through streets, police officers who blocked the moving traffic, animals, and Indians.

In Erikson's view, sex differences in the play constructions of children are to be understood in terms of "the ground plan of the human body," meaning that at least in these preadolescent children, the experience of forthcoming sexual maturation strongly influences the playful use of space in elaborating interior and exterior configurations. Stated differently, the spatial tendencies determining these two kinds of productions, Erikson believes, are analogous to sexual anatomy: boys emphasize erectile, projectile, and active motifs whereas girls employ enclosure, protection, and receptivity (albeit with the ever-present threat of forceful intrusion). On a more theoretical level, Erikson proposes that it is the somatic design of the female body, the *inner space* of its womb and vagina, that determines the identity formation of women and makes it different from that of men. The anatomical plan of the female body signifies a biological, psychological, and ethical commitment to take care of human infancy. The core problem of female fidelity is the girl's disposition of this commitment. Clearly, these interpretations seem to agree with Freud's dictum that "anatomy is destiny," with the implication that sex roles are innate and resistant to change.

Quite understandably, Erikson has attracted considerable negative criticism from feminists because of his views on identity development in women (Chesler, 1972; Doherty, 1973). These critics have noted, for instance, that there is no justification for concluding that sex differences in the play constructions of children are determined by, or even related to, anatomical differences. For them, a simpler and more realistic explanation rests with what children have already learned about toys and play in a society which gives boys trucks, guns, and microscopes, and girls doll houses, dolls, and other items redolent of impending motherhood. Given the existence of sex-linked differences in socialization, it is not possible to know the extent to which innate factors contribute to sex differences in personality and behavior in later childhood.

In response to his critics, Erikson (1975) points out that he never said psychological differences between the sexes were determined solely by anatomical facts. Human physiology, while setting limits on potentials, always interacts with cultural and experiential factors to produce a given behavioral outcome. Accordingly, what males and females do with their masculine and feminine potentials is not rigidly controlled by their sexual anatomy, but is subject to the influence of personality variables, expected social roles, and life goals.

Research on Ego Identity versus Role Confusion

As has been noted, Erikson (1968a) devotes more theoretical attention to the period of adolescence than any other psychosocial stage in his epigenetic conception of the life cycle. Our selection of the two representative studies reported below reflects the fact that the majority of studies published to date, sparse as they are in number, deal almost exclusively with this phase of Erikson's comprehensive account of human development.

In describing the various elements of ego-identity development, Erikson has explained how either weak identification or overidentification with the same-sexed parent may be detrimental to the young person's psychosocial adjustment. Dignan (1965) predicted that, for females, "ego identity is weak with poor maternal identification, strong with good maternal identification, and poor again with over-identification which borders on the pathological (pp. 477–478)." In this study, 182 female college freshmen and sophomores and their mothers served as subjects. Two test instruments were developed to provide indices of ego identity and maternal identification, respectively. The first instrument, labeled "The Ego-Identity Scale" by Dignan, consisted of fifty true-false statements constructed on the basis of the writings of Erikson and others who have critically examined and developed the construct of ego identity. This scale tapped seven different areas relevant to a sense of ego identity: (1) sense of self, (2) uniqueness, (3) self-acceptance, (4) role expectations, (5) stability, (6) goal-directedness, and (7) interpersonal relations. Two sample items of this scale are: "I know I'm not perfect but I prefer to be as I am" (self-acceptance) and "People seldom mistake me for another girl" (uniqueness). The measure of maternal identification, based on a semantic differential instru-ment, consisted of having both the students and their mothers rate ten concepts (e.g., myself, father, mother) on a series of nine bipolar adjective scales (e.g., happy-sad; rugged-delicate; hot-cold). In a single testing session, all students completed the ego-identity scale and rated the ten concepts according to standard instructions (i.e., self-evaluation). During this session the students also rated the same semantic differential concepts as they believed their mothers would. Mothers of the subjects received, completed, and returned the semantic differential instrument by mail. Two measures of maternal identification, assumed similarity and real similarity, were derived from the semantic differential ratings. Assumed similarity was determined by comparing the degree to which the student rated her mother as similar to herself, whereas real similarity was based upon the degree of actual similarity between the student's self-ratings and the mother's self-ratings.

The results of this study are presented in Figure 4-3. The hypothesis that ego identity would be positively related to maternal identification was statistically supported when analyzed in terms of the assumed similarity measure. A similar trend was found by Dignan for ego-identity scores and real similarity, although the relationship failed to reach statistical significance. Accordingly, Dignan concluded: "These findings suggest that identity formation is more closely related to the girl's subjective experience of mother-daughter similarity than to any objective likeness of thought between them (p. 482)."

In a unique study, Waterman, Buebel, and Waterman (1970) provided ad-ditional evidence for the empirical adequacy of Erikson's concept of "identity crisis." Basing their study on the epigenetic principle, these investigators reasoned that degree of success in resolving the identity crisis should be positively correlated with levels of the previously developed ego components: basic trust, autonomy, initiative, and industry. In the first part of the study, an interview technique devised by Marcia (1966) was used to assess level of ego identity. The interviews, taped and scored independently by at least two judges, included questions pertaining to the

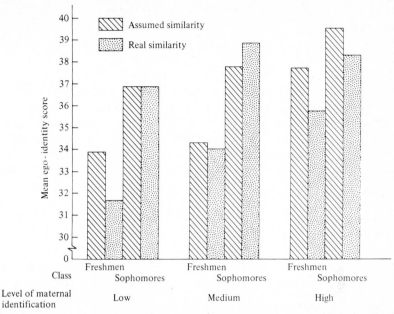

Figure 4-3 Mean ego-identity scores as a function of three levels and two measures of maternal identification and two levels of class standing. Note: $N = 20$ for ego-identity scores based on assumed similarity; $N = 15$ for ego-identity scores based on real similarity. (*Adapted from Dignan, 1965.*)

subject's occupational choice and the nature and content of his political belief system. The questions elicited information about the presence or absence of a crisis in each of these areas, in addition to determining the subject's degree of commitment to his ideas. Ninety-two male freshmen at a private college served as subjects. Rotter's (1966) "Internal-External Locus of Control" scale was used to measure the subjects' degree of autonomy. This scale indicates the extent to which an individual believes that events are under his or her control (i.e., internality), as opposed to believing that events are determined by factors such as fate, chance, powerful others, and the complexity of the social world (i.e., externality). As a measure of basic trust, subjects completed Rotter's (1967) "Interpersonal Trust" scale, a measure of the extent to which others can be relied upon. It was predicted that subjects with high developmental levels of ego identity would have higher scores on the internal-external control scale (greater internality) and show a greater degree of interpersonal trust than subjects with developmentally lower ego identity. Based on interview protocols, subjects were assigned to high, mixed, or low identity levels, depending on their judged level of ego-identity development. As hypothesized, subjects high on ego identity showed the greatest degree of internal control (autonomy), while subjects low on ego identity were the least internal. However, no support was found for the predicted relationship between level of ego identity and degree of basic trust. In the second part of their study, Waterman et al. tested the same relationships derived from the epigenetic principle, except that this time measures of psychosocial development specifically constructed within an Erik-sonian framework were used. Eighty-seven male college students were administered a series of self-report scales constructed to measure both successful and unsuc-cessful resolutions of the first five psychosocial stages. It was predicted that scores on the ego-identity scale would be positively correlated with scores for basic trust, autonomy, initiative, and industry. Consistent with Erikson's theory, all correla-tions were significant in the expected direction (r's ranged between +.43 for identity-basic trust and +.24 for identity-industry). Collectively, the findings reported by Waterman et al. support the Eriksonian hypothesis that successful coping with the identity crisis is related to positive outcomes of the previous psychosocial crises.

Adult Development: Turning Points in Midstream

In addition to greatly enriching our understanding of the nature and complexity of the journey from birth to old age, Erikson's theory has generated empirical interest in adult development (Vaillant, 1977). Let us briefly consider a research example of this relatively new and burgeoning interest in the process of adult development—a topic which is clearly an outgrowth of Erikson's theoretical insights.

In the 1970s Daniel Levinson (1978) and a team of researchers began an intensive investigation of the psychological and social changes occurring in adult life. The participants in this study were forty American men between the ages of 35 and 45, an age span which Levinson identifies as a turning point in a person's life, the move from early to middle adulthood. The men came from four occupational subgroups: hourly workers in industry, business executives, university biologists, and novelists. They also represented a diversity of social class backgrounds, racial and ethnic origins, and educational levels. Thirty-two of the forty men were in their first marriage; of the eight who had been divorced, three had not remarried and five were in their second marriage. Levinson admits a compelling reason, in addition to research design and sampling considerations of a professional nature, for deciding to limit the study to men: "In all candor, however, I must admit to a more personal reason for the choice: I chose men partly because I wanted so deeply to understand my own adult development (1978, p. 9)."

In-depth *biographical interviews* with each man in his home or work place constituted the heart of Levinson's method of study. These tape-recorded interviews usually lasted an hour or two and were held at weekly intervals over a span of two to three months. Moreover, the majority of men completed a follow-up interview approximately two years after the initial interviewing. The main objective of the interviews was to reconstruct the "life stories" of the men from childhood to the present. Accordingly, information about a wide range of topics was gathered during the interviewing phase of the study, including family background, current marriage and family life, important relationships with men and women, education, occupational choice and work history, hobbies and use of leisure time, involvement in religious, political, and ethnic groups, illness, death, and loss of loved ones, and key turning points in the life course. As Levinson notes: "At various key times we tried to pull together a picture of the man's life as a whole: how the various components of his life were interrelated at that time; how the life pattern at age 34, say, had emerged from the past and what were his hopes, fears, plans and imaginings for the future (1978, p. 15)."

The next stage of Levinson's research consisted of preparing biographies for each of the men. Specifically, Levinson and his collaborators immersed themselves in the interview material and gradually worked toward an intuitive understanding of each man and his life as it evolved over the years. In turn, as the preparation of each biography took form, the formation of specific concepts and ways of thinking about adult development were advanced and consolidated into a developmental perspective on adulthood.

As a result of going back and forth between the interviews and interpretive analysis, and aided by theoretical concepts as they existed at a given time, Levinson was eventually able to identify several age-linked adult developmental periods. The pivotal concept linking these various periods of male adult development is what Levinson calls the "individual life structure." The concept refers to the underlying pattern or design of a person's life at a given period. In Levinson's view, the life structure of a person is best understood in terms of the conscious *choices* made and how the person deals with their consequences. The important choices in adult life have to do with occupation, marriage and family, friends, leisure, involvement in religious, political, and community life, and immediate and long-range goals.

According to Levinson, a person's basic life structure evolves through an orderly sequence of stages during the adult years. The essential character of the sequence is a series of alternating *stable* (structure-building) and *transitional* (structure-changing) periods, usually lasting four to eight years each, during which one builds, modifies, and rebuilds the structure of one's life. Each period is characterized by various tasks which must be performed if successful transition is to be made to the next set of tasks. In Levinson's view, a transitional period marks the end of the existing life structure and creates the possibility for a new one. The primary task of every transitional period is to question and reappraise the existing life structure, to explore various possibilities for change in self and world, and to move toward commitment to the crucial choices that form the basis for a new life structure in the ensuing period.

The first transitional period, for example, is termed the *early-adult transition* (ages 17 to 22). The main tasks confronting the individual here are to terminate existing relationships with important others, to consolidate an initial adult identity, and to make and test some preliminary choices for adult living. Another transition period occurs at about the age of 30—a time when one either confirms the choices one has made or sets off in other directions. But by far the most disruptive juncture occurs for men when they cross the meridian age of 40 and into *midlife transition*. This is a period of great uncertainty accompanied by a sense of urgency about time. More specifically, at this time a majority of men come to the realization that their lives are half over, that they will never fulfill their youthful dreams, or, even if they did, that these dreams did not bring the magical sense of completeness they had expected. Whatever the traumatic event—or even without one—every man, Levinson insists, faces a midlife crisis that forces him to appraise his past and prepare for a seemingly uncertain future.

In addition to making external changes in his life, Levinson believes, the middle-aged male must rebuild "the internal aspects" of his life structure; he must consciously shape his own individuality as a mature adult. Basically, a man redefines himself in relation to youth and old age, seeking new sources of vitality while preserving the judgment and perspective that come with maturity. He must also come to terms with the task of *deillusionment*, a term used by Levinson to refer to the painful process through which a person is stripped of those long-held assumptions and beliefs about himself and the world which are not true. At the same time, Levinson discovered that some men do very little questioning or searching during the midlife transition. They are apparently untroubled by questions regarding the meaning and purpose of their lives. Other men realize that their life structure is changing, but the process is not a painful one. But for the vast majority of men this is a time of great turmoil within the self and with the world. They question nearly every aspect of their lives and feel that they must make modest or profound changes in their life structures if they are to cope effectively with the tasks of middle adulthood.

While Levinson speculates further about other significant developmental periods occurring within Erikson's psychosocial stage of middle adulthood, space does not permit description of them here. The interested reader is referred to Levinson's (1978) *The Seasons of a Man's Life*. We do hope, however, that our brief description of Levinson's research has captured something of the excitement and curiosity within contemporary psychology surrounding the Erikson-based notion that personality continues to develop over the adult years, often by way of predictable stages, tasks, and crises.

APPLICATION: ADOLESCENCE IN AMERICA OR "WHO AM I?"

Erikson has applied his theoretical views to such fascinating and diverse topics as children's play behaviors (1937), childhood in American Indian tribes (1945), juvenile delinquency (1957), identity problems of black youth (1964b), dissent in youth (1970a), and various historical figures such as Luther (1958), Hitler (1963a), Gandhi (1969), and Jefferson (1974). In particular, he has stressed various social-emotional experiences influencing adolescent personality development in American society. More than any other personologist, Erikson is credited with elaborating the concept of ego identity and establishing a place for it in current studies of the adolescent personality.

There is no dearth of published material on adolescence today. Young persons who want to know why they think, feel, or do what they do can find a wide variety of "answers" offered in numerous books, newspaper articles, magazines, and TV discussion programs. Along with other professionals, psychologists have contributed to this burgeoning wealth of information by proposing theories and concepts that highlight specific dimensions of adolescent experience and also illuminate the general psychological significance of this life stage. Examples range from G. Stanley Hall's historical biogenetic view of the "storm and stress" aspects, through Otto Rank's emphasis on the need for independence, to the cultural relativism proposed by the anthropologists Margaret Mead and Ruth Benedict (Muuss, 1962). Erikson, however, seems to identify, capture, and articulate an essential element that all others have missed.

From Erikson's viewpoint, the fundamental question confronting the adolescent is "Who am I?" More abstractly, the young person must develop a sense of personal identity, of stable selfhood, so that experienced past and anticipated future are meaningfully connected. In a rigidly patterned culture (e.g., Chinese) with many prescribed social roles, such identity problems are minimized since there are relatively few options available. By comparison, American society offers a much wider latitude of potential life-styles to its young people, and American adolescents are more vulnerable to identity problems precisely because they have more options. According to Erikson's perspective, it is the democratic system in America that poses special problems in this regard since democracy requires "self-made identities." In American society, then, young people bear considerable individual responsibility for defining who and what they are.

When democracy is coupled with the technological sophistication of our social world, identity crises are further intensified. Our technology demands an extended period of formal education. In primitive cultures, one can become a witch doctor by heredity alone; in America, it takes years of study to become a psychiatrist or clinical psychologist. Such prolonged education, often involving financial dependence upon one's parents during the college years, markedly extends adolescence. Further, considering the exceedingly rapid social change in which basic values and norms are continually questioned (Toffler, 1970), the young person's identity problems become immeasurably more complicated. American adolescents have not only more time to search for their identities but also more alternatives from which to select.

Five major areas of contemporary American adolescent behavior that can be interpreted, at least in part, as manifestations of the identity crisis are discussed below. They are (1) the problem of vocational choice, (2) conflict with parents, (3) peer-group membership, (4) love relationships, and (5) alcohol and drug use.

The Problem of Vocational Choice   Erikson believes that the inability to settle on an occupational identity is a source of great concern to many young people. Simply stated, the adolescent must define who she or he *is* before a decision on what she or he wishes to become is possible. Since different life-styles accompany different occupations in our society, selecting a vocation is, in reality, selecting a whole way of life. To make a wise choice, people must have an accurate view of themselves as well as a reasonably good estimate of where they might best "fit" in the occupational world. In the final analysis, an individual's vocational choice may well represent a definition and expression of the kind of person that she or he wishes to become (Ziegler, 1973).

Adolescent vocational indecision, then, often reflects a more fundamental indecisiveness about personal identity. This is especially true for young women who, because of their biological potential for bearing children, are faced with the choice of wife and mother roles versus other career goals (or some combination of the two). Some women who opt for the former may eventually believe they have no ego identity apart from their marital role. Because traditional society has often dictated passive acceptance of "feminine" values and aspirations, contemporary adolescent women experience significant vocational conflict in the struggle for identity achievement. By the same token, young men are subjected to intense pressure to select an occupational career and are more susceptible than women to the potentially disruptive effects of competing for lucrative jobs: a sense of integrity and personal worth often hangs in the balance.

Conflict with Parents   One need not study personality theory to know that parents often resist or try to curtail independence in their adolescents. A typical example would be the case of the 16-year-old whose father vetoes his Saturday evening request for the family car (both knowing that the car will be in the garage anyway at that time). In this situation, the adolescent may feel or say "Look, damn it, I'm no longer the kid whose diapers you used to change and whose nose you used to wipe—I'm a *person* in my own right and I expect to be treated as such!"

Underlying many superficially different conflicts of this type is the adolescents' feeling that their parents simply do not recognize their individuality. Thus, they will often counterattack (i.e., test the limits of their freedom) to prove they are psychologically separate entities. Some rebellion against parental authority and values is often essential if a deeper sense of individuality and self-confidence is to develop. To this end, adolescents must often define and express their ego identity *against* parental standards and expectations, suggesting that some degree of parent-adolescent conflict is inevitable. The outcomes of such conflicts will vary. However, if the adolescent can find a satisfactory path toward an independent identity, then it is likely that serious problems will be avoided. From an Eriksonian perspective, it seems that parents must relinquish their control voluntarily if young persons are to move toward full realization of their unique potentials.

Peer-Group Membership   Rejecting parents as models in establishing their identity, adolescents often seek in their peers an alternative source of support as they reorganize their conceptions of themselves. In our culture, peer-group bonds are particularly strong during this period; they often affect the adolescent's values and attitudes more than parents, schools, religious institutions, or any other social influence. Such groups help to reassure individuals at a time when they are undergoing dramatic internal changes. By communicating their own feelings as well as sharing vicariously in the experiences of peers, adolescents are able to cope with otherwise confusing and sometimes frightening situations.

Erikson (1963a) has noted that the cliquishness and uniformity of dress and gesture so often observed in adolescent groups are really defenses against identity confusion. If young persons are uncertain about who they are, dressing and acting like their friends provides some sense of internal stability and security. Moreover, wearing apparel, hairstyles, and music serve to symbolize their separateness from parents and the associated adult world. Membership in a peer group also provides exposure to new and different ideologies—political, social, economic, and religious. Erikson believes that the appeal of various ideologies and alternative life-styles for adolescent groups is largely based upon the identity search. In part, they are searching for new personal values to replace childhood rules. Furthermore, learning to believe in and act upon a new set of social values while experimenting with and possibly rejecting an old ideology can strengthen the adolescent's emerging sense of identity.

Love Relationships   Erikson argues that through love relationships adolescents are often able to clarify some of their identity confusion:

> To a considerable extent adolescent love is an attempt to arrive at a definition of one's identity by projecting one's diffuse ego image on another and by seeing it thus reflected and gradually clarified. This is why so much of young love is conversation (1963a, p. 262).

Thus, depending upon the reactions they receive, adolescents may be able to resolve some of their uncertainties. Intimate, understanding love relationships also permit the young person self-expressions that otherwise have no social outlet. Hopes, dreams, aspirations, and ideals can be explored along with disappointment, fear, guilt, and disillusionment. At the same time, such relationships enable young people to learn how to conduct themselves in new situations, explore their sexual conceptions of themselves, experiment with overt sex to some degree, and thus prepare for later, riskier exposures of self in more involved sexual encounters. Individuals must, according to Erikson, know who they are and who they want to become before they can enter into permanent relationships involving adult responsibilities (e.g., marriage).

Alcohol and Drug Use   The extraordinary range of drugs known to be currently available, the most widely used of which is alcohol, makes it clear that there are no simple explanations of the factors which lead to their use or abuse by adolescents. The immediate and long-term effects of alcohol, opium, morphine, heroin, barbiturates, cocaine, amphetamines, hallucinogens, and marijuana vary so immensely as to make pointless a search for just one underlying reason for their use. Yet there can be little doubt that the use and abuse of alcohol and other drugs among adolescents continues to be an uncomfortable reality. To illustrate, studies done throughout the 1970s indicate that alcoholism is steadily increasing among the adolescent population (U.S. Dept. of Health, Education, and Welfare, 1974) as is the use of marijuana (National Institute on Drug Abuse, 1975). More specifically, a survey of a large sample of both private and public high schools across the country cited in the latter publication revealed that almost half of the 16,000 seniors questioned had used marijuana at least once.

Depending on the person and the drug, the motive that initiates and sustains drug use among young people may range from curiosity, thrill seeking, peer pressure and acceptance, escape from stress, and rebellion against authority to more philosophical rationales such as desire for self-knowledge, self-improvement, creativity, spiritual enlightenment, or expansion of consciousness. When these motives are considered in terms of Erikson's theory, a case can be built for their relation to an underlying sense of identity confusion. Young people who do not know who they are might find alcohol and drug-related experiences attractive in exploring the outer boundaries of selfhood; they may think that they can find a dimension of themselves which evades them in the sober, "straight" world.

Using alcohol and drugs may also temporarily relieve the emotional stresses accompanying the identity crisis. Beset by vocational indecision, parental conflict, and fragile love relationships, young persons may see such drugs as a vehicle for momentarily stepping outside themselves; marijuana, in particular, functions like alcohol in this respect. Moreover, when adolescents are surrounded by a drug-using peer group, so crucial to their identity search, it is easy to understand how they could be "pressured" toward drugs, especially if their group status is contingent upon drug use. A person with an established sense of ego identity could resist such pressure; the Eriksonian adolescent would probably find it difficult not to conform.

It would be erroneous to assume that all facets of adolescent behavior can be explained in terms of Erikson's identity concept. Nonetheless, the concept of identity crisis furnishes an excellent theoretical perspective from which to view the diversity of psychological problems displayed during this period of life. By attempting to identify the mainstreams of psychosocial development, Erikson has made a rich and valuable contribution to personological theory.

SUMMARY

Erik Erikson's psychosocial theory, developed within a psychoanalytic framework, emphasizes the importance of ego psychology, developmental change throughout the life cycle, and understanding personality against the background of social and historical forces. In contrast to Freud, Erikson regards the ego as an autonomous personality structure; his theory focuses on ego qualities that emerge at various developmental periods.

Erikson asserts that ego development proceeds through a series of universal stages. In his epigenetic conception of human development, each stage in the life cycle has an optimal time to emerge. The sequential unfolding of these life stages is a function of the individual's biological maturation interacting with his expanding social radius.

In Erikson's view, eight psychosocial stages characterize the human life cycle. Each is marked by a particular kind of crisis or turning point in the person's life. The eight stages, depicted in terms of the essential psychosocial conflicts associated with each, are as follows: (1) basic trust versus mistrust, (2) autonomy versus shame and doubt, (3) initiative versus guilt, (4) industry versus inferiority, (5) ego identity versus role confusion, (6) intimacy versus isolation, (7) generativity versus stagnation, and (8) ego integrity versus despair. The individual's personality is determined by the resolutions of these conflicts.

Erikson's theory is rooted in his basic assumptions about human nature. His psychosocial theory reflects (1) a strong commitment to the assumptions of holism, environmentalism, and changeability and (2) a moderate commitment to the assumptions of determinism, rationality, objectivity, proactivity, heterostasis, and knowability.

Erikson's theory has thus far generated very little research. However, illustrative research pertinent to Erikson's theory concerning children's play constructions, adolescent ego identity, and adult development crises was described in this chapter.

Application of Erikson's theory to an understanding of adolescence in American society was discussed in the concluding section of the chapter. Diverse areas of contemporary adolescent behavior—the problem of vocational choice, conflict with parents, peer-group membership, love relationships, and alcohol and drug use—were interpreted as partial reflections of the identity crisis.

BIBLIOGRAPHY

Chesler, P. *Women and madness.* Garden City, N.Y: Doubleday, 1972.

Ciaccio, N. A test of Erikson's theory of ego epigenesis. *Developmental Psychology*, 1971, **4**, 306–311.

Coles, R. *Erik H. Erikson: The growth of his work.* Boston: Little, Brown, 1970.

Dignan, M. Ego identity and maternal identification. *Journal of Personality and Social Psychology*, 1965, **1**, 476–483.

Doherty, M. Sexual bias in personality theory. *The Counseling Psychologist*, 1973, **4**, 67–74.

Erikson, E. Configurations in play—Clinical notes. *Psychoanalytic Quarterly*, 1937, **6**, 139–214.

Erikson, E. Childhood and tradition in two American Indian tribes. In *The psychoanalytic study of the child.* Vol. 1. New York: International Universities Press, 1945, pp. 319–350.

Erikson, E. Growth and crises of the healthy personality: VI. Identity versus self-diffusion. In M. Senn (Ed.), *Symposium on the healthy personality* II: *Problems of infancy and childhood.* New York: Josiah Macy, Jr. Foundation, 1950, pp. 134–140.

Erikson, E. *Young man Luther: A study in psychoanalysis and history.* New York: Norton, 1958.

Erikson, E. *Childhood and society* (2d ed.). New York: Norton, 1963a.

Erikson, E. (Ed.). *Youth: Change and challenge.* New York: Norton, 1963b.

Erikson, E. *Insight and responsibility.* New York: Norton, 1964a.

Erikson, E. Memorandum on identity and Negro youth. *Journal of Social Issues*, 1964b, **20**, 29–42.

Erikson, E. *Identity: Youth and crisis.* New York: Norton, 1968a.

Erikson, E. Life cycle. *International Encyclopedia of the Social Sciences.* New York: Crowell Collier and Macmillan, 1968b, **9**, 286–292.

Erikson, E. *Gandhi's truth.* New York: Norton, 1969.

Erikson, E. Reflections on the dissent of contemporary youth. *Daedalus*, 1970a, **99**, 154-176.

Erikson, E. Autobiographic notes on the identity crisis. *Daedalus*, 1970b, **99**, 730–759.

Erikson, E. *Dimensions of a new identity: The 1973 Jefferson lectures in the humanities.* New York: Norton, 1974.

Erikson, E. *Life history and the historical movement.* New York: Norton, 1975.

Erikson, E. *Toys and reasons.* New York: Norton, 1977.

Erikson, E. (Ed.). *Adulthood.* New York: Norton, 1978.

Erikson, E., & Erikson, K. Confirmation of the delinquent. *Chicago Review*, 1957, **10**, 15–23.

Evans, R. *Dialogue with Erik Erikson*. New York: Harper & Row, 1967.

Levinson, D., Darrow, C., Klein, M., Levinson, M., & McKee, B. *The seasons of a man's life*. New York: Knopf, 1978.

Lifton, R. (Ed.). *Explorations in psychohistory*. New York: Simon and Schuster, 1974.

Maier, H. *Three theories of child development: The contributions of Erik H. Erikson, Jean Piaget, and Robert R. Sears, and their applications*. New York: Harper & Row, 1965.

Marcia, J. Development and validation of ego-identity status. *Journal of Personality and Social Psychology*, 1966, **3**, 551–558.

Muuss, R. *Theories of adolescence*. New York: Random House, 1962.

National Institute on Drug Abuse. *Marijuana and health: Fifth annual report to the U.S. Congress*. Rockville, Md.: National Institute on Drug Abuse, 1975.

Newman, B., & Newman, P. *Development through life: A psychosocial approach*. Homewood, Ill.: Dorsey, 1975.

Rotter, J. Generalized expectancies for internal versus external control of reinforcement. *Psychological Monographs*, 1966, **80** (1, Whole no. 609).

Rotter, J. A new scale for the measurement of interpersonal trust. *Journal of Personality*, 1967, **35**, 651–655.

Toffler, A. *Future shock*. New York: Random House, 1970.

U.S. Department of Health, Education, and Welfare. *Alcohol and health*. M. Chafetz, Chairman of the Task Force. Washington, D.C.: U.S. Government Printing Office, 1974.

Vaillant, G. *Adaptation to life*. New York: Little, Brown & Co., 1977.

Waterman, C., Buebel, M., & Waterman, A. Relationship between resolution of the identity crisis and outcomes of previous psychosocial crises. *Proceedings of the Annual Convention of the APA*, 1970, **5**, 467–468.

Ziegler, D. Distinctive self and occupational member concepts in different occupational preference groups. *Journal of Vocational Behavior*, 1973, **3**, 53–60.

SUGGESTED READINGS

Breger, L. *From instinct to identity: The development of personality*. Englewood Cliffs, N.J.: Prentice-Hall, 1974.

Erikson, E. Youth: Fidelity and diversity. Humanitas: *Journal of the Institute of Man*. 1972, **8**, 21–35.

Erikson, K. (Introducer). *In search of common ground: Conversations with Erik H. Erikson and Huey P. Newton*. New York: Norton, 1973.

Loevinger, J. The meaning and measurement of ego development. *American Psychologist*, 1966, **21**, 195–206.

Loevinger, J., & Wessler, R. *Measuring ego development*. Vol. 1. San Francisco: Jossey-Bass, 1970.

Orlofsky, J., Marcia, J., & Lesser, I. Ego identity status and the intimacy versus isolation crisis of young adulthood. *Journal of Personality and Social Psychology*, 1973, **27**, 211–219.

Roazen, P. *Erik H. Erikson: The power and limits of his vision*. New York: Free Press, 1976.

Toder, N., & Marcia, J. Ego-identity status and response to conformity pressure in college women. *Journal of Personality and Social Psychology*, 1973, **26**, 287–294.

DISCUSSION QUESTIONS

1 In what way is Erikson's theory different from Freud's?
2 Do you agree with Erikson that ego identity versus role confusion is the central crisis of adolescence? Do you believe that you have experienced this crisis to any degree? If so, can you see how it may have affected other areas of your life, e.g., career choice, relationships with parents, love relationships?
3 Erikson maintains that ego identity is a lifelong struggle. Do you agree? If so, what are some of the identity problems that might be faced by a person as he or she enters young adulthood, middle adulthood, and old age?
4 What kinds of changes do you think are most needed in family life in our society to help more children to become competent adults?
5 Erikson's views on sex differences have provoked much criticism from the feminist movement. How much of any observed behavioral differences between the sexes do you consider to be anatomically based and how much to be the result of social roles imposed on females and males? More specifically, with regard to the ego-identity crisis, does being male or female affect the nature of the crisis? Has this occurred in your own life?

GLOSSARY

Autonomy The inner sense that one is a self-governing person, able to exert some influence over those events that affect one's life.

Basic Trust The inner feeling that one's social world is a safe and stable place and that caring others are nurturant and reliable.

Care The psychosocial virtue accruing from generativity that enables a person to feel that someone or something matters.

Competency The psychosocial strength stemming from a sense of industry which enables a person to feel that she or he is able to deal effectively with the environment.

Despair The feeling evident among old people that life has been a series of unfulfilled opportunities and missed directions.

Ego Identity The totality of self-perceptions which confer upon one a sense of uniqueness and continuity over time.

Ego Integrity The feeling of fulfillment at the culmination of the life cycle as one takes stock of one's life, including job, accomplishments, and children.

Ego Psychology A theoretical view of personality that has its origins in psychoanalytic theory, but has evolved new perspectives and ways of understanding human behavior that are significant departures from Freud's original theory. Emphasizes the ego (rationality) rather than the id as the basis of human behavior and functioning.

Epigenetic Principle The assumption that human development proceeds in terms of a series of invariant stages that are universal to humanity and that each stage is accompanied by a crisis that arises from biological maturation and social demands made upon a person at that stage.

Fidelity The psychosocial virtue issuing from a sense of ego identity that enables a young person to perceive and act in terms of an ideology despite its contradictions and limitations.

Generativity Accompanying middle age, it reflects a concern for the welfare of the next generation and the type of society in which that generation will live and work.

Guilt   Feelings of unworthiness and self-doubt experienced by children whose parents are unwilling to allow them the opportunity of completing tasks on their own.

Hope   The psychosocial virtue accompanying a sense of basic trust which serves as the foundation for perceiving meaning in one's existence.

Identity Crisis   In Erikson's theory, a period of time during which a young person struggles with such questions as "Who am I?" and "Where am I going?" The young person plagued by an identity crisis often lacks a clear idea of his or her social roles and assumes whatever role seems appropriate to a given situation.

Industry   Corresponding to the school age, it reflects a concern with being on the move, learning new skills, and completing tasks on one's own.

Inferiority   Feelings of self-doubt and incompetence resulting from a lack of industry; a low sense of self-worth.

Initiative   Associated with the play age, it reflects an active interest in the work of others, trying out new things, and the inner sense that one is able to undertake activities.

Intimacy   Associated with young adulthood, it includes sexuality, deep relationships with others, and a commitment to one's fellow beings.

Isolation   Feelings of social emptiness and futility resulting from the failure to attain intimacy.

Life Cycle   The sequence of psychosocial stages from birth to death.

Love   The psychosocial virtue issuing from a sense of intimacy which enables the young person to commit himself or herself to others and to abide by such commitments, even though they may require self-denial and compromise.

Mistrust   A sense of fear, suspicion, and apprehension in the infant toward the world in general and people in particular due to a style of maternal care which is inadequate or rejecting.

Mutuality   A term used by Erikson to represent the notion that the needs and capacities of different generations are interdependent.

Psychohistory   A type of inquiry which attempts to relate a person's major life themes to particular historical events and circumstances.

Psychosocial Crisis   A critical period in an individual's life, engendered by physiological maturation and social demands, which has the potential for either a positive or negative outcome.

Psychosocial Moratorium   A period during late adolescence when a person is allowed some delay in assuming adult roles and responsibilities.

Shame   The child's sense of rage turned inward upon the self because he or she has not been allowed to exercise autonomy by the parents.

Stagnation   A state of self-absorption in which only the individual's personal needs are of central concern.

Will Power   The psychosocial virtue accompanying autonomy which enables a child to exercise free choice as well as self-restraint.

Henry A. Murray (*Public Relations Department, News Office, Harvard University*)

Chapter 5

Henry Murray: A Need Theory of Personality

Many students are first drawn to the study of psychology by the question "What makes people tick?" Psychology seeks to explain why people behave as they do, what drives them, and what is "underneath" their behavior. These are really questions of *motivation* and, to that extent, are in some way dealt with by all personality theorists. But some theorists are more closely identified than others with motivation as a dynamic, energizing, and directing force within persons. Henry Murray is clearly one of these theorists. Having evolved a *need theory* of personality into a personological system over several decades, Murray qualifies as one who has addressed himself pointedly to the question of the internal motivational forces that guide and direct human activities. Central to this theory is a great emphasis on neurophysiological processes as the source of human functioning. Stated simply, Murray (1953) believes that the anatomical center of personality is the brain—the site of our emotions, the seat of consciousness, and the repository of memory traces, concepts, attitudes, needs, beliefs, and value systems.

Murray's need theory of personality is basically a modification of Freudian theory. Like Freudian theory it places heavy emphasis on unconscious motivational forces. Yet unlike classical psychoanalysis, Murray gives as much weight to conscious as to unconscious motives. In this respect he is similar to the ego psychologists (see Erikson, Chapter 4), and his theory is equally suitable for understanding normal and abnormal behavior. Finally, in common with more contemporary cognitive social-learning theorists (see Bandura, Chapter 7), Murray believes that the individual and his or her environment must be considered together as an interaction. It is evident that Murray has provided us with a highly inclusive theory of human personality.

BIOGRAPHICAL SKETCH

Henry Alexander Murray was born in New York City on May 13, 1893. His parents were quite wealthy and owned a home on what is now the site of Rockefeller Center. Summer holidays were spent with a sister and brother on a Long Island beach.

Murray was also afforded the opportunity to accompany his parents on four trips to Europe during his childhood.

From an early age, Murray was afflicted with strabismus (a visual defect commonly known as crossed eyes). He was operated on at the age of 9 to correct the condition. Unfortunately, a mistake made by the surgeon made matters worse, and he was left without stereoscopic vision. This visual defect prevented him from playing well at tennis, golf, or any such game because he could not focus both eyes on the ball. Oddly enough, he remained unaware of the defect until he was in medical school, when a professor asked him if he had had difficulty playing childhood games. Murray also stuttered as a child.

Following prep school at Croton, Murray enrolled at Harvard University, where he received his B.A. in history in 1915. He attended one psychology lecture as an undergraduate and found the professor so boring that he walked out of class and never returned. In 1919, Murray received his medical degree from Columbia College of Physicians and Surgeons, ranking first in his graduating class. He also secured an M.A. in biology from Columbia and then returned to Harvard where he divided his time between research and an instructorship in physiology. After two years of surgical internship at the Presbyterian Hospital in New York City, he was appointed assistant and then associate member of the Rockefeller Institute for Medical Research, where he conducted embryological research.

In 1924-1925, Murray took a year's leave of absence to study biology and biochemistry at Trinity College, Cambridge, England. He was awarded a Ph.D. in physiological chemistry from Cambridge University in 1927. It was during his year abroad that Murray first became interested in medical psychology. He credits his attraction to professional psychology to a period of analytic work, including a brief personal analysis, with Carl Jung in Zurich, Switzerland. In later years, reflecting upon his personal conversations with Jung, he wrote:

> We talked for hours, sailing down the lake and smoking before the hearth of his Faustian retreat. "The great floodgates of the wonder-world swung open," and I saw things that my philosophy had never dreamt of. Within a month a score of bi-horned problems were resolved, and I went off decided on depth psychology. I had experienced the unconscious, something not be be drawn out of books (Murray, 1940, p. 153).

Swept away with enthusiasm for psychoanalysis, Murray returned to the Rockefeller Institute as an associate for one year, in addition to studying at various New York psychiatric clinics. In 1927, he accepted an invitation from Morton Prince to return to Harvard University, this time to teach psychology and to be assistant director of the newly founded Harvard Psychological Clinic. Murray assumed leadership of the clinic in 1928 and was appointed assistant professor of abnormal psychology, followed by promotion to associate professorship in 1937. During the period from 1928 to the onset of World War II, Murray collaborated on research in personology that proved to be both creative and fruitful. This work culminated in the publication of *Explorations in Personality* (1938), still a classic in the field. Under his stimulating guidance, psychoanalytic theory was submitted to vigorous empirical investigation. He was also one of the charter members of the

Boston Psychoanalytic Institute, where in 1935 he completed training under Franz Alexander and Hans Sachs (two members of Freud's inner circle) which enabled him to practice psychoanalysis part-time.

Murray left Harvard in 1943 to become a major and then a lieutenant colonel in the Army Medical Corps. He was assigned to the Office of Strategic Services to develop screening and selection methods for OSS espionage personnel who were about to embark upon "cloak-and-dagger" missions in the European theater. His wartime research, which took him to Britain, France, and China, resulted in the publication of *Assessment of Men* (1948), a compilation of the work in which he and his coworkers successfully applied ingenious psychological techniques in selecting OSS personnel. At the war's end, Murray was awarded the Army's Legion of Merit for his services.

In addition to his other pursuits, Murray has made a lifelong commitment to the study of literature. Since 1925, he has studied the life and literary works of Herman Melville, and in 1949 he published an edition of Melville's *Pierre,* to which he added a lengthy discussion of the psychology of creative writing. The next year he rejoined the Harvard faculty as professor of clinical psychology in the newly formed Department of Social Relations.

Aside from his theoretical conceptions of personality, perhaps Murray's best-known achievement is the development (with Christiana Morgan) of the Thematic Apperception Test, a projective assessment device still widely used. He also conducted research on fear, humor, dreams, religion, and mythmaking. In September 1961, he received the American Psychological Association's Distinguished Scientific Contribution Award for his theoretical and practical contributions to the understanding of the complexity of human behavior. He was awarded the Gold Medal Award of the American Psychological Foundation in 1969. After thirty-six years of teaching and research, Murray retired from the Harvard faculty in 1962, having been named professor emeritus of clinical psychology. His foremost professional aim has been the development of a comprehensive personological system for the representation and explanation of the unfolding series of events that constitute an individual's life history. His accomplishments in this domain of theory and practice were celebrated in a volume of essays (*The Study of Lives: Essays on Personality in Honor of Henry A. Murray*) written by admiring colleagues and edited by one of his former students, Robert W. White, which was presented to him on his seventieth birthday.

WHAT IS PERSONALITY?

Murray provided several answers to this question in his various writings. Certain of Murray's definitions of personality are so intricately couched in his total theory as to be virtually impossible to understand apart from it. Other definitions, such as the following, are more immediately comprehensible: "Personality may be biologically defined as the governing organ, or superordinate institution of the body. As such, it is located in the brain. No brain, no personality (Murray, 1951a, p. 267)." Murray's various definitions of personality all stress that it is a hypothetical entity, rather than something of real physical substance. Personality is not the brain itself, but the hypothetical structure of the mind. As a fairly gross example, if a person's head were opened for inspection, his personality could not be "seen." If, however, his brain was then removed from his head, he would immediately be rendered "personality-less." Personality, while itself hypothetical, is completely and utterly dependent on brain processes in Murray's system.

Rooting personality in brain processes carries with it some definite theoretical implications. For instance, one always "has" a personality since one always has a brain. And, for Murray, personality represents a process of development from birth to death (Murray, 1968). Further, since brain processes largely integrate, organize, and regulate the rest of the individual's physical functioning, it follows that personality would do about the same thing in the behavioral domain. More specifically, Murray believes that personality integrates and directs the person's behavior. It is what accounts for the recurring, stabilizing elements in behavior that help individuals adapt to their environment. Stated another way, personality is what makes you today basically the same kind of person that you were yesterday. Same brain, same personality.

To highlight the intimate relationship between cerebral physiology and personality, Murray (1938) coined the term *regnancy*. The physiological and neurological brain activities underlying personality functioning are termed *regnant processes*. In Murray's scheme, all personality variables can ultimately be reduced to their regnant-process underpinnings. By way of illustration, take a well-known personality variable such as "need for achievement." People differ noticeably on this variable. For example, one college student with a high need for achievement would drive hard to get her "A's" and raise her grade point average as high as possible. Another student with a low achievement need might be less motivated to do so. While Murray recognizes that this and other needs could be measured without reference to the brain (see the "Application" section of this chapter), he strongly argues that all such psychological variables were founded in regnant processes. Although some personality variables can be measured on a purely *psychological* level (e.g., by personality tests), they cannot be fully accounted for without reference to the brain. Murray's concept of personality, then, is intimately tied to brain processes. Everything on which personality depends exists in the brain—emotional states, unconscious memories, beliefs, fears, attitudes, and values.

NEED THEORY

Reading the works of Henry Murray is truly a mind-boggling experience, not only because of the numerous theoretical concepts that he proposes but also because of the detailed classifications of these concepts that he develops. Rather than give passing notice to many of these varied and sundry ideas, valuable though they are, primary attention here is devoted to the three central theoretical concepts that seem most accurately to reflect Murray's unique view of human beings: *need, press,* and *thema.*

Need: What Drives People

The very title of this chapter indicates that *need* is central in Murray's theorizing. Murray is recognized as a major personality theorist primarily because of his extensive efforts to demonstrate the pervasive effects of needs on human actions. This raises the logical question "What is a need?" Consistent with his conception of personality, Murray (1938) defined "need" as a hypothetical construct which stands for a force in the brain region, a force either internally or externally instigated which organizes other psychological processes.

For example, need for achievement (labeled "nAchievement" and probably the most widely studied of all needs in Murray's system) is a *construct*, meaning a convenient fiction or hypothetical concept. It does not exist in the sense that one can see, feel, smell, or taste it (no personality theory concept does). However, nAchievement is an extremely useful abstraction for purposes of describing and explaining what may underlie and direct a person's activities. Second, nAchievement represents a force in the brain region. While the state of present day science does not allow precise delineation of the physiochemical nature of such a force, Murray conceived it to be activated from either within or without. College students with high nAchievement, for example, could either seek out situations in which they could achieve or simply be confronted by outside events that would heighten their achievement motivation, e.g., a professor suggests that the student consider preparing his or her term paper for submission to a professional journal for publication. Third, nAchievement, like all Murray's needs, also serves to organize various psychological processes, such as *perception*. The high nAchievement student *perceives* a final examination as an opportunity to achieve; a low nAchievement person would perceive it in other terms, e.g., a threat, waste of time, game, etc. Needs, then, organize the way people perceive, think, feel, and act.

How Many Needs Are There?   After an elaborate series of investigations at the Harvard Psychological Clinic in the 1930s, Murray proposed a list of twelve "viscerogenic" (physiological) needs and twenty-eight "psychogenic" (nonphysical) needs as the basis for human behavior. Examples from the long list of psychogenic needs, those which occupy a major place in Murray's theory, are presented in Table 5-1. Word changes have been made to avoid some of the unique and not readily understandable terms coined by Murray. Note that all needs in Murray's theory are always preceded by the lower case "n," as in "nDominance."

One of the major tasks confronting any personality theory is to explain how people fundamentally differ from one another. Murray's answer lies in the realm of needs, since his need listing does not imply that all people experience all needs to the same degree. In his system, some people may never experience certain needs in their lifetime while the actions of other persons are constantly dominated by these same needs. Some individuals may be attracted to a particular need or set of needs and express the remaining needs only infrequently. Then, too, other people may experience the entire range of needs within a relatively brief time period in their lives. As an intellectual exercise, the reader is invited to reexamine the exemplar needs presented in Table 5-1 and simply assess how important each is in his or her

Table 5-1   Illustrative List of Murray's Psychogenic Needs

Need	Definition or behavioral example
nAchievement	To accomplish something difficult. To master, manipulate, or organize physical objects, human beings, or ideas as rapidly and independently as possible. To overcome obstacles and attain a high standard. To improve oneself and excel. To rival and surpass others.
nAffiliation	To draw near and enjoyably cooperate or reciprocate with an allied other—one who resembles the subject or likes the subject. To please and win the affection of a cathected other. To remain loyal to a friend.
nDominance	To control one's human environment. To influence or direct the behavior of others by suggestion, persuasion, or command. To convince others of the correctness of one's opinion.
nExhibition	To make an impression. To be seen and heard. To excite, fascinate, entertain, shock, or amuse others. To attract attention by mannerisms, gestures, or emphatic speech. To monopolize the conversation.
nInfavoidance	To avoid humiliation. To quit embarrassing situations which may lead to belittlement. To refrain from action because of fear of failure. To associate with inferiors. To conceal a disfigurement.
nNurturance	To give sympathy, and gratify the needs of a helpless person. To assist a person in danger. To feed, help, support, console, protect, comfort, and heal.
nOrder	To put things in order. To achieve cleanliness, arrangement, organization, balance, neatness, tidiness, and precision.
nPlay	To act for "fun," without further purpose. To engage in enjoyable, stressless, "make-believe" activity. To devote spare time to sports, dancing, drinking, parties, cards.
nSex	To form and further an erotic relationship. To have sexual intercourse.
nSuccorance	To have one's needs gratified by the sympathetic aid of an allied object. To be supported, sustained, protected, advised, guided, and indulged. To exaggerate an injury. To remain close to a devoted protector. To always have a supporter.

Source: Adapted from Murray, 1938, pp. 152–266.

own behavior. Then take a few other persons whom you know reasonably well and carry out the same assessment. While this exercise is admittedly less than scientific in terms of personality measurement, it should intuitively reveal how Murray's need theory can be used to account for individual differences.

When is a Need Present?   Given that needs are hypothetical constructs rather than directly observable phenomena, how does the personologist know when a particular need is operative in behavior? On what basis is behavior attributed to a need for achievement, dominance, exhibition, etc.? To grapple with this important theoretical question, Murray (1938) proposed *five criteria by which needs can be recognized.* First is the consequence or end result of the mode of behavior involved. To illustrate, let's carry through with the example of college students with high nAchievement. They consistently get an "A" on the final, turn in the best term papers, or do the highest quality class projects. The second criterion is the kind of pattern of behavior involved. These students thoroughly prepare for examinations, work hard in the library or lab, and forgo activities directly conflicting with their scholastic achievement, e.g., drinking or carousing immediately before exams.

The selective perception of and response to a group of circumscribed stimulus objects constitutes Murray's third criterion. High nAchievement students pay particular attention to important aspects of lectures, books, or other assigned readings that will help them master the subject matter and do well in each course. Fourth is the expression of a characteristic emotion or feeling, e.g., "I want to do well," "I *need* to do well," "I want an "A" in this course so much I can taste it!" Finally, Murray's fifth criterion is the manifestation of satisfaction associated with the attainment of a certain effect or the manifestation of dissatisfaction associated with the failure to attain a certain effect. Attaining an "A" should result in "Wow!" (or an equivalent verbal expression) and a feeling of satisfaction. Depending on the colorfulness of the student's vocabulary, failure to attain the much-wanted grade may result in expressions often represented in comic books and other pornography-free publications by the terms "Blank!" or "Blankety blank blank!"—expressions of deep disappointment and dissatisfaction. The same five criteria, of course, can be applied with equal cogency to any of the needs on Murray's lengthy list.

Kinds of Needs Murray devoted a great deal of time and energy to developing a variety of schemes for classifying types of needs. While his complete need taxonomy is too exhaustive to present here, it may be useful to examine a few of the distinctions Murray made. One illustration has already been mentioned— viscerogenic and psychogenic needs. In Murray's system, *viscerogenic* or primary needs stem from the tissue requirements of the person. Reflecting the universal biological requirements for human life, this category includes needs for food, water, air, urination and other such necessary, life-sustaining activities. *Psychogenic* or secondary needs derive from viscerogenic needs and would include among them the needs depicted in Table 5-1. Interestingly, Murray argued that some psychogenic needs may become extremely influential and even assume priority over viscerogenic needs in certain situations. Examples might be the high nAchievement business executive who neglects his health to earn $10 million a year, or the high nNurturance altruist who risks her life to save another's.

A second illustration of Murray's need classifications, proactive and reactive, is based on the origin of the need. *Proactive* needs are aroused by some change of state occurring within the person. Common experience suggests that the need for food falls in this category. To illustrate, a person who is hungry looks for food, and doesn't wait to react to an advertisement for a steak dinner to satisfy the hunger need. By contrast, *reactive* needs are evoked by environmental stimuli. They are often instigated by situations that are unsought, unexpected, and dissatisfying, e.g., the need to avoid freezing temperatures. As with any other classification system, however, some needs can be perceived as falling in both categories. The need for sex is a good example; sometimes nSex appears to be a function of the time interval since the last sexual outlet (proactive), while at other times it seems to rise directly in response to environmental "sex objects" (reactive).

Overt and covert needs constitute another of Murray's categories. *Overt* (manifest) needs are allowed free expression by society. For example, in American society one can freely express nAchievement, nAffiliation, or nOrder. On the other hand, *covert* (latent) needs are not permitted open expression by the culture. Instead, they remain partly or completely unconscious and find their outlets primarily in dreams, fantasies, projections, and neurotic symptoms. Depending on social norms, nAggression, nSex, and nSuccorance could easily fall in this category. Interestingly, the implication here is that overt needs in one society may be covert in another. Anthropological findings seem to bear this out, in that need-based behaviors vary widely from culture to culture.

A final distinction within Murray's need categories is that of effect versus modal. An *effect* need is linked with some direct or specific goal state. A student enrolled in a personality theory course, for example, usually is motivated toward some identifiable goal (e.g., passing the course, fulfilling a requirement for graduation). The need or needs involved (e.g., achievement) are directed toward some tangible result. *Modal* needs, by contrast, are those in which experienced satisfaction is present to some degree throughout the activity rather than linked only to its end result (Murray, 1951a). An illustration would be playing or listening to music. Or a student may actually come to *enjoy learning* about personality theory in the process of completing the course! Murray describes this as the *sheer pleasure function*—the need to attain a high degree of excellence or perfection of performance. In Murray's system, then, the pleasure derived from doing something just for the sake of doing it can be just as important as the end result obtained.

How Needs Interact   There is constant dynamic interplay among needs in Murray's theory. Persons are by no means static entities in this system; the world within is characterized by continuous cooperation and conflict among forces. Again, however, the principles elaborated by Murray to describe the organization and interplay of needs are simply too numerous to catalog here. A few samples of these principles follow.

The principle of *prepotency* serves as a good beginning example. In Murray's view, needs are arranged in a hierarchy of prepotency or urgency. Murray (1951a) describes prepotent needs as those which come to the fore with the greatest urgency if they are not satisfied. The need to avoid physical danger, for example, is more compelling (i.e., has greater prepotency) than nNurturance. A man does not go to the assistance of another if a person holding a gun to his head commands otherwise. Consequently, needs are ordered in terms of their relative importance in assuring a person's survival—the order being determined less by the person than by the nature of the need itself.

The principle of *fusion* is a second illustration. Whenever a single course of action satisfies two or more needs simultaneously, there is a fusion of needs. For instance, a person might satisfy both nAffiliation and nNurturance through a single activity, e.g., joining a social sorority or doing volunteer hospital work. Fusion, then, does not mean that the two needs become identical. Rather, they complement one another in that they both are satisfied by the same behavior.

Subsidiation is another of Murray's principles governing need interaction. Basically, the principle states that certain needs are satisfied only through the fulfillment of other less demanding needs. In brief, a subsidiary need serves to gratify another need. As an illustration, consider the student who consistently displays admiration and conformity toward a professor (a deference need). Through the subsidiary nDeference, the student may really be attempting to gratify a more hidden nAchievement, i.e., to get an "A". Of course, all students who respond to professors in this way are not so motivated; some professors are actually worthy of admiration!

A fourth and final illustration of Murray's interaction principles is *conflict*. Needs of about equal strength may often be in conflict with one another and thus produce tension. Murray believes that much of human misery and most neurotic behavior are direct results of such inner conflict. Consider, for example, the plight of the young person with strong needs for autonomy and independence who also wants to get married. The various needs that push such a person toward marriage are in direct conflict with the need to come and go freely. Obviously, tension and a great deal of uncertainty can result. One hopes that such a young person might be able to resolve the conflict by finding in a marital partner the kind of individual who will allow great autonomy in the relationship. Unfortunately, all need conflicts do not lend themselves to such ready resolution.

Careful thought about the latter three principles will reveal that true needs cannot be readily inferred by casually observing behavior. Human actions may result from two or more needs (fusion), one need operating in the service of another (subsidiation), or a compromise or lack thereof among incompatible needs (conflict). While needs motivate behavior, it is not always easy to determine what needs are motivating what behavior. In Murray's system, you can't tell a book by its cover! Murray did, however, propose a novel and highly useful means of assessing needs, the Thematic Apperception Test, which will be discussed in a subsequent section of this chapter.

Press: The Person's Environment   Needs are always gratified or thwarted in some environmental context. Thus, to be comprehensive, Murray's theory must describe aspects of the outer world that aid or impede need satisfaction. His concept of *press* (the plural is also press) fulfills the requirement of describing the dynamic attributes of an object—how an object can affect a subject or person. Specifically, Murray describes press as follows: "The press of an object is what it can do to the subject or for the subject—the power it has to affect the well-being of the subject in one way or another (1938, p. 121)." As an example, take aggression press (called pAggression in Murray's system). When people find themselves in an environment surrounded by others who assault, criticize, or belittle them, pAggression is present. Such press can do a great deal to a person in terms of blocking need satisfactions. Very few needs can be gratified in such an environment. Yet for masochistic, guilt-ridden, and self-punishing people, this type of press may actually work in terms of need satisfaction. They like it. In Murray's theory, press in the form of persons or objects may either facilitate or block an individual's efforts to gratify his or her needs.

Varieties of Press   Murray draws an important distinction between alpha and beta press in his system. *Alpha press* represents persons, objects, or events as they actually exist in reality. For example, alpha pAggression reflects the fact that there actually are people in one's environment harboring and acting upon hostile feelings toward oneself. *Beta press*, on the other hand, represents the environment as subjectively *perceived* and *experienced* by the individual. Beta pAggression, then, means that the person sees hostility in those around him. According to Murray, it is the beta aspect of press which exerts the greater influence on behavior since that is what is felt, interpreted, and responded to by the person.

In well-balanced individuals, there is good correspondence between alpha and beta press. What you see is what you get. By contrast, serious discrepancy between the two types of press can result in *delusional* thinking. The paranoid patient, for example, experiences a high degree of beta pAggression without there really being corresponding alpha pAggression. Thus, she or he manifests a delusion of persecution, thinking that people are actively plotting against her or him when in fact they are not.

Aside from these two basic aspects of press, Murray (1938) developed several lists of specific press terms which he believes to represent significant sources of influence on a person's life. Again, Murray was consistently thorough and detailed here; Table 5-2 presents a few illustrations from his exhaustive listings. As in pAggression, each specific variety of press is preceded by a lowercase "p" in his system.

Need-Press Relationships   A person is a dynamic moving force in Murray's theory. Needs are constantly interacting with press to mold behavior. Thus, people's actions can never be fully understood by reference to their need states alone. Nor can we explain their behavior simply as a product of their environment alone. Both needs and press, and particularly the relationships between the two, must be taken into account in attempting to understand a person.

Table 5-2   Common Forms of Press

Press	Definition or behavioral example
pAffiliation	Companions who are friendly
pAggression	Others who assault, criticize, or belittle one
pCounteraction	Being attacked either verbally or physically
pDominance	Persons or obstacles which restrain or prohibit one
pLack	Living in a state or poverty
pRecognition	Competing for awards and honors
pRejection	Being refused membership in a club or organization

As an illustration, let's consider the seven sample forms of press listed in Table 5-2 and see how they might interact with just one need. Specifically, take the case of a young business executive with very high nAchievement. He drives himself endlessly, works hard, and is completely willing to "play the game" in order to get ahead. In fact, his nAchievement is so high that everything else in his life is secondary to it; our young man sees everything in terms of his goal to reach the top.

Of the kinds of press depicted in Table 5-2, pAffiliation and pRecognition probably would greatly facilitate the satisfaction of this expression of nAchievement. Having companions around who are friendly (pAffiliation) could conceivably help one get ahead, especially if they are bosses! An environment which presses him to compete for awards and honors (pRecognition) could hardly be more ideal for a high nAchievement person of this type, e.g., annual award for personally generating the highest sales volume. On the other hand, pAggression, pRejection, pCounteraction, and pDominance would appear to work against gratifying his nAchievement. Office companions who assault, criticize, or belittle him (pAggression), attack him verbally or physically—perhaps for outselling them—(pCounteraction), or restrain and prohibit his efforts (pDominance) certainly do not facilitate his climb up the ladder of success. Moreover, being refused membership in a club or organization (pRejection) necessary for recognition in a particular field could seriously frustrate his achievement strivings.

The precise impact of pLack seems more open to alternative interpretations in this case. For example, living in a state of poverty could block nAchievement if a person must "moonlight" at another job to make ends meet. In this situation, she might be forced to forgo the chance to attend night classes needed to further her career. When viewed developmentally, however, pLack could be seen as facilitating this type of nAchievement. There are many instances in which having lived in poverty as a child strongly prompts an individual to drive for high achievement later in life. Basically, she has made up her mind early to achieve later so that she will never be forced to live in poverty again.

More generally, then, needs interact with press to produce and guide behavior. The above example is restricted to only one need in possible relation with seven forms of press. When the great variety of needs interacting with the numerous press forms is imagined, the truly dynamic picture of individuals that Murray portrayed is strikingly revealed. In his theory, human behavior is indeed complex, produced by many interacting forces, and subject to both internal and external pressures.

Thema: The Interaction

Thema is Murray's theoretical concept that formally links need to press. It essentially refers to the interaction between press and need resulting in a particular behavioral episode. As an illustration, let us suppose that a high school student who earns a final grade of "A" in his math course is subjected to pAggression: another student in the course publicly and with obvious hostile intent makes fun of him and calls him derogatory names, e.g., "brown-noser." Such pAggression may instigate nAggression in our "A" student, prompting him to punch the name-caller in the mouth ("behavioral episode"). Murray's term "thema" refers to these kinds of press-need interactions resulting in specific behavioral episodes. As such, the concept represents a more comprehensive unit of analysis for personality study than either need or press alone; essentially, it gives coherence to the individual's behavior.

In the above "behavioral episode" example of a thema in action, one form of press instigated one need on one occasion. But human behavior is rarely so simple. For instance, the student involved may not react this way to all forms of pAggression but only that which emanates from a few of his classmates. Further, all people do not characteristically respond to pAggression in this fashion. Some withdraw from it, others try to overlook it, and still others may even accept it to alleviate their guilt. Theoretically, then, Murray required a more elaborate concept than thema to represent complex, ongoing person-environment interactions. His term "serial thema" largely accomplishes this purpose.

A *serial thema* reflects more than one need-press interaction. Specifically, it represents some combination of the simple themas underlying a person's behavior. Suppose, for example, that our fist-swinging high schooler *always* reacted to pAggression in this way. Murray's serial thema concept could then be employed here to reflect the fact that, for this student, various forms of pAggression always instigate nAggression, which in turn is characteristically expressed physically, e.g., fighting. In brief, we have here a characteristic way in which the person interacts with aspects of the environment, based on the underlying serial thema.

Conceivably, the student may not consistently handle pAggression in this manner. When pressed by male peers, he may punch—but he might respond to parental or teacher pAggression with deference. Nonetheless, these different situations represent simple themas which can be combined to form a serial thema, the central core of which is various reactions to aggression press. Serial themas, then, represent the more complex, varied, and ongoing need-press relationships underlying behavior.

Unity Thema: The Key to Uniqueness Each person is, in a profound sense, like no other. Many personologists acknowledge this fact, and some formally attempt to account for it. While Murray recognized that individual uniqueness was the product of many interacting factors, he singled out one as the essential key to an individual's uniqueness. He termed this key the *unity thema* (Murray, 1938).

In Murray's theory, the unity thema refers to the person's basic and individual pattern of need-press relationships. Viewed as a kind of underlying reaction system, it is largely an unconscious force originating in early childhood experience. Murray believed that, with intense study, it is possible to identify a person's unity thema, which, in effect, renders him or her different from other people. Once identified, the unity thema allows one to make sense of the person's various behaviors, which otherwise would seem inconsistent and unintelligible.

In essence, the unity thema constitutes the *psychological core* of the individual. It provides the fundamental continuity in personality over time. For example, while there are many things that might have changed within John Doe over the past ten years, Murray would argue that he is still fundamentally the same person that he was then. And in spite of future changes, he basically will continue to be that same person ten years from now. Why? Because there is a unique constellation of dominant needs inextricably linked to certain kinds of press to which he was exposed in early life. This fundamental set of need-press relationships is fixed and goes on to become the pervasive and dominant force in an individual's personality. Without it there would be no meaning or coherence to his behavior. In this sense, Murray's unity thema is the closest his system comes to defining the psychological essence of a person. Since it is constituted of need-press patterns particular to a given individual, the unity-thema stands as the "key to the uniqueness" of personality.

HOW PERSONALITY DEVELOPS

Murray focused much theoretical attention on the development of personality. While the various concepts that he employed in this respect are too numerous to catalog here, suffice it to say that, in one sense, Murray regarded the history of the personality as *being* the personality (Murray & Kluckhohn, 1953). What a person is today directly reflects her or his past history. And more—Murray argued that personality can never be understood outside a time dimension. It is not enough to describe what needs are interacting with what press at what time. To be understood, persons must be reviewed as constantly developing entities against the background of both their past history and future goals. To understand who an individual is, one must understand where she has been and where she intends to go as a person.

Childhood Complexes

Building upon the foundations laid by Freud and other psychoanalysts, Murray focuses on events and experiences of early childhood and the behavior patterns that are formed during these crucial years. More specifically, he divides childhood into five stages, each of which is characterized by a pleasurable condition that is inevitably frustrated or terminated during the individual's maturation and socialization. Each of these stages leaves its mark on personality in the form of *complexes*—groups of traits and styles derived from the imprints of the various stages—which unconsciously determine the course of the individual's subsequent development. According to Murray, everyone develops these five complexes because everyone progresses through the same five stages of development. There is, therefore, nothing pathological about them, except when they reach extreme proportion. When they are carried to an extreme, the person remains more or less fixated at one level of development, and is therefore unable to progress toward adult maturity.

   The five pleasurable conditions or stages of childhood and their correlated complexes are:

   1   The secure, passive, and dependent existence   *Claustral complex*
within the womb

2 The sensuous enjoyment of sucking good nourishment from the mother's breast or the bottle	*Oral complex*
3 The enjoyments of pleasurable sensations accompanying defecation	*Anal complex*
4 The pleasant sense impression accompanying urination	*Urethral complex*
5 The pleasurable excitations that arise from genital pleasures	*Castration complex*

Claustral Complex   The claustral complex, of which Murray has identified three specific types, stems from the uterine or prenatal experience of the individual. In the *simple claustral* complex, the desire to return to the prenatal state takes the form of seeking womblike enclosures. This type of person is usually passive and dependent, oriented toward the past, and resistant to novelty or change. He or she would likely prefer remaining under the bedcovers in the morning, having a secret hiding place, or living in a secluded part of town. The second claustral complex, the *insupport* complex, involves basic insecurity and anxiety over helplessness. Fears of insupport are commonly expressed as fears of open spaces, falling, drowning, earthquakes, fires, and loss of family support. The *egression* complex centers around fears of suffocation and confinement. Accordingly, the person who displays this complex has a strong preference for wide open spaces and fresh air, and for movement, travel, and change. She or he also possesses a strong need for autonomy.

Oral Complex   The oral complexes, of which there are three varieties, are derived from events associated with early feeding experiences. The *oral succorance* complex involves oral activity in combination with passive and dependent tendencies. This complex also manifests itself in the form of sucking, eating, kissing, and the desire for some nurturant figure from whom one can passively receive nourishment, protection, praise, sympathy, love, and care. When oral biting activities become associated with the need for aggression, the *oral aggression* complex is displayed. The behavior involved in this complex includes spitting, biting, shouting, and a general ambivalence toward authority figures. Finally, the *oral rejection* complex reveals itself in the form of spitting, vomiting, closing the lips tightly, stuttering, fearing oral infection (as from kissing), loss of appetite, and a general aversion to dependency relationships.

Anal Complex   Like Freud, Murray believes that anal complexes are derived from events associated with the act of defecation and toilet training. There are two such anal complexes recognized by Murray: one concerned with ejection of feces (anal rejection complex) and one with the retention of feces (anal retention complex). The *anal rejection* complex centers around preoccupation with defecation, enjoyment of anal humor, and an interest in feceslike material (dirt, plaster, clay). This type of person is usually dirty and disorganized. When the need for aggression becomes a part of this complex, the person's activities take a distinctly hostile and destructive turn, as with the subject who reported "I found an old can of paint and proceeded to smear our car all up and there were many other things like it

(Murray, 1938, p. 382)." In the *anal retention* complex there are strong tendencies to hoard things, to fear robbery, to be obstinate and negativistic, and to obsessively order possessions. There is also a strong need for order and cleanliness (one is reminded here of Freud's description of the anal character).

Urethral Complex   Although Murray (1938) originally considered the urethral complex unimportant, he later became convinced that it plays a key role in the lives of many people. He has also suggested that this complex be called the *Icarus complex*, named after the mythical Greek figure who, despite his father's warnings, flew so close to the sun that the wax holding together his artificial wings melted. Behavioral characteristics displayed by the Icarian individual include preoccupation with fire, excessively high ambitions that melt in the face of failure, craving for admiration, exaggerated self-esteem, and a history of bedwetting.

Castration Complex   Freud, as you may recall, traced much of adult neurotic anxiety to the childhood fear of castration. Murray, on the other hand, believes that the complex should be interpreted in a more limited and literal fashion as simply "anxiety evoked by the fantasy that the penis might be cut off (1938, p. 385)." He also believes that such a fear usually results from fantasies associated with infantile masturbation and the parental prohibitions that may have accompanied it. And as might be expected, the adult personality characteristics associated with this complex are similar to those of Freud's phallic stage. Thus Murray, like Freud, argues for the critical importance of early childhood as the ultimate root of adult personality development.

Proceeding: Behavior in Time

Murray divided the individual's past history into temporal units, or subject-subject or subject-object interactions, which he termed *proceedings*—segments of time in which behavior patterns are carried through from beginning to end. His longitudinal view of personality, perhaps most fundamentally expressed in this theoretical concept, was that a sample of behavior must be observed over a sufficient period of time in order to be properly studied. Instantaneous records, such as a photograph taken during the expression of a particular emotion, are abstractions from reality and, in this sense, distort it (Murray, 1951b). A photograph cannot tell us what led up to the event, which needs are associated with the emotional expression, or what the person did afterwards. Behavior, to be understood, must be analyzed in terms of a time dimension.
       Murray distinguished two types of proceedings—internal and external. An *internal proceeding* involves some segment of time during which individuals are absorbed in their private world of feelings, images, and ideas. Examples would be daydreaming, interpreting the symbolic meaning of a movie, solving a math problem, or figuring out Henry Murray's theory. By contrast, an *external proceeding* involves a stretch of time during which the person is actively engaged in dealing with the environment in terms of observable motor and/or verbal behavior. Playing tennis, registering for a course, participating in a class discussion, and going

to lunch with friends are illustrations. While internal proceedings have only a scarcely appreciable behavioral aspect, then, external proceedings are marked by their overt or observable behavioral character (Murray, 1968). Although he placed equal emphasis on both for understanding personality, Murray felt that the latter could more readily be studied by personologists because of their greater "observability." In particular, he believed that *interpersonal* or *dyadic* proceedings were very fruitful for personality study, e.g., the interaction between parent and child, sister and brother, wife and husband, teacher and student. In basic theoretical terms, such proceedings allow for the observation of the behavioral aspects of a person's need-press relationships in a time dimension.

Space does not permit consideration of Murray's additional developmental units for behavioral analysis. The basic point here is simply that personality, to be properly understood, must be seen in a time dimension in Murray's system. This idea inevitably leads to a broader question—what are the developmental forces that determine the formation of personality?

Personality Formation

In describing how personality is formed, Murray employed four sets of determinants—constitutional, group membership, role, and situational (Murray and Kluckhohn, 1953).

Constitutional Determinants The person's total physical makeup at any given time is what Murray means by constitutional determinants of personality. Included in this category would be such factors as the individual's age, sex, body type, skin pigmentation, physical strength, disabilities, and conformity of physique to the culturally fashionable type. But these constitutional forces do not act in a vacuum. Rather, in Murray's system, they are differentially important according to the person's social environment.

As an illustration, consider the male in our culture who is and always has been thin, fragile, and physically weak. By themselves, these constitutional factors play little or no part in Murray's scheme of personality development. But placed in a social context, they can assume great importance. For example, this male will never successfully play football and have the opportunity to develop whatever aspects of personality he might if he were able to participate in this sport. Because of his physique, he will never make the high school team, much less run against the defensive line of the Pittsburgh Steelers. Further, assuming that he attends a high school in which football types are most popular with females, our hypothetical male could experience pRejection on these grounds alone. Thus, he may be led to develop his personality, or satisfy his needs, in other ways, e.g., strive for high grades. While constitutional factors are part of personality determination, then, their precise effects upon the person are a function of their constant interactions with the environment.

Group Membership Determinants The social groups to which an individual belongs or aspires to belong also contribute to molding personality in Murray's system. Among these determinants are such groupings as familial, ethnic, religious, racial, political, regional, and socioeconomic ones. Belonging to any one or more of these groups affects personality primarily because membership carries with it exposure to a particular social environment and value system. Thus, certain needs will be both developed differently and expressed differently depending upon these external variables.

An example requiring little elaboration would be the potential differences in personality development between a suburban, middle-class child and an urban-ghetto, poor child as a function of the differences in their social environments and accompanying value systems alone. On a broader cultural level, most middle-class citizens of the United States, regardless of their regional, occupational, and religious differences, have developed certain motivational structures and behavior patterns which distinguish them somewhat from Norwegians, Italians, Chinese, or any other cultural group. The individual's culture and the groups within it are accorded special significance by Murray in determining personality development.

Role Determinants   Role determinants of personality are viewed by Murray as a special subclass of group membership determinants but are treated separately here because they are so potent in differentiating individuals within a group. The culture prescribes how roles necessary to group life are to be enacted, and the personality formation of individuals becomes intimately bound up with the roles ascribed to them (e.g., sex) as well as those which they select (e.g., occupation).

As an illustration, consider the traditional female sex role in our culture. Many little girls, solely because they are females, are taught in various ways to be subservient to males, not to manifest nAchievement in certain directions, and to acquire those characteristics designed to make them the "good" wives and mothers of the future. The female sex role, then, fosters certain directions of personality development while seriously curtailing others. Needs compatible with this role are allowed free expression by society—e.g., nSuccorance—while the expression of needs incompatible with it are frowned upon—e.g., nDominance (particularly over chauvinistic males). To some extent, all other roles perform about the same kind of personality-formation function in Murray's theory.

Situational Determinants   This group of personality determinants is made up of the day-to-day experiences of the individual, which for the most part are capricious and unpredictable. Situational determinants may include things that have happened a thousand times as well as those that happen only once—provided they are not uniform for a whole group (Murray and Kluckhohn, 1953). Accordingly, this is an omnibus category of factors shaping personality, including such diverse elements as interpersonal contacts of brief duration, family constellations (e.g., oldest in a five-child family), friendships with particular individuals, and divorced parents.

What seems of particular interest here is that random occurrences which happen only once may set in motion a whole chain of subsequent events that may profoundly affect personality development. Consider, for example, the random or "chancy" way that a person may meet his or her marital partner. The initial event does not, of course, immediately and directly change personality. But it may initiate what will become a deep, involved, and extraordinary intimate relationship that will decisively affect subsequent personality formation. These types of determinants, unique to one's life situation, may play an extremely important part in helping shape the kind of person one will become.

MURRAY'S BASIC ASSUMPTIONS CONCERNING HUMAN NATURE

Although Murray's need theory has been heavily influenced by the psychoanalytic tradition, there are distinct elements of humanism in his thinking (Maddi and Costa, 1972). This blend of psychoanalysis and humanism makes for an interesting profile of basic assumptions (graphically portrayed in Figure 5-1).

Freedom-Determinism   Even though Murray (1962) believes that human beings possess a small margin of freedom in making decisions, for the most part he endorses a deterministic point of view. Murray's behavioral determinants include both the person (needs) and the environment (press). He advocates a kind of biosocial determinism in which internal changes or external stimuli evoke an existing need. This need, brought on by the perceived external force, then instigates behavior to satisfy it. Thus, individuals are pushed by needs and pulled by press, with the primary goal being the satisfaction of needs.

Take nExhibition as an example. Suppose that a young man, because of his past learning experiences, has developed a high need for exhibition. Put him in a situation that he perceives as calling for exhibition—e.g., a fraternity party—and he will try mightily to be exciting, entertaining, amusing, shocking, or, more generally, to exhibit himself psychologically to others. For Murray, this person has some flexibility (freedom) in deciding how he might "exhibit" in this situation, but that he

	Strong	Moderate	Slight	Midrange	Slight	Moderate	Strong	
Freedom							■	Determinism
Rationality	■							Irrationality
Holism		■						Elementalism
Constitutionalism				■				Environmentalism
Changeability						■		Unchangeability
Subjectivity		■						Objectivity
Proactivity		■						Reactivity
Homeostasis	■							Heterostasis
Knowability				■				Unknowability

Figure 5-1   Murray's position on the nine basic assumptions concerning human nature.

will strive to exhibit is entirely outside his voluntary control. It is the interaction between need and press that determines a person's behavior in any given situation.

It will also be recalled that Murray has always stressed the physiological processes which underlie behavior (concept of regnancy). He considers the brain as the locus of the personality—the place where it is. The implication is that brain processes ultimately determine behavior. Only a staunch determinist could hold such a position.

Rationality–Irrationality   Although he recognizes traces of irrationality in human behavior, Murray invests people with a large measure of rationality. The irrational side of life is seen most vividly when a person engages in inconsistent or self-defeating behavior; for instance, when a student refuses to study for final exams, a motorist speeds through a red light in heavy traffic, a patient ignores a physician's advice, or an adolescent takes drugs with known dangerous side effects. The usual reaction to such actions is "Why did I do that—that's not like me." Despite such instances of apparent irrationality, Murray is convinced that rationality more often characterizes human activities. Human beings think, anticipate, plan, and pursue long-range goals.

Murray's strong stand on rationality is best seen in his *serial* conception of human behavior. In an aspect of his complex theory not previously covered here, Murray clearly asserted that an adult is quite capable of (1) organizing a set of subgoals leading to an important future goal (*serial program*); (2) employing creative strategies to avoid or minimize need-press demands that may conflict with long-range goals (*schedules*); and (3) establishing long-term plans and their priorities (*ordination*). Organisms that can consciously direct their behavior over time in such an ordered fashion must be highly rational.

Because people differ in terms of needs, press, and especially prior learning experiences, one person may not be as rational as another in conducting his or her life. A culturally deprived person, for example, may have relatively less opportunity than an affluent person to learn to make long-term plans or even to understand why such plans are necessary. Thus, he or she probably will be less able to make logical decisions affecting his or her life-style. Nonetheless, Murray maintains that the adult's functioning is characteristically rational, being governed by long-term objectives, plans of action, and philosophies of life.

Holism–Elementalism   Early in his theorizing, Murray set forth as his goal the complete understanding of the whole person: "Personality is a temporal whole and to understand a part of it one must have sense, though vague, of the totality (Murray, 1938, p. 4)." This insistence upon the wholeness of the individual, of course, is a common orientation among humanistic personologists. His various definitions of personality, stressing the interrelatedness of dynamically organized brain and psychological processes, also imply a holistic emphasis. Conversely, Murray recognizes the importance of avoiding the vagueness of holistic concepts insofar as they encourage "those lazy white elephants of the mind—huge, catchall, global concepts signifying nothing (Murray, 1959, p. 19)." This view makes Murray critical of personality explanations which do not include some reference to personality's component parts.

Murray's theory constitutes a rich and highly detailed attempt to bridge the gap between holism and elementalism. In so doing, he construes personality in a hierarchical way, including both general and specific "components." For example, the "unity thema" concept is quite broad while "need" is much more narrow. For Murray, then, it is impossible to understand the wholeness of personality without at least some reference to its specific parts, suggesting that his commitment to holism is less than extreme.

Constitutionalism–Environmentalism   Murray assumes that behavior cannot be understood unless the dynamic interaction between persons and their environments is taken into account. In this scheme, constitution and environment are given equal emphasis. Murray's early training in medicine, biology, and physiological chemistry made him appreciate the importance of constitutional factors underlying behavior. His central theoretical concept of *need*, rooted in brain processes, clearly reflects this orientation. Further, all psychological events depend on organized brain processes in Murray's system—"No brain, no personality."

On the environmental side of the coin are Murray's four determinants of personality. Of these—constitutional, group membership, role, and situational— three deal with external influences. For one who has been strongly indoctrinated in Freudian theory, Murray assigns a significant role to sociocultural factors: "A person is an emergent entity *of* and *in* a certain physical, social and cultural milieu (Murray and Kluckhohn, 1953, p. 6)." Thus, persons cannot be properly understood apart from their surroundings—constitutional and environmental forces combine to produce behavior.

Changeability–Unchangeability   Murray appears at least moderately committed to the unchangeability assumption. The key concept in his theory which reflects this assumption is that of unity thema, the person's basic and individual pattern of need-press relationships. For Murray, unity thema (formed early in life) constitutes the psychological core of an individual's personality over time. This basic core of personality is fixed and remains unaltered throughout a person's life.

But Murray's commitment to the unchangeability assumption is less than complete. Indeed, he finds it necessary to account for overall personality formation in terms of constitutional, group membership, role, and situational determinants— all of which are operative throughout the individual's life. Some acknowledgment of personality change is thus implied in such a formulation. Consequently, perhaps the best way to understand the relationship of changeability and unchangeability in Murray's system is this: the core of personality, unity thema, is fixed early in life and remains unaltered thereafter (unchangeability); other aspects of personality are open to some change throughout life by way of the four sets of personality formation determinants. On the question of *fundamental* personality change over time, then, Murray leans at least moderately in the direction of unchangeability.

Subjectivity–Objectivity Murray seems moderately committed to subjectivity, as indicated by the following statement: "The need to describe and explain varieties of inner experience decided the original, and, I predict, will establish the final orientation of psychology (Murray, 1938, p. 470)." Murray's theory includes several important concepts for understanding human subjective experience, e.g., needs, unity thema. Even environmental influences are seen from a subjective perspective—beta press, representing a person's unique interpretation of external forces, exerts a decisive influence upon his or her behavior. What is in objective reality (alpha press) is important in Murray's system, but what is privately experienced and interpreted as well as subjectively felt is the dominant factor accounting for human behavior.

Be that as it may, Murray falls short of making a fetish of subjectivity. His major theoretical concern is with motivation rather than subjective experience per se. For Murray, needs cut across people and, more generally, behavior can be described adequately without relying unduly upon individual subjectivity. External, objective factors (e.g., sociocultural determinants), while always subject to individual interpretation, are nevertheless prominent in his scheme. All things considered, however, Murray appears to believe that subjective factors are more potent determinants of behavior (though just a bit more) than are external, objective variables.

Proactivity–Reactivity In line with his humanistic leanings, Murray is moderately committed to a proactive view of human nature. He feels that people are capable of generating (self-initiating) their own behavior, particularly as it relates to future goals and aspirations. The fact that the human being is more of a "proactor"—an active agent in dealing with the environment—than a "reactor"—simply responding when stimulated—is what in Murray's judgment helps to make human beings uniquely different from lower organisms. An animal's behavior is largely governed by external forces over which it has no control as well as by the necessity of promptly reacting to biological need states. Conversely, there is an "inner-directedness" to human behavior that goes far beyond the demands of the immediate social-physical environment. This is best understood in terms of the individual's pursuit of life goals (schedules and serial programs) which provide a sense of purpose and self-enhancement. Persons are thus somewhat future-oriented in Murray's system.

However, Murray does recognize the existence of both proactive and reactive needs. Acknowledgment of reactive needs clearly suggests that no individual is entirely free of immediate reality demands—all persons must respond to physiological and environmental pressures if they are to survive. Furthermore, Murray's need-press account of behavior, stressing the instigating effects of press upon need, logically requires a reactive view of human nature. Hence, Murray's commitment to proactivity is less than complete.

Homeostasis–Heterostasis Murray strongly favors a homeostatic conception of human behavior. He argues that needs lead to tension which, in turn, leads to tension reduction. It is Murray's belief that reducing need tension comes closest to an "all-embracing" principle of personality. This simple need-reduction model, however, applies only to negative needs in Murray's theory, e.g., need to avoid aversive stimuli. As for positive need systems, Murray insists that a tensionless state itself is not satisfying, as Freud assumed, but rather that the process of reducing tension creates satisfaction. We are satisfied to the degree that we are able to reduce the tensions which we experience. For example, the hungrier people are, the more likely they will be to enjoy their favorite dinner. In fact, some people deliberately work up an appetite so that they can increase the bliss of eating. Thus, Murray's homeostatic view of motivation is not limited to simple tension reduction but is expanded to include the *generation of tension* as well. Individuals first generate the tensions of positive need systems so that they can subsequently enjoy the process of reducing them. This "generation of tension–reduction of tension" formula repre- sents an ongoing motivational pattern as opposed to an end state, a way of life rather than a final goal (Murray and Kluckhohn, 1953). It is the nature of human beings to constantly generate and reduce various need-related tensions. Murray's view of motivation, while a significant variation on the homeostatic theme, nonetheless reveals the assumption of homeostasis at its base.

Knowability–Unknowability   An important key to understanding Murray's position on this assumption is found in the statement: "Every man is in certain respects, a. like all other men, b. like some other men, c. like no other man (Kluckhohn and Murray, 1953, p. 53)." Murray regards the scientific disciplines of anthropology, biology, and psychology as potentially able to discover most if not all that there is to know about people in categories a and b. To this important extent, he supports the knowability side of the continuum.

However, in category c, individual uniqueness, Murray considers the potential contributions of psychology to be much more limited. Why? Murray's answer is that since individuals are unique, there will always be a subjective, idiosyncratic element in each person that will elude scientific explanation, given a science of psychology concerned with all people. In other words, scientific concepts cannot encompass all aspects of human personality, since it is a practical impossibility for science to study the idiosyncracies of every individual in the human race even if the appropriate scientific methods were available to do so. Murray quotes Aristotle in this regard: "It is the part of an educated man to seek exactness in each class of subjects only so far as the nature of the subject admits (1954, p. 453)."

The nature of Murray's subject, humankind, admits only a partial degree of exactness (knowability) through scientific methods. This is especially true when the personologist strives to explain why every person is in certain respects like no other person. Despite his efforts to develop a science of persons, then, Murray is a humanist who appears doubtful about the capacity of science to establish meaningful laws of individual behavior. When his position is viewed in total, Murray is not markedly inclined to either pole of the knowability–unknowability assumption.

EMPIRICAL VALIDATION OF
NEED THEORY CONCEPTS

What evidence is there to support Murray's personological system? In attempting to answer this question, one must distinguish between research that is an outgrowth of Murray's conceptions of personality and research aimed at determining his theory's empirical validity. Despite his significant contribution to personality assessment, there is an alarming absence of studies designed to test specific predictions derived from his theoretical formulations. Thus, at present, there is little basis on which to evaluate the empirical validity of Murray's concepts directly.

This assessment does not imply that he has failed to stimulate interest among personologists concerning certain variables outlined in his theory. There is, for instance, a voluminous literature on nAchievement (McClelland, 1961, 1965; Feacher and Simon, 1972; Lenney, 1977). But this research cannot be regarded as indicative of the empirical existence of his list of needs. Most of this research treats nAchievement simply as an avenue for investigating theoretical variables outside the domain of Murray's system.

Murray's professional life has involved deep commitment to the scientific study of personality. He has conducted studies examining the effects of fear on personality judgments (Murray, 1933) and clairvoyance phenomena in dreams (Murray and Wheeler, 1936), and he has made a psychological interpretation of Melville's novel *Moby Dick* (1951b). Fascinating as they are to read, such reports do not clarify the empirical adequacy of his position. Murray would undoubtedly agree. Nonetheless, his pioneering efforts to develop a comprehensive and detailed science of persons has inspired many psychologists to devise new and effective procedures for understanding human motivational processes (Murstein, 1963).

Why hasn't Murray's theory attracted others to evaluate its empirical status? Perhaps the most commonly cited reason is that his concepts are limited to elaborate descriptions, rather than explanations, of human behavior. His rich taxonomy of needs is seen by many personologists as a bewildering array of overlapping classifications largely devoid of theoretical utility (Maddi, 1963). Furthermore, it has been noted (Hall and Lindzey, 1978) that Murray has offered no explicit psychological assumptions linked to his concepts, rendering no testable consequences based on the theory. It has also been argued by some that Murray has neglected to specify how needs relate to other aspects of personality and how needs develop within an individual. Overall, it is safe to conclude that his various theoretical concepts need to be made more coherent and explicit before they can be properly tested. While these kinds of criticisms may be leveled against any personality theorist, they do constitute a partial explanation of why Murray's position has failed to capture research attention.

Another plausible explanation of why Murray's theory has not received the empirical attention it deserves is offered by Epstein (1979):

> The answer to the question of what kept Murray's theory and approach to conducting research from exerting the influence they deserved is that the field was not ready for

them. The field was ready instead for the laboratory experiment. The zeitgeist dictated that for the next 40 years a narrow conception of science was to prevail, epitomized by the one-shot, 50-minute laboratory experiment, in which all sources of incidental variation could presumably be controlled and people could be treated as interchangeably as different samples of the same chemical (p. 650).

Speculating about future directions in personological research, however, Epstein predicts that there will be an increase in investigations patterned after the approach adopted by Murray at the Harvard Psychological Clinic some forty years ago. Let us now see what this approach is.

Murray's Approach to Research

Murray has steadfastly insisted that predicting human behavior is an impossible task, an attitude clearly compatible with his theoretical emphasis on the complexity and uniqueness of the individual. Nonetheless, he keeps at it. Based on his humanistic respect for individuality, he has approached personality research from an *idiographic* perspective. Specifically, Murray believes that a scientific appraisal of human personality must be based on intensive, multifaceted studies of persons as individuals, as opposed to a search for common tendencies in groups of people. In fact, he deplores any assessment of behavior in which the results reflect group differences, statistical averages, or summary relationships between specific measures of personality. Murray contends that this latter approach, *nomothetic* in nature, fails to account for the complex subtleties of individuals and their relationships with others.

At the same time, he argues that the future development of a coherent science of persons can evolve if the tested methods of experimental specialists are integrated with those of personologists into what he calls a "multiform assessment program" (Murray, 1963). Toward this end, he has proposed two rules which would govern the activities of personological investigators. First, all investigators would use the same limited sample of subjects. The advantage of this procedure in Murray's judgment is that investigators would have at their disposal not only the results of other experiments but also the massive accumulation of data obtained through the assessment process in general. This recommended strategy would be something akin to a central information file from which competent investigators would select or contribute relevant data. The second rule (possessing even greater potential significance for personality researchers) would require two series of meetings of experimentalists and clinicians: one series to formulate the personality profile of each subject, and another to establish plausible explanations of the individual differences observed in each experiment taken as a unit. The goal of this second meeting would be to explain, with a reasonable degree of accuracy, the individual's behavior in everyday life. Additionally, Murray has argued that the *ecological validity* of psychological experiments (i.e., their generalizability to natural settings) would be greatly enhanced if experimental settings could more closely approach the individual's real world. While these are lofty ideals for any investigator, they serve as guiding principles for Murray's own research efforts.

What Are Harvard Men Really Like? Murray's principal contribution to personality research resulted from an exhaustive study of fifty college males conducted under his auspices as director of the Harvard Psychological Clinic. These young men were extensively studied for several months by a staff of experienced investigators representing the disciplines of psychiatry, psychology, anthropology, and sociology. The techniques employed in this longitudinal study included projective and objective personality tests, behavioral observations and ratings, in-depth interviews, and a variety of experimental procedures: the students were really put through the mill! Below is a partial listing of methods used in this multiform clinical assessment program:

1 Autobiographical Sketch (family and personal history, school and college experiences, sexual development, future goals, self-appraisal).
2 Present Dilemmas (discussion of personal problems and solutions for them).
3 Predictions and Sentiments Test (measurement of the similarity between one's prediction of economic, political, social, scientific, etc., events and one's hopes regarding such events).
4 Musical Reverie Test (report of thought processes elicited by phonograph music).
5 Abilities Test (self-report measures of such abilities as mechanical, social, artistic, and theory-creative).
6 Memory for Failures Test (recall of failure and successes in solving jigsaw puzzles).

After gaining a comprehensive picture of the student's personality using these and other procedures, the interdisciplinary team would study each student and then share their information and observations in a case conference setting, or "diagnostic council." Rigorous debate followed by a majority vote would then be used as the basis for developing an integrated account of each student's personality. Presently this approach to personality assessment would be regarded as unscientific, but personology then was in its infancy and Murray was exploring alternatives. By the same token, it would be erroneous to think that Murray's complicated theory can be verified merely by studying the needs of a group of fifty Harvard undergraduates. Harvard students do not necessarily reflect the rest of the world. In other words, unless the observations upon which Murray's theory rests are representative of the general population, its validity is likely to be restricted if not totally suspect.

Achievement Motivation in Women: The Motive to Avoid Success

Of all the needs catalogued by Murray, nAchievement is undoubtedly the one that has been studied most extensively (Weiner, 1972). Although Murray is not directly associated with achievement motivation research and theory, he did much to encourage other personologists to examine this important human motive. A prime beneficiary is David McClelland, whose efforts to establish a systematic theory of achievement motivation based on scientific inquiry clearly reflects Murray's formative guidance. Unfortunately, however, virtually all of the research conducted until the early 1960s on achievement motivation was confined to males. In 1958, for instance, an 873-page compilation of available data and theory concerning achievement and related motives appeared: research on females was limited to a single footnote. In that footnote, sex differences were referred to "as perhaps the most persistent unresolved problem in research on nAchievement (Atkinson, 1958)." Consider also what one critic said, in retrospect, about McClelland's 1961 book, *The Achieving Society:*

> He talks about achievement motivation in the Quakers, the Turks, and Ancient Greeks, the Apaches and the Commanches, the Saudi Arabians, and the Vikings of Iceland. He describes achievement motivation in Poland, Argentina, Pakistan, Bulgaria, Australia, and the USSR. He finds expression of achievement strivings in vases, in flags, in the Peloponnesian War, in Russian children's readers, in the use of motors, in Zen Buddhism, and in doodles. But there is not a single reference to achievement motivation in women (Lesser, 1973, p. 202).

Since the mid-1960s, research and theory focusing on achievement motivation in women has gained considerable momentum. One particular theme emerging from this burgeoning literature is that women, more than men, are ambivalent about the role that achievement strivings should play in their lives (French and Lesser, 1964; Lenney, 1977; Lesser, Krawitz, and Packard, 1963). Such ambivalence is attributed in large part to the conflict between women's desires for achievement and conditioned sex-role stereotypes that cause the "femininity" and appropriateness of such desires to be questioned.

Perhaps the most relevant research dealing with the achievement quandaries of women is the work of Matina Horner (1973). She has theorized that women, unlike men, have a *motive to avoid success,* a fear that achievement will lead to negative consequences, e.g., competition with men, loss of femininity, and the possibility of social rejection. As a result of such fear, women typically experience anxiety in achievement-oriented situations, and this may lead them to avoid success in a career. Competent men, on the other hand, do not experience this conflict because achievement and masculinity in Western society are seen as compatible. For Horner, the motive to avoid success is a stable personality characteristic which develops early in life when the girl assimilates the standards of sex-role identity.

To test her theory, Horner (1973) asked female and male undergraduates to write a story to a verbal cue designed to elicit the disposition to avoid success. For females the cue given was: "After first-term finals, Anne finds herself at the top of her medical school class." The verbal cue for males was identical except that the name of the story character was changed to "John." The stories were then scored for the presence of fear of success imagery based on statements showing: (1) fear of social rejection (losing one's friends or eligibility as a dating partner, or experiencing loneliness or unhappiness due to success); (2) concern about one's normality or femininity (feeling guilty or concerned about success and questioning one's femininity); and (3) denial of responsibility for the success (changing the contents of the story, distorting, or refusing to believe what has happened).

Systematic analysis of the stories written by the subjects revealed that women often expressed ambivalence or conflict over Anne's success. More than 65 percent of the women in the study wrote stories that contained high fear of success imagery (i.e., imagery describing unpleasant events after a success experience), whereas only 8 percent of the men did! The following story, written by a woman, illustrates her concern about not being normal: "Anne is completely ecstatic but at the same time she feels guilty. She wishes that she could stop studying so hard, but parental and personal pressures drive her. She will finally have a nervous breakdown and quit med school and marry a successful young doctor (Horner, 1973, p. 226)." Another frequently occurring response of females reflected concern about social rejection as a result of Anne's success. Here is an example:

> Anne has a boyfriend Carl in the same class and they are quite serious. Anne met Carl at college and they started dating around their soph years in undergraduate school. Anne is rather upset and so is Carl. She wants him to be higher scholastically than she is. Anne will deliberately lower her academic standing the next term, while she does all she subtly can to help Carl. His grades come up and Anne soon drops out of med school. They marry and he goes on in school while she raises their family (Horner, 1973, p. 227).

A final category of responses to Anne's success story involved the bizarre. Here is an excerpt from one such response: "She starts proclaiming her surprise and joy. Her fellow classmates are so disgusted with her behavior that they jump on her in a body and beat her. She is maimed for life (Horner, 1973, p. 226)."

Horner's pioneering research on fear of success motivation was conducted in 1965. In the years that followed, dozens of follow-up studies were done all over the country and the world—Yugoslavia, Italy, Norway, the West Indies. All of this work by no means confirmed Horner's earlier results (Shaver, 1976), with one contradictory finding being that a high percentage of men also revealed motivation to avoid success. (Hoffman, 1974). Nonetheless, in addition to demonstrating how a particular need might profitably be studied, Horner's research serves as a compelling illustration of the awesome power that society's sex roles wield in restraining persons from even wanting to reach their full human potentials.

APPLICATION: THE THEMATIC APPERCEPTION TEST

The Thematic Apperception Test or TAT was developed by Morgan and Murray (1935) as one method of exploring unconscious thoughts and fantasies. It is currently one of the most popular *projective techniques* (the meaning of this term will be clear shortly) used by clinical psychologists and is second only to the Rorschach inkblot test in terms of the amount of research it has stimulated (Buros, 1972). Its primary areas of application are clinical diagnosis and motivational research.

The TAT consists of a set of thirty black-and-white pictures (some fairly realistic and some quite symbolic) and one blank card. Most of the pictures have one or several people in them who are engaged in some ambiguous action. For example, one picture depicts a young man standing with downcast head buried in his arm, with the figure of a seminude woman lying in bed behind him. A second picture depicts the huddled form of a boy on the floor against a couch with his head bowed on his right arm. On the floor beside him is a revolver (Murray, 1943). Somewhat different sets of pictures are available for children, adolescents, and minority groups. The task of subjects is to make up as dramatic or interesting a story as they can for each picture. In the story they are to tell what has led up to the scene depicted on the card, what is happening at the moment, and what the outcome will be. In short, the story should have a past, present, and future. They also are instructed to describe what the characters in their stories are thinking and feeling. Their imagination is taxed to the limit if they are shown the blank card, since they must first imagine a picture on it and then construct a related story! Typically, twenty cards are administered one at a time to a subject in two separate testing sessions, and he or she is allotted an average of five minutes per story. The examiner usually records each story verbatim, occasionally requesting the subject to clarify or expand some portion of the narrative.

The assumptions underlying projective techniques (e.g., Rorschach, TAT) reflect the influences of psychoanalytic theory, specifically projection. The review of Freudian theory (Chapter 2) described projection as a defense mechanism whereby individuals unconsciously attribute their own thoughts, needs, or characteristics to other persons or objects in their environment. Although this is the sense in which "projection" has been commonly used, it is not precisely what Murray meant by the term in the projective test situation. The TAT is a storytelling test, in a sense a game of "make-believe," a situational task in which subjects are encouraged to give free rein to their imagination and say whatever comes into their minds. Thus, Murray stresses that in projective testing we are dealing with *imaginative* projection rather than with Freudian projection per se. The thoughts or feelings which the subject gives are not necessarily negative or totally foreign to his or her personality. Rather, they are all those expressions that one has in relation to a specific card.

It is assumed that imaginative projection is maximal if the stimulus material is ambiguous—the more unstructured something is, the more likely subjects are to reveal something of themselves in interpreting it. The TAT deliberately furnishes subjects with a series of unstructured stimuli (pictures) that they are expected to "structure" ("What is going on here?"). How they interpret these stimuli largely depends on aspects of their personality, i.e., their individual readiness to perceive in a certain way (their apperception). The idea is that because there is no established meaning, any meaning that the subject gives the story must come from within and should therefore reveal something about the subject's innermost feelings and desires. In short, it is assumed that the stories subjects tell reflect their own dominant needs, emotions, and conflicts; without being aware of the process, they identify with the principal characters in the pictures and thereby reveal themselves.

As might be expected, scoring and interpretation of the TAT requires considerable skill and training. Even though a few quantitative scoring systems exist, in actual practice many clinicians invent their own systems of analysis. This is because there are no right or wrong answers to the TAT cards. Murray (1943) recommends that the subject's responses be studied to determine if there are predominant *themes* repeated throughout many of the stories. This method of TAT interpretation, primarily content-oriented and qualitative in nature, is comparable to the psychoanalyst's interpretation of a patient's associations. That is, the interpreter looks for major motivations (or needs), conflicts, and strategies used to resolve conflicts and satisfy needs.

In Murray's system, the content of TAT stories is analyzed into two parts: (1) the force or forces emanating from the "hero" and (2) the force or forces emanating from the environment. The hero is the character with whom the subject has identified himself or herself—the character whose point of view is adopted and whose motives and feelings are most intimately portrayed. Murray also suggests that the examiner direct attention to the hero's outstanding traits, e.g., intelligence, leadership, dominance. Once the hero or heroes have been identified, the examiner analyzes the forces (needs) within the hero and the environmental forces (press) acting upon her or him. In other words, TAT stories are interpreted in terms of needs, such as those for achievement, aggression, and sex, and of press, such as physical danger and rejection by loved ones. The interaction of hero need and environmental press together with the outcome of a single story constitutes a *simple thema*. *Complex themas* (interlocked simple themas forming a sequence) are inferred from common themes that permeate several stories. Murray's need-press approach to TAT interpretation is thus concerned with questions such as these: Do subjects act on the environment or are they controlled by it? Are they active or passive? Do they overcome obstacles in the path of achievement or does the environment block them? Do others help or hinder them? Do they respond to frustration with aggression or withdrawal? Are they dominant or submissive?

According to Murray, careful TAT interpretation can answer these kinds of questions. However, TAT stories are never to be understood as literal translations of the subject's behavior in everyday life. Murray (1943) distinguished two levels of functioning in this regard: *first-level functioning,* physical and verbal behavior (actual overt needs), and *second-level functioning,* ideas, plans, fantasies, and dreams about behavior. TAT content belongs in the latter category. Moreover, it is primarily a symbolic rather than a literal representation of this level of functioning. Thus, TAT stories represent working hypotheses for the interpreter rather than proved facts; they require verification by other methods. The psychologist's interpretations of TAT stories, which provide a window to the subject's private world of experience, also rely heavily upon a knowledge of personality theory as well as a highly developed sense of clinical intuition. Translation of these interpretations to actual subject behavior, even under the best of circumstances, is exceptionally difficult and hazardous.

A greater appreciation of the psychological significance of TAT stories can be gained by way of illustration. Below are excerpts from a story told by a male college student in response to a TAT card depicting a young boy contemplating a violin which rests on a table in front of him:

> This is a boy seated in his room gazing at the violin . . . (pause) His parents bought it for him and want him to learn to play it well . . . they *expect* this of him. They are

always expecting something of him. He is looking at the thing and he doesn't want to play it . . . besides, it's a nice day, the window is open, and he hears his friends playing outside. He *resents* his parents for making him do this. (pause) It's hard to see what he's going to do. Maybe he'll try to play it for awhile, but if he still hates it, he may check out by way of the window (laughs)—it's on the first floor.

This student gave a number of other stories with a similar theme. The heroes consistently felt "pressed" by the expectations of significant others in the environment, especially parents and teachers. The heroes also felt a great need to escape their difficult life situations; yet the outcomes of many stories were difficult for the student to articulate, e.g., "It's hard to see what he's going to do." As counseling progressed, he began to understand how deeply pressured by his parents he felt. The student felt that his parents expected him to attend college and do quite well, and he experienced their high expectations as both anxiety-provoking and overly constricting. Furthermore, he indicated a strong desire to escape his situation in two ways: by leaving college and by having occasional suicidal impulses (e.g., "but if he still hates it, he may check out by way of the window . . .)". While the feeling of being "pushed" was very evident in this case, lesser intensities of the same kind of feeling are experienced by many psychologically healthy college students.

In sharp contrast are excerpts from a story constructed by another male college student in response to the same TAT card:

The boy in this picture often daydreams about his future accomplishments—he's doing so now. He's using the violin to stimulate his thinking. The kid is day-dreaming about the time when he'll become a world-famous violinist—another Isaac Stern. He diligently goes to his room every day to practice with this idea in mind. He's always felt that he could accomplish something worthwhile—becoming a great violinist is what he has decided to do. It's hard to stop a person like this. As far as the ending of this story goes, I think he'll make it. The boy will continue to practice until he achieves his ambition.

This student, a subject in a pilot study of certain TAT variables, presented other stories with similar achievement themes. Heroes consistently had high aspiration; they worked at something important with energy and persistence, striving to reach their objectives in life. They were seen as ambitious, persuasive, and creative. Environmental obstacles were either not present (as in this story) or rather easily overcome by the hero. The subject in this case had an excellent scholastic record. He was bright, purposeful, and self-confident. He knew who he was and where he wanted to go. At the time he was tested, he was applying to outstanding law schools, with a view to becoming a lawyer and then eventually entering politics.

The striking differences between the two students' responses above reflect significant personality differences. Murray's theoretical concepts of need, press, thema, and individual uniqueness thus come alive in TAT stories. In the hands of a skilled examiner, such stories are gateways to an understanding of the operation of Murray's hypothesized personality dynamics in any given individual. Although the TAT is far from perfect as a psychometric tool and is certainly not a magic key that will automatically unlock the doors to the unconscious, it has proved to be a productive and flexible method which has added significantly to our understanding of human motivation.

SUMMARY

Murray portrays personality as the hypothetical integrating agent within individuals that serves to organize and stabilize their behavior over time. In this scheme, all psychological events are functionally dependent upon underlying brain processes; without a brain, there would be no personality.

Murray's central theoretical concept—need—represents a force in the brain region which organizes psychological processes and behavior. There are various means of classifying needs in Murray's theory, such as viscerogenic-psychogenic, proactive-reactive, overt-covert, and effect-modal. Further, needs are organized and interrelated according to such principles as prepotency, fusion, subsidiation, and conflict.

Needs constantly interact with environmental forces (press) to produce behavior. Different need-press combinations that characterize a person's behavior are called themas. Moreover, each person's uniqueness resides in the basic underlying pattern of his or her individual need-press relationships: the unity thema.

Murray maintains that personality is deeply embedded in a time dimension, and portrays its roots in early childhood complexes. To represent behavioral continuity over time, he employs concepts such as "proceeding" (a temporal unit of either subject-subject or subject-object interaction). Murray also believes that as personality develops, it is powerfully influenced by four major groups of determinants: constitutional, group membership, role, and situational.

Murray's basic assumptions about human nature reflect an interesting blend of psychoanalytic and humanistic elements in his thinking. Need theory is based upon (1) a strong commitment to the assumptions of determinism, rationality, and homeostasis; (2) a moderate commitment to the assumptions of holism, unchangeability, subjectivity, and proactivity; and (3) a midrange position on the constitutionalism–environmentalism and knowability–unknowability assumptions.

While Murray has had enormous influence on personality assessment, there is an absence of empirical studies directly designed to test aspects of his theory. Murray's own idiographic approach to personality research, the multiform clinical assessment program, was described in this chapter along with an intriguing and provocative study of achievement motivation in women.

One major application of need theory is the Thematic Apperception Test. The TAT is currently among the most widely used projective techniques in clinical diagnosis and motivational research.

BIBLIOGRAPHY

Atkinson J. (Ed.). *Motives in fantasy, action and society: A method of assessment and study.* Princeton, N.J.: Van Nostrand, 1958.

Atkinson, J., & Raynor, J. *Personality, motivation, and achievement.* New York: Wiley, 1978.

Buros, O. (Ed.). *The seventh mental measurements yearbook.* Highland, N.J.: Gryphon Press, 1972.

Epstein, S. Explorations in personality today and tomorrow: A tribute to Henry A. Murray. *American Psychologist,* 1979, **34,** 649–653.

Feather, N., & Simon, J. Luck and the unexpected outcome: A field replication of laboratory findings. *Australian Journal of Psychology,* 1972, **24,** 113–117.

French, E., & Lesser, G. Some characteristics of the achievement motive in women. *Journal of Abnormal and Social Psychology,* 1964, **68,** 119–128.

Hall, C., & Lindzey, G. *Theories of personality* (3d ed.). New York: Wiley, 1978.

Hoffman, L. Fear of success in 1965 and 1974: A follow-up study. *Journal of Consulting and Clinical Psychology,* 1974, **42,** 353–358.

Horner, M. A psychological barrier to achievement in women: The motive to avoid success. In D. McClelland & R. Steele (Eds.), *Human motivation: A book of readings.* Morristown, N.J.: General Learning Press, 1973.

Kluckhohn, C., & Murray, H. Personality formation: The determinants. In C. Kluckhohn, H. Murray, & D. Schneider (Eds.), *Personality in nature, society, and culture* (2d ed.). New York: Knopf, 1953, pp. 53–67.

Lenney, E. Women's self-confidence in achievement settings. *Psychological Bulletin,* 1977, **84,** 1–13.

Lesser, G. Achievement motivation in women. In D. McClelland & R. Steele (Eds.), *Human motivation: A book of readings.* Morristown, N.J.: General Learning Press, 1973.

Lesser, G., Krawitz, R., & Packard, R. Experimental arousal of achievement motivation in adolescent girls. *Journal of Abnormal and Social Psychology,* 1963, **66,** 59–66.

Maddi, S. Humanistic psychology: Allport and Murray. In J. Wepman & R. Heine (Eds.), *Concepts of personality.* Chicago: Aldine, 1963, pp. 162–205.

Maddi, S., & Costa, P. *Humanism in personology: Allport, Maslow, and Murray.* Chicago: Aldine Atherton, 1972.

McClelland, D. *The achieving society.* Princeton: Van Nostrand, 1961.

McClelland, D. N achievement and entrepreneurship: A longitudinal study. *Journal of Personality and Social Psychology,* 1965, **1,** 389–392.

McClelland, D. *Assessing human motivation.* New York: General Learning Press, 1971.

Morgan, C., & Murray, H. A method for investigating fantasies: The Thematic Apperception Test. *Archives of Neurology and Psychiatry,* 1935, **34,** 289–306.

Murray, H. The effect of fear upon estimates of the maliciousness of other personalities. *Journal of Social Psychology,* 1933, **4,** 310–329.

Murray, H. *Explorations in personality: A clinical and experimental study of fifty men of college age.* New York: Oxford University Press, 1938.

Murray, H. What should psychologists do about psychoanalysis? *Journal of Abnormal and Social Psychology,* 1940, **35,** 150–175.

Murray, H. *Thematic Apperception Test manual.* Cambridge, Mass.: Harvard University Press, 1943.

Murray, H. Introduction. In H. Melville, *Pierre, or the ambiguities.* New York: Farrar Straus, 1949, pp. xiii–ciii.

Murray, H. Some basic psychological assumptions and conceptions. *Dialectica,* 1951a, **5,** 266–292.

Murray, H. In nomine diaboli. *New England Quarterly,* 1951b, **24,** 435–452.

Murray, H. Toward a classification of interaction. In T. Parsons & E. Shils (Eds.), *Toward a general theory of action.* Cambridge: Harvard University Press, 1954, pp. 434–464.

Murray, H. Preparations for the scaffold of a comprehensive system. In S. Koch (Ed.), *Psychology: A study of a science.* Vol. 3. New York: McGraw-Hill, 1959, pp. 7–54.

Murray, H. The personality and career of Satan. *Journal of Social Issues,* 1962, **28,** 36–54.
Murray, H. Studies of stressful interpersonal disputations. *American Psychologist,* 1963, **18,** 28–36.
Murray, H. Personality: II. Contemporary viewpoints, components of an evolving personological system. In D. Sills (Ed.), *International encyclopedia of the social sciences.* New York: Macmillan and Free Press, 1968, Vol. 12, pp. 5–13.
Murray, H., & Kluckhohn, C. Outline of a conception of personality. In C. Kluckhohn, H. Murray, & D. Schneider (Eds.), *Personality in nature, society, and culture* (2d ed.). New York: Knopf, 1953, pp. 3–49.
Murray, H., & Wheeler, D. A note on the possible clairvoyance of dreams. *Journal of Psychology,* 1936, **3,** 309–313.
Murstein, B. *Theory and research in projective techniques.* New York: Wiley, 1963.
Office of Strategic Services Assessment Staff. *Assessment of men.* New York: Rinehart, 1948.
Shaver, P. Questions concerning fear of success and its conceptual relatives. *Sex Roles,* 1976, **2,** 305–320.
Weiner, B. *Theories of motivation: From mechanisms to cognition.* Chicago: Markham Publishing Co., 1972.
White, R. (Ed.). *The study of lives: Essays on personality in honor of Henry A. Murray.* New York: Atherton, 1963.

SUGGESTED READINGS

Dailey, C. *Assessment of lives.* San Francisco: Jossey-Bass, 1971.
Hall, M. A conversation with Henry A. Murray. *Psychology Today,* 1968, **4,** 56–63.
Murray, H. American Icarus. In A. Burton & R. Harris (Eds.), *Clinical studies of personality.* New York: Harper Torchbooks, 1966, Vol. 2, pp. 615–641.
Murray, H. *Encounter with psychology.* San Francisco: Jossey-Bass, 1969.

DISCUSSION QUESTIONS

1 Describe the principles which govern the interrelationship and operation of needs as outlined by Murray. Cite some examples in your everyday routine in which your behavior is influenced by your needs. Finally, cite three important themas that you can detect underlying your own behavior.

2 Could you live a normal, healthy existence without any direct gratification of your achievement and affiliation needs? What kinds of press currently operate in your life to facilitate or impede satisfaction of these needs? Are these alpha or beta press?

3 How useful do you find Murray's concept of unity thema as a key to understanding the uniqueness of a person? Do you sense that each individual has such a "psychological core" and that, if you know a person well enough, you can discover it? Give an example by describing a person you know well in terms of a unity thema.

4 Do you agree with the findings of the Horner study cited in this chapter which suggest that women fear success more than men? Have there been any changes in the achievement strivings of women and men since the advent of the feminist movement? Cite reasons for your answer.

5 Describe Murray's approach to personality research. What might be some problems in following Murray's general approach in terms of establishing generalizable laws and principles of human behavior?

GLOSSARY

Alpha Press   Persons, objects, or events that objectively exist in an individual's immediate environment.

Beta Press   The environment as subjectively experienced and perceived by an individual.

Complex   A group of traits, acquired in early life, which play a significant role in shaping an individual's later development.

Covert Need   A type of need which is not allowed open expression by society, thus remaining partly or completely unconscious and finding its expression in dreams or fantasies.

Effect Need   A type of need that leads an individual to a direct and identifiable goal.

External Proceeding   A period of time during which an individual is actively involved in dealing with the environment in terms of observable motor or verbal behavior (e.g., fixing a car or talking to a friend).

Fusion   The process by which two or more needs are simultaneously satisfied by a single course of action.

Internal Proceeding   A period of time during which an individual is absorbed in his or her inner feelings, images, and thoughts (e.g., solving a math problem).

Modal Need   A type of need which is satisfied through the activity it arouses rather than any goal it leads to (e.g., playing music).

Motive to Avoid Success   The fear that achievement strivings will lead to negative consequences (e.g., loss of femininity, social rejection). It is developed in early life when a child assimilates sex-role standards and is evident in both men and women. Also called *fear of success.*

Need   A hypothetical construct (i.e., convenient fiction) which stands for a force in the brain region, a force which organizes all psychological processes so as to transform in a certain direction an existing, unsatisfying situation.

Need Theory   A personality theory formulated by Murray which emphasizes the motivational forces that instigate and direct human behavior.

Overt Need   A type of need which is allowed free expression by society (e.g., nAffiliation).

Prepotency   The principle that needs are arranged in a hierarchy of urgency.

Press   Term used to represent the impact of environmental stimuli upon the individual (see *alpha* and *beta press*).

Proactive Need   A type of need which is aroused by a change of state or condition occurring within the individual (e.g., need for food).

Proceeding   A segment of time in which behavior patterns (person-object interactions or person-person interactions) are carried through from beginning to end. For Murray, proceedings constitute the basic data of the personologist.

Psychogenic Need   A type of need characterized by a lack of direct connection with any specific organic processes or physical satisfactions (e.g., needs for recognition, dominance, and autonomy).

Reactive Need   A type of need aroused by some environmental event or stimulus (e.g., need to avoid extreme temperatures).

Regnancy   Concept used by Murray to indicate interrelationship between neurophysiological activities in the brain and psychological processes.

Serial Thema   A combination of need-press interactions giving rise to overt behavior.

Subsidiation   Principle governing need interaction which states that certain needs are satisfied only through the satisfaction of other, less demanding, needs.

TAT   Abbreviation for Thematic Apperception Test, a projective test consisting of a series of pictures for which the subject makes up stories. The TAT is often used to explore the individual's unconscious thoughts, fantasies, and motives.

Thema   The interaction between an instigating situation (press) and a particular need, producing a behavioral episode.

Unity Thema   A single pattern of related needs and press, derived from infantile experience, that gives meaning and coherence to the individual's behavior. Murray considers a person's unity thema as the "key" to his or her unique nature.

Viscerogenic Need   A type of need which is linked to the biological requirements of a person (e.g., need for urination, sleep, and food).

B. F. Skinner (*Photo by Jill Krementz*)

B. F. Skinner:
A Behavioristic-Learning
Theory of Personality

Much of our behavior is either learned or modified by learning. Through learning we acquire knowledge, language, attitudes, values, manual skills, fears, personality traits, and insights into ourselves. Accordingly, the discovery of the laws of learning can be viewed as one of the key avenues to understanding the reasons for our actions. One of the most prolific of all psychologists who have devoted themselves to the goal of explaining, predicting, and controlling human behavior is B. F. Skinner. Building on the work of Pavlov, Watson, and Thorndike, Skinner has become the leading present-day exponent of a behavioristic-learning approach to psychology. Based on the premise that nearly all behavior is directly governed by environmental contingencies of reinforcement, his efforts have provided the foundation for a science of behavior unparalleled in the history of modern thought. In the eyes of many, Skinner is the most influential psychologist of our time.

BIOGRAPHICAL SKETCH

Burrhus Frederic Skinner was born March 20, 1904, in Susquehanna, Pennsylvania, a railroad town in the northeastern part of the state. His father practiced law. He recalls his early years as occurring in a warm and stable environment where learning was esteemed, discipline prevailed, and rewards were given when deserved:

> I was never physically punished by my father (a lawyer) and only once by my mother. She washed my mouth out with soap and water because I had used a bad word. My father never missed an opportunity, however, to inform me of the punishments which were waiting if I turned out to have a criminal mind. He once took me through the county jail, and on a summer vacation I was taken to a lecture with colored slides describing life in Sing Sing. As a result I am afraid of the police and buy too many tickets to their annual dance (Skinner, 1967, pp. 390–391).

As a boy, Skinner spent many hours designing and building things—roller-skate scooters, steerable wagons, merry-go-rounds, blow guns, kites, model air-planes, and similar gadgets. He also worked for years on the design of a perpetual motion machine (which perpetually failed). This boyhood fascination with me-chanical inventions foreshadowed his later concern with modifying observable behavior:

> Some of the things I built had a bearing on human behavior. . . . At one time my mother started a campaign to teach me to hang up my pajamas. Every morning while I was eating breakfast she would go up to my room, discover that my pajamas were not hung up, and call to me to come up immediately. She continued this for weeks. When the aversive stimulation grew unbearable, I constructed a mechanical device that solved my problem. A special hook in the closet of my room was connected by a string-and-pulley system to a sign hanging above the door to the room. When my pajamas were in place on the hook, the sign was held high above the door out of the way. When the pajamas were off the hook, the sign hung squarely in the middle of the door frame. It read: "Hang up your pajamas!" (Skinner, 1967, p. 396).

In high school, Skinner earned money by lettering advertising show cards, played in a jazz band, and with three other boys organized an orchestra that performed two nights a week in a local movie theater. He also reports that he liked school and acquired a sound education in literature, mathematics, and the natural sciences from a fine few teachers.

Skinner received his B.A. degree in English literature in 1926 from Presbyte-rian-founded Hamilton College, a small liberal arts school in upstate New York. He notes, however, that he never really adjusted to student life. In addition to being disappointed by the lack of intellectual interest shown by his fellow students, he was quite disenchanted with some of the curriculum requirements (such as compulsory attendance at chapel). His participation in several escapades designed to embarrass those faculty members the students found to be arrogant led to threats of expulsion by the college president, but he was permitted to graduate. It is interesting to note that Skinner did not take any psychology courses as an undergraduate.

Following college, Skinner returned to his parents' home, now Scranton, Pennsylvania, and attempted to become a writer. Spurred on by an encouraging letter from the eminent poet Robert Frost, he built a study in the attic and sat down to write. The results were disastrous. "I fretted away my time. I read aimlessly, built model ships, played the piano, listened to the newly-invented radio, contributed to the humorous column of a local paper but wrote nothing else, and thought about seeing a psychiatrist (Skinner, 1967, p. 394)."

Eventually he gave up writing as a career and moved to New York City, at one point living in Greenwich Village as a bohemian. Reflecting on his personal failure as a writer, Skinner observes:

> I had failed as a writer because I had nothing to say, but I could not accept that explanation. It was literature which must be at fault . . . . A writer might portray human behavior accurately, but he did not therefore understand it. I was to remain interested in human behavior, but the literary method had failed me; I would turn to the scientific (Skinner, 1967, p. 395).

Skinner entered the psychology graduate program at Harvard University in 1928. He specialized in the area of animal behavior and was awarded the Ph.D. degree in 1931. Although he did not follow in the footsteps of any particular faculty member, he did take course work under E. G. Boring, Carroll Pratt, W. J. Crozier, and Henry A. Murray. Vividly aware that he was far behind in a new field, he set up a rigorous study schedule and adhered to it for almost two years:

> I would rise at six, study until breakfast, go to classes, laboratories, and libraries with no more than fifteen minutes scheduled during the day, study until exactly nine o'clock at night and go to bed. I saw no movies or plays, seldom went to concerts, had scarcely any dates, and read nothing but psychology and physiology (1967, p. 398).

From 1931 to 1936, he continued to work at Harvard, the first two years supported by a National Research Council Fellowship and the last three years as a Junior Fellow in the prestigious Harvard Society of Fellows. His research endeavors focused on the nervous system of animals.

Skinner began his teaching career at the University of Minnesota in 1936, remaining there until 1945. This was a period of remarkable productivity and established Skinner as one of the leading behaviorists in the United States. During the years 1942–1943, he conducted war research sponsored by General Mills, Inc., and was a Guggenheim Fellow in 1944–1945. In the fall of 1945 he accepted the chairmanship of the psychology department at Indiana University, a position he held until 1947, when he rejoined Harvard as William James Lecturer. The following year Skinner was promoted to Professor of Psychology at Harvard, and in 1958 he became Edgar Pierce Professor of Psychology.

Dr. Skinner is a member of a great number of professional and honorary societies. He has also been accorded many honors by his fellow psychologists. He was awarded the Warren Medal by the Society of Experimental Psychologists in 1942, an honorary Sc.D. by Hamilton College in 1951, and the American Psychological Association (APA) Distinguished Scientific Contribution Award in 1958. He is one of a handful of psychologists who have received the President's Medal of Science and is a 1971 recipient of the APA's Gold Medal Award with the following citation: "To B. F. Skinner—pioneer in psychological research, leader in theory, master in technology, who has revolutionized the study of behavior in our time (American Psychologist, 1972, January, p. 72)." Responding to his many accolades, Skinner says: "Many notes in my files comment on the fact that I have been depressed or frightened by so-called honors. I forgo honors which would take time away from my work or unduly reinforce specific aspects of it (1967, p. 408)."

The volume of work that Skinner has published is gigantic: his books include *The Behavior of Organisms* (1938); *Walden Two* (1948a, requiring only seven weeks to write); *Science and Human Behavior* (1953); *Verbal Behavior* (1957); *Schedules of Reinforcement* (1957, with C. B. Ferster); *Cumulative Record* (1961); *The Technology of Teaching* (1968); *Contingencies of Reinforcement* (1969); *Beyond Freedom and Dignity* (1971); *About Behaviorism* (1974); and *Particulars of My Life* (1976). Perhaps best known among college students is Skinner's *Walden Two,* a novel depicting the creation of a miniature utopian community based on the control of behavior through psychological principles of reinforcement. Twin Oaks, a functioning commune in rural Virginia, is currently implementing the kind of social life proposed by Skinner in this book (Kinkade, 1973). In addition, *A Festschrift for B. F. Skinner,* edited by Dews (1970)—a collection of edited papers—was presented to Skinner on his sixty-fifth birthday. His autobiography appears in Volume 5 of the *History of Psychology in Autobiography* (Skinner, 1967, pp. 385–413).

Skinner's dominant area of interest is the experimental analysis of behavior. He has worked primarily with infrahuman organisms, usually rats or pigeons, but has also applied the principles of operant conditioning, among other things, to the study of adult psychotics and autistic children, an analysis of human language, and the design of teaching machines. In addition to the widely known "Skinner box," a device used to study the operant behavior of animals, he designed a temperature-controlled crib (often referred to as a "baby box") which he and his wife occasionally used with one of their infant daughters. Moreover, he has developed a number of instructional machines to facilitate learning from kindergarten through college. Skinner's many and significant contributions have made him a pivotal figure in contemporary psychology.

SKINNER'S APPROACH TO PSYCHOLOGY

Most personological theorists share two perspectives: (1) a commitment to the study of persistent differences among people and (2) a reliance on hypothetical constructs to account for the variety and complexity of human behavior. These perspectives constitute the mainstream, if not the essence, of virtually all theorizing about personality to date. Throughout most of his career, Skinner questioned whether abstract theories are necessary or desirable or whether they should be abandoned in favor of an approach based solely on observed relationships between behavior and its consequences (1950). He insisted that psychology, particularly the field of learning, is not sufficiently advanced to justify efforts devoted to grand-scale, formalized theory building. Second, he also contended that there is no need for theory-directed research since it provides "explanations of observed facts which appeal to events taking place in different terms and measured, if at all, in different dimensions (Skinner, 1961, p. 39)." Finally, Skinner suggested that theories of human behavior often give psychologists a false sense of security about their state of knowledge, when in fact they do not comprehend the relationships between ongoing behavior and its environmental antecedents.

In light of Skinner's apparent antitheoretical position, it is questionable whether he should be included in a volume concerned with personality theories. Fortunately, Skinner now admits to being a psychological theorist, thus justifying our presentation of his system as illustrative of a behavioristic-learning approach to the study of personality. In one interview he noted:

> I defined theory as an effort to explain behavior in terms of something going on in another universe, such as the mind or the nervous system. Theories of that sort I do not believe are essential or helpful. Besides, they are dangerous; they cause all kinds of

trouble. But I look forward to an overall theory of human behavior which will bring together a lot of facts and express them in a more general way. That kind of theory I would be very much interested in promoting, and I consider myself to be a theoretician (Evans, 1968, p. 88).

Furthermore, he has asserted that whether some experimental psychologists approve or not, experimental psychology is inevitably committed to the task of constructing a theory of behavior (Skinner, 1969). While Skinner's view of such a theory is far different from that of most personologists, it nonetheless is essential to the scientific understanding of human behavior.

Out with Autonomous Man!

Skinner passionately rejects all explanations of behavior based on the presumed existence of an indwelling agent (a little man or *homunculus*), the self, the unconscious, or any other hypothetical entity referring to events which "lie under the skin." Such mentalistic and intrapsychic mechanisms, he notes, originated in primitive animism but persist because there is ignorance of the environmental conditions governing behavior. In Skinner's words:

> Autonomous man serves to explain only the things we are not yet able to explain in other ways. His existence depends upon our ignorance, and he naturally loses status as we come to know more about behavior. . . . We do not need to try to discover what personalities, states of mind, feelings, traits of character, plans, purposes, intentions, or the other prerequisites of autonomous man really are in order to get on with a scientific analysis of behavior (1971, pp. 12–13).

Skinner's objection to the use of such hypothetical constructs or inner causes is not that they are inappropriate phenomena for psychologists to study but rather that they are shrouded in terminology that makes objective definitions and empirical tests impossible. In the history of science, he observes, it has usually been necessary to completely abandon such conceptions rather than modify them to a form which permits empirical study. To explain why a competent student flunks out of college, we might easily say "because he had a strong fear of failure," "because he lacked motivation," or "because he cut classes as a result of an unconscious fear of success." Such hypotheses about the student's dismissal from college may sound like explanations, but Skinner warns that they explain nothing unless the motives involved are explicitly defined and unless the antecedents of flunking out are established.

Thus, if a so-called mentalistic (unobservable) concept is invoked to explain behavior, it must be translatable into terms relevant to the experimental operations involved in investigation and measurement. To settle for less would be to resort to the very armchair philosophizing that Skinner so vehemently deplores. One could start with what can be observed (i.e., the incident of flunking out) and then determine whether additional explanations augment the understanding of the behavior in question. If a competent student flunks out of college, is it not more illuminating to examine what environmental variables preceded that behavior than to propose as its cause some mental entity that cannot be objectively identified? For instance, did dormitory noise disrupt her sleep so that she could not study effectively? Did she work forty hours per week and thus lack the time to study? Or did she play on the varsity basketball team whose schedule forced her to miss numerous classes and exams? These questions clearly reveal that Skinner places responsibility for the individual's actions on environmental circumstances rather than the autonomous person within.

Skinner also believes that the mental, or intentional, explanation of events brings curiosity to an end. He says:

> We can see the effect in casual discourse. If we ask someone, "Why did you go to the theatre?" and he says, "Because I felt like going," we are apt to take his reply as a kind of explanation. It would be much more to the point to know what has happened when he has gone to the theatre in the past, what he heard or read about the play he went to see, and what other things in his past or present environments might have induced him to go (as opposed to doing something else), but we accept "I feel like going" as a sort of summary of all this and are not likely to ask for details (1971, p. 10).

In Skinnerian psychology, then, no attempt is made to ask questions or to infer processes about the individual's inner state. It is considered irrelevant for a scientific explanation of behavior. To avoid the notion that describing is explaining, Skinner contends that the human organism is an unopened box (an "empty organism"), and hence that all variables (motives, drives, conflicts, attitudes, emotions, etc.) which mediate the inputs and outputs of behavior should be discarded from the domain of psychological inquiry. These organismic variables add nothing to our understanding of human activity and only serve to delay the development of a scientific study of behavior. According to Skinner, adequate explanations can be accomplished without recourse to any constructs other than those accounting for the functional relationships between various stimulus conditions (tangible characteristics of the environment affecting the individual) and behavioral responses overtly emitted by the individual. However, Skinner does not categorically reject the study of inner events. Indeed, he believes that psychologists must provide adequate explanations of private events, but the events studied must be capable of being reliably and objectively measured. That is, so-called private events are an acceptable part of psychological science to the degree that they can be externalized and objectively measured. It is this emphasis on objectivity that earmarks Skinner's attempt to recognize the legitimacy of internal events.

Down with Physiological-Genetic Explanations!

Unlike many contemporary psychologists, Skinner does not believe that the ultimate answers to the questions of psychology will be found in the laboratory of the physiologist. This disregard for physiological-genetic conceptions of behavior is based largely on the conviction that they do not facilitate behavioral control. Skinner explains his aversion to "physiologizing" by noting:

> Even when it can be shown that some aspect of behavior is due to season of birth, gross body type, or genetic constitution, the fact is of limited use. It may help us in predicting

behavior, but is of little value in an experimental analysis or in practical control because such a condition cannot be manipulated after the individual has been conceived (1975, p. 371).

Thus, Skinner does not oppose recognition of the biological-genetic elements of behavior but rather ignores them because they are not (at least currently) amenable to modification through manipulation.

What Behavioral Science Should Be

In his approach to the study of people, Skinner assumes that all behavior is lawfully determined, predictable, and able to be brought under environmental control. To understand behavior is to control it, and vice versa. He is unalterably opposed to any admission of free will or any other "volitional," uncaused event. Human beings, in his system, are machines—highly complicated ones, but machines nonetheless. While he is by no means the first psychologist to propose a mechanistic approach to the study of behavior (Watson advocated throwing out mentalistic concepts in the 1920s), his formulation is exceptional in that he carries the idea to its logical conclusion. To Skinner, the science of human behavior is basically no different from any other data-oriented natural science; thus, its goals are the same—prediction and control of the phenomena studied (overt behavior in this case).

Additionally, Skinner argues that since all science advances from the simple to the complex, it is logical to study infrahumans prior to studying humans. The former enables the psychologist to discover more easily the basic processes and principles of behavior. Among other advantages, the researcher is able to exert more precise control over the conditions influencing an animal's environment and to collect data over longer periods of time. There is, of course, a serious question as to how much of the findings uncovered by studying one species (e.g., rats) are truly applicable to another species (e.g., humans). Skinner, however, advocates the use of lower species as experimental subjects because he believes there is ample evidence showing definite relationship between principles of behavior established at that level and their application to human functioning. To illustrate, the recent development of teaching machines and programmed learning are direct products of Skinner's work in the animal laboratory.

Unlike most current psychological research, Skinner's work stresses a thorough analysis of a single organism's behavior. Skinner believes that the study of a single organism is appropriate because laws governing such organisms are identical to the laws which govern all organisms. Thus, while the behavior of individual rats, pigeons, or people may vary, the basic scientific laws controlling that behavior do not. By studying *one* rat, *one* pigeon, or *one* person, Skinner argues that such basic laws can be uncovered and generalized to other organisms.

This orientation, often referred to as the *single-subject experimental design,* does not require the traditional statistical techniques (i.e., inference) that most students learn in their psychological training. Instead of seeking to make statistical predictions about the behavior of the nonexistent average individual, Skinner strongly argues that psychological science should attempt to predict and determine experimentally the influence of one or more controlled variables upon a specified component of an individual organism's behavior in a controlled environment. This approach requires a nonstatistical strategy which yields laws relevant to real individual behavior. This, says Skinner, is what psychology as a behavioral science should have as its aim. Skinnerian psychology might be summarized by a statement Skinner (1956) quotes from Pavlov: "Control your conditions and you will see order."

In keeping with his behavioristic approach, Skinner advocates a *functional analysis* of the behaving organism. In such an analysis the psychologist strives to establish exact, real, and specifiable relationships between the organism's observable behavior (responses) and the environmental conditions (stimuli) that control or determine it. The variables employed must be external, visible, and defined in quantitative terms. It is the cause-and-effect relationships emerging from a functional analysis which become the laws of behavioral science. The practical goal is to be able to manipulate the environmental (independent) variables from which predictions are made and then to measure the resulting changes in behavior (dependent variables). Thus, one can work within the boundaries of a natural science and yet discover laws relevant to the behavior of individual organisms.

Personality Viewed from a Behavioristic Perspective

We have now examined some of the reasons why Skinner adopts an experimental approach to the study of behavior. But what about the study of personality? It is completely lost in Skinner's uncompromising emphasis on a functional, cause-and-effect analysis of behavior? Simply stated, the answer to the latter question is "No," provided that established scientific criteria are met. As we have seen, for instance, Skinner does not accept the idea of a personality or self that instigates and directs behavior. He considers such an approach a vestige of primitive animism, a doctrine that presupposed the existence of something akin to spirits within the body which moved it (Skinner, 1974). Nor would he accept so-called "dead-end" explanations of behavior such as this: "Why did Rev. Jones and some 980 members of the People's Temple Church kill themselves in the jungle of Guyana? —Because they were emotionally disturbed."

From Skinner's behavioristic perspective, the study of personality involves a systematic and rigorous examination of the idiosyncratic learning history and unique genetic background of the individual:

> In a behavioral analysis, a person is an organism . . . which has acquired a repertoire of behavior. . . . [He] is not an originating agent; he is a locus, a point at which many genetic and environmental conditions come together in a joint effect. As such, he remains unquestionably unique. No one else (unless he has an identical twin) has his genetic endowment, and without exception no one else has his personal history. Hence no one else will behave in precisely the same way (Skinner, 1974, pp. 167–168).

For Skinner, then, the study of personality involves the discovery of the unique pattern of relationships between the behavior of an organism and its reinforcing consequences, as opposed to the study of the presumed properties of some hypothetical internal "spirit" (personality) which is thought to instigate an individual's behavior.

OPERANT BEHAVIOR

In formulating a system of behavior, Skinner (1938) distinguishes two types of behavioral responses: respondent and operant. In its simplest terms, *respondent behavior* (also known as classical or Pavlovian conditioning) refers to a specific kind of response which is elicited by a known stimulus, the latter always preceding the former in time. Familiar respondents include pupillary constriction or dilation to changes in light stimulation, knee jerk to a hammer tapped on the patellar tendon, shivering to cold, and salivation to food. In each of these examples, the relationship between the stimulus (light stimulation, hammer, etc.) is involuntary and spontaneous—it always occurs. In fact, the same stimulus elicits the same response from all organisms of the same species. Thus, respondent behavior usually entails *reflexes* involving the autonomic nervous system. However, at a higher level, respondent behavior may also be learned. For example, the professor who perspires profusely and has "butterflies in his stomach" prior to delivering an important lecture is manifesting respondent behavior.

In the early 1900s Ivan Pavlov, the famous Russian physiologist and Nobel Prize winner, first discovered, while studying the physiology of digestion, that respondent behavior can be conditioned. He observed that meat powder placed in the mouth of a hungry dog always evokes salivation. In this case, salivation is an unlearned response or, as Pavlov called it, an *unconditioned response* (UCR). It is elicited by the meat powder which, in this instance, is termed the *unconditioned stimulus* (UCS). Pavlov's great discovery was that if a previously neutral stimulus is repeatedly paired with the unconditioned stimulus, eventually the neutral stimulus acquires the capacity to elicit the unconditioned response when it is presented alone *without* the unconditioned stimulus. For example, if a bell is rung each time immediately before the meat powder reaches its mouth, gradually a dog will begin to salivate upon hearing the bell, even if the meat powder is no longer presented. The new response, salivation to the bell sound, is termed a *conditioned response* (CR), while the previously neutral eliciting stimulus, the bell, is known as the *conditioned stimulus* (CS). If, on subsequent trials, meat powder is regularly omitted, the magnitude of the salivary response gradually decreases until it ceases to occur when the conditioned stimulus (bell) is presented. This process, known as *extinction* of the conditioned response, demonstrates that reinforcement (meat powder) is essential for both the acquisition and maintenance of respondent learning.

A well-known experiment conducted by Watson and Rayner (1920) illustrates the phenomenon of human classical conditioning. These investigators conditioned an emotional fear response in Albert, an 11-month-old child. Prior to the experiment it was determined that Albert showed no fear reactions to a number of stimuli—cotton; burning newspapers; masks with and without hair; and several animals including a rabbit, rat, dog, and monkey. Likewise, he had never been seen in a state of fear or rage. Watson and Rayner's procedure was to present a tame white rat (conditioned stimulus) together with a loud noise (unconditioned stimulus) produced by striking a long steel bar with a claw hammer just behind Albert's back. After the rat and the frightening sound were paired seven times, a strong fear response (CR)—crying and falling over—was elicited when the rat alone was presented. Subsequent tests indicated that Albert had generalized his fear reactions to a wide range of stimuli including a short-haired dog, sealskin coat, Santa Claus mask, and even Watson's hair. Cruel though this case may seem, it does reveal how similar fears (of strangers, dentists, and doctors) may be acquired through the process of classical conditioning.

Although Skinner has incorporated many of the principles of Pavlovian conditioning into his system, he does not believe that the major portion of human behavior is composed of simple reflexes or conditioned responses. According to Skinner (1953), most human social behavior falls into a second class, that of behavior freely *emitted* by an organism. Because this type of behavior implies an active organism that "operates" upon its environment, controlling the environment and being controlled by it, Skinner labeled the responses *operants*. Operant behavior (produced by instrumental or operant conditioning) is determined by the events that follow the response. That is, a behavior is followed by a consequence and the nature of the consequence modifies the organism's tendency to repeat the behavior in the future. For instance, riding a bicycle, playing the piano, throwing a ball, kissing, and writing one's name are considered operant response patterns, or operants, since they are controlled by the consequences which follow their respective performances. They are voluntary, learned responses for which an identifiable stimulus does not exist. If the outcomes or consequences of the response are favorable to the person, then the likelihood of the operant being emitted again in the future is thereby increased. When this happens, the consequence is said to be *reinforcing* and the operant response which has been affected by the reinforcement (in the sense that it is more likely to occur) has been conditioned. The strength of a positive reinforcing stimulus is thus defined in terms of its effects on the subsequent frequency of the response which immediately preceded it.

Alternatively, if the outcomes of responses are unfavorable or nonreinforcing, then the likelihood of the operant occurring again is decreased. For example, you will soon stop smiling at a person whose consistent response to your smile is a scowl. In other words, operant behavior may be controlled by another class of consequences called negative reinforcers or *aversive stimuli.* By definition, these stimuli weaken the behavior that produces them and strengthen the behavior that removes them. If a person consistently scowls, you will eventually try to avoid him or her altogether.

In order to study operant behavior in the laboratory, Skinner devised a deceptively simple type of procedure called the free *operant method.* In this procedure, a semistarved rat is placed in an experimental chamber (commonly referred to as the Skinner box) which is empty except for a lever and a food dish at one end of it. (Isolation is required in order to minimize the effects of extraneous influences.) At first, the rat will normally exhibit a variety of operants: walking, sniffing, scratching, grooming, and urinating. Such responses are not elicited by any recognizable stimulus; they are spontaneously emitted. Eventually, in the course of its exploratory activity, the rat will strike the lever, causing a pellet of food to be automatically delivered to the dish. Because the response of lever pressing has an initially low probability of occurrence, it must be considered purely accidental with regard to feeding; that is, we cannot predict when the rat will press the lever, nor can we make the rat do it. However, by depriving it of food, say, for twenty-four hours, we can ensure that the lever-pressing response will eventually have a high probability of occurrence in this particular situation. This is done through a method called *magazine training,* whereby the experimenter delivers a food pellet each time the rat presses the lever. It can then be observed that the rat spends more time in the vicinity of the lever and the feeding dish until, in due course, it is pressing the lever at an ever-increasing rate. Lever pressing thus quickly becomes the rat's most frequent response under conditions of food deprivation. In the operant conditioning situation, then, the rat's behavior is instrumental (i.e., operates upon the environment) in producing the reinforcement (food). If nonreinforced trials now occur, that is, if food fails to appear consistently following the lever-pressing response, the rat eventually stops pressing and undergoes *experimental extinction.*

Now that we have covered the nature of operant conditioning, it may be helpful to consider an example of it encountered in almost any family with young children—the operant conditioning of crying behavior. Whenever young children are in obvious pain, they cry, and the parents' immediate reaction is to express attention and other positive reinforcements. Since attention is reinforcing for the child, the crying response naturally becomes conditioned. However, crying may occur even when pain is absent. Most parents believe that they can discriminate between crying due to pain and crying evoked by the desire for attention, yet many parents persist in reinforcing the latter.

Is it possible for parents to eliminate conditioned crying behavior or is the child destined to be a "crybaby" the rest of his life? A case study reported by Williams (1959) illustrates how conditioned crying was extinguished in a 21-month-old child. Due to serious illness during the first 18 months of life, the child had received considerable attention from his concerned parents. In fact, because of his screaming and crying when put to bed, the parents or an aunt, who lived with the family, stayed in his bedroom until he went to sleep. These bedside vigils usually took from 1½ to 2 hours. By remaining in the room until he fell asleep, the parents were undoubtedly providing positive reinforcement for the maintenance of the child's crying behavior. He had his parents under perfect control. To extinguish this objectionable behavior, the parents were instructed to leave the child awake in the bedroom by himself and to ignore any subsequent crying. Within a period of seven nights, the crying behavior had virtually disappeared. By the tenth night, the child even smiled as his parents left the room and could be heard making happy sounds as he fell asleep. A week later, however, the child immediately began screaming when his aunt put him to bed and left the room. She returned to the room and remained there until the child went to sleep. This one instance of positive reinforcement was sufficient to necessitate going through the entire extinction process a second time. By the ninth night the child's crying was finally extinguished and Williams reported that no remission occurred within a two-year follow-up period.

How to Quantify Operant Behavior

In Skinner's view, functional laws of behavior are best developed by focusing on factors which increase or decrease the probability of a response occurring over time, rather than by establishing which specific stimuli instigate a response. Thus, Skinner contends that the most useful and significant source of psychological data is the organism's *rate of responding* (i.e., the number of responses emitted in a given unit of time). As an easily identifiable measure of operant conditioning, it yields an orderly account of the individual organism's behavior as it occurs. Referring to a previous example, every time the rat presses the lever, a pen is activated by an electric timer making a mark on a constantly moving paper tape recording the response. This automated device, called a *cumulative recorder,* provides students of operant behavior with a *cumulative response record* of the organism's response rate. In addition to recording responses automatically, the apparatus enables the investigator to examine how variables, such as the kind and amount of reinforcement or punishment, affect operant behavior over extended periods of time. Skinner's method of obtaining data affords the psychologist a powerful means of controlling behavior.

Schedules of Reinforcement

The essence of operant conditioning relies on the fact that, all other things being equal, reinforced behavior tends to be repeated, whereas behavior that is nonreinforced or punished tends not to be repeated or is extinguished. Hence, the concept of reinforcement occupies a key role in Skinner's theory.

The rate at which operant behavior is acquired and maintained is a function of the schedule of reinforcements employed. A *schedule of reinforcement* is, in brief, a rule stating the contingencies under which reinforcements will be delivered. The simplest and most obvious contingency rule would be to reinforce the organism every time it emits the correct or desired response. This schedule, utilized by Skinner in his early research, is termed *continuous reinforcement* and is commonly used at the outset of all operant conditioning when the organism is learning to acquire the correct response. In most everyday-life situations, however, this is neither a feasible nor an economical way to maintain the desired response, since reinforcement of behavior does not usually occur on a uniform or regular basis. Most human social behavior is reinforced only intermittently. A baby cries many times before it elicits the mother's attention. A young man proposes matrimony many times before his proposal is honored. A scientist tries many approaches before arriving at a correct solution to a difficult problem. In each of these instances, a number of unreinforced responses occurs before one of them is reinforced.

Skinner (1956) humorously relates that he initially discovered the possibility of using *intermittent reinforcement* schedules as the solution to a practical problem.

He had automated his experimental apparatus so that each bar press released one pellet of rat food from a magazine (a kind of storage container). Skinner himself manufactured his own food pellets through a laborious and painstaking process. At one point in his research the pellet supply was near depletion and more time was needed to replenish it. The easiest solution was to reduce the number of reinforcements. Skinner adds: "There were two results: (a) my supply of pellets lasted almost indefinitely, and (b) each rat stabilized at a fairly constant rate of responding (1956, p. 226)." Impressed by this regularity, Skinner and his coworkers embarked on a series of investigations of various intermittent reinforcement schedules.

In Skinner's system, many different reinforcement schedules are possible, but they all can be categorized according to two basic dimensions: (1) the individual is reinforced only after a fixed or irregular *time interval* has elapsed since the previous reinforcement (called *interval* reinforcement schedules) and (2) the individual is reinforced only after a fixed or irregular *number of responses* have been made since the previous reinforcement (called *ratio* reinforcement schedules). In terms of these two dimensions, the following four basic schedules of reinforcement are most extensively studied by students of operant conditioning.

A *fixed-ratio* (FR) schedule is one in which the reinforcement is given only after the organism has emitted a predetermined or "fixed" number of responses. To illustrate, a rat may be rewarded after every third lever-pressing response, every fifth response, every tenth response, or on whatever schedule is desired, with the intervening responses never being rewarded. The ratio designates the number of unreinforced to reinforced responses (e.g., if the FR is 8:1, the rat emits seven unreinforced responses and is reinforced on the eighth). FR reinforcement generates extremely high operant levels, since the more the organism responds, the more reinforcement it receives. This schedule is fairly common in everyday life and exercises considerable control over behavior. For many jobs, employees are paid partly or even exclusively according to the number of units they produce or sell. In industry, this system is known as piecework pay. FR schedules may also control the behavior of professors when they are required to publish a specified number of research articles per year in order to receive salary increases, promotions, lighter teaching loads, and sabbatical leaves. In academia, this reinforcement system is known as "publish or perish."

When reinforcement is supplied only after an established, or "fixed," period of time has elapsed since the previous reinforcement, without regard to the response rate of the organism, it is referred to as a *fixed-interval* (FI) schedule. For example, a rat that is rewarded every two minutes, even if it presses the lever only once during this interval, is on an FI-2 schedule. On the human level, FI schedules are operative in paying salaries for work done by the hour, day, week, or month. Similarly, giving a child a weekly allowance constitutes an FI form of reinforcement. At one time pediatricians recommended that infants be fed on an FI schedule (e.g., every four hours). Universities typically operate in terms of an FI time schedule. Examinations are administered on a regular basis and reports of academic progress are issued at designated time intervals.

Skinner has noted that an FI reinforcement schedule is characterized by a pattern in which the rate of responding gradually increases with time and then sharply accelerates near the end of the interval. This particular pattern of response, called a *fixed-interval scallop,* occurs because the time for reinforcement is fast approaching. Consider, for example, the student who loafs through the semester and then dramatically accelerates her work as deadlines for term papers and final exams approach. Interestingly, FI schedules also yield low rates of responding immediately after the reinforcement has been obtained, a phenomenon called *postreinforcement pause.* This is evidenced by the student who experiences difficulty in studying after a midterm exam since a long interval will elapse before the next exam occurs. He literally pauses in his studies.

When the number of responses required for reinforcement is varied randomly around some designated average value, the organism is said to be on a *variable-ratio* (VR) schedule. In a VR-20 schedule, for instance, a rat is rewarded for every twentieth lever-pressing response on the average, but sometimes the sixth response is reinforced, sometimes the thirty-first, and so on. The VR schedule produces an extremely high and constant response rate inasmuch as the organism does not know precisely when the next reinforcement will be forthcoming. Perhaps the most dramatic illustration of the operation of this schedule at the human level is gambling behavior. Consider the actions of a person operating a slot machine, or one-armed bandit. These devices are constructed so that reinforcement (i.e., money) is distributed according to the number of times a person pays to pull the handle. However, the payoffs are unpredictable, irregular, and rarely yield a return surpassing what the gambler invests. This explains why owners of gambling casinos receive far more reinforcement than do their patrons.

Another commonplace example of behavior on a VR schedule is the door-to-door salesperson who quickly learns that the more she knocks on doors, the more she earns. Perhaps she makes twenty house calls but does not sell even one subscription. Then she takes large-volume orders from two homemakers in succession, providing her with sufficient incentive to ensure that her behavior will not be extinguished. It should not be surprising that many salespeople adopt the attitude "If at first you don't succeed, try, try again." Persistence brings reward. Extinction of behavior acquired on a VR reinforcement schedule is extremely slow. Thus, a gambler compulsively feeds coins into a machine, even though the returns are slim, in the conviction that next time she or he will "hit the jackpot." Such persistence is typical of the behavior generated by VR reinforcement schedules.

Finally, when reinforcements are contingent on some stated time interval but the intervals between reinforcements are irregular and cannot be anticipated, the organism is said to be on a *variable-interval* (VI) schedule. Although reinforcement in this condition is a function of time alone, the organism must make an appropriate response after the interval is over in order to receive reinforcement again. Thus, a rat performing on a VI five-minute schedule might be rewarded for lever pressing after eight minutes, two minutes, six minutes, and four minutes. The averages of these four intervals is five minutes. It is generally true that response rates under VI schedules are a direct function of the interval length employed, with short intervals generating high rates and long intervals generating low rates. However, VI reinforcement also tends to establish steady response rates and is slow to extinguish because the organism cannot precisely anticipate when the next reinforcement will come.

Illustrations of true VI schedules are not common in our culture, although several variations can be observed. A parent, for example, may praise a child's behavior on a rather random basis, thus assuring that the child will continue to behave appropriately during nonreinforced intervals. The child has no way of knowing when the next reinforcement will occur. Professors who give "pop quizzes" are also depending upon a VI schedule. Students can be expected to maintain a relatively stable rate of studying under these conditions.

Superstitious Behavior: Conditioning by Chance

As we have already seen, operant conditioning is mediated by a *causal-temporal* relation between the organism's behavior and the consequences which it produces, i.e., the organism operates upon its environment to generate consequences (Skinner, 1953). Often, however, the association between a response and the outcome which follows its expression is purely accidental. For example, a gambler shouts "Come on baby" while throwing dice, and a winning roll occurs. Or a tennis player insists that she use a particular racket while competing in a major tournament, and she goes on to win all her matches. In both cases an adventitious connection between the two events may result in the person's behaving in the future as though the connection were causal. Closer inspection reveals that the behavior-reinforcement contingency is merely coincidental. This type of conditioning, in which there is an apparent (but nonfunctional or chance) relationship between response and reinforcement, Skinner (1948b) calls *superstitious behavior.*

It is unlikely that saying "Come on baby" or using a particular tennis racket will consistently be followed by a favorable outcome on every occasion that they occur but, as previously noted, the intermittent reinforcement of operant responses leads to the acquisition and maintenance of very stable behavior patterns. Thus, superstitious behavior abounds in any setting where chance reinforcements are likely. Athletes seem especially susceptible to the ritualistic effects of this phenomenon. Baseball players often perform unique hat ceremonies before they position themselves in the batter's box; bowlers sometimes twist in indescribable gyrations as their balls travel down the alley; and golfers adopt unaccountable stances while attempting to putt. Such idiosyncratic actions become the embarrassing trademarks of many outstanding athletes simply because they were formerly connected with fortuitous reinforcement.

Superstitious behavior, according to Skinner, is not necessarily the result of the individual's own conditioning history. Much of it is handed down from one generation to the next in the form of folklore, myth, and, in certain primitive cultures, magic. In our own culture, for instance, many people believe that walking under a ladder, seeing a black cat cross their path, breaking a mirror, or making a decision on Friday the thirteenth bring "bad luck." While many such persons have never directly experienced bad fortune under these conditions, the ideas persist as superstition since they have been transmitted and occasionally reinforced through the social context of their culture.

Successive Approximation: How to Get the Mountain to Come to Mohammed

Skinner's first attempts at operant conditioning were directed to responses normally emitted at moderate or high frequency, e.g., pigeons' key pecking and rats' bar pressing. However, it soon became evident that the standard procedure for operant conditioning (i.e., the experimenter waits until the animal makes the correct response before it is reinforced) was ill suited for vast numbers of complex operant responses whose probability of spontaneous occurrence was near zero. In the realm of human behavior, for example, it is doubtful that the general strategy of operant conditioning would be successful in establishing verbal behavior in autistic children. In order to alleviate this problem, Skinner devised a procedure by which experimenters could efficiently and rapidly accelerate the time required to condition almost any behavior within the repertoire and capabilities of the organism. This procedure is referred to as the *method of successive approximation* or *shaping*.

As is often the case in science, Skinner's discovery that behavior could be rapidly conditioned by reinforcing a series of successive approximations occurred accidentally. He and a group of colleagues were working on a wartime project and, in one of their lighter moments, they decided to teach a pigeon to bowl. Skinner relates the following story:

> The pigeon was to send a wooden ball down a miniature alley toward a set of toy pins by swiping the ball with a sharp sideward movement of the beak. To condition the response, we put the ball on the floor of an experimental box and prepared to operate the food magazine as soon as the first swipe occurred. But nothing happened. Though we had all the time in the world, we grew tired of waiting. We decided to reinforce any response which had the slightest resemblance to a swipe—perhaps at first, merely the behavior of looking at the ball—and then to select responses which more closely approximated the final form. The result amazed us. In a few minutes, the ball was caroming off the walls of the box as if the pigeon had been a champion squash player (1961, p. 138).

Thus, the technique of shaping consists of reinforcing progressively closer approximations of the operant behavior the experimenter wishes to condition. To revert to an earlier example, if a hungry rat is placed in a Skinner box, eventually it presses the bar, and sooner or later it learns that pressing the bar brings a pellet of food. By utilizing the method of successive approximations, the psychologist could markedly shorten the time required to condition this response. The first reinforced response might be any movement that orients the rat toward the end of the box where the lever is mounted. Next, the rat must approach the area of the lever before it is reinforced. Reinforcement is then reserved only for responses that bring the animal into contact with the lever. Finally, only the correct response, actual bar pressing, is reinforced. Thereafter, every bar press is rewarded and bar pressing grows in frequency. This step-by-step process—whereby one response is reinforced and then replaced by another which more closely resembles the desired behavior—greatly increases the range of possible operants which can be brought under the psychologist's control.

The shaping technique has also been applied to several different kinds of human operant responses. Isaacs, Thomas, and Goldiamond (1960) have reported an especially dramatic demonstration of the effectiveness of this method. These investigators, all therapists, wanted to reinstate verbal behavior in a hospitalized catatonic schizophrenic patient who had been mute for nineteen years. Shaping occurred accidentally when one of the therapists dropped a package of gum while searching for some cigarettes in his pocket. He noted that this incident caused the patient's eyes to move in the direction of the gum. Thus, he had a simple response from which to start shaping the desired behavior. For the first two weeks the therapist and patient met privately, during which time the therapist held up a stick of gum and waited until the patient noticed. When this response occurred, the patient was given the gum. This was followed by two weeks in which the therapist held the gum as before but demanded that the patient's lips move before giving it to him. By the end of four weeks, presentation of the gum as reinforcement readily elicited eye and lip movements, and a vocalization "resembling a croak." Thereafter followed two more weeks of shaping in which the therapist required the patient to say "gum, gum" in order to receive the reward. At the end of six weeks the patient was able to say spontaneously "gum please." Subsequently, the patient responded to questions regarding his age and name in group therapy sessions. Aside from the therapeutic benefits this patient derived from having some of his verbal behavior reinstated, the reader should note that shaping plays a crucial role in the way children acquire speech. Beginning with rather crude forms of babbling in infancy, the child's verbal behavior is gradually shaped until it comes to resemble the language of adults. The reader is referred to Skinner's *Verbal Behavior* (1957) for a more detailed behavioral analysis of the development of language.

Conditioned Reinforcers

Like almost all contemporary learning theorists, Skinner recognizes two types of reinforcement—primary and secondary. A *primary* reinforcement (also referred to as *unconditioned* reinforcement) is any event or object which possesses inherent reinforcing properties. Thus, it does not require prior association with other reinforcement in order to satisfy physiological needs and drives. Specifically, food for a hungry person and water for a thirsty one are primary reinforcers. Their reward value to the organism is independent of learning. A *secondary* or *conditioned* reinforcement, on the other hand, is any event or object which acquires its reinforcing qualities through close association with a primary reinforcement in the past conditioning history of the organism.

A slight alteration in the standard operant conditioning procedure demonstrates how a neutral stimulus can acquire reinforcing powers for other behavior. When a rat is trained to bar-press in a Skinner box, a tone comes on momentarily (as the animal makes the response), followed by a pellet of food. In this case, the tone acts as a *discriminative stimulus,* i.e., the animal learns to respond only in the presence of the tone since it signals the arrival of the food reward. After the animal has acquired this specific operant response, extinction is begun: when it bar-presses neither the food nor the tone appears. In time the rat ceases to bar-press altogether. Next, the tone is presented whenever the animal engages in bar pressing, but the food pellet is withheld. Despite the absence of the primary reinforcer, the animal learns that bar pressing elicits the tone so it continues to respond persistently, thereby overcoming the extinction phase of the experiment. In other words, the stabilized rate of bar pressing reflects the fact that the tone is now functioning as a conditioned reinforcing agent. The exact rate of responding depends on the strength of the tone as a conditioned reinforcer (i.e., the number of times the tone was associated with the primary reinforcer, food, during the acquisition phase of conditioning). Skinner has demonstrated that practically any neutral stimulus may become reinforcing in its own right if it is connected with other stimuli that have primary reinforcing properties. Hence, the phenomenon of conditioned reinforcement greatly increases the range of possible operant conditioning, particularly in reference to human social behavior. Stated in another way, if everything we learned had to be contingent upon primary reinforcement, the occasions for learning would be very restricted and the complex variety of human activity would not exist.

A significant feature of conditioned reinforcement is its propensity to become generalized when paired with more than one primary reinforcement. Money is an especially conspicuous example. It is obvious that money cannot nourish any of our primary drives. Yet, through the establishment of a cultural exchange system, money is a powerful and robust agent for obtaining a host of basic gratifications, e.g., food, clothing, housing, education, medical aid, and sex. Other kinds of generalized conditioned reinforcers suggested by Skinner (1953) include *attention, approval, affection*, and *submission of others*. These so-called *social reinforcers* (because they involve the behavior of other people) often act in subtle and intricate ways but are essential to the maintenance of our behavior in a variety of situations. Attention is a simple case. The example of a child who gains attention by feigning illness or misbehaving is familiar. Children often are noisy, ask ridiculous questions, interrupt adult conversations, show off, tease younger siblings, and wet their beds as a means of attracting attention. The attention of an attractive other— parent, teacher, loved one—is an especially effective generalized reinforcer which may promote strong attention-getting behavior.

A still stronger generalized reinforcer is social approval. For example, many people spend a great deal of time preening themselves before a mirror, hoping to elicit an approving glance from their spouses or dates. Both women's and men's fashions are subject to approval and remain in vogue only as long as social approval is forthcoming. High school students compete for the varsity team in athletics or participate in extracurricular events (drama, debate, school newspaper) in order to procure approval from parents, peers, teachers, and neighbors. Good grades in college are positively reinforcing because they have been followed in the past by parental praise and approval. As powerful conditioned reinforcers, satisfactory grades also foster studying behavior and the pursuit of higher academic goals.

Finally, many simple verbal responses enhance a sense of self-approval and esteem, for example, "That's right," "Good going," or "Excellent job."

Skinner (1953) has pointed out that conditioned reinforcers are extremely potent in the control of human behavior. He has also noted that since each person is subjected to a unique history of conditioning, it is improbable that all people will be governed by the same reinforcers. For example, some people are strongly reinforced by entrepreneurial success; others are more readily rewarded by affectionate responses; and still others derive reinforcement from athletic, academic, or musical accomplishments. The possible variations in behavior maintained by conditioned reinforcers are endless. Accordingly, the understanding of human conditioned reinforcers is far more complex than the understanding of a food-deprived rat bar pressing for the reinforcing properties of a tone.

Controlling Behavior through Aversive Stimuli

We have stressed how operant responses are acquired and maintained through the presentation of stimuli (food, money, affection, grades) that are regularly associated with positive reinforcement. In Skinner's view, however, a great deal of human behavior is controlled by the use of *aversive stimuli,* that is, painful, unpleasant, obnoxious, or anxiety-arousing consequences associated with certain responses made by the individual. Two commonly employed methods of aversive control are *punishment* and *negative reinforcement.* Since these terms are often used synonymously to describe the conceptual properties and behavior effects of aversive control, Skinner has offered the following distinction: "You can distinguish between punishment, which is making an aversive event contingent upon a response, and negative reinforcement, in which the elimination or removal of an aversive stimulus, conditioned or unconditioned, is reinforcing (Evans, 1968, p. 33)." Thus, punishment refers to any aversive stimulus or event whose presentation follows and depends upon the occurrence of some operant response. Skinner notes that it is the most common technique of behavioral control in modern life. Some simple examples are these: if children misbehave, they are spanked or scolded; if students cheat on an exam, they are dismissed from the course or school; if adults are caught stealing, they are fined or imprisoned. Instead of strengthening the response it follows, punishment decreases, at least temporarily, the probability that the response will occur again. The intended purpose of punishment is to induce people not to behave in given ways.

Unlike punishment, negative reinforcement generates and maintains operant behavior which allows the organism to terminate, escape, or avoid an aversive stimulus whenever it is administered. Any behavior that prevents an aversive state of affairs thereby tends to increase in frequency and is said to be negatively reinforced. *Escape* behavior is such a case. An animal will tend to repeat whatever behavior it is performing (e.g., pressing a lever, moving to the other side of a cage) if the behavior is associated with cessation of painful electric shock. Likewise, a person who escapes from the hot sun by moving indoors is more likely to move indoors when the sun is again hot. It should be noted that escaping from an aversive stimulus is not the same as avoiding it, since the aversive stimulus which is avoided is not physically present. Consequently, another way of dealing with aversive conditions is to behave in ways which prevent their occurrence—to learn to avoid them. This strategy is referred to as *avoidance* learning. For example, the rat in the Skinner box can learn to bar-press in order to *avoid* onset of an electric shock. Avoidance behavior can also be illustrated by drug addicts who develop clever and adroit schemes to maintain their habits and thereby shun the aversive consequences of being incarcerated.

Skinner (1971) staunchly opposes the application of all forms of behavioral control based on aversive stimuli. For one thing, because of its threatening nature, the tactic of punishing unwanted behavior may generate undesirable emotional and social side effects. Severe and debilitating anxiety, behavioral inhibition, and antisocial actions are just a few of the possible negative by-products of punishment. The threat imposed by aversive controls may also encourage individuals to develop patterns of behavior which are even more objectionable than the ones for which they were initially punished. Consider, for example, the parent who tries to suppress a child's dislike for and poor performance in school by physically punishing her or him. Later, in the parent's absence, the child may adopt other behaviors which are more maladaptive—playing hookey, becoming a dropout, vandalizing school property. Regardless of the outcome, it is clear that punishment has failed to instill desirable behavior in the child. While punishment may temporarily inhibit inappropriate or maladaptive responses, Skinner's main objection is that it does not contribute to the permanent extinction of the responses from a person's behavioral repertoire. Behavior that is punished is likely to reappear as soon as the aversive conditions are withdrawn; therefore, punishment is quite ineffective as a means of thwarting socially undesirable behavior.

In place of aversive types of behavioral control, Skinner recommends alternative techniques to eliminate undesirable behavior. Extinction is one technique of getting rid of objectionable behavior. However, it is usually of limited effectiveness because it is so time-consuming and does not indicate to the person what she or he must do in order to receive positive reinforcement. Accordingly, the most preferred method advocated thus far by Skinner is to condition incompatible behavior by employing positive reinforcement. He argues that positive reinforcers do not generate the negative by-products associated with aversive stimuli; hence, they are more suitable in shaping the individual's behavior. A brief example suggests a possible application of this method. Convicted felons are subjected to intolerable conditions in many penal institutions (witnessed by several prison riots in the country over the past few years). It is obvious that most attempts to rehabilitate the criminal have failed miserably, a conclusion supported by the high rate of recidivism or recurring offenses. Skinner's approach would be to arrange environmental conditions within prisons so that behavior resembling that of law-abiding citizens is positively reinforced, e.g., reinforcing the criminal for learning socially adaptive skills, values, and attitudes (Boslough, 1972). This type of penal reform would require a team of behavioral experts knowledgeable in the principles of learning, personality, and psychopathology. In Skinner's view, such reform could be effectively implemented with the currently existing resources available to psychologists trained in the methods of behavioristic psychology.

Stimulus Generalization and Discrimination

A logical extension of the principle of reinforcement is that behavior strengthened in one stimulus situation is likely to recur when the organism encounters other situations that resemble the original one. If this were not so, our behavioral repertoires would be so severely limited and chaotic that we would probably spend most of our waking moments relearning how to respond appropriately in each new stimulus situation. In Skinner's system, the tendency of reinforced behavior to extend to a variety of related settings is called *induction* or *stimulus generalization.* This phenomenon can be readily observed in everyday life. For example, a child who has been rewarded for learning the subtleties of good manners at home will usually generalize this behavior to appropriate situations outside the home environment; such a child does not need to learn how to behave politely in each new social setting. Stimulus generalization may also result from painful or aversive experiences. A young woman who has been sexually assaulted by a stranger may generalize her shame and hostility to all persons of the opposite sex because they remind her of the physical and emotional trauma imposed by the stranger. Similarly, a single frightening or unpleasant experience with a person belonging to an identifiable ethnic group (whites, blacks, Hispanics, Japanese) may be sufficient grounds for a person to stereotype and thus avoid all future social contact with all such group members.

Although the capacity to generalize responses is an important aspect of much of our everyday social interaction, it is equally apparent that adaptive behavior requires the ability to make fine discriminations in different situations. *Stimulus discrimination,* the obverse of generalization, is the process of learning how to respond appropriately to various environmental stimuli. Examples are legion. A motorist survives the rush hour by discriminating between red and green traffic lights. A child learns to discriminate between the family pet and a vicious dog. An adolescent learns to discriminate between behavior which results in peer approval and behavior which irritates or alienates others. A diabetic readily learns to discriminate between foods containing high and low amounts of sugar. Indeed, practically all intelligent human behavior is contingent upon the ability to make discriminations.

Discrimination is acquired through reinforcement of behavioral responses in the presence of some stimuli and nonreinforcement of them in the presence of other stimuli. Discriminative stimuli thus enable us to anticipate the probable outcomes associated with emitting a particular operant response in different social situations. Accordingly, individual differences in discriminative ability are dependent upon unique histories of differential reinforcement. Skinner would argue that healthy personality development results from a blend of generalization and discrimination capacities: we regulate our behavior so as to maximize positive reinforcement and minimize punishment. Let us now turn attention to the philosophic assumptions underlying Skinner's behavioristic-learning theory.

SKINNER'S BASIC ASSUMPTIONS CONCERNING HUMAN NATURE

Because he rejects the traditional concept of internal personality variables as causes of behavior, Skinner presents a conception of human beings radically different from that of most personologists. Moreover, his basic assumptions about human nature tend to be both strong and explicit. Skinner's positions on these assumptions are graphically depicted in Figure 6-1.

Freedom–Determinism   Skinnerian man is completely determined by his conditioning history. More specifically, the individual's behavior is a product of prior reinforcements; one does what one has been reinforced to do. Individual differences in behavior result exclusively from variable reinforcement histories, since freedom is not even acknowledged in the experimental analysis of behavior. In fact, Skinner has long argued that the deterministic assumption is an absolute necessity for scientifically studying human behavior:

> If we are to use the methods of science in the field of human affairs, we must assume that behavior is lawful and determined. We must expect to discover that what a man does is the result of specifiable conditions and that once these conditions have been discovered, we can anticipate and to some extent determine his actions (Skinner, 1953, p. 6).

In Skinner's system an infant has an infinite number of possibilities for behavior acquisition. It is parents first who principally reinforce and thus shape development in specific directions; in turn, the infant will behave contingent upon their rewards. Behavior consistently followed by nonreinforcement will not be strengthened. Gradually, as her development proceeds, the child's behavior is

	Strong	Moderate	Slight	Midrange	Slight	Moderate	Strong	
Freedom							■	Determinism
Rationality				Not applicable				Irrationality
Holism							■	Elementalism
Constitutionalism							■	Environmentalism
Changeability	■							Unchangeability
Subjectivity							■	Objectivity
Proactivity							■	Reactivity
Homeostasis				Not applicable				Heterostasis
Knowability	■							Unknowability

Figure 6-1   Skinner's position on the nine basic assumptions concerning human nature.

"shaped" into patterns as a direct function of her ongoing conditioning experiences. In more traditional, "non-Skinnerian" terms, her "personality" is emerging.

As the child's social world expands, other reinforcement sources are more central in affecting behavioral development. School, athletic, and peer-group experiences are especially powerful sources of reinforcement. The principle of behavior determination by reinforcement remains the same—it is only the kinds and sources of reinforcement that change. Sexual and occupational types of reinforcement occur later. By the time adulthood is reached, the person behaves in a characteristic fashion because of his or her unique conditioning history; the person's behavior can be expected to change only as a consequence of the contemporary reinforcement contingencies to which she or he is exposed. Throughout the entire developmental process, previously reinforced behaviors drop out of the person's response repertoire as a result of either nonreinforcement or punishment from the current social environment. Skinnerian man, then, has no freedom to choose his behavior; rather, his behavior is molded exclusively by external reinforcements.

Rationality–Irrationality   As noted previously, Skinner views the human organism as an "unopened box." That the box may eventually prove to contain rational and/or irrational processes may be an interesting speculation—but neither possibility has anything to do with explaining human behavior. For Skinner, behavior is a function only of its consequences or of lawful stimulus-response relationships. What goes into the box, what comes out of the box, and what follows therefrom are the only relevant variables needed in analyzing behavior—not what may or may not occur inside. The principles of behavior, uncovered by means of this functional approach, apply equally to rats, pigeons, and human beings; the latter's presumably more highly developed rational processes are simply not relevant in behavior causation. Because both extremes of the rationality–irrationality dimension refer to hypothetical internal processes that underlie behavior, this assumption plays no important role in Skinner's thinking. It is not really applicable to his position.

Holism–Elementalism   What is traditionally referred to by others as "personality" is translated by Skinner to mean nothing more than a collection of behavior patterns that are characteristic of a given individual. These behavior patterns can be further reduced to specific responses—all of which have been acquired through conditioning. An individual's personality, then, is composed of relatively complex but nonetheless independently acquired responses. To understand behavior, one need only understand the person's conditioning history. Most clearly, in Skinner's system behavior is composed of specific elements (responses).

A further indication of Skinner's basic elementalism is revealed in his approach to the study of behavior. He exhaustively examines the conditions under which single responses are acquired and modified, e.g., rats pressing bars, pigeons pecking disks. The unit of analysis in Skinner's experimental work is focused upon single response acquisition. Such an approach demands a commitment to the underlying elementalist assumption that behavior can be understood only by detailed analysis of its constituent parts.

In Skinner's view, individual personality differences are nothing more than what meets the eye—individual differences in behavior. Harry's "personality" is distinguishable from Joe's only insofar as Harry characteristically behaves differently than Joe. Each personality is constructed over time—element by element—people differ only because their individual conditioning histories differ. This elementalistic view is in sharp contrast to holistic conceptions that tend to portray individual uniqueness in terms of some single, unifying, and idiosyncratic factor underlying the person's behavior, e.g., Murray's unity thema. In opposition to gestalt psychology, then, Skinner believes that the whole is the sum of its parts.

Constitutionalism–Environmentalism   That Skinner has spent his entire professional life studying how behavior is modified by environmental effects clearly implies a wholehearted commitment to environmentalism. While he recognizes that constitutional factors limit a person, these factors are largely ignored in accounting for the individual's behavior. Instead, Skinner portrays the person as supremely subject to environmental whim; characteristic ways in which he or she learns to behave (personality) result exclusively from situationally based reinforcement contingencies (conditioning). Skinnerian man is a product of the environment.

In explaining how people differ from one another, Skinner places little reliance upon constitutional variation. Following the lead of earlier behaviorists (e.g., Watson), Skinner envisions environmental variation as the basic cause of individual differences. Baldly, he asserts: "The variables of which human behavior is a function lie in the environment (Skinner, 1977, p. 1)." Thus, Beverley and Susan differ from one another not primarily because of their unique constitutions but because of the different environments to which they have been exposed. If their environments had been interchanged at birth, their personalities at age 20 would also have been interchanged.

Changeability–Unchangeability   There is no ambiguity about where Skinner stands on this issue: he is strongly committed to the view that human behavior is changeable throughout life. Yet, as revealed in an interview conducted in 1977, he disagrees with most developmentally oriented personologists about what conditions and factors instigate behavioral change. Specifically, Skinner asserts: "Psychological growth is not a naturally occurring process that emerges from the individual (APA Monitor, 1977, p. 6)." Instead, he argues that changes in people's behavior over the life span are due to variations in their environments—as the environment varies in terms of its reinforcing properties, so also does the behavior which is, after all, under its direct control. Unlike developmental stage theorists such as Erikson, then, Skinner would explain life crises in terms of the environment changing but leaving the individual behind—left with a repertoire of behaviors inadequate to obtain reinforcement in the new situation. From this perspective, developmental changes mainly reflect alterations in the contingencies of reinforcement throughout the life cycle.

Despite his differences with developmental stage theorists, Skinner nonetheless shares their general emphasis on behavioral change. But consistent with the rest of his position, he views changes in behavior as resulting from environmental changes, e.g., since Harry's behavior is a product of his environment, it will change over his lifetime in proportion to the degree of change taking place in his environment over his lifetime. And the central focus of behavioristic-learning theory is the study of those forces which produce behavior change. Thus, Skinner's commitment to the changeability assumption appears quite strong, and seems to underlie the entire thrust of his scientific work in psychology.

Subjectivity–Objectivity   Skinner's approach to the organism as an unopened box suggests an unequivocal commitment to the objectivity assumption. One does not need to look into the box to explain its behavior. Consistent with much of behaviorism, Skinner argues that human activities can be explained solely in terms of objective stimulus-response relationships. Input occurs, output results —that which follows output (reinforcement) determines the likelihood that it will again follow similar inputs in the future. What the person may presumably think or feel about incoming stimuli or outgoing responses is irrelevant when explaining his or her behavior.

Subjective experience is not only totally irrelevant in Skinner's system, but references to it are held to be the main source of confusion in contemporary psychology. Skinner contends that the constructs portraying inner experience used by all other personologists in this text (e.g., Freud's "ego," Adler's "striving for superiority," Erikson's "identity crisis," Murray's "need") simply obfuscate the issue of behavior explanation. These mentalistic concepts are nothing more than explanatory fictions superimposed upon the real external causes of human actions. And the most significant of these fictitious internal agents is the concept of personality itself! While his system allows for the description and explanation of both the similarities and differences among persons (just as does any other personality theory), Skinner can accomplish these objectives without any reference to "personality." Objectivity is an all-important assumption underlying this system; Skinner has taken Watson's earlier rejection of "mind" to its logical conclusion.

Proactivity–Reactivity   Skinner's account of human behavior in stimulus-response and response-reinforcement terms emphasizes an underlying commitment to the reactivity assumption. A person's behavior, in his system, is largely a function of external stimulus control. Such reactivity is most evident in classical conditioning, where responses are automatically elicited by stimuli immediately preceding them in time. Pavlov's dogs *react* (salivate) to the sound of a bell; humans *react* in much the same way to the sight and smell of turkey on Thanksgiving.

But even in operant conditioning there is clear evidence of reactivity. While the organism's responses appear to be "freely" emitted, it cannot be assumed that they are proactively based. Certainly the rat bar pressing in a Skinner box is not internally generating its behavior in a future-oriented fashion. Rather, operant responses seem to suggest the "active" more than the "proactive" nature of the organism. All the individual's actions are triggered by some stimulus events, however subtle or elusive, with the majority of these initiating stimuli being external. As Lundin states, operant responses "are under some form of stimulus control, usually from the external environment, and the problem for the psychologist is to discover what the stimuli are and under what conditions the operant response has developed (1963, pp. 266–267)." On close inspection, people are totally reactive in Skinner's theory.

Homeostasis–Heterostasis   Both extremes of this dimension refer to the nature and properties of internal motivational states that presumably cause behavior. A person acts to reduce internal tensions or to seek growth and self-actualization. According to Skinner, there is no necessity to speculate about the properties of such hypothetical inner states—they are irrelevant, superfluous concepts used to explain behavior. Only external agents actually cause behavior. Wondering about the nature of motives is like wondering what kind of spirit within a tree causes its branches to bend in the wind. Skinner takes no position on either side of this dimension—both homeostasis and heterostasis are irrelevant assumptions in his system.

How then does Skinner account for motivated behavior? What causes an organism's behavior to change while the environment remains relatively constant? To answer these questions, it is necessary only to examine rat behavior in the Skinner box. Suppose that a rat who has learned to bar-press for food pellets is deprived of food for two days. It can be observed that it will bar-press more often, eat more vigorously when permitted, and prefer food to water. A more "mentalistic" theorist would ascribe the rat's behavior to the hunger motive. To Skinner, however, the term "hunger" has no meaning or status apart from the fact that it designates a relationship between groups of external stimuli and observable responses. Hunger is simply a convenient word to describe the relation of certain objective operations (depriving the animal of food) to the occurrence of certain responses (e.g., more frequent or vigorous bar pressing). Hunger as a presumed internal motivational state does not cause behavior; the environmental operations actually *produce* the behavior. Consistent with his overall position, Skinner does not rely on inner motives to explain behavior. Thus, he assumes nothing about the particular properties (homeostatic versus heterostatic) of such motives.

Knowability–Unknowability   Skinner's strong stands on the assumptions of determinism and objectivity logically require an equally strong commitment to the knowability assumption. He insists that behavior is determined by external, objective factors; these factors can be elucidated by means of rigorous scientific investigation; therefore, all of human behavior (nature) is ultimately knowable in scientific terms.

Skinner's total commitment to man's knowability through science is unmistakable—he devoted an entire book to the subject (*Science and Human Behavior*), the theme of which is a clear, logically consistent, and exhaustively detailed argument for a natural science of human behavior. In addressing himself to behavior as a scientific subject matter, he stated:

> Behavior is a difficult subject matter, not wholly because it is inaccessible, but because it is extremely complex. Since it is a process, rather than a thing, it cannot easily be held still for observation. It is changing, fluid, and evanescent, and for this reason it makes great technical demands upon the ingenuity and energy of the scientist. But there is nothing essentially insoluble about the problems which arise from this fact (Skinner, 1953, p. 15).

While studying behavior is difficult, science clearly has the potential to unravel all such problems. Skinner argues further that science can do so only when its practitioners rid themselves of the mythological concept of man as a free, responsible agent who internally initiates his or her actions. In effect, scientists' *basic assumptions* about human nature hinder them in studying behavior. To apply scientific methodology profitably to human behavior, it is necessary to view people as objectively determined. Stated another way, Skinner seems to believe that a true science of behavior will be fully developed only when other psychologists adopt his particular basic assumptions about human nature!

Let us now turn to some illustrative research generated by this highly stimulating and provocative position.

EMPIRICAL VALIDATION OF BEHAVIORISTIC-LEARNING THEORY CONCEPTS

It would be a monumental task simply to highlight the vast number of animal and human studies that empirically validate the behavioristic principles of operant conditioning. More than any other contemporary theorist, Skinner has both provided and stimulated massive amounts of experimental data to support his conceptual formulations of behavior. Furthermore, he has been extremely successful in attracting a large group of adherents who have carried on and extended his efforts to develop a scientifically based approach to behavior. Another indication of the accelerating impact of Skinner's work is the growing number of psychology graduate programs where students are trained in the methods and applications of operant conditioning (Bennasi and Lanson, 1972). The Universities of Kansas, Oregon, Illinois, North Carolina at Chapel Hill, and Pennsylvania State University and the State University of New York at Stony Brook are currently at the forefront of this movement (Goodall, 1972, p. 59). There is no question that Skinner's behavioristic-learning position has generated widespread attention in basic and applied fields of American psychology.

The following discussion examines the methodological characteristics of Skinner's approach to behavioral research and concludes with several illustrations of how his principles have been validated in the context of clinical treatment. Students and interested readers who wish to explore these aspects of Skinner's position in more detail are directed particularly to the following texts: *Operant Learning: Procedures for Changing Behavior* (Williams, 1973); *Behavior Therapy; Techniques and Empirical Findings* (Rimm & Masters, 1979); *Cumulative Record* (Skinner, 1961); and *Handbook of Operant Behavior* (Honig and Staddon, 1977). *The Journal of the Experimental Analysis of Behavior, The Journal of Applied*

Behavior Analysis, and *Behavior Research and Therapy* also publish reports of experimental research relevant to the empirical verification and behavioral application of Skinnerian concepts.

When compared with the mainstream of present-day behavioral research, Skinner's methodological strategy is quite unconventional. First, as previously noted, his experimental analysis of behavior concentrates on the single subject as opposed to the more prevalent method of selecting a group of subjects as the focus of study. This reliance on a single-subject research design reveals Skinner's fundamental belief that psychological science should ultimately lead to precise and quantifiable laws which are applicable to actual individual behavior.

A second identifiable feature of Skinner's methodological orientation is his automated experimental apparatus and well-defined control over the conditions under which the individual's behavior is observed and recorded. In the typical experimental setting, an investigator would proceed through the following steps: (1) initially establish a baseline measure of stable response rates, e.g., a cumulative record of a rat's spontaneous rate of pressing a lever; (2) introduce a treatment or controlling variable, e.g., a fixed-interval reinforcement schedule; and (3) withdraw that variable after some level of performance has been attained in order to measure and determine its effect upon the behavior under investigation. Any changes in operant behavior which occur as a result of introducing and then withdrawing the treatment variable can thus be reliably attributed to that variable.

Skinner adopts a *molecular* approach to the study of behavior. Reflecting his elementalistic assumption, he believes that the logical place to begin is with the simplest, most basic ingredients of the organism's behavior. Building on his understanding of simple behavioral events, the psychologist can then direct attention to the more complex activity of the organism. Complex behavior in Skinner's approach is nothing more than the summation and integration of its component parts.

Skinner depends primarily on the use of infrahuman species (notably rats and pigeons) as the source of data for establishing empirical laws of learning. As implied earlier in this chapter, he defends his choice of lower organisms as experimental subjects on the grounds that it enables the psychologist to exert greater control over the conditions and variables affecting the behavior under study than would be the case for human subjects. At the same time, Skinner does not hesitate to suggest that principles of behavior demonstrated for infrahumans have direct application to phenomena of interest to the human-oriented psychologist. This assertion reflects an assumption made by practically all Skinnerians, specifically, that laboratory-derived findings are generalizable to the entire animal kingdom, including humans. It should come as no surprise that most personologists consider the notion of generalization of principles based on the study of lower organisms to be untenable.

Finally, it should be stressed that the research conducted by Skinner and his followers is exclusively focused on variables amenable to change or modification through manipulation of environmental stimuli. Accordingly, much of the recent research emanating from Skinner's theoretical system is pertinent to our understanding of personality development.

Skinner's current status in psychological science is apparent in the many active domains of research directly affected by his behavioristic principles. The major areas include (1) psychopharmacology, or the study of the effects of drugs on behavior; (2) educational technology, including programmed instruction devices and classroom contingency management systems; (3) psycholinguistics and the acquisition of verbal behavior; (4) industrial management, including employee morale and job satisfaction; and (5) therapeutic treatment of psychological problems, e.g., alcoholism, drug addiction, mental retardation, juvenile delinquency, childhood autism, phobias, speech disorders, obesity, and sexual disorders. These examples indicate the extent to which operant techniques can be applied effectively outside the "artificial" conditions of the experimentally isolated subject.

Behavior Therapy and the Token Economy: A Research Illustration

Although he is not a clinical psychologist, Skinner's views concerning operant conditioning and behavioral control have had considerable impact on modifying the behavior of severely disturbed individuals (e.g., Ayllon and Azrin, 1965; Atthowe and Krasner, 1968). Indeed, his approach to behavior change or modification has been instrumental in establishing a new breed of behavior therapists in this country.

Coined by Skinner and Lindsley (1954), "behavior therapy" approaches psychotherapy with experimentally established principles and methods derived from behavioristic-learning theory. The details of this form of psychological treatment are well beyond the scope of this book (see O'Leary and Wilson's *Behavior Therapy: Application and Outcome,* 1975, for a comprehensive description of behavior therapy methods and techniques). However, the underlying premise upon which this therapy is practiced is relatively simple—psychological disorders have been *learned* through some faulty history of conditioning. Therefore, the task facing the Skinnerian behavior therapist is to pinpoint those of the patient's maladaptive behaviors ("symptoms") that are to be eliminated, specify the desired new behaviors, and determine the reinforcement schedules that are required to shape the desired behaviors. These objectives are accomplished by creating an environment in which the patient's attainment of the "good things in life" are made contingent on performing adaptive or socially desirable behaviors. Thus, behavior therapy is a logical extension of the principles of operant conditioning through which many adjustment problems may be effectively eliminated.

The development of what is called a *token economy* illustrates one procedural application of behavior therapy. In a token economy, patients, usually hospitalized adults manifesting severe behavioral disturbances, are rewarded with tokens (i.e., conditioned reinforcers) for engaging in various activities that are deemed desirable. The token is simply a stimulus, like a plastic chip or a numerical rating, which represents something for which certain desired items or activities may be exchanged. Thus, patients might be rewarded for engaging in such routine activities as cleaning their rooms, mopping floors, feeding themselves, completing a work assignment, or interacting with their fellow patients. The tokens they receive for participating in such activities are then exchanged at a later date for a variety of desired incentives, e.g., candy, cigarettes, clothing, entertainment, leaving the ward for a walk, or a private meeting with the hospital psychologist.

How effective is a token economy in abolishing maladaptive behavior and establishing adaptive behavior? A study conducted by Atthowe and Krasner (1968) suggests a most favorable answer. These two clinicians made the first attempt to institute a token reinforcement program in a psychiatric ward of a Veterans Hospital in Palo Alto, California. Its purpose "was to change the chronic patients' aberrant behavior, especially that behavior judged to be apathetic, overly dependent, detrimental, or annoying to others (Atthowe and Krasner, 1968, p. 37)." The patients (N = sixty) selected had a median age of 57 and had been hospitalized for a median number of twenty-two years. Most had been previously diagnosed as chronic schizophrenics; the remainder were classified as brain-damaged.

The study extended across twenty months and consisted of three distinct phases. The first six months served as a baseline or operant period during which the investigators recorded daily the frequency of target behaviors which were to be subsequently extinguished. This was followed by a three-month shaping period during which the patients were gradually prepared to participate in the token economy (i.e., instructed about the types of activities they must perform in order to receive and exchange tokens for items in the hospital canteen). Finally, during the experimental period, which continued for eleven months, patients received tokens for performing specified desirable behaviors involving self-care, attendance at activities, interaction with others, or demonstration of responsibility. The token used was a plastic file card (similar to a credit card) which came in seven colors, with different exchange values assigned to the different colors. Whenever possible, each patient was given a token immediately after completing the desired activity, accompanied by an expression of social approval from a hospital attendant (e.g., the words "fine job" or a smile).

The results indicated a significant increase in reinforced "desirable" behaviors and a general improvement in patient initiative, activity, responsibility, and social interaction. Figure 6-2 shows, for instance, how attendance at group activities increased and decreased as a function of token reinforcement level. During the operant baseline period, the average hourly attendance rate per week was 5.8 hours per patient. With the introduction of the token economy, this rate increased to 8.4 hours for the first month and averaged 8.5 hours throughout the experimental period. Moreover, the rate increased to 9.2 hours during a three-month span within the experimental period when the reinforcing value of the tokens was raised from one to two tokens per hour of attendance.

A second set of findings reported by Atthowe and Krasner focuses on the number of infractions committed by patients. Ordinarily many hospitalized patients refuse to get out of bed in the morning, make their beds, or leave the bedroom area by a specified time, thus necessitating the help of extra personnel. Immediately prior to the introduction of the token economy, the number of infractions in these three areas was recorded for a one-week period. This yielded an average of seventy-five infractions (or a little more than one per patient) per week. A token was then

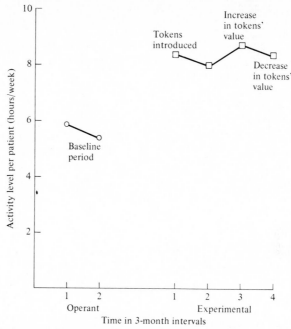

Figure 6-2 Attendance at group activities as a function of tokens given for the activity. (*Adapted from Atthowe and Krasner, 1968, p. 39.*)

given daily, contingent upon not having a recorded infraction in any of these areas. As seen in Figure 6-3, the number of infractions dropped following the establishment of the contingency program. The unexpected rise in infractions during the fourth week (increased to thirty-nine) of the token economy was not explained by the investigators. During the last six months of the experimental period, the frequency of infractions averaged nine per week (not indicated in Figure 6-3).

Atthowe and Krasner also report that significant behavioral gains were made in other areas of the patient's life in the hospital setting. They note: "At the beginning of the study, there were 12 bed-wetters, 4 of whom were classified as "frequent" wetters and 2 were classified as "infrequent". . . . At the end of the experimental period no one was wetting regularly and, for all practical purposes, there were no bed-wetters on the ward (1968, p. 40)."

Despite the impressive behavioral changes demonstrated in this clinical research program, it is not altogether clear whether the changes in behavior were a function of the specific reinforcement procedures used. For example, the possibility exists that patients who participate in a token economy are merely responding to the interest, enthusiasm, attention, and hopeful expectancies of the hospital staff. Advocates of behavior therapy strongly insist that this type of interpretation is not valid, and that the change in patient behavior is a direct result of the shaping and contingency methods they employ. One study which clearly supports this contention is that of Ayllon and Azrin (1965). They found that performance of desired behaviors directly fluctuated as a function of the presence or absence of token rein-

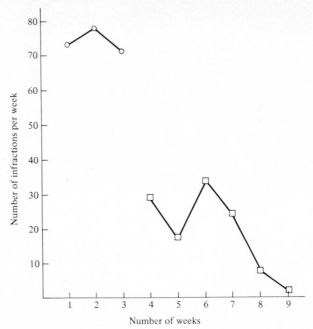

Figure 6-3 Number of infractions in performing morning routines. (*Adapted from Atthowe and Krasner, 1968, p. 41.*)

forcements. Based on six specific experiments of the token economy, they concluded:

> The reinforcement procedure was effective in maintaining desired performance. In each experiment, the performance fell to a near-zero level when the established response-reinforcement relation was discontinued. On the other hand, reintroduction of the reinforcement procedure restored performance almost immediately and maintained it at a high level for as long as the reinforcement procedure was in effect (1965, p. 381).

Thus, it seems safe to conclude that a token economy can alter the behavior of psychotics in a constructive direction within a hospital setting. More significantly, it illustrates a particularly interesting and rigorous test of the validity of Skinnerian principles in the context of one of humanity's greatest social problems. And finally, it should also be recognized that token economies have not been restricted to mental hospital settings—they have also been used extensively in classroom situations with "normal" children, delinquents, and the mentally retarded (Kazdin and Bootzin, 1972; O'Leary and Drabman, 1971). Manuals are available for parents and teachers about token economies aimed at eliminating fear, hyperactivity, and negativistic behavior in children (Patterson and Gullion, 1971).

The effectiveness of token economies in highly structured and controlled settings such as psychiatric wards is unquestionable. Nonetheless, enthusiasm for token economies has diminished somewhat in recent years. It seems that behaviors acquired in the token economy situation do not always generalize well to situations in which the token economies are not in effect. People will learn new behaviors in order to obtain tokens, but will not perform those behaviors when the tokens are no longer available. In one study, for instance, schoolchildren who learned task-oriented behavior in a token program were identified as needing the same kind of help a few months after the program was over (Walker, Mattson, and Buckley, 1969). There is even evidence that behaviors learned in token systems during one part of the day may not spontaneously occur during another part of the day (Becker, Madsen, Arnold, and Thomas, 1967). Accordingly, if psychologists are to take full advantage of token economy procedures, they must establish how behavior learned in token economies can be maintained after the token program has ended. At present, the state of token economies as employed in controlled settings may best be summed up by Levine and Fasnacht, who note: "Tokens do lead to powerful learning, but the learning may, in fact, be token (1974, p. 820)."

Treating Marital Discord: Tokens for Husbands and Wives

Another intriguing research illustration of how operant conditioning principles have been applied to the treatment of behavioral problems is in the area of marital discord. Stuart (1969) called it an *operant interpersonal* approach to marital treatment, because it is based on the assumption that the pattern of interaction (especially communication) existing between spouses is present because it is the most reinforcing of available alternatives. Thus, a husband who spends long hours watching football on TV, or with the "boys," is doing so because these activities are more reinforcing to him than time spent with his wife. From this perspective, a successful marriage is one in which both partners work to maximize mutual and equitable rewards while minimizing individual costs. An unsuccessful marriage, by contrast, is one in which "each partner reinforces the other at a low rate and each is therefore relatively unattractive to and unreinforced by the other (Stuart, 1969, p. 675)." It follows that a marriage hovering on the brink of divorce might be saved, if not enriched, by encouraging each partner to dispense reinforcement to the other more frequently.

The operant interpersonal approach to reviving troubled marriages seeks to establish a situation in which the frequency and intensity of mutual reinforcement is increased. One particular type of contractual arrangement between spouses aimed at meeting this objective is known as the *good faith contract*. Here, each partner commits himself or herself to increase the frequency of a specific target behavior in exchange for a reward, with the understanding that such change is not dependent upon the actions of the other. For example, a wife might agree to manage and balance the family checking account, her targeted change, in return for any number of reinforcements, such as a goodbye kiss in the morning or a night of bridge with the gals once a week. At the same time the husband might agree not to work overtime, his targeted change, for which he would earn reinforcements such as a neatly pressed shirt or a night of poker with the guys once a week. Tokens are an ideal medium for such reinforcement because they are given immediately and can be redeemed later for the specific consequences that the recipient desires.

The effectiveness of the good faith contract in helping couples to improve their level of marital satisfaction is revealed in a study by Stuart (1969). The study involved four couples who had sought treatment as a last-ditch effort prior to filing for a divorce. In each instance, the wife expressed the wish that her husband would converse with her more fully, or at least that he would not "close me out of his life even when he is at home (Stuart, 1969, p. 678)." At the outset of treatment, each couple identified the level of intensity of the conversation that would be positively reinforcing to the wife, and this was rehearsed during treatment sessions. The wife was then instructed to purchase a kitchen timer which she could carry with her about the house. She was also instructed to set the timer as soon as her husband entered and to give him one token when the bell rang after each hour in which he conversed at the agreed-upon level. In the event he failed to behave at the criterion level for conversation by the end of the first thirty minutes of each hour, she had to notify him of this and offer constructive suggestions as to how his performance could be improved. Conversational tokens earned by the husband for talking to his wife were given for a wide variety of possibilities, ranging from intense conversation at one extreme to the wife's feeling free to interrupt her husband with a question at the other extreme. The tokens were redeemable at the husband's request "from a menu stressing physical affection. . . . Husbands were charged three tokens for kissing and 'lightly petting' with their wives, five tokens for 'heavy petting,' and 15 tokens for intercourse (Stuart, 1969, p. 679)." (See Discussion Question 4 at the end of this chapter for some issues raised by this particular treatment strategy.) Each spouse also completed a self-report inventory measuring the extent of his or her own satisfaction in and commitment to the marriage at the start of treatment and at two follow-up periods. Results indicated that the use of good faith contracting is quite effective in bringing about desired behavioral changes. Specifically, Stuart found that the rates of conversation and sexual intercourse increased sharply after the start of treatment and continued through six- and twelve-month follow-up periods. In addition, all four couples expressed increased satisfaction with their marriages at the conclusion of ten weeks of therapy. The level of satisfaction continued to increase at six and twelve month follow-ups.

Although Stuart's results are suggestive of the efficacy of good faith contracting in the treatment of marital difficulties, the lack of a control group as well as total reliance upon self-report data rather than objective behavioral data precludes definitive interpretation. Accordingly, Jacobson (1977) undertook a more rigorous investigation of the effectiveness of contingency contracting in relieving marital distress, and obtained results essentially confirming Stuart's earlier findings. While (as with many other behavior therapy techniques) some would find this approach to this particular problem superficial and perhaps even offensive, the positive results obtained do offer promise for the treatment of a serious situation that appears to be reaching epidemic proportions in contemporary society. Readers interested in expanding their knowledge of this exciting area are advised to read *Marriage and Marital Therapy: Psychoanalytic, Behavioral and Systems Theory Perspectives,* edited by Paolino and McCrady (1978).

APPLICATION: THE WORLD AS A BIG SKINNER BOX

As noted, Skinnerian principles have been applied to an incredible array of phenomena ranging from teaching machines for schoolchildren to the treatment of hospitalized psychotics. Any of the various applications of Skinner's position is sufficiently important to warrant further discussion here. But so far the most significant and far-reaching application of all is spelled out in his 1971 book *Beyond Freedom and Dignity*. In this work, Skinner emerges as a futurist and carefully outlines how entire cultures and social institutions may be consciously designed in strict accordance with his behavioristic principles. He theoretically leaps from simple rat behavior in the operant box to complex human behavior in society with the ease of an Olympic high-jumper. In the words of T. George Harris, describing this B. F. Skinner manifesto, "All the world's a box (1971, p. 33)."

Skinner's book, predictably, has stimulated and challenged his many followers while further alienating, outraging, and possibly even frightening his adversaries. It has brought him public attention far beyond the traditional scope of psychology. He appeared on the cover of *Time* magazine (Sept. 20, 1971) and has made appearances on several major United States television shows. He has been the center of a storm of controversy, receiving criticism from poets, philosophers, theologians, psychologists, and even politicians! Others have compared the significance of his work to that of Darwin. And how does Skinner react to this publicity, unprecedented for a psychology professor? "My hat still fits," he said in a *Psychology Today* interview (Hall, 1972, p. 68). And why shouldn't it? Consistent with his position, anyone with Skinner's genetic endowment and unique conditioning history could have done the same!

Beyond Freedom and Dignity is divided into nine chapters. Each is briefly discussed below.

A Technology of Behavior   In this first chapter, Skinner argues convincingly that all the major problems confronting the modern world involve human behavior. Population, nuclear war, famine, disease, ghettos, and pollution—all relate to the action or inaction of human beings. While science ultimately holds the keys for solving these problems, physics and chemistry alone will not suffice. What is needed is a technology of behavior.

Yet, even in the face of problems that threaten the very survival of the human race, the science of human behavior progresses at a snail's pace. Skinner contends that the necessary technology of behavior cannot be established until scientists (and the rest of us) discard our outmoded conceptions of human actions as internally caused:

> Unable to understand how or why the person we see behaves as he does, we attribute his behavior to a person we cannot see, whose behavior we cannot explain either but about whom we are not inclined to ask questions. . . . The function of the inner man is to provide an explanation which will not be explained in turn. . . . He is not a mediator between past history and current behavior, he is a *center* from which behavior emanates. He initiates, originates, and creates. . . . We say that he is autonomous— and, so far as a science of behavior is concerned, that means miraculous (1971, p. 14).

To properly understand human behavior, we must look toward its antecedents —toward the *environment* (here the basic assumptions of environmentalism, objectivity, and reactivity again rear their heads). A true behavioral technology will emerge only when we put aside the erroneous concept of autonomous man and come to grips with the selective function of the environment in behavior causation (determinism assumption). But the most troublesome features of autonomous man that prevent his conceptual demise are his presumed "freedom" and "dignity."

Freedom   The persistent and fallacious belief that people, by nature, are or could be free is nourished by what Skinner terms the "literature of freedom." This literature "consists of books, pamphlets, manifestoes, speeches, and other verbal products designed to induce people to act to free themselves from various kinds of intentional control (p. 30)." In reality, our perennial struggle for freedom is not the result of the will to be free but rather of the behavioral tendency to avoid or escape from aversive environmental stimuli. The literature of freedom has as its targets all "controllers" of human behavior, e.g., governments, organized religions, economic systems, formal education, and parents. While it has encouraged escape from or attack upon all such controllers, the literature of freedom has at the same time erroneously branded any semblance of control as aversive.

Skinner addresses himself to this point as follows:

> Those who manipulate human behavior are said to be evil men, necessarily bent on exploitation. Control is clearly the opposite of freedom, and if freedom is good, control must be bad. What is overlooked is control which does not have aversive consequences at any time. Many social practices essential to the welfare of the species involve the control of one person by another, and no one can suppress them who has any concern for human achievements (p. 41).

In brief, Skinner argues that humanity can never be totally freed of environmental control but only from certain kinds of aversive control. To improve the human condition, people must cease the futile search for freedom and focus scientific attention on drastic modification of social structures (reward systems in the culture). In his words, "to make the social environment as free as possible of aversive stimuli we do not need to destroy that environment or escape from it; we need to redesign it (p. 42)."

Dignity   Total commitment to Skinner's version of societal redesign rests squarely on the premise that human behavior is environmentally determined. Accordingly, one cannot legitimately be either praised or blamed for one's actions; the human being (whose autonomy is purely mythological) is not responsible for his or her activities—the environment is. And herein lies the downfall of dignity. As long as autonomous man can be credited for achievements and castigated for failures, dignity is possible. But if the environment is responsible for behavior, there is no room for the concept of human dignity or worth. And, as Skinner points out, the more that we know about the real causes of behavior, the less these causes can be attributed to autonomous man:

> It is in the nature of scientific progress that the functions of autonomous man be taken over one by one as the role of the environment is better understood. A scientific conception seems demeaning because nothing is eventually left for which autonomous

man can take credit. And as for admiration in the sense of wonderment, the behavior we admire is the behavior we cannot yet explain. Science naturally seeks a fuller explanation of that behavior; its goal is the destruction of mystery (p. 58).

The concept of human dignity is concerned with preserving due credit and admiration. Defenders of the concept (the "literature of dignity") oppose behavioral scientific and technological advances because they directly threaten the illusion of autonomous man's individual responsibility and dignity. Hence, dignity stands in the way of further human achievement. If we are to build the safe, sane, and controlled Skinnerian world of the future, humanity's ego-gratifying but illusory concept of dignity must be discarded along with that of freedom. In short, the salvation of humanity lies only "beyond freedom and dignity."

Punishment   An additional negative consequence of the literatures of freedom and dignity is that they have acted in part to preserve the concept of punishment as a perfectly justifiable and effective means of dealing with human behavior. If people are truly responsible for their own behavior, then parents, governments, and religions are justified in meting out all sorts of punishments for bad conduct, crimes, and sins. Skinner argues against punishment systems not only because they stem from a false concept of human behavior but also because they are largely ineffective:

> A person who has been punished is not thereby simply less inclined to behave in a given way; at best, he learns how to avoid punishment. Some ways of doing so are maladaptive or neurotic. . . . Other ways include avoiding situations in which punished behavior is likely to occur and doing things which are incompatible with punished behavior (p. 81).

The issue raised here by Skinner is one of controllability—punishment, in addition to being occasionally horrendous, is simply not all that effective in controlling human behavior. Skinner contends that our task is to make life less punishing by designing a society that need not resort to punishment to control the behavior of its members. But, once again, the literature of freedom and dignity (with their primary emphasis upon autonomous man) stand in the way. Punishment is erroneously seen in these literatures as a means of making "better people." Skinner instead exhorts us to "accept the fact that all control is exerted by the environment and proceed to the design of better environments rather than of better men (p. 82)."

Alternatives to Punishment   The champions of freedom and dignity do not confine themselves to punishment as a means of controlling behavior. Other largely ineffective alternatives to punishment are practiced precisely because they allow autonomous man to exercise a presumed freedom and to achieve an illusory dignity. Among the various practices of this type cataloged by Skinner are "permissiveness," "guidance," and "changing minds." Permissiveness, or the abandonment of policy, is ineffective because it simply leaves the control to other aspects of the environment. Guidance fails because behavior changes as a result of externally arranged contingencies, rather than the inner unfolding of human potentialities. Attempts to change minds are simply misdirected if the real purpose is to change behavior. Striking at the heart of the matter, Skinner explains why the measures employed by the defenders of freedom and dignity are ineffective:

> The apparent freedom respected by weak measures is merely inconspicuous control. When we seem to turn control over to a person himself, we simply shift from one mode of control to another (p. 97). . . . The fundamental mistake made by all those who choose weak methods of control is to assume that the balance of control if left to the individual, when in fact it is left to other conditions. The other conditions are often hard to see, but to continue to neglect them and to attribute their effects to autonomous man is to court disaster (p. 99).

By their inability to see that behavior is controlled by external contingencies rather than by autonomous man, the advocates of freedom and dignity encourage the misuse of controlling practices and thereby block progress toward an effective technology of behavior. Again Skinner's message is clear—the quality of human life will only be significantly enhanced when people consciously redesign their social environments in accordance with the principles of behavioristic science.

Values But who is to decide what is for the good of humanity? How will the new technology of behavior be used, by whom, and for what ultimate purpose? Skinner recognizes in these questions the fundamental issue of *values* raised by his radical proposals for societal redesign. He responds by asserting that questions about values are really questions about reinforcements:

> To make a value judgment by calling something good or bad is to classify it in terms of its reinforcing effects (p. 105). . . . Things are good (positively reinforcing) or bad (negatively reinforcing) presumably because of the contingencies of survival under which the species evolved (p. 104). . . . The only good things are positive reinforcers, and the only bad things are negative reinforcers (p. 107).

Supposedly, then, the question of values raised by the proponents of freedom and dignity largely resolves itself. The things that have become "good" in the course of evolution (meaningful work, material possessions) can be scientifically used to induce people to behave for "the good of others." However, Skinner warns that the "good" things must not become excessively available—people will rebel by challenging them and turning to things good only for themselves. He would then react "by intensifying the contingencies which generate behavior for the good of others or by pointing to previously neglected individual gains, such as those conceptualized as security, order, health, wealth, or wisdom (pp. 125–126)." Skinner's broad objective is, from the vantage point of his followers, benign—to create a balanced society in which each person is maximally reinforced.

The Evolution of a Culture But the creation of a behaviorist utopia requires an understanding of how cultures, or social environments, evolve. On this score, Skinner seems to be in fundamental agreement with a kind of "social Darwinism": "A culture, like a species, is selected by its adaptation to an environment: to the extent that it helps its members to get what they need and avoid what is dangerous, it helps them to survive and transmit the culture (p. 129)." Cultural practices, like species traits in Darwin's theory, may be initiated accidentally (mutation), but they persist because they have an adaptation value. The survival of a culture, like that of a species, depends upon evolving practices (traits) which enable it to deal with the physical environment as well as to compete successfully with other cultures. Ultimately, a culture's value can only be judged by one criterion—survival. To ensure survival, the culture must somehow encourage its members to work for this objective, i.e., people must be reinforced for their efforts to help the culture survive. The challenge for the "cultural designer" here is to accelerate the development of practices which bring the remote consequences of an individual's behavior into more direct play. If people are not reinforced by such remote consequences, they will have no reason to work for the survival of the culture. Hence, the culture will fail. The role of behavioral technology in ensuring the survival of the culture is quite clear: "Explicit design promotes that good by accelerating the evolutionary process, and since a science and a technology of behavior make for better design, they are important 'mutations' in the evolution of a culture (p. 144)."

The Design of a Culture In this most lengthy chapter of his book, Skinner argues strongly for the behavioristic design of cultures:

> A culture is very much like the experimental space used in the analysis of behavior. Both are sets of contingencies of reinforcement. A child is born into a culture as an organism is placed in an experimental space. Designing a culture is like designing an experiment; contingencies are arranged and effects noted. In an experiment we are interested in what happens, in designing a culture with whether it will work (p. 153).

All the world is indeed a box! However, Skinner allows that cultures are significantly more complex "boxes" than his operant conditioning chambers and that human behavior, equally, is more complex than rat bar pressing. Be that as it may, the underlying scientific principles governing the variables in both instances remain the same. Skinner emphatically contends that we now know enough about the experimental analysis of behavior to apply its technology to cultural design.

Clearly, objections to this proposal are raised on many sides, and Skinner attempts to answer these criticisms. For example, what of those who simply "wouldn't like" living in a totally controlled culture? Skinner translates this objection as follows: "'The culture would be aversive and would not reinforce me in the manner to which I am accustomed (p. 163).'" Further, "'I wouldn't like it' is the complaint of the individualist who puts forth his own susceptibilities to reinforcement as established values (p. 164)." Skinner replies, "The problem is to design a world which will be liked not by people as they now are but by those who live in it (p. 163)." While there is bound to be resistance to cultural change, people cannot resist positive reinforcement. As the designed culture evolves, individuals will change as their lives become progressively more reinforcing. After all, in the final analysis, happiness is positive reinforcement.

A danger in this controlled new world is how to control the controller. The answer here, says Skinner, is effective countercontrol. The controller must live fully within the designed culture and thus be wholly susceptible to the important consequences of her or his behavior. In essence, all control is really reciprocal; the challenge for the cultural designer is to build into the culture effective avenues for such reciprocity. Literally, controllers can never be permitted to get beyond the reach of the countercontrol measures available to the controllees.

Skinner concludes by arguing that scientific cultural design is our only means of survival:

> Our culture has produced the science and technology it needs to save itself. It has the wealth needed for effective action. It has, to a considerable extent, a concern for its own future. But if it continues to take freedom or dignity, rather than its own survival, as its principal value, then it is possible that some other culture will make a greater contribution to the future (p. 181). Like Milton's Satan, we will find ourselves in hell with no consolation other than the illusion that "here at least we shall be free (p. 182)."

What Is Man?   Skinner devotes the last chapter of his book to completing the demolition of the idea of autonomous man. His basic assumptions of environmentalism and objectivity are strikingly evident when he argues against the existence of autonomous man and his miraculous mental attributes:

> It is in the nature of an experimental analysis of human behavior that it should strip away the functions previously assigned to autonomous man and transfer them one by one to the controlling environment (p. 198). . . . The picture which emerges from a scientific analysis is not of a body with a person inside, but of a body which *is* a person in the sense that it displays a complex repertoire of behavior (p. 199).

But what of the nobility of the human being which has been cherished for centuries?

> . . . whereas the traditional view supports Hamlet's exclamation, "How like a god!" Pavlov, the behavioral scientist, emphasized "How like a dog!" But that was a step forward. . . . Man is much more than a dog, but like a dog he is within range of a scientific analysis (p. 201).

In brief, Skinner argues that "No theory changes what it is a theory about (p. 213)." That there presently is a scientifically outmoded but still prevalent conception of the human being as a free, dignified, and internally responsible agent is no reason to continue to cherish such an ultimately destructive illusion. While Skinner's view of human beings is deeply offensive to those who hold such a conception, he obviously believes his own position to be more accurate. The human being is not demolished in his view—only human autonomy. And this, Skinner argues, is necessary for our survival as a species. A culture based on a scientific conception of humanity is our main hope for a future. As Skinner puts it in concluding his work: "A scientific view of man offers exciting possibilities. We have not yet seen what man can make of man (p. 215)."

What is the real significance of *Beyond Freedom and Dignity?* As we approach the final years of this century, we stand on the brink of disaster and possibly even species extinction. Is Skinner a scientific-age savior who alone is pointing the way for humanity to save itself? Or can it be argued that many significant human problems have been brought about precisely because our social, moral, and educational systems have worked against each individual's realization of the full extent of his or her freedom and dignity? If so, then Skinner is leading us further down the path of developing a race of human robots in the manner of Huxley's *Brave New World* or Orwell's *1984*.

Psychologists and others differ sharply on the answers to these questions. One might ask why, since the evidence is equally available to all. Our answer is the theme of this book. Individuals react differently to Skinner's proposals fundamentally because they hold different basic assumptions about the nature of the human being. One who believes that human beings are free, subjectively oriented, and heterostatically motivated could never accept Skinner's ideas for social reform. Regardless of the ultimate "truth" of his position, however, B. F. Skinner has made a profound mark upon contemporary personology that will not soon fade away.

SUMMARY

Skinner's behavioristic-learning approach to personality is characterized by a rejection of an inner "autonomous" man as the cause of human actions and a disregard for physiological-genetic explanations of behavior. Skinner contends that behavior is lawfully determined, predictable, and environmentally controlled. Further, he holds that the fundamental principles underlying human behavior are most readily discerned by studying lower organisms, e.g., rats, pigeons.

Skinner has focused most of his scientific attention upon operant behavior, i.e., behavior which is emitted by, rather than elicited from, the organism. In a professional lifetime of operant conditioning research, Skinner has shown quantification of such behavior, indicated the lawful control of various reinforcement schedules, conditioned reinforcers, and aversive stimuli, demonstrated the shaping of operant behavior through successive approximation, and indicated its extension and appropriate adaptation to new stimuli (stimulus generalization and discrimination). No other personologist has done more than B. F. Skinner to empirically demonstrate lawful behavior-environment relationships.

Skinner's basic assumptions about human nature are strong and explicit. Behavioristic-learning theory reflects a strong commitment to determinism, elementalism, environmentalism, changeability objectivity, reactivity, and knowability. The basic assumptions of rationality–irrationality and homeostasis–heterostasis are not applicable to Skinner's position since he rejects internal sources of behavior.

Behavioristic-learning theory has generated more experimental research than any other personological system. Both the amount and diversity of this research is enormous. Skinner's own approach to behavioral research is characterized by concentration upon single subjects, automated equipment and well-defined control over experimental conditions, emphasis on molecularity, use of infrahumans, and focusing upon environmentally modifiable variables. One research illustration related to Skinner's position deals with behavior therapy and the token economy, while another discussed in this chapter focuses upon a behavioral treatment of marital discord.

Current applications of Skinnerian principles are numerous and far-reaching. Perhaps the most significant application to date is Skinner's attempt to outline how entire cultures can be designed in accordance with operant conditioning principles. This idea is presented in detail in his highly controversial book *Beyond Freedom and Dignity.*

BIBLIOGRAPHY

American Psychologist, January, 1972, **27**, 72.

American Psychological Association. A chat with Skinner. *APA Monitor,* 1977, **8**, 6.

Atthowe, J., & Krasner, L. Preliminary report on the application of contingent reinforcement procedures (token economy) on a "chronic" psychiatric ward. *Journal of Abnormal Psychology,* 1968, **73**, 37–42.

Ayllon, T., & Azrin, N. The measurement and reinforcement of behavior of psychotics. *Journal of the Experimental Analysis of Behavior,* 1965, **8**, 357–384.

Becker, W., Madsen, C., Arnold, C., & Thomas, D. The contingent use of teacher attention and praising in reducing classroom behavior problems. *Journal of Special Education,* 1967, **1**, 287–307.

Bennasi, V., & Lanson R. A survey of the teaching of behavior modification in colleges and universities. *American Psychologist*, 1972, **27**, 1063–1069.

Boslough, J. Reformatory's incentive plan works. *Rocky Mountain News*, December 24, 1972, p. 13.

Dews, P. (Ed.). *Festschrift for B. F. Skinner.* New York: Appleton-Century-Crofts, 1970.

Evans, R. *B. F. Skinner: The man and his ideas.* New York: Dutton, 1968.

Goodall, K. Who's who and where in behavior shaping. *Psychology Today,* June 1972, 58.

Hall, E. "My hat still fits." *Psychology Today,* November 1972, 68.

Harris, T. All the world's a box. *Psychology Today,* August 1971, 33–35.

Honig, W., & Staddon, J. (Eds.). *Handbook of operant behavior.* Englewood Cliffs, N.J.: Prentice-Hall, 1977.

Isaacs, W., Thomas, J., & Goldiamond, I. Application of operant conditioning to reinstate verbal behavior in psychotics. *Journal of Speech and Hearing Disorders,* 1960, **25**, 8–12.

Jacobson, N. Problem solving and contingency contracting in the treatment of marital discord. *Journal of Consulting and Clinical Psychology,* 1977, **45**, 92–100.

Kazdin, A., & Bootzin, R. The token economy: An evaluative review. *Journal of Applied Behavior Analysis,* 1972, **5**, 343–372.

Kinkade, K. *A Walden two experiment: The first five years of Twin Oaks community.* New York: William Morrow, 1973.

Levine, F., & Fasnacht, G. Token rewards may lead to token learning. *American Psychologist,* 1974, **29**, 816–820.

Lundin, R. Personality theory in behavioristic psychology. In J. Wepman & R. Heine (Eds.), *Concepts of personality.* Chicago: Aldine, 1963, pp. 257–290.

O'Leary, K., & Drabman, R. Token reinforcement programs in the classroom. *Psychological Bulletin,* 1971, **75**, 379–398.

O'Leary, K., & Turkewitz, H. Marital therapy from a behavioral perspective. In T. Paolino and B. McCrady (Eds.), *Marriage and marital therapy: Psychoanalytic, behavioral and systems-theory perspectives.* New York: Bruner-Mazel, 1978.

O'Leary, K., & Wilson, G. *Behavior therapy: Application and outcome.* Englewood Cliffs, N.J.: Prentice-Hall, 1975.

Paolino, T., & McGrady, B. (Eds.). *Marriage and marital therapy: Psychoanalytic, behavioral and systems-theory perspectives.* New York: Bruner-Mazel, 1978.

Patterson, G., & Gullion, M. *Living with children.* Champaign, Ill.: Research Press, 1971.

Rimm, D., & Masters, J. *Behavior therapy: Techniques and empirical findings* (2d ed.). New York: Academic Press, 1979.

Skinner, B. F. *The behavior of organisms: An experimental analysis.* New York: Appleton-Century-Crofts, 1938.

Skinner, B. F. *Walden two.* New York: Macmillan, 1948a.

Skinner, B. F. Superstition in the pigeon. *Journal of Experimental Psychology,* 1948b, **38,** 168–172.

Skinner, B. F. Are theories of learning necessary? *Psychological Review,* 1950, **57,** 193–216.

Skinner, B. F. *Science and human behavior.* New York: Macmillan, 1953.

Skinner, B. F. A case history in scientific method. *American Psychologist,* 1956, **11,** 221–233.

Skinner, B. F. *Verbal behavior.* New York: Appleton-Century-Crofts, 1957.

Skinner, B. F. *Cumulative record.* New York: Appleton-Century-Crofts, 1961.

Skinner, B. F. Autobiography of B. F. Skinner. In E. Boring & G. Lindzey (Eds.), *History of psychology in autobiography* (Vol. 5). New York: Appleton-Century-Crofts, 1967, pp. 387–413.

Skinner, B. F. *The technology of teaching.* New York: Appleton-Century-Crofts, 1968.

Skinner, B. F. *Contingencies of reinforcement: A theoretical analysis.* New York: Appleton-Century-Crofts, 1969.

Skinner, B. F. *Beyond freedom and dignity.* New York: Knopf, 1971.

Skinner, B. F. *About behaviorism.* New York: Knopf, 1974.

Skinner, B. F. *Particulars of my life.* New York: Knopf, 1976.

Skinner, B. F. Why I am not a cognitive psychologist. *Behaviorism,* 1977, **5,** 1–10.

Skinner, B. F., & Ferster, C. *Schedules of reinforcement.* New York: Appleton-Century-Crofts, 1957.

Skinner, B. F., & Lindsley, O. *Studies in behavior therapy, status reports II and III.* Office of Naval Research, Contract N5 ORI-7662, 1954.

Stuart, R. Operant-interpersonal treatment for marital discord. *Journal of Consulting and Clinical Psychology,* 1969, **33,** 675–682.

Walker, H., Mattson, R., & Buckley, W. Special class placement as a treatment alternative for deviant behavior in children (Monograph 1). Department of Special Education, University of Oregon, Eugene, 1969.

Watson, J., & Rayner, R. Conditioned emotional reactions. *Journal of Experimental Psychology,* 1920, **3,** 1–14.

Williams, C. The elimination of tantrum behavior by extinction procedures. *Journal of Abnormal and Social Psychology,* 1959, **59,** 269.

Williams, J. *Operant learning: Procedures for changing behavior.* Monterey, Calif.: Brooks/Cole, 1973.

SUGGESTED READINGS

Carpenter, F. *The Skinner primer: Beyond freedom and dignity.* New York: Free Press, 1974.

Kazdin, A. *Behavior modification in applied settings.* Homewood, Ill.: Dorsey, 1975.
Matson, R. *Without/within: Behaviorism and humanism.* Belmont, Calif.: Wadsworth, 1973.
Skinner, B. F. Behaviorism at fifty. In T. Wann (Ed.), *Behaviorism and phenomenology.* Chicago: University of Chicago Press, 1964, pp. 79–108.
Skinner, B. F. Will success spoil B. F. Skinner? *Psychology Today,* June 1972, 65–72; 130.

DISCUSSION QUESTIONS

1 From what you know about B. F. Skinner's early life, can you see any factors that might have led him in the direction of developing the kind of theory of human behavior that he did? Indeed, can Skinner's own theory-construction behavior be explained in reinforcement terms? How?
2 Now that you have read about schedules of reinforcement, can you detect how these different schedules operate in your own life? Give one example of how each reinforcement schedule—fixed-ratio, fixed-interval, variable-ratio, and variable-interval—operates to maintain different aspects of your behavior.
3 How much do you agree with Skinner's basic assumptions about human nature—his basic image of the human being? If you do agree, what are some of the important implications for what *you* fundamentally are as a person and how you should thus live your life.
4 In the operant treatment of marital discord study described in this chapter, husbands earned tokens by conversing with their wives which they could then exchange for sexual intercourse with their wives. Do you think that is right? Does such a treatment approach, regardless of its efficacy, perpetuate constraining male and female sex roles, e.g., male as active and desirous of sex, female as passive dispenser of occasional sexual favors? Or does this approach merely reflect the reality of most married people's sexual relationship?
5 What do you think of the utopia that Skinner outlines in *Beyond Freedom and Dignity?* Can the creation of such a society be achieved? Would the pressing problems of contemporary society vanish in this new world? Could you live happily in it? Above all, is the creation of such a society desirable in terms of facilitating human development? Why or why not?

GLOSSARY

Behaviorism   A school of psychology founded by J. B. Watson, whose members believe that the only scientifically valid subject matter for psychology is observable and measurable behavior.
Behavior Therapy   A collection of therapeutic techniques that seek to change behavior through reliance on principles of operant conditioning.
Classical Conditioning   Basic form of learning in which a previously neutral stimulus is paired with a stimulus that naturally elicits a response so that the neutral stimulus comes to elicit the same response. For example, a child hears an angry voice paired with a spanking and subsequently responds to an angry voice in fear.
Conditioned Response   A response similar to an unconditioned response which is elicited by a previously neutral stimulus.
Conditioned Stimulus   A stimulus which acquires the capacity to elicit particular responses through repeated pairing with another stimulus capable of eliciting such responses.
Continuous Reinforcement   Schedule of reinforcement in which the organism is rein-

forced every time it emits the desired or correct response. Also called a 100 percent schedule of reinforcement.

Discriminative Stimulus   A stimulus (cue) whose presence indicates that some particular form of behavior will or will not be reinforced.

Extinction   The process through which conditioned responses are weakened and eventually eliminated when no longer reinforced.

Fixed-Interval Schedule   Reinforcement schedule in which the first response that occurs after an absolute amount of time has elapsed is reinforced.

Fixed-Ratio Schedule   Reinforcement schedule in which the first response following an absolute number of responses is reinforced.

Functional Analysis   The establishment of specifiable relationships between the organism's behavior and the environmental conditions that control it.

Intermittent Reinforcement   Reinforcement schedule in which reinforcers are applied to given responses occasionally or intermittently.

Negative Reinforcement   Any stimulus that maintains or strengthens the occurrence of a response which leads to the removal or termination of an aversive stimulus.

Operant Behavior   Responses freely emitted by an organism, the frequency of which is strongly affected by the application of various reinforcement schedules.

Operant Conditioning   A form of learning in which a correct response or change of behavior is reinforced and becomes more likely to occur (also called instrumental conditioning).

Positive Reinforcement   Stimulus associated with behavior that increases the probability of the occurrence of the behavior.

Primary Reinforcement   Any event or object which possesses inherent reinforcing properties (also referred to as *unconditioned reinforcement*).

Punishment   Presentation of aversive stimuli following a behavior considered undesirable that results in a decrease in the performance of that behavior.

Reinforcement   In classical conditioning, the association formed through repeated pairing of the conditioned stimulus and the unconditioned stimulus; in operant conditioning, the association that is formed when an operant response is followed by a reinforcing stimulus.

Respondent Behavior   A specific response which is elicited by a known stimulus, the latter always preceding the former in time.

Schedule of Reinforcement   Rule stating the contingencies under which reinforcements will be delivered.

Secondary Reinforcement   Any stimulus which acquires reinforcing properties through close association with a primary reinforcement in the past conditioning history of the organism.

Single-Subject Experimental Design   Attempt to establish basic laws of behavior by studying the influence of one or more controlled variables upon a specific component of a single organism's behavior in a controlled environment.

Skinner Box   A small experimental chamber that Skinner invented in order to study principles of operant conditioning.

Stimulus Discrimination   Process of learning how to respond appropriately to various environmental stimuli.

Stimulus Generalization   The tendency of reinforced behavior to extend to a variety of related settings.

Superstitious Behavior   Type of conditioning in which there is an apparent but chance connection between a response and a reinforcement.

Token Economy   A behavior therapy program, usually employed in an institutional setting, in which patients are rewarded with tokens for performing appropriate behaviors. The tokens can later be exchanged for goods or services.

Unconditioned Response   The natural, automatic response elicited by an unconditioned stimulus.

Unconditioned Stimulus   Any stimulus possessing the capacity to elicit reactions from organisms in the absence of prior conditioning.

Variable-Interval Schedule   Reinforcement schedule in which the first response performed after the passage of a variable interval of time (varying around some average value) is reinforced.

Variable-Ratio Schedule   Reinforcement schedule in which reinforcement is delivered only after the completion of a variable number of responses (the number of responses which must be completed varies around some average value).

Albert Bandura

Chapter 7

Albert Bandura: A
Social-Learning Theory
of Personality

Personological conceptions of human nature have generally emphasized either *dispositional* or *situational* factors as the basis for explaining why people behave as they do. Proponents of the former view maintain that the principal causes of behavior are found within the individual in the form of instincts, drives, needs, traits, and other intrapsychic forces. Those favoring the latter view insist that behavior is acquired, maintained, and modified through the impact of environmental influences as mediated by the individual's learning history. In recent years, however, personality psychologists have begun to theorize that human behavior is governed by a complex interplay between inner processes and environmental forces. Such theorizing, the product of the individual and collective efforts of many psychologists, has culminated in what may be called a *social-learning perspective* and is perhaps best singularly illustrated by the work of Albert Bandura.

According to Bandura's social-learning view, psychological functioning is best understood in terms of a continuous reciprocal interaction among behavioral, cognitive, and environmental influences. This means that behavior, personal factors, and social forces all operate as interlocking determinants of one another— that behavior is influenced by the environment but that people also play a role in creating the social milieu and other circumstances that arise in their daily transactions. Moreover, unlike Skinner, who is almost entirely concerned with learning by direct experience, Bandura places primary emphasis on the role of *observational learning* in behavioral acquisition. Indeed, the most distinctive feature of Bandura's theory is the belief that most of our behavior is learned by observing other people and modeling our behavior after theirs:

> Psychological theories have traditionally assumed that learning can occur only by performing responses and experiencing their effects. In actuality, virtually all learning phenomena resulting from direct experience occur on a vicarious basis by observing other people's behavior and its consequences for them. The capacity to learn by

observation enables people to acquire large, integrated patterns of behavior without
having to form them gradually by tedious trial and error (Bandura, 1977, p. 12).

BIOGRAPHICAL SKETCH

Albert Bandura was born on December 4, 1925, in the town of Mundar (pop. 600)
in the province of Alberta, Canada. The son of wheat farmers of Polish heritage,
he attended a high school that had only twenty students and two teachers. Largely
obliged to educate himself, as were his classmates, Bandura recalls that this self-
education was such that virtually every graduate went on to a successful professional career. Little other published information is available on his childhood.

After high school, Bandura attended the University of British Columbia in
Vancouver, where he received his B.A. degree in 1949. He then enrolled in graduate
study at the University of Iowa, believing its psychology department to be the most
forward-looking at the time. He was awarded an M.A. in 1951 and a Ph.D. in 1952.
Bandura next served a year's clinical internship at the Wichita Kansas Guidance
Center, following which he accepted a position in the psychology department at
Stanford University, where he has remained ever since.

Throughout his career, Bandura has been actively engaged in the development
of a social-learning approach to the study and understanding of personality. He has
also maintained an impressive record of scholarship, publishing several books and
countless research articles in professional journals. His early books, *Adolescent
Aggression* (1959) and *Social Learning and Personality Development* (1963), were
written in collaboration with Richard H. Walters, his first Ph.D. student. Then he
published *Principles of Behavior Modification* (1969), an extensive review of the
psychosocial principles that govern behavior. In 1969, Bandura was named a
Fellow of the Center for Advanced Study in the Behavioral Sciences at Stanford
University. He used that year both to write his book *Aggression: A Social-Learning
Analysis* (1973) and, by his own admission, to study the subculture of the daily
volleyball games played by the highly competitive fellows at the center. He has also
published a module entitled *Social-Learning Theory* (1971), an abbreviated treatment of the key concepts that help to explain behavior. Bandura's most recent book
(at the time of this writing), *Social-Learning Theory* (1977), presents a concise
overview of the recent theoretical and experimental advances in the field of social
learning.

Bandura has been frequently recognized for his contributions to psychology.
He received the Distinguished Scientist Award in 1972 from the American Psychological Association and in 1973 the Distinguished Scientific Achievement
Award from the California Psychological Association. He was also elected president of the American Psychological Association in 1973.

After over twenty-five years on the Stanford faculty, Bandura still teaches two
undergraduate courses, one a seminar in personality change and the other on the
psychology of aggression. He reports being invigorated by both the teaching and
research of today, as opposed to his own undergraduate days when "it was mostly

the study of the literature of the dead (Kiester and Cudhea, 1974, p. 31." Bandura and his wife, Virginia, live with their two daughters near the Stanford campus. Sierra Club members, they enjoy spending a weekend backpacking through the high country of Yosemite National Park. The couple also delights in the opera and symphony, with their favorite Friday night diversion a visit to one of San Francisco's fine restaurants.

Today Albert Bandura is recognized as the premier figure of social-learning theory, one of the pioneers of behavior modification, and a renowned scholar in theories of aggression. He is one of a handful of thinkers who have moved into the mainstream of personality theory from its individualistic, Freudian roots toward a broader view of how people develop patterns of behavior in interface with their surroundings. His views have had a widespread impact on his colleagues, especially in the clinical and developmental areas, and thus merit our special attention.

BASIC TENETS OF SOCIAL-LEARNING THEORY

The study of Bandura's social-learning approach to personality must begin with an overview of his assessment of how other theories have sought to explain the causes of human behavior. In this way we can contrast his theory with the others presently available.

Out with Inner Forces!

Bandura notes that until recently the most common view, popularized by various psychodynamic doctrines, depicted people's behavior as arising from an assortment of inner processes (e.g., drives, impulses, needs, and other motivational forces) often operating below the threshold of awareness. Although this view gained widespread professional and popular acceptance, it is open to question on both conceptual and empirical grounds. Bandura describes the conceptual limitations of such theories this way:

> The inner determinants often were inferred from the behavior they supposedly caused, resulting in description in the guise of explanation. A hostile impulse, for example, was derived from a person's irascible behavior, which was then attributed to the action of an underlying hostile impulse. Similarly, the existence of achievement motives were deduced from achievement behavior; dependency motives from dependent behavior; curiosity motives from inquisitive behavior; power motives from domineering behavior; and so on. There is no limit to the number of motives one can find by inferring them from the kinds of behavior they supposedly produce (1977, p. 2).

In addition, psychodynamic theories disregard both the enormous complexity and the diversity of human responses. According to Bandura, an internal motivator cannot possibly account for the marked variation in the frequency and strength of a given behavior in different situations, toward different persons, and in different social roles. How a mother reacts to a child at home one day compared to the next, how she reacts to her daughter as opposed to her son in a comparable situation, and how she reacts when her husband is present rather than when she is alone with a child is a case in point. The empirical adequacy of psychodynamic formulations has also been questioned. At the risk of oversimplification, experimental personologists contend that while such theories may offer intriguing interpretations of events that have already occurred, they lack the power to predict how people will behave in a given situation (Mischel, 1968). For these reasons, it eventually became evident that if we were ever to improve our understanding of human behavior, we had to improve our explanatory systems (theories) along both conceptual and empirical lines.

Behaviorism from the Inside

Advancements in learning theory shifted the focus of causal analysis from the hypothetical inner forces of the psychodynamic mold to external influences on responsiveness (e.g., B. F. Skinner's position). Human behavior was extensively analyzed in terms of the social stimuli that evoke it and the reinforcing consequences that maintain it. But to Bandura, such a drastic explanatory shift was something like throwing the baby out with the bath water. The internal "baby" that should have been retained and emphasized was, for Bandura, people's cognitive processes; in other words, behaviorism neglected determinants of people's behavior arising from their cognitive processes. For Bandura, human beings possess superior capabilities that provide them with some measure of self-direction. To the extent that traditional behavior theories could be faulted, it was for providing an incomplete rather than an inaccurate account of human behavior.

From Bandura's perspective, people are neither driven by intrapsychic forces nor buffeted by environmental ones. Instead, the causes of human behavior are to be understood in terms of a continuous reciprocal interaction of behavioral, cognitive, and environmental influences. In this approach to analyzing the causes of behavior, which Bandura has termed *reciprocal determinism,* dispositional and situational factors are considered to be interdependent causes of behavior. Thus, one and the same event can be a stimulus, a response, or an environmental reinforcer, depending on where in the sequence the analysis arbitrarily begins (see Figure 7-1). Moreover, while behavior is influenced by the environment, the environment is also partly a product of a person's own making, so that people can exercise *some* influence over their own behavior. Thus, in Bandura's view, people are not simply reactors to external stimulation. Because of their extraordinary capacity to use symbols, human beings are able to think, create, and plan—cognitive processes that are constantly revealed through overt actions.

Figure 7-1 Schematic representation of reciprocal determinism. *B* signifies behavior, *P*, the cognitive and other internal events that can affect perceptions and actions, and *E*, the external environment. *(Adapted from Bandura, 1978.)*

Beyond Reinforcement

Traditional learning theorists generally stress reinforcement as a necessary condition for the acquisition, maintenance, and modification of behavior. Skinner, for example, contends that changes in behavior occur as a result of our direct experiences with the rewarding and punishing consequences that follow our actions. Responses that are rewarded tend to be repeated; those that are punished tend to be discarded. While Bandura accepts this view, he maintains that it does not fully account for the ways in which our behavior is acquired, maintained, or altered. In his view, most human behavior is not controlled by immediate external reinforcement. As a result of prior experiences, people come to expect that certain kinds of behavior will have the effects they value, others will produce undesired outcomes, and still others will have little appreciable impact. Our behavior is therefore regulated to a large extent by *anticipated consequences* (Bandura, 1971). For example, as homeowners we do not wait until we experience the trauma of a burning house to buy fire insurance. Instead, we rely on information gained from others about the potentially devastating consequences of lacking fire insurance in making our decision to purchase it. Similarly, we do not wait until caught in a blinding snowstorm or a torrential rainstorm to decide what to wear on a venture into the wilderness. Nor if we are failing a psychology course do we usually wait until after the final examination to begin studying for it. In each instance, we can imagine the consequences of being inadequately prepared and take precautionary steps. Through our capacity to represent actual outcomes symbolically, future consequences can be translated into current motivators that influence behavior in much the same way as potential consequences. Our higher mental processes thus provide us with the capability for both insight and foresight.

Finally, Bandura also believes that new patterns of behavior can be acquired *in the absence of external reinforcement*. He notes that much of the behavior we eventually display is acquired through the influence of example: we simply attend to what others do and then repeat their actions. This emphasis on *learning by observation* or example, rather than by direct reinforcement, is the most distinctive feature of Bandura's theory. It will be discussed fully in the next major section of this chapter.

Self-Regulation and Cognition in Behavior

Another distinguishing feature of social-learning theory is the prominent role it assigns to the unique human capacity for *self-regulation*. By arranging their immediate environment, by creating cognitive supports, and by producing consequences for their own actions, people are able to exercise some influence over their behavior. To be sure, self-regulative functions are created and not infrequently supported by environmental influences. Having external origins, however, does not diminish the fact that, once established, self-generated influences partly govern which actions one performs. Furthermore, Bandura contends that our superior intellectual capacity to engage in symbolic thought provides us with a powerful means of dealing with our environment. Through *verbal* and *imaginal representa-*

tions we process and preserve experiences in ways that serve as guides for future behavior. Our ability to form images of desirable futures fosters behavioral strategies designed to lead us toward long-range goals. On the strength of our symbolizing powers, we can solve problems without having to resort to actual, overt trial-and-error behavior, and we can thus foresee the probable consequences of different actions and modify our behavior accordingly. To illustrate, a child anticipates that if she breaks her younger sister's toy, she will cry, bring out their mother to investigate the commotion, blame the toy-breaker, and institute some form of punishment. Realizing the probable consequences, the child would probably choose to play with her own toys, thus avoiding parental wrath and keeping intact positively reinforcing maternal approval. In other words, the child's ability—rooted in her symbolic powers—to foresee the consequences of different actions enables her to behave appropriately.

Let us now examine the kind of observational learning that Bandura believes to be so central to these various facets of human behavior.

LEARNING THROUGH MODELING

Learning would be quite laborious, not to mention inefficient and potentially dangerous, if we had to depend exclusively on the outcome of our own actions to guide us. For instance, suppose a motorist had to rely solely on immediate consequences (e.g., being hit by another vehicle, running over a child) in order to learn not to go through an intersection against a red light at the peak of rush-hour traffic. Fortunately, verbal transmission of information and observation of competent models (i.e., other people) provide the basis for the acquisition of most complex human behaviors. Indeed, Bandura maintains that virtually all learning phenomena resulting from direct experience can occur on a vicarious basis by observing other people's behavior and its consequences for them. We do not need to experience terminal cancer, for example, to appreciate the emotional upheaval it causes, since we have seen others stricken by the disease, read accounts of those dying, and seen dramas about the struggles. Thus, to ignore the role of observational learning in the acquisition of new behavior patterns is to ignore a uniquely human capacity.

Each of us has had the experience of struggling with a problem only to find that it is ridiculously easy after seeing someone else solve it. The observation factor is the key. Children learn by watching, whether it is to enjoy studying, to do household chores, or to play certain games. They may also learn, through observation, to be aggressive, or altruistic, or cooperative, or even obnoxious. In many instances the behavior modeled must be learned in essentially the same way it is performed. Riding bicycles, skateboarding, typing, and dental surgery, for example, permit little, if any, departure from essential practices. However, in addition to transmitting specific response patterns, modeling influences can create innovative behavior. Should a child learn to share jelly beans with her dolly, it is but a short leap for her to share toys with peers, attention with her baby brother, chores with her mother, and later in life, time with her church and money with many unfortunate people she has never met. Through the modeling process, observers extract common features from seemingly diverse responses and formulate rules of behavior that enable them to go beyond what they have seen or heard. Bandura describes this facet of learning through modeling in the following way: "By synthesizing features of different models into new amalgams, observers can achieve through modeling novel styles of thought and conduct. Once initiated, experiences with the new forms create further evolutionary changes. A partial departure from tradition eventually becomes a new tradition (1974, p. 864)."

According to Bandura, one forms a cognitive image of how certain behaviors are performed through the observation of a model, and on subsequent occasions this coded information (stored in long-term memory) serves as a guide for one's action. Furthermore, Bandura believes that because people can learn what to do from example, at least in approximate form, they are spared the burden of needless mistakes and time-consuming performance of inappropriate responses.

Processes of Observational Learning

The key assumption of social-learning theory is that modeling influences generate learning chiefly through their informative function (Bandura, 1977). That is, during exposure, observers (learners) acquire mainly symbolic representations of the modeled activities which serve as prototypes for both appropriate and inappropriate behavior. According to this formulation, summarized schematically in Figure 7-2, observational learning is governed by four interrelated components or processes: *attentional, retention, motor reproduction,* and *motivational* processes. Viewed from this theoretical perspective, learning by observation emerges as an actively judgmental and constructive process, rather than a mechanical, copying process of monkey see, monkey do. The four component processes outlined by Bandura (1977) are considered next.

1   Attentional Processes: Perceiving the Model   Bandura notes that a person cannot learn much by observation unless she or he attends to, or accurately perceives, the salient cues and distinctive features of the model's behavior. In other words, it is not sufficient for a person merely to see the model and what it is doing; rather, the individual must attend to the model with enough perceptual accuracy to extract the relevant information to use in imitating the model. Attentional processes thus influence what is selectively perceived in the model to which one is exposed and what is acquired from such exposure. Any professor can verify that the presence of a

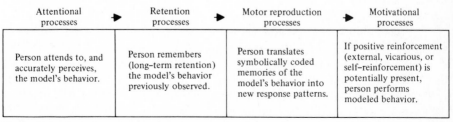

Attentional processes	Retention processes	Motor reproduction processes	Motivational processes
Person attends to, and accurately perceives, the model's behavior.	Person remembers (long–term retention) the model's behavior previously observed.	Person translates symbolically coded memories of the model's behavior into new response patterns.	If positive reinforcement (external, vicarious, or self–reinforcement) is potentially present, person performs modeled behavior.

Figure 7-2 Component processes governing observational learning. (*Adapted from Bandura, 1977.*)

student in class in no way guarantees that student's assimilation of the presented material. Spring fever, a nasty cold, room temperature, a late night preceding the class, daydreaming, or myriad other possibilities may cause the student to "lose" the train of thought (or never even get on the train), thereby vitiating the learning process.

Several factors, some involving the observer, others involving the modeled activities, and still others involving the structural arrangement of human interactions, can greatly influence the modeling process, i.e., the likelihood that a bit of exemplary behavior will be attended to by the observer. Bandura (1977) indicates that among the attentional determinants influencing modeling, *associational patterns* are of utmost importance. The people with whom one regularly interacts, either by preference or imposition, restrict the types of behavior that will be observed and hence learned most thoroughly. Opportunities for learning altruistic behavior, for example, differ markedly for members of assaultive gangs or religious groups. Similarly, within any social group some individuals are likely to command greater attention by virtue of their status and assigned roles than others. The functional value accompanying the behaviors displayed by different models (i.e., who metes out rewards and punishments) is therefore highly influential in determining which models people will observe and thus emulate and which they will ignore. Attention to models is also governed by their interpersonal attractiveness. Models who personify charismatic qualities are generally sought out, while those who demonstrate displeasing qualities are usually ignored or rejected. The fact that many black adolescents from Harlem sneer at the values of the white middle class illustrates this truth. Moreover, ample evidence suggests that we tend to be more strongly influenced by models who are similar to ourselves (in life-styles and goals) than by models who differ from us in obvious and significant ways (Rosenkrans, 1967).

Other research has shown that models who appear high in competence, who are alleged experts, or who are celebrities or superstars command greater attention than models who lack these attributes (Rosenbaum and Tucker, 1962). Advertisers of everything from popcorn poppers to feminine products capitalize on this idea, utilizing television personalities, football superstars, and financial wizards to hawk their products. In general, any set of characteristics that causes a model to be perceived as intrinsically rewarding for prolonged periods of time increases the probability of more careful attention to the model, and, consequently, the probability of modeling.

2   Retention Processes: Remembering the Model   The second process involved in observational learning concerns long-term retention of activities that have been modeled at one time or another. Simply put, a person cannot be affected much by observation of a model's behavior if he or she has no memory of it. Indeed, without the capacity to recall what the model did, the observer is unlikely to demonstrate any enduring behavioral change.

In order for a person to benefit from the behavior of a model when it is no longer present to serve as a guide, the model's responses must be coded into some symbolic form (e.g., words or images) that may later be recalled to duplicate the performance. Bandura proposes two main internal representational systems as the means by which the model's behavior is retained and converted into later action. The first is *imagery*. As the person is observing modeling stimuli, a process of sensory conditioning produces relatively enduring and easily retrievable images of what has been seen. The mental images are formed so that any reference to events previously observed immediately calls forth a vivid image or picture of the physical stimuli involved. Bandura suggests that this is an everyday phenomenon and accounts for one's ability to "see" an image of a person one had lunch with last week or an image of the activities (tennis, cycling, golfing) one engaged in last summer. In passing, it should be noted that visual imagery plays a central role in observational learning during early developmental stages when linguistic skills are lacking, as well as in learning behavior patterns that do not lend themselves readily to verbal coding.

The second representational system involves the *verbal* coding of previously observed events. While observing the model, a person might verbally recite to himself or herself what the model is doing. These subvocal descriptions (codes) can later be rehearsed internally, without an overt enactment of the behavior; for example, a person might silently "talk through" the steps involved in mastering a complicated motor skill, e.g., downhill skiing. In effect, the person is silently rehearsing a sequence of modeled activities to be performed at a later time, and, when she or he wishes to perform the skill, the verbal code will provide the relevant cues. Bandura maintains that observational learning is greatly facilitated by such verbal codes because they carry considerable information in an easily stored form.

3   Motor Reproduction Processes: Translating Memories into Behavior

The third basic component involved in observational learning consists of translating the *symbolically coded memories* into appropriate action. Despite the fact that a person may have carefully formed and retained symbolic representations of a model's behavior and rehearsed that behavior numerous times, he or she may still be unable to enact the behavior correctly. This is especially true for highly skilled motor acts that require the execution of many individual responses for their skillful performance, e.g., driving, skiing, playing an instrument, or piloting a plane. The fine or delicately balanced movements involved may be learned by watching someone else (perhaps with the aid of slow-motion audio-visual reproduction), and the symbolic representation of the model's behavior may be repeated silently a number of times, but the translation into actual behavior will likely be clumsy and uncoordinated at first. Mere observation in such instances is not sufficient to ensure a smooth and coordinated performance of the act. Persistent practice in performing the motor movements (and self-corrective adjustment on the basis of informative feedback) is essential if one is to perfect the behavior. Of course, observing and intentionally rehearsing certain behaviors may facilitate learning, for one is at least able to begin to perform the necessary movements based on what had been earlier observed. This silent rehearsal is helpful with skills such as driving but may not be as useful with more complicated skills, such as diving from a ten-meter springboard.

4 Motivational Processes: From Observation to Action The fourth and final component involved in modeling concerns *reinforcement* variables. These variables influence observational learning by exerting selective control over the types of modeling cues to which a person is most likely to attend, and they also affect the degree to which a person tries to translate such learning into overt performance.

Bandura is careful to point out that no matter how well people attend to and retain the modeled behavior or how much ability they possess to perform the behavior, they will not perform it without sufficient incentive or motivation to do so. In other words, a person can acquire, retain, and possess the capabilities for skillful execution of modeled behavior, but the learning may seldomly be activated into overt performance if it is negatively sanctioned or otherwise unfavorably received. A woman who believes herself "queen of the kitchen" may exclude her husband from all cooking duties despite the fact that he talks to her nightly while she prepares dinner. His reliance on her culinary skills is total until she becomes ill. Prompted by the motivation of an empty stomach and whining children, he may execute the modeled behavior of fixing dinner. His attentional and retentional behavior will no doubt increase in the future as his mind stumbles to recall where the peanut butter or sauerkraut is kept.

Generally speaking, if positive incentives are presented, modeling or observational learning is promptly translated into action. Moreover, not only does positive reinforcement enhance the likelihood of overt expression or actual performance of the behavior in question, it also influences the person's attentional and retentional processes. In everyday life, we rarely pay attention to something or somebody if no incentive impels us to—and when little attention has been paid, there is virtually nothing to retain! We may often ride with the same friend to a specific destination, yet become confused or even lost when we are required to drive the route ourselves. We have not paid attention to the route previously travelled because we have not had to—someone else was driving the car. Once we come to depend on ourselves to reach the place we want, we retain the directions.

One way in which a person's desire to attend to, retain, and perform a modeled behavior may be influenced is through the anticipation of reinforcement or punishment for so doing. The observation that another's behavior brings about positive reward, or prevents some aversive condition, can be a compelling incentive to attend to, retain, and later (in a comparable situation) perform that behavior. In this case, the reinforcement is experienced vicariously, after which the person can anticipate that enactment of the same behavior will lead to similar consequences. A child may spontaneously sweep the porch, vacuum his or her room, or set the table, thereby anticipating grateful smiles and appreciative words for his or her considerate actions. As this example suggests, the child's anticipation of reinforcement was effective in initiating the helping behavior.

REINFORCEMENT IN OBSERVATIONAL LEARNING

Bandura believes that while reinforcement often serves to facilitate the learning process, it is not necessary in order for learning to occur. There are many other factors, he notes, other than reinforcing consequences of behavior that can influence what people will or will not attend to. We do not have to be reinforced, for example, to attend to fire sirens, flashes of lightening, putrid smells, and novel stimuli. In fact, when our attention to modeled activities is gained through the sheer impact of physical stimuli, the addition of positive incentives does not enhance observational learning. This fact is borne out by research showing that children who watched a model on television in a room darkened to minimize distractions later displayed the same amount of imitative learning regardless of whether they were told in advance that such imitations would be rewarded or given no prior incentives to learn the modeled performances. In short, reinforcement can aid modeling, but it is not vital to it (Bandura, 1971).

More specifically, Bandura considers the notion of human behavior as *exclusively controlled* by its external consequences to be too restrictive: "If actions were determined solely by external rewards and punishments, people would behave like weather vanes, constantly shifting in radically different directions to conform to the whims of others (Bandura, 1971, p. 27)." More to the point, while social-learning theory does acknowledge the powerful role played by extrinsic feedback (i.e., learning by directly experienced reinforcement), it posits a broader range of reinforcement influences. People are not only influenced by the experiences produced by their actions; they also regulate their behavior on the basis of observed consequences as well as those they create for themselves. These two forms of reinforcement control—*vicarious* and *self-monitored*—will be discussed shortly.

Bandura's treatment of the role of reinforcement in observational learning reveals his cognitive orientation. He proposes that external reinforcement seldom operates as the automatic determiner of behavior. More often, it serves two other functions, as *information* and as *incentive*. Reinforcement following a given response indicates, or at least enables the individual to form hypotheses about, what the correct response is. This informative, or feedback, function can operate whether the reinforcement is experienced directly or vicariously. To take one example, witnessing someone else punished for a certain deed is as informative as being punished oneself. In addition, reinforcement informs us what to expect as a result of making the correct or incorrect response. The student who aspires to become a physician during high school and then discovers that she can earn excellent grades (reinforcement) in her college premed courses is a case in point. This kind of information—usually called incentive—is essential if we are to correctly anticipate the probable consequences of our actions and to regulate our behavior accordingly. Indeed, without the capacity for anticipatory or foresightful behavior, people would likely act in ways that might prove highly unproductive, if not perilous. Fortunately, however, one is constantly observing, thinking, forming hypotheses and expectations, and eventually deciding what to do in Bandura's theory—based on probable consequences conveyed by environmental stimuli as well as on what one wants to do.

Vicarious Reinforcement

It is evident from the preceding discussion that people can profit immensely from the observed successes and failures of others, as well as from their own direct experiences. Indeed, as social beings, we repeatedly attend to the actions of others and the situations in which they are rewarded, ignored, or punished. Consider, for instance, a child who observes a friend reprimanded for interrupting the teacher. This experience will likely inhibit interrupting, unless of course the observing child expects that the consequences in his or her case will be different, e.g., by seeing different consequences in the home, or being told that similar behavior will not be punished. Or, consider the waitress or waiter who sees fellow workers generously tipped for a friendly smile and cheerful chatter with the patrons. This experience will no doubt enhance her or his tendency to smile and chatter with subsequent customers as well. As these two examples illustrate, the observed or vicarious consequences (rewards and punishments) accruing to the actions of others often play an influential role in regulating our behavior. Accordingly, the study of *vicarious reinforcement* is critical to the understanding of conditions governing human behavior.

In general, vicarious reinforcement is operative whenever an observer witnesses an action of a model who experiences some external outcome which the observer perceives to be contingent on the model's earlier action. *Vicarious positive reinforcement* is said to occur when observers increase behavior for which they have seen others reinforced, whereas *vicarious punishment* occurs when observed negative consequences reduce people's tendency to behave in similar or related ways. In each instance, the information conveyed by observed consequences enables the observer to determine whether a particular externally administered reinforcer will serve as a reward or punishment. Thus, if one sees people rewarded for doing something, one is more likely to do it; if one sees them punished for doing it, one is less likely to do it.

How Does Vicarious Reinforcement Work?

Just how vicarious reward and punishment operate to instigate or inhibit an observer's behavior is no simple issue. Indeed, Bandura (1971; 1977) has proposed six regulatory mechanisms, or functions, through which vicarious reinforcement can affect the thoughts, feelings, and actions of observers; these functions are termed informative, motivational, emotional learning, influenceability, modification of model status, and valuation, respectively. Let us briefly illustrate them.

In the first of these mechanisms, the *informative function,* the learner, through observing what happens to a model for some particular kind of behavior, guides his or her own behavior accordingly, e.g., a student who observes a fellow student's detected plagiarism on a term paper being severely punished will not be inclined to plagiarize in similar situations. The second mechanism, the *motivational function,* involves the arousal of observer expectations as the result of having seen others reinforced, e.g., a female student observing the reinforcements accruing to a female professor may thereby increase her own motivation to pursue an independent, self-sufficient, and similarly rewarding life-style and career. The *emotional-learning function* refers to emotional arousal or general heightening of responsiveness that takes place in observational-learning situations, e.g., a child's observation of a sibling spanked arouses fear and anxiety; the fear, in turn, suppresses not only the specific responses the child made, but any response from the observer—he or she may turn attention elsewhere or flee the anxiety-arousing situation entirely. In the *influenceability function,* the learner's susceptibility to direct reinforcement is increased through observation of the model's responses to similar reinforcements, e.g., the student who observes another student excited and happy about receiving an "A" in a difficult course thereby becomes more susceptible to the reinforcing properties of "A's" in her or his own difficult courses. The *modification of model status function* means that a model's social status can rise or fall as a function of being rewarded or punished. This factor is also assumed by Bandura to affect observational learning, e.g., an athlete praised by the coach for a good performance thereby rises in status on the team; other team members will thus be more inclined to emulate this performance. And finally, the mechanism termed *valuation function* refers to situations in which reinforcement applied to a model alters the observer's perceived valuation of both the reinforcing agent and the model, e.g., an otherwise law-abiding person may be provoked to break the law without remorse by watching what he or she believes to be unjust punishment applied to a model for breaking that law. Together, these six regulatory mechanisms help to explain how reinforcement applied to one person can powerfully affect learning in another.

Self-Reinforcement

Thus far we have considered how people regulate their behavior on the basis of external consequences that they either observe or experience firsthand. In particular, we have noted that both direct, external reinforcement and vicarious reinforcement exert a powerful influence over the ways in which we acquire, maintain, and modify our behavior. From the perspective of social-learning theory, however, many of our actions are governed by self-imposed reinforcement. Indeed, Bandura argues that behavior is extensively *self-governed* through *self-produced consequences* for one's own actions.

According to the concept of self-reinforcement, human actions are not at the mercy of external influences. Instead, people possess self-reactive capacities that allow them to exercise control over their own feelings, thoughts, and actions—behavior is therefore regulated by the interplay of self-generated and external sources of influence (Bandura, 1977).

Self-reinforcement is evident whenever people set standards of performance or achievement and proceed to reward or punish themselves for attaining, exceeding, or falling short of their own expectations. In preparing a book or writing a journal article for publication, for example, authors do not require the presence of someone looking over their shoulders and reinforcing each sentence until a satisfactory manuscript is produced. Rather, they possess an internalized standard of what constitutes an acceptable end product and engage in continuous self-corrective editing that often exceeds accepted standards. Some authors in fact impose such stringent self-editing standards that they are literally paralyzed in their own writing efforts. In most other areas of functioning, people similarly judge and evaluate their own behavior and reward and punish themselves. They congratulate themselves for their own characteristics and actions; they praise or debunk their own accomplishments; and they self-administer social and material rewards and punishments from the enormous array available to them.

In Bandura's view, human beings are far less dependent upon external support systems than lower animals because they are uniquely endowed with symbolizing and self-reactive capacities. Accordingly, the admission of self-reinforcement processes in learning theory greatly enhances the explanatory power of reinforcement principles as they apply to human behavior.

How Self-Regulation Occurs

Self-reinforcement involves a process whereby individuals improve and maintain their own behavior by giving themselves rewards over which they have control whenever they attain certain self-imposed standards of performance. Since both negative as well as positive self-reactions are possible, Bandura uses the more inclusive term *self-regulation* to encompass both the enhancing and reducing effects of self-evaluative influences.

From Bandura's perspective, self-regulated incentives increase performance mainly through their motivational function. That is, by making self-gratification or tangible rewards conditional upon realizing certain accomplishments, individuals motivate themselves to expend the effort needed to attain the desired performance. The individual's level of self-induced motivation aroused by this means usually varies according to the type and value of the incentives and the nature of the performance standards. In social-learning theory, there are three component processes involved in the self-regulation of behavior by self-produced consequences: self-observation, judgmental, and self-response processes.

Human behavior typically varies along a number of *self-observation* dimensions, e.g., the quality or rate of one's responses. The functional significance of these dimensions depends on the type of activity in question. For example, track and field performances are judged in terms of time and distance. Artistic endeavors, on the other hand, are generally evaluated on the basis of esthetic value and originality. Social behavior, by contrast, is commonly judged in terms of dimensions such as sincerity, deviance, ethicalness, and a host of other evaluative qualities.

The second component involved in the self-regulation of behavior is the *judgmental* process. It is often the case that whether a given performance will be regarded as commendable and hence rewardable or unsatisfactory and hence punishable depends upon the personal standards against which it is evaluated. In general, those actions that measure up to internal standards are judged positively whereas those that fall short of the mark are judged negatively. Of course, absolute measures of the adequacy of one's performance are often lacking. The time in which the 100-meter backstroke is swum, the number of points earned on a psychology exam, or the amount given to a charitable organization may not convey sufficient information for self-appraisals even when compared against an internal standard. In these and many other instances, the adequacy of performance must be defined relationally, i.e., by comparing them with those of others. To illustrate, consider the student who scores 85 points on a psychology test and who strives to be in the upper 5 percent of her class. Clearly, her score would provide no basis for making either a positive or negative self-assessment unless she knew the scores of her fellow students. In the case of still other activities and tasks, the adequacy of one's performance may be defined in terms of standard norms or the accomplishments of reference groups.

The individual's previous behavior also provides a standard against which the adequacy of ongoing performance may be judged. Here it is self-comparison that supplies the benchmark of adequacy or inadequacy. Bandura suggests that past performance influences self-appraisal principally through its impact on goal setting. "After a given level of performance is attained, it is no longer challenging, and new self-satisfactions are sought through progressive improvement. People tend to raise their performance standards after success and to lower them to more realistic levels after repeated failure (1977, p. 132)."

Evaluation of activities constitutes another important factor in the judgmental component of self-regulation of behavior. It is obvious, for instance, that people expend little or no effort in activities that have no personal relevance for them. Rather, it is in those areas of life affecting one's well-being and self-esteem that self-appraisal activates persistent effort and commitment. Additionally, the way people perceive the causes of their behavior strongly influences self-appraisal. Most people feel a sense of pride and pleasure for the accomplishments which they attribute to their own ability and effort. Conversely, they seldom derive much satisfaction when they attribute their success to external factors such as luck or chance. The same holds true for judgments of failure and blameworthy conduct. People tend to respond self-critically to poor performances for which they view themselves responsible but not to failures which they perceive to be due to mitigating circumstances or insufficient abilities. Performances that are deemed to have no personal relevance do not elicit any reactions one way or another. For example, should an individual achieve first-chair trumpet, he would likely believe that practice and true ability brought him the reward. However, the same person would take little pride in the accomplishment if he felt his conductor-father awarded him the position based on something other than ability. Should he be denied the honor, he might justify his poor performance with the idea that he was experiencing the flu during the tryouts. The drummer viewing all this from afar has no more than a passing interest in the whole affair.

Bandura (1977) maintains that a wide spectrum of human behavior is regulated through self-evaluative consequences as expressed in the form of self-satisfaction, self-pride, self-dissatisfaction, and self-criticism. Thus, the third and final component involved in behavioral self-regulation concerns *self-response* processes, particularly self-evaluative reactions. Other things being equal, positive self-appraisals of performance give rise to rewarding self-reactions, whereas negative appraisals inspire punishing self-responses. Moreover, "self-evaluative reactions acquire and retain their rewarding and punishing value through correlation with tangible consequences. That is, people usually engage in self-gratifications after achieving a sense of self-pride, whereas they treat themselves badly when they judge themselves self-critically (Bandura, 1977, p. 133)."

Three additional aspects of self-regulation of behavior through self-managed incentives warrant our brief attention: (1) How are self-monitoring reinforcement systems acquired? (2) How effective are they in regulating behavior? (3) What sustains them? Let us consider each of these issues in turn.

Learning Self-Regulation   Standards for self-reward and punishment can be acquired in a variety of ways. One of these is through the process of *differential* or *selective reinforcement*. People frequently learn how to evaluate their behavior in terms of how others have reacted to it. Parents and other significant socializing figures adhere to certain rules or standards of what constitutes acceptable behavior. Early in life children learn that if these rules of behavior are followed, they are rewarded; if ignored, they are punished for violating them. Indeed, parents are usually pleased and respond approvingly when children attain or exceed desired standards and displeased when their performances fall short of the valued level. The child who has been scolded by her mother for hitting a younger sibling over the head with a block associates the withdrawal of the mother's love with her aggressive act. Eventually she internalizes both her mother's standard (aggression is bad) and the punishment (withdrawal of love). Thus, when she behaves aggressively in the future, or is tempted to do so, she withdraws her own love from herself. In short, she feels *self-guilt*. The result of such differential or selective treatment is that children eventually come to respond to their own behavior in self-approving and self-condemning ways, depending on whether it deviates from or conforms to the evaluative standards set by others.

Modeling represents another influential means by which self-evaluative standards may be learned. The procedure used by Bandura to study this process typically requires having children observe models performing a task in which the models adopt either high or low performance for self-reward. When models achieve or surpass the self-imposed standard, they reward themselves tangibly and voice self-praise; but when their performances fall short of their self-prescribed standard, they deny themselves available rewards and react self-critically. The observers (children) subsequently perform the same task alone, and the performance levels for which they reward or punish themselves are recorded. Numerous experiments employing this research design reveal three findings concerning the influence of models in the establishment of self-reinforcing systems: (1) children tend to adopt evaluative standards displayed by exemplary models; (2) they judge their own performances relative to those standards; and (3) they then serve as their own reinforcing agents.In one study, for instance, two groups of children participated in a miniature bowling game with adult models (Bandura and Kupers, 1964). In one condition, the children observed a model reward himself with candies only for superior performances. In another condition, they observed a model reward himself for mediocre performances. Following exposure to the models, the children were left alone to play with no models present. The results indicated that the children exposed to models who set high performance standards later rewarded themselves only sparingly and only when they matched or exceeded the criterion, whereas those who were exposed to the low-standard model rewarded themselves quite generously, even for mediocre performances. By contrast, children who had no prior exposure to models did not reward themselves selectively for different levels of achievement.

Regulating Behavior through Self-Produced Consequences   According to Bandura, people not only respond to their own behavior in self-rewarding and self-punishing ways, they also regulate their behavior through self-produced consequences. Indeed, a central premise of social-learning theory is that without self-generated influences, people's efforts involving task-oriented activities would be difficult to sustain. To illustrate, consider an experiment conducted by Bandura and Perloff (1967) in which the relative effectiveness of self-monitored versus externally applied reinforcement was compared. In this investigation, children worked at a manual task—cranking a wheel—and earned scores depending on the number of cranking responses they performed. The apparatus was constructed in such a way that the more effort they expended, the higher the scores they could achieve. Specifically, eight cranking responses were required to attain a score of 5, sixteen responses to achieve a score of 10, twenty-four responses to attain a score of 15, and a total of thirty-two cranking responses to reach the maximum score of 20. In the self-reward condition, children selected which of these standards they would strive for and proceeded to reward themselves with tokens redeemable for prizes whenever they achieved their self-defined goals. In the externally reinforced condition, other children were individually matched with subjects in the self-reward group and were *given* the same standards that the self-rewarders set for themselves; they were rewarded by others whenever they attained the predesignated levels. A third group of children worked at the same task but received the rewards in advance, while a fourth group of children performed without receiving any rewards at all. All children performed the task alone, and the number of cranking responses they performed until they wished to discontinue the activity served as the dependent measure of industrious behavior.

The results showed that children assigned to the externally rewarded and self-rewarded groups were more than twice as productive as children who got their rewards in advance or got no rewards. An even more striking result was the prevalence with which children in the self-rewarded group imposed upon themselves stringent performance demands. Although they worked alone and were allowed to select any goal they desired, not a single child chose the lowest standard, which required the least amount of effort. Many of these children, in fact, selected the highest level of achievement as the minimal performance meriting self-reward. Moreover, Bandura and Perloff found that nearly a third of the children raised their initial standard to a higher level without a corresponding increase in amount of self-reward, thereby demanding of themselves additional work for the same recompense.

Why did the children in the self-reward condition demand of themselves high levels of performance when no one compelled them to do so? Although the experiment was not designed to answer this question, Bandura (1977) offers the following plausible explanation. To begin, it will be recalled that most children internalize achievement standards through modeling and the evaluative reactions of others. Furthermore, they are likely to have experienced criticism on various occasions for being self-satisfied with performances deemed by others to be unworthy. Thus, under conditions where children are provided opportunities to maximize their material gains by engaging in behavior that has low self-regard value, conflicting tendencies are likely to be aroused. In this case, Bandura suggests that children are inclined to optimize their rewards for minimum effort by simply lowering their achievement standards. At the same time, however, reward for mediocre performances evokes self-disapproval, which, if sufficiently strong, may inhibit undeserving self-compensation. Evidently, then, children are willing to deny themselves rewards over which they have control rather than incur self-reproof for unmerited self-reward. (Perhaps this is something like Groucho Marx's classic comment, "Any social club that will accept me, I don't want to belong to!") The explanation is consistent with the fact that many of the children in the study just cited aspired to goals that required considerable effort at minimum material gain. In a broader context, Bandura suggests that whenever people engage in activities having little or no self-evaluative consequences, they tend to put forth the least amount of effort for each tangible self-reward.

Sustaining Self-Reward Systems   According to Bandura, four interrelated factors serve to maintain the regulation of behavior through self-imposed incentives —negative sanctions, predictive situational determinants, personal benefits, and modeling supports.

1   Negative Sanctions: The Headaches of Undeserved Rewards   Adherence to performance standards for self-reward are partly maintained by a variety of periodic social influences. For example, rewarding oneself for either inadequate or undeserving performances often results in negative reactions from others. A case in point is the professor who treats himself to a lengthy vacation despite the fact that he failed to meet his department's yearly publication quota and who subsequently evokes the contempt of his more deserving colleagues. Such a negative sanction may well deter him from taking another undeserved break the following year under similar conditions.

2   Predictive Situational Determinants: Avoiding the Headaches   Most people are able to predict the probable consequences of undeserved self-rewards and are thus able to deny themselves such rewards until their performance standards are met. In light of the example just given, for instance, our professor is likely to know that he will jeopardize future promotions, merit raises, and harmonious colleague interactions if he takes another vacation prior to fulfilling his research commitments. Acting on the basis of this knowledge, he will no doubt redouble his efforts to achieve his goals and then reward himself by taking the highly desired vacation.

3   Personal Benefits: Getting What You Earn   The desire to reduce or eliminate aversive behavior is still another way by which self-prescribed reinforcement may be sustained. Consider, for example, a student who is motivated to improve his or her study habits to avoid failing so that academic life will be personally more rewarding. Or a heavy smoker who curtails smoking to avoid lung cancer. Personal benefits derived from self-directed change are also evident in the case of valued activities. People often strive, through conditional self-rewards, to improve their skills in tasks they wish to master and to enhance their competencies in dealing with the demands of day-to-day living. Such self-imposed discipline is especially evident among persons engaged in solitary creative activities. By making self-reward contingent upon completion of a specified task, they ensure their progress toward long-range goals. Thus, an author who decides she must complete thirty pages a week for her book will reward herself with a ski weekend if the task is done.

4 Modeling Supports: Success Thrives on Company A final factor serving to maintain self-reinforcing behavior involves the influence of supportive models. Since our behavior is partly governed by modeling stimuli, it follows that seeing others successfully manage their behavior through self-reward contingencies would facilitate our adherence to self-imposed contingencies. In everyday life, modeling supports usually consist of reference groups whose influence on an individual is realized through a system of common behavioral norms for self-reinforcement. The obese person who joins a diet workshop in order to lose weight is a case in point. By seeing others lose weight through the aid of self-imposed rewards, one's own efforts to curb overeating are strengthened.

Until now the discussion has focused on the question of what supports self-reinforcing actions. However, as Bandura well recognizes, an adequate social-learning theory must also account for such puzzling questions as why people deny themselves available rewards, why they demand of themselves high levels of performance when no one compels them to do so, and why they inflict punishment upon themselves. Clearly, these are challenging questions requiring explanation, and Bandura readily admits that they have by no means been sufficiently studied. What follows are a set of tentative interpretations offered by Bandura.

Why Do We Punish Ourselves? In the social-learning view, people tend to engage in self-deprecatory and other distressing thoughts when they function inadequately or violate their own internal standards of conduct. This tendency is repeatedly experienced throughout the course of socialization and involves the following sequence of events: *transgression–internal distress–punishment–relief.* In this process, transgressive behavior arouses anticipatory fear and self-condemnation that often persist until the person is reprimanded. Punishment, in turn, not only terminates anguish over the transgression and possible social repercussions, it also tends to restore the approval of others. Accordingly, self-administered punishment can provide relief from thought-produced distress and apprehension which may last longer and be more painful than the actual reprimand itself.

Self-punishing responses persist because they alleviate thought-created anguish and attenuate external punishment. By criticizing and belittling themselves for reprehensible moral actions, people stop tormenting themselves about their past behavior. Similarly, self-criticism may reduce disconcerting thoughts about faulty or disappointing performance. Still another reason for self-punitive behavior is that it often serves as an effective means of downplaying negative reactions from others. In other words, when certain actions are likely to evoke disciplinary measures, self-punishment may be the "lesser of two evils." Finally, verbal self-punishment can be used to encourage compliments from others. By criticizing and debunking themselves, individuals can get others to articulate their positive qualities and abilities, and to offer reassuring statements that sustained effort will produce future successes.

Although self-punishment can serve to end or at least reduce thought-produced distress, it can also intensify personal distress. In fact, excessive or prolonged self-punishment based on inordinately severe standards of self-evaluation may give rise to chronic depression, feelings of apathy and worthlessness, and lack of purpose. This is tragically evident in persons who suffer considerable self-devaluation as a result of a loss in ability due to aging or some physical handicap but who continue to adhere to their original standards of performance. They may belittle themselves and their achievements so severely that they eventually become apathetic and abandon activities that formerly brought them great personal fulfillment. Behavior which is the source of self-produced distress may also facilitate the development of various forms of abnormal behavior. To illustrate, some people whose efforts generate a continuing sense of inadequacy and failure may resort to alcoholism or drug addiction as a way of coping with their environment. Others protect themselves from feelings of self-contempt by escaping into a world of grandiose thinking, where they attain in delusional fantasy what is unattainable in reality. Still others are driven by self-generated tyranny to suicide.

We now conclude our account of Bandura's theoretical concepts by briefly considering the role of self-evaluation and self-conception in social-learning theory.

Self-Evaluation and Self-Concept   As we have already seen, self-evaluative and self-reinforcing functions occupy a central position in social-learning theory. In addition to giving humans a capacity for self-direction, self-evaluation serves as the basis for feelings of satisfaction and worth. Specifically, the extent to which individuals experience both satisfaction and dissatisfaction is determined not only by their achievements but also by the standards against which their achievements are judged. Thus, objectively identical accomplishments may make one person highly fulfilled but leave another quite disappointed because of differing evaluative standards. For instance, a final grade of "B" may leave one student elated while another is deeply disappointed.

From Bandura's perspective, *self-esteem* is defined in terms of discrepancies between a person's actual behavior and the standards he or she has adopted as indicative of personal worth. People who hold themselves in low self-esteem do so because their behavior falls short of self-prescribed standards. Part of the tragedy here is that many people who judge themselves negatively are in fact quite competent but live in continual agony since their best efforts are rarely considered by them to be good enough. On the other hand, people who hold themselves in high self-esteem do so because their behavior matches or exceeds self-created standards. The same line of reasoning may be extended to individual differences in *self-conception*. Viewed from the framework of social-learning theory, negative self-concept reflects a history of frequent negative self-evaluation, i.e., a tendency to devalue oneself. Conversely, positive self-concept reflects an enduring disposition to engage in positive self-evaluation, i.e., a tendency to judge oneself favorably.

Let us now consider the basic assumptions about human nature underlying social-learning theory.

BANDURA'S BASIC ASSUMPTIONS CONCERNING HUMAN NATURE

In terms of the basic theoretical positions that can be taken within psychology, Bandura is often portrayed as a "moderate behaviorist." Yet social-learning theory as it is epitomized in Bandura's work suggests a different image of the human being from that espoused by John B. Watson, traditional stimulus-response behaviorists, or, in particular, B. F. Skinner (often termed a "radical behaviorist"). One strong indication of this difference is the central role given to cognition in social-learning theory, an internal thinking process the existence of which is denied in Skinnerian psychology. But Bandura's most essential differences from other varieties of behavioristic theory (especially Skinner) can best be appreciated by considering his positions on the basic assumptions about human nature (Figure 7-3).

Freedom–Determinism   Bandura's position on this dimension can best be conceptualized as falling midway between the extremes of freedom and determinism. The key to an understanding of his position lies in his concept of *reciprocal determinism* (Bandura, 1978), the continuous interplay of behavior, the person, and the environment in all human activity: "Because people's conceptions, their behavior, and their environments are reciprocal determinants of each other, individuals are neither powerless objects controlled by environmental forces nor entirely free agents who can do whatever they choose (Bandura, 1978, pp. 356–357)."

From the viewpoint of social-learning theory, then, people can be considered somewhat free insofar as they can influence future environmental conditions by regulating their own behavior (Bandura, 1974). This they do largely by means of cognitive processes and self-reinforcement. Still, the environment affects people as much as people affect the environment. To illustrate, one's cognitive development and self-reinforcement standards are at least partially determined by environmental influences. Thus, in social-learning theory, the relationship between person and environment is truly *bidirectional:* people shape environments while environments simultaneously shape people. This continuous interplay of forces allows for both a measure of freedom *and* determinism in Bandura's underlying conception of human nature.

Rationality–Irrationality   Bandura's distinctiveness from traditional behaviorism in general, and from Skinner in particular, can be traced to his strong

	Strong	Moderate	Slight	Midrange	Slight	Moderate	Strong	
Freedom				■				Determinism
Rationality	■							Irrationality
Holism						■		Elementalism
Constitutionalism							■	Environmentalism
Changeability	■							Unchangeability
Subjectivity				■				Objectivity
Proactivity				■				Reactivity
Homeostasis			Not applicable					Heterostasis
Knowability	■							Unknowability

Figure 7-3   Bandura's position on the nine basic assumptions concerning human nature.

commitment to the rationality assumption, reflected clearly in the powerful cognitive thrust of his entire theoretical position. To illustrate, recall part of a quotation cited earlier: "The extraordinary capacity of humans to use symbols enables them to engage in reflective thought, to create, and to plan foresightful courses of action in thought rather than having to perform possible options and suffer the consequences of thoughtless action (Bandura, 1978, p. 345)." Spoken like a true cognitive psychologist—a personologist with the rationality assumption firmly implanted in the foundation of his or her theoretical structure.

Rationality is patently evident in Bandura's central theoretical concept, that of *modeling*, or *observational learning*. Without the ability to form and store in memory cognitive images of observed behaviors, modeling would be impossible. Moreover, Bandura's treatment of reinforcement emphasizes its informative and incentive functions, as opposed to construing external reinforcement as an automatic determiner of behavior. Stated simply, reinforcement in Bandura's theory (whether direct or vicarious) gives a person something to think about in generating future behavior—again, a cognitive concept quite foreign to Skinnerian theory (Skinner, 1977). Thus, the central place and pervasiveness of cognition in social-learning theory reveals the rationality assumption at its base.

Holism–Elementalism   Much more in line with traditional behaviorism is Bandura's moderate commitment to the elementalism assumption. To illustrate, nowhere in Bandura's theory is there a global construct absolutely vital to the explanation of behavior (such as the construct of "self" or "self-concept" in phenomenological theory). Indeed, when Bandura speaks of self-evaluation, he consistently argues against a global approach to its conceptualization and measurement. But more important, modeling can only be understood in terms of its component subfunctions: "Understanding how people learn to imitate becomes a matter of understanding how the requisite subfunctions develop and operate (Bandura, 1974, p. 864)." However, the requisite subfunctions—discriminative observation, memory encoding, coordinating ideomotor and sensorimotor systems, judging probable consequences for matching behavior (Bandura, 1974)—are themselves reasonably broad and complex concepts. Thus, while Bandura appears to believe that behavior is best understood through its constituent parts, the constituents are not particularly molecular. For this reason, his underlying commitment to elementalism might best be judged as moderate.

Constitutionalism–Environmentalism   As the very name "social-learning theory" implies, Bandura's work is mainly concerned with the social environment and the learning processes through which environment has an impact upon behavior. When placed on the constitutionalism–environmentalism scale, then, Bandura's theory leans heavily toward environmentalism. Yet in social-learning theory, the environment lacks the awesome and automatic control over behavior that it possesses in Skinnerian theory. Instead, in accordance with Bandura's (1978) doctrine of reciprocal determinism, people affect their environments as much as their environments affect them. Through self-regulation and cognition, the direct effects of the environment are considerably modified, since there is a constant interaction among behavioral, cognitive, and environmental factors. Nonetheless, Bandura (1971) clearly invests the environment with considerable potency in the production and modification of human behavior, although it is not seen as the sole or automatic cause of that behavior. In opposition to the relative absence of constitutionalism in Bandura's thinking, however, environmentalism clearly is the more dominant assumption underlying social-learning theory. Furthermore, in terms of our basic assumptions model, the particular interplay of rationality and environmentalism at the root of Bandura's position seems in large measure responsible for the unique cognitive orientation of social-learning theory against the historical background of the behavioristic tradition in psychology.

Changeability–Unchangeability   A personologist whose central theoretical concept is that of modeling would necessarily seem strongly committed to the changeability assumption. For the entire thrust of modeling deals with how people learn and how they acquire and change their behavior. And in Bandura's system, as people mature, they gain progressively greater control over the direction that such behavior changes take with the aid of self-reinforcement and environment arrangement to yield more positive reinforcement. Thus, people arrange the external inducements for desired behavior, they evaluate their performances, and they serve as their own reinforcing agents (Bandura, 1974).

Instead of focusing his theoretical attention upon internal variables that persist and characterize an individual's behavior over time, Bandura attends closely to the processes of behavior change. A strong commitment to an underlying assumption of changeability is thus implied, one which Bandura shares with other theorists who emphasize learning, be they of the behavioristic persuasion or not.

Subjectivity–Objectivity   The continuous interplay between person and environment in social-learning theory, especially as it is emphasized in Bandura's doctrine of reciprocal determinism, reflects a nice blending of the subjectivity and objectivity assumptions. On the subjectivity side, people do not indiscriminately absorb the objective influences impinging upon them. Rather, these influences are processed through private and presumably subjective, internal factors (i.e., cognitive structures) before they affect behavior. Further suggestions of subjectivity are found in Bandura's concept of self-evaluative standards; because of differences in such standards among people, *objectively identical* situations may be perceived and responded to differently by any two individuals. Thus, Bandura acknowledges the role of private experience in human activity.

But Bandura by no means ventures into the subjective world of the person with the abandon of a phenomenologist; he treads cautiously, like a reformed behaviorist peering into the depths of an unexplored and possibly scientifically unacceptable jungle of subjective experience. Insofar as possible, Bandura makes considerable efforts to anchor all internal constructs to objective, observable factors. And while people do influence the environment in social-learning theory, it cannot be forgotten that the environment (objective factors) also influences people's behavior. Thus there appears to be equal room for both subjectivity and objectivity in the household of social-learning theory.

Proactivity–Reactivity The person in social-learning theory continually reacts to external influences, but *reacts proactively!* To understand this apparent paradox, consider a previously cited assertion of Bandura's: "Behavior is . . . regulated by the interplay of self-generated and external sources of influence (Bandura, 1977, p. 129)." Essentially, this statement again reflects his doctrine of reciprocal determinism, a doctrine encompassing equal parts of both the proactivity and reactivity assumptions.

In Bandura's system, people react to external influences by observing and then processing these influences through their cognitive structures. People observe, think, plan, and anticipate the probable external consequences of their actions. Indeed, in social-learning theory, it is fair to say that the behavior of people is governed more by their reactions to *anticipated* consequences than by their reactions to past or present external consequences (Bandura, 1974). A person generates behavior in a future-oriented fashion (proactivity), but primarily as a reaction to the anticipated consequences of his or her actions (reactivity). Thus, the basic assumptions of proactivity and reactivity blend together in social-learning theory.

Homeostasis–Heterostasis The basic issue involved in this assumption dimension is the nature and properties of the motives presumed to underlie behavior. Do people act to reduce tensions and maintain internal equilibrium, or is human behavior fundamentally directed toward personal growth and self-actualization? In Bandura's theory, there is an apparent lack of speculation about these questions, and in no case does the basic issue discernibly affect the nature of his theoretical constructs: one can model many kinds of behaviors regardless of the nature of the possible motives underlying one's own behavior or that of the model.

This is not to say that Bandura rejects the concept of motivated behavior. He does not; he simply conceptualizes motivation in a fashion which does not readily lend itself to a homeostasis–heterostasis type of analysis. More specifically, rather than dwelling on the properties of presumed inner motives, Bandura (1977) instead analyzes motivation in terms of antecedent, incentive, and cognitive inducements, all potentially verifiable by experimentation. To understand this position better, the reader need only recall the previous discussion of the role of motivation in observational learning (see again Figure 7-2) as well as in self-regulation. Motivation is definitely present in social-learning theory, but it is couched largely in terms of cognitive structures and various types of reinforcement (e.g., external, vicarious, and self-reinforcement). Thus, unless one is willing to stretch things unduly, the homeostasis–heterostasis assumption dimension is not directly applicable to Bandura's position.

Knowability–Unknowability Bandura clearly assumes that human nature is knowable. Indeed, the knowability assumption pervades all his work, from the respect he consistently shows for empirical data, through his attempts to construct theoretical concepts open to empirical test, to his own prolific contributions to scientific research. To provide but one illustration, while Bandura employs internal cognitive structures in explaining behavior, he clearly believes that such internal processes must eventually be tied to observable actions in a complete account of human behavior (Bandura, 1974). In effect, such ties would necessarily place all hypothesized internal variables within the domain of scientific knowability, since they could be observed and presumably measured. Moreover, in Bandura's theory, there are no allusions to mysterious variables beyond scientific comprehension and no real attempt to transcend the realm of what many consider to be proper psychological science. Thus, like the broad behavioristic tradition from which social-learning theory has in part emerged, Bandura is strongly committed to the assumption that human nature is ultimately knowable through science.

Let us now turn to the empirical testing of social-learning concepts.

EMPIRICAL VALIDATION OF SOCIAL-LEARNING THEORY CONCEPTS

Bandura's social-learning position has generated an impressive amount of evidence in support of its basic concepts and principles. As might be expected, most of the research has focused on validating the role of observational learning in the acquisition, maintenance, and modification of human behavior. This research has greatly enhanced our knowledge of how parental modeling practices influence children's social development, how language and thought processes are acquired, and how self-reinforcement can be used in the treatment of a variety of psychological problems. Additionally, Bandura himself has conducted numerous studies concerning the importance of observational learning in the acquisition and modification of aggressive behavior (Bandura, 1973). These contributions coupled with countless empirical findings in related areas of personality functioning (e.g., sex-role development, helping behavior, social skills) are already an integral part of contemporary psychology. In general, then, Bandura's theory has a high degree of empirical support and there is every reason to expect a continued growth of interest in it.

In this chapter section we shall consider illustrative studies pertaining to (1) the effects of observing televised violence on children's aggressive behavior and (2) the role which observational learning plays in the development of self-control. These are but two of the many areas in which Bandura's theory has been the focus of and impetus for vigorous scientific inquiry. Before proceeding, however, let us briefly examine Bandura's overall approach to empirical research.

Bandura's Methodological Orientation

We have already considered a few examples of the way in which Bandura obtains data for his social-learning theory. Essentially, he operates as an inductive scientist, setting up testable hypotheses that emerge from his general theory and then collecting data from individuals and groups to validate the theory. The basic methodology of studies on observational learning requires the subject merely to observe, but not to act out, the behavior of a model and then later to be tested for similar behaviors in the setting previously occupied by the model. Bandura has also made an extensive effort to introduce into experimental settings conditions comparable to a real social environment. Because of this, his work is often generalizable to socially relevant issues. Moreover, of all the theories discussed in this text, Bandura's is clearly based on the broadest range of subjects (preschoolers to adults), another factor that allows the theory's empirical findings to be generalized to the real world. The studies of observational-learning processes and their pervasive influence on human behavior are well-controlled investigations, conducted in the tradition of experimental social psychology.

Bandura's theoretical position, however, has by no means escaped criticism. Some contend that the theory has difficulty explaining how various cognitive variables operate to influence behavior, and indeed that such cognitive constructs are unnecessary for behavior explanation (Skinner, 1974). Others argue that the theory is incomplete in that it neglects to indicate how the various components of observational learning contribute to the phenomenon of modeling (Bavelas, 1978). Despite these and other conceptual problems, the reaction of research person-ologists to Bandura's theory has been most enthusiastic.

Violence on Television: Aggressive Models in Every Living Room

Obviously not all observational learning leads to socially acceptable outcomes. Indeed, people can learn undesirable and antisocial forms of behavior through the same processes which foster the development of cooperation, sharing, and effective problem solving skills. Violence as portrayed in the mass media, especially on television, has long been suspected of having such a negative impact.

Beginning with a series of laboratory studies by Bandura and his colleagues in the 1960s (e.g., Bandura, Ross, and Ross, 1963), a considerable body of evidence has been gathered about the effects of televised violence on social behavior. This literature, reviewed several times (Bandura, 1973; Berkowitz, 1965; Bryan and Schwartz, 1971; Geen, 1978; Goranson, 1970), indicates that prolonged exposure to televised violence can have at least four different effects on viewers: (1) it teaches aggressive styles of conduct, (2) it lowers restraints on aggressive behavior, (3) it desensitizes and habituates people to violence, and (4) it shapes people's images of reality, upon which they base many of their actions. Evidence shows, too, that once acquired, imitative aggression tends to be fairly persistent over long periods of time. Hicks (1965), for example, tested young children for modeled aggression both immediately after observation of a simulated program of aggressive acts and again six months later. Relative to children who had not been exposed to the program, those who had been exposed made more imitative responses even after the long lapse in time. In a subsequent study, Hicks (1968) showed a retention of more than 60 percent of the model's aggressive acts two months after observation and of 40 percent as long as eight months afterward. Nor is the modeling effect of television mayhem limited to the very young. Both laboratory and controlled field studies, in which adolescents and young adults are repeatedly shown either violent or non-violent fare, disclose that exposure to filmed violence shapes the form of aggression and typically increases interpersonal aggression in everyday life (Hartman, 1969;

Leyens, Camino, Parke, and Berkowitz, 1975; Friedrich and Stein, 1973; Steuer, Applefield, and Smith, 1971). Moreover, adults who pursue a life of crime improve their criminal skills by patterning their behavior after the ingenious styles portrayed in the mass media (Hendrick, 1977; Heller and Polsky, 1975). There is no doubt, then, that observation of violence such as that depicted in movies and television contributes to aggressive styles of behavior.

These findings are cause for alarm considering the fact that most Americans, particularly children, watch at least two hours of commercial television per day and more on weekends (Liebert and Schwartzberg, 1977). In a study conducted under the auspices of the National Commission on the Causes and Prevention of Violence, for example, programs on all three major networks were monitored for one week in both 1967 and 1968. The results (Baker and Ball, 1969) revealed that some form of violence occurred in eight out of every ten programs (nine out of ten weekend children's hour programs), with an average of five violent episodes per hour. More recently, Slaby, Quarfoth, and McConnachie (1976) reported that children's television cartoons averaged 21.5 violent acts per hour. We may safely infer from these findings that a person who watches television for several hours a day is exposed to a heavy diet of violence.

It is important from the standpoint of observational learning to note that whether or not aggression that is learned through modeling will actually be performed by the subject depends upon both the perceived consequences of the model's behavior for the model and the consequences of aggression for the observer. If, for instance, an observer sees that a model is punished for aggression, this may inhibit overt aggression even though the observer has thoroughly learned the response and is fully capable of performing it. Furthermore, whether a learned response is enacted depends to some extent on whether the observer is rewarded for doing so. Both of these contingencies are clearly demonstrated in an experiment by Bandura (1965).

In that investigation, nursery school boys and girls were shown films in which a male model performed aggressive acts.

> The films began with a scene in which an adult male model walked up to an adult-size plastic Bobo doll and ordered him to clear the way. After glaring for a moment at the noncompliant antagonist the model exhibited four novel aggressive responses each accompanied by a distinctive verbalization.
>
> First, the model laid the Bobo doll on its side, sat on it, and punched it in the nose while remarking, "Pow, right in the nose, boom, boom." The model then raised the doll and pommeled it on the head with a mallet. Each response was accompanied by the verbalization "Sockeroo . . . stay down." Following the mallet aggression the model kicked the doll about the room, and these responses were interspersed with the comment, "Fly away." Finally, the model threw rubber balls at the Bobo doll, each strike punctuated with "Bang." This sequence of physically and verbally aggressive behavior was repeated twice (Bandura, 1965, pp. 590–591).

The consequences which affected the model in the film constituted the major independent variable. Specifically, one group of children viewed the film, as described above, but with the addition of a final scene in which the model was rewarded for his aggressive actions (the *model-rewarded* condition). A second group of children also observed the basic film, but with an added scene in which the model was punished because of his actions (the *model-punished* condition). And a third group of children watched the film, but observed *no consequences* affecting the model because of his actions. Next each child was escorted into an experimental room which contained an assortment of toy materials (e.g., balls, a pegboard, plastic farm animals, and miniature doll family), including a Bobo doll. The child was subsequently left alone for ten minutes and his or her behavior was periodically recorded by judges who were situated behind a one-way vision screen. As predicted, children who had seen the aggressive model punished emitted fewer imitative aggressive behaviors than those who had seen the model either rewarded or unaffected. Furthermore, boys displayed much more imitative aggression than girls. Later on, however, the experimenter reentered the room and offered each child an attractive reward (fruit juice and sticker pictures) in exchange for performing the responses previously carried out by the model. This addition of an incentive for the child obliterated the effects of the model's reward or punishment and also greatly reduced the sex differences. In other words, children of both sexes in all three conditions had learned the model's responses almost equally well. Rewards to the child encouraged the performance of these learned responses.

If we grant the possibility that media violence can have harmful effects on children under such circumstances, what steps can we take to modify and control the depiction of aggressive behavior? Bandura (1973) has put forth many recommendations. He suggests, for example, that on a personal level parents model nonaggressive forms of behavior for their children and reward nonviolent behavior. In addition, they should try to curtail their children's exposure to violence in the media by monitoring the content of such programs in advance. Although these efforts may help to reduce violence to some extent, Bandura does not assume that his recommendations would automatically eliminate the problem.

> Like so many other problems confronting man, there is no single grand design for lowering the level of destructiveness within a society. It requires both individual corrective effort and group action aimed at changing the practices of social systems. Since aggression is not an inevitable or unchangeable aspect of man but a product of aggression-promoting conditions operating within a society, man has the power to reduce his level of aggressiveness. Whether this capability is used wisely or destructively is another matter (Bandura, 1973, p. 323).

And finally, it should be at least briefly noted that the effects of television are not all bad. Indeed, there are a large number of studies conducted within the social-learning tradition demonstrating the positive effects of television on the prosocial behavior of viewers, e.g., altruistic behavior, friendliness, self-control, diminishing fears (see Rushton, 1979, for an excellent review of this literature).

Delay of Gratification: Waiting for Rewards

Another particularly interesting illustration of observational learning research involves the phenomenon of self-control. There are, in fact, many different types of self-control, but we shall consider only one in this section: delay of gratification.

Delay of gratification may be defined as the self-imposed postponement of an immediate, smaller reward in favor of a larger, more valuable reward in the future. An example would be a child who forgoes buying candy in order to save her money for a ten-speed bike. Still another example would be a student who decides not to drop out of college for a reasonably good job now, but instead persists under difficult economic circumstances in order to obtain a better paying position afterwards. It goes without saying that the ability to delay some small immediate reward for the sake of a larger more valued reward for which one must wait is a crucial factor in determining happiness in our achievement-oriented society.

The influential role of modeling variables in the development of the ability to delay gratification has been the focus of numerous investigations (Mischel, 1974). It has been shown, for example, that people who have a preference for delayed rewards grow up in homes where parents emphasize the importance of achievement and encourage self-reliance and independence. In addition, evidence indirectly suggests that the parents of such people model the delay of reward for them. A study by Bandura and Mischel (1965), now considered a classic, serves to illustrate how a willingness to delay gratification can be influenced through observational learning.

In the initial phase of the experiment, a large group of children (8 to 10 years of age) were administered a series of paired rewards. In each of these pairs they were asked to select either a small immediate reward or a larger postponed reward (e.g., a small candy bar which they could have immediately or a larger one that required waiting one week). On the basis of this pretest assessment, those children who characteristically preferred either high delay of reward or low delay of reward were selected for the succeeding phases of the experiment. The purpose of the experiment itself was to demonstrate that these initial preferences could be changed through exposure to an appropriate adult model who made choices between immediate and postponed rewards. The experiment also compared the relative magnitude and stability of changes in delay-of-reward behavior as a function of exposure to real-life and symbolic (written) modeling cues.

Children from each of the extreme groups (who predominantly displayed either delayed-reward or immediate-reward preference) were then assigned to one of three conditions. In one treatment children observed a *live* adult model who exhibited delay-of-reward choices that were counter to their own self-reward pattern. For example, if the child was initially high in delay preferences, the adult model chose immediate rewards. Conversely, children who preferred immediate gratification during the pretest period observed a model who chose delayed, larger rewards. Models also gave verbal statements about their choices. For instance, when the choice was between a plastic chess set obtainable immediately and a more expensive wooden set available a week later, the low delay-of-reward model commented: "Chess figures are chess figures. I can get much use out of the plastic ones right away (Bandura and Mischel, 1965, p. 701)." In the second condition, children were similarly exposed to a model displaying delay-of-reward behavior opposite to their own, with the exception that the modeling cues were presented in *written* form (i.e., symbolic modeling) rather than "live." In a final condition, children had no exposure to any models.

The children's own choices to have immediate or delayed gratification were tested immediately after they had observed the model (in the model's absence). Figure 7-4 shows the mean percentage of immediate-reward responses produced by the high-delay children on each of three test periods as a function of treatment conditions. It is evident that the subject's choices were strongly influenced in the direction of the choices made by the model they had observed. Specifically, children who had shown a predominantly delayed-reward pattern displayed an increased preference for immediate and less valuable rewards as a function of observing models favoring immediate gratification; conversely, while not addressed in Figure 7-4, those who had exhibited a marked preference for immediate rewards likewise increased their willingness to wait for more valuable but delayed reinforcers following exposure to models displaying high-delay behavior. Moreover, the effects of the treatment persisted when the subjects were administered a subsequent delay-of-reward measure one month later. The effects of seeing the model's written responses were similar to those of watching "live" models, although less pronounced and less generalized. Collectively, these findings are impressive when we consider the fact that observing the model actually reversed a predisposition that the child brought to the experimental setting.

Can such learning influence older people? Stumphauzer (1972) reports a similar experiment involving young prison inmates. The model in this instance was a highly respected inmate who had served more time. Exposure to this model's delay-of-reward behaviors produced a substantial increase in the subjects' delay of gratification. Furthermore, the change was found to last through at least a one-month follow-up. So it would seem that adults as well as children are subject to the influence of models. Indeed, it should be recognized that these are but a few of the many experiments that strongly support Bandura's central theoretical con-

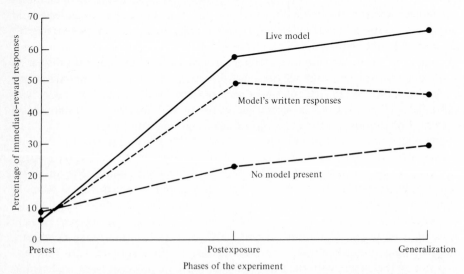

Figure 7-4 Mean percentage of immediate-reward responses by high-delay children on each of three test periods for each of three experimental conditions. (*Adapted from Bandura and Mischel, 1965, p. 702.*)

cept of observational learning. Criticisms of Bandura's theory notwithstanding, his concepts have generated and been supported by a wealth of empirical data. Let us now turn to an important application of social-learning theory: self-control.

APPLICATION: "POWER TO THE PERSON"—
SELF-DIRECTED BEHAVIOR CHANGE

People have always shown an interest in managing their own lives. Indeed, a key factor in achieving an effective and fulfilling life in our complex society is the ability to exert control over our actions. Unfortunately, however, far too many individuals seem to lack adequate self-management skills and thus are not living as effectively as they might. To illustrate, some people eat too much, others smoke or drink too much, others are painfully shy, and still others have poor study habits. Most, if not all, of these people would like to change their unwanted behavior, but they simply don't know how. Some rely on "willpower" while others seek professional help, frequently to no avail. Implicit in social-learning theory, however, is the promise of *self-control,* a scientifically based means of systematically changing one's behavior in desired directions—what Mahoney and Thoresen (1974) have called "power to the person." Looking ahead, it is entirely possible that self-control may prove to be the most far-reaching practical application of Bandura's entire theoretical position.

To appreciate this point, one need only recall Bandura's doctrine of reciprocal determinism, especially as it relates to his position on the freedom–determinism dimension. Essentially, this doctrine asserts that people shape their environments while their environments simultaneously shape their behavior. If this is so, when added to the assumptions that human beings are basically rational, that human nature is knowable through science, and that people can and do change, then the possibilities of self-control are almost limitless. Obviously we cannot control all events and all accidents, and we may be limited by a lack of talent or motivation and, occasionally, good fortune. But, within very broad limits, it is possible for each of us to increase the control we exercise over our behavior and our lives—to direct ourselves toward our chosen goals. Thus, Bandura depicts us as somewhat free to change in directions of our choice, provided that we know enough about the relationships between people and their environments.

What Is Self-Control?   Self-control as it is employed within a social-learning context is considered to be "exhibited when a person engages in a behavior whose previous probability has been less than that of alternatively available responses (Mahoney and Thoresen, 1974, p. 22)." For example, self-control is evidenced if you formerly smoked cigarettes and no longer do so, or if you ate excessively in the past and now maintain a more modest and reasonable diet. In self-control, then, the desired response (not smoking, eating moderately) often involves immediately unpleasant but ultimately desired consequences, while alternative responses (smoking, eating excessively) involve immediately pleasant but ultimately aversive results.

In accordance with Bandura's concept of reciprocal determinism, self-control does not lie exclusively within the province of either inner forces (e.g., willpower) or outer forces (e.g., external reinforcement in the Skinnerian sense). Rather, self-control is embedded in a person's reciprocal interaction with the environment in a carefully planned fashion. To see how this process works, let us examine three basic elements in self-control.

Basic Elements in Self-Control: Know Thyself, Thy Environment, and How the Two Interact.

Mahoney and Thoresen (1974) suggest that there are three basic elements in behavioral self-control, namely, *self-observation, environmental planning,* and *behavior programming.*

Self-Observation   In the self-control literature, *self-observation* can best be understood as the systematic gathering of information about the factors that influence one's actions. In effect, the individual must become a sort of personal scientist, not only monitoring her or his actions but also recording their occurrence for the purposes of feedback and evaluation. To illustrate, a person who is attempting to curtail smoking systematically counts the number of cigarettes smoked per day or during a specified period, a dieter keeps a daily weight chart over several months, or a shy person counts the number of times per day that efforts to initiate a conversation were attempted. As these examples suggest, observation of self in social-learning theory is quite unlike the kind of global self-understanding emphasized in other theoretical positions, e.g., Freud's emphasis on insight into unconscious processes, Rogers' stress on being open to one's experience, the importance in yoga and Zen of focusing one's attention on inner experience. Rather, self-observation emphasizes the detailed counting, charting, and evaluating of specific responses, either overt (observable) or covert (unobservable). The essential rationale behind self-observation is that an individual must first get a clear fix on the frequency of a target behavior (including its eliciting cues and consequences) before he or she can efficiently control it.

To illustrate, suppose that a college student has developed what are known as "poor study habits." That is, his less than meteoric academic success thus far is due not to any lack of intelligence but simply to the fact that he does not study properly. Now he wants to change these habits. To do so effectively, he must first systematically observe what those study habits really are. The act of systematically observing a particular behavior—in this case, studying or not studying—sensitizes the student to himself. In turn, the systematic recording of one's own behavior provides feedback on gradual changes that might otherwise go unnoticed. It is surprising what people can miss about their daily routines simply because they do not attend to them.

The types of self-observation devices that can be employed are limited only by the imagination of people who use them. For example, a *behavioral diary* can be kept in which a person records the occurrence of a desired behavior (e.g., assertive responses to others) along with remarks about relevant antecedent cues and consequences. Or a person can keep a *behavior graph* or *chart* of eating responses or weight fluctuations. Still another popular self-observation device is the *miniature counter*—hand-held, pocket, or wrist devices that allow an individual to keep an ongoing count of the frequency of a given behavior (e.g., number of cigarettes smoked). Any device that will help the individual systematically to observe and record the behavior targeted for change can be useful in this respect.

For the college student wishing to change his study habits, systematic observation of studying behavior is the first step in a self-control approach. He might employ a wall chart to record the actual time spent studying per day and where it was spent. In addition, he could keep a daily record in a behavioral diary of the judged effectiveness of his studying in relation to the surrounding circumstances, e.g., does he attend more to the material in the morning or evening, in his room or in the library, when seated at a desk or lying down, in brief spaced intervals of study time or longer concentrated periods?

Such detailed records are very beneficial, indeed essential, if one is to achieve desired behavior change. For in Bandura's view, what an individual is really doing with these detailed self-observation procedures is learning to understand the reciprocal person-environment relationship so central in his theory. Furthermore, self-observation is not only an assessment procedure in self-control; there is at least some research to show that behavior can change simply as a result of observing it (Kazdin, 1974). Thus, study habits may markedly improve simply as a consequence of their careful observation. But such changes tend to be short-lived unless self-observation is supplemented by other self-control strategies.

Environmental Planning   A second major self-control strategy, *environmental planning,* involves changing the environment so that either the stimuli preceding a behavior or the consequences following it are changed (Mahoney and Thoresen, 1974). Instead of facing temptation, then, the individual is enabled to avoid the tempting situation in the first place or, perhaps, to be punished for yielding to it.

Two major subtypes of environmental planning are recognized: stimulus control and prearrangement of response consequences. In *stimulus control,* the individual rearranges stimulus cues that prompt undesired responses and/or establishes cues that will elicit desired responses. The all-too-common situation of obese people attempting to reduce their overeating serves as an excellent illustration. Viewed in terms of social-learning theory, overeating is nothing more than a bad habit; it is eating without physiological hunger in response to environmental cues, and it is sustained by immediate pleasant consequences. Through careful self-observation, it is possible to identify the cues for overeating, e.g., guzzling beer and munching pretzels while watching television, eating excessively in response to emotional upset, eating because it's there (placing too much food on the plate and finishing it to avoid waste). Once these cues are accurately identified, it becomes possible to dissociate the eating response from them, e.g., one drinks diet soda or consumes nothing while watching television, develops alternative responses to emotional tension (muscle relaxation, meditation), or learns to serve smaller, more appropriate portions and to chew more thoroughly. For the doubting reader, there has been empirical research available for some time to show that people trained to detect and alter such maladaptive eating cues can significantly reduce their weight and sustain their weight loss (Stuart and Davis, 1972). And such evidence is also available to support the self-control of other undesired behaviors (e.g., smoking) through stimulus-control procedures (Mahoney and Thoresen, 1974).

The second subtype of environmental planning, *prearrangement of response consequences*, involves the systematic altering of one's environment so that pleasant consequences follow desired responses while unpleasant consequences follow undesired responses. For example, the drug *disulfiram* (more popularly known as *antabuse*) has been used in the treatment of alcoholism. Antabuse, when mixed with even small quantities of alcohol, produces severe nausea and vomiting. Thus, the recovering alcoholic, by the simple expedient of taking the drug each morning, thereby assures dire consequences for any drinking behavior in the next twenty-four hours. Such prearrangement of response consequences most certainly reduces the chances that a person will give in to the temptation of drinking during that period. Unfortunately, however, this self-control strategy isn't foolproof: one can simply fail to prearrange response consequences and thereby nullify the strategy, e.g., many alcoholics simply stop taking antabuse, wait twenty-four hours, and start drinking again (Lubetkin, Rivers, and Rosenberg, 1971). Nonetheless, in the case of many other, less powerful habitual responses, persistent use of prearranged response consequences can prove beneficial to the person.

How might environmental planning apply to the student with poor study habits? Suppose through self-observation our exemplar student discovers that he studies most effectively early in the evening in one particular area of the college library. Employing stimulus control, he might then arrange to arrive at that library area each evening at six and do nothing but study (no letter writing or daydreaming). The minute he begins to engage in behaviors incompatible with studying, he gets up and leaves the area so that he will not associate being in that area with these other behaviors. Moreover, to ensure initial maintenance of the stimulus-control program, he could begin with small blocks of study time (e.g., twenty minutes) or content goals (e.g., seven text pages) and then gradually increase them. Finally, using prearrangement of response consequences, he could decide beforehand to reward himself if he sticks to his studying regime (e.g., going out with friends, having a pizza, going to a movie) or to punish himself if he does not (e.g., deny himself the aforementioned pleasures). In effect, the student is systematically applying Bandura's doctrine of reciprocal determinism; he is purposefully shaping the environment so that it in turn will shape his behavior in desired directions.

Behavioral Programming   The third self-control strategy identified by Mahoney and Thoresen (1974), *behavioral programming,* involves systematically altering the consequences of a behavior instead of changing its eliciting cues. As such, behavioral programming seems to represent a more detailed version of what was described above as prearrangement of response consequences. The details follow.

Self-Contracts   If there is any essential difference between New Year's resolutions for behavioral change and self-control strategies, that difference lies in systematic planning—specifying the details of implementing and evaluating a self-change program. In other words, if an individual is to program her behavior effectively, she must do so systematically. An excellent vehicle toward this end is the *self-contract,* an agreement with oneself (preferably in writing) specifying the relevant target behaviors and response consequences (rewards and punishments) involved in the self-control program.

The terms for such contracts should be clear, consistent, positive, and fair. There should also be a provision for periodic review of contract terms to be sure that they are reasonable; many people initially set their self-change goals too high, which leads to unnecessary discouragement and abandonment of the self-control program. Moreover, to maximize effectiveness, at least one other person should participate. Likewise, the consequences in self-contracts should be individualized in terms of rewards and punishments. Finally, the rewards and punishments should be immediate, frequent, and attend actual performance—not verbal promises or stated intentions (Homme, C'de Baca, Cottingham, and Homme, 1968). An example of a self-contract that might be employed in altering study habits can be found in Figure 7-5.

Self-Rewards and Punishments   According to Bandura's position, if people want to structure their environments to shape their own behavior in desired directions, then they must build relevant reward and punishment contingencies into their environments. Further, since behavior is controlled by its consequences, it behooves the individual to arrange these consequences beforehand to effect desired behavior change.

If we consider the issue of rewards and punishments in a social-learning context, there is scope for both types of rewards and both types of punishments (Mahoney and Thoresen, 1974). Reward of any type (just as in Skinner's system) increases the frequency of a behavior associated with it. Two types of reward are possible: positive and negative. *Positive reward* refers to a situation in which a response is strengthened by a positive consequence, e.g., in the self-contract on study habits depicted in Figure 7-5, Jack's improved studying behavior is rewarded by pizzas, movies, Mike's praise, and Mike's shoe shining. Moreover, there is likely to be covert self-reward also operating in this situation, i.e., Jack is going to feel better about himself because he is successfully engaged in this undertaking. And who knows? His grades may also improve as a result—more overt positive reward! In contrast, *negative reward* (called negative reinforcement in Skinner's system) occurs in those situations in which a response is strengthened by the removal or avoidance of a negative (aversive) consequence, e.g., if Jack continues his good studying behavior, he avoids Mike's criticism, shining Mike's shoes, and other associated aversive consequences. Further, on a covert level, he will also probably escape or avoid negative thoughts about himself, e.g., "I'm a loser—I'm in college, I have potential, and I'm not living up to it because I can't develop good study habits."

In behavioral programming, punishment of any type decreases the frequency

SELF-CONTRACT

Date: *September 15, 1980*
Self: *Jack Wilson*
Other: *Mike Thompson*

Goal: *To improve my study habits*

Agreement

Self: *I agree to go to the designated area in the college library at 6:00* P.M. *on five evenings per week and to devote my time there exclusively to studying.*

Others: *Mike Thompson (my roommate) agrees to praise me whenever he observes me doing this and criticize me whenever I do not.*

Consequences

Provided by Self:
(if contract is kept) *If I stick to the above agreement, I will reward myself with a pizza every Wednesday evening and a movie on the weekend.*

(if contract is broken) *If I do not keep the above agreement during a particular week, I will shine both pairs of my roommate's shoes on Wednesday evening instead of having a pizza, and I will not go to a movie that weekend.*

Provided by Other:
(if contract is kept) *Mike will (1) praise me for systematically studying in the library, and (2) shine my shoes each week that I keep the contract.*

(if contract is broken) *For each week that I fail to keep the contract, Mike is authorized to (1) criticize me, (2) insist that I shine his shoes, (3) eat pizza and make derogatory remarks while watching me shine his shoes, and (4) refuse to lend me his car on the weekend.*

Signed *Jack Wilson*

October 15, 1980
Review Date   *Mike Thompson*
                   Witness

Figure 7-5 Self-contract for study habit improvement. (*Adapted from Mahoney and Thoresen, 1974.*)

of a behavior associated with it. Two types of punishment can also be distinguished: positive and negative. The term *positive punishment* applies to those situations in which a response is suppressed or weakened by the removal or avoidance of a positive (pleasant) consequence, e.g., if Jack lapses back into poor study habits in any week, he loses pizza, a movie, and access to Mike's car on the weekend. On a covert level, he will also tend to lose some of the good feelings he has been developing about himself. Finally, *negative punishment* refers to those situations in which a response is suppressed due to its subsequent negative (aversive) consequences, e.g., Jack's poor studying behavior will result in Mike's criticism, his shining Mike's shoes, and other aversive consequences. Covertly, Jack is also likely to experience negative self-thoughts as a result of his undesired behavior.

For best results in behavioral programming, whether the target behavior is study habits, smoking, overeating, drinking, shyness or whatever, it is preferable not to rely on one reward or punishment strategy alone. A combination of these various strategies in most instances constitutes the best approach, as in our illustration. For further reading on self-control procedures, the reader is referred to Mahoney and Thoresen's *Self-Control: Power to the Person* (1974), Goldfried and Merbaum's *Behavior Change Through Self-Control* (1973) and Martin and Poland's *Learning to Change: A Self-Management Approach to Adjustment* (1980).

In conclusion, it seems clear that Bandura's theory offers rich and exciting possibilities for scientifically based self-control, possibilities which, at this point, may have only begun to be realized. Indeed, because of his successful efforts to steer elements of the behavioristic movement in a cognitive direction, the firm grounding of his theory in empirical research, and the numerous actual and potential applications of his ideas, Albert Bandura's social-learning theory is a central force in personology today, one not likely to fade in importance in the foreseeable future.

SUMMARY

Albert Bandura's social-learning theory depicts psychological functioning in terms of the continuous reciprocal interaction of behavioral, cognitive, and environmental influences. This conception of human behavior casts people into a role of neither pawns controlled by external forces nor free agents able to become whatever they choose; rather, the reciprocal interplay of behavioral and environmental forces is highlighted, a fluid, dynamic process in which cognitive factors play a central role in the organization and regulation of human activity.

Bandura's major theoretical concept is that of modeling, or learning through observation. A key assumption here is that modeling influences generate learning chiefly through their informative function, a depiction of learning which clearly reflects the cognitive orientation of Bandura's theory. Furthermore, observational learning is governed by four interrelated factors—attentional, retention, motor reproduction, and motivational processes.

Bandura's treatment of reinforcement in observational learning also reflects his cognitive orientation. In social-learning theory, external reinforcement often serves two functions—information and incentive—for the individual. Additionally, Bandura emphasizes the role of vicarious reinforcement, the observation of others being reinforced, and self-reinforcement, in which people reinforce their own behavior.

Self-regulation, or how people regulate their behavior, is also an important feature of social-learning theory. In self-regulation, the major processes of self-observation, judgment, and self-evaluation are highlighted. Finally, in describing self-regulation, Bandura discusses such issues as how it is learned, how behavior is monitored through self-produced consequences, the conditions which sustain self-reward systems, why people punish themselves, and the role of self-evaluation and self-concept in the process of self-regulation.

While Bandura is often characterized as a moderate behaviorist, his basic assumptions about human nature suggest a different view of the person from that espoused by Watson, traditional stimulus-response behaviorists, and particularly B. F. Skinner. Social-learning theory reflects (1) a strong commitment to the assumptions of rationality, environmentalism, changeability, and knowability; (2) a moderate commitment to the elementalism assumption; and (3) a midrange position on the freedom–determinism, subjectivity–objectivity, and proactivity–reactivity dimensions. The homeostasis–heterostasis assumption does not apply to Bandura's position, since he conceptualizes motivation in a fashion that does not readily lend itself to this type of analysis.

Bandura's theory has been well-researched, and there is ample empirical support for it. In this chapter, research dealing with the effects of observing televised violence on children's aggressiveness and the role of observational learning in the development of self-control was presented.

In the concluding chapter section, social-learning concepts were applied to the phenomenon of self-control. Three basic elements involved in behavioral self-control were described—self-observation, environmental planning, and behavior programming—along with illustrations designed to demonstrate how self-control could operate in one's own life.

BIBLIOGRAPHY

Baker, R., and Ball, S. *Violence and the media: A staff report to the national commission on the causes and prevention of violence.* Washington D.C.: U.S. Government Printing Office, 1969.

Bandura, A. Influence of models' reinforcement contingencies on the acquisition of imitative responses. *Journal of Personality and Social Psychology,* 1965, **1**, 589–595.

Bandura, A. *Principles of behavior modification.* New York: Holt, Rinehart and Winston, 1969.

Bandura, A. *Social-learning theory.* New York: General Learning Press, 1971, 1–46.

Bandura, A. *Aggression: A social-learning analysis.* Englewood Cliffs, N.J.: Prentice-Hall, 1973.

Bandura, A. Behavior theory and the models of man. *American Psychologist,* 1974, **29**, 859–869.

Bandura, A. *Social-learning theory.* Englewood Cliffs, N.J.: Prentice-Hall, 1977.

Bandura, A. The self system in reciprocal determinism. *American Psychologist,* 1978, **33**, 344–358.

Bandura, A., and Kupers, C. The transmission of patterns of self-reinforcement through modeling. *Journal of Abnormal and Social Psychology,* 1964, **69**, 1–9.

Bandura, A., and Mischel, W. Modification of self-imposed delay of reward through exposure to live and symbolic models. *Journal of Personality and Social Psychology,* 1965, **2**, 698–705.

Bandura, A., and Perloff, B. Relative efficacy of self-monitored and externally imposed reinforcement systems. *Journal of Personality and Social Psychology,* 1967, **7,** 111–116.

Bandura, A., Ross, D., and Ross, S. Imitation of film-mediated aggressive models. *Journal of Abnormal and Social Psychology,* 1963, **66,** 3–11.

Bandura, A., and Walters, R. *Adolescent aggression.* New York: Ronald, 1959.

Bandura, A., and Walters, R. *Social learning and personality development.* New York: Holt, Rinehart and Winston, 1963.

Bavelas, J. *Personality: Current theory and research.* Monterey, Calif.: Brooks/Cole, 1978.

Berkowitz, L. The concept of aggressive drive: Some additional considerations. In L. Berkowitz (Ed.), *Advances in experimental social psychology.* Vol. 2. New York: Academic Press, 1965, pp. 301–329.

Bryan, J., and Schwartz, T. Effects of film material upon children's behavior. *Psychological Bulletin,* 1971, **75,** 50–59.

Friedrich, L., and Stein, A. Aggressive and prosocial television programs and the natural behavior of preschool children. *Monographs of the Society for Research in Child Development,* 1973, **38,** (4) Serial No. 151.

Geen, R. Some effects of observing violence upon the behavior of the observer. In B. Maher (Ed.), *Progress in experimental personality research.* Vol. 8. New York: Academic Press, 1978, pp. 49–92.

Goldfried, M., and Merbaum, M. (Eds.). *Behavior Change Through Self-Control.* New York: Holt, Rinehart and Winston, 1973.

Goranson, R. Media violence and aggressive behavior: A review of experimental research. In L. Berkowitz (Ed.), *Advances in experimental social psychology.* Vol. 5. New York: Academic Press, 1970.

Hartman, D. Influence of symbolically modeled instrumental aggression and pain cues on aggressive behavior. *Journal of Personality and Social Psychology,* 1969, **11,** 280–288.

Heller, M., and Polsky, S. *Studies in violence and television.* New York: American Broadcasting Companies, 1975.

Hendrick, G. When television is a school for criminals. *TV Guide,* January 29, 1977, pp. 4–10.

Hicks, D. Imitation and retention of film-mediated aggressive peer and adult models. *Journal of Personality and Social Psychology,* 1965, **2,** 97–100.

Hicks, D. Effects of co-observer's sanctions and adult presence on imitative aggression. *Child Development,* 1968, **39,** 303–309.

Homme, L., C'de Baca, P., Cottingham, L., & Homme, A. What behavioral engineering is. *Psychological Record,* 1968, **18,** 425–434.

Kazdin, A. Self-monitoring and behavior change. In M. Mahoney & C. Thoresen, *Self-control: Power to the person.* Monterey, Calif.: Brooks/Cole, 1974, pp. 218–246.

Kiester, E., and Cudhea, D. Albert Bandura: A very modern model. *Human Behavior,* September 1974, 27–31.

Leyens, J., Camino, L., Parke, R., and Berkowitz, L. Effects of movie violence on aggression in a field setting as a function of group dominance and cohesion. *Journal of Personality and Social Psychology,* 1975, **32,** 346–360.

Liebert, R., and Schwartzberg, N. Effects of mass media. In *Annual Review of Psychology.* Vol. 21. Palo Alto, Calif.: Annual Reviews, 1977.

Lubetkin, B., Rivers, P., & Rosenberg, C. Difficulties of disulfiram therapy with alcoholics. *Quarterly Journal of Studies on Alcohol,* 1971, **32,** 168–171.

Mahoney, M., & Thoresen, C. *Self-control: Power to the person.* Monterey, Calif.: Brooks/Cole, 1974.

Martin, R., and Poland, E. *Learning to Change: A Self-Management Approach to Adjustment*. New York: McGraw-Hill, 1980.

Mischel, W. *Personality and assessment*. New York: Wiley, 1968.

Mischel, W. Processes in delay of gratification. In L. Berkowitz (Ed.), *Advances in experimental social psychology*. Vol. 7. New York: Academic Press, 1974.

Rosenbaum, M., and Tucker, I. Competence of a model and the learning of imitation and nonimitation. *Journal of Experimental Psychology*, 1962, **63**, 183–190.

Rosenkrans, M. Imitation in children as a function of perceived similarity and vicarious reinforcement. *Journal of Personality and Social Psychology*, 1967, **7**, 307–315.

Rushton, J. Effects of prosocial television and film material on the behavior of viewers. In L. Berkowitz (Ed.), *Advances in experimental social psychology*. Vol. 12. New York: Academic Press, 1979, pp. 321–351.

Skinner, B. F. *About behaviorism*. New York: Knopf, 1974.

Skinner, B. F. Why I am not a cognitive psychologist. *Behaviorism*, 1977, **5**, 1–10.

Slaby, R., Quarfoth, G., and McConnachie, G. Television violence and its sponsors. *Journal of Communication*, 1976, **26**, 88–96.

Steuer, F., Applefield, J., and Smith, R. Televised aggression and the interpersonal aggression of preschool children. *Journal of Experimental Child Psychology*, 1971, **11**, 442–447.

Stuart, R., & Davis, B. *Slim chance in a fat world: Behavioral control of obesity*. Champaign, Ill.: Research Press, 1972.

Stumphauzer, J. Increased delay of gratification in young prison inmates through imitation of high-delay peer-models. *Journal of Personality and Social Psychology*, 1972, **21**, 10–17.

Thoresen, C., and Mahoney, M. *Behavioral self-control*. New York: Holt, Rinehart and Winston, 1973.

SUGGESTED READINGS

Bandura, A. *Psychological modeling: Conflicting theories*. Chicago: Aldine-Atherton, 1971a.

Bandura, A. Psychotherapy based upon modeling principles. In A. Bergin and S. Garfield (Eds.), *Handbook of psychotherapy and behavior change*. New York: Wiley, 1971b.

Bandura, A. Self-reinforcement: Theoretical and methodological considerations. *Behaviorism*, 1976, **4**, 135–155.

Bandura, A. Self-efficacy: Toward a unifying theory of behavioral change. *Psychological Review*, 1977, **84**, 191–215.

Parke, R. (Ed.). *Recent trends in social learning theory*. New York: Academic Press, 1972.

Watson, D., and Thorp, R. *Self-directed behavior: Self-modification for personal adjustment* (2d ed.). Belmont, Calif.: Wadsworth, 1977.

DISCUSSION QUESTIONS

1 Now that you have studied his theory, do you believe that Bandura is truly a behaviorist? In considering this question, compare and contrast Bandura's position with that of Skinner. Is contemporary behaviorism sufficiently broad to accommodate both positions?

2 Think of a particular skill that you have learned through modeling. Can you see how each

of the four component processes—attentional, retention, motor reproduction, and motivational—played a part in this observational-learning process? Be specific—give an example of each. Now repeat this exercise by citing a particular personality characteristic that you have; can it too be understood in terms of observational learning?

3 Take the same skill that you cited for the above question and show how vicarious reinforcement played a part in its acquisition. Do the same with the personality characteristic that you also cited.

4 What are some important implications of the studies of violence on television discussed in this chapter? Do you believe that watching such violence on television over the years has affected you in any way? What do you think a parent's attitude should be toward his or her child's watching violence on television?

5 Pick a specific aspect of your behavior that you would like to change—something that you're not doing now that you'd like to do (e.g., "I'd like to be able to start conversations with members of the opposite sex") or a present behavior that you'd like to curtail (e.g., "I overeat, and I wish I didn't"). Based upon the application section on self-directed behavior change, describe how you might employ the three basic elements in self-control—self-observation, environmental planning, and behavior programming—to effect the desired change in your behavior. Be specific—give concrete examples of each basic element.

GLOSSARY

Anticipated Consequence   The expectancy, based on prior experience, that performance of a certain behavior will lead to a specific outcome.

Attentional Processes   The salient cues of a model's behavior which govern which aspects of the model an observer will attend to and thus what will be acquired by the observer.

Behavioral Programming   A type of self-control strategy whereby the individual self-administers rewards for engaging in a particular behavior (e.g., a student studies three hours for an exam and rewards herself by watching her favorite television program).

Cognitive Processes   Those mental processes which provide us with the capability for both insight and foresight.

Delay of Gratification   The self-imposed postponement of an immediate reward in favor of a larger, more valuable reward in the future.

Dispositional Factor   Any factor residing within a person which is assumed to be relatively enduring and causally related to overt behavior (e.g., instinct, trait, need).

External Reinforcement   A reinforcing environmental stimulus that immediately follows the occurrence of a particular behavior (e.g., social approval, money, attention).

Imaginal Representation   Mental image a person has formed from a previously observed event or modeled activity. For Bandura, imagery enables the observer to retain the model's behavior and convert it into subsequent action, e.g., the person can "see" the image of his or her tennis teacher demonstrating how to serve a month ago.

Modeling   Form of learning in which one learns by watching someone (the model) perform the desired or correct response (see also *observational learning*).

Motivational Processes   A component of observational learning having to do with reinforcement variables which exert selective control over the types of modeling cues to which a person is likely to attend; such variables influence the degree to which a person tries to enact behaviors based on observational learning.

Motor Reproduction Processes   A component involved in observational learning which consists of translating symbolically coded memories of modeled behavior into appropriate action. For Bandura, "silent rehearsal" of the model's behavior is of definite help in perfecting motor skills such as driving a car.

Observational Learning   The process through which the behavior of one person, an observer, changes as a function of being exposed to the behavior of another, the model (also called imitative learning).

Reciprocal Determinism   Term used by Bandura to reflect the notion that the causes of human behavior are to be understood in terms of the continuous reciprocal interaction of behavioral, cognitive, and environmental influences.

Retention Processes   A component of observational learning having to do with long-term memory of what a model did. Bandura maintains that one cannot be much affected by observational learning if one has no memory of it.

Self-Contract   An agreement made with oneself, usually stated in writing, specifying target behaviors and response consequences in a self-control program.

Self-Regulation   The human being's capacity to exert influence over his or her own behavior.

Self-Reinforcement   The process whereby individuals improve and maintain their own behavior by giving themselves rewards over which they have some control.

Situational Factor   Any factor in the environment which has an influence on an individual's behavior (e.g., membership in a reference group).

Social-Learning Theory   A theory of personality formulated by Bandura which emphasizes that behavior occurs as a result of a complex interplay between inner, or cognitive, processes and environmental influences.

Verbal Coding   An internal representational process whereby a person silently rehearses a sequence of modeled activities to be performed at a later time.

Vicarious Reinforcement   Any change in a person's behavior due to observing a model being reinforced or punished for the same behavior. For instance, a child refrains from crying as a result of seeing his sister scolded by his mother for crying.

Gordon W. Allport

Gordon Allport: A Trait Theory of Personality

No two people are completely alike. Thus, no two people react identically to the same psychological situation or stimulus. Perhaps this fact is the most compelling and fundamental issue confronting the student of personality. Indeed, every personality theory, in one way or another, must deal with the enigma of individual differences if it is to remain a viable commodity in the marketplace of psychological science. Gordon Allport is a personologist who regards the explanation of an individual's uniqueness as the paramount goal of psychology. Allport's emphasis on the uniqueness of the person is, however, only one of the features of his position. In addition, there is a strong focus on the ways in which internal cognitive and motivational processes influence and cause behavior.

Allport's theory represents a blend of humanistic and personalistic approaches to the study of human behavior. It is humanistic in its attempts to recognize all aspects of the human being, including the potential for growth, transcendence, and self-realization. It is personalistic in that its objective is to understand and predict the development of the real individual person (Allport, 1968b). Further, as a theoretician, Allport may be broadly described as an eclectic because he incorporates insights from philosophy, religion, literature, and sociology, blending such ideas into an understanding of the uniqueness and complexity of personality. In fact, Allport's belief that each person's behavior derives from a particular configuration of personal *traits* is the trademark of his orientation to personology.

BIOGRAPHICAL SKETCH

Gordon Willard Allport, the youngest of four brothers, was born in Montezuma, Indiana, in 1897. His father, a country doctor, moved the family to Ohio shortly after Gordon's birth, and the youngest Allport received his early education in the Cleveland public schools. He characterized his family life as marked by trust and affection, along with a strong emphasis on the Protestant work ethic:

> My mother had been a school teacher and brought to her sons an eager sense of philosophical questioning and the importance of searching for ultimate religious

answers. Since my father lacked adequate hospital facilities for his patients, our household for several years included both patients and nurses. Tending office, washing bottles, and dealing with patients were important aspects of my early training . . . Dad was no believer in vacations. He followed rather his own rule of life, which he expressed as follows: "If every person worked as hard as he could and took only the minimum financial return required by his family's needs, then there would be just enough wealth to go around." Thus it was hard work tempered by trust and affection that marked the home environment (Allport, 1967, pp. 4–5).

Allport was scholarly from an early age; he described himself as a social isolate who was skilled with words but poor at sports. One of his classmates, in a show of contempt, once said: "Aw, that guy swallowed a dictionary" (1968a, p. 378). Although he finished second highest academically in his high school graduating class of one hundred students, Allport insisted that he was "a good routine student, but definitely uninspired . . . about anything beyond the usual adolescent concerns" (Allport, 1968a, p. 379). Allport pursued undergraduate study at Harvard University at the urging of his older brother Floyd, who was then a graduate student in psychology at the same university. Going to college was a real intellectual awakening for the small town boy from the Midwest:

Almost overnight my world was remade. My basic moral values, to be sure, had been fashioned at home. What was new was the horizon of intellect and culture I was now invited to explore. . . . First and foremost was the pervading sense of high standards. . . . At the first hour examinations I received an array of D's and C's. Profoundly shattered, I stiffened my efforts and ended the year with A's (Allport, 1967, p. 5).

Although he took several psychology courses at Harvard, Allport majored in economics and philosophy. He also participated in a number of volunteer service projects during his undergraduate years. After receiving his B.A. degree in 1919, he accepted an offer to teach sociology and English at Robert College, Istanbul, Turkey. The following year he won a fellowship for graduate study in psychology at Harvard. Before returning to the United States, however, he decided to visit another brother who was working in Vienna at the time. While there, he wrote a letter to Sigmund Freud announcing that he was in Vienna and implying that Freud would no doubt be glad to meet him.

On the day of their meeting, Freud ushered Allport into his inner office and sat down, saying nothing, and waited for Allport to speak. The silence grew longer and Allport became uncomfortable under the intense, steady gaze of the world-famous psychoanalyst. Finally, desperate for something to say, Allport blurted out an incident he had witnessed on the streetcar ride to Freud's home. He reported that he had seen a small boy who displayed an obvious fear of dirt. Throughout the ride the boy complained to his mother: "I don't want to sit there . . . don't let that dirty man sit beside me" (Allport, 1968a, p. 383). The mother appeared to Allport to be domineering, extremely neat, and "well-starched," and he assumed that Freud would readily see the point of the story, namely, that the boy's abhorrence of dirt was a result of his mother's obsession with cleanliness. Freud, however, observing the prim and proper young man sitting across from him, kindly remarked: "And was that little boy you?" (Allport, 1968a, p. 383). Allport was flabbergasted but managed to change the subject. The incident left a deep impression on him, however; it made him suspicious of the deep probing into the unconscious that was the basis of psychoanalysis. He also came away from the experience convinced that psychologists might understand people better if they devoted more attention to their manifest, conscious motives rather than probing into their unconscious natures.

Allport received his Ph.D. in psychology in 1922, at the age of 24. His thesis research focused on an examination of the traits of personality and was the first such study done anywhere in the United States. During the next two years, supported by a Sheldon Traveling Fellowship, Allport studied at the universities of Berlin and Hamburg in Germany and Cambridge in England. Returning from Europe, he served as an instructor for two years in Harvard's Department of Social Ethics. There he offered what was probably the first course ever given in personality in the United States. Allport married Ada Lufkin Gould in 1925. They had one child, Robert.

In 1926 Allport accepted the position of assistant professor of psychology at Dartmouth College, where he stayed until 1930. In that year, he was invited by Harvard to return at the same rank in the Department of Social Relations. He was promoted to Professor of Psychology in 1942 and held this position until his death on October 9, 1967. During his long and distinguished career at Harvard, Allport influenced several generations of students through his popular undergraduate course. He also came to be considered to be the "dean of American personality study."

Allport actively participated in numerous professional and honorary organizations. During World War II he served on the Emergency Committee in Psychology, an organization specializing in problems of civilian morale and rumor. He was a representative of the American Psychological Association (APA) on both the National and Social Science Research Council, and a director of the National Commission for the United Nations Educational, Scientific, and Cultural Organization. Between 1937 and 1949, Allport was editor of the *Journal of Abnormal and Social Psychology*. He was president of the APA in 1937, of the Eastern Psychological Association in 1943, and of the Society for the Psychological Study of Social Issues in 1944. He was a recipient of the Gold Medal from the American Psychological Foundation in 1963 and received the APA's Distinguished Scientific Contribution Award in 1964, which had the following citation:

> For reminding us that man is neither a beast nor a statistic, except as we choose to regard him so, and that the human personality finds its greatest measure in the reaches of time. This is to say that, while life may have its crude beginnings, it has its noble endings too, and there is a line that leads from one to the other—a line that graphically portrays the character of the individual, and of mankind as well. This is what he taught his students. He taught them also to respect scholarship and to abhor the massive ignorance of the fortuitous researcher. And because so many of them learned their lessons well, the name of Gordon Allport has become a hallmark of the well-turned curriculum vitae (*American Psychologist,* 1964, p. 942).

Allport was a prolific writer. Among his widely known publications are *Personality: A Psychological Interpretation* (1937); *The Individual and His Religion* (1950); *Becoming: Basic Considerations for a Psychology of Personality* (1955); *Personality and Social Encounter* (1960); *Pattern and Growth in Personality* (1961); and *Letters from Jenny* (1965). He also coauthored two widely used personality tests; *The A-S Reaction Study* (with F. H. Allport, 1928) and *A Study of Values* (with P. E. Vernon, 1931; revised with G. Lindzey in 1951 and again in 1960). A complete list of his writings may be found in *The Person in Psychology* (Allport, 1968a). His autobiography is presented in Volume 5 of *A History of Psychology in Autobiography* (1967, pp. 3–25).

PERSONALITY AS A "SOMETHING"

The term "personality" is not easily defined. In fact, its precise meaning varies considerably from theory to theory. According to some theorists (e.g., Skinner), personality as such does not even exist—it is really a superfluous term that some people unfortunately find useful in describing behavior. For other theorists (e.g., Freud), personality includes deep, dark recesses of the mind that very few people, including the subject, even know about. Allport was quite dissatisfied with this state of affairs and expended a great deal of energy in constructing his own definition of personality. If he was going to spend a professional lifetime studying the functioning of personality, he first wanted to at least have a preliminary idea of what it is!

In his first book, *Personality: A Psychological Interpretation,* Allport devoted an entire chapter to a review of the many different notions of personality offered by theologians, philosophers, poets, sociologists, and psychologists, and concluded that an adequate synthesis of existing definitions might be expressed in the phrase "what a man really is" (1937, p. 48). What this definition possesses in the way of comprehensiveness it certainly lacks in precision. Recognizing this, Allport went a step further and asserted that "personality is something and does something. . . . It is what lies behind specific acts and within the individual" (1937, p. 48). Eschewing the notion of personality as merely a hypothetical entity, then, Allport argued that it definitely is an existing "something" within the person. At least in Allport's system, personality is alive, well, and functioning.

The question remains, however, "What is the nature of this *something?*" Allport (1937) answered by offering a precise definition of personality which he subsequently modified slightly to read as follows: "Personality is the dynamic organization within the individual of those psychophysical systems that determine his characteristic behavior and thought" (1961, p. 28). What does all this mean? First, the phrase "dynamic organization" suggests that human behavior is constantly evolving and changing; a person is not a static entity in Allport's theory, although there is an underlying mental system that integrates and organizes the various elements of personality. As Allport used the phrase, "psychophysical systems" means that both "mind" and "body" elements must be considered when describing and studying personality. Personality, then, reflects all of what a human being is. The inclusion of the term "determine" is a logical consequence of Allport's psychophysical orientation. Basically, the implication is that personality is made up of "determining tendencies" which, when aroused by appropriate stimuli, give rise to actions through which the individual's true nature is revealed. (These "determining tendencies"—traits in Allport's theory—will subsequently be discussed at length.) The word "characteristic" in Allport's definition simply highlights the paramount importance that he attached to individual uniqueness. Each person is truly an entity unto herself or himself in this personological system. Finally, the phrase "behavior and thought" is a blanket designed to cover everything the person does. Allport believed that personality may express itself in some way in virtually all observable human actions.

In arriving at his conceptual definition, Allport noted that the terms *character* and *temperament* have often been used as synonyms for personality. This seems particularly true when considering the layman's use of these terms. Allport explains how each may be readily distinguished from the concept of personality. The word "character" traditionally connotes a moral standard or value system against which the individual's actions are evaluated. For example, whenever another person is considered of "good character," a personal judgment as to the social and/or ethical desirability of his or her personal qualities is really the topic. Character thus is actually an ethical concept. Or, as Allport (1961) put it, character is personality *evaluated;* personality is character *devaluated.* Character, then, should not be considered as some special region contained within personality.

Temperament, by contrast, is the "raw material"—along with intelligence and physique—out of which personality is fashioned. Allport considered the term particularly useful in referring to the characteristic and largely hereditary aspects of a person's emotional nature, e.g., susceptibility to emotional stimulation, customary strength and speed of response, prevailing mood state, fluctuation and intensity of moods (Allport, 1961). Representing one aspect of an individual's genetic endowment, temperament limits the development of personality. Temperamentally speaking, you certainly "can't make a silk purse out of a sow's ear" in Allport's system. Like any good definition of personality, then, Allport's concept states clearly both what it *is* and what it *is not.*

WHAT A PERSONALITY THEORY SHOULD BE

Before considering those concepts that are most uniquely identified with Allport's theory, it will be instructive to examine his five requirements for an adequate personality theory. Specifically, Allport (1960) insisted that:

1 *A truly adequate theory of human behavior must regard the human personality as centered in the organism.* This raises the question "Where else would it be?" In fact, other theorists have in effect placed personality outside the person by equating it with social roles or interpersonal relationships. Concerning the former, *role theory,* as proposed by sociologists and anthropologists, explains personality as nothing more than one's membership in a group and the situationally defined roles one is expected to adopt. According to this approach, any given person, say, Adam, for example, is known only by the roles he enacts—Adam is only a college student, son, consumer, church attender, part-time drug pusher, and so on. Allport was quick to chide such theorists, arguing that these situational factors should not obscure the more central idea that Adam's traits, values, and other internal factors account for his conduct in everyday life. If Adam is to be truly understood, he must be considered as a self-contained unit rather than as the social impression he makes on others, his reputation, or how people react to him.

   2   *A complete theory of personality regards the organism as replete, not empty.* Readers who have been converted to Skinner's view of the human being by the previous chapter would find Allport's second requirement patently absurd. Representing the antithesis of Skinner's position, Allport argued that we must assume a "well-stocked" organism, not an empty one, if we are to advance in personality theorizing. Whereas Skinner believes environmental events shape the "empty" organism, Allport believes personality is something that is located within the organism: "Any theory of personality pretending adequacy must be dynamic and, to be dynamic, must assume a well-stocked organism" (Allport, 1960, p. 26). To explain Adam's behavior, then, the personologist must postulate some set of dispositions existing within him. In other words, one must understand what's happening psychologically within Adam in order to comprehend his observable behavior. Most major personality theories today, Allport's included, represent highly systematic attempts to accomplish such a person-centered objective.

   3   *An adequate theory must regard motivation as normally a fact of present structure and function, not simply as an outgrowth of earlier forces or experience.* Motivationally speaking, Adam is not a prisoner of his past. He does not forever drag the chains of his early childhood experiences to rattle through his every adult action. Instead, Allport believed that an adequate personality theory should portray Adam as he is now, as a 20-year-old college student, and interpret his motivation accordingly. Suppose, for example, that Adam is a psychology major contemplating clinical psychology as a career. Some Freudians would have us believe that this vocational preference is due to Adam's frustrated and now repressed childhood curiosity about sex. He is unconsciously motivated to pursue clinical psychology so that he can spend a professional lifetime probing the intimate and lurid details of patients' sex lives.

   In Allport's scheme of things, this is, in a word, nonsense. While Allport would admit that childhood experiences certainly contribute to the direction of personal development, he also would argue that a psychologically healthy Adam has a vocational preference understandable in terms of more contemporary and adult motives, e.g., a desire to help disturbed individuals therapeutically, a keen interest in simply understanding human behavior for its own sake, or an effort to fulfill oneself as a person. Allport elaborated this requirement considerably in his theoretical concept of *functional autonomy* (to be discussed subsequently). Basically Allport believed that the confusion between the historical roots of motives and the contemporary functioning of motives is the most stultifying of all misconceptions that mar current personality theories. The motives of people must be understood as they are now rather than as they were in the historical past. Thus, an adequate theory must allow for the forward thrust or futuristic bent of personal motives that normally characterizes healthy adults.

   4   *In order for a theory to be adequate it must employ units of analysis capable of living synthesis.* This requirement stipulates that personality must somehow be broken down into definable units (segments, aspects, factors) for study, but that the units themselves must be of such a nature as to permit their reconstruction, capturing that holistic quality of "dynamic organization" which is at the heart of Allport's definition of personality. For example, to account for the personality of Humpty Dumpty, it would indeed be necessary for a theory first to break him into pieces. However, an adequate personality theory would be able to put Humpty Dumpty together again, dynamically—into a "living synthesis."

But what of the "pieces"—what is their nature? Allport rejected units of analysis such as attitudes, values, needs, and drives because they fail to reconstruct, when synthesized, the vital and intrinsic nature of personality organization within the individual. Instead, Allport remained true to his own definition of personality involving an enduring psychophysical organization *unique* to each person. Consequently, he suggested that theorists have no choice but to rely upon units of analysis which are *peculiar to the individual*—specifically, a system of generalized action tendencies or traits. Adam, then, can be best understood by studying the individual trait system representing the unique, dynamic pattern of organization characterizing his life.

  5   Finally, *a theory must allow adequately for, but not rely exclusively upon, the phenomenon of self-consciousness.* To portray Adam accurately, an adequate personality theory must recognize that he is consciously aware of himself. In fact, this self-consciousness is the most concrete evidence Adam has of his personal identity. Further, Adam's awareness of himself, at least to some extent, makes him an active agent in the shaping of his destiny. To the extent that he knows the ship, he can navigate it through various seas. Finally, it is precisely this aspect of personality, self-consciousness, that most clearly separates humans from other species. Humans are conscious of their own consciousness; lower organisms are not. A truly human theory of personality, while not preoccupied by this fact, recognizes it fully.

CONCEPT OF TRAIT

This chapter started with the assertion that no two people are completely alike. Any one person behaves in a consistent and different fashion from all others. Allport's explanation for this is found in his concept of *trait*, which he regarded as the most valid "unit of analysis" for representing what people are like and how they differ from one another behaviorally.

What is a trait of personality? Allport begins by defining it as a "neuropsychic structure having the capacity to render many stimuli functionally equivalent, and to initiate and guide equivalent (meaningfully consistent) forms of adaptive and expressive behavior (1961, p. 347)." In simpler terms, *a trait is a predisposition to respond in an equivalent manner to various kinds of stimuli.* Traits, in effect, are psychological entities that render many stimuli as well as many reponses equivalent. Many stimuli may evoke the same response, or many responses (perceptions, interpretations, feelings, actions) have the same functional meaning in terms of the trait. To illustrate this concept, Allport (1961) cites the case of a fictitious Mr. McCarley whose leading trait is a "fear of communism." For him, this trait renders equivalent the social stimuli of Russians, black and Jewish neighbors, liberals, most college professors, peace organizations, the United Nations, and so forth. All are perceived and labeled as communists. In addition, such a trait triggers hostile response sequences which are equivalent in their capacity to reduce the perceived threat of communism. Mr. McCarley might support nuclear war against Russians, write hostile letters to the local newspaper about blacks, vote for extreme right-wing political candidates and policies, join the Ku Klux Klan or John Birch Society, criticize the UN, and/or participate in any one of a number of other equivalent hostile responses. Figure 8-1 shows schematically the range of possibilities.

Needless to say, an individual may sincerely engage in a number of these activities without necessarily possessing undue hostility or fear of communism. Additionally, everyone who votes for right-wing candidates or opposes the UN does not necessarily fall in the same personological category. However, this example shows that one's traits are organized and expressed on the basis of perceived similarities. That is, many stimulus situations, because of their perceived equivalence, arouse a certain trait which then initiates a variety of behavioral responses which are equivalent in giving expression to the trait. It is this conception of equivalence of stimuli and responses, united and mediated by a trait, that constitutes Allport's theory of personality organization. In essence, traits serve to integrate theoretically what would otherwise be dissimilar stimuli and responses.

According to Allport, traits are not linked to a small number of specific stimuli or responses; rather, they are relatively generalized and enduring. By uniting responses to numerous stimuli, traits produce fairly broad consistencies in behavior. A trait is what accounts for the more permanent, enduring, transsituational features of our behavior. It is a vital ingredient of our "personality structure." At the same time, traits may also be focal in nature. For example, the trait of dominance may be aroused only when the individual is in the presence of specific others, his or her children, spouse, or intimate acquaintances. In each case he or she immediately becomes ascendant. However, the trait of dominance is not activated in the event that the individual discovers a $10 bill on the floor of a neighbor's home. Such a stimulus would arouse the trait of honesty (or dishonesty as the case may be). It would not arouse dominance. Allport thus admits that personality traits are

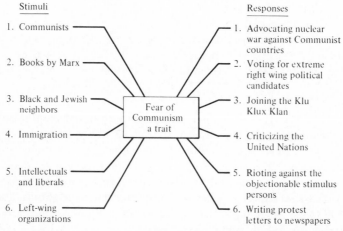

Figure 8-1 The generality of a trait as determined by equivalence of stimuli that arouse it and by equivalence of responses that it produces. (*Adapted from Allport, 1961, p. 322.*)

embedded within social situations, adding, "any theory that regards personality as stable, fixed, invariable is wrong" (1961, p. 175). As an analogy, water can have the shape and texture of a liquid, a solid (ice), or some substance along the continuum (snow, hail, sleet). It is the degree of environmental warmth that determines its physical form.

It should be emphasized, however, that traits do not lie dormant waiting to be aroused by external stimuli. In fact, the individual may actively seek stimulus situations that encourage the expression of her traits. A person with a strong disposition toward sociability not only responds in a charming manner when in a group of people but also seeks out company when she is alone. In other words, the individual is not a passive "reactor" to the situation, as B. F. Skinner might suggest; rather, the situations in which she is likely to find herself are often those in which she has actively placed herself. Specifically, Allport suggests that traits and the situation interact to produce behavior. The two components are functionally interdependent. Like Bandura (Chapter 7), then, Allport also recognizes that behavior is regulated by interactions between personal dispositions and situational variables.

The "Traits" of Traits

In Allport's system, traits themselves may be said to have "traits" or defining characteristics. Shortly before his death, Allport (1966) published an article entitled "Traits Revisited" in which he summarized all that he had learned in response to the question "What is a trait of personality?" In this article, he proposed that eight basic criteria define a personality trait:

1 *A trait has more than nominal existence.* Personality traits are not fictions; they are a very real and vital part of one's existence. Every person possesses inside his or her skin these "generalized action tendencies"—it is the psychologist's task to discover what they are. Aside from "fear of communism," other readily defined traits would be such things as "fear of capitalism," "introversion," "extraversion," "aggressiveness," "meekness," "honesty," "dishonesty," and a whole possible host of others. Allport's main point here is that these personal characteristics are *real*—they actually exist in people and are not simply theoretical make-believe.

2 *A trait is more generalized than a habit.* Traits tend to cut across situations and thereby account for the more permanent, enduring, and general features of our behavior. Habits, while enduring, refer to more narrow and limited types of tendencies and are thus less generalized in terms of the situations which may arouse them or the responses which they evoke. For example, a child learning to brush her teeth may continue to do so for some time only because she is encouraged by her parents. This is a habit. However, with the passing of years, brushing one's teeth not only becomes habitual but is woven into a broader system of habits, viz., a *trait* of personal cleanliness. To some extent, then, a trait is the product of integrating numerous specific habits that serve the same adaptive function for the person. Traits embrace two or more interdependent habits.

3 *A trait is dynamic or at least determinative in behavior.* Traits underlie behavior—they *cause* behavior. In Allport's system, traits do not lie dormant waiting to be aroused by external stimuli. Rather, they motivate one to seek

stimulus situations in which to manifest one's traits. For example, a college student with a strong "sociability" trait does not just sit around and wait to go to parties to be sociable. She actively seeks out parties so that she can express this sociability trait. Traits, then, guide and direct an individual's actions. Because traits can, in effect, cause behavior, they can be considered "derived motives."

4 *A trait's existence may be established empirically.* If they're real, psychologists ought to be able to prove that they are. While traits as such can never be directly observed (how can you "see" sociability?), Allport believed that they could be verified scientifically. Specifically, evidence for the existence of traits may be derived from observations of repeated actions by the subject, case histories or biographies, or statistical techniques that determine the degree of coherence among separate responses. Some interesting approaches to establishing a trait's existence empirically will be discussed in the "Empirical Validation" section of this chapter.

5 *A trait is only relatively independent of other traits.* To paraphrase a well-known saying, "No trait is an island." Traits overlap. There is no rigid boundary separating one trait from another. Rather, the personality is comprised of a network of overlapping traits only *relatively* independent of one another. To illustrate, Allport (1960) cites a study in which it was found that the traits of insight and humor are highly correlated with one another. Clearly, these are separate traits, but they nonetheless are somehow related. While it is scientifically impossible to draw causal conclusions from such correlational data, one might speculate that if a person possessed a high degree of insight, he or she would undoubtedly perceive the ludicrous aspects of the human condition and be led to develop a well-rounded sense of humor. Much more likely from Allport's viewpoint, however, is that traits overlap primarily because of the organism's tendency to react to events in an integrated fashion.

6 *A trait is not synonymous with moral or social judgment.* Despite the fact that many traits (e.g., sincerity, loyalty, greed) are subject to conventional social judgment, they still represent true traits of personality. Ideally, one would first discover traits as they exist in a given individual and then seek neutral, devalued words to identify them. In Allport's opinion, personologists should be studying *personality*, not *character*.

7 *A trait may be viewed in light of either the personality that contains it or its distribution in the population at large.* Take autoeroticism as an illustration. Like any other trait, it has both *unique* and *universal* aspects. When viewed uniquely, autoeroticism could be studied in terms of the role it plays in a given individual's personality. Conversely, this trait could be studied "universally" by constructing a reliable and valid "autoeroticism scale" and determining how people differ on it. This latter approach is called "differential psychology," or the psychology of individual differences.

8 *Acts or even habits that are inconsistent with a trait are not proof of the nonexistence of the trait.* As an illustration, consider Eve Smith who is characteristically neat in terms of her personal appearance; with never a hair out of place and her attire impeccable, she indubitably possesses the trait of neatness. But one would never know this by examining her desk, room, or car. Her personal belongings in each case are carelessly arranged, cluttered, and downright sloppy. Why the apparent contradiction? From an Allportian frame of reference, there are three possible explanations. First, not everyone will show the same degree of integration in respect to a given trait—what is a major trait for one person may either be a minor or nonexistent trait for another person. Here, Eve's trait of neatness is less major than it might be for someone else, in terms of its pervasiveness. In Eve's case, neatness may be restricted to her person. Second, the same individual may possess contradictory traits, e.g., Eve is *neat* with respect to her personal appearance and *slovenly* with regard to her belongings. Usually, however, contradictory traits are of unequal strength; considered as a whole, Eve should be able to be characterized as more neat than slovenly. Third, there are instances where a person's actions are simply unrelated to the trait; rather, they are products of stimulus situations or momentary attitudes. If Eve is running to catch a plane, for example, she may not care whether her hair blows all over the place or her clothing becomes disheveled in the process. Therefore, to observe that not all Eve's actions are consistent with an underlying disposition of neatness is no proof that the disposition does not exist within her.

Types of Traits: Pervasiveness within a Personality

As has been indicated, traits are determining tendencies, or predispositions to respond consistently over time and across situations. Even Eve Smith's rather circumscribed trait of neatness in her personal appearance should be manifested practically any time she "personally appears" any place. But must a person who has a certain trait *always* exhibit it? If he or she does not, how are the varying degrees of a trait's generality judged?

Facing this issue, Allport proposed that traits may be classified into the following threefold and somewhat overlapping category system according to the degree to which they are pervasive and dominant in a person's life:

1 Cardinal Traits   If a trait is extremely pervasive, so pervasive that almost all a person's activities can be traced to its influence, it is a *cardinal trait* in Allport's system. This highly generalized disposition cannot remain hidden unless, of course, it happens to be something like seclusiveness, in which case its possessor might become a hermit, whose traits were known to no one. In other instances, however, this kind of master sentiment or ruling passion makes its possessor famous or infamous. Allport insisted that very few people possess a cardinal trait.

The meaning of a cardinal trait may be readily grasped by considering the many trait adjectives derived from historical and fictional characters, e.g., when someone is referred to as being a chauvinist, Machiavellian, Don Juan, Scrooge, or Joan of Arc. Or consider that Albert Schweitzer was said to have had one cardinal disposition in his life—"reverence for every living organism." Similarly, Leo Tolstoy was said to have been endowed with a burning passion for the "oversimplification of life." Finally, most of Sigmund Freud's adult life could be said to be characterized by a consuming "interest in psychology," in uncovering the nature of man's deepest motivations. The theme of the lives of these individuals reveals the all-pervasive quality of cardinal traits.

2 Central Traits   Less pervasive but still quite generalized characteristics of the individual are what Allport termed *central traits*—the so-called building blocks of personality. These traits might best be regarded as those attributes which would be stressed in writing a carefully defined letter of recommendation, e.g., outgoing, sentimental, attentive, sociable, or vivacious. Specifically, central traits are those tendencies that a person often expresses that people around him can readily discern. In a rather hypothetical manner, Allport asked: "How many central traits does the average individual possess?" He approached this question by asking ninety-three students "to think of some one individual of your own sex whom you know well" and "to describe him or her by writing words, phrases, or sentences that express fairly well what seem to you to be the essential characteristics of this person" (1961, p. 366). Ninety percent of the students listed between three and ten essential characteristics: the average number listed was 7.2. Allport thus concluded that the number of central dispositions by which a personality can be described is surprisingly small, perhaps no more than five to ten. Sometimes from the vantage point of the person himself, his central traits may be perceived as very few indeed. H. G. Wells once commented that there were only two dominant themes in his life: interest in an ordered world society and sex. This example should shed light on the meaning of central, as opposed to cardinal, traits (and on H. G. Wells).

   3 Secondary Traits   Dispositions which are less conspicuous, less generalized, less consistent, and thus less relevant to the definition of a personality are called *secondary traits*. Food preferences, specific attitudes, and other situationally determined characteristics of the person would be classified under this rubric. Consider, for instance, a person whose central traits are dominance and assertiveness, which he manifests in practically every interpersonal encounter. This person might also have as a secondary trait submissiveness, which he displays only in relation to police who dutifully stop him for speeding, running red lights, and ignoring stop signs ("Yes, officer," "No, officer," "You're right, officer," etc.). According to Allport, an individual possesses a great many more of these than of the other trait types; hence, an individual must be known quite intimately in order to discern these secondary traits.

Common versus Individual Traits

Allport also distinguished between common and individual traits. The former, *common traits* (also called *dimensional* or *nomothetic* traits) includes any generalized disposition to which most people within a given culture can be reasonably compared. We might say, for example, that some people are more assertive than others or that some people are more polite than others. The logic for assuming the existence of common traits is that members of a given culture are subject to similar evolutionary and social influences; therefore, they develop roughly comparable modes of adjustment. Examples include proficiency in the use of language, political and/or social attitudes, value orientations, anxiety, and conformity. The majority of people within our culture could be measurably compared with one another on these common dimensions.

   According to Allport, what usually (but not invariably) results from such trait comparisons among individuals is a normal distribution curve. That is, when common trait test scores are plotted on a graph, they approximate a bell-shaped curve, with the bulk of cases piling up as average scores in the middle and the rest

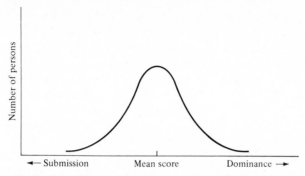

Number of persons

← Submission   Mean score   Dominance →

Figure 8-2 The distribution of scores based on a test measuring the dominance–submission trait continuum.

tapering off toward the extremes. Figure 8-2 illustrates this situation for the common trait "dominance-submission." The dimensionality of common traits, then, allows the personologist to compare one individual with another along meaningful psychological dimensions (as one might for common physical characteristics such as height and weight).

While regarding such cross-comparisons as legitimate and useful, Allport (1968a) also believed that traits never occur in any two people in exactly the same way. The psychological pervasiveness and expression of dominance for Linda is unique to her. To this extent, Linda's dominance cannot really be compared with Susan's. *Individual trait* (also called *personal dispositions* or *morphological traits*), then, designate those characteristics peculiar to the individual which do not permit comparisons among individuals. It is these "genuine and neuropsychic units that guide, direct, and motivate specific acts of adjustment" (1968a, p. 3). Always operating in unique ways within each person, this category of traits most accurately pinpoints the personality structure of any given individual, the organized focuses of his or her life. For Allport, then, the true personality surfaces only when individual traits are examined, using such resources as a person's case history, diary, letters, and other such personal documents. Consequently, the common trait of dominance can be profitably studied by comparing Linda, Susan, and everybody else on some meaningful yardstick (e.g., a dominance test or scale). But dominance as an individual trait can only be understood by studying its unique functioning in Linda, in Susan, and in everyone else considered one at a time, which, for Allport, was the only real way to understand individual personalities.

THE PROPRIUM: A REAL SELF?

No personologist, least of all Allport, believes that personality is a mere bundle of unrelated traits. Personality embodies a unity, consistency, and integration of traits. It is therefore reasonable to suppose that there is an overall principle that unifies traits, attitudes, values, motives, and experiences. For Allport, the problem of identifying and describing the nature of personality integration requires an all-inclusive construct such as the self, ego, or style of life. Formerly, in less scientific days, people called it a soul. But all these terms had accumulated too many ambiguous connotations and semantic ambiguities for Allport's taste. So he introduced a new term—the *proprium.*

Allport's humanistic orientation to personality is nowhere more clearly revealed than in his concept of proprium, defined as "the self-as-known—that which is experienced as warm and central, as of importance" (1968a, p. 4) It's the "me" part of subjective experience. It's selfhood.

For Allport, the proprium represents the positive, creative, growth-seeking, and forward-moving quality of human nature. This point is highly significant, for this view of the person represented a radical departure from the deterministic portrait painted by many psychoanalysts or the stimulus-response robot image promulgated by many behaviorists. The influence of the true humanists in psychology—e.g., Abraham Maslow—had yet to be felt when Allport conceived his theory, yet much that he wrote about selfhood has a contemporary humanist-Maslowian ring to it. This important turn in the development of personality theory will be more fully appreciated when the reader proceeds to Chapters 10 and 11 (Maslow and Rogers).

While Allport conceived of the proprium as including all aspects of personality that contribute to a sense of inward unity, as marking the consistency associated with the individual's traits, intentions, and long-range goals, he did not regard it as a "thing." It is not separable from the person as a whole. Above all, it is not a homunculus. Rather, Allport (1955) used the term to refer to those functions that make for the peculiar unity and distinctiveness of personality. Moreover, he identified at least seven different aspects of "selfhood" which are involved in the development of the proprium. These so-called *propriate functions* develop gradually (are not innate), and their eventual synthesis constitutes the "me" as an object of subjective knowledge and feeling. The following propriate functions of personality are presented in order of their sequential appearance in the growing child. (When studying these, the reader is urged to attempt to relate them to *him- or herself,* so that Allport's concept of the proprium will become more intuitively clear.)

1 The Sense of Bodily Self   A sense of one's own body, including bodily sensations, attests to one's existence and therefore remains a lifelong anchor for self-awareness. Emerging around the age of 15 months, one's bodily sense is so basic that most adults are unaware of it—it assumes importance only when pain or illness strike (e.g., one is usually unaware of one's little finger until it is smashed in a door). A dramatic example of how the natural intimacy of bodily functions can readily become alien is seen in the following exercise. First, imagine yourself sucking blood from a cut in your finger; then picture yourself sucking blood from a bandage around your finger. What was formerly perceived as belonging intimately to your body instantly becomes cold and disgusting. Presumably, most adults retain a very infantile conception of their bodies; otherwise examples of this sort would not be so unpalatable.

2 The Sense of Self-Identity   The second aspect of the proprium to unfold, self-identity, is most evident when, through language, the child recognizes himself or herself as a distinct and constant point of reference. Unquestionably, the most important anchorage for one's self-identity is one's own name, e.g., "That's Tommy (me) in the mirror." Clothing, toys, and other precious possessions also strengthen this sense of identity, but identity is not firmly established all at once. For instance, a 2-year-old may be unaware that he is cold, feels tired, or needs to eliminate. Fantasy and reality are often blurred and the former often dominates play life.

3 The Sense of Self-Esteem or Pride   Essentially, self-esteem is an individual's evaluation of herself or himself. The urge to want to do everything for oneself and take all the credit is one of the most conspicuous aspects of a 2-year-old's behavior. Parents frequently consider this the age of negativism, since the child resists almost any adult proposal as a threat to integrity and autonomy. Later, by the age of 4 or 5, self-esteem acquires a competitive flavor, reflected by the child's delighted "I beat you!" when she or he wins a game.

4 The Sense of Self-Extension   From approximately 4 to 6 years of age, the proprium is elaborated through self-extension, that is, the sense that although other people and things are not inside my physical body, they are still very much a part of me—they are "mine." With it comes jealous possessiveness, e.g., "This is *my* ball," "I *own* the doll house." *My* mommy, *my* sister, *my* dog, *my* house are regarded as warm parts of oneself and are to be guarded against loss, especially against takeover by another child. Later, we extend our loyalties to our families, our churches, and our nation; we can also become preoccupied with material possessions in this respect.

5 The Self-Image   How others view "me" is another aspect of selfhood that emerges during childhood. Now is the time when the child realizes that parents expect him or her to be "good" while at times he or she is "naughty." As yet, however, the child has no clearly developed conscience, nor any image of how she or he would like to be as an adult. Allport writes: "In childhood the capacity to think of oneself as one is, as one wants to be, and as one ought to be is merely germinal" (1961, p. 123).

6 The Sense of Self as a Rational Coper   Between 6 and 12 years of age, the child begins to fully realize that he or she has the rational capacity to find solutions to life's problems and thereby cope effectively with reality demands. Reflective and formal thought appear, and the child begins to think about thinking. But the child does not yet trust himself or herself to be an independent moral agent, but rather dogmatically believes that his or her family, religion, and peer group are *right;* this stage of propriate development reflects intense moral and social conformity.

7 Propriate Striving Allport believed that the core problem for the adolescent is the selection of an occupation or other life goal. The adolescent knows that the future must follow a plan and, in this sense, her or his selfhood assumes a dimension entirely lacking in childhood (Allport, 1961). Pursuing long-range goals, having a sense of directedness and intentionality in striving for defined objectives, imparting to life a sense of purpose—this is the essence of propriate striving, although it may be quite elementary in the adolescent.

Examples of propriate striving include all forms of behavior that serve self-enhancement. The artist, the scientist, the parent—all strive for goals that are, strictly speaking, unattainable but which unify personality to make life meaningful. In Allport's words:

> Propriate striving confers unity upon personality, but it is never the unity of fulfillment, of repose, or of reduced tension. The devoted parent never loses concern for his child; the devotee of democracy adopts a life-long assignment in his human relationships. The scientist, by the very nature of his commitment, creates more and more questions, never fewer. Indeed the measure of our intellectual maturity, one philosopher suggests, is our capacity to feel less and less satisfied with out answers to better and better problems (1955, p. 67).

Although the emergence of propriate striving is described in terms of discrete stages, Allport felt that the various aspects of the proprium do not function separately. Several, even all of them, can function simultaneously, as the following example illustrates:

> Suppose that you are facing a difficult and critical examination. No doubt you are aware of the butterflies in your stomach (bodily self); also of the significance of the exam in terms of your past and future (self-identity); of your prideful involvement (self-esteem); of what success or failure may mean to your family (self-extension); of your hopes and aspirations (self-image); of your role as the solver of problems on the examination (rational agent); and of the relevance of the whole situation to your long-range goals (propriate striving). In actual life, then, a fusion of propriate states is the rule (Allport, 1961, p. 137).

FUNCTIONAL AUTONOMY: THE PAST IS PAST

Basic to Allport's trait theory is the underlying idea that personality is a dynamic (motivated) growing system. In fact, Allport held that "any theory of personality pivots upon its analysis of the nature of motivation (1961, p. 196)."

Allport proposed that an adequate theory of human motivation must meet four requirements. First, it must recognize the *contemporaneity of motives*. While knowledge about a person's past helps to reveal the present course of her or his life, Allport believed that such historical facts are useless unless they can be shown to be dynamically active in the present. In his words, "Past motives explain nothing unless they are also present motives" (1961, p. 220). Thus, it is the current state of the individual—not what happened during toilet training or weaning—that is central.

Second, it must be a *pluralistic theory, allowing for motives of many types.* Many theorists, hoping to unravel the complex nature of human motivation, have suggested that all motives are reducible to one type, e.g., a few basic drives, the unconscious, or self-actualization. Being a true eclectic, Allport felt that there is some truth in all these formulations of motivation, adding, "Motives are so diverse in type that we find it difficult to discover the common denominator" (1961, p. 221). Thus, many motivational concepts must be used if we are to understand motivation. Third, such a theory must *ascribe dynamic force to the individual's cognitive processes,* especially to the individual's long-range intentions and plans. For Allport, the most significant question one can ask a person in order to understand his or her personality is "What do you want to be doing five years from now?" or "What are you trying to do with your life?" An adequate theory of motivation must therefore address itself to what sort of future a person is trying to bring about. And fourth, the theory must *allow for the concrete uniqueness of motives.* In contrast to theorists who assume a schedule of motives common to all, Allport insisted that the study of motivation must focus on how motives function in unique ways in the individual organism.

The concept of *functional autonomy* of motives provides, in Allport's view, the necessary foundations for a theory of motivation which satisfies the four criteria specified above. This is undoubtedly the best-known and most controversial of the concepts contained within Allport's theoretical system. In many ways it constitutes the core of trait theory.

The principle of functional autonomy states that adult motives are not related to the earlier experiences in which they originally appeared. The past is past—no strings. A person's present motives are functionally autonomous, *independent* of whatever might have brought them into existence originally. Put another way, the personality is divorced from its past; our bonds to the past are historical, not functional. What you are today, you are today—you are not motivationally bound to your past history. Obviously, one can see how such a view of motivation would anger psychoanalysts and behaviorists alike, with their respective strong emphases upon early childhood developmental stages and conditioning experiences as crucial to contemporary adult personality functioning.

Functional autonomy clearly means that a given form of behavior may become an end or goal in itself despite the fact that it may originally have been adopted for some other reason. As an example, consider a young woman who wants to become a veterinarian. As a youngster she liked to catch frogs, dissect them, and examine their organs. Furthermore, her parents happened to operate a pet store and encouraged her to pursue an interest in reptiles. Finally, to complete the example, her peers would bring their pet frogs to her for advice. Her teachers praised such knowledge and encouraged its development, so that she eventually became a celebrity in the local frog-raisers' subculture.

Now it may be quite true that our young woman first began cutting up frogs as the result of encouragement from her father. It's also quite conceivable that all the praise from teachers and recognition from peers could have powerfully reinforced her interest in animals, broadening and deepening it. But now she is 23, in veterinary school, has taken numerous courses in biology and animal behavior, and is simply interested in veterinary medicine for its own sake. She lives it and is self-motivated to pursue it as a career. In Allport's system, it is assumed that the original motives are entirely lost. What was formerly a means to an end has now become an end in itself. The young woman's present drive to become a veterinarian is functionally autonomous of earlier motives.

Other illustrations of functional autonomy include (1) the retired sailor who aches to return to the salt air and sea; (2) the skilled craftsman who perfects his product even though his income no longer depends on the extra effort; (3) the musician who yearns to blow a trumpet again after an enforced absence; (4) the miser who continues to amass money while living in poverty; and (5) the economically secure businessman who makes himself sick in order to further expand the business and gross $20 million a year. In each example the original basis for the motive has been removed or displaced, yet the motive remains. In other words, the original reason for the behavior is missing, yet the behavior persists. This is the essence of functional autonomy.

Two Kinds of Autonomy

Some years after initially formulating the concept of functional autonomy, Allport distinguished between two levels, or types, of functional autonomy. The first, *perseverative functional autonomy,* refers to reverberatory, or feedback, mechanisms in the nervous system that are governed by simple neurological principles. Processes in this category of functional autonomy are neurologically self-maintaining; they help to keep the organism going. Illustrations are infrahuman perseverative activity (e.g., mollusks that burrow in the sand on the beach as a function of the movements of the tide and continue the same rhythm when placed in a laboratory); "circular mechanisms," such as the infant's babbling and other repetitive actions, and the marked inclination of people to satisfy their drives in familiar and routine ways (e.g., eating at th same times each day, sleeping in a familiar bed, suffering from acute homesickness during vacations).

In contrast to the "circular-feedback" processes that characterize perseverative autonomy, *propriate functional autonomy* refers to the individual's acquired interests, values, attitudes, and intentions. Propriate autonomy, essential to the integration of adult personality, significantly contributes to the person's striving for a congruent self-image and an enriching style of life. It is what impels an individual to respond to life's challenges, resulting in the attainment of progressively higher levels of authentic maturity and growth. Once again, Allport proposed a concept that is a precursor of much of contemporary humanistic thinking about human nature. For example, propriate autonomy clearly suggests that we need not be constantly rewarded (reinforced) to sustain our efforts:

> How hollow to think of Pasteur's concern for reward, or for health, food, sleep, or family, as the root of his devotion to his work. For long periods of time he was oblivious of them all, losing himself in the white heat of research. And the same passion is seen in the histories of geniuses who in their lifetime received little or no reward for their work (Allport, 1961, p. 236).

Propriate functional autonomy, then, is a distinct step above merely "keeping the person going." It represents the striving for values and goals, the perception of the world in terms of those values and goals, and the sense of responsibility one takes for one's life. Again, the concept is quite in line with a humanistic conception of personality.

As might be expected, the notion of functional autonomy of motives has been the target of considerable controversy and attack. Not only are those of psychoanalytic and behavioristic persuasion ruffled by it, but personologists of other theoretical persuasions would simply like to see some of the issues that this concept raises adequately addressed. For example, how does functional autonomy evolve? Precisely how does a motive divest itself of its childhood origin and still continue as a motive? How does a motive evolve? In actuality, Allport never explained this developmental process so central to the viability of the functional autonomy concept.

Another problem is that Allport never specified exactly what relationship, if any, there was between childhood and adult functionally autonomous motives. Is there a relation between childhood experience and adult motivation? If so, what is it? If not, what prevents everything one does as a child from somehow becoming a propriate striving in adulthood—why do certain developmental experiences in the lives of people seem important? Besides frogs, Beth liked kites too. Why isn't she interested in becoming an airplane pilot today?

Principles of Propriate Autonomy

Allport's posture in response to such questions was that the phenomenon of functional autonomy will never be understood until the neurophysiological processes involved are understood. However, he did attempt a clarification of the psychological processes underlying the incorporation of motives into the proprium. Specifically, the process of propriate autonomy is governed by three principles. The first of these is the *principle of organizing the energy level.* This principle states that propriate autonomy is possible because the energy level possessed by an individual is in excess of that required to satisfy survival needs, drives, and demands for immediate adjustment. Here Allport suggests that we require adequate outlets to consume these available energies and to supplement the routine motives of survival and drive satisfaction, e.g., a productive man, now retired, channels his energies into new interests and activities. The second principle, the *principle of mastery and competence,* states that the essence of human nature is to master and extract meaning from the environment and to orient oneself toward future aspirations. Hence, whatever increases or enhances one's competence will become functionally autonomous. Allport's third principle, that of *propriate patterning,* asserts that the autonomy of motives emerges *because the self-structure of man demands it*—the essential nature of the human being innately presses toward a relative unification of life. As a consequence of this trend toward unification, Allport noted that human behavior is primarily proactive, intentional, and unique. In brief, then, functional autonomy is "a way of stating that men's motives change and grow in the course of life because it is the nature of man that they should do so. Only theorists wedded to a reactive, homeostatic, quasi-closed model of man find difficulty in agreeing" (Allport, 1961, pp. 252–253). Conversely, only theorists wedded to a *proactive, heterostatic,* quasi-open model of man easily agree with the functional autonomy concept. Once again, then, it becomes evident that regardless of the important but surface theoretical disagreements among personologists on a given theory or concept, the fundamental differences among them lie in the realm of their basic assumptions about human nature.

WHAT IS A HEALTHY PERSON?

Unlike many personologists whose theories grew out of their work with neurotic or deviant personalities, Allport never practiced psychotherapy, nor did he consider clinical observations to be relevant to personality theorizing. He simply refused to believe that neurotic and psychologically healthy people really had much in common. In fact, he seemed to feel that most other personologists of his day could not even identify a healthy personality, and, worse still, that there was little concerted theoretical effort to define or describe one. A person was "healthy" if he or she did not have enough evident neurotic symptoms or money to consult a psychoanalyst. So Allport began a long search to uncover an adequate definition and description of the healthy personality, or what he termed the "mature personality." When viewed historically, Allport pioneered efforts that ultimately led to the rejection by many contemporary personologists of the concept of personality built around psychopathology. He helped to focus attention on some *positive* human attributes, such as self-esteem and competence.

During his search, it quickly became obvious to Allport that different cultures have different concepts of what constitutes healthy behavior. Despite this fact, Allport maintained that some people approximate an "ideal" personality more closely than others, at least as far as the values of Western culture are concerned. He gradually came to view healthy personality development as a growing and active process by which an individual assumes responsibility for his or her life and develops in a unique and personal way. The emergence of personal maturity is a continuous and lifelong process of *becoming* (Allport, 1955). He concluded that positive mental health has six components:

1 *The mature person will have a widely extended sense of self.* Healthy people can get "outside" of themselves. They are not forever stuck in the psychological rut of narrow activities related only to their own needs and desires. Instead, they *care.* They participate meaningfully in work, family, various human relationships, hobbies, political and social issues, religion, or whatever else they experience as valuable. Each activity requires authentic ego involvement and commitment resulting in some direction to life. For Allport, self-love is a prominent factor in everyone's life, but it need not dominate one's life-style.

2 *The social adjustment of the mature person is characterized by a warm relating of self to others.* There are two kinds of interpersonal warmth subsumed under this criterion—*intimacy* and *compassion.* The intimate aspect of warmth is seen in a person's capacity to show deep love for family and close friends unencumbered by possessive and jealous feelings. Compassion is reflected in a person's ability to tolerate differences (concerning values or attitudes) between the self and others, which allows the person to show profound respect and appreciation for the human condition and a sense of kinship with all people.

   3   *Emotional security* or *self-acceptance is another feature of the mature personality.* The well-rounded individual has a fundamentally positive self-image so that he can tolerate frustrating or irritating events as well as his own shortcomings without becoming inwardly bitter or hostile. He *accepts* himself as a person. Such an individual also deals with his emotional states (e.g., depression, anger, ineptness) in such a way that they do not interfere with the well-being of others. For example, if his sex drive is up that day, he doesn't go out and rape somebody; if he is angry, he doesn't fly off the handle at the first person he sees. Finally, the healthy person expresses his beliefs and feelings with consideration for those of others; he is secure enough not to be threatened by his own emotional expressions or by theirs.

   4   *The mature person is also marked by realistic perception, skills, and assignments.* Healthy persons see things as they are, not as they wish them to be. They are in full contact with reality; they do not continually distort it perceptually to fit their needs and fantasies. Moreover, healthy people possess appropriate skills for solving objective problems. By being problem-oriented, they can lose themselves in their work, provisionally setting aside personal desires and impulses while a task takes precedence. Allport quotes Harvey Cushing, the famous brain surgeon, to convey this aspect of maturity: "The only way to endure life is to have a task to complete" (1961, p. 290). Mature people, then, perceive other persons, objects, and situations for what they are; they possess sufficient skills to deal with reality; and they strive for personally important and realistic goals.

   5   *The mature person is capable of self-objectification* and of *insight in humor.* Socrates observed that there is one paramount rule for achieving the good life: "Know thyself." Allport called this "self-objectification." By it, he means that the mature person will know herself as an "object" and will understand the differences between what she is, what she would like to be, and what others think of her. Humor is an important ingredient in self-insight because it prevents pompous self-glorification and just plain phoniness. It allows a person to see and appreciate the utterly ludicrous aspects of her own or anyone else's life situation. Humor, as Allport saw it, is the ability to laugh at the things one cherishes (including oneself) and still cherish them.

   6   Finally, *a unifying philosophy of life earmarks the healthy adult.* Healthy people can "put it all together" with a clear, consistent, and systematic way of seeing meaning in their lives. A person does not have to be an Aristotle to do this—one simply needs a value system that will present one with a dominant goal, theme, or object that makes one's life meaningful. Different people may develop different central values around which their lives will purposefully revolve (see the "Application" section of this chapter for further discussion of this point). They may choose the pursuit of truth, social welfare, religion, or whatever—there is no one best value or philosophy in Allport's opinion. Rather, Allport's point is that a mature person has a set of deeply held values which serves as a unifying foundation for his or her life. A unifying philosophy of life therefore provides a kind of overriding value orientation which gives meaning and significance to practically everything one does.

Allport admits that relatively few adults achieve full maturity in the way he describes. However, he did consider these six criteria to offer a reasonably accurate and comprehensive picture of what personal maturity is like in our culture.

Attention is now shifted to the basic assumptions underlying this trait theory of personality.

ALLPORT'S BASIC ASSUMPTIONS CONCERNING HUMAN NATURE

Allport waged a lifelong battle against the basic psychoanalytic and behavioristic conceptions of human nature. Of his humanistic persuasion, he wrote:

> Some theories of becoming are based largely upon the behavior of sick and anxious people or upon the antics of captive and desperate rats. Fewer theories have derived from the study of healthy human beings, those who strive not so much to preserve life as to make it worth living (Allport, 1955, p. 18).

The reasons underlying Allport's objections to psychoanalysis and behaviorism are readily apparent when considering his basic assumptions about human nature (Figure 8-3).

Freedom–Determinism With the exception of Alfred Adler, Allport supported the concept of human freedom more than any other personologist examined thus far in this volume. This position is illustrated in a published conversation between Allport and Richard Evans: "I would say that we have more freedom than most of today's psychology admits. I would not, however, argue for the absolute, untrammeled freedom espoused by some of the existentialists. The answer lies somewhere in the middle course" (Evans, 1971, p. 59).

The emphasis on freedom found in Allport's theory is most clearly revealed in his portrayal of personality development. Specifically, Allport viewed human growth as an active process of "becoming" in which the individual takes some responsibility for charting the course of his or her life. At least part of the "dynamic organization" so essential to Allport's definition of personality is thus self-determined.

	Strong	Moderate	Slight	Midrange	Slight	Moderate	Strong	
Freedom			■					Determinism
Rationality	■							Irrationality
Holism		■						Elementalism
Constitutionalism				■				Environmentalism
Changeability					■			Unchangeability
Subjectivity			■					Objectivity
Proactivity	■							Reactivity
Homeostasis							■	Heterostasis
Knowability		■						Unknowability

Figure 8-3 Allport's position on the nine basic assumptions concerning human nature.

However, Allport's trait concept puts serious limits on the absolute degree of freedom in human behavior. That is, once traits are formed in a person, they largely determine his or her perceptions and actions. As explained earlier, traits are potent governors of both selection of and responses to various stimuli. Human actions are thus initiated and guided by specific traits. Allport further believed that situational determinants play a central role in influencing an individual's behavior. Thus, while granting significantly more free choice to man than is characteristically encountered in either psychoanalysis or behaviorism, Allport's overall commitment to freedom in human behavior is best judged as slight.

Rationality–Irrationality   Allport was extremely committed to the assumption that human beings are rational organisms. In fact, he spent considerable effort disputing the Freudian emphasis upon unconscious, irrational elements in human behavior (Allport, 1961). He agreed with Freud that such forces dominate the mental lives of the emotionally disturbed—this, in fact, is what distinguishes disturbed from healthy individuals. But Allport argued that Freud erred in assuming that unconscious processes dominate the functioning of sound and healthy people. Mature, well-balanced people are fully capable of conscious, rationally based actions; they live their lives in terms of goals, long-range plans, and an overall philosophy—all of which are founded upon rationality.

The belief in human rationality underscores practically all Allport's theoretical formulations. For example, he insisted that one important criterion of an adequate theory of motivation is that it ascribe dynamic force to the individual's cognitive processes, such as thinking, planning, and intending (Allport, 1961). Allport also considered the recognition of the self as a rational coper (i.e., the realization that one can solve problems by thinking) to be an integral part of proprium development. Finally, it will be recalled that Allport described the mature person as one who possesses realistic perception, skills, and assignments. This clearly implies that such people know where they are going and how to get there. If he or she develops and functions along normal lines, the Allportian person is exquisitely rational.

Holism–Elementalism   Allport's theory reflects an intricate interweaving of the holism and elementalism assumptions, although the former is considerably stronger in his system. To appreciate this counterbalance of forces, consider that Allport's unit of analysis is the "trait." People are studied largely in terms of their exhibited traits, which seems to be a straightforward, elementalist approach to personological research. Yet Allport argued that personality will never be totally understood by examining each trait separately. While he believed that some system of "dimensions or conceptual schemata" (traits) was necessary to study personality, Allport maintained that a trait must ultimately be related to the total pattern of personality of which it is a part (Evans, 1971).

Underlying the various elements (traits), then, is a unifying, holistic entity—the proprium—which includes all aspects of personality that contribute to inward unity (Allport, 1955). Moreover, the most essential ingredient in this totality of personality is propriate striving (Allport, 1961). Rather than merely a static unity at any given time, a person is depicted as continually seeking inward unity by striving for distant goals, objectives, and ideals. While he recognized the empirical necessity of studying "elements" in personology, Allport believed that such elements can never be properly understood apart from the more holistic frame of reference of propriate striving.

Constitutionalism–Environmentalism   Allport strikes a near-perfect balance between constitution and environment in his conception of human nature. Specifically, he believed that genetic and environmental factors are equally influential in determining human behavior. In fact, Allport (1961) argued that no feature or act of the human personality is without both genetic and environmental influences.

According to Allport, neither heredity alone nor environment alone determines the way personality is fashioned. Instead, it is through the reciprocal influence of heredity and environment that intelligence, interests, aptitudes, values, or any other personality characteristics emerge. Also, Allport suggested that one's temperament (representing constitutional factors) sets limits upon external influences, while broad social and cultural forces, in turn, modify temperament. Although he conceded that psychology still has much to learn about the precise operations of constitutional and environmental influences upon behavior (Evans, 1971), Allport regarded both as of equal importance in human functioning.

Changeability–Unchangeability   Allport's theory reflects an equal mixture of the changeability and unchangeability assumptions. A clue to the former is found in the phrase "dynamic organization" so central to his definition of personality (Allport, 1961). This phrase strongly suggests that, whatever personality is, there is at least some room for it to grow and evolve during the course of a lifetime. But the real key to changeability in trait theory is found in Allport's conception of motivation. In his system, people are depicted as forward-moving, future-oriented, and growing. And, as we noted in the first chapter, one important reflection of the changeability assumption in any theory is a major concept that explains how people may be discontinuous with their past. Allport has just such a concept—that of functional autonomy. According to this conception of motivation, an individual's motives can change during his or her life and, in this sense, so can the individual.

But this is not the whole story, for the unchangeability assumption is equally evident in Allport's theory. One need only consider its title—a *trait* theory of personality—to grasp this idea. Traits are what account for the enduring aspects of a person's behavior; they explain why behavior remains relatively stable over time and across situations. To focus attention on such a concept suggests that there are at least some important things about people which remain fairly stable over time. And, as was also noted in Chapter 1, the unchangeability assumption is likely to reveal itself in concepts of unchanging core personality structures that underlie the individual's behavior throughout life. Allport's trait concept nicely fits this description. And his construct of the proprium as the subjective center of personality still further suggests an ongoing underlying stream of stability. Thus, along the continuum of changeability–unchangeability, Allport's overall position is best judged as midrange.

Subjectivity–Objectivity While Allport was passionately interested in the uniqueness of the individual personality, he did not regard subjective experience (subjectivity) as particularly critical in understanding individuality. Specifically, in his morphogenic approach to personality study (to be elaborated in the following section), he considered uniqueness to be of paramount importance, but in his system it is to be found in the dynamic organization of individual *traits* rather than in the quality of one's subjective experience. There is, then, a difference between the concepts of *uniqueness* and *subjectivity*. Allport strongly emphasizes the former in his theory while manifesting at best only a slight commitment to the latter.

The subjectivity assumption surfaces when Allport's concept of the proprium is examined. Referring to the focal point of one's personal sense of existence, the proprium identifies all the regions of personal life that one regards as peculiarly one's own. In effect, the proprium aids the individual in drawing distinctions between matters of subjective importance and matters of fact. Yet, while Allport's proprium contains within it the seeds of subjectivity, he did not regard subjectivity as the key to understanding a person. For him, the world of subjective experience is only one component of many that constitute the complexity of personality. Psychology, in Allport's opinion, will become truly scientific only when it can deal fully with the issue of individual uniqueness.

Proactivity–Reactivity In describing the concept of propriate striving, Allport (1961) noted that directedness, or intentionality, is the cement which holds a person's life together. That is, in order to function well, an individual needs a defining objective toward which she or he is striving. The assumption of proactivity evident in this description is even more unmistakable when Allport speaks of propriate patterning: "the essential nature of man is such that it presses toward a relative unification of life (never fully achieved). . . . As a consequence of this quest—which is the very essence of human nature—we note that man's conduct is to a large degree proactive. . . ." (Allport, 1961, p. 252).

We live in a world of future goals, life ambitions, and strivings which are generated from within, according to Allport. Functional autonomy serves to demolish reactive ties to the past; propriate striving negates any account of behavior merely in terms of reactions to present stimuli. Allport's commitment to the proactivity assumption is strong and explicit.

Homeostasis–Heterostasis Allport recognized the validity of homeostatic drives as the primitive and animal-like part of human motivation. But he (1961) cited Cannon, the originator of the homeostasis concept, as acknowledging that tension reduction does not account for all human conduct. Basically, Cannon believed that once a person's essential needs were answered through homeostasis, she or he was free to seek the "priceless unessentials." Allport, revealing his heterostatic assumption, felt that these "priceless unessentials" are the most conspicuous features of the human personality. More specifically, he writes:

> The healthy child and adult are continually building up tensions . . . and are going way beyond the basic, safety level of homeostasis. New experiences, which most of us crave,

cannot be put in terms of tension-reduction, nor can our desire to acquire knowledge for its own sake, to create works of beauty and usefulness, nor to give and receive love. . . . (Allport, 1961, p. 90).

Allport's assumption of heterostasis is further expressed in his theoretical account of propriate functional autonomy, which, you may recall, involves the principles of "organizing the energy level," "mastery and competence," and "propriate striving." If these previously discussed principles are now considered within a heterostatic framework, persons must be viewed as motivated toward growth and unification. In fact, this sort of motivation is one example of human phylogenetic uniqueness. There is a strong commitment to heterostasis throughout Allport's theory.

Knowability–Unknowability   Like most other humanistically minded personologists, Allport was less than optimistic about the ultimate power of psychological method and theory to unravel the mystery of human behavior. More to the point, he believed that although it is possible to study empirically specific aspects of our behavior and functioning, science alone could not provide total understanding of human nature. As an illustration, Allport (1966) advocated what he termed "heuristic realism" as the basic empirical approach to personality study. Briefly, this doctrine holds that inasmuch as within every individual there inhere generalized action tendencies or traits, it is psychology's task to discover what they are. Because traits are never directly observed but only inferred, however, there are major scientific obstacles to uncovering their true nature. Yet the persistent "heuristic realist" presses onward. While he knows that his efforts probably will not wholly succeed, because of both the complexity of personality and the inadequacy of present methods for its study, he prefers to believe that the nature of personality is partly or approximately knowable (Allport, 1966).

In effect, Allport maintained that personality can be studied empirically—but one defined "limb" at a time. The degree to which science can eventually put these appendages together to form the complete person, which Allport holistically believes is there, remains a largely unanswered question. Furthermore, Allport's morphogenic approach to personality research, emphasizing as it does, normal individual development, renders it difficult to grasp human nature as a whole because it studies people one at a time. Perhaps Allport said it best in concluding his discussion of the "heuristic realism" approach to the study of the person: "Along the way we regard him as an objectively real being whose tendencies we can succeed in knowing—at least in part. . . ." (Allport, 1966, pp. 8–9). Thus, Allport's commitment to the knowability assumption is less than complete.

EMPIRICAL VALIDATION OF TRAIT THEORY CONCEPTS

To what extent have psychologists demonstrated the empirical validity of Allport's theoretical conceptions of personality? An exhaustive search of the relevant literature indicates that Allport has stimulated almost no research to empirically validate his trait theory concepts to date. Several sophisticated writers in per-sonology agree (Hall and Lindzey, 1978; Ryckman, 1978; Maddi and Costa, 1972). Although Allport's is certainly a comprehensive personological system, it seems that almost no one has taken the time or trouble to test the empirical validity of its concepts. In an empirical discipline like psychology, no theory will endure unless it generates testable predictions based on its major constructs. Allport's theory is no exception.

Several factors account for the paucity of research bearing on Allport's theory. First and foremost, the theory is populated with rather vague and ill-defined concepts and relational statements. Concepts such as propriate striving, self as rational coper, and personal disposition do not readily lend themselves to opera-tional definitions. Second, Allport neglected to specify the ways in which his trait concepts are related to his formulations about the development of the proprium. In fact, the various developmental stages of the proprium are described in general terms, and there is little attempt to specify precisely the variables that control the emergence, maintenance, and modification of the phenomena of the self. Given these obstacles, it remains very difficult to design adequate empirical tests of Allport's theory.

Although trait theory has failed in the heuristic sense, it has definitely been of considerable stimulus value for other domains of psychological study. Through collaboration with colleagues and students, for example, Allport has contributed significantly to the literature on expressive behavior (e.g., Allport and Cantril, 1934; Allport and Vernon, 1960; Estes, 1938; Huntley, 1940; Zweigenhaft and Marlowe, 1973). "Expressive behavior" refers to the style in which an individual performs behavioral acts, e.g., facial expression, gait, voice, and handwriting. More recent research focusing on the criteria of psychological maturity, children's imagery, self-esteem, humor, social perception, rumor, and prejudice also partially reflects, although only indirectly, the influence of Allport's theoretical interests. These and other empirical contributions are listed in the extensive bibliography accompanying Allport's *Personality and Social Encounter* (1960). The Allport-Vernon-Lindzey (1960) *Study of Values* (3d ed.), a scale designed to assess six separate value orientations possessed by an individual, also documents the con-tinuing influence of Allport. This scale, to be discussed in the "Application" section, is still regarded as a highly respectable method of measuring values and has been used extensively in various research in recent years.

If frequency of citations in major texts on personality theory were a valid measure of stimulus value, Allport would receive a gold star. A scan of the author indexes of fifteen personality textbooks published since 1975 reveals that each contains no fewer than five references to Allport. His theoretical concepts may not have inspired much empirical study, but contemporary personologists seem unable to ignore the total impact of his thinking.

Allport's Approach to Research: Illustrative Studies

Allport argued that personality research should always be guided by methods that allow for the reliable and valid study of individual life-styles. Specifically, he advocated the *morphogenic* (also called *idiographic*) approach to personality study whereby the uniqueness of each person is the primary goal of psychological investigation. While he did not abandon a belief in the usefulness of *nomothetic* approaches (which emphasize that a science of personality should seek to establish general laws of human functioning), Allport (1968b) argued for the increased study of individual patterns of growth to illuminate the nature of personality. His commitment to the study of individual uniqueness was unmistakable:

> Psychology is truly itself only when it can deal with individuality. It is vain to plead that other sciences do not do so, that they are allowed to brush off the bothersome issue of uniqueness. The truth is that psychology is assigned the task of being curious about human persons, and persons exist only in concrete and unique patterns. . . .
>
> We study the human person most fully when we take him as an individual. He is more than a bundle of habits, more than a point of intersection of abstract dimensions. He is more than a representative of his species, more than a citizen of the state, more than an incident in the movements of mankind. He transcends them all. The individual, striving ever for integrity and fulfillment, has existed under all forms of social life— forms as varied as the nomadic and feudal, capitalist and communist. No society holds together for long without the respect man shows to man. The individual today struggles on even under oppression, always hoping and planning for a more perfect democracy where the dignity and growth of each personality will be prized above all else (Allport, 1961, p. 573).

Although morphogenic methods are easy neither to devise nor to employ, Allport (1962) considered things such as personal documents—including diaries, autobiographies, letters, open-ended questionnaires, and verbatim recordings of interviews—to have obvious research applicability. However, he insisted that such procedures should not be used to the exclusion of proved nomothetic methods. Indeed, the bulk of his own empirical investigations followed the more conventional nomothetic approach. In the remaining pages of this section, two studies illustrating Allport's orientation toward personality research will be discussed. The first reveals how personal documents may be used to establish the existence of individual traits, while the second deals with the relationship between religiosity and prejudice, a topic that captivated Allport's theoretical imagination.

Letters from Jenny: A Morphogenic Trait Study   The value of morphogenic methods as a means of determining an individual's outstanding traits is best illustrated in Allport's *Letters from Jenny* (1965). This case study was based on the personal correspondence of a middle-aged woman named Jenny Grove Masterson who wrote, during the last 11 years of her life, some 300 letters to a young married couple living and teaching in an Eastern college town: "The tie of friendship extended back to the time when the husband (Glenn) had been the roommate of Jenny's son (Ross) at college, about ten years before the beginning of the correspondence. . . . The correspondence begins in earnest in March, 1926, and continues without interruption . . . until Jenny's death in October, 1937" (Allport, 1965, p. v). Allport acquired Jenny's letters in the 1940s and he subsequently used them as pedagogical material for stimulating class discussions in his personality course at Harvard. Of specific interest here, however, are the various clinical and quantitative analyses of these personal documents made by Allport and his students.

Allport's (1942) first empirical assessment consisted of listing Jenny's essential characteristics as perceived by thirty-nine clinical judges who read her letters in sequence. Labeled *content analysis,* this procedure resembles a commonsense, or impressionistic, approach to personality study. The results were expressed in the form of a series of 198 descriptive adjectives that clustered into eight distinct groups of "commonsense" traits. Baldwin (1942), one of Allport's students, extended the content analysis of Jenny's letters to include a more elaborate and statistical treatment of the data. Using a method that he called *personal structure analysis,* he instructed raters to count the number of times particular topics and themes (e.g., money, art, women, nature) occurred in each of the letters and to correlate such categories of thought that clustered together. In brief, Baldwin's study revealed that Jenny's personality was described quite accurately in terms of the eight central traits which had emerged from Allport's prior analysis.

More recently, Paige (1966), yet another of Allport's protégés, conducted a still more quantified analysis of Jenny's letters. He used a computer program (called the General Inquirer) specifically designed to recognize and "tag" certain designated adjectives in the letters that were used in conjunction with each other. For example, any terms Jenny used to express aggression, hostility, and opposition were coded together under the tag category "Attack." The program also provided the frequency with which various tag words in a given letter were associated with all others in the same letter. Paige then subjected these to a statistical technique known as factor analysis. Based on this computerized evaluation of the document, eight highly stable trait factors were identified as descriptive of Jenny. These factorially derived traits are very similar to those which were obtained from the previous studies. Table 8-1 lists in parallel fashion the clusters obtained by content analysis based on a careful reading of the series, along with the factors, obtained by Paige in his factorial study.

Allport interpreted the similarity of the two lists (derived from two divergent types of analysis) as indicative of the validity of his conclusions about Jenny's

Table 8-1   Central Traits in Jenny's Personality as Determined by Impressionistic and Factor-Analytic Methods of Assessment

Commonsense traits	Factorial traits
1 Quarrelsome-suspicious, aggressive	1 Aggression
2 Self-centered (possessive)	2 Possessiveness
3 Sentimental	3 Need for affiliation, need for family acceptance
4 Independent-autonomous	4 Need for autonomy
5 Esthetic-artistic	5 Sentience
6 Self-centered (self-pitying)	6 Martyrdom
7 (No parallel)	7 Sexuality
8 Cynical-morbid	8 (No parallel)
9 Dramatic-intense	9 ("Overstate")

Source: Adapted from Allport, 1966, p. 7.

personality-trait structure: "In spite of the differences in terminology the general paralleling of the two lists establishes some degree of empirical check on both of them. We can say that the direct common-sense perception of Jenny's nature is validated by quantification, coding, and factoring" (Allport, 1966, pp. 7–8).

While Allport considered personal documents to be the most revealing method for the intensive study of the single life, such documents do have their shortcomings. For one thing, we must know the author's motivation for writing the document so that we can judge how much validity to attach to it and the extent to which it characterizes the author's life. Another problem is the lack of information about the author's formative years. But recognizing the shortcomings of this approach, much rich material can nonetheless be gleaned concerning the dynamics of a single life.

Religion and Prejudice: Are They Related?   During the later years of his career, Allport became vitally interested in the individual's religious life, particularly as it relates to ethnic prejudice. As noted earlier, Allport considered religion as one source of a unifying philosophy of life. The research problem is this: many investigations have established that church attenders harbor more ethnic prejudice, on average, than nonattenders. This finding might suggest that religion encourages prejudice. At the same time, however, it is assumed that all great religions teach equality, brotherhood, and compassion. Indeed, many ardent workers for human rights (e.g., Mahatma Gandhi, Albert Schweitzer, Martin Luther King, Jr.) were known to be religiously motivated. This could suggest that religion as such breaks down prejudice. The situation, then, is paradoxical: "Religion makes for prejudice; it also unmakes prejudice" (Allport, 1966, p. 5).

In attempting to resolve the paradox, Allport (1966) tentatively assumed that two contrasting but measurable forms of religious orientation exist. An *extrinsic orientation* involves religious devotion not as a value in its own right but rather as an instrument in the service of motives such as personal comfort, security, status, or social support. Extrinsically oriented religious people use religion to satisfy other needs. On the other hand, an *intrinsic orientation* regards faith as a supreme value in its own right. An intrinsically religious person, Allport adds, "takes seriously the commandment of brotherhood that is found in all religions, and seeks a unification of being" (1966, p. 6). A self-report questionnaire (called the Religious Orientation Scale) was constructed to measure these two opposing orientations toward religion. Two scale items follow, with possible response alternatives ranging from strongly agree to strongly disagree. Endorsement of the first statement is indicative of an extrinsic religious orientation, while endorsement of the second is indicative of an intrinsic religious orientation:

> One reason for my being a church member is that such membership helps to establish a person in the community.

> I try hard to carry my religion over into all my other dealings in life.

The utility of Allport's distinction between extrinsic and intrinsic orientations was determined by correlating religious orientation scores with various measures of ethnic prejudice for several different samples of Protestant and Catholic church-

Table 8-2   Correlations between Measures of Religious Orientation among Churchgoers and Various Scales of Ethnic Prejudice

Denominational sample	Religious orientation	Target of prejudice	r
Unitarian ($N = 50$)	Extrinsic type	Anti-Catholic	+.56
	Intrinsic type	Anti-Catholic	−.36
	Extrinsic type	Anti-Mexican	+.54
	Intrinsic type	Anti-Mexican	−.42
Catholic ($N = 66$)	Extrinsic type	Anti-Negro	+.36
	Intrinsic type	Anti-Negro	−.49
Nazarene ($N = 39$)	Extrinsic type	Anti-Negro	+.41
	Intrinsic type	Anti-Negro	−.44
Mixed* ($N = 207$)	Extrinsic type	Anti-Semitic	+.65

Source: Adapted from Allport, 1966, p. 7.
*From Wilson (1960).

goers. As shown in Table 8-2, for each sample studied extrinsicness of orientation is positively related to prejudice (i.e., those who agree with extrinsically worded items` tend toward greater prejudice), whereas intrinsicness of orientation is negatively related to prejudice (i.e., those who agree with intrinsically worded items tend toward absence of prejudice).

Ironically, an earlier study by Wilson (1960) found that subjects who endorse both intrinsic and extrinsic items are the most prejudiced of all! Allport designated such individuals "inconsistently proreligious," noting that they simply like religion; for them, it has social desirability. This interesting research area, although not a direct outgrowth of Allport's trait theory, provides a basis for evaluating the religious sentiment and its role in the dynamics of ethnic prejudice.

Let us now consider an application of Allport's theory.

APPLICATION: THE STUDY OF VALUES

Allport stressed that a mature person needs a unifying philosophy of life to make sense of his or her existence. An individual's philosophy is founded upon *values*—basic convictions about what is and is not of real importance in life. Believing that a person's efforts to find order and meaning in his or her existence are governed by values, Allport worked hard to identify and measure basic value dimensions. The success of his effort is evident in the well-known personality test that he helped significantly to develop—the *Study of Values*—which was originally published in 1931 and is currently in its third edition (Allport, Vernon, and Lindzey, 1960). Within the context of trait theory, this instrument illustrates Allport's ability to dissect an enormously complex component of personality (values) into empirically measurable terms.

To accomplish this difficult task, Allport needed a conceptual model that could account for value differences among persons. He found the required model in the work of Eduard Spranger, a European psychologist. In his book *Types of Men,* Spranger (1922) outlined six major value-types. Conceived as the basic alternative value directions evidenced in human life, not as six main types of people, these values are found to varying degrees in all of us; we construct the unity of our lives around them (Allport, 1961). Hence, no one person falls exclusively under any one value category; rather, different value combinations are more or less salient in the lives of different individuals. From an Allportian perspective, these values are best described as deep-level traits.

Following are Spranger's basic value types, as depicted in the *Study of Values* manual (Allport, Vernon, and Lindzey, 1960).

1 The Theoretical   The theoretical person is primarily concerned with the discovery of *truth.* He or she assumes a "cognitive" attitude in pursuing this objective, seeking only to observe and to reason. In so doing, the theoretical individual searches for fundamental identities and differences, rejecting any considerations of beauty or utility. Since his or her interests are basically rational, critical, and empirical, the theoretical person is necessarily an intellectual, frequently a scientist or philosopher. Such a person need not, however, attain a high level of achievement, since Spranger believed that one's true values are revealed in interests and intentions rather than through concrete achievements. What theoretical persons want most is to order and systematize their knowledge.

2 The Economic   The economic individual places highest value upon what is *useful.* He or she is thoroughly "practical" and conforms closely to the stereotype of the successful American businessperson. Rooted originally in the satisfaction of bodily needs (self-preservation), the economic value gradually extends to the everyday affairs of the business world—the production, marketing, and consumption of goods, the elaboration of credit, and the accumulation of tangible wealth. The economic person is interested in making money.

In their personal lives, economic individuals are likely to confuse luxury with beauty. Moreover, in their relations with others, economic persons tend to be interested in surpassing them in wealth rather than in understanding (theoretical), serving (social), or dominating (political) them. But, above all, the economic individual values what is practical and useful. He or she wants education to be such and regards unapplied knowledge as waste. Many great feats of engineering and technology have resulted from the demands that economic persons have made upon science.

3 The Aesthetic   The aesthetic person places highest value on *form* and *harmony.* Judging each single experience from the standpoint of grace, symmetry, or fitness, he or she perceives life as a procession of events, with each individual impression enjoyed for its own sake. Such an individual need not be a creative artist but is aesthetic to the degree that his or her chief interest is in the artistic episodes of life.

In direct opposition to the theoretical value, the aesthetic individual agrees with Keats that truth is beauty and with Mencken that to make a thing charming is a million times more important than to make it true. Such persons oppose the economic value, seeing manufacturing, advertising, and trade as wholesale destructions of their most primary values. In social affairs, aesthetic individuals are interested in persons but not in their welfare; they tend toward individualism and self-sufficiency in their dealings with others.

4 The Social   The highest value of the social type is *love of people*. Since the *Study of Values* focuses only upon the altruistic or philanthropic aspects of love (as opposed, for example, to conjugal or familial love), social persons prize others as ends and are themselves kind, sympathetic, and unselfish. Such a person is likely to experience the theoretical, economic, and aesthetic attitudes as cold and inhuman, regarding love as the only suitable form of human relationship. In its purest form, the social attitude is selfless and is closely related to the religious value.

5 The Political   The dominant interest of the political individual is *power*. Vocational activities of this type of person are not necessarily confined to the realm of politics, since leaders in any field generally place a high value on power. Because competition and struggle are inherent in all life, many philosophers have argued that power is the most universal and fundamental human motive. In fact, some of the early writings of Alfred Adler, as you may recall, reflect this point of view. However, for Spranger there are clear individual differences in the power value. For certain personalities, direct expression of this motive overrides all others in that they yearn for personal power, influence, and renown above all else.

6 The Religious   Religious individuals place their highest value upon *unity*. Fundamentally mystical, they seek to understand and experience the world as a unified whole. Spranger describes the religious person as one who is permanently oriented toward the creation of the highest and absolutely satisfying value experience. There are, however, different modes of seeking this level of experience. For instance, some religious persons are "immanent mystics," i.e., individuals who find religious meaning in the affirmation and active participation in life, while others are "transcendental mystics," striving to unite themselves with a higher reality by withdrawing from life, e.g., monks. Regardless of the particular type of expression, the religious person basically seeks unity and higher meaning in the cosmos.

To concretize these six types, consider the following. Suppose that six individuals, each representing one of the dominant value orientations, are walking together through the woods on a sunny fall afternoon. The theoretical individual might be contemplating the basic biological principles underlying tree growth; the economic person could be wondering how much money could be made by chopping down some of the trees, converting them to toothpicks, and marketing them; the aesthetic would probably be having a peak experience running to and fro among the leaves experiencing the beauty of the surroundings; the social person might simply be happy that five other people are present; the political individual would undoubtedly be walking in front of the group periodically insisting that the others follow his or her path through and out of the woods; and the religious person might be sublimely

Sample item from Part I

If you should see the following news item with headlines of equal size in your morning paper, which would you read more attentively? *(a)* PROTESTANT LEADERS TO CONSULT ON RECONCILIATION; *(b)* GREAT IMPROVEMENTS IN MARKET CONDITIONS

Sample item from Part II

In your opinion, can people who work in business all the week best spend Sunday
a. trying to educate themselves by reading serious books.
b. trying to win at golf or racing.
c. going to an orchestral concert.
d. hearing a really good sermon.

Figure 8-4 Sample items from the *Study of Values* test. (*Allport, Vernon, and Lindzey, 1960.*)

contemplating the nature of the underlying ultimate reality of which these people and woods are a profound expression.

It is again worth noting that, while Spranger described these six in terms of "ideal types," he did not imply that a given person falls exclusively under any single one of them. Rather, they are to be understood as basic ways in which persons in varying degrees orient, perceive, experience, and evaluate their personal world. Each individual can be characterized by a specific *pattern* of values as well as by her or his dominant value orientation.

Allport attempted to assess the relative strength of these six values in any given individual by means of the *Study of Values* test. Developed and standardized with college students, the test consists of forty-five questions and requires about twenty minutes to complete. Two sample questions are found in Figure 8-4. As a self-administered pencil-and-paper inventory, it can be taken in a group or individually.

Part I of the test consists of thirty relatively "controversial" statements or questions with two possible alternative answers provided for each. The subject's task is to select the alternative in each instance that is relatively more acceptable to her or him. In so doing, the testee has three points to distribute between the two alternatives for each item. For example, if one *strongly* agrees with alternative *a* and disagrees with *b*, one assigns three points to the former and zero points to the latter. Should one *slightly* prefer *a* to *b,* one would assign two points to *a* and one to *b*. These two situations would of course be reversed if one's preference was for alternative *b* over *a*. In this fashion, one is permitted to indicate not only one's preference but also, in at least approximate form, the *relative* strength of these preferences. To clarify this procedure, the reader is advised to reexamine the first item in Figure 8-4 and then answer it personally. As one might imagine, alternative *a* reflects the religious value while *b* reflects the economic.

Part II of the test is made up of the remaining fifteen questions. Four alternatives, much like a multiple-choice examination, are provided for each question. Unlike the typical "multiple-guess" test, however, the *Study of Values* asks the subject to order the four alternatives in terms of relative preferences, assigning a numerical value of 4 to the first choice, 3 to the second, and so on. Consistent with Part I of the test, this response format is designed to elicit the relative strengths of the person's preferences. Again, the reader is advised to carry out this process with the second item in Figure 8-4 to gain a more intuitive sense of what this test is like.

Since there are basically two alternative answers to each of the first thirty questions and four alternatives to each of the remaining fifteen items, there are 120 possible responses in Parts I and II of this instrument, twenty of which refer to each of the six values. When one's scores on each value dimension are summed, they may be plotted on a profile so that one can see one's standing on the six values simultaneously. These profiles are particularly helpful for classroom demonstration and counseling.

How adequate is the *Study of Values* as a personality test? Allport himself noted that Spranger's conception of values, while useful, tends to present a flattering view of human nature. For example, it does not allow for valueless, hedonistic, expedient, or sensuous philosophies that obviously pervade the lives of some people. Referring again to the second question in Figure 8-4, some subjects may really believe that a person who works hard all week might best spend Sundays drinking beer or watching pornographic films! But given this limitation, how well does the *Study of Values* measure what it was designed to measure? To answer this question, psychologists resort to data on the *reliability* (consistency, or freedom from chance error of measurement) and *validity* (the degree to which a test measures what it purports to measure) of the instrument. Generally, the reliability and validity data reported by the test authors are acceptable. For instance, subjects who retake the *Study of Values* one or two months after an original testing tend to achieve scores quite similar to their original ones (reliability) while average scores on the six values differ in expected directions for different occupational groups (validity), e.g., business students score highest on the economic value, art and design students on the aesthetic value, and clergymen on the religious value (Allport, Vernon, and Lindzey, 1960).

Another aspect in evaluating a personality test is its utility. Allport, Vernon, and Lindzey (1960) suggest various ways that the *Study of Values* can be used in classroom demonstration, counseling, research, vocational guidance and selection. In fact, this test has been widely employed over the years in these diverse areas. In sum, this instrument is a deceptively simple, straightforward, and highly useful approach to the assessment of certain fundamental and broad personality traits (values), based on the assumption that the subject is largely consciously motivated and rational. In this respect, it accurately reflects Gordon Allport's theory of personality and basic view of human beings.

SUMMARY

Gordon Allport's trait theory represents a blend of humanistic and personalistic approaches to the study of human behavior. Believing that the explanation of an individual's uniqueness is the paramount goal of psychology, Allport viewed personality as the dynamic organization of those internal psychophysical systems that determine a person's characteristic behavior and thought. Within the individual, personality is real; it is "what a person really is."

Allport regarded the *trait* as the most valid unit of analysis for understanding and studying personality. In his system, traits are predispositions to respond in an equivalent manner to various kinds of stimuli. In short, traits account for a person's behavioral consistency over time and across situations. They may be classified under one of three headings—cardinal, central, or secondary—according to their degree of pervasiveness within a personality. Allport also distinguished between common and individual traits, the former being generalized dispositions to which most people within a given culture can be compared, whereas the latter refer to personal dispositions peculiar to an individual which do not permit comparisons with others.

The overall construct that unifies traits and provides direction for the person's life is termed the *proprium*. This concept essentially refers to the "self-as-known," including all aspects of personality that contribute to an inward sense of unity. Another of Allport's personality concepts, his best-known and most controversial, is that of *functional autonomy*. This principle asserts that adult motives are not related to the earlier experiences in which they originally appeared. Allport further distinguished between perseverative functional autonomy (reverberatory, or feedback, mechanisms in the nervous system) and propriate functional autonomy (the individual's acquired interests, values, attitudes, and intentions). In essence, the latter allows for the development of the truly mature person, the salient characteristics of which Allport carefully delineated.

Allport's profound disagreements with the psychoanalytic and behavioristic conceptions of human nature are clearly evident in his basic assumptions. Trait theory reflects (1) a strong commitment to the assumptions of rationality, proactivity, and heterostasis; (2) a moderate commitment to the holism and knowability assumptions; (3) a slight commitment to the assumptions of freedom and subjectivity; and (4) a midrange position on the constitutionalism–environmentalism and changeability–unchangeability dimensions.

While trait theory has stimulated almost no research to date in support of its core constructs, Allport himself made some interesting empirical contributions to the personological literature. He advocated the morphogenic approach to personality study, which is directed toward uncovering the uniqueness of each individual. One such study, *Letters from Jenny*, was described, along with an illustration of Allport's more traditional, nomothetic research in the area of personal religious orientation and prejudice.

One useful application of Allport's theory, the *Study of Values*, is a self-report personality test. Based upon Spranger's value types, it assesses the relative strength of each of six basic values in the individual's life: theoretical, economic, aesthetic, social, political, and religious. Persons can be characterized by their dominant value orientation or by their particular patterns of values.

BIBLIOGRAPHY

Allport, G. *Personality: A psychological interpretation.* New York: Holt, Rinehart and Winston, 1937.

Allport, G. *The use of personal documents in psychological science.* New York: Social Science Research Council. Bulletin **49**, 1942.

Allport, G. *The individual and his religion.* New York: Macmillan, 1950.

Allport, G. *Becoming: Basic considerations for a psychology of personality.* New Haven, Conn.: Yale University Press, 1955.

Allport, G. *Personality and social encounter: Selected essays.* Boston: Beacon Press, 1960.

Allport, G. *Pattern and growth in personality.* New York: Holt, Rinehart and Winston, 1961.

Allport, G. The general and the unique in psychological science. *Journal of Personality,* 1962, **30,** 405–422.

Allport, G. (Ed.). *Letters from Jenny.* New York: Harcourt, Brace & World, 1965.

Allport, G. Traits revisited. *American Psychologist,* 1966, **21,** 1–10.

Allport, G. Autobiography. In E. Boring & G. Lindzey (Eds.). *A history of psychology in autobiography.* Vol. 5. New York: Appleton-Century-Crofts, 1967, 1–25.

Allport, G. *The person in psychology: Selected essays.* Boston: Beacon Press, 1968a.

Allport, G. Personality: Contemporary viewpoints (1). In D. Sills (Ed.), *International encyclopedia of the social sciences.* New York: Macmillan and Free Press, 1968b.

Allport, G., & Allport, F. *A-S reaction study.* Boston: Houghton Mifflin, 1928.

Allport, G., & Cantril, H. Judging personality from voice. *Journal of Social Psychology,* 1934, **5,** 37–55.

Allport, G., & Vernon, P. *Studies in expressive movement* (3d ed.). Boston: Houghton Mifflin, 1960.

Allport, G., Vernon, P., & Lindzey, G. *A study of values* (3d ed.). Boston: Houghton Mifflin, 1960.

American Psychologist, 1964, **19,** 942–945.

Baldwin, A. Personal structure analysis: A statistical method for investigating the single personality. *Journal of Abnormal and Social Psychology,* 1942, **37,** 163–183.

Bischof, L. *Interpreting personality theories* (2d ed.). New York: Harper & Row, 1970.

Estes, S. Judging personality from expressive behavior. *Journal of Abnormal and Social Psychology,* 1938, **33,** 217–236.

Evans, R. Gordon Allport: A conversation. *Psychology Today,* April 1971, 55–59, 84, 86, 90, 94.

Hall, C., & Lindzey, G. *Theories of personality* (3d ed.). New York: Wiley, 1978.

Huntley, C. Judgments of self based upon records of expressive behavior. *Journal of Abnormal and Social Psychology,* 1940, **35,** 398–427.

Maddi, S., & Costa, P. *Humanism in personology: Allport, Maslow, and Murray.* Chicago: Aldine-Atherton, 1972.

Paige, J. Letters from Jenny: An approach to the clinical analysis of personality structure by computer. In P. Stone (Ed.), *The general inquirer: A computer approach to content analysis.* Cambridge, Mass.: MIT Press, 1966.

Ryckman, R. *Theories of personality.* New York: Van Nostrand, 1978.

Spranger, E. *Lebensformen* (3d ed.). Halle: Niemeyer, 1922. (Trans.: P. Pigors, *Types of men.* Halle: Niemeyer, 1928.)

Wilson, W. Extrinsic religious values and prejudice. *Journal of Abnormal and Social Psychology,* 1960, **60,** 286–288.

Zweigenhaft, R., & Marlowe, D. Signature size: Studies in expressive movement. *Journal of Consulting and Clinical Psychology,* 1973, **40,** 469–473.

SUGGESTED READINGS:

Allport, G. *The nature of prejudice.* Cambridge, Mass.: Addison-Wesley, 1954.

Allport, G. The open system in personality theory. *Journal of Abnormal and Social Psychology,* 1960, **61,** 301–310.

Gormly, J., & Edelberg, W. Validity in personality trait attribution. *American Psychologist,* 1974, **29,** 189–193.

Maddi, S. Humanistic psychology: Allport and Murray. In J. Wepman & R. Heine (Eds.), *Concepts of personality.* Chicago: Aldine, 1963, pp. 162–205.

DISCUSSION QUESTIONS

1 Select any person that you know well and list his or her essential personality characteristics. Do these characteristics appear to be what Allport means by "central traits"? How useful is the concept of "central traits" for describing a person in everyday terms?

2 List what you believe to be your own essential personality characteristics or central traits. Does this list *fully* capture your own intuitive sense of self, i.e., your subjective sense of who you are as a total person? Or do you also find Allport's concept of "proprium" necessary to describe your total personality? What precisely does the concept of proprium add to your personality description that was missing from your list of central traits?

3 What do you think of Allport's concept of "functional autonomy"? Can people really cut their motivational ties to the past, or is this concept a theoretical illusion? Bolster your argument with examples that you have observed.

4 How well do Allport's six characteristics of a "mature personality" fit your own idea of what constitutes a healthy personality? Can you think of any features a healthy personality might possess that are not in any way related to Allport's six characteristics?

5 Rate yourself on the six values described in the application section of this chapter— theoretical, economic, etc.—how high or low are you on each of these values? Consider also how well your value pattern fits with your present choice of occupation. Does the field that you've chosen to enter satisfy these values?

GLOSSARY

Bodily Self   That aspect of the proprium based on the individual's perception of his or her body. Allport considered it to be a lifelong anchor for self-awareness.

Cardinal Trait   A characteristic so pervasive that virtually all of a person's activities can be traced to its influence.

Central Trait   A characteristic of the individual that influences his or her behavior in a variety of settings. Allport viewed central traits as the "building blocks" of personality.

Character   Term used to refer to a moral standard or value system against which an individual's actions are evaluated.

Common Trait   Any generalized disposition against which most people within a given culture can reasonably be compared (also called *nomothetic trait*).

Extrinsic Religious Orientation   Term used by Allport to characterize a person who uses religion to satisfy his or her need for comfort, security, status, or social approval.

Functional Autonomy   Process whereby a given form of behavior becomes an end or goal in itself despite the fact that it may originally have been adopted for another reason. What was formerly a means to an end becomes an end in itself.

Idiographic View   Approach to personality study whereby the uniqueness of each person is the primary goal of investigation.

Individual Trait   Trait unique to the individual (also called *personal disposition*).

Intrinsic Religious Orientation   Term used by Allport to characterize a person who regards religious values as an integral part of his or her life and conducts his or her life in accordance with them.

Nomothetic View   Scientific approach to the study of personality that seeks to establish general laws of human functioning.

Propriate Striving   The individual's motivation to enhance self through the pursuit of important, long-range goals. Such motivation involves an increase, not a decrease, in level of tension.

Proprium   Term which refers to all the various aspects of a person that make her or him unique. It also represents the positive, creative, and forward-moving quality of human nature.

Psychophysical System   An integral part of Allport's definition of personality which suggests that both mental and physical factors must be considered when we seek to understand human functioning.

Secondary Trait   Peripheral characteristic of an individual, such as a specific food preference.

Self-Acceptance   The individual's tolerance for frustrating or irritating events as well as recognition of her or his personal strengths.

Self as Rational Coper   Term used to describe a person's realization that he or she can cope effectively with reality demands and achieve personal goals.

Self-Esteem   The favorableness of one's self-image.

Self-Extension   The feelings one has about one's material possessions. Such feelings are an integral part of a person's self-image.

Self-Identity   One's recognition of oneself as a distinct and constant point of reference relative to others.

Self-Image   The diversity of roles one plays in order to gain the approval of others and to manage their impressions of who and what one is.

Self-Objectification   Ability to know oneself objectively and to recognize one's strengths and weaknesses.

Study of Values   Self-report personality test used to measure six basic value dimensions, or types.

Temperament   The raw materials (intelligence and physique) of which personality is molded.

Trait Theory   Theoretical conception of personality that postulates the existence of underlying dispositions or characteristics that initiate and direct behavior. Traits are typically inferred from overt behavior.

George A. Kelly

George Kelly: A Cognitive Theory of Personality

It is a fundamental fact of life that human beings are thinking animals. Indeed, man's intellectual processes are so self-evident that all personality theories in some way acknowledge their effects on behavior. George Kelly, a practicing clinical psychologist, was the first personologist to emphasize the cognitive or knowing aspects of human existence as the dominant feature of personality. According to his theoretical system, the *Psychology of Personal Constructs*, a person is basically a *scientist*, striving to understand, interpret, anticipate, and control the personal world of experience for the purpose of dealing effectively with it. This view of human behavior as scientist-like is the hallmark of Kelly's theory:

> Mankind, whose progress in search of prediction and control of surrounding events stands out so clearly in the light of the centuries, comprises the men we see around us every day. The aspirations of the scientist are essentially the aspirations of all men (Kelly, 1955, p. 43).

Kelly admonished his fellow psychologists not to proceed as if their subjects were passive "reactors" to external stimuli. He reminded them that their subjects also behave like scientists, inferring on the basis of the past and hypothesizing about the future. His own thinking, highly original and different from the dominant forms of psychological thought prevalent in America in his day, has greatly contributed to recent major innovations in cognitive personality theory.

BIOGRAPHICAL SKETCH

George Alexander Kelly was born in Perth, Kansas, on April 28, 1905, the only child of farm parents. His father was a Presbyterian minister who turned to farming because of ill health. Kelly's early education was limited to a one-room country school. His parents later sent him to Wichita, Kansas, where in the course of four years he attended four different high schools. Kelly's parents were religiously devout, hardworking, and firmly opposed to evils such as drinking, card playing, and dancing. Kelly's family was imbued with traditional Midwestern values and aspirations, and Kelly himself was afforded considerable attention as an only child.

Kelly pursued undergraduate study for three years at Friends University, followed by one year at Park College, where he received his B.A. degree in physics and mathematics in 1926. Originally he had sought a career in mechanical engineering but, partly because of his experience in intercollegiate debates, he shifted his interests to social problems. He majored in educational sociology at the University of Kansas, minoring in labor relations and sociology. He wrote a thesis based on a study of the distribution of leisure-time activities of workers in Kansas City and was awarded an M.A. degree in 1928. The following year Kelly had divergent teaching responsibilities; he was a part-time instructor in a labor college in Minneapolis; he conducted classes in public speech for the American Bankers' Association; and he taught an Americanization class for prospective citizens. He next joined the faculty of a new public junior college in Sheldon, Iowa, where he met Gladys Thompson; they were married in 1931 and subsequently had two children. After a year and a half in Iowa, including a brief spell as an aeronautical engineer in Wichita, Kelly obtained an exchange fellowship to study at the University of Edinburgh in Scotland. There, in 1930, he earned a bachelor's degree in education and was permitted to take examinations over two years of graduate work after only nine months in residence. Under the direction of Sir Godfrey Thomson, a prominent statistician and educator, his thesis dealt with the prediction of teaching success. That same year he returned to the United States to enroll as a psychology doctoral candidate at the State University of Iowa. In 1931 Kelly was awarded the Ph.D. degree, having written a dissertation on common factors in speech and reading disabilities.

Kelly's career as an academic psychologist began at Fort Hays Kansas State College. There he rose to become an associate professor of psychology in 1943. During his twelve-year period he developed a program of traveling psychological clinics that allowed both him and his students opportunities to implement new approaches to behavior problems encountered in the state's school system. This experience also stimulated numerous ideas that were later incorporated into his formulations of personality and psychotherapy. In particular, it was during this period that Kelly abandoned the Freudian approach to understanding personality. His clinical experiences taught him that people in the Midwest were more victimized by prolonged drought, dust storms, and economic setbacks than by libidinal forces.

During World War II, as a naval aviation psychologist, Kelly headed a training program for local civilian pilots. His interest in aviation continued at the Bureau of Medicine and Surgery of the Navy in Washington, D.C., where he remained in the Aviation Branch until 1945. That year he was appointed associate professor at the University of Maryland.

The war's end created considerable demand for clinical psychologists because large numbers of American military personnel were returning home plagued with a variety of personal problems. Indeed, World War II was the single most important factor contributing to the development of clinical psychology as an integral part of the health sciences. Kelly became a prominent figure in this evolution. In 1946 he attained national status when he became professor and director of clinical psychology at Ohio State University. In his twenty years there, Kelly completed his major theoretical contributions to psychology. For the first few years of this period, his efforts focused on the reorganization and administration of the graduate program in clinical psychology. Within a few years he piloted this program to the forefront of graduate training in the United States.

In 1965 Kelly departed for Brandeis University, where he was appointed to the Riklis Chair of Behavioral Science. This position, a professor's dream come true, allowed him complete freedom to pursue his own scholarly interests. One year later, on March 6, 1966, he died at the age of 62. At the time of his death, Kelly was assembling a volume composed of the numerous papers he had delivered in the previous decade. Under the editorship of Brendan Maher, a former student, a revised version of this work appeared posthumously in 1969.

In addition to his distinguished career as a teacher, scientist, and theorist, Kelly held many positions of leadership among American psychologists. He served as president of both the Clinical and Counseling Divisions of the American Psychological Association. He was also instrumental in formulating the American Board of Examiners in Professional Psychology, an organization devoted to the further upgrading of professional psychologists, and served as its president from 1951 through 1953. He received invitations to teach and lecture at universities throughout the world. During the concluding years of his life, Kelly contributed much of his time to international affairs. For example, financed by a grant from the Human Ecology Fund, he and his wife traveled around the world during 1960–1961 applying his personal construct theory (to be discussed shortly) to the resolution of international problems.

Although he published less extensively than other major personologists, Kelly exerted a lasting influence through his training of clinical psychologists. In the short span of three years (1952–1955), for instance, twelve doctoral dissertations at Ohio State were addressed to research implications and applications of his theory. Kelly's best-known scholarly contribution is a two-volume work published in 1955 entitled *The Psychology of Personal Constructs.* These volumes describe his theoretical formulations of personality and their clinical ramifications. Students who wish to pursue other aspects of Kelly's work might be interested in the following books: *Inquiring Man: The Theory of Personal Constructs* (Bannister and Fransella, 1971); *Clinical Psychology and Personality: The Selected Papers of George Kelly* (edited by Maher, 1969); *Perspectives in Personal Construct Theory* (edited by Bannister, 1970).

CORNERSTONES OF COGNITIVE THEORY

The central theme of this volume is that any personality theory necessarily involves certain philosophical assumptions about human nature. That is, the way a personologist chooses to view his or her subject matter, the human organism, will largely determine his or her model of the person. Unlike most personologists, George Kelly explicitly acknowledged that all conceptions of human nature, including his own, are founded on basic assumptions. Kelly developed his personal constructs theory on the basis of a single philosophical assumption—constructive alternativism.

Constructive Alternativism

Now that people of all ages are exploring alternative life-styles and ways of understanding things, George Kelly's vintage-1955 theory appears to have been curiously ahead of its time. Kelly's underlying philosophy, constructive alternativism, furnishes a dazzling array of options for people seeking alternatives to the commonplace. In fact, the philosophy practically demands that people do so.

As a doctrine, constructive alternativism asserts that all present interpretations of the universe are subject to revision or replacement. Nothing is sacred. There are no politics, religions, economic principles, social mores, or even college administrative policies that are absolutely and unalterably "right." All would be changed if people simply saw things differently. Kelly argues that there is no such thing as an "interpretation-free" view of the world. A person's perception of reality is always subject to interpretation; in Kelly's philosophy, objective reality or absolute truth are figments of the imagination. Truth, like beauty, exists only in the mind of the beholder.

Since events exist in the human mind alone, it follows that there are various ways to construe them. To illustrate, consider the event of a girl taking money from her mother's purse. What does it signify? The event is simple: money has been removed from the purse. However, if we ask a child therapist to interpret the event, she or he may give an elaborate account of the girl's feelings of rejection by the mother—rejection itself the result, perhaps, of the mother's frustration at having to stay home and raise a daughter instead of pursuing her own career goals. If we ask the mother, she may say that her daughter is "bad" and untrustworthy. The girl's father may suggest that she is "undisciplined." Grandfather may consider the event a childish prank. The girl herself may regard it as reflecting her parents' unwillingness to provide her with a sufficient allowance. While the event itself obviously cannot be undone—the money was taken—its meaning is open to alternative interpretations. Any event, then, can be viewed from a wide variety of perspectives. Persons have a dazzling choice of options available when interpreting the inner world of experience or the outer world of practical affairs. Kelly summarized his commitment to constructive alternativism in the following way: ". . . whatever nature may be, or howsoever the quest for truth will turn out in the end, the events we face today are subject to as great a variety of constructions as our wits will enable us to contrive (1970, p. 1)."

The intriguing nature of constructive alternativism can be understood more clearly if it is contrasted with one of Aristotle's traditional philosophic principles. Aristotle first put forth the principle of identity: A is A. A thing is itself in objective reality; it is open to only one valid interpretation. For example, assume that a person's behavior is produced by one motive or set of motives only. If the personologist does not understand that person's motives, that is her or his problem (and mistake), not the subject's. By contrast, Kelly would argue that *A is what one construes as A!* Reality is what one construes as reality; events can always be viewed from a wide variety of perspectives. In this scheme of things, then, there is no one true or valid way of interpreting a person's behavior. Whether one is attempting to understand another person's behavior, one's own, or the nature of the universe, there are always "constructive alternatives" open for consideration.

Furthermore, the concept of constructive alternativism clearly implies that our behavior is never totally determined. We are always free to some extent to revise or replace our interpretation of events. Yet Kelly also believes that some of our thoughts and behavior are determined by antecedent events. For, as will become increasingly evident, cognitive theory is constructed on a joint freedom–determinism base. In Kelly's words, "Determinism and freedom are inseparable, for that which determines another is, by the same token, free of the other" (1955, p. 21).

People as Scientists

Kelly's theory is a contemporary cognitive approach to the study of personality, one which emphasizes the manner in which individuals perceive and interpret people and things in their environments. Construct theory thus focuses on the processes that enable people to understand the psychological terrain of their lives. From this cognitive perspective, Kelly proposed a model of personality based on the analogy of a person *as a scientist*. Specifically, he theorized that, like the scientist who studies her or him, the human subject also generates working hypotheses about reality with which she or he tries to anticipate and control the events of life. To be sure, Kelly did not propose that every person is literally a scientist who attends to some limited aspect of the world and employs sophisticated methods to gather and assess data. That analogy would have been foreign to his outlook. But he did suggest that all persons are scientists in that they formulate hypotheses and follow the same psychological processes to validate or invalidate them as those involved in a scientific enterprise (Kelly, 1955). Thus, the basic premise underlying personal construct theory is that science constitutes a refinement of the aims and procedures by which each of us works out a way of life. The aims of science are to predict, to modify, and to understand events (i.e., the scientist's main goal is to reduce uncertainty). Not only the scientist, every person shares these same aims. We are all motivated to anticipate the future and make plans based on expected outcomes.

To concretize this model of the human being, consider the example of a student who encounters a new professor on the first day of class (assuming that she has no previous knowledge of the professor's "reputation"). Based on limited data (perhaps fifty minutes of class time), the student perceives and interprets the professor to be "fair." Kelly's word for this process is *construe;* the student "construes" fairness in the professor. Essentially, what's happening is that the student is generating a hypothesis about the professor that will help her anticipate and control events involving that course. Specifically, if the student's hypothesis proves "valid," the professor can be expected to assign a reasonable amount of reading, give decent examinations, and grade fairly. Should the professor's subsequent behavior differ markedly, the student would then need an alternative hypothesis, e.g., the prof is unfair, the prof is a nurd, or whatever. The point is that the student (like all of us) needs a useful and consistent means of anticipating events affecting her life if she is to function effectively.

In developing this theory of personal constructs based on the analogy of the person as a scientist, Kelly was amazed to discover the contrast between views the psychologist uses to explain his or her own behavior and those used to explain the behavior of research subjects. He described this discrepancy as follows:

> It is as though the psychologist were saying to himself, "I, being a psychologist, and therefore a scientist, am performing this experiment in order to improve the prediction and control of certain human phenomena; but my subject, being merely a human organism, is obviously propelled by inexorable drives welling up within him, or else he is in gluttonous pursuit of sustenance and shelter" (1955, p. 5).

Kelly rejected the tunnel-vision notion that only the psychological scientist wearing a lab coat and behaving like a scientist is concerned with predicting and controlling the course of events in life. Rather than viewing the human organism as some kind of unwilling and unthinking blob of protoplasm, Kelly credited the human subject with the same aspirations as the so-called scientific psychologist. This notion, namely that the psychologist is no different from the subject she or he studies, epitomizes Kelly's personal construct theory of personality. It reveals Kelly's belief that no being can lay claim to more intelligent and rational powers than any other.

To treat all persons as if they were scientists leads to a number of important consequences for Kelly's theory. Foremost, it suggests that people are fundamentally oriented toward future rather than past or present events in their lives. In fact, Kelly (1955) maintained that all behavior can be understood as anticipatory in nature. He also noted that one's outlook on life is transitory, insofar as it is rarely the same as it was yesterday or will be tomorrow. In attempting to anticipate and control future events, one's view of reality is constantly being tested: "Anticipation is not merely carried on for its own sake; it is carried on so that future reality may be better represented. It is the future which tantalizes man, not the past. Always he reaches out to the future through the window of the present" (Kelly, 1955, p. 49).

A second consequence following from the analogy of the person as a scientist is that this person has the capacity to actively represent his or her environment rather than merely passively respond to it. Just as the psychologist rationally formulates and revises theoretical notions about phenomena, so can a layperson interpret and reinterpret, construe and reconstrue, his or her environment. For Kelly, then, life is characterized by the continuous struggle to make sense of the tangible world of experience; it is this quality of life that enables persons to shape their own destiny. One need not be an enslaved victim of one's past history or present situation— unless one decides to construe oneself in such a way. In short, a person is not controlled by present events (as Skinner suggests) or past ones (as Freud proposed) but rather *controls* events depending on the questions raised and the answers found.

PERSONAL CONSTRUCT THEORY

The heart of Kelly's cognitive theory lies in the manner in which individuals perceive and interpret people and things in their environments. Labeling his approach *personal construct theory*, Kelly focused on the psychological processes which enable the person to order and understand the events of his or her life.

Constructs: Templets for Reality

Scientists formulate theoretical constructs to describe and explain the events with which they are concerned. In Kelly's personological system, the key theoretical construct is the term *construct* itself:

> Man looks at his world through transparent patterns or templets which he creates and then attempts to fit over the realities of which the world is composed. The fit is not always very good. Yet without such patterns the world appears to be such an undifferentiated homogeneity that man is unable to make any sense out of it (Kelly, 1955, pp. 8–9).

It is these "transparent patterns or templets" which Kelly designated *personal constructs*. Stated otherwise, a construct is a category of thought by which the individual construes, or interprets, his or her personal world of experience. It represents a consistent way for the person to make sense of some aspect of reality in terms of similarities and contrasts. Examples of personal constructs include "excitable versus calm," "refined versus vulgar," "intelligent versus stupid," "good versus bad," "religious versus nonreligious," and "friendly versus hostile." These constructs are ones which many people use to construe events in their daily lives.

As an illustration of constructs in action, let's examine how different people might construe the same event. The event in question is that a recent college graduate, instead of pursuing his earlier plans to attend medical school, packs up his guitar and goes off with his companion and lover to live in a hippie commune. The young man's father might construe this event as "distressing" or "embarrassing," while his mother construes him to be "living in sin" ("sinful"). His college counselor, well-grounded in Eriksonian theory, thinks that he is "searching for his identity," and his sociology prof believes that he's simply "rejecting the norms of a consumption-oriented society." The young man himself construes the event as "natural," as "the right thing for me to do at this time." Which is it? In Kelly's theory, there is no way to tell. Kelly's point is simply that, for each of us, reality is filtered through different templets or constructs—that we need in order to understand the world in a consistent fashion.

According to Kelly, a person predicts and controls personal experiences by construing their replications. This process is significant in that it provides a tangible basis for expecting what kinds of events are likely to occur and for interpreting their meaning. In the initial stages of construing, one notes the general flow of events and tentatively interprets them. One then recognizes a pattern, or repetition of the events, within one's field of experience. Finally, one places a structure and meaning on the events that have been experienced. This temporal process of experiencing, interpreting, and structuring is called *construing:* it accounts for a person's capacity to generalize experiences in an orderly and meaningful fashion. Constructs are thus relevant to prediction and control because they provide one with expectations with which to anticipate subsequent events. In the absence of constructs, life would be chaotic; one would have no consistent way to make sense of the world. If one were unable to form expectations about the future, current events would also be incomprehensible. The existence of personal constructs thus enables one to impose some order and predictability upon the world.

Consistent with his model of humans as scientists, Kelly maintained that once a person hypothesizes that a given construct will adequately anticipate and predict some event in his or her environment, he or she will then test that hypothesis against events that have not yet occurred. If the construct leads to an accurate prediction of the environment (i.e., helps the person to anticipate events correctly), the person retains it. Conversely, if a prediction is disconfirmed, the construct from which it was derived is likely to undergo some revision or may even be eliminated altogether (recall our earlier example of the professor initially construed as "fair"). The validity of a construct, then, is tested in terms of its *predictive efficiency,* of which there are varying degrees.

Kelly also theorized that all personal constructs are inherently *bipolar* and *dichotomous* in nature—that the essence of human thought is to perceive life's experiences in black versus white terms, not shades of gray. More specifically, in experiencing events, a person observes that certain events seem similar to each other (they share common properties) and different from other events. One notices, for example, that some people are fat and some are skinny, some are black and some are white, some are affluent and some are poor, some things are dangerous to touch and some are not. It is this cognitive process of observing similarities and differences that leads to the formation of personal constructs. Thus, at least three elements (events or things) are needed to form a construct: two of the construct elements must be perceived as similar to each other, while the third element must be perceived as different from these two, e.g., Danny and Betty are *honest;* Dick is not.

The way in which two elements are construed to be similar or alike is called the *construct* or *similarity* pole of the construct dimension; the way in which they are contrasted with the third element is called the *contrast* pole of the construct dimension. Every construct thus has a similarity pole and a contrast pole. The thrust of personal construct theory is to discover how people interpret and anticipate their experiences in terms of similarities and contrasts.

However, Kelly neglected to elaborate on the processes by which an individual comes to construe his or her experiences along particular lines, i.e., *why* are John's constructs different from Burt's? He simply did not consider the issue of individual differences vis-a-vis the origin and development of personal constructs. This is understandable insofar as Kelly's theory is *ahistorical*, placing no special emphasis upon the individual's early experiences. However, constructs must come from somewhere, and it seems most reasonable to assume that they are a product of the individual's past history. It is likely that differential histories of environmental experiences account for the variability among individual construct systems.

Formal Properties of Constructs

Kelly proposed that certain formal properties characterize all constructs. First, a construct resembles a theory in that it encompasses a particular domain of events. This *range of convenience* consists of all events for which a particular construct may be relevant or applicable—that is, a given construct has relevance for some events but not for others. The construct dimension "scholarly versus not scholarly," for example, is quite applicable to understanding a vast array of intellectual and scientific accomplishments but is hardly appropriate for construing the relative merits of being married or single. Kelly noted that the predictive efficiency of a construct is seriously jeopardized whenever it is generalized beyond the range of events for which it was intended. Thus, all constructs have a limited range of convenience, though the scope of the range may vary widely from construct to construct. The construct "good versus bad" has a wide range of convenience since it applies to most situations requiring personal evaluation. In contrast, the construct "virginity versus prostitution" is substantially narrower in scope.

Each construct also has a *focus of convenience,* that is, a point or area within the construct's range of convenience where it is maximally useful in construing certain events. For instance, one person's construct of "honest versus dishonest" might have as its focus of convenience keeping one's hands off other people's money and property. Another person may apply the same construct to politics. Hence, a construct's focus of convenience is always specific to the individual employing the construct.

Permeability-impermeability is another dimension along which constructs vary. A permeable construct admits to its range of convenience elements not yet construed within its boundaries, whereas an impermeable one, while embracing events that made up its original formulation, remains closed to the interpretation of new experiences. There are relative degrees of permeability and impermeability. One student's construct of "competent versus incompetent" teachers might be sufficiently permeable to account for any new instructor he encounters. That is, after interacting with any new instructor for some time, the student could construe her or him as either competent or incompetent; the construct is completely permeable. But another student may use the same construct in a totally impermeable way, insisting that competent teachers no longer exist—that the last competent one was her third grade teacher who is now dead. Thus, the distinction between competent and incompetent teachers is no longer relevant for her. All teachers are incompetent! Note that permeability is relevant only to a given construct's range of convenience; a construct is impermeable by definition to any experience beyond its range of convenience. Hence, "competent versus incompetent" has no meaning when judging the taste of one's favorite drink.

Types of Constructs   Kelly also suggested that personal constructs can be classified according to the nature of the control they implicitly exercise over their elements. A construct which freezes ("preempts") its elements for membership exclusively in its own realm Kelly termed a *preemptive* construct. This is a type of pigeonhole construct; what has been placed in one pigeonhole is excluded from any other. Preemptive construing may be likened to the "nothing but" kind of thinking characteristic of a rigid person. Ethnic labels illustrate the use of preemptive constructs. For instance, if a person is identified as a Chicano, then she or he may be thought of by some as nothing but a Chicano. Or, to a lesser degree, once a professor has been labeled as "hard-nosed," some students may disregard the possibility of thinking of him or her in other ways, e.g., as a person with tender feelings for his or her children, artistic hobbies, or social reform pursuits. Preemptive thought represents a kind of denial of the right of both others and ourselves to re-view, reinterpret, and see in a fresh light some part of the world around us (Bannister and Fransella, 1971).

A *constellatory* construct permits its elements to belong to other realms concurrently but fixes their realm memberships. That is, once an event is subsumed under one construct, its other characteristics are fixed. Stereotyped or typological thinking illustrates this type of construct. For example, constellatory thinking accepts "if this man is a pro football player, he must be brutal, insensitive, and dumb." Here, the athlete may be considered as something other than an athlete, but there is no latitude as to what else he may be considered. By definition, constellatory constructs restrict one's chances of adopting alternative views; once we assign a person to a given category, we then attribute a cluster or constellation of other characteristics to him or her.

A construct which leaves its elements open to alternative constructions is called a *propositional* construct. This type of construct directly contradicts preemptive or constellatory constructs since it allows the person to be open to new experiences and adopt alternative views of the world. In this instance, construing someone as a football player is propositional to the extent that other personal attributes do not necessarily follow. Accordingly, propositional thinking is flexible thinking. The person is continuously open to new experience and is capable of modifying existing constructs. While it is tempting to "construe" preemptive and constellatory constructs as undesirable and propositional constructs as desirable, Kelly clearly stated that such is not necessarily true. If one used propositional constructs only, one would have an extremely difficult time getting along in the world since one could not reach pressing decisions.

As an illustration, consider a baseball game in which the ball is speedily coming in the direction of your head. You could begin to construe the ball propositionally, considering and reconsidering it from all perceptual angles. As it smacked you in the face, you might then see that it would have been far better in this circumstance to construe the ball preemptively, i.e., this event is a baseball coming at my head and nothing else! However, Kelly believed that, to avoid intellectual rigor mortis, one must be able to engage in propositional thinking. Without it, a person would be doomed to a sterile, unchanging, and stereotyped mode of perceiving reality. Hence, preemptive, constellatory, and propositional forms of thinking are all necessary to construe events. Propositional thinking is simply a contrast to preemptive and constellatory ways of making sense of reality.

There are several ways in which constructs can be categorized or typed. For example, there are *comprehensive* constructs, which subsume a relatively wide spectrum of events, and *incidental* constructs, which subsume a small range of events (i.e., have a much narrower range of convenience). There are *core* constructs that govern a person's basic functioning and *peripheral* constructs that may be altered without serious modification of the core structure. Finally, some constructs are *tight* insofar as they lead to unvarying predictions, whereas others are *loose* in that they lead an individual to arrive at different predictions under similar conditions.

Personality: The Personologist's Construct?

Kelly never offered an explicit definition of the term "personality." However, he discussed the concept in general terms in one paper, stating that personality is "our abstraction of the activity of a person and our subsequent generalization of this abstraction to all matters of his relationship to other persons, known and unknown, as well as to anything else that may seem particularly valuable" (1961, pp. 220–221). Kelly thus believed that personality is an abstraction made by personologists of the psychological processes they observe in others. It is not a separate entity to be discovered by them. Furthermore, Kelly argued that personality is by its very nature embedded in a person's interpersonal relationships. Meshing these two ideas and adding one of our own, a more pointed definition of personality within Kelly's system is possible; specifically, an individual's personality is nothing more or less than his or her construct system. One uses constructs to interpret one's world of experience and to anticipate future events; indeed, personality consists of the constructs one uses to anticipate the future. To understand another person involves knowing something about the constructs he or she employs, the events subsumed under these constructs, and the way in which they are organized in relation to one another to form a construct system. In short, to know someone's personality is to know how she or he construes personal experience.

Motivation: Who Needs It?

Psychologists have traditionally used the concept of motivation to explain two aspects of behavior: (1) why people are active (behave) at all and (2) why their activity takes one direction rather than another. In Kelly's judgment, the term "motivation" assumes that humans are by nature static beings and act only when some special enlivening force prods them. In contrast, Kelly outrightly repudiated the notion that *humans are inactive or reactive* by nature and behave only when set into motion by some internal or external force. For Kelly (1958), people are motivated for no other reason than that they are alive. In fact, life itself is seen as a form of process or movement; human beings represent one species of such all-pervasive movement. Following from this reasoning, no special concepts (e.g., drives, needs, instincts, rewards, motives) are required to understand what produces or motivates human behavior.

Kelly's objection to the concept of motivation came from his experience as a practicing therapist. He found that it makes virtually no difference, in terms of helping clients, whether or not one attributes a set of motives to them. Motivational concepts are interpretations that therapists place on their clients' behavior. They may be useful for predicting someone's behavior (e.g., Anjie is lazy and, therefore, probably won't finish her term paper), but they are useless for understanding and helping a person because they reflect the way the *therapist,* rather than the client, thinks about the world. Furthermore, Kelly noted that motivational statements usually reveal more about the speaker than about the person whose motives are in question: "When we find a person who is concerned about motives, he usually turns out to be the one who is threatened by his fellowmen and wants to put them in their place" (Kelly, 1969, p. 77).

Kelly summarized the state of modern motivation theories and contrasted them with his own position in the following way:

> Motivational theories can be divided into two types, push theories and pull theories. Under push theories we find such terms as drive, motive, or even stimulus. Pull theories use such constructs as purpose, value, or need. In terms of a well known metaphor, there are pitchfork theories on the one hand and the carrot theories on the other. But our theory is neither of these. Since we prefer to look to the nature of the animal himself, ours is probably best called a jackass theory (1958, p. 50).

Personal construct theory construes the human being to be an active and struggling organism simply by virtue of being alive and "motivation," therefore, to be a redundant construct.

Since Kelly rejected motivation to account for human activity, how did he explain its direction? The explanation is presented in his fundamental postulate, discussed below.

A POSTULATE AND SOME COROLLARIES

The formal structure of personal construct theory is both economical and parsimonious in that Kelly advanced his central tenets by using one fundamental postulate and eleven elaborative corollaries. After we describe his basic postulate, we will discuss those corollaries that most appear to add to our account of Kelly's position presented up to now.

Channelizing Processes

Each personality theorist seems to have a language of his or her own when describing human behavior. Kelly is no exception, as can be seen in his *fundamental postulate: "A person's processes are psychologically channelized by the ways in which he anticipates events"* (1955, p. 46). A typical response to this postulate by an uninitiated Kelly reader might be "Huh?" Let us therefore break it down for better understanding since it is central to his formal system.

Roughly translated, the fundamental postulate stipulates that how a person predicts future occurrences determines his or her behavior. In other words, we function in terms of our expectations about events. It also means that Kelly is primarily interested in the whole individual rather than any part of her or him (e.g., intergroup relations). The word "processes" suggests that a person is basically a behaving, changing organism, not an inert substance pushed and pulled by internal or external forces (recall Kelly's "jackass" view of human motivation).

Kelly's fundamental postulate also reveals that his system is psychological in scope, that its range of convenience is limited to understanding human behavior. "Channelized" means that behavior is relatively stable across time and situations. Kelly (1955) conceived of a person's processes as operating through a network of pathways as opposed to fluttering about in an unpredictable void. The word "ways" is synonymous with *constructs,* while the pronoun "he" highlights the individuality of construing. Concerning this latter point, Kelly (1955) noted that each individual erects and characteristically uses different ways (constructs), and it is the way one chooses that channelizes one's processes. Finally, the phrase "anticipates events" conveys the predictive and motivational features intrinsic to cognitive theory. Like a scientist, a person seeks to predict reality to facilitate the anticipation of events affecting his or her life. This notion is what accounts for the directionality of human activities in Kelly's scheme. In this system, persons look at the present so that they may anticipate the future through the unique templet of their personal constructs.

Individuality and Organization

The basic theme set forth in Kelly's fundamental postulate is elaborated in various corollaries. Of these, the *individuality corollary* appears particularly helpful in understanding the uniqueness of personality: "Persons differ from each other in their construction of events" (Kelly, 1955, p. 55). For Kelly, no two people, whether they be identical twins or supposedly similar in outlook, will approach and interpret the same event in exactly the same way. Each person construes reality through his or her unique personal construct "goggles." Hence, differences between people are rooted in their construing events from different perspectives.

Examples abound. Consider the traditional differences of opinion between political liberals and conservatives on such issues as welfare, military spending, abortion, taxation, forced racial integration, pornography, and capital punishment. Or reflect on why students may disagree with professors, professors with department chairpersons, department chairpersons with deans, and everybody with college presidents. Or what is popularly called the "generation gap"—the fundamental differences of viewpoint between parents and their offspring—a situation which, in Kelly's theory, might more properly be labeled a "personal construct gap." In all these instances, persons are in disagreement because each is operating from a different construct system. No wonder there is such lack of accord among people— from Kelly's vantage point, they are not even talking about the same things!

In addition to the individuality of personal constructs, Kelly also maintained that constructs are organized within persons in different ways. This is clearly asserted in his *organization corollary:* "Each person characteristically evolves, for his convenience in anticipating events, a construction system embracing ordinal relationships between constructs" (1955, p. 56). This corollary indicates that persons organize their personal constructs hierarchically to minimize incompatibilities and inconsistencies. Perhaps even more important, it implies that people differ not only in the number and kinds of constructs they use to view the world but also in the ways in which they organize their constructs.

For Kelly, the organization of systems of constructs is essentially a logical one: constructs are ordered in a pyramidal structure so that some constructs are either superordinate or subordinate in relation to other parts of the system. (Of course, a construct may be quite independent of all others in the person's repertoire.) A *superordinate* construct subsumes other constructs, whereas a *subordinate* construct is one that is included in another (superordinate) construct. For example, for some people, the construct "good versus bad" subsumes within its two poles the two poles of the construct "sexy versus nonsexy." In this instance, the former construct is superordinate to the latter. To illustrate, consider a male-chauvinist type in the process of construing the playmate of the month in *Playboy* magazine. He would most probably construe her as "sexy" and hence, superordinately speaking, "good." But even in the most blatant male chauvinist's construct system, "good" usually incorporates more than "sexy." For example, he may also construe the interview of the month in the same magazine as "good" because, to him, it is "insightful." In this case, then, the constructs "sexy versus nonsexy" and "insightful versus noninsightful" are both subordinate to the "good versus bad" superordinate construct. The basic point is that people evolve different hierarchies of personal constructs. What is a superordinate-subordinate construct relationship in one person's system is not necessarily the same as that in another's system. According to Kelly, only by knowing an individual's mode of organizing constructs can one make meaningful statements about his or her behavior.

To Construe or Not to Construe: That Is the Question

From Kelly's perspective, the translation of cognition into behavior in any situation depends upon the construct a person uses to construe the relevant events and which end of the dichotomous construct he or she applies. Kelly's *choice corollary* describes how people make these selections: "A person chooses for himself that alternative in a dichotomized construct through which he anticipates the greater possibility for extension and definition of his system" (1955, p. 64). Specifically, if one is confronted with a choice (i.e., a situation in which one must use one's constructs in one way or another), one will opt for the alternative that is most likely to enhance either one's understanding of the world or clarify one's present construct system. In other words, one will choose the construct pole that renders the event most understandable—the one that will contribute most to the predictive efficiency of one's construct system. Kelly called this the *elaborative choice*.

The choice corollary also suggests that one's construct system is elaborated in the direction of either *definition* or *extension*. In the case of definition, one chooses the alternative with the greater probability of validating aspects of experience that have already been fairly accurately construed. That is, one wagers a relatively safe bet as to how things will turn out, based on previous experience, and then observes the evidence. If the anticipated event does occur and the construct system is confirmed, then the construct becomes consolidated and clear-cut by virtue of its having led to a correct prediction. In extension, one chooses that alternative which has the greater likelihood of broadening one's understanding of events (increasing the construct's range of convenience) in new and different ways. If the prediction is correct, then the construct is validated and becomes, at least temporarily, more comprehensive. Thus, if enough is known about the structure of a person's construct system to predict his or her choices in terms of that system, then it is also possible to predict the person's behavior to some extent.

Kelly characterized the difference between definition and extension as one of *security* or *adventure*. Persons must continuously decide which of these two modes will further articulate their personal constructs. College students, for example, must often choose whether to take courses similar to ones they have previously taken—courses in which satisfactory grades are somewhat assured—or whether to take unfamiliar courses where failure is a risk but which offer possibilities of broadening their knowledge and understanding of the world. A "snap" course in a familiar subject represents "security" while organic chemistry, for most students, is an "adventure." In this instance, if a student chooses the alternative that minimizes risk, then the construct system (if validated) is further consolidated and defined. However, if a student opts for the alternative that will extend her or his system, this invites greater risk: she or he may not be able to correctly anticipate events, i.e., might flunk. Of course, the likelihood of acquiring additional understanding which will serve in future predictions is increased.

Kelly did not suggest that the individual seeks certainty, reinforcement, and/or the avoidance of pain in elaborating personal constructs. People simply seek to anticipate events while validating and extending construct systems. Literally, they strive to increase the range of convenience of their construct systems.

Although Kelly detailed the basis for recognizing whether a person defines or extends his or her construct system, there is scant empirical evidence or theoretical rationale as to why or when one kind of choice will be favored over another. Possibly when one feels secure and confident in predicting events correctly and can even risk being wrong, one will more likely choose to extend one's construct system. In contrast, if one feels insecure and inadequate in correctly predicting events, one will be more likely to choose definition.

C-P-C Cycle   Kelly presented various models to illustrate the process whereby cognition is translated into action. One of particular importance is called the *circumspection-preemption-control* (C-P-C) *cycle,* which involves a sequential progression from construction to overt behavior. In the first phase of the C-P-C cycle, the *circumspection* phase, an individual considers a number of different constructs as they relate to a particular situation—that is, she contemplates the various possibilities facing her in a propositional fashion. This is analogous to looking at all sides of the question. (Recall that a propositional construct is open to new experiences.) The *preemption* phase follows when the individual reduces the number of alternative constructs (hypotheses) to ones most appropriate to the problem. Here she decides which of the preemptive alternatives to use. Finally, during the *control* phase of the cycle, she decides on a course of action and its accompanying behavior. The choice is made, in other words, based on an estimate of which alternative construct is most likely to lead to extension and definition of the system.

As an illustration of the C-P-C cycle, consider the case of a young woman just entering college. She surveys her situation, considering a wide variety of constructs. There are a great many ways in which she *could* construe herself in relation to this new situation (circumspection). However, if she is eventually to graduate, the situation must be preempted in terms of the construct "student"; she must predominately construe herself as a college student before she can consistently act accordingly, e.g., attend classes, study seriously, pass examinations (preemption and then control). However, if, instead, the young woman continues to think of herself as only "Mary Highschooler, the goof-off," or "Daddy's little girl," or "Star local lover—seducer of men," she will never get to engage in the behaviors necessary to the successful completion of college.

Kelly noted that a person may go through a number of C-P-C cycles before he or she decides to act. He cites Hamlet as the classic example of a person who, after preemption ("To be, or not to be; that is the question . . ."), could not decide on the final choice and instead returned to the circumspection phase of the cycle. The notion of the C-P-C cycle is consistent with Kelly's conviction that the alternatives we see before us are of our own making and reflect the constructs we use to construe the situation. Thus, if we could only change our constructs, we could literally change our lives; the options in Kelly's system are dazzling. Kelly also contended, however, that since the world is multidimensional and a person possesses a number of different dimensions in his or her construct system, the dimensions must be sorted, until there is a single dichotomous choice to be made before the person can act. In Kelly's view, only when a person says "this and this only is the important dimension" is she or he ready to act. Ultimately, then, one must construe in order to behave intelligently.

Change in a Construct System

A construct system enables an individual to anticipate events as accurately as possible. It follows, then, that a construct system changes in relation to its inability to correctly anticipate the unfolding sequence of events. In this regard, Kelly postulated that a change in one's construct system occurs most often when one is exposed to novel or unfamiliar events which do not conform to one's existing system of constructs. Accordingly, the *experience corollary* states: "A person's construct system varies as he successively construes the replication of events" (1955, p. 72).

Also called the *learning corollary,* it suggests that a personal construct system is a set of hypotheses about the world that are perpetually being tested by experience. The feedback one receives on how well these hypotheses helped to predict the future leads to a modification of constructs which, in turn, are used as new hypotheses to progressively change the system. Those constructs found to be useful are retained, whereas those that are not are revised or discarded. Thus, for Kelly, a construct system undergoes successive revision with the ebb and flow of its validational fortunes.

For Kelly, a person's *experience* is the reconstruction of his or her life based upon revisions of his or her constructs as they are affected by events in time. This means that a person gains little or no experience if after having observed a succession of events he or she still construes the events in the same way. If, for example, a professor has been teaching for ten years and is still presenting the same lectures in the same way that she did in her first year, Kelly would question whether she has really had ten years of teaching experience. On the other hand, if what she taught during her first year led her to alter and improve her teaching in her second year and successively through the tenth year, she could legitimately claim to have had a decade of teaching experience.

Kelly's *modulation corollary* specifies the conditions under which changes occur in a construct system: "The variation in a person's construction system is limited by the permeability of the constructs within whose range of convenience the variants lie" (1955, p. 77). As discussed earlier, "permeability" refers to the degree to which a construct can assimilate novel experiences and events within its range of convenience. Thus, this corollary implies that the more permeable (open) a person's superordinate constructs, the greater the possible variation (systematic change) within the substructures they subsume. If one has no superordinate constructs for construing change, then change cannot occur within one's system. One is psychologically rigid. Consequently, a person must not only be capable of construing new events or reconstruing old ones, but also of construing change itself. In other words, since modification of a construct or a set of constructs is an event for oneself, one must have some conceptual framework in which the changes in one's system can be construed. Otherwise, change cannot take place, although chaos might.

By way of way of illustration, consider a 21-year-old male who construes his relationship to his mother in such a way that he still reacts to her as "Mommy's little boy," i.e., overdependently. Obviously, he is going to have a great deal of trouble in life unless he can change this construction of the relationship. The young man is in luck if he happens to have a permeable superordinate construct like "mature versus immature" which he can apply to this situation. If he does, he can begin to construe himself as "mature" and thus begin to respond differently to his mother, i.e., less dependently. In essence, he reconstrues his relationship to his mother in terms of his application of the construct "mature" to himself.

Social Relationships and Personal Constructs

If, as Kelly asserted in his individuality corollary, people differ as a result of the way they interpret situations, then it follows that they may be similar to others to the extent that they construe experiences in similar ways. Birds of a feather construe together. This idea is explicit in Kelly's *commonality corollary:* "To the extent that one person employs a construction of experience which is similar to that employed by another, his psychological processes are similar to those of the other person" (1955, p. 90). Thus, if two people view the world in the same way (i.e., are similar in their constructions of personal experiences), they are likely to behave in similar ways. The essential point to note is that people are similar neither because they have experienced similar events nor because they manifest similar behavior: they are similar because events have approximately the same psychological meaning for them. In line with his cognitive orientation, Kelly's emphasis is upon construing rather than past experience or observable behavior.

Interestingly, this notion implies that the similarities evident among members of a particular culture are not behavioral similarities alone. More fundamentally, Kelly (1955) believed that people who belong to the same cultural group construe their experiences in much the same way. So, for example, in understanding the culture of a primitive tribe that practices rain dances, it is not enough to observe the peculiarities of the rain dance alone. One must see that the members of this culture all possess the construct "rain god," who occasionally responds favorably to their ritualistic importunings. Or, closer to home, the differences in our own society between members of the "middle class" and "counterculture" cannot be explained in terms of dress, hair length, music preferences, and other such behaviors alone. In Kelly's system, the basic difference lies in the way each group commonly construes its experience. Consider, for example, the classic "middle class" versus "counterculture" constructions of drugs, money, work, religion, morality, material goods, meaning of life. These are fundamental differences in construing, not just overt behavior.

Another important aspect of Kelly's theory of personal constructs deals with relationships between people and their construct system. This is formally defined in the *sociality corollary,* which specifies the conditions necessary for an effective interpersonal relationship: "To the extent that one person construes the construction processes of another, he may play a role in a social process involving the other person" (1955, p. 95). This corollary stipulates that social interaction consists primarily of one person trying to understand how another person perceives and interprets his or her environment. This differs from the assumption that people can only interact when they have similar construct systems or are in some sense similar people. For Kelly, harmonious social interaction requires that one person psychologically place himself or herself in the shoes of another so that he or she is better able to understand and predict the other's present and subsequent behavior. To "role-play" your father, for instance, it would be necessary to understand how he views things (including yourself) through *his* constructs and to structure your actions appropriately. Playing a role in relation to another person does not necessarily mean agreeing with him or her, as parent-child relationships readily attest. As indicated by the commonality corollary, it is far easier to understand how another person thinks if one shares similar outlooks, but it is not essential for effective role playing.

Kelly's use of "role" should not be confused with usage of the term in sociological role theory. For the sociologist, a role is a unit of the social structure to which individuals are recruited (e.g., police officer, union president, train conductor). A role in Kelly's system, however, is defined as a "pattern of behavior that follows from a person's understanding of how the others who are associated with him in his task think" (1955, pp. 97–98). This definition suggests that significant social interaction does not automatically exist because two or more people are communicating with one another or are involved in a common task. Role enactment requires that at least one of the interacting individuals have some perception of the other person's ways of seeing things. Thus, based on the understanding of what the other person is doing and thinking in relation to oneself, one engages in an interpersonal activity. Roles need not be reciprocal (i.e., the person enacting the role need not be construed by the person or persons toward whom the role is directed) in order for a person to become involved in a social relationship. The other person need not enter into a role relationship with the construing individual. Indeed, our society is dominated by one-sided role relationships (e.g., teacher-student, doctor-patient, lawyer-client, employer-employee). In this regard, Kelly noted that an optimal relationship involves mutual understanding of one another's views on life, as in the case of a healthy relationship between wife and husband.

According to Kelly, it is intrinsically satisfying to have one's social predictions about other people confirmed. We have certain ideas about what others expect of us. When we act in accordance with these ideas and discover that we have correctly predicted the expectations of others, we are strongly encouraged toward further socialized behavior.

Kelly's sociality corollary has profound relevance for the field of human relations. In particular, it offers a potentially unifying link between individual and social psychology. The implicit notion that a lasting and genuine human relationship cannot develop until at least one person attempts to see the other through the other's glasses may explain those problems people have in communicating with each other in situations ranging from everyday discourse (parents, relatives, friends, teachers) to international affairs. A better world may ultimately depend upon the capacity of human beings (particularly heads of state) to sensitively and accurately construe one another's construction processes.

Let us now consider the basic assumptions about human nature underlying cognitive theory.

KELLY'S BASIC ASSUMPTIONS CONCERNING HUMAN NATURE

Kelly's philosophic position of constructive alternativism denies any objective reality independent of human construction systems. Reality is what we construe it to be. When applied to human nature, Kelly's doctrine asserts that persons are fundamentally whatever they construe themselves to be. Differences among personality theorists concerning human nature, then, were seen by Kelly as reflections of the unique construct systems with which they construed their subject matter. Kelly himself, of course, was no exception to this principle. Using the approach taken to all theorists in this text, however, Kelly's constructs about humanity may be construed as actually reflecting his basic assumptions concerning human nature. His positions, discussed below, are depicted in Figure 9-1.

Freedom–Determinism   In Kelly's theory, human beings are both free *and* determined. Paradoxically, man is depicted as *freely determining* his own behavior. As Kelly neatly puts it:

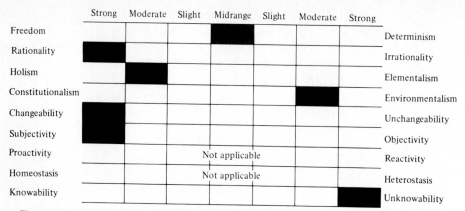

Figure 9-1 Kelly's position on the nine basic assumptions concerning human nature.

> This personal construct system provides him with both freedom of decision and limitation of action—freedom, because it permits him to deal with the meaning of events rather than forces him to be helplessly pushed about by them, and limitation, because he can never make choices outside the world of alternatives he has erected for himself (1958, p. 58.)

In other words, human beings have an enormous range of constructs from which to choose in interpreting events, but—once selected—their constructions determine their behavior. Humans operate behaviorally only within the boundaries of the constructs they employ. A person facing a new event, for example, is free to use or not use the construct "good–bad" in construing it. Should she decide to employ it, she will automatically use that pole of the construct through which she anticipates greater extension and definition of her system (*choice corollary*), and her behavior will necessarily follow therefrom. However, she is free not to use the "good–bad" construct; she may opt to construe the new event in other terms, thereby establishing different self-imposed boundaries resulting in different behaviors. Of course, a person may construe and reconstrue the event throughout her lifetime, thus allowing the freedom–determinism cycle underlying her behavior to manifest itself again and again. Freedom and determinism are inextricably interwoven in Kelly's theory.

Rationality–Irrationality Kelly's exceptionally strong commitment to the rationality assumption pervades every aspect of his theory. This assumption plays a more central part in Kelly's system than in any other presented in this text. Fundamentally regarding man as "man the scientist," Kelly portrays human beings as constantly engaged in the process of intellectually construing the world around them. Kelly's man does not desire to love the world, nor to conquer it; he basically wants to *know* the world or at least to construe it. For Kelly to construe individuals in this fashion, for him to regard personality as a construct system, absolutely requires as a philosophical precursor the basic assumption of rationality. In fact, Kelly's cognitive theory could not exist as a viable "constructive alternative" without the rationality assumption as its base.

Holism–Elementalism Kelly is moderately committed to a holistic view of human nature. While his unit of analysis, the construct, appears at first glance to reflect an elementalist approach to the study of humanity, Kelly does not suggest that a person can ever adequately be understood "one construct at a time." Instead, he refers repeatedly to a construct system, unique to each person, in which constructs are related to one another in an organized individual manner. The person is depicted as forever using his or her total system in construing the events of everyday life. Thus, to understand a person, it is necessary to understand his or her entire construct system.

Student A's construct of "good," for example, as applied to his or her psychology professor, might merely be subordinate to his or her construct of "entertaining," whereas the "good" construct of student B in this same situation may be subordinate to "intellectually stimulating." One could never appreciate this difference simply by studying in isolation the "good" constructs of A and B. The myriad of additional construct interrelationships within a system would also be missed in an element-by-element approach. Nevertheless, constructs can in fact be studied individually; in this sense, Kelly adopts a less than complete commitment to the holistic assumption.

Constitutionalism–Environmentalism Kelly is noticeably inclined toward the environmentalism pole of this dimension. While he never addressed himself directly to the constitutional versus environmental origins of personal constructs, there is simply no acknowledgment of constitution in Kelly's theory. On the other hand, the environment is theoretically ubiquitous; Kelly's person is construing and reconstruing it all the time. Personal constructs are presumably abstracted from experience, employed to anticipate environmental events, and modified or discarded if they do not help to predict these events. Thus, the ultimate function of the individual's personal construct system is to interpret the surrounding world.

Yet in Kelly's theory, the environment is not invested with the awesome determinative power that it is in Skinner's system. The cognitive person interprets, evaluates, hypothesizes about, construes, and reconstrues the environment, rather than simply being molded by its effects. This is because this person is, unlike Skinner's, fundamentally cognitive and rational. The environment is certainly there in Kelly's system, but never to the point of being overwhelming to the construer. Kelly's commitment to environmentalism is thus best described as moderate.

Changeability–Unchangeability Kelly's theory is permeated by novelty, motion, and change. Life is seen as constant movement, with all events subject to reinterpretation in light of different constructs. This kinetic awareness reflects Kelly's basic assumptions concerning human nature, especially his strong commitment to changeability.

As noted earlier, Kelly viewed personality makeup in terms of an individual's construct system. The changeability assumption is perhaps most clearly evidenced by the fact that Kelly found it necessary to explain how change occurs in a construct system. Specifically, people change their construct systems as they successively construe the replication of events (the experience corollary). In our terminology of basic assumptions, this means that an individual's personality can change over time as a function of experience. And Kelly's modulation corollary partly explains how: a person's construct system can change to the degree that his or her constructs are permeable. The more permeable the constructs, the more events they can subsume within their range of convenience and the greater the latitude for change in the overall system.

Kelly thus seems to imply that not all people are capable of change to the same degree. For example, a person who does not revise his or her constructs in light of ongoing events (i.e., one who lacks true "experience" in Kelly's sense), largely because these constructs lack permeability, is not going to change very much over time. Such an individual will go through life construing and behaving in one rigid fashion, regardless of the ongoing flow of events. But a person with permeable constructs who can construe change can truly profit from experience—such a person is capable of constant, profound, and constructive change throughout life. Because Kelly clearly recognized the possibility of such change and attempted to explain how it occurs, he must be judged to be strongly committed to the changeability assumption.

Subjectivity–Objectivity   Kelly contended that human beings live in a highly subjective world of personal constructs. People may construe and reconstrue external events however they wish, but they nonetheless remain encapsulated within their subjective constructive systems. Each individual views reality through a templet of personal constructs, and the templets are unique to each person.

Objective external factors can have no uniform or standardized effects upon the individual because they are always construed by him or her in idiosyncratic ways. What is a "worthwhile" experience to one person is "anxiety-provoking" to another; what is "relevant" for one may be simply "superficial" in another's construct system. Objective reality (assuming there is such a thing) is always filtered through a person's constructive apparatus—reality is what one construes as reality. Thus, each person lives in a unique constructive world of his or her own making. To be sure, that world can change, but only to the extent that one is willing to reconstrue it. Kelly is firmly committed to the subjectivity assumption. In fact, the particular blend of the rationality and subjectivity assumptions appears to contribute heavily to the unique character of Kelly's theory.

Proactivity–Reactivity   The proactivity–reactivity assumption is fundamentally an issue of *motivation:* Do human beings internally generate their own behavior or is their behavior a reaction to external stimuli? Since Kelly regards motivation as a redundant construct, he makes no assumption about its proactive versus reactive nature. For Kelly, humans are neither proactive nor reactive—they are simply alive. To be alive is to be active; life *is* a form of movement. Hence, Kelly's person finds it unnecessary to internally generate his or her behavior since, by simply being alive, he or she is already behaving. Relying on the environment to reactively stimulate behavior is equally unnecessary. Because of Kelly's unique position on motivation, then, the proactivity–reactivity assumption is not applicable.

Homeostasis–Heterostasis   This assumption also refers essentially to a basic motivational question: Do people behave to reduce drives and maintain internal harmony or is their behavior directed toward growth and self-actualization? For Kelly, neither category applies. Instead, in Kelly's view, people seek to develop and organize coherent construct systems so that they can accurately anticipate future events. In so doing, the person engages in *elaborative choice,* i.e., he or she always chooses that alternative that seems to lead to the greater extension and definition of his or her construct system (*choice corollary*). To the heterostatically oriented, this may sound suspiciously like growth and self-actualization. On the other hand, champions of homeostasis might argue with equal cogency that persons always choose in this fashion because they are attempting to reduce inner uncertainties about the world. Kelly himself, however, took no position on this motivational issue. Motivation is a nonessential concept in his view. As a basic assumption about human nature, then, the homeostasis–heterostasis issue is not applicable to Kelly's system.

Knowability–Unknowability   For all practical purposes, human nature is scientifically unknowable in Kelly's theory. He rejects the prevalent philosophical position of *realism,* which asserts that there is an objective reality independent of our perception of it. Within the framework of realism, the ultimate task of science is to discover the nature of that reality. Each science has a "range of convenience"— for personology, it is the nature of human beings. Eschewing realism, Kelly put forth his own epistemological doctrine of constructive alternativism (actually a version of philosophical nominalism) which holds that only individual events have reality. Objective reality has no existence apart from our constructions of it. Launched from this basic premise, science can never "discover" objective reality, since there is none to discover! For psychology, human nature can never really be known but only alternatively construed.

The obvious question, then, becomes why bother with science? Kelly's answer is that scientific theories serve as differentially useful construct systems in the process of explaining events. Some are more efficacious than others in this regard— only future events will tell—but the more durable theories have served well as constructive alternatives. Consider personality theories as an example. Freud construed human beings in terms of unconscious motivation; Adler discerned a style of life; Erikson discovered psychosocial stages of ego development; Murray perceived needs; Skinner observed instrumentally conditioned responses; Bandura saw observational learning; and Allport sensed traits underlying behavior. And Kelly? Kelly construed constructs.

By implication, Kelly's personal construct theory carries within it the seeds of its own demise. Since reality remains open to alternative constructions, there will come a day when the events presently construed by Kelly's theory will be better anticipated by some other personological construct system. He recognized this and, with disarming candor, admitted it. In discussing the various ways in which personal construct theory has been categorized by responsible scholars, he concluded that "It has also been classified as nonsense, which indeed, by its own admission, it will likely some day turn out to be (Kelly, 1970, p. 10)." By virtue of his philosophic position, then, Kelly assumes that human nature is unknowable through science.

EMPIRICAL VALIDATION OF COGNITIVE THEORY CONCEPTS

To what extent has the psychology of personal constructs generated evidence supporting the empirical validity of its major theoretical concepts? This question was the focus of a comprehensive literature survey conducted by Bonarius (1965) who, on the basis of evaluating more than ninety published studies stimulated by Kelly's ideas or directly related to them., concluded that it would be premature to assume that Kelly's basic theory had been validated at that point. However, close inspection of these studies reveals that most pertain to a test that Kelly developed, the Role Construct Repertory Test (commonly called the Rep Test), rather than to his theoretical concepts per se. The truth is that the Rep Test has captured more research attention than the theory of which it is an integral part. While Kelly's theory has not been subjected to much empirical validation then, he has exerted a significant influence upon personological research primarily through the development of the Rep Test.

More recent sources also support the impression that Kelly's theory itself has not received much research attention. For instance, the personality chapters in the *Annual Review of Psychology* (published yearly and consisting of evaluations by experts of progress in both traditional and new areas of psychology), 1970 through 1978, cite Kelly in the author index of only one issue. *The Handbook of Personality Theory and Research* (edited by Borgatta and Lambert, 1968), a lengthy volume reflecting the current status of personality theory and research, does not mention any work by Kelly or his followers. Accordingly, it appears that there has been no systematic attempt to test the validity of Kelly's major theoretical concepts. Since the vast majority of the existing Kelly-related research employs the Rep Test (e.g., Adams-Webber, 1970; Guertin, 1973; Sechrest, 1968), let's briefly examine its rather interesting nature before considering any investigations prompted by Kelly's theory.

Role Construct Repertory Test: Assessing Personal Constructs

Kelly (1955) developed the *Role Construct Repertory Test* to identify the important constructs a person uses to construe significant people in his or her life. More importantly, the Rep Test was originally devised as a diagnostic instrument to assist the therapist in understanding a client's construct system and the way the client uses it to structure his or her personal and material environment. Unfortunately, the format of the Rep Test does not readily lend itself to traditional psychometric assessment; no data for its reliability, validity, or standardization are in a form that enables a potential user to apply the test routinely. But then, there was very little that was traditional about Kelly. Thus, although the Rep Test was developed out of Kelly's theory, studies pertaining to its clinical and research applications are not indicative of the underlying validity of the theory itself.

Many forms of the Rep Test, individual and group, exist, but one procedure is basic to all of them. The subject is presented a *Role Title List* of twenty to thirty different role definitions of persons assumed to be of personal importance to her or him. For each role, the subject is asked to write the name of a person known personally who best fits the role description. Some of the roles that typically appear on a role title list are shown in Table 9-1.

The names assigned to these designated roles are called *figures*. After the role title list has been completed, the examiner presents the subject with the names of three figures who had been mentioned as filling these roles, asking him or her to state which two are alike in some important way but different from the third. For example, the subject might be asked to compare and contrast the persons he has named for sister, brother, and mother. In considering the triad, he might decide that brother and sister are similar in that they are "calm" but different from mother, who

Table 9-1   Role Title List Definitions for the Gridform of the Rep Test

	Role titles	Definitions
1	*Self*	Yourself
2	*Mother*	Your mother or the person who has played the part of a mother in your life
3	*Father*	Your father or the person who has played the part of a father in your life
4	*Brother*	Your brother who is nearest your own age, or if you have no brother, a boy near your own age who was most like a brother to you during your early teens
5	*Sister*	Your sister who is nearest your own age or, if you have no sister, a a girl near your own age who was most like a sister to you during your early teens
6	*Spouse*	Your wife (or husband) or, if you are not married, your closest present friend of the opposite sex
7	*Accepted teacher*	The teacher who influenced you most when you were in your teens
8	*Rejected teacher*	The teacher whose point of view you found most objectionable when you were in your teens
9	*Boss*	An employer, supervisor, or officer under whom you worked during a period of great stress
10	*Doctor*	Your physician
11	*Pitied person*	The person whom you would most like to help or for whom you feel most sorry
12	*Rejecting person*	A person with whom you have been associated, who, for some unexplained reason, appeared to dislike you
13	*Happy person*	The happiest person whom you know personally
14	*Ethical person*	The person who appears to meet the highest ethical standards whom you know personally
15	*Intelligent person*	The most intelligent person whom you know personally

Source: Adapted from Kelly, 1955, p. 227.

is "hyperactive." Thus, the construct dimension elicited from this "sort" is that of "calm versus hyperactive." This procedure is repeated with several other triads (usually twenty to thirty) to determine how the subject categorizes and differentiates these persons. All the roles are used approximately equally in triads, so that the sampling of the subject's construction system is not biased. Based on the verbal content of the elicited constructs, the psychologist can then formulate hypotheses about the way the subject perceives and copes with significant persons in life. This form of the Rep Test is called the *Listform* and is administered individually.

Kelly also devised a *Gridform* of the Rep Test (illustrated in Figure 9-2). The procedure for administering this form of the test consists of presenting the subject with a specially prepared grid or matrix in which the significant figures in his or her life are listed on one axis and the various sorts he or she is required to make are listed on the other axis. The subject inserts the names of persons who fit each role in the space on the form corresponding to those illustrated at the top of Figure 9-2 (i.e., after reading the brief role definition of each). He is then instructed to enter the first row of the matrix to the columns where three people designated by circles are located. These circles designate the three figures whom the subject is to consider in the first sort.

In Figure 9-2, for instance, row 1 of the matrix contains circles in the squares under columns 9, 10, and 12 (i.e., "Boss," "Doctor," and "Rejecting Person"). The subject is instructed to decide how two of them are alike in some important respect

Self	Mother	Father	Brother	Sister	Spouse	Accepted teacher	Rejected teacher	Boss	Doctor	Pitied person	Rejecting person	Happy person	Ethical person	Intelligent person	Sort No.	Construct pole	Contrast pole
1	2	3	4	5	6	7	8	9	10	11	12	13	14	15			
							√	⊗	⊗		O			√	1	Authorities	Nonauthority
O	O	O													2		
	O						O					O			3		
		O										O		O	4		
			O							O			O		5		
O					O	O									6		
	O	O								O					7		
O		O	O												8		
										O			O	O	9		
				O			O					O			10		
								O		O		O			11		
												O	O	O	12		
	O	O												O	13		
				O			O	O							14		
O	O									O					15		

Figure 9-2 Illustration of Grid Form of the Rep Test. (*Adapted from Kelly, 1955, p. 270.*)

that differentiates them from the third. Once he has decided how two of the figures are alike but different from the third, he inserts an "X" in the two circles which correspond to the two persons who are similar. The third circle is left blank. Next, the subject writes a word or brief phrase that indicates how these two figures are alike in the column marked "Construct pole." In the column marked "Contrast pole" he writes a word or brief phrase that tells how the third figure is different from the other two. As depicted in Figure 9-2, boss and doctor are seen as alike in terms of being "authorities" whereas rejecting person is seen as being a "nonauthority." Finally, the subject examines the remaining figures in the first row (those not considered in the sort which elicited the construct dimension) and puts a check mark in the square of each if the construct pole characteristic can be used to construe that figure. This procedure is continued until the subject has completed each of the remaining rows. Each succeeding presentation of a triad generates a construct dimension. The end result is a grid with the figures at the top, the various constructs in the right-hand columns, and a pattern of voids and check marks inside the rectangle. The reader may find it an intellectually interesting and self-revealing exercise to complete Figure 9-2 with his or her own constructs.

How to Construe Rep Test Results   The end product of the Rep Test, regardless of the way in which it is administered, is a sample of the individual's personal construct system and the way it is used. Results of the Listform are generally subjected to a clinical analysis in which the examiner considers (1) the number and variety of constructs elicited, (2) the substance and tone of the constructs, (3) the way in which various figures are related to the constructs and to one another, and (4) additional characteristics of the subject's constructs such as their permeability, looseness or tightness, and communicability. This is fundamentally a subjective interpretation of Rep Test results allowing the examiner to become acquainted with the ways the subject construes others in her life and how she anticipates the future. Kelly (1961) devised a mathematical scheme (nonparametric factor analysis) for analyzing the Gridform so that it is less susceptible to interpretative error or bias. In brief, this type of statistical analysis reduces the grid to a few basic construct dimensions which capture most succinctly the dominant world views of the subject.

Another way of construing Rep Test results has been proposed by Bieri (1961). This investigator suggests that by inspecting the pattern of checks across the various rows of the Gridform one can determine the relative *complexity–simplicity* of an individual's construct system. A pattern of similar check marks signifies a small number of constructs and thus an undifferentiated view of others (cognitive simplicity). On the other hand, a pattern of dissimilar check marks indicates a large number of constructs and thus a highly differentiated view of others (cognitive complexity). According to Bieri, cognitively simple persons are likely to ignore information which denies or contradicts the impression they have of others. They oversimplify and show a lack of versatility in their interpersonal relationships. By contrast, cognitively complex persons are likely to code the full range of nuances and subtleties in another's personality, including their inevitable contradictions. They are also better able to predict the behavior of others than those who are cognitively simple (Bieri, 1955).

Schizophrenic Thought Disorder: A "Destructive" Alternative

One illustrative use of the Rep Test is found in studies of schizophrenic thought disorders. Clinical descriptions of schizophrenia generally stress that it is marked by language and thought disturbances. Confusion and vagueness of ideas, use of new words with idiosyncratic meanings (*neologisms*), and unusual shifts in the direction of thought are quite commonly observed. In construct theory terms, schizophrenics are employing an overly loose and inconsistent construct system for construing their experiences. Their ideas about people are both poorly integrated and unstable in that they suffer from a relative lack of structure and consistency. Since the Rep Test provides a method of assessing degree of cognitive structure and organization in construing other people, it offers a promising approach for understanding the nature of the disordered thinking characteristic of schizophrenia.

Bannister and Fransella (1966) hypothesized that schizophrenics use overloose and highly inconsistent constructs. Additionally, they sought to establish a clinically economic and adequately standardized grid test for detecting the presence of schizophrenic thought disorder. The subjects for this study consisted of six different groups: (1) thought-disordered schizophrenics, (2) non-thought-disordered schizophrenics, (3) normals, (4) neurotics, (5) organics (i.e., organic brain damage), and (6) depressives. Each subject was individually presented with an array of eight passport-type photographs of strangers and instructed to rank-order them on six constructs that normal people usually consider highly interrelated. Specifically, subjects were asked to rank all eight photographs from the *most kind* to the *least kind*. This procedure was then repeated with the same photos using the constructs *stupid, selfish, sincere, mean,* and *honest.* Immediately after the subjects completed the test, they were asked to retake it, using the same photographs and rank-ordering them for the same constructs. They were also told that this was not to test their memory but that they should undertake the second test as if they were doing it for the first time.

Bannister and Fransella computed two statistical measures from each subject's test protocol—one for *intensity* and one for *consistency.* The intensity score reveals how closely the subject ranked the photos on one construct relative to his rankings on the other constructs. A high intensity score indicates that the subject has rank-ordered as if the constructs he has judged are related, whereas a low intensity score indicates that he has treated them as relatively independent characteristics. The consistency score reflects the degree to which the subject has maintained the pattern of relationships between his constructs from Grid Test I to Grid Test II. In effect, it is a test-retest correlation indicating the degree to which the subject on retest uses the constructs in the same way she or he did on the original test.

It was predicted that thought-disordered schizophrenics would have lower intensity and consistency scores than subjects in the other five groups. The results

Table 9-2 Means and Standard Deviations of Intensity and Consistency Scores for Six Groups of Subjects

	Thought-disordered schizophrenics	Normals	Non-thought-disordered schizophrenics	Depressives	Neurotics	Organics
Intensity X	728	1,253	1,183	1,115	1,383	933
Standard deviation	369	339	390	456	517	524
Consistency X	0.18	0.80	0.73	0.75	0.74	0.73
Standard deviation	0.39	0.34	0.34	0.41	0.45	0.47

Source: Adapted from Bannister and Fransella, 1966, p. 98.

provided substantial support for these predictions. Table 9-2 presents the means and standard deviations for intensity and consistency for the six groups. This table reveals that the constructs of the thought-disordered schizophrenics were considerably less highly interrelated (i.e., lower intensity) than were those of the other groups, and that their immediate test-retest reliability (i.e., consistency) was also significantly lower.

A second experiment conducted by Bannister and Salmon (1966) examined the question of whether schizophrenics are disordered across their entire construct system (i.e., are equally perplexed by every aspect of the world in which they live) or whether they are disordered in a more focal sense (i.e., are perplexed by some aspects of life more than others). This question was investigated by administering two grid forms of the Rep Test to thought-disordered schizophrenics and normal controls. The first, a "people" form, used passport-type photographs of strangers and, as in the preceding study, subjects ranked the photos on each of six psychological constructs. The second form of the test, an "object" form, required subjects to rank a set of fifteen objects (e.g., English bowler hat, loaf of bread) on six constructs (e.g., curved–straight, heavy–light). Subjects completed both forms of the test in the same experimental session so that both the degree of structure and stability of the pattern of construct interrelationships across elements could be assessed.

Bannister and Salmon reported that while schizophrenics did not differ from normal controls in their construing of objects, they were vastly less stable and consistent in their construing of people. This finding suggests that schizophrenic thought disorder may not be diffuse but, rather, may be particularly related to interpersonal constructs. That is, it is interpersonal construing that has been damaged in thought disorder. Contemplating results such as those considered in these two experiments, Bannister (1963) proposed a theory of schizophrenic thought disorder based on a *serial invalidation* hypothesis. In brief, this theory suggests that thought disorder is the outcome of being consistently wrong in one's predictions, so that a gross loosening of one's construct system is the ultimate form of psychological adjustment. This type of research is just one example of the heuristic value of Kelly's theory. To reiterate, however, experimental evidence in support of Kelly's central theoretical propositions is quite limited. Perhaps investigators will remedy this situation in the future so that the scientific worth of cognitive theory can be judged more clearly.

APPLICATION: EMOTIONAL STATES, PSYCHOLOGICAL DISORDERS, AND FIXED-ROLE THERAPY

Kelly's personal construct theory represents a cognitive view of behavior; the human being is depicted as a scientist, that is, as someone who is continuously engaged in predicting and controlling the events that occur in his or her environment. Yet this personological system emerged, in the main, from *clinical psychology,* a professional discipline devoted to the understanding and treatment of psychological disturbances. Kelly's ultimate goal was to create a more scientific approach to the difficult work of clinical psychology. In fact, Volume 2 of *The Psychology of Personal Constructs* (1955) is subtitled "Clinical Diagnosis and Psychotherapy," while an entire chapter in Volume 1 describes Kelly's own particular psychotherapeutic approach, fixed-role therapy. How, then, does a fundamentally *cognitive, intellectually oriented* theory of personality apply to the everyday realities encountered by a clinical psychologist—emotional states, psychological health and disorder, and psychotherapy?

Emotional States   Kelly retained but redefined several traditional psychological concepts of emotion in terms relevant to cognitive theory. For example, he defined *anxiety* as the awareness "that the events with which one is confronted lie outside the range of convenience of one's construct system (1955, p. 495)." Thus, the vague feeling of apprehension and helplessness commonly labeled as anxiety is, for Kelly, a result of being aware that one's available constructs are not applicable to anticipating the events one encounters. Kelly emphasized that it is not the fact that one's construct system is not functioning that is anxiety-provoking; one is not anxious merely because one's anticipations are inaccurate. Anxiety is created (experienced) only when one realizes that one has no constructs with which to interpret an event. Kelly often facetiously referred to a person in this state as being "caught with his constructs down." Under such circumstances an individual cannot predict, hence cannot fully comprehend what is happening or solve the problem.

This view of anxiety is far different from the Freudian conception of the neurotically anxious individual as a victim of unconscious conflicts and dammed-up instinctual energy. Rather than being threatened by the breakthrough of sexual and aggressive impulses into consciousness, the anxious person is really overwhelmed by events which she or he can neither understand nor anticipate. Viewed in this manner, psychotherapy assists a client either in acquiring new constructs, which will enable him or her to better predict the troublesome events, or in making his or her existing constructs more permeable, so they admit new experiences to their range of convenience.

Guilt, another emotional state often alluded to in personality theories, is defined by Kelly as the perception of apparent dislodgment of the self from one's core role structure. The guilty person is aware of having deviated from the important roles (self-images) by which she or he maintains relationships to others. For example, a college student who construes himself as a scholar will feel guilty if he spends too much time at the local beer house with his roommates, thus violating the most basic aspect of his role as a scholar, namely studying. Presumably a student who construes himself as a playboy would not experience such guilt.

Still another familiar emotional experience, *threat,* is viewed by Kelly as the awareness that one's construct system is about to be drastically altered by what has been discovered. One feels threatened when a major shakeup in one's personal constructs is imminent. Threat does psychological violence to the person. The thought of one's own death is perhaps the most formidable type of threat, unless a person construes it as basic to his or her life's meaning.

Hostility, a final illustration of emotional states, is defined as the "continued effort to extort validational evidence in favor of a type of social prediction which has already proved itself a failure" (Kelly, 1955, p. 510). Traditionally considered a disposition to behave vindictively toward or inflict harm upon others, hostility in Kelly's system is merely an attempt to hold onto an invalid construct in the face of contradictory (invalidating) evidence. The hostile person, rather than resign himself to the fact that his expectations about other people are unrealistic and therefore in need of revision, tries to make others behave in ways which fit his expectations. Consider, for example, the reaction of a father who discovers that his college-aged daughter is living the life of a "sexually liberated" woman. No matter how compelling the contrary evidence, the angry father persists in his belief that she is his "little girl." Changing one's constructs is difficult, threatening, and sometimes even impossible. How much better it would be if one could change the world, rather than one's way of viewing it, so that it would conform to one's preconceptions. Hostility represents just such an attempt.

Psychological Health and Disorder   Each day clinical psychologists deal with the realities of psychological health and disorder. How are these concepts to be understood within Kelly's theory? Turning first to health, four distinct characteristics define the well-functioning person from Kelly's perspective. First, and perhaps most important, healthy persons are willing to evaluate their constructs and to test the validity of their perceptions of other people. In other words, such people test the predictions derived from their personal constructions of social experiences. Second, healthy persons are able to discard their constructs and reorient their core role systems whenever they appear to be invalid. In Kelly's terminology, their constructs are permeable, meaning not only that they can admit when they are wrong, but also that they can update their constructs when their life experiences so dictate. The third characteristic of personal soundness is a desire to extend the range, scope, and coverage of one's construct system. In Kelly's view, healthy people remain open to new possibilities for personal growth and development. The fourth and final characteristic of psychological health is a well-developed repertoire of roles; one is healthy to the extent that one can effectively play a variety of social roles and comprehend the perspectives of one's counterplayers.

Kelly also took a unique stance in relation to psychological disorders, reconstruing them in terms of cognitive theory. For him, a psychological disorder is "any personal construction which is used repeatedly in spite of consistent invalidation" (1955, p. 831). Psychological disturbances thus represent the apparent failure of a person's construct system to achieve its purpose. Or, more to the point, psychological disorders involve anxiety and the individual's repeated efforts to regain the sense of being able to predict events. Caught up in a lack of capacity to predict, the disturbed individual searches frantically for new ways of construing the events of his world. Or he may swing in the opposite direction and rigidly adhere to the same predictions, thereby keeping his personal construct system intact in the face of repeated failures. In either case, the maladjusted person cannot anticipate events with much accuracy and hence fails to learn about or cope with the world.

Kelly interpreted psychological disturbances in accordance with his own unique set of diagnostic constructs. *Dilation* serves as a good example of one such construct in terms of which psychological disorders can be viewed. In Kelly's theory of psychopathology, dilation occurs when a person has no superordinate constructs to organize her perceptual field. Having abandoned or lost governing constructs, the individual then attempts to broaden (dilate) her constructs and to reorganize them at a more bizarre and comprehensive level of plausibility. What happens? Kelly suggested that the disorders traditionally labeled *mania, depression,* and *paranoia* result. Traditionally, *mania* has been understood as a psychotic state in which the patient's thinking is overinclusive (patient is unable to preserve conceptual boundaries, and so thought becomes less accurate, more vague, and overly general) while her affect often appears euphoric. Manic patients are forever frantically beginning a variety of projects and activities that they will never finish, talking feverishly about their plans in grandiose terms all the while. They jump from topic to topic and make sweeping generalizations with few substantive ideas. In Kelly's view, the manic person's exploration has simply outrun her conceptual organization. She is left with "loose constructions" of reality, and her excitement represents a kind of frenzied attempt to cope with a rapidly dilating perceptual field.

Another psychopathological response to anxiety is *depression.* Depression tends to occur in people who have *constricted* their perceptual field (i.e., narrowed their interests to a smaller and smaller area). The depressed patient has profound difficulty in making even the simplest everyday decisions. Overwhelmed by the immensity of his problems, the depressed person often contemplates suicide—the ultimate act of constriction. Depression, then, represents a psychological disorder in which people attempt to construe their experiences from the opposite side of the dilation construct: constriction.

Dilation is also focal in the case of the paranoid patient. As classically conceived, *paranoia* is a serious disorder involving only one cardinal symptom—an extremely well-systematized delusion, usually of persecution. The paranoid earnestly but erroneously believes that others are intentionally "out to get her," a feeling often accompanied by a delusion of grandeur, the false belief that one is a special or divine person. Why else would so many people be actively plotting against one? There are a variety of ways of construing reality, and paranoia is simply one of the less fortunate and less predictively efficient alternatives. The paranoid has a well-developed persecution construct; as she elaborates upon it, she is led farther and farther afield. Armed with a comprehensive persecution construct, the paranoid simply proceeds to dilate her whole perceptual field, gradually construing most people and events in persecution terms.

Other diagnostic constructs and descriptions of related disorders may be found in Volume 2 of Kelly's 1955 major work.

Fixed-Role Therapy   While many of the therapeutic methods described by Kelly (1955) are compatible with those used in other clinical schemes (including psychoanalysis), there are two distinguishing features of his approach: first, his conception of what the goal of psychotherapy should be and, second, the development and practice of fixed-role therapy.

Kelly discussed the nature and task of therapeutic change in terms of the development of better construct systems. Since disorders involve using constructs in the face of consistent invalidation, psychotherapy is directed toward the psychological reconstruction of the client's construct system so that it is more workable. But more than this, it is an exciting process of scientific experimentation. The therapy room is a laboratory in which the therapist encourages the client to develop and test new hypotheses, both within and outside the clinical situation. The therapist is highly active—constantly prodding, pushing, and stimulating the client to try new constructs on for size. If they fit, the client can use them in the future; if not, other hypotheses are generated and tested. Science is thus the model clients use in reconstructing their lives. Along with this, it is the therapist's task to make validating data (information feedback) available, against which the client can check his own hypotheses. By providing these data in the form of responses to a wide variety of the client's constructions, the clinician actually gives the client an opportunity to validate his constructs, an opportunity which is not normally available to him (Kelly, 1955).

Kelly went beyond this unique interpretation of psychotherapy to develop his own specific brand, *fixed-role therapy*. Fixed-role therapy maintains that, psychologically, human beings are not only what they construe themselves to be but also what they do. In general terms, the therapist sees her role as one of encouraging and helping the client to perceive and construe himself in new ways and to act accordingly, thereby becoming a new, more effective person.

How does fixed-role therapy actually work? It begins by having the client write a sketch of himself in the third person. The sketch has no detailed outline, and the client is given only the following instructions. Note how the instructions elicit objectivity, minimize threat, and allow the client freedom of expression.

> I want you to write a character sketch of Harry Brown, just as if he were the principal character in a play. Write it as it might be written by a friend who knows him very *intimately* and very sympathetically, perhaps better than anyone even really could know

him. Be sure to write it in the third person. For example, start out by saying, Harry Brown is . . . (Kelly, 1955, p. 323).

Careful study of Harry Brown's self-characterization will uncover many of the constructs he habitually uses in construing himself and his relationships to significant others. What is then needed is a tailor-made means of helping Harry revise his personal construct system. The vehicle for accomplishing this objective is called the *fixed-role sketch*. Based on the self-characterization, it is essentially a personality role description of a fictional individual, preferably compiled by a group of experienced clinicians. The fictional person is given a name other than the client's and furnished with a construct system that, it is judged, it would be therapeutically beneficial for Harry to act out. The sketch is not designed to "remake" Harry but, rather, to invite him to explore, experiment, and—more to the point—*reconstrue* himself and his life situation. In short, the fixed-role sketch is designed to stimulate the client to reconstrue his experiences so that he will become better able to deal with them effectively.

In the next phase of fixed-role therapy, the therapist presents the fixed-role sketch to the client, making an *acceptance check* to determine if the client understands and accepts it as representing a person he would like to be (Patterson, 1973). The client is then directed to *act as if he were that person* for the next two weeks. He reads the sketch at least three times a day and tries to think, act, talk, and *be* like the fictional character portrayed in the sketch. If, for instance, the character is Archie Bunker, then the client is told the following: "For a few weeks you are to try to forget who you are or who you ever were. You *are* Archie Bunker. You behave like him. You think and feel like him. You do the things you think he would do. You even have his interests and you enjoy the things he would enjoy." While we will refrain from speculating about who could possibly benefit from aspiring to Archie Bunker's construct system, the point is simply that the client is asked to temporarily suspend being himself so that he can discover new aspects of himself. During this period, therapist and client meet often to discuss the latter's problems in enacting the role sketch. There may also be some rehearsing of the sketch during therapy sessions so that therapist and client are able to examine the new construct system firsthand. Through techniques such as role playing, the client is encouraged to apply the sketch character's constructs in his social relationships, work situation, family pattern, and other important life settings. Throughout this period, the therapist treats the client as if he were actually the character in the sketch.

To what end? As is the case with most forms of psychotherapy, the results are mixed. While some clients respond favorably to Kelly's unorthodox approach, others do not. Ideally, the Kellian client is provided with a golden opportunity to begin to reconstrue herself and her life under expert therapeutic guidance. She can explore constructive alternatives, retaining useful constructs and rejecting unworkable ones. Rather than dredge up her past, she need only learn to reconstrue the present (including herself) so that she can better anticipate the future. Kelly remained optimistic that a more functional construct system would emerge from this entire therapeutic process.

Clearly, then, the psychology of personal constructs is applicable to realms of human experience far removed from those traditionally considered to be cognitive. For instance, emotional states, psychological health and disorder, and psychotherapy can all be construed from Kelly's novel perspective. If George Kelly's purpose in developing his theory was, as he sometimes noted, to stimulate, excite, and open our minds to the incredible array of life's possibilities, he has indeed succeeded.

SUMMARY

George Kelly's cognitive theory is based on the philosophical position of constructive alternativism, which holds that reality is what one construes it to be. Accordingly, an individual's perception of reality is always subject to interpretation and modification. Man is a "scientist," constantly generating and testing hypotheses about the nature of things so that adequate predictions of future events can be made.

Persons comprehend their worlds through transparent patterns, or templets, called *constructs*. Each individual has a unique construct system (personality) which he or she uses to construe or interpret experience. Kelly theorized that all constructs possess certain formal properties: range of convenience, focus of convenience, and permeability–impermeability. Kelly also recognized various types of constructs: preemptive, constellatory, propositional, comprehensive, incidental, core, peripheral, tight, and loose.

Kelly's theory is formally stated in terms of one fundamental postulate and eleven elaborative corollaries. The former stipulates that a person's processes are psychologically channelized by the ways in which she or he anticipates events, while the corollaries explain how a construct system functions, changes, and influences social interaction.

Kelly was much more cognizant of and explicit about the philosophical underpinnings of personality theory than most personologists. His position is nonetheless founded upon his basic assumptions concerning human nature. Cognitive theory reflects (1) a strong commitment to the assumptions of rationality, changeability, subjectivity, and unknowability; (2) a moderate commitment to the assumptions of holism and environmentalism; and (3) a midrange position on the freedom–determinism dimension. The proactivity–reactivity and homeostasis–heterostasis assumptions do not apply to Kelly's position, since he regarded motivation as a redundant construct.

Although Kelly's theoretical concepts have directly stimulated little research to date, he devised a personality instrument, the Rep Test, which has been widely employed in a variety of studies. The Rep Test assesses personal constructs; in this chapter, its use is illustrated in two investigations of schizophrenic thought disorder.

Kelly's personal construct theory is applicable to behavioral domains far beyond those traditionally defined as cognitive. In the concluding chapter section, Kelly's theory was applied to the everyday concerns of the clinical psychologist—emotional states, psychological health and disorder, and psychotherapy.

BIBLIOGRAPHY

Adams-Webber, J. An analysis of the discriminant validity of several repertory grid indices. *British Journal of Psychology,* 1970, **60,** 83–90.

Bannister, D. The genesis of schizophrenic thought disorder: A serial invalidation hypothesis. *British Journal of Psychiatry,* 1963, **109,** 680–686.

Bannister, D. (Ed.). *Perspectives in personal construct theory.* New York: Academic Press, 1970.

Bannister, D., & Fransella, F. A grid test of schizophrenic thought disorder. *British Journal of Social and Clinical Psychology,* 1966, **5,** 95–102.

Bannister, D., & Fransella, F. *Inquiring man: The theory of personal constructs.* Baltimore: Penguin Books, 1971.

Bannister, D., & Salmon, P. Schizophrenic thought disorder: Specific or diffuse? *British Journal of Medical Psychology,* 1966, **39,** 215–219.

Bieri, J. Cognitive complexity-simplicity and predictive behavior. *Journal of Abnormal and Social Psychology,* 1955, **51,** 263–268.

Bieri, J. Complexity-simplicity as a personality variable in cognitive and preferential behavior. In D. Fiske & S. Maddi (Eds.), *Functions of varied experience.* Homewood, Ill.: Dorsey, 1961.

Bonarius, J. Research in the personal construct theory of George A. Kelly: Role construct repertory test and basic theory. In B. Maher (Ed.), *Progress in experimental personality research.* New York: Academic Press, 1965, pp. 1–46.

Borgatta, E., & Lambert, W. (Eds.). *Handbook of personality theory and research.* Chicago: Rand McNally, 1968.

Guertin, W. Factor analysing two sorts of Kelly's personal construct productions. *Journal of Personality Assessment,* 1973, **37,** 69–71.

Kelly, G. *The psychology of personal constructs.* Vols. 1 and 2. New York: Norton, 1955.

Kelly, G. Man's construction of his alternatives. In G. Lindzey (Ed.), *Assessment of human motives.* New York: Rinehart and Winston, 1958, pp. 33–64.

Kelly, G. *A nonparametric method of factor analysis for dealing with theoretical issues.* Unpublished manuscript. Mimeograph, Ohio State University, 1961.

Kelly, G. *Clinical psychology and personality.* In B. Maher (Ed.), *Clinical psychology and personality: The selected papers of George Kelly.* New York: Wiley, 1969.

Kelly, G. A brief introduction to personal construct theory. In D. Bannister (Ed.), *Perspectives in personal construct theory.* New York: Academic Press, 1970, pp. 1–29.

Maher, B. (Ed.). *Clinical psychology and personality: The selected papers of George Kelly.* New York: Wiley, 1969.

Patterson, C. *Theories of counseling and psychotherapy* (2d ed.). New York: Harper & Row, 1973.

Sechrest, L. The psychology of personal constructs: George Kelly. In J. Wepman & R. Heine (Eds.), *Concepts of personality.* Chicago: Aldine, 1963, pp. 206–233.

Sechrest, L. Personal constructs and personal characteristics. *Journal of Individual Psychology,* 1968, **24,** 162–166.

SUGGESTED READINGS

Adams-Weber, J. *Personal construct theory: Concepts and applications.* New York: Wiley-Interscience, 1979.

Forgus, R., & Shulman, B. *Personality: A cognitive view.* Englewood Cliffs, N.J.: Prentice-Hall, 1979.

Kelly, G. Europe's matrix of decision. In M. Jones (Ed.), *Nebraska symposium on motivation,* 1962, pp. 83–125.

Kelly, G. *A theory of personality.* New York: Norton, 1963.

Kelly, G. Personal construct theory as a line of inference. *Journal of Psychology,* 1964a, **1,** 80–93.

Kelly, G. The language of hypotheses: Man's psychological instrument. *Journal of Individual Psychology,* 1964b, **20,** 137–152.

Kelly, G. A threat of aggression. *Journal of Humanistic Psychology,* 1965, **5,** 195–201.

Mancuso, J. (Ed.). *Readings for a cognitive theory of personality.* New York: Holt, Rinehart and Winston, 1970.

Mancuso, J. Current motivational models in the elaboration of personal construct theory. In J. Cole (Ed.), *Nebraska symposium on motivation.* Lincoln, Neb.: U. of Nebraska Press, 1976, pp. 43–98.

DISCUSSION QUESTIONS

1 What do you think of Kelly's philosophy of constructive alternativism? Do you believe that reality is what one construes to be reality? If so, what implications does this philosophy have for your life? For example, are your "headaches" largely of your own making (because of the way in which you construe things)? Viewed in this fashion, can you reconstrue things to lighten the unnecessary psychological burdens that you now carry? How?

2 A difficult exercise: If you had only one word to describe your feeling about your entire life to this point, what would that word be? Write it down. Now write down its opposite. Can you see how this construct dimension plays a part in the way you construe events in various areas of your life, e.g., human relationships, school, work?

3 Do you believe that "personality" is "the personologist's construct"? If so, might this explain why we have such different theories of personality? What then is the relationship between personologists' constructs and their basic assumptions concerning human nature?

4 Complete the Gridform of the Rep Test in Figure 9-2 with your own constructs. Does this exercise help you to understand your own constructs as well as precisely what is meant by the term "construct" itself? How?

5 What do you think of Kelly's fixed-role therapy? Do you believe that certain kinds of clients would respond to it better than others? What kinds of clients and why?

GLOSSARY

Anxiety Feeling of dread and apprehension which results from being aware that one has no constructs by which to interpret an event.

Choice Corollary The proposition that, when confronted with a choice, a person will opt for the alternative that is most likely either to enhance his or her understanding of reality or to clarify his or her present construct system.

Circumspection-Preemption-Control Cycle The process by which cognition of an event is translated into overt behavior.

Commonality Corollary The proposition that individuals are similar to one another to the extent that they interpret experiences in similar ways.

Constellatory Construct Type of construct that permits its elements to belong to other realms concurrently; however, once the elements are identified in a particular way, they are fixed. Stereotyped thinking illustrates this type of construct.

Constructive Alternativism Kelly's fundamental assumption that human beings are capable of revising or changing their interpretation of events. Objective reality and absolute truth are figments of one's imagination.

Experience Corollary The proposition that an individual's construct system changes in relation to its inability to correctly predict the unfolding sequence of events; those constructs found to be useful are retained, whereas those that are not are revised or discarded.

Fixed-Role Therapy Type of psychotherapy developed by Kelly and aimed at helping clients to reconstrue themselves and their life situations. Clients are encouraged to develop and test new roles, both within and outside the therapeutic setting.

Fixed-Role Sketch Description of the personality of a fictional individual designed to help client construe himself or herself in a different manner so that he or she will be better able to deal with various life situations.

Focus of Convenience A point or area within a construct's range of convenience at which it is maximally useful in construing certain events; it is always specific to the individual employing the construct.

Guilt Awareness of having deviated from the important roles by which one maintains relationships to others.

Hostility The attempt to hold on to an invalid construct in the face of contradictory evidence. A hostile person attempts to make others behave in ways which fit her or his unrealistic expectations.

Individuality Corollary The proposition that differences between people are rooted in their construing events from different perspectives.

Modulation Corollary The proposition that an individual's construct system will change to the extent that he or she is capable of construing new events or reconstruing old events.

Organization Corollary The proposition that an individual's constructs are arranged hierarchically so as to minimize incompatibilities and inconsistencies.

Permeability Dimension concerned with the question of whether new elements will or will not be admitted within the boundaries of a construct. A permeable construct is one that allows new information into its context; an impermeable one cannot.

Personal Construct A category of thought by which the individual interprets or construes her or his personal world of experience. At least three elements are needed to form a construct; two of the elements must be perceived as similar to each other, while the third element must be perceived as different from these two.

Predictive Efficiency The extent to which a construct is useful in enabling a person to correctly predict and anticipate some event in his or her environment.

Preemptive Construct Type of construct which freezes ("preempts") its elements for membership exclusively in its own realm. Use of ethnic labels illustrates the use of preemptive constructs.

Propositional Construct Type of construct that allows a person to be open to new experiences and to adopt alternative views of the world.

Range of Convenience All the events for which a particular construct may be relevant or applicable.

Role Construct Repertory Test Test developed by Kelly to assess the important constructs a person uses to construe significant people in her or his life.

Sociality Corollary The proposition that harmonious interpersonal relationships depend upon the participants' reciprocal understanding of each others' construct systems.

Threat Awareness that one's construct system is about to be drastically changed.

Abraham H. Maslow

Abraham Maslow: A Humanistic Theory of Personality

The three distinct psychological revolutions that dominate personological thought today have all occurred in the twentieth century. The first, that of *psychoanalysis,* presents an image of man as a creature of instinct and conflict. This bleak conception of human nature emerged from Freud's study of mentally disturbed individuals and, at least until recently, emphasized unconscious and irrational forces as the controlling factors in behavior. *Behaviorism,* the second revolution, characterizes man as a flexible, malleable, and passive victim of external stimuli—the permanent pawn of environmental fate. As epitomized by B. F. Skinner, behaviorism emphasizes the essential similarity of men and animals, stressing learning as the major explanation for human behavior. More recently, a third revolution has swept psychology. This new brand, the *humanistic,* or *third force,* movement, has given rise to a radically different image of human nature, namely, that persons are basically good and worthy of respect, and that they will move toward realization of their potentialities if environmental conditions are right. It is generally acknowledged that Abraham Maslow is the spiritual father of humanism in American psychology. His self-actualization theory of personality, based on the study of healthy and creative individuals, clearly illustrates the humanistic perspective:

> Human life will never be understood unless its highest aspirations are taken into account. Growth, self-actualization, the striving toward health, the quest for identity and autonomy, the yearning for excellence (and other ways of phrasing the striving "upward") must now be accepted beyond question as a widespread and perhaps universal tendency (Maslow, 1970, pp. xii–xiii).

All in all, Maslow's humanistic theory—emphasizing as it does the uniqueness of the individual, the importance of values and meaning, and the potential for self-direction and personal growth—has had a major influence on contemporary thought about human behavior.

BIOGRAPHICAL SKETCH

Abraham Harold Maslow was born April 1, 1908, in Brooklyn, New York. His parents were uneducated Jewish immigrants from Russia who dreamed of a better life for their son than theirs had been. Maslow, the eldest of seven children, was strongly encouraged by his parents to be academically successful, yet by his own admission he experienced considerable loneliness and suffering during most of his childhood and early adolescence: "With my childhood, it's a wonder I'm not psychotic. I was a little Jewish boy in the non-Jewish neighborhood. It was a little like being the first Negro enrolled in the all-white school. I was isolated and unhappy. I grew up in libraries and among books, without friends" (Maslow, 1968, p. 37). One might speculate that Maslow's desire to help people live more enriching lives had its origins in his desire to live better himself. Not only did he spend numerous hours in cloistered study, he also experienced the practical side of life, working many summers for his family's barrel manufacturing company, which his brothers still operate today.

Maslow began his college education by trying to specialize in law because of pressure from his father. Two weeks of study at City College of New York convinced him that he couldn't become a lawyer, and with his father's reluctant approval, he undertook a more eclectic course of study at Cornell University. In his junior year Maslow transferred to the University of Wisconsin, where he subsequently received all his formal academic training in psychology, obtaining his B.A. degree in 1930, his M.A. in 1931, and his Ph.D. in 1934. While still an undergraduate, Maslow married Bertha Goodman, his high school sweetheart. Getting married was an extremely important event in Maslow's life. "Life didn't really start for me," he reported, "until I got married and went to Wisconsin" (1968, p. 37).

Maslow's decision to study psychology at Wisconsin was largely affected by the behaviorism of John Watson. Maslow explains:

> I had discovered J. B. Watson and I was sold on behaviorism. It was an explosion of excitement for me. . . . Bertha came to pick me up and I was dancing down Fifth Avenue with exuberance; I embarrassed her, but I was so excited about Watson's program. It was beautiful. I was confident that here was a real road to travel, solving one puzzle after another and changing the world. . . . I was off to Wisconsin to change the world. But off to Wisconsin because of a lying catalog. I went there to study with Koffka, the psychologist; Dreisch, the biologist; and Meiklejohn, the philosopher. When I showed up on campus, they weren't there. They had just been visiting professors, but the school put them in the catalog anyway (1968, p. 37).

Despite the intense disappointment and disillusionment he must have felt, Maslow completed his doctoral work under the guidance of Harry Harlow. Incredible as it may seem today, his Ph.D. dissertation was an observational study of sexual and dominance characteristics of *monkeys!* Actually, this study marked the beginning of Maslow's abiding interest in sexuality and affection, which later shifted to humans. Maslow always considered sex research, especially the study of homosexuality, as essential to a profound understanding of humanity.

After serving on the Wisconsin faculty as Assistant Instructor in Psychology (1930–1934) and Teaching Fellow in Psychology (1934–1935), Maslow became a Carnegie Fellow at Columbia University, remaining there from 1935 through 1937. While at Columbia he worked as a research assistant for the eminent learning theorist E. L. Thorndike. He next served as Associate Professor at Brooklyn College until 1951. Maslow described New York City during this period, particularly the late 1930s and early 1940s, as the center of the psychological universe. It was here that he personally encountered the cream of European intellectuals who were forced to flee from Hitler. Erich Fromm, Alfred Adler, Karen Horney, Ruth Benedict, and Max Wertheimer were a few of those whom Maslow sought out to enhance his understanding of human behavior. The informal conversations and challenging experiences afforded by such distinguished scholars played an enormous role in shaping the intellectual foundations for Maslow's later humanistic views. He was also psychoanalyzed during this time.

Maslow's enthusiasm for behaviorism literally vanished when the first of two daughters was born. "Our first baby changed me as a psychologist. It made the behaviorism I had been so enthusiastic about look so foolish I could not stomach it anymore. . . . I'd say that anyone who had a baby couldn't be a behaviorist" (Maslow, 1968, p. 55). Evidently, the complex behavior displayed by Maslow's own children convinced him that behavioristic psychology was more relevant to understanding rodents than humans.

World War II markedly changed the direction of Maslow's professional life. For him the war epitomized the prejudice, hatred, and baseness of mankind. The experience of witnessing a parade shortly after Pearl Harbor was the turning point in Maslow's career.

> As I watched, the tears began to run down my face. I felt we didn't understand—not Hitler, nor the Germans, nor Stalin, nor the communists. We didn't understand any of them. I felt that if we could understand, then we could make progress. I had a vision of a peace table, with people sitting around it, talking about human nature and hatred and war and peace and brotherhood. . . . That moment changed my whole life and determined what I have done since. Since that moment in 1941 I've devoted myself to developing a theory of human nature that could be tested by experiment and research (Maslow, 1968, p. 54).

In 1951 Maslow was appointed chairman of the Psychology Department at Brandeis University and held that position until 1961, after which he continued as professor of psychology. During this period Maslow became the foremost spokesperson of the humanistic movement in American psychology. In the spring of 1969 he took a leave of absence from Brandeis to become the first resident fellow of the W. P. Laughlin Charitable Foundation in Menlo Park, California. This nonacademic post allowed him complete freedom to pursue his interests in the philosophy of democratic politics and ethics. But on June 8, 1970, at the age of 62, Maslow died of a heart attack, after a chronic history of heart disease.

Maslow was affiliated with a number of professional and honorary societies. He served on the council of the Society for the Psychological Study of Social Issues and was president of the Massachusetts State Psychological Association. As a member of the American Psychological Association he was president of the Division of Personality and Social Psychology, president of the Division of Esthetics, and was elected president of the entire association for 1967–1968. Maslow was also a founding editor of both the *Journal of Humanistic Psychology* and the *Journal of Transpersonal Psychology,* and he served as consulting editor of numerous other scholarly periodicals. Maslow was vitally interested in growth psychology and, toward the end of his life, he supported the Esalen Institute in California and other groups involved in the human potential movement.

The majority of Maslow's books were written within the last ten years of his life and include *Toward a Psychology of Being* (1962); *Religions, Values, and Peak Experiences* (1964); *Eupsychian Management: A Journal* (1965b); *The Psychology of Science: A Reconnaissance* (1966); *Motivation and Personality* (1970, 2d edition); and *The Farther Reaches of Human Nature* (1971, a collection of articles previously published by Maslow in various psychological journals). A volume compiled with the assistance of his wife and entitled *Abraham H. Maslow: A Memorial Volume* was published posthumously in 1972.

BASIC TENETS OF HUMANISTIC PSYCHOLOGY

The term "humanistic psychology" was coined by a group of psychologists who in the early 1960s joined under the leadership of Abraham Maslow to establish a viable theoretical alternative to the two most influential intellectual currents in psychology —psychoanalysis and behaviorism. Unlike the others, humanistic psychology is not a single organized theory or system; it might better be characterized as a movement (i.e., a collection or convergence of a number of lines and schools of thought). Maslow called it *third force psychology.* Although proponents of this movement represent a wide range of views, they do share certain fundamental conceptions of human nature. Practically all these shared concepts have deep roots in the history of Western philosophical thinking (Durant, 1977). More specifically, humanistic psychology is heavily steeped in European existential philosophy and psychology as developed by such thinkers and writers as Kierkegaard, Sartre, Camus, Binswanger, Boss, and Frankl. The American psychologist, Rollo May, has also been influential in promoting existential thought in the United States.

Existential philosophy is concerned with man as an individual and the unique problems of human existence. Man is literally one who exists as being-in-the-world, consciously and painfully aware of his own existence and eventual nonexistence (death). Rejecting the notion that a person is either a product of hereditary (genetic) factors or environmental influences (particularly early ones), existentialists believe that each person carves out his or her own destiny; one creatively fashions *essence* (what one is) from the fact of *existence* (that one is). Since there are no cause-effect relationships in human behavior, the individual has complete freedom of choice, and each person alone is responsible for his or her existence. In a profound sense, then, "life is what you make it." What each of us makes of our existence is up to us.

Human beings, determining what they will or will not do, are free to be whatever they want to be. This does not mean that given freedom of choice, one will necessarily act in one's best interest. Having the freedom to choose does not ensure that all the choices will be wise ones. If this were so, people would not be afflicted with misery, alienation, anxiety, boredom, guilt, and a host of other self-imposed ailments. For the existentialists, the question is whether or not one can live an authentic (honest and genuine) life. Because existential philosophy believes each person is responsible for his or her actions, it appeals to humanistic psychology; humanistic theorists also stress that each individual is the chief determinant of his or her behavior and experience. The human being is a conscious agent—experiencing, deciding and freely choosing his or her actions. Humanistic psychology, then, takes as its basic model the responsible human being freely making choices among the possibilities that are open. As Sartre often put it: "I *am* my choices."

Perhaps the most important concept which humanistic psychologists have extracted from existentialism is that of *becoming*. A person is never static; he or she is always in the process of becoming something different. A college student is decidedly different from the record-swapping, giggling teenager of four years ago. And four years from now she or he may be radically different as a contributing member of society. Accordingly, it is the individual's responsibility as a free agent to realize as many of his or her potentialities as possible; only by actualizing these can one live a truly authentic life. Thus, in the existential-humanistic view, the quest for an authentic existence requires more than the fulfillment of biological needs and of sexual and aggressive instincts. Conversely, people who refuse to become have refused to grow; they have denied themselves the full possibilities of human existence. Humanistically speaking, this is a tragedy and a distortion of what human beings can be, since Maslow regarded this process of becoming, or self-actualization, as inherent in human nature.

Despite the high value placed on becoming, humanistic psychologists recognize that the quest for a meaningful and fulfilling life is not an easy one. This is especially true in an age of profound cultural change and conflict, where traditional beliefs and values no longer provide adequate guidelines for the good life or for finding meaning in human existence. In a bureaucratic society the individual tends to be depersonalized and submerged in the group. Thus, some people become alienated and estranged—strangers to themselves and to other men and women. Other people lack "the courage to be"—to break away from old patterns, to stand on their own, and to seek new and more fulfilling pathways to greater self-actualization. They prefer to rely upon some outside authority to advise them on how to behave and what to believe. But the freedom to shape our essence can be a blessing as well as a curse: humanistic psychologists maintain that this predicament can challenge us to make something worthwhile of our lives. We must all accept responsibility for making choices and directing our own destiny. For whether any of us asked to be born or not, here we are in the world and we are responsible for one human life—our own. To flee from our freedom and responsibility is to be inauthentic, to show bad faith, and ultimately to live in despair.

Finally, existentialism stresses human consciousness, subjective feelings and moods, and personal experiences as they relate to one's existence in the world of other people. This outlook may be designated in a shorthand way as the *phenomenological,* or "here-and-now," perspective. Existentialists and humanists alike emphasize subjective experience as the primary phenomenon in the study of human nature. Both theoretical explanations and overt behavior are secondary to experience itself and its meaning to the experiencer. In this vein, Maslow (1966) wrote: "The basic coin in the realm of knowing is direct, intimate, experiential knowing" (p. 46) and "There is no substitute for experience, none at all" (p. 45).

Scattered throughout his various theoretical writings Maslow set forth his brand of humanistic psychology. As will become increasingly evident, his personological theory sharply contradicts theories dominant for the past half century.

The Individual as an Integrated Whole   One of the most fundamental aspects of humanistic psychology—and Maslow's version of it—is that each individual must be studied as an integrated, unique, organized whole. Maslow felt that for too long psychologists had concentrated upon minute analyses of separate events, neglecting the basic aspects of the whole person and his or her nature. In a commonplace metaphor, psychologists studied the trees, not the forest. In fact, Maslow's theory was primarily developed as a revolt against those theories (especially behaviorism) that deal in bits and pieces of behavior while ignoring the person as a unified whole.

In Maslow's theory, motivation affects the individual as a *whole* rather than just in part:

> In good theory there is no such entity as a need of the stomach or mouth, or a genital need. There is only a need of the individual. It is John Smith who wants food, not John Smith's stomach. Furthermore, satisfaction comes to the whole individual and not just to a part of him. Food satisfies John Smith's hunger and not his stomach's hunger. . . . when John Smith is hungry, he is hungry all over (Maslow, 1970, pp. 19–20).

For Maslow, then, the central characteristic of personality is its unity and totality.

Irrelevance of Animal Research   Advocates of humanistic psychology recognize a profound difference between human and animal behavior. For them, human beings are more than just animals; they are special kinds of animals. This is in sharp contrast to behaviorism, which relies heavily on infrahuman research. Unlike the behaviorists, who emphasize humanity's continuity with the animal world, Maslow regarded the human being as different from all other animals. He believed that behaviorism and its accompanying philosophies have "dehumanized" the individual, leaving little more than a machine composed of chains of conditioned and unconditioned reflexes. Hence, animal research is irrelevant to the understanding of human behavior because it ignores those characteristics that are uniquely human, e.g., ideals, values, shame, courage, love, humor, art, jealousy, and, equally important, what it takes to produce poetry, music, science, and other works of the mind. Highly significant from a humanistic perspective, then, is the fact that there are no rat, pigeon, monkey, or even dolphin personologists—only humans have the capacity to theorize about humans.

Man's Inner Nature   Freud's theory implicitly assumed that man basically has an evil character, that human impulses, if not controlled, will lead to the destruction of others as well as the self. Whether this view is accurate or not, Freud placed little faith in human virtue, and speculated pessimistically on the course of human destiny. Those who endorse a humanistic view advocate quite another position, i.e., that human nature is essentially good—or, at the very least, neutral. One might not be able to appreciate this view while being mugged in Central Park; however, from the humanistic perspective, the evil, destructive, and violent forces in people arise from a bad environment rather than from any inherent rottenness on their part.

Human Creative Potential   The primacy of human creativity is perhaps the most significant concept of humanistic psychology. Maslow (1950) merits the distinction of being the first to call attention to the fact that the most universal characteristic of the people he studied or observed was creativeness. Describing it as a characteristic common to human nature, Maslow (1970) viewed creativity as potentially present in all people at birth. It's natural—trees sprout leaves, birds fly, humans create. However, sad to say, Maslow also recognized that most human beings lose it as they become "enculturated" (formal education stamps out a lot of it). Happily, some few individuals hold on to this fresh, naïve, and direct way of looking at things or, if they number among the majority who lose it, are able to recover it later in life. Maslow theorized that since creativity is potential in anyone, it requires no special talents or capacities. One need not write books, compose music, or produce art objects to be creative. Comparatively few people do. Creativity is a universal human function and leads to all forms of self-expression. Thus, for example, there can be creative homemakers, disc jockeys, shoe sales-persons, business executives, and even college professors!

Emphasis on Psychological Health   Maslow consistently argued that none of the available psychological approaches to the study of behavior does justice to the *healthy* human being's functioning, mode of living, or life goals. In particular, he strongly criticized Freud's preoccupation with the study of neurotic and psychotic individuals. Quite simply, Maslow considered orthodox psychoanalytic theory to be one-sided and lacking in comprehensiveness, since it was grounded in the abnormal or "sick" part of human behavior. He felt that psychology had concentrated on the negative side of human nature (i.e., its frailties and shortcomings), ignoring humanity's strengths and virtues. For example, the nature of graduate students would hardly become evident by studying high school dropouts exclusively. In fact, such a study would be much more likely to discover what graduate students are *not* like than what they are like. To correct this deficiency, Maslow and those sympathetic to the humanistic movement focused attention on the psychologically healthy person and the understanding of such a person in terms other than comparison with the mentally ill. In short, it was Maslow's belief that one cannot understand mental illness until one understands mental health. Stated more baldly, Maslow (1970) argued that the study of crippled, stunted, immature, and unhealthy specimens can yield only a "crippled" psychology. He strongly urged the study of self-actualizing, psychologically healthy persons as the basis for a more universal science of psychology. In brief, humanistic psychology considers self-fulfillment to be the main theme in human life—a theme never uncovered by studying disturbed individuals alone.

MASLOW'S HIERARCHICAL THEORY OF MOTIVATION

Maslow believed that much of human behavior can be explained by the individual's tendency to seek personal goal states that make life rewarding and meaningful. In fact, motivational processes are the heart of his personality theory. Maslow (1970) depicted the human being as a "wanting animal" who rarely reaches a state of complete satisfaction. If nirvana exists, it is temporary. In Maslow's system, as one personal desire is satisfied, another surfaces to take its place. When a person satisfies this one, still another clamors for satisfaction. It is characteristic of human life that people are almost always desiring something.

Maslow proposed that human desires (i.e., motives) are innate and that they are arranged in an ascending hierarchy of priority or potency. Figure 10-1 is a schematic representation of this need-hierarchy conception of human motivation. The needs are, in order of potency: (1) basic physiological needs; (2) safety needs; (3) belongingness and love needs; (4) self-esteem needs; and (5) self-actualization needs, or the need for personal fulfillment. Underlying this scheme is the assumption that low-order, prepotent needs must be at least somewhat satisfied before an individual can become aware of or motivated by higher-order needs.

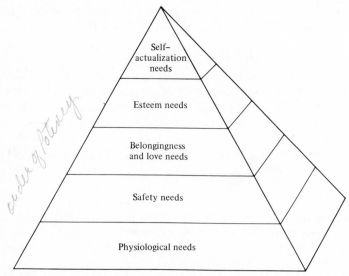

Figure 10-1 A schematic representation of Maslow's need-hierarchy theory.

That is, as one general type of need is satisfied, another higher-order need emerges and becomes operative. For example, if one is starving to death, one urgently needs food and drink before one is able to worry about higher-order needs. Gratification of needs lower in the hierarchy allows for awareness of and motivation by needs higher in the hierarchy, i.e., physiological needs must be met before safety needs become salient; both physiological and safety needs must be satisfied *to some degree* before the needs for belongingness and love emerge and press for satisfaction, and so forth. For Maslow, this sequential arrangement of basic needs in a hierarchy of lesser or greater potency is the chief principle or organization underlying human motivation. He posited that the hierarchy of needs is species-wide and that the farther up the hierarchy a person is able to go, the more individuality, humanness, and psychological health he or she will display.

Maslow acknowledged that there may be exceptions to this hierarchical arrangement of motives. For instance, he noted that some creative people have pursued the development and expression of their special talents despite serious hardships and social ridicule. There are also people whose values and ideals are so strong that they are willing to suffer hunger or thirst or even die rather than renounce them. For example, social reformers have continued their struggles despite harrassment, jail sentences, physical deprivation, and, often, certain death. In general, however, the lower the need in the hierarchy, the greater its strength or priority tends to be.

Let's examine each of Maslow's need categories.

Physiological Needs   The most basic, powerful, and obvious of all human needs is the need for physical survival. Included in this group are the needs for food, drink, oxygen, activity and sleep, sex, protection from extreme temperatures, and sensory stimulation. These physiological drives are directly concerned with the biological maintenance of the organism and must be gratified at some minimal level before the individual is motivated by higher-order needs. Put another way, a person who fails to satisfy this basic level of needs won't be around long enough to attempt to satisfy higher-level needs.

Admittedly, the social and physical environment in American culture provides for the satisfaction of primary needs for most persons. However, if one of these needs remains unsatisfied, the individual rapidly becomes dominated by it, so that all other needs quickly disappear or become secondary. The chronically hungry person will never strive to compose music, construct personological theories, or build a brave new world. Such a person is too preoccupied with getting something to eat. Maslow adds:

> For our chronically and extremely hungry man, Utopia can be defined simply as a place where there is plenty of food. He tends to think that, if only he is guaranteed food for the rest of his life, he will be perfectly happy and will never want anything more. Life itself tends to be defined in terms of eating. Anything else will be defined as unimportant. Freedom, love, community feeling, respect, philosophy, may all be waved aside as fripperies that are useless, since they fail to fill the stomach. Such a man may fairly be said to live by bread alone (1970, p. 37).

Physiological needs are crucial to the understanding of human behavior. The devastating effects on behavior produced by a lack of food or water have been chronicled in numerous experiments and autobiographies. For example, in the Nazi concentration camps of World War II, it was common for prisoners subjected to prolonged deprivation and torture to relinquish their moral standards, steal food from each other, and in other ways surrender the values they had held under normal conditions (Bettelheim, 1943). Another terrifying example of the behavioral effects of prolonged food deprivation occurred when a Peruvian airliner crashed deep in the jungle of South America in 1970. Trapped with a dwindling supply of food, the survivors, including a Catholic priest, resorted to eating the victims of the crash. This incident illustrates how even deeply ingrained social and moral taboos can give way to biological drives under life-threatening conditions. Without a doubt, physiological needs dominate human desires, forcing themselves on one's attention before higher-order goals can be pursued.

Safety needs   Once the physiological needs have been satisfied, an individual becomes concerned with a new set, often called the *safety* or *security* needs. The primary motivating force here is to ensure a reasonable degree of certainty, order, structure, and predictability in one's environment. Maslow suggested that the safety needs are most readily observed in infants and young children because of their relative helplessness and dependence on adults. Infants, for instance, respond fearfully if they are suddenly dropped or startled by loud noises or flashing lights. Experience and education eventually neutralize such apparent dangers, e.g., "I am not afraid of thunder and lightning because I know something about them." The urgency of safety needs is also evident when a child experiences bodily illnesses of various kinds. A child with a broken leg will temporarily experience fears, have nightmares, and manifest a need for protection and reassurance not evident before the accident.

Another indication of the need for safety is the child's distinct preference for some kind of dependable, undisrupted routine. According to Maslow, young children function more effectively in a family setting which has at least a skeletal outline of rigidity, which can be not only anticipated for the present but projected into the future. If such elements are absent in the environment, a child will feel insecure, anxious, and mistrustful, seeking out those areas of life which offer the most stability. Maslow further noted that parents who apply only unrestricted, permissive child-rearing practices do not satisfy a child's safety needs. Not to require a child to go to bed at a certain time or to eat at somewhat regular intervals will only cause confusion or fright. The child then has nothing stable in the environment upon which to depend. Maslow cited parental quarreling, physical assault, separation, divorce, and death within the family as particularly harmful to a child's sense of well-being. In effect, these factors render the child's environment unstable, unpredictable, and hence unsafe.

Safety needs also exert an active influence beyond childhood. The preference for a job with tenure and financial protection, the establishment of savings accounts, and the acquisition of insurance (e.g., medical, unemployment, old age) may be regarded as motivated in part by safety seeking. At least in part, religious and philosophic belief systems may also be interpreted in this fashion. Religions and philosophies help a person to organize his or her world and the people in it into a coherent and meaningful whole, thus making the person feel "safe." Other expressions of the need for safety occur when individuals are confronted with real emergencies, e.g., war, crime waves, floods, earthquakes, riots, societal disorganizations and similar conditions.

Maslow further maintained that certain types of neurotic adults (especially obsessive-compulsive neurotics) are predominantly motivated by the search for safety. Some neurotics behave as if a great catastrophe were imminent, frantically attempting to stabilize their world in a neat, disciplined, orderly fashion so that new contingencies may not appear. The neurotic's safety needs "often find specific expression in a search for a protector, or a stronger person on whom he may depend, perhaps a Fuehrer" (Maslow, 1970, p. 42).

Belongingness and Love Needs   The *belongingness* and *love* needs constitute the third hierarchical level. These needs emerge primarily when the physiological and safety needs have been met. An individual motivated on this level longs for affectionate relationships with others, for a place in his or her family and/or reference groups. Group membership becomes a dominant goal for the individual. Accordingly, a person will feel keenly the pangs of loneliness, social ostracism, friendlessness, and rejection, especially when induced by the absence of friends, relatives, a spouse, or children. Students who attend college far from home fall prey to the effects of belongingness needs, striving with great intensity to be recognized within a group regardless of its size.

Despite the sparsity of empirical data concerning the belongingness and love needs, Maslow insisted that their behavioral effects are potentially disruptive in a highly mobile society such as the United States. America has become a land of nomads (approximately 45 million Americans, about one-fifth of the population, change their addresses at least once a year), a nation of people who are rootless, alienated, indifferent to community and home problems, and afflicted with shallowness in personal relationships. In Maslow's view, the widespread social mobility brought about by industrialization is a key factor in accounting for the phenomenal popularity of *encounter groups* and other forms of personal growth groups. Such groups, he writes, are

> motivated by this unsatisfied hunger for contact, for intimacy, for belongingness and by the need to overcome the widespread feelings of alienation, aloneness, strangeness, and loneliness, which have been worsened by our mobility, by the breakdown of traditional groupings, the scattering of families, the generation gap, the steady urbanization and disappearance of village face-to-faceness, and the resulting shallowness of American friendship (Maslow, 1970, p. 44).

Maslow also held that rebellious youth groups are motivated to some extent by the profound need for "groupiness," for intimate contact, for real togetherness "in the face of a common enemy, any enemy that can serve to form an amity group simply by posing an external threat (Maslow, 1970, p. 44)." University administrators and political figures often serve as excellent "common enemies" in this respect.

Maslow rejected the Freudian notion that love and affection are derived from sublimated sexual instincts; to Maslow, love is not synonymous with sex. Rather, he contended that mature love involves a healthy, loving relationship between two people, which includes mutual respect, admiration, and trust. Maslow also stressed that a person's needs for love involve both giving and receiving love. Being loved and accepted is instrumental to healthy feelings of worth. Not being loved generates futility, emptiness, and hostility.

In brief, it was Maslow's contention that the belongingness and love needs are often frustrated in American society, resulting in maladjustment and pathology. Love and affection are regarded with ambivalence, as if a taboo existed on tenderness. Many people are reluctant to disclose themselves in intimate relationships, since they fear rejection. Maslow concluded that there is mounting evidence to prove a substantial correlation between affectionate childhood experiences and a healthy adulthood. Such data, in his judgment, add up to the generalization that love is a basic prerequisite of healthy development of the human being: "We can say that the organism is so designed that it needs . . . love, in the same way that automobiles are so designed that they need gas and oil" (Maslow, 1970, p. 176).

Self-Esteem Needs   When one's needs for being loved and for loving others have been reasonably gratified, their motivating force diminishes, paving the way for *self-esteem* needs. Maslow divided these into two subsidiary sets: self-respect and esteem from others. The former includes such things as desire for competence, confidence, personal strength, adequacy, achievement, independence, and freedom. An individual needs to know that he or she is worthwhile—capable of mastering tasks and challenges in life. Esteem from others includes prestige, recognition, acceptance, attention, status, fame, reputation, and appreciation. In this case people need to be appreciated for what they can do, i.e., they must experience feelings of worth because their competence is recognized and valued by significant others.

Again, the hierarchical nature of Maslow's view of motivation needs to be kept in mind. One seeks self-esteem only after one's love and belongingness needs are satisfied. One quickly reverts from level four to level three if level-three need satisfaction is suddenly jeopardized. For example, consider a person who, thinking her love needs are in good order, busies herself with becoming a business tycoon. Suddenly and unexpectedly, her husband leaves her. Immediately she casts aside all aspects of self-esteem and becomes consumed in an effort to regain her husband, i.e., satisfy her love needs. Once this relationship is restored or a suitable alternative developed, however, she is free to reconcern herself with the business world.

Satisfaction of the self-esteem needs generates feelings and attitudes of self-confidence, self-worth, strength, capability, and the sense of being useful and necessary in the world. In contrast, the thwarting of these needs leads to feelings and attitudes of inferiority, ineptness, weakness, and helplessness. These negative self-perceptions, in turn, may give rise to basic discouragement, a sense of futility and hopelessness in dealing with life's demands, and a low evaluation of self vis-à-vis others. Maslow emphasized that the most healthy self-esteem is based on earned *respect* from others rather than on fame, status, or adulation. Esteem is the result of effort—it is earned. Hence, there is a real psychological danger of basing one's esteem needs on the opinions of others rather than on real ability, achievement, and adequacy. Once a person relies exclusively upon the opinions of others for self-esteem, she or he is in psychological jeopardy. To be solid, self-esteem must be founded on one's *actual* worth, not on external factors outside one's control.

Self-Actualization Needs   Finally, if all the foregoing needs are sufficiently satisfied, the need for self-actualization comes to the fore. Maslow characterized *self-actualization* as the desire to become everything that one is capable of becoming. The person who has achieved this highest level presses toward the full use and exploitation of his or her talents, capacities, and potentialities. Self-actualization is a person's desire for self-improvement, his or her drive to make actual what he or she is potentially. In short, to self-actualize is to become the kind of person one wants to become—to reach the peak of one's potential: "A musician must make music, an artist must paint, a poet must write, if he is to be at peace with himself. What a man can be, he must be. He must be true to his own nature" (Maslow, 1970, p. 46).

Movement in this direction, however, is by no means easy or automatic. In fact, Maslow believed that we often fear "our best side, . . . our talents, . . . our finest impulses, . . . our creativeness" (1962, p. 58). In other words, self-actualization generates fulfillment, but it also generates fear of responsibilities and the unknown.

Self-actualization need not take the form of creative and artistic endeavors. A parent, an athlete, a student or teacher, or an ardent laborer may all be actualizing their potentials in doing well what each does best; specific forms of self-actualization vary greatly from person to person. It is at this level of Maslow's need hierarchy that individual differences are greatest.

As an illustration of self-actualization in action, suppose that Mark is taking a personality course as part of a long-term plan to become a clinical psychologist. Other theorists could probably explain why he selected this vocational alternative. For example, Freud might say it's related to his deeply repressed childhood curiosity about sex, while Adler might see it as an attempt to compensate for some childhood inferiority. Murray might argue that it's an outgrowth of his attempts to satisfy nAchievement and nNurturance. Skinner, on the other hand, may say it's a product of his conditioning history, while Bandura could relate it to social-learning variables. And Kelly may feel that it all depends on how he construes it. Maslow, however, would argue that Mark might be moving toward becoming the kind of person that he really wants to become, i.e., he is pulled toward this career objective by the need for self-actualization.

Now, further, suppose that Mark has passed the numerous psychology graduate courses, completing the required 2000-hour internship, done a doctoral dissertation, and finally obtained a Ph.D. in clinical psychology. Then somebody offers him a job as a police detective in Brooklyn. The job pays extremely well, provides excellent fringe benefits (Blue Cross, Blue Shield, great vacation time), and *guarantees* steady employment and security for life. Would he take it? If his answer is yes, go back three spaces to level two (safety needs)—psychologically, that's where he's at. If he wouldn't take it,why wouldn't he? Certainly not because the job lacks social value: Brooklyn could function better and longer without psychologists than without police detectives. From Maslow's perspective, one issue is that "what a man can be, he must be." Given his interests and aspirations, Mark would simply have no chance for self-actualization in this job. He would probably hold out instead for a job as a clinical psychologist so that he could develop his capacities, become the kind of person that he really wants to become, and, in brief, self-actualize. Maslow's doctrine of self-actualization is exciting and refreshing because it makes a person *look up* to what he or she *can be*—and thus live with zest and purpose.

Why Can't All People Achieve Self-Actualization?

According to Maslow, most, if not all, of mankind needs and seeks inner fulfillment. His own research led him to conclude that the impulse toward realizing one's potentialities is both natural and necessary. Yet only a few—usually the gifted—ever achieve it (less than 1 percent of the population Maslow estimated). In part, he believed that this extremely unfortunate state of affairs exists because many people are simply blind to their potential; they neither know that it exists nor understand the rewards of self-enhancement. Rather, they tend to doubt and even fear their own abilities, thereby diminishing their chances of becoming self-actualized. In addition, the social environment often stifles self-fulfillment.

One example is the cultural stereotype of what is masculine and what is not. Such human qualities as sympathy, kindness, gentleness, and tenderness are frequently discouraged because of the cultural tendency to consider such characteristics "unmasculine." Or worse, consider the overwhelming and stifling effects that the traditional female role has upon the psychological development of women (Monahan, Kuhn, and Shaver, 1974). Following from such considerations, actualization of the highest potentials—on a mass basis—is possible only under "good conditions." Or, more directly, people will generally need a "facilitative" society in which to maximize their human potentials to the fullest. At this point in history, there is no society that fully facilitates the self-actualization of all its members, although, admittedly, some are far superior to others in terms of providing opportunities for individual self-fulfillment.

A final obstacle to self-actualization mentioned by Maslow is the strong negative influence exerted by the safety needs. The growth process demands a constant willingness to take risks, to make mistakes, to break old habits. This requires courage. It follows that anything that increases the individual's fear and anxiety also increases the tendency to regress toward safety and security. It is also evident that most people exhibit strong tendencies to continue specific habits—to persist in past behavior. Realization of one's full potential therefore requires an openness to novel ideas and experiences. Maslow maintained that children reared in a secure, warm, friendly atmosphere are more apt to acquire a healthy taste for the growth process. In short, under healthy conditions (where the individual's basic need satisfactions are not endangered), growth is rewarding and the individual will strive to become the best that he or she is able to become. In other words, people who fail to develop their true potential—to become what they as individuals could become—are reacting to the deprivation of their basic needs. If more people are to achieve self-actualization, then, the world needs to be changed to permit more widespread opportunities for people to satisfy their lower-level needs. Obviously, this task would require a major reorganization of many of our social institutions and political structures.

DEFICIT MOTIVATION VERSUS GROWTH MOTIVATION

In addition to his hierarchical conception of motivation, Maslow (1955) distinguished two broad categories of human motives: *deficit* motives and *growth* motives. The former (also designated *deficiency* or *D motives* by Maslow) reflect little more than the lower needs in Maslow's motivational hierarchy, especially those concerned with the organism's physiological and safety requirements. The exclusive aim of deprivation motivation is to fend off organismic tension arising from deficit states, e.g., hunger, cold, insecurity. In this sense, D motives are urgent determiners of behavior. According to Maslow (1962), deficit motives share five criteria: (1) their absence produces illness (using hunger as an example, if a man does not eat, he will get sick); (2) their presence prevents illness (if he eats properly, he won't get sick because of it); (3) their restoration cures illness (there's no cure for starvation like food); (4) under certain complex free-choice conditions, they are preferred by the deprived person over other gratifications (if he is starving, he will choose food over sex); and (5) they are found to be inactive or functionally absent in the healthy person (healthy people are fortunate enough that their behavior is not constantly dominated by a quest for food).

In contrast to D-type motives, growth motives (also designated *metaneeds* and *being* or *B motives*) are distant goals associated with the inborn urge to actualize one's potentials. The objective of growth motives, or metaneeds (*meta* means "beyond," or "after"), is to enrich living by enlarging experiences, thus increasing the joy of being alive. Growth motivation does not involve the repairing of deficit states (i.e., tension reduction) as much as the expansion of horizons (i.e., tension increase). Taking a course in organic chemistry, for example, just because one wants to know about it is more reflective of B- than D-type motivation. Growth or B-type motives come into play chiefly after the D motives have been satisfied. A person would certainly not be interested in taking organic chemistry if she were starving to death.

More recently, Maslow (1967a) proposed that metaneeds are as instinctive or inherent in people as the deficit motives. Thus, they too must be satisfied if psychological health is to be maintained and the fullest growth achieved. Otherwise, an individual may become psychologically "sick." The "illnesses" resulting from failure to achieve one's fullest humanness or growth Maslow labeled "meta-pathologies" (Maslow, 1967a). Such psychological states as apathy, alienation,

Table 10-1   Maslow's Metaneeds and Metapathologies

Metaneeds (B-values)	Metapathologies
Truth	Mistrust, cynicism, skepticism
Beauty	Vulgarity, loss of taste, bleakness
Uniqueness	Loss of feeling of self and individuality, feeling oneself to be interchangeable or anonymous
Perfection	Hopelessness, nothing to work for, chaos, unpredictability
Justice	Anger, lawlessness, total selfishness, cynicism
Playfulness	Grimness, depression, loss of zest in life, cheerlessness
Goodness	Hatred, repulsion, disgust, reliance only upon self and for self
Simplicity	Overcomplexity, confusion, bewilderment, loss of orientation

Source: Adapted from Maslow, 1971, pp. 318–319.

depression, and cynicism are just a few examples of what Maslow meant by this higher level of psychic disturbance. In humanistic psychology, not only is the person more highly regarded than in psychoanalysis or behaviorism, he or she is even endowed with *psychological disorders* of a distinctly higher class! Table 10-1 presents examples of Maslow's metaneeds along with the specific metapathologies that result from metaneed frustration.

Maslow also theorized that metaneeds, or growth motives, possess equal value; thus, they have no generalized hierarchy. Consequently, one can be easily substituted for another when a person's life circumstances so dictate. People who are metamotivated are devoted to working for truth, for beauty, for goodness, for law and order, for justice, and for perfection. Maslow described metamotivated people as follows:

> For more highly evolved persons, "the law" is apt to be more a way of seeking justice, truth, goodness, etc., rather than financial security, admiration, status, prestige, dominance, masculinity, etc. When I ask the questions: which aspects of your work do you enjoy most? What gives you your greatest pleasures? When do you get a kick out of your work? etc., such people are more apt to answer in terms of intrinsic values, of transpersonal, beyond-the-selfish, altruistic satisfactions, e.g., seeing justice done, doing a more perfect job, advancing the truth, rewarding virtue and punishing evil, etc. (1971, p. 310).

In sum, the motivational life of self-actualizers is not only quantitatively different but also qualitatively different from that of non-self-actualizers. Whereas ordinary people are motivated by basic need gratifications, self-actualizing people strive to grow to perfection and to develop more and more fully in their own style. In sharp contrast to Skinner's *Beyond Freedom and Dignity,* then, Abraham Maslow's view of persons might aptly be termed "beyond determinism and homeostasis."

MASLOW'S BASIC ASSUMPTIONS CONCERNING HUMAN NATURE

As was emphasized earlier, humanistic psychology differs sharply from both psychoanalysis and behaviorism in terms of its basic image of human nature. In fact,

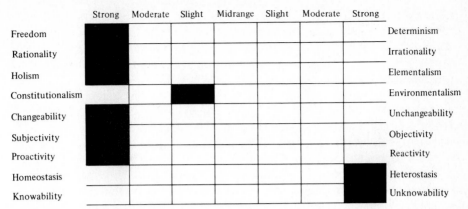

Figure 10-2   Maslow's position on the nine basic assumptions concerning human nature.

humanistic psychology was born largely out of protest against the images of humanity prevalent in psychoanalytic and behavioristic circles. The profound differences separating these other "forces" from humanistic theory are most evident when considering the basic assumptions concerning human nature espoused by each. Careful examination of Maslow's basic assumptions (depicted in Figure 10-2), particularly when contrasted with those of Freud and Skinner, should prove illuminating in this respect.

Freedom–Determinism   Although hesitant to accept the idea of total freedom propounded by influential existentialists, Maslow pretty much approximates their belief. In his system, the human being is fundamentally free and responsible for his or her own behavior. This freedom is manifest in whether one decides to satisfy one's needs, how one chooses to satisfy them, and, specifically, how one gropes toward self-actualization. A person *decides* what her or his potentialities are and how she or he will actualize them.

In Maslow's theory, the older a person becomes and the higher he or she climbs on the need ladder, the more freedom that person has. For example, infants aren't really "free" because they are dominated by physiological needs; they don't actually "decide" when to eat, sleep, or eliminate. But their potential is already present in their nature. As people mature, they move up the need hierarchy and progressively fashion their own individuality. In effect, they begin to create themselves—they carve out the kind of person they wish to become from a host of possibilities. The higher they progress on the need ladder, the more free they are of pressing D-type motivation and hence the more free they are as persons to create their own destinies. Furthermore, *each person* has the potential to actualize himself or herself in his or her own way. Maslow's commitment to the underlying freedom assumption is really very strong indeed.

Rationality–Irrationality   When considering Maslow's position on the rationality assumption, it is important to remember that he regards animal research as largely irrelevant for human psychology. One major reason for this rejection is that an animal lower on the phylogenetic scale does not consciously review past experiences, think about present circumstances, consider future possibilities, and then cognitively decide on a course of action. An average human being, however, engages in this activity daily. So, in Maslow's theory, rationality is a central feature of human makeup and conduct.

While Maslow allows for irrationality—seen in conflict among needs, compulsions, inconsistencies in behavior, and unconscious processes—human conduct, to him, is largely governed by rational forces. As one instance of this conviction, Maslow (1966) considered a person's conscious self-report of his or her own subjective experience as valid data for scientific study. No personologist supports an "introspective method of inquiry" unless she or he thinks that the person giving it is sufficiently rational and self-aware to understand and report the reasons for his or her behavior. At the same time, however, Maslow (1970) accepted data from projective techniques (e.g., Thematic Apperception Test and Rorschach) which are designed to tap unconscious, irrational aspects of personality. But irrational processes do not dominate most people's lives. The basic thrust of Maslow's theory presents a picture of human beings who *rationally* make decisions and strive to actualize their potential. Maslow's commitment to rationality is strong.

Holism–Elementalism   It is difficult to imagine a theorist more committed to the holism assumption than Abraham Maslow. As noted earlier, one of the basic tenets of humanistic psychology is of "the individual as an integrated whole." Even among humanistic psychologists, he stands out in terms of the extent to which holism characterizes his theory (Maddi and Costa, 1972).

Earlier Maslow was quoted in this respect, observing that "it is John Smith who wants food, not John Smith's stomach" (Maslow, 1970, pp. 19–20). It can now be observed that, in this theory, it is also *John Smith* who wants safety, *John Smith* who wants self-esteem, and, above all, *John Smith* who wants self-actualization. All aspects of personality are intertwined and fused in Maslowian man. The individual as a totality is the only valid object for psychological study—no bits and pieces for Maslow! His position on the holism assumption is indeed extreme.

Constitutionalism–Environmentalism   The heavy existentialist-type emphasis upon freedom running throughout Maslow's theory almost makes the issue raised by this assumption irrelevant. If people are largely free to shape themselves and creatively determine their own destinies, then neither constitution nor environment play a significant role in molding human behavior. Of the two, however, Maslow is inclined to give constitution slightly more weight. *Physiological needs,* obviously constitutional in origin, are the basis for his entire need-hierarchy conception of human motivation. Yet he seems to use this concept more to recognize the biological communality of humanity than to explain individual differences in personality, e.g., Kathryn and Eleanor are similar in that they both have physiological needs, but the essential personality difference between them is not constitutional—it lies much more in the realm of how each freely chooses to satisfy needs and to self-actualize.

Further traces of constitutionalism are found in Maslow's concepts of B-motives and self-actualization itself. In discussing these earlier in the chapter, terms like "inborn urge," "instinctive," and "inherent in humanity" were used. Indeed, Maslow regarded the drive toward actualizing one's potentials as an inherent aspect of *what a person is,* rather than what he or she learns. This drive is inborn. Maslow (1962) also recognized the influences of early environment on personality development, but seemed to give weight to this factor only when it was a devastatingly destructive force contributing to a later emotional disturbance. On balance, Maslow leans slightly toward constitutionalism, but in no way does he emphasize it. Because of his strong position on the freedom assumption, his commitment to constitutionalism is only slightly greater than it is to environmentalism.

Changeability–Unchangeability To appreciate Maslow's position on this assumption, one needs to understand the relationship between freedom and growth motivation in humanistic theory. As noted earlier, Maslow believed that people are largely free to fashion their own destinies. Also central to his theory is the notion that individuals are forever striving for personal growth—with the concept of self-actualization at the pinnacle of the need-hierarchy pyramid. Freedom and growth motivation interact in humanistic theory, and change occurs in the individual's personality makeup over time. That is, as the person continues to ascend the need hierarchy, he or she becomes progressively more free to chart the directions of his or her personal growth. As these directions are charted and followed, the person necessarily undergoes change. So in Maslow's theory, people have the capacity to decide what kind of persons they wish to become; as they continue to grow in various directions, personality changes necessarily take place.

In humanistic theory, personality change might best be thought of as movement toward the actualization of one's potentials. Even though some of these potentials may be innate, the degree to which one actualizes them, as well as how one decides to do so, is largely a matter of personal choice. So in the constant process of moving from D- to B-type motives, people are continually making choices about the direction of their lives and are thereby changing in the process. Viewed in this light, Maslow's commitment to the changeability assumption is indeed strong.

Subjectivity–Objectivity The existential, phenomenological, "here-and-now" perspective in Maslow's theory clearly reveals a strong allegiance to the subjectivity assumption. While not elevating it to the apex of importance that his fellow humanistically inclined colleague Carl Rogers does (see next chapter), Maslow obviously believed that human subjective experience constitutes the cardinal data of psychological science. People cannot be understood without reference to their private world; subjective experience is more important than observable behavior for psychology.

While he posited a hierarchical set of needs common to humanity, Maslow (1964) argued that these needs are specific to each individual and will thus be expressed in a unique way. For example, while both Ayn and Betty have a need for self-esteem, each will *subjectively experience* and attempt to satisfy this need in a different way. One may enhance her position as a mother so that others will recognize her outstanding parenthood, while the other may derive self-esteem from a career outside the home. Finally, it should be noted that the word "self" in Maslow's key phrase "self-actualization" is firmly rooted in the subjectivity assumption. According to humanistic psychology, each person is constantly working toward the actualization of a unique self which only he or she alone can subjectively experience and appreciate.

Proactivity–Reactivity Rejecting practically any kind of situational determinism, Maslow (1970) clearly advocates a proactive view of humanity. The Maslowian person does not behave in response to external stimuli; he or she *acts* rather than *reacts*. Maslow depicts people as attempting to satisfy broad internal need states; these needs generate their behavior.

Maslow's exceedingly strong adherence to the proactivity assumption is most evident in his central concept of self-actualization. *There can be no external stimuli for self-actualization. By its nature, self-actualization is a proactive concept.* Persons are pictured as oriented toward the future, aware of their potentials, and forever striving to bring them into being. In fact, the only way that a person can self-actualize is through internally generated actions. To achieve self-actualization, a person *must act*. Persons, then, are highly proactive in Maslow's system.

Homeostasis–Heterostasis Maslow is strongly inclined toward the heterostatic assumption; the image of the individual pushing on to greater and greater heights of psychological growth is an integral part of Maslow's theory. Yet Maslow recognizes two categories of human motivation: D- and B-type motives. Examination of these clearly indicates that D (deficit) motives are homeostatically based, while B (growth) motives are obviously heterostatic. Thus a human being doesn't strive for growth all the time—part of human life necessarily involves tension reduction.

But Maslow did not achieve recognition in psychology because of his account of D motives. Others, particularly animal psychologists, had already studied these thoroughly. No—instead, Maslow seems to treat D motives as almost a necessary theoretical evil. They are something that have to be recognized, worked through, and dealt with successfully on one's way to becoming fully human. And how does one become fully human? By rising above D-level functioning and working toward growth and self-realization. In Maslow's theory, a human being is an animal that has its eyes on the sky. The entire thrust of his theory points to the individual rising above those motives that form a link with the rest of the animal kingdom and seeking growth and personal fulfillment. Such a conception of personality could not exist without a solid foundation in the heterostasis assumption.

Knowability–Unknowability D. O. Hebb (1974) has observed that humanistic psychology as a whole tends to confuse two very different ways of knowing about man—science and literature. The first is objective, careful, and circumscribed; the second is intuitive, immediate, and perhaps overly global. Whether one agrees or disagrees with Hebb's assessment, it is clear that a theory which regards human beings as free and subjective will have a difficult time achieving ultimate knowledge of its subject matter through traditional scientific methodology. Maslow's is precisely such a theory.

Implicit in Maslow's writings is a humanistic image of man that cannot be fully captured by traditional modes of scientific inquiry. Persons are unknowable in this sense. And so, to approach a more comprehensive understanding of human nature, we will either have to look beyond the traditional ken of science or restructure psychological science to incorporate subjective, intuitive concepts befitting the nature of the subject. As a psychologist, Maslow unequivocally favored the latter. In fact, he chastised psychology and its graduate training for studying "Dry bones. Techniques. Precision. Huge mountains of itty-bitty facts, having little to do with the interests that brought the students into psychology" (Maslow, 1956, p. 229). Instead, as the "spiritual father" of the humanistic movement, Maslow wanted a drastically redefined psychology—one that would address itself squarely to his image of humanity. One is forced to conclude that this is because the Maslowian person is simply unknowable within the traditional domain of psychological science. Thus the third force movement emerged.

EMPIRICAL VALIDATION OF HUMANISTIC THEORY CONCEPTS

To date, efforts aimed at verifying Maslow's humanistic conceptions of personality have focused primarily on two areas: (1) the hierarchy of needs and (2) the concept of self-actualization. Empirical attention has been given to only these two areas because they constitute the greater part of Maslow's contributions to personology. Regrettably, other aspects of Maslow's theory have received virtually no empirical support. In particular, there is no evidence to substantiate the notion that the various metaneeds emerge or become dominant once the basic needs have been gratified. At the same time, however, it should be emphasized that Maslow's metamotivational theory has had a decided impact on the thinking of many investigators in a variety of disciplines. Furthermore, not only has he encouraged personological researchers to consider the positive aspects of human nature, he has also forced some of them to reconsider their own limited conception of the scientific enterprise as applied to human behavior. Specifically, Maslow admonished his fellow psychologists for inevitably stressing "elegance, polish, technique, and apparatus [which] has, as a frequent consequence [led to] a playing down of meaningfulness, vitality, and significance of a problem and of creativeness in general" (1970, p. 11). As a result, he has helped some researchers to view science as an enterprise in which appropriate techniques are used to tackle important questions rather than as a method in which sophisticated techniques are used to examine minutiae.

Are Needs Arranged in a Hierarchy?   As previously discussed, Maslow proposed that human needs are arranged in a dominance hierarchy with the gratification of lower, deficit needs a prerequisite to the emergence of higher, growth-related needs. This idea has received considerable attention in theoretical and applied writings on human motivation (e.g., McGregor, 1960; Porter, 1961), yet relatively few attempts have been made to test it empirically. Many studies have included measures of the needs described by Maslow, but most investigators, having assumed the validity of need-hierarchy theory, used the measures only to examine other issues.

With few exceptions, empirical support for Maslow's need-hierarchy conception of motivation is based on the study of physiological and safety needs. For example, numerous psychological reports substantiate the dominating and disrupting effects of severe cold, hunger, thirst, and fear (Keys, Brozek, Henschel, and Mickelson, 1950). It seems well documented that survival needs and those involving pain and threat (e.g., anxiety and insecurity) can dominate the organism's behavior under severe conditions and remain secondary at other times. To this extent, Maslow's hierarchy of needs has received support. However, hierarchical needs lying above the physiological and safety levels (e.g., belongingness and love, self-esteem) have seldom been studied by personologists with an eye to validating Maslow's concepts.

Other evidence supporting Maslow's views of motivation comes from organizational research. To illustrate, Porter (1961) found that high-level executives are more concerned with esteem needs and self-actualization than lower-status managers in an industrial setting. Most personologists question the value of such research since it relies upon cross-sectional methodology which excludes the study of behavior *over a period of time*. And, as Maddi and Costa (1972) point out, the crucial test of Maslow's theory would require a longitudinal design (one that examines behavior over time), since Maslow's view states that as lower-level needs become satisfied, the next higher-level need in the hierarchy comes to the fore. Studies involving such longitudinal assessment of need-hierarchy theory are not yet evident in psychological journals and texts.

In one of the few direct empirical tests of need-hierarchy theory, Graham and Balloun (1973) advanced two hypotheses. The first hypothesis stated that "the level of satisfaction of any given need should be negatively correlated with desire for satisfaction of that need" (p. 99). The second predicted that "in any pairwise comparison of needs at different levels in the hierarchy, satisfaction with the lower order need should be greater than for the higher order need" (p. 99).

The subjects ($N = 37$) for this study were preselected to represent the general population in terms of such variables as age, education, and income. Home interviews with each subject were then conducted by trained interviewers. Two methods were used to collect data specific to the hypotheses. First, subjects were asked to *describe the most important things in their lives*. Answers to this open-ended question, recorded verbatim, were subsequently rated by several psychology graduate students in terms of the amount of desire expressed for physiological, security, social, and self-actualization needs. Ratings were made separately for each need level and were expressed on a five-point scale ranging from "very high" to "little or no" desire. An example of an interview protocol rated high on desire for

Table 10-2   Product-Moment Correlations between Satisfaction and Desire for Maslow's Needs

Satisfaction	Desire			
	Physiological	Security	Social	Self-actualization
Physiological	−.57	−.21	−.24	−.20
Security	−.40	−.66	−.25	−.11
Social	−.22	−.27	−.72	−.18
Self-actualization	−.09	−.04	−.17	−.42

Source: Adapted from Graham and Balloun, 1973, p. 103.

self-actualization follows: "I feel that self-growth, self-improvement is a lifetime challenge for myself as an individual" (p. 100). A concern for the fulfillment of security needs is reflected in the following statement: "I think the most important thing is money, house, food, clothing and transportation" (p. 101).

A second measure consisted of having subjects provide self-report ratings of present *satisfaction and of improvement wanted* for each of the four needs. Subjects expressed their level of satisfaction on a five-point scale ranging from "very satisfied" to "very unsatisfied." A four-point scale ranging from "none" to "very much" was used to assess the amount of improvement desired.

The first hypothesis was tested by computing product-moment correlations between level of satisfaction and desire for satisfaction as furnished by the direct self-report rating scales (measure 2). Table 10-2 presents the correlation matrix obtained from these indexes. It can be readily seen that the direction and magnitude of the diagonal correlations confirmed the predicted relationship between satisfaction and desire. For example, the more satisfied the subjects reported being about their security needs, the less improvement they desired ($r = -.66$). Hypothesis 1, therefore, was supported.

The second hypothesis was examined independently for each need measure. Mean scores computed from ratings of the interview protocols (measure 1) are shown in Table 10-3.

These data are based on ratings of the degree of concern shown for physiological, security, social, and self-actualization needs in subjects' descriptions of the most important things in their lives. Since low mean values indicate high levels of expressed concern, it can be seen that level of concern follows a hierarchical pattern which corresponds to the ordering of needs as proposed by Maslow. Table 10-3 also contains mean scores computed from subjects' ratings of their present level of satisfaction with each need (measure 2). Again, it is readily apparent that the ordering of mean values approximates what would be expected from need-hierarchy theory, although the mean satisfaction rating for the social need did not conform to the predicted pattern. In sum, the results of Graham and Balloun's investigation support Maslow's theory concerning the relationships between satisfaction and desire as well as the hierarchical ordering of human needs. Such results, however, require replication before confidence can be placed in these aspects of Maslow's theory. Moreover, there is need for greater precision concerning the exact

Table 10-3   Mean Scores for Interview Protocol and Satisfaction Ratings

Need	Mean Interview protocols	Satisfaction
Physiological	14.23	4.14
Security	12.69	3.35
Social	9.09	3.73
Self-actualization	7.20	3.00

Source: Adapted from Graham and Balloun, 1973, pp. 104 and 106.

amount of gratification the individual must experience before the next-higher need will emerge.

Is Self-Actualization Real or Not?   The basic view of human nature espoused by Maslow and other humanistic psychologists is highly positive (some might say "rosy"). They not only emphasize humanity's innate potential for creativity and personal growth but are also optimistic about the realization of these human potentials given favorable environmental conditions. Allied to this image is the belief that a person is imprisoned by different layers of circumstances which do not always allow him or her to attain full humanness. Thus, if self-actualization is to be achieved, the individual must transcend the restraints of society and his or her deficit needs and assume responsibility for becoming whatever he or she is capable of becoming. Empirical validation for this conception of human nature is tenuous at best, and what little does exist comes from Maslow's (1950) own study of self-actualizing people.

In a modestly conducted informal study (regrettably informal, considering the speculative weight it was subsequently required to support), Maslow examined the characteristics of forty-nine famous and prominent people who, he felt, personified the ideal of psychological health. The individuals studied were selected from his personal friends and acquaintances, from public figures living and dead, and from college students. These were people who by all conventional standards appeared to have lived self-actualized lives and thus achieved genuine maturity. Notably, they showed no tendencies toward neurotic, psychotic, or other gross psychological disorders. At the same time, there was considerable evidence of self-actualization— loosely defined by Maslow as evidence that the person appeared to be fulfilling herself or himself and to be doing the best that she or he was capable of doing. Maslow justified his lack of methodological rigor in selecting subjects this way:

> If we want to answer the question how tall can the human species grow, then obviously it is well to pick out the ones who are already tallest and study them. If we want to know how fast a human being can run, then it is no use to average out the speed of a "good sample" of the population; it is better to collect Olympic gold medal winners and see how well they can do. If we want to know the possibilities for spiritual growth, value growth, or moral development in human beings, then I maintain that we can learn most by studying our most moral, ethical, or saintly people (Maslow, 1969, p. 726).

Abiding by this rationale, Maslow's research relied heavily upon observation rather than hypothesis testing, with the resulting observations admittedly subjective in nature. Moreover, by focusing on a relatively small and select group of subjects, he deviated markedly from sampling theory, the orthodox conception of statistics. Nonetheless, his assessment of the self-actualized person and the kinds of motives which characterize him or her has captured the imagination of personologists and laypersons alike.

Maslow divided his subjects into three categories. Examples of the first category, "fairly sure cases," included Jefferson, Lincoln, Spinoza, Einstein, and Eleanor Roosevelt. Category two of "partial cases" consisted of five contemporary individuals who fell short somewhat of self-actualization but still could be used for study. Their names were not revealed. Finally, a "potential or possible cases" category included people who appeared to be striving toward self-actualization but who never quite attained it, e.g., Franklin, Whitman, G. W. Carver, Renoir, Pablo Casals, and Adlai Stevenson. Maslow regarded all these individuals as rare specimens of psychological health who could be used as touchstones to explore the farther reaches of human nature.

The data accumulated on these persons did not consist of the usual gathering of discrete facts; rather it involved the gradual development of global or holistic impressions of the sort that one forms of new friends and acquaintances. Specifically, Maslow obtained biographical information relevant to each subject (much like a case history) and, whenever possible, he questioned friends and relatives. In many cases it was impossible for him to question or test his older subjects, although such measures were carried out with the younger ones. Hence, quantitative analysis of the data was impossible. This procedure yielded a list of fifteen salient characteristics or traits of self-actualizing people which will be discussed in the "Application" section of this chapter. Despite its inadequacies and technical flaws (discussed next), this study serves as the foundation for Maslow's idea of the self-actualizing person as a model of optimal psychological health.

The crucial flaw in Maslow's study is the procedure he used to select his sample of self-actualizers (Smith, 1973). In effect, Maslow chose people for whom he personally had the highest admiration as human specimens. His empirical definition of self-actualization thus rests solely on his own implicit values. One may well question whether these characteristics pertain to a psychological process called self-actualization or are merely the reflections of Maslow's particular value system. The array of characteristics that he reports must, then, be considered not as a factual description of self-actualizing people but rather as a reflection of Maslow's personalized conception of ideal human values. In short, the dice are loaded in favor of Maslow's own values.

Other methodological problems also make it difficult to evaluate Maslow's claim that his self-actualizing subjects represent the best possible specimens of the human race. Foremost is the question of *how* they were studied. What were their ages, sex distributions, marital status, number of children, socioeconomic levels, and places of residence? Were they exceedingly bright, highly educated, favorably employed? Is it possible that some factor such as intelligence, talent, or privileged background may have made them unrepresentative of the general populace and, therefore, a *biased* sample from which to generalize about the species? Unfortunately, basic questions such as these cannot be answered from the available data. In light of these problems, it is easy to see why Maslow's descriptive account of the metapsychology of the self-actualizing being has been criticized for the relative vagueness of its concept, "looseness" of its language, and sheer lack of evidence related to its basic contentions (Cofer and Appley, 1964).

Measuring Self-Actualization   Lack of an adequate instrument to measure self-actualization originally blocked any attempts to validate Maslow's major assertions. However, with the recent development of the Personal Orientation Inventory (POI: Shostrom, 1965, 1966) as a reliable and valid measure of self-actualization, empirical research relating to Maslow's theory is now being pursued at an accelerating rate (Tosi and Hoffman, 1972). The POI, a self-report questionnaire, was devised in strict accordance with Maslow's thinking and provides an assessment of an individual's degree of self-actualization. It consists of 150 two-choice comparative value and behavior judgments. For each set of items, the subject must choose one of the two as most relevant to her or him. The response format and sample items are illustrated as follows:

a I live by the rules and standards of society.
b I do not always need to live by the rules and standards of society.
a It is better to be yourself.
b It is better to be popular.

The items are scored to measure two major areas of personal and interpersonal development: one dealing with effective use of time (*time competence*) and the other with the extent to which one depends upon oneself or others in making judgments (*inner direction*). In addition, there are ten complementary subscales designed to measure conceptually important elements of self-actualization: *Self-actualizing values, existentiality, feeling reactivity, spontaneity, self-regard, self-acceptance, nature of man, synergy, acceptance of aggression*, and *capacity for intimate contact*.

Since the POI first appeared, there has been increasing evidence of its construct validity (Fox, Knapp, and Michael, 1968; Shostrom, 1966, 1973; Raanan, 1973). These studies have shown that the test does differentiate between groups of individuals nominated by personologists as representing different categories of self-actualization and non-self-actualization. A study by McClain (1970) illustrates how the POI has been validated as a measure of an individual's level of positive mental health. He examined the personalities of thirty guidance counselors who were attending a summer counseling institute. Their scores on the POI, administered during the first week of the institute, indicated that they were a psychologically healthy group. A composite self-actualization score for each counselor was then derived from the evaluations of the three staff members who knew him or her most intimately. One of these was a practicum supervisor who supervised only six counselors. He reviewed the taped counseling sessions with his counselors and thus was able to become acquainted with each one in terms of his or her personality dynamics and ways of behaving in personal confrontations. Second was a group-process leader who also had six counselors in his group. The group sessions focused on sensitivity training, enabling the staff leader to know the counselors in his group in depth. Third was a clinical psychologist who studied each of the thirty counselors by means of self-report and projective personality instruments.

At the end of the nine-week session, these staff members reviewed a long list of characteristics of self-actualizers summarized from Maslow's various writings. Based on these characteristics, each staff member rated each counselor in his charge along a six-point scale for overall self-actualization. The three staff ratings for each counselor were summed for a composite rating which was then correlated with the POI scales. The correlations between the POI scores and the composite behavioral ratings for self-actualization by staff members are given in Table 10-4. Of a total of twelve correlations, nine were statistically significant in the predicted direction. These data are offered as evidence that the POI does measure self-actualization among normal adults.

The POI has also been studied in relationship to other standardized measures of personality. For instance, the inner-support scale (measuring whether one's orientation is toward self or others) correlates positively with the autonomy scale and negatively with the abasement scale of the Edwards Personal Preference Schedule (Grossack, Armstrong, and Lussiev, 1966). Further, certain POI scales correlate positively with various measures of creativity (Braun and Asta, 1968). The majority of the POI scales also are positively correlated with academic achievement among college students (LeMay and Damm, 1968).

Several investigators have sought to determine whether or not responses to the POI are influenced by the tendency to present oneself in a socially desirable light. Fisher and Silverstein (1969) and Foulds and Warehime (1971) found that instructions to "fake good" actually yielded lower self-actualization scores in subjects! These findings suggest that the POI is remarkably resistant to faking—a problem which unfortunately plagues many other self-report personality questionnaires. In

Table 10-4   Product-Moment Correlations between Counselor Personal Orientation Scores and Composite Ratings for Self-Actualization

POI scale	r	p
Time competence	.40	.05
Inner-support	.69	.01
Self-actualizing value	.41	.05
Existentiality	.43	.02
Feeling reactivity	.45	.02
Spontaneity	.53	.01
Self-regard	.36	ns
Self-acceptance	.56	.01
Nature of man constructive	.23	ns
Synergy	.32	ns
Acceptance of aggression	.42	.05
Capacity for intimate contact	.42	.05

Source: Adapted from McClain, 1970, p. 22.

summary, then, the POI seems well suited for research on self-actualization; as data continue to accumulate, they should shed progressively more empirical light on Maslow's central theoretical construct.

APPLICATION: FOOD FOR THOUGHT ON HOW TO SELF-ACTUALIZE

For anyone attracted to humanistic psychology, the attainment of self-actualization epitomizes the ideal life-style. In this section some ideas will be offered on how one might accomplish this laudable objective. Of course, as with any ideal psychological state, e.g., mental health, nirvana, cosmic consciousness, self-actualization cannot be attained simply by following pat prescriptions propounded by "experts." Nonetheless, to the extent that the concept of self-actualization is *real*, there should be clear ways in which it can be applied to each person. It is in this spirit that this chapter section is offered—food for thought, not "prescriptions."

The first requirement for becoming a self-actualized person is to satisfy the first four levels of needs in Maslow's hierarchy. That, for many of us, would take the rest of our lives! But for those who do go on from there, developing self-actualization on one's own can best be facilitated by studying the characteristics of healthy, self-actualizing adults. In this way, one has some standard against which to measure one's progress; one can see what to modify in one's own personality development. Maslow (1950, 1970) listed fifteen salient characteristics of self-actualizers in his unique study discussed earlier. In spite of the methodological problems of this study, the characteristics that emerged from it make intuitive sense when related to the concept of psychological well-being.

What Are Self-Actualizers Like?

Maslow lists fifteen notable characteristics of his self-actualizing persons, some which may or may not be applicable to each reader. They are presented as follows along with appropriate examples.

1 Efficient Perception of Reality   Perhaps the most universal characteristic of these superior people is their unusual ability to perceive other people correctly and efficiently, to see reality *as it is* rather than *as they wish it to be*. They have a better perception of reality and more comfortable relations with it. They are less emotional and more objective about their perceptions; they do not allow their desires and hopes to distort their observations. Because of their superior perception, self-actualizing people are more readily able to detect the fake, the phony, and the dishonest in others. Maslow discovered that this ability to see more efficiently extended to many other areas of life, including art, music, science, politics, and philosophy. For example, an informal survey indicated that self-actualizers are more accurate in their predictions of future events.

The self-actualized or psychologically healthy (Maslow equated the two) individual's perception is also less distorted by expectations, anxieties, stereotypes, false optimism, or pessimism. Maslow labeled this nonjudgmental type of perception *"being* or *B-cognition."* Self-actualizers are really "with it" in a profound sense; they are *realists.* Finally, the self-actualizer is able to tolerate ambiguity and uncertainty more easily than others. She is generally unthreatened and unfrightened by the unknown; she accepts it, is comfortable with it, and often is even more attracted by it than by the known.

2 Acceptance of Self, Others, and Nature   The healthy person displays a sense of respect for self and others. Without feeling undue concern, he or she accepts his or her own nature in a stoic style, with all its shortcomings, frailties, and weaknesses. There is also freedom from overriding guilt, crippling shame, and debilitating anxiety. Maslow writes:

> One does not complain about water because it is wet, or about rocks because they are hard, or about trees because they are green. As the child looks out upon the world with wide, uncritical, undemanding, innocent eyes, simply noting and observing what is the case, so does the self-actualizing person tend to look upon human nature in himself and in others (1970, p. 156).

Self-acceptance is also vividly expressed at the physiological level. Self-actualizers have hearty appetites, sleep well, and enjoy their sex lives without unnecessary inhibition. Basic biological processes (e.g., urination, pregnancy, menstruation, growing old) are considered part of nature and are graciously accepted.

3 Spontaneity, Simplicity, Naturalness   The behavior of self-actualizing people is marked by spontaneity and simplicity, by an absence of artificiality or straining for effect. This does not imply consistently unconventional behavior. It is the person's *inner life* (thoughts, impulses, etc.) that is unconventional, natural, and spontaneous. Their unconventionality is not intended to impress others and may even be suppressed in order not to distress others, so that they may even abide by ceremonies and rituals. Thus, they may conform if it means protecting themselves or others from pain or injustice. For this reason, if it suits their purposes, self-actualizers may in fact tolerate practices within educational institutions that they regard as unnecessary, repetitive, or mind-debilitating. However, the self-actualizer refuses to be hampered or inhibited by social convention when it seems to interfere with an act that he or she considers to be important or basic. In other words, if the self-actualizer becomes keenly absorbed in a personally vital project or task, he or she may, for its sake, ignore normally accepted rules. One consequence of this characteristic is that such a person's ethical codes do not necessarily correspond to those of her or his milieu.

4 Problem Centering   Without exception, Maslow found his subjects to be committed to some task, duty, vocation, or beloved job which they regarded as important. That is, they are not ego-centered but rather oriented toward problems beyond their immediate needs, problems to which they are dedicated in the sense of a mission in life. In this sense, they live to work rather than work to live; their work is subjectively experienced as a defining characteristic of themselves.

Self-actualizers are also deeply concerned with philosophic and ethical issues. Accordingly, they live and work within the widest frame of reference, tending to devote themselves to nonpersonal "missions" or tasks. Such a life-style denotes a lack of concern for the trivial and petty, thus making life far more bearable not only for the self-actualizers but for all who are associated with them.

5 Detachment: Need for Privacy   This kind of individual prefers solitude and privacy and even seeks it to a greater extent than the average person. In social encounters he or she is often viewed by "normal" people as aloof, reserved, snobbish, and cold. This is because self-actualizers do not *need* other people in the usual sense of friendship. They rely completely upon their inner resources and remain unruffled by that which produces turmoil in others.

This quality of detachment encompasses other aspects of behavior as well. For instance, since they are able to concentrate more intensely than ordinary people, they may become absentminded and oblivious to outer surroundings. They remain calm and serene during periods of personal misfortune. Maslow explained that this comes in part from the self-actualizer's tendency to stand by his or her own interpretation of situations instead of relying upon what other people think or feel about matters.

6 Autonomy: Independence of Culture and Environment   As characteristics already discussed would suggest, self-actualizing people are not dependent for their main satisfactions on the physical and social environment. Rather, they rely on their own potentialities and latent resources for growth and development. For example, truly self-actualizing college students do not really *need* the "right" academic atmosphere on campus to learn. They can learn anywhere because they have *themselves*. Of course, some campus "atmospheres" may be better than others in this respect; the point here is that the self-actualizer does not require a particular type of environment before he or she can learn, or, for that matter, do almost anything else. In this sense, the self-actualizer is a self-contained unit.

Healthy people also have a high degree of self-direction and "free will." They regard themselves as self-governed, active, responsible, and self-disciplined agents in determining their own destinies. They are strong enough to be oblivious to others' opinions and affection; thus, they shun honors, status, prestige, and popularity. Such extrinsic satisfactions are perceived as less significant than self-development and inner growth. Of course, attaining this point of relative independence depends upon having been loved and respected in the past, e.g., satisfying lower-level needs.

7 Continued Freshness of Appreciation   Maslow discovered that healthy, mature adults exhibit a capacity to appreciate even the most ordinary events in their lives with a sense of newness, awe, pleasure, and even ecstasy. They seldom become bored with life experiences:

> Thus for such a person, any sunset may be as beautiful as the first one, any flower may be a breathtaking loveliness, even after he has seen a million flowers. The thousandth baby he sees is just as miraculous a product as the first one he saw. . . . For such

people, even the casual workaday, moment-to-moment business of living can be thrilling, exciting, and ecstatic (Maslow, 1970, p. 163).

8 Peak or Mystic Experiences   Maslow observed that self-actualizing individuals commonly had what he called *peak experiences* (also termed "oceanic feeling"). This term refers to moments of intense excitement and high tension as well as to those of relaxation, peacefulness, blissfulness, and stillness. Representing the most ecstatic moments of life, such occurrences usually come from love and sexual climax, bursts of creativity, insight, discovery, and fusion with nature. These people can "turn on" without artificial stimulants. Just being alive turns them on.

For Maslow, peak or mystic experiences are not necessarily religious or spiritual in nature. He found that "peakers" feel more in harmony with the world, lose their self-awareness or transcend it, feel simultaneously more powerful and more helpless than before, and become less conscious of time and space. According to Maslow, the peak experiences that really change a person come about when they are earned. "The person comes to some glorious insight as the result of a year of sweating on a psychoanalytic couch; or a philosopher who has been working for fifteen years at some problem comes to an illumination" (Hardeman, 1979, p. 24). Undoubtedly, peak experiences can also be experienced through books, music, art, intellectual endeavors, and human relationships generally.

9 Social Interest   Even though self-actualizers are sometimes troubled, saddened, and even enraged by the shortcomings of the human race, they experience a deep feeling of kinship with humanity. Consequently, they have a genuine desire to help improve the lot of their fellows. This nurturant attitude is evidenced by a feeling of compassion, sympathy, and affection for all humanity. Oftentimes this is a special kind of brotherhood, like the attitude of an older brother or sister toward younger siblings. Adler and Erikson also emphasize the dimension of social interest in their respective accounts of psychological health, e.g., Adler's "social interest," Erikson's "generativity."

10 Interpersonal Relations   Self-actualizing people tend to form deeper and closer personal relationships than those of the "average" adult. Similarly, those with whom they associate are likely to be healthier and closer to self-actualization than the average person. That is, self-actualizers are more inclined to associate closely with others of similar character, talent, and capacity ("birds of a feather"). Usually their circle of intimate friends is small, since befriending in the self-actualizing style demands a great deal of time. One of Maslow's subjects said it this way: "I haven't got time for many friends. Nobody has, that is, if they are to be real friends (Maslow, 1970, p. 166)." They also have especially tender feelings for children and are easily touched by them.

Maslow noticed that many of the relationships that these people develop are one-sided. It is not unusual for them to attract admirers, disciples, and worshipers —individuals who, in effect, demand more than they give. When forced into these distressing and distasteful relationships, self-actualizers are kind and pleasant but try to avoid them as gracefully as possible. However, this does not imply a lack of social discrimination. In fact, they may become very harsh with those who deserve it, particularly people who are hypocritical, pretentious, or unduly indignant.

11 Democratic Character Structure   Maslow described his subjects as being "democratic" in the deepest sense. Since they are free of prejudice, they tend basically to respect all persons. Further, they are willing to learn from anybody who is able to teach them, irrespective of class, education, age, race, or political beliefs. At the same time, Maslow discovered that self-actualizers do not indiscriminately equalize all human beings: "These individuals, themselves elite, select for their friends elite, but this is an elite of character, capacity, and talent, rather than of birth, race, blood, name, family, age, youth, fame, or power" (Maslow, 1970, p. 168).

12 Discrimination between Means and Ends   In their day-to-day living, self-actualizing individuals show less confusion, inconsistency, and conflict than the average person about what is right or wrong, good or bad. They have definite moral and ethical standards, although very few of them are religious in the orthodox sense of the term. Maslow's subjects also showed an unusually keen ability to discriminate between ends (goals) and the means for accomplishing those ends. On the other hand, they often enjoy the means, or instrumental behavior leading to a goal, which more impatient persons would dislike. That is, they are more likely to appreciate doing something for its own sake, the "doing itself" (Maslow, 1970).

13 Sense of Philosophical Humor   Another characteristic common to Maslow's subjects was a distinct preference for philosophical or cosmic humor. Whereas the average person may enjoy humor that pokes fun at another's inferiority, that hurts or ridicules someone, or that is "off-color," the healthy person typically finds humor expressing the foolishness of humanity in general most appealing. Lincoln's humor serves as a relevant example. His jokes always had something to convey, a purpose beyond just producing a laugh. They often dealt with a parable or fable. According to Maslow, philosophical humor usually elicits more of a smile than a laugh.

14 Creativeness   Not surprisingly, Maslow found that, without exception, creativity was more prominent in self-actualizers than in others. However, the creativeness manifested by his subjects was different from unusual talent or genius as reflected in poetry, art, music, or science. Maslow likened it to the natural creativeness found in children. This kind of self-actualizing creativity appears in everyday life as an expression of a personality which is perceptive, spontaneous, and "childlike." It does not necessarily involve the writing of books, composing of music, or production of art objects. It may be humble in nature and can touch virtually all the person's activities. Basically, it revolves around the discovery of things new and novel that depart from conventional ideas.

15 Resistance to Enculturation   Finally, Maslow observed that his superior subjects are in harmony with their culture and yet maintain a certain inner detachment from it. Essentially autonomous beings, they make their own decisions, even if they are at odds with popular opinion. This resistance to enculturation does not mean that self-actualizers are unconventional in all realms of behavior. For instance, they remain well within the limits of conformity concerning choice of clothes, speech, food, and the manner of doing things, which are not really important enough to prompt objection. However, they can become extremely independent and unconventional when they feel basic issues are involved. Self-actualizers also manifest a calm, long-term commitment to cultural improvement. Although cognizant of society's imperfections, they accept the fact that social change can be slow and painstaking but is best achieved by working within the system.

Self-Actualizers Aren't Angels

The preceding discussion may have invited the illusion that self-actualizers are a race of supermen and wonderwomen so far above the rest of humanity as to approach perfection. Maslow clearly refuted this. As *imperfect* human beings, self-actualizers are just as susceptible to silly, nonconstructive, and wasteful habits as the rest of humanity. They, too, can be obstinate, irritable, boring, petulant, selfish, or depressed, and they are by no means immune from superficial vanity, undue pride, and partiality to their own friends, family, and children. Temper outbursts are not unusual. Maslow also found his subjects capable of displaying a certain "surgical coldness" when confronted with interpersonal difficulties:

> The man who found that a long-trusted acquaintance was dishonest cut himself off from this friendship sharply and abruptly and without any observable pangs whatsoever. Another woman who was married to someone she did not love, when she decided on divorce, did it with a decisiveness that looked almost like ruthlessness. Some of them recover from the death of people close to them so easily as to seem heartless (Maslow, 1970, p. 175).

Moreover, self-actualizers are not free from guilt, anxiety, sadness, and self-doubt. Their intense concentration may produce a lack of tolerance for idle gossip and light conversation. In fact, they may use language or engage in behavior that is distressing, shocking, or insulting to others. Finally, their kindness toward others may leave them vulnerable to exploitative relationships, e.g., becoming deeply involved with neurotics, bores, and unhappy people. Despite such imperfections in their makeup, Maslow's healthy subjects remind us that humanity's potential for psychological growth is far greater than has yet been attained.

Perhaps a more fundamental question to consider is whether it is even possible to become a healthy person in an imperfect society? Or, as Maslow asked, "How good a human being does society permit?" While this question is open to empirical research, the mere existence of self-actualizing people suggests that human beings are more improvable than most people believe. And that is precisely the legacy that

Maslow wished to leave to psychology. He desperately wanted a better world, an improvement in the human condition, and a society that would allow us to elevate ourselves and our treatment of one another to a truly *humanistic* level based on knowledge gained from psychology. In fact, for Maslow, this is the ultimate value of psychology: "If we die in another war or if we continue being tense and neurotic and anxious in an extended cold war, then this is due to the fact that we don't understand ourselves and we don't understand each other. Improve human nature and you improve all. . . . We need psychology. . . ." (Maslow, 1956, p. 227).

SUMMARY

Humanistic psychology, or the third force movement, has given rise to an image of humanity in psychology radically different from that of either psychoanalysis or behaviorism. Heavily influenced by existential philosophy, humanistic psychology has as its basic tenets the individual as an integrated whole, the irrelevance of animal research, the perception of the person as a basically good, creative being, and an emphasis on the study of psychological health.

One major statement of humanistic psychology, the theory of Abraham Maslow, depicts human motivation in terms of a hierarchy of ascending priorities. Lower (more basic) needs in the hierarchy must be satisfied before higher-level needs emerge as dominant energizing forces in the individual's behavior. In order of potency, Maslow's hierarchy of human needs is: (1) physiological; (2) safety; (3) belongingness and love; (4) self-esteem; and (5) self-actualization. The humanistic nature of Maslow's theory is epitomized in the self-actualization level, the highest fulfillment of self.

Maslow's basic assumptions concerning human nature are reasonably strong and generally explicit. Maslow's humanistic theory reflects (1) a strong commitment to the assumptions of freedom, rationality, holism, changeability, subjectivity, proactivity, heterostasis, and unknowability and (2) a slight commitment to the constitutionalism assumption.

Empirical research generated by Maslow's theory has tended to fall into two main areas: (1) the hierarchy of needs, and (2) the concept of self-actualization. Illustrative studies reflecting each of these areas, including one of Maslow's own, were discussed in this chapter.

In the concluding chapter section, some ideas stemming from Maslow's work were offered to further detail his self-actualization concept. Fifteen notable characteristics of self-actualizing persons were listed and discussed.

BIBLIOGRAPHY

Abraham H. Maslow: A memorial volume. Monterey, Calif: Brooks/Cole, 1972.

Bettelheim, B. Individual and mass behavior in extreme situations. *Journal of Abnormal and Social Psychology,* 1943, **38,** 417–452.

Braun, J., & Asta, P. Intercorrelations between the Personal Orientation Inventory and the Gordon Personal Inventory scores. *Psychological Reports,* 1968, **23,** 1197–1198.

Cofer, C., & Appley, M. *Motivation: Theory and research.* New York: Wiley, 1964.

Conversation with Abraham H. Maslow. *Psychology Today,* 1968, **2,** pp. 35–37; 54–57.

Crosson, S., & Schwendiman, G. *Self-actualization as a predictor of conformity behavior.* Unpublished manuscript. Marshall University, 1972.

Durant, W. Humanism in historical perspective. *The Humanist,* January/February 1977, **37,** 24–26.

Fisher, G., & Silverstein, A. Simulation of poor adjustment on a measure of self-actualization. *Journal of Clinical Psychology,* 1969, **25,** 198–199.

Foulds, M., & Warehime, R. Effects of a "fake good" response set on a measure of self-actualization. *Journal of Counseling Psychology,* 1971, **18,** 279–280.

Fox, J., Knapp, R., & Michael, W. Assessment of self-actualization of psychiatric patients: Validity of the Personal Orientation Inventory. *Educational and Psychological Measurement,* 1968, **28,** 565–569.

Graham, W., & Balloun, J. An empirical test of Maslow's need hierarchy theory. *Journal of Humanistic Psychology,* 1973, **13,** 97–108.

Grossack, M., Armstrong, T., & Lussiev, G. Correlates of self-actualization. *Journal of Humanistic Psychology,* 1966, **6,** 87.

Hardeman, M. A dialogue with Abraham Maslow. *Journal of Humanistic Psychology,* 1979, **19,** 23–28.

Hebb, D. What psychology is about. *American Psychologist,* 1974, **29,** 71–79.

Keys, A., Brozek, J., Henschel, A., & Mickelson, H. *The biology of human starvation.* Minneapolis: University of Minnesota Press, 1950.

LeMay, M. & Damm, V. The Personal Orientation Inventory as a measure of self-actualization of underachievers. *Measurement and Evaluation in Guidance,* 1968, 110–114.

McClain, E. Further validation of the Personal Orientation Inventory: Assessment of self-actualization of school counselors. *Journal of Consulting and Clinical Psychology,* 1970, **35,** 21–22.

McGregor, D. *The human side of enterprise.* New York: McGraw-Hill, 1960.

Maddi, S., & Costa, P. *Humanism in personology: Allport, Maslow, and Murray.* Chicago: Aldine-Atherton, 1972.

Maslow, A. *Self-actualizing people: A study of psychological health. Personality symposia: Symposium #1 on values.* New York: Grune & Stratton, 1950, pp. 11–34.

Maslow, A. Deficiency motivation and growth motivation. In M. Jones (Ed.), *Nebraska symposium on motivation.* Lincoln, Neb.: University of Nebraska Press, 1955.

Maslow, A. A philosophy of psychology. In J. Fairchild (Ed.), *Personal problems and psychological frontiers.* New York: Sheridan House, 1956.

Maslow, A. *Toward a psychology of being.* Princeton: Van Nostrand, 1962.

Maslow, A. *Religions, values and peak experiences.* Columbus, Ohio: Ohio State University Press, 1964.

Maslow, A. Criteria for judging needs to be instinctoid. In M. Jones (Ed.), *Human motivation: A symposium.* Lincoln, Neb.: University of Nebraska Press, 1965a, pp. 33–47.

Maslow, A. *Eupsychian management: A journal.* Homewood, Ill.: Irwin-Dorsey, 1965b.

Maslow, A. *The psychology of science: A reconnaisance.* New York: Harper & Row, 1966.

Maslow, A. A theory of metamotivation: The biological rooting of the value-life. *Journal of Humanistic Psychology,* 1967a, **7,** 93–127.

Maslow, A. Self-actualization and beyond. In J. Bugental (Ed.), *Challenges of humanistic psychology.* New York: McGraw-Hill, 1967b.

Maslow, A. Toward a humanistic biology. *American Psychologist,* 1969, **24,** 724–735.

Maslow, A. *Motivation and personality* (2d ed.). New York: Harper & Row, 1970.

Maslow, A. *The farther reaches of human nature.* New York: Viking, 1971.

Monahan, L., Kuhn, D., & Shaver, P. Intrapsychic versus cultural explanations of the fear of success. *Journal of Personality and Social Psychology,* 1974, **29,** 60–64.

Porter, L. A study of perceived need satisfactions in bottom and middle management jobs. *Journal of Applied Psychology,* 1961, **45,** 1–10.

Raanan, S. Test review. *Journal of Counseling Psychology,* 1973, **20,** 477–478.

Shostrom, E. An inventory for the measurement of self-actualization. *Educational and Psychological Measurement,* 1965, **24,** 207–218.

Shostrom, E. *Manual: Personal Orientation Inventory.* San Diego: Educational and Industrial Testing Service, 1966.

Shostrom, E. Comment on a test review: The Personal Orientation Inventory. *Journal of Counseling Psychology,* 1973, **20,** 479–481.

Smith, B. On self-actualization: A transambivalent examination of a focal theme in Maslow's psychology. *Journal of Humanistic Psychology,* 1973, **13,** 17–33.

Tosi, D., & Hoffman, S. A factor analysis of the Personal Orientation Inventory. *Journal of Humanistic Psychology,* 1972, **12,** 86–93.

SUGGESTED READINGS

Chiang, H., & Maslow, A. *The healthy personality* (2d ed.). New York: Van Nostrand, 1977.

Child, I. *Humanistic psychology and the research tradition: Their several virtues.* New York: Wiley, 1973.

Goble, F. *The third force: The psychology of Abraham Maslow:* New York: Pocket Books, 1970.

Hampden-Turner, C. *Radical man: The process of psychosocial development.* Garden City, N.Y.: Anchor Books, 1971.

Jourard, S., & Landsman, T. *Healthy personality: An approach from the viewpoint of humanistic psychology* (4th ed.). New York: Macmillan, 1980.

King, M. *For we are: Toward understanding your personal potential.* Reading, Mass.: Addison-Wesley, 1975.

Oakland, J., Freed, R., Lovekin, A., Davis, J., & Camilleri, R. A critique of Shostrom's Personal Orientation Inventory. *Journal of Humanistic Psychology,* 1978, **18,** 75–85.

Shaffer, J. *Humanistic psychology.* Englewood Cliffs, N.J.: Prentice-Hall, 1978.

DISCUSSION QUESTIONS

1 Of the three dominant movements in twentieth-century psychology—psychoanalysis, behaviorism, and humanistic psychology—which is closest to your own view of personality and human behavior? Why? Can you see any relationship between your theoretical preference and your own basic assumptions concerning human nature? Explain.

2 One of the basic tenets of humanistic psychology is the irrelevance of animal research. Do you agree with this idea? Why? If not, specify exactly what we have learned about human behavior from the study of lower organisms.

3 How would you evaluate Maslow's hierarchical theory of motivation? Does his portrayal of motivation make sense in terms of understanding your own behavior and that of others? Give some examples.

4 In Maslow's account of self-esteem needs, there are two subsidiary sets: self-respect and esteem from other people. If you *had to* make a choice, which of these two need sets

would you consider to be most important in maintaining your own psychological health? Explain.

5 Describe the ideal society that would be *most* conducive to the attainment of self-actualization for the greatest number. How does that society basically differ from the one described by B. F. Skinner in *Beyond Freedom and Dignity*?

GLOSSARY

Becoming Developmental process whereby an individual assumes responsibility as a free agent to realize as many of his or her potentials as possible.

Belongingness Need Basic need that motivates a person toward affectionate relationships with others. Gratification of this need is found through friends, family life, and membership in groups and organizations.

Deficiency Motive (*D*-motive) Basic need aimed at eliminating organismic tension, especially those needs arising from physiological and safety demands. For Maslow, deficiency needs must be satisfied before a person can progress toward self-actualization.

Existential Philosophy Philosophical view that each person is responsible for his or her own life.

Growth Motive Higher-level needs (metaneeds) associated with the inborn urge to actualize one's potentials. Growth motives emerge only if basic needs have been satisfied. They increase the joy of being alive.

Hierarchy of Needs The arrangement of the needs from lowest to highest in terms of their potency.

Humanistic Psychology Type of psychology primarily focused on the study of healthy and creative individuals. Humanistic psychologists emphasize the uniqueness of the individual, the quest for values and meaning, and the freedom inherent in self-direction and self-fulfillment. Also called *third force* psychology.

Metapathology Term used by Maslow to indicate psychological disorders (e.g., apathy, depression, cynicism) resulting from failure to satisfy one's metaneeds.

Meta Value Those higher aspects of life pursued by self-actualizing individuals. Included are such values as truth, goodness, beauty, justice, and perfection.

Peak Experience State in which the individual feels intense excitement and/or relaxation. Such a state is often accompanied by a feeling of power and confidence, a profound sense that there is nothing one could not accomplish or become.

Personal Orientation Inventory (POI) Self-report personality questionnaire designed to assess an individual's degree of self-actualization.

Physiological Need Most basic and powerful of all human needs, it includes the need for water, food, oxygen, sleep, etc.

Safety Need Basic need that motivates an individual to establish a reasonable amount of order, structure, and predictability in his or her environment.

Self-Actualizers Individuals who have satisfied their deficiency needs and developed their potentials to the extent that they can be considered supremely healthy human beings.

Self-Actualization The desire to become all that one is capable of becoming—to become the kind of person that one wants to become and thus live a meaningful and fulfilling life.

Self-Esteem Need Basic need that motivates an individual to gain recognition and esteem from others.

Carl R. Rogers

Carl Rogers:
A Phenomenological
Theory of Personality

Phenomenology is the study of the individual's subjective experience, feelings, and private concepts as well as his or her personal views of world and self. As a disciplined effort to explain why each of us experiences and relates to the world as we do, phenomenological psychology today has one of its most articulate spokesmen in Carl Rogers. For Rogers, behavior is utterly dependent upon how one perceives the world—that is, behavior is the result of immediate events as they are perceived and interpreted by the individual. Such an approach to personology emphasizes the self and its characteristics. Indeed, Rogers' theory is often referred to as a *self* theory of personality because, for him, "the best vantage point for understanding behavior is from the internal frame of reference of the individual himself" (Rogers, 1951, p. 494).

BIOGRAPHICAL SKETCH

Carl Ransom Rogers was born January 8, 1902, in Oak Park, Illinois, a suburb of Chicago. He was the fourth of six children, five of whom were boys. His father was a civil engineer and contractor who achieved financial success in his profession, so the family was economically secure throughout Rogers' childhood and early youth. When he was 12 years old, Rogers' parents moved to a farm west of Chicago, and it was in this rural setting that he spent his adolescence. The family members were self-reliant yet inwardly dependent upon one another, and there is no impression of actual joy or contentment among its members. Rogers recalls his boyhood years structured by a strict and uncompromising religious and ethical atmosphere. He describes his parents as sensitive and loving, but nonetheless devoutly and dogmatically committed to fundamentalist religious views:

> I think the attitudes toward persons outside our large family can be summed up schematically in this way: Other persons behave in dubious ways which we do not approve in

our family. Many of them play cards, go to movies, smoke, drink, and engage in other activities—some unmentionable. So the best thing to do is to be tolerant of them, since they may not know better, and to keep away from any close communication with them and live your life within the family (Rogers, 1973, p. 3).

Rogers recalls that his parents' condescending attitude toward others outside the home characterized his own behavior throughout elementary school. Having no close friends beyond the family, he spent much time in solitary pursuits, especially reading. This pattern of social isolation continued throughout Rogers's high school years. He attended three different high schools, none for more than two years, commuting long distances by train to each one, so that he was never able to participate in extracurricular activities with other students. However, Rogers was an outstanding student during his preparatory years. He received straight "A" grades in almost all his courses and did his best work in English and science. Despite his election as president of his junior class, he had only one date in high school—to attend a senior class dinner. Summer vacations were consumed by long hours of tiring work on the farm:

> I rode a cultivator all day long, usually being assigned to the cornfield at the far end of the farm which was full of quack grass. It was a lesson in independence to be on my own, far away from anyone else. . . . It was a type of responsibility experienced by few young people today (Rogers, 1967, p. 347).

College represented the first break in this solitary existence. Rogers enrolled at the University of Wisconsin in 1919, the school which both his parents and three older siblings had attended. He chose scientific agriculture as his initial field of study and roomed with his older brother Ross at a YMCA dormitory. Following his family's religious tradition, he became very active in church work and was the leader of a boys' club. During his sophomore year, Rogers attended a Christian youth conference which had as its slogan "Evangelize the world in our generation." This experience encouraged him to study for the ministry. The following year an event occurred which changed the direction of his life: He was selected as one of ten United States college students to attend a World Student Christian Federation Conference in Peking, China. Abroad for more than six months, he observed a range of religious and cultural attitudes far different from his own. This experience not only liberalized Rogers' outlook on life but caused him to question the divinity of Jesus. This trip also marked Rogers' declaration of independence from the intellectual and religious ties with his home, which was done, it might be noted, with a minimum of emotional upheaval. Following his sojourn in the Orient, Rogers returned to Wisconsin and completed his B.A. degree in history in 1924. At this point he had had only one psychology course—by correspondence!

Following graduation, despite strong parental objections, Rogers married Helen Elliott, a Wisconsin classmate whom he had known since childhood. (They subsequently had two children, David and Natalie.) That summer the newlyweds set out in a Model-T Ford for Union Theological Seminary, a liberal religious institution in New York City. Rogers found life in New York stimulating and exciting: "I made friends, found new ideas, and fell thoroughly in love with the whole experience" (Rogers, 1967, p. 353). While at Union Seminary, Rogers first realized that the goal of helping distressed persons was one that the ministry and mental health professions shared. About then he became disenchanted by the academic courses in religion—a disenchantment augmented by his growing skepticism about specific doctrines. At the end of his second year he transferred from the seminary to Teachers College, Columbia University, to pursue graduate study in clinical and educational psychology. He received a fellowship at the emerging Institute of Child Guidance and spent a rewarding year there from 1927 to 1928. Rogers obtained his M.A. in 1928 and his Ph.D. in clinical psychology in 1931. Under the supervision of Goodwin Watson, his doctoral dissertation culminated in a test for measuring personality adjustment in children which, incredibly, is still being sold by the thousands today, according to Rogers (1974).

Upon receiving his doctoral degree, Rogers accepted a position as staff psychologist at the Child Study Department of the Society for the Prevention of Cruelty to Children in Rochester, New York. For the next decade Rogers was very active in applied psychological service for delinquent and underprivileged children. He was also instrumental in forming the Rochester Guidance Center, of which he emerged as director despite strong feelings that the office should be held by a psychiatrist. As a result of publishing a highly successful volume entitled *Clinical Treatment of the Problem Child* in 1939, Rogers accepted a faculty appointment in the psychology department at Ohio State University in 1940. The move into academia brought Rogers wide recognition in the burgeoning field of clinical psychology. He attracted many talented and critical graduate students and began to publish numerous articles detailing his views on psychotherapy and how it might be empirically investigated. Rogers' text *Counseling and Psychotherapy: Newer Concepts in Practice* (1942) represented the first major alternative to psychoanalytic therapy.

From 1945 to 1957 Rogers was Professor of Psychology and Director of Counseling at the University of Chicago. This position enabled him to establish a counseling center for undergraduates where professional staff and graduate students worked as equals. During this period he completed his major work, *Client-Centered Therapy: Its Current Practice, Implications, and Theory* (1951), a book detailing the theory underlying his approach to interpersonal relations and personality change. All in all, it was a very active period for both clinical work and research in psychotherapy with a strong client orientation.

In 1957 Rogers returned to his alma mater, the University of Wisconsin, where he held joint appointments in the departments of psychology and psychiatry except for the year 1962–1963, which he spent as a fellow at the Center for Advanced Study in the Behavioral Sciences at Stanford. He subsequently initiated an intensive research program utilizing psychotherapy with schizophrenic patients in a state mental hospital. Unfortunately, this research program encountered several problems and proved to be far less successful than Rogers had anticipated. Several staff members were opposed to Rogers' client-centered approach, data mysteriously disappeared, and findings indicated that schizophrenics in the program showed little improvement when compared with patients exposed to routine hospital activities. Rogers' major disappointment, however, focused on the university's psychology department and its narrow and, to him, punitive approach to the training of doctoral students. He discovered that psychology graduate students were required to memorize vast amounts of trivia that had nothing to do with the real world of professional psychology (Rogers, 1968).

Rogers resigned from his academic post in 1964 to become a fellow in residence at the Western Behavioral Sciences Institute (WBSI) in La Jolla, California, a nonprofit organization devoted to humanistically oriented research in interpersonal relationships. In 1968 he left WBSI to take a position with the Center for Studies of the Person, also situated in La Jolla. He continues there at the present time. Rogers' affiliation with this group has led him to apply his theoretical concepts of personality growth to industrial organizations and school systems. He is also actively involved in the encounter group movement as a means of facilitating human growth and potential.

Like many other personality theorists, Carl Rogers is a member of numerous scholarly societies. He was president of the American Academy of Psychotherapists in 1956, vice president of the Orthopsychiatric Association in 1944, president of the American Association for Applied Psychologists in 1944, and president of the American Psychological Association in 1946–1947. Rogers was awarded the APA's Distinguished Scientific Contribution Award in 1956 and was the recipient of the APA Distinguished Professional Contribution Award in 1972. The citation for the latter reads:

> His commitment to the whole person has been an example which has guided and challenged the practice of psychology in the schools, in industry, and throughout the community. By devising, practicing, evaluating, and teaching a method of psychotherapy and counseling which reaches to the very roots of human potentiality and individuality, he has caused all psychotherapists to re-examine their procedures in a new light. Innovator in personality research, pioneer in the encounter movement, and a respected gadfly of organized psychology, he has made a lasting impression on the profession of psychology (*American Psychologist,* 1973, p. 71).

Rogers has written several books on counseling and personality, including *Psychotherapy and Personality Change* (with R. Dymond, 1954), *On Becoming a Person: A Therapist's View of Psychotherapy* (1961), *Freedom to Learn: A View of What Education Might Become* (1969), *Carl Rogers on Encounter Groups* (1970), *Becoming Partners: Marriage and Its Alternatives* (1972), and *Carl Rogers on Personal Power* (1977). His autobiography appears in *A History of Psychology in Autobiography* (Volume 5, 1967, pp. 341–384). Carl Rogers is unquestionably one of the most influential American psychologists living today.

ROGERS' VIEW OF HUMAN NATURE

Rogers' ideas of human nature, like Freud's, grew out of his experiences in working with emotionally disturbed people. The major impetus to his psychological thinking, he admits, is the continuing clinical experience with individuals who perceive themselves, or are perceived by others to be, in need of personal help. Since 1928, for a period now approaching thirty years, I have spent probably an average of 15 to 20 hours per week, except during vacation periods, in endeavoring to understand and be of therapeutic help to these individuals. . . . From these hours, and from my relationships with these people, I have drawn most of whatever insight I possess into the meaning of therapy, the dynamics of interpersonal relationships, and the structure and functioning of personality (Rogers, 1959, p. 188).

On the basis of his clinical experience, Rogers has concluded that the innermost core of human nature is essentially purposive, forward-moving, constructive, realistic, and quite trustworthy. He regards the person as an active force of energy oriented toward future goals and self-directed purposes, rather than a creature pushed and pulled by forces beyond his or her control. Such a point of view clearly implies the faith of a Rousseau in the inherent goodness of human nature—a belief that if the innate potential of this nature is allowed to unfold and blossom, optimal personal development and effectiveness will result.

Rogers contends that Christianity has nourished the belief that man is innately evil and sinful. Moreover, it is his contention that this negative view of humanity has been reinforced by Freud, who presented a portrait of the person with an id and an unconscious which would, if permitted expression, manifest itself in incest, homicide, thievery, rape, and other horrendous acts. According to this view, humanity is basically and fundamentally irrational, unsocialized, selfish, and destructive of self and others. Rogers (1957a) agrees that people occasionally express a variety of bitter and murderous feelings, abnormal impulses, and bizarre and antisocial actions, but he contends that at such times they are not behaving in concert with their true inner natures. Thus, when people are functioning *fully*, when they are free to experience and to satisfy their inner natures, they show themselves to be positive and rational creatures who can be trusted to live in harmony with themselves and others. Aware that his view of human nature may be considered to be nothing more than naïve optimism, Rogers indicates that his conclusions are based on almost thirty years of psychotherapeutic experience. He declares:

I do not have a Pollyanna view of human nature. I am quite aware that out of defensiveness and inner fear individuals can and do behave in ways which are incredibly cruel, horribly destructive, immature, regressive, anti-social, and harmful. Yet one of the most refreshing and invigorating parts of my experience is to work with such individuals and to discover the strongly positive directional tendencies which exist in them, as in all of us, at the deepest levels (Rogers, 1961, p. 27).

In sum, Rogers has a profound (almost religious) sense of respect for human nature. He posits that the human organism has a natural tendency to move in the direction of differentiation, self-responsibility, cooperation, and maturity. The expression of this basic nature, according to Rogers, allows for the continuation and enhancement of the individual and the species. It should be noted that such assumptions about human nature appear throughout Rogerian theory and are closely identified with the humanistic movement in personology.

ACTUALIZING TENDENCY AS LIFE'S MASTER MOTIVE

In line with his positive view of human nature, Rogers hypothesizes that all behavior is energized and directed by a single, unitary motive which he calls the *actualizing tendency*. This represents "the inherent tendency of the organism to develop all its capacities in ways which serve to maintain or enhance the person" (Rogers, 1959, p. 196). Thus, the primary motive in people's lives is to actualize, maintain, or enhance themselves—to become the best self that their inherited natures will allow them to be. This basic actualizing tendency is the *only* motivational construct postulated in Rogers' theoretical system. Rogers (1963) felt that there was nothing to be gained from postulating specific motives—such as hunger, sex, and competence—and using these hypothetical motives to explain the why of behavior. Take hunger as an illustration. Traditionally, psychology has regarded it as a separate drive or motive, a thing unto itself. In Rogers' system, hunger is just one specific expression of the master motive underlying human existence; specifically, it serves to "maintain" the person. If you don't believe this, stop eating. You will come to believe it in less than a week—or die trying. Or consider sex as a motive. Sex serves to "enhance" the person. This requires no elaboration. Or the need for achievement—Murray's nAchievement. In Rogers' system, such a need can easily be construed as one expression of the actualizing tendency. A person seeks achievement as a way of fulfilling his or her potential as a human being.

Certain definitive characteristics mark the actualizing tendency. First, it is rooted in the physiological processes of the entire body (i.e., it is a *biological fact,* not a psychological tendency). At an organic level this inborn tendency involves not only the maintenance of the organism by meeting deficiency needs (air, food, water) but also the enhancement of the organism by providing for development and differentiation of the body's organs and functions, its growth and continual regeneration. Of even greater significance for the human personality is the motivating force which the actualizing tendency provides for increased autonomy and self-reliance, for enlarging one's field of experience, and for being creative.

Secondly, the actualizing tendency does not merely aim at tension reduction (the preservation of life processes and the pursuit of comfort and quiescence). It also involves *tension increase.* Instead of seeing all behavior as having the discharge of tension as its goal, Rogers views behavior as motivated by the individual's need to develop and improve. A person is governed by a growth process in which potentialities and capacities are brought to realization. Additionally, Rogers maintains that the actualizing tendency is common to *all* forms of life—it is characteristic not only of human beings, or only of animals, but of all living things. It is the essence of life.

Rogers himself neglects to give many concrete behavioral examples of the actualizing tendency, but it might be characterized in terms of wanting to achieve or accomplish something that makes one's life more enriching and satisfying (e.g., getting good grades, obtaining a job promotion, striving to be imaginative, helping underprivileged children). One can think of numerous other examples of Rogers' actualizing principle. For instance, a young child learning to walk is impressive by virtue of her tenacity—she really "hangs in there" and actualizes. She falls backward, buckles at the knees, bumps her head, and smashes her nose. Yet eventually she walks. Similarly, tennis players strive to perfect their forehand and backhand, golfers their putting and driving, college professors their publication records, and adolescents their identities. This movement toward self-development is often accompanied by struggle and pain, but because the urge is compelling, the person perseveres despite the pain he or she may have to endure. In short, it is Rogers' conviction that virtually everything that humans do is aimed at increasing their competence, or actualizing themselves.

According to Rogers, the actualizing tendency serves as a criterion against which all one's life experiences are evaluated. Specifically, in the course of actualizing themselves, individuals engage in what Rogers describes as an *organismic valuing process*. Experiences that are perceived as maintaining or enhancing the self are sought after and valued positively. A person derives a feeling of satisfaction from such positive experiences. Conversely, experiences which are perceived as negating or opposing the maintenance or enhancement of the self are valued negatively and avoided. The organismic valuing process enables a person to evaluate experiences in light of whether they facilitate or impede his or her basic actualizing tendency. Accordingly, the natural tendency is to approach actualizing experiences and avoid those perceived to be otherwise.

Research presented by Davis (1933) on dietary self-selection provides some scientific evidence in support of Rogers' organismic valuing hypothesis. The study investigated the capacity of young children to naturally alter their eating habits when nutritional imbalances exist. Using an array of thirty unmixed and unseasoned foods from which the children could freely choose, Davis demonstrated that over a 4½-year span, children maintained themselves on balanced diets. They were kept under medical supervision, and were judged to be not only healthy but remarkably free of digestive upsets. These findings are quite consistent with Rogers' notion of an organismic valuing process, i.e., that a child "knows" which foods and experiences are good for her or him and which are bad.

The most critical aspect of the actualizing tendency from the standpoint of personality is the individual's drive toward self-actualization. In the context of Rogerian theory, the *self-actualizing tendency* is what gives a forward thrust to life, involving all movement of a person in the direction of complexity, self-sufficiency, and maturity. Self-actualization is the process of becoming a more competent person. For Rogers, no special motivational constructs (i.e., specific drives) are required to understand why a human being is active; every person is inherently motivated simply by being alive. Motives and drives do not account for the activity and goal-directedness of the organism. Humanity is basically active and self-actualizing by virtue of its nature.

It must be emphasized that self-actualization is not a final state of perfection. For Rogers, one never becomes self-actualized enough to abandon the motive altogether. There are always more talents to develop, more skills to enhance, more efficient and pleasurable ways to satisfy biological drives. It is possible, however, to speak of some people as engaging in the self-actualizing process to a greater degree than others; they have moved further toward functioning in a self-fulfilling, creative, autonomous manner.

ROGERS' PHENOMENOLOGICAL POSITION

It has already been noted that Rogers' theory is illustrative of the phenomenological approach to personality. A *phenomenological* position holds that what is real to an individual (i.e., what reality is thought, understood, or felt to be) is that which exists within that person's *internal frame of reference,* or subjective world, including everything in his or her awareness at any point in time. It follows that an individual's perceptions and experiences not only constitute that person's reality but also form the basis for his or her actions; one responds to events in accordance with how one perceives and interprets them. For example, a thirsty man stranded in the desert will run as eagerly to a pool of water that is a mirage as to a real pool. Similarly, two people observing an identical set of circumstances may later recall two very different outcomes, which is often the case with "eyewitness" accounts of unidentified flying objects, traffic accidents, and other unexpected events.

Phenomenological psychology asserts as its basic doctrine that the psychological reality of phenomena is exclusively a function of the way in which they are perceived. A person's senses do not directly mirror the world of reality; instead, effective reality is reality as it is observed and interpreted by the reacting organism. Each individual, then, according to Rogers (1959, pp. 222–223), construes reality in accordance with his or her private world of experience, and this experiential world can be completely known *only* to the individual. A final point here is that Rogers (1951), unlike Kelly, avoids making any assertions about the nature of "objective" reality. He concerns himself only with *psychological reality* (i.e., how the person perceives and experiences the world), leaving objective reality to the philosophers.

One important implication of a phenomenological perspective for a theory of personality is that the best understanding of a person's behavior is obtained through observation of his or her internal frame of reference. To explain why an individual thinks, feels, and behaves in a given way, it is necessary to know how that person perceives and interprets the world. Subjective experience is thus the key to understanding behavior. This means that the most important object of psychological study is a person's subjective experiences, because these experiences alone are the ultimate causal agents of behavior.

Subjective Experience and Behavior

The relationship between experience and behavior is vividly illustrated in the case of paranoia. As may be recalled from our brief mention of it in the Kelly chapter, *paranoia* is a serious psychological disturbance marked by a *fixed delusion,* typically of persecution. Now paranoids have been known to shoot people for no apparent reason (unlike most mental patients, classic paranoids are often dangerous to others). For instance, a paranoid individual may believe that "the communists" are actively plotting to do her in. She perceives communists all over the place, reading into the behavior of others various innuendoes and cryptic "messages" reflecting the fact that they are "in" on the conspiracy. But the fact of the matter is that this individual is a shoe clerk in the middle of North Dakota and, most probably, the Kremlin is not all that interested in her. But *she* thinks it is, and she interprets the world accordingly. Finally, in the face of this truly frightening world of subjective experience populated by imaginary enemies conspiring against her, she decides to shoot some of them first, either to protect herself or to teach them a lesson.

Newspapers frequently report these tragic incidents as inexplicable, and after some digging, they eventually describe the perpetrator as a "loner." You'd be a "loner" too if you perceived most people around you to be enemies plotting to kill or otherwise harm you. And the behavior *is* inexplicable—unless one happens to look at the world from the paranoid's frame of reference. Her behavior is a direct product of, and cannot be understood without reference to, the private world in which she lives. While this example may seem to overstate the case, Rogers' position is that we *all* live in private worlds of subjective experience and that the relationship between these worlds and our overt behavior is the same for us as for the unfortunate paranoid. The relationship between experience and behavior is the essential theme in Rogers' phenomenological position.

In terms of predicting behavior, Rogers maintains that a person acts in accordance with his or her impression of events. He thus advocates abandoning Skinner's notion that the regularities of behavior can be explained in terms of a person's response to the objective stimulus situation—rather, it is *his or her interpretation* of the stimulus situation and of its personal meaning that governs his or her behavior. What is critical in life is the perception of things: it is what eggnog tastes like to me, what love and anger feel like to me, what a particular person means to me. It follows that no one can properly claim that his or her sense of reality is necessarily better or more correct than that of anyone else; no one has the right to impose his or her reality upon others.

For the most part, Rogers rejects Freud's position that historical aspects or derivatives of behavior are the primary factors underlying personality. Behavior is not determined by something that occurred in the past. Instead, Rogers emphasizes the necessity of understanding the individual's relationship to the environment as he or she now exists and perceives it. It is one's present interpretation of past experiences rather than their factual existence that influences current behavior. If Rogers were asked, for instance, "What causes that person to act in such a hostile way?" he would respond, "He views the world as a dangerous place and considers himself unloved and unlovable." Rogers would not respond, "He was deprived and neglected when he was a child."

The significance of this *ahistorical* view is that it is unnecessary to retrace a distant past in order to discover why an individual is behaving as he or she is today. To be sure, Rogers recognizes that past experiences exert an influence on the meaning of present experiences. However, he insists that current behavior is always affected by present perception and interpretation. Moreover, Rogers believes that ongoing behavior is strongly affected by how people foresee their future (note the similarity to Kelly's personal construct system here). For instance, if a young woman regards herself as a socially unappealing person who has experienced difficulty with men, her present dilemma is not so much due to past failures as it is to her perceived anticipation of future failures. She is governed by a self-fulfilling prophecy, namely, that she will be unable to interest men because of her lack of social charm. Changing her negative self-image would presumably result in more rewarding heterosexual experiences in the future. Thus, Rogers favors the notion that personality should be studied within a "present-future" framework.

Finally, Rogers' choice of a phenomenological approach to personality theory reflects his belief that the complexity of behavior can only be understood by reference to the entire person. In other words, Rogers espouses a *holistic* view of personality, the view that a person behaves as an integrated organism and that his or her unity cannot be derived from atomistic (i.e., reductionistic) approaches to behavior. As will become evident in the ensuing discussion, Rogers' commitment to a holistic point of view is manifest in practically every facet of his thought.

Concept of Self: Who Am I Anyway?

The self is the most important construct in Rogers' theory of personality; indeed, the concept of self is indispensable to an appreciation of Rogers' view of human behavior. Surprisingly, however, this emphasis on self was not always so paramount. Rogers recalls that he began his clinical work with the notion that the concept of self was a vague, scientifically meaningless word that had disappeared from the psychologist's vocabulary with the departure of the introspectionists. However, his clients persisted in expressing their problems and attitudes in terms of the self, and gradually he realized that self was a significant element in human experience and that the client's goal was to become her or his "real self."

The self or self-concept (Rogers uses the terms synonymously) is defined as

> the organized, consistent conceptual gestalt composed of perceptions of the characteristics of the "I" or "me" and the perceptions of the relationships of the "I" or "me" to others and to various aspects of life, together with the values attached to these perceptions. It is a gestalt which is available to awareness though not necessarily in awareness (Rogers, 1959, p. 200).

In other words, the self is a differentiated portion of the individual's *phenomenal* or *perceptual field* (defined as the totality of experience) and consists of the conscious perceptions and values of the "I" or "me." The self-concept denotes the individual's conception of the kind of person he or she is. The self-concept is one's image of oneself. Especially included are awareness of being (what I *am*) and awareness of function (what I can *do*).

The self-concept includes not only one's perceptions of what one is like but also what one thinks one ought to be and would like to be. This latter component of the self is called the *ideal self*. The ideal self represents the self-concept that the individual would most like to possess. It is basically equivalent to the superego in Freudian theory.

Rogers' notion of the self may be further understood in terms of its various properties and functions. To begin, Rogers posits that one's self-conception follows the general laws and principles of perception established in scientific psychology. This means that the conception of self is consistent with what has traditionally been a basic domain of experimental psychology. Second, Rogers views the self-concept as being configurational in nature, meaning that it represents an organized, coherent, and integrated pattern of self-related perceptions. Thus, for example, although the individual's self is fluid and constantly changing as a result of new experiences, it always retains a patterned, gestaltlike quality. No matter how much people change over time, they always retain a firm internal sense that they are still the same person at any moment in time. Rogers goes on to suggest that the self-concept is not a homunculus, or "little man in the head" who controls a person's actions. The self does not regulate behavior; instead, it symbolizes the individual's existing body of conscious experience. Finally, the conglomeration of experience and perception known as the self is, in general, conscious and admissible to awareness. Rogers believes that a concept of the self that incorporates unconscious mentation could not yield an operational definition and would therefore not be amenable to research, a necessity in his system.

Development of the Self-Concept

Unlike other clinic-based theorists such as Freud, Adler, and Erikson, Rogers does not devote much attention to personality development per se and has not worked out a specific timetable of critical stages through which one passes in acquiring a self-concept. Instead, he concerns himself with the ways in which evaluations of an individual by others, particularly during infancy and early childhood, tend to promote the development of a positive or negative self-image.

The neonate perceives all experience as unitary, whether produced by bodily sensations or by external stimuli such as the movement of a mobile in the crib. The infant is not aware of himself or herself as a separate being, as an "I"; therefore he or she makes no distinction between what is "me" and what is "not me." Hence, early in life self is a nonentity (does not exist); only the unitary, all-encompassing, and un-differentiated phenomenal field is present. However, out of the general tendency toward differentiation which is a part of the actualizing process, a child gradually begins to distinguish herself or himself from the rest of the world. It is this process of differentiating the phenomenal field into that which is recognized and felt as part of oneself and that which is not part of oneself that accounts for the emergence of the individual's self-concept in Rogers' theory.

Rogers postulates that when the self is first formed, it is governed by the organismic valuing process alone. In other words, the infant or child evaluates each new experience in terms of whether it facilitates or impedes his or her innate actualizing tendency. For instance, hunger, thirst, cold, pain, and sudden loud noises are negatively valued, since they interfere with the maintenance of biological integrity. Food, water, security, and love are positively valued; they favor the en-hancement of the organismic tendency. In a sense, the organismic valuing process is a monitoring system that keeps the human infant on the proper course of need satisfaction. Infants evaluate their experiences according to whether or not they like them, whether they are pleasing or displeasing, and so on. Such evaluations result from their spontaneous responses to direct experiences, i.e., they are completely "natural."

The structure of self is subsequently shaped through interaction with the environment, particularly the environment composed of significant others (e.g., parents, siblings, relatives). In other words, as the child becomes socially sensitive and as his or her cognitive and perceptual abilities mature, his or her self-conception becomes increasingly differentiated and complex. To a large extent, then, the content of one's self-concept is a social product. Elements important in self-concept development follow.

Need for Positive Regard   Rogers contends that all persons possess a basic desire to experience attitudes such as warmth, respect, admiration, love, and acceptance from significant people in their lives. This *need for positive regard* develops as the awareness of self emerges, and it is pervasive and persistent. It is first seen in the infant's need to be loved and cared for, and is subsequently reflected in the person's satisfaction when approved by others and frustration when disapproved. Rogers indicates that positive regard may be either learned or innately given to all persons, and although he prefers the former explanation (i.e., that it is a secondary, learned motive), its origin is irrelevant to his theory. An intriguing aspect of positive regard is its reciprocal nature; that is, when an individual views himself or herself as satisfying another's need for positive regard, he or she necessarily experiences satisfaction of his or her own need.

Rogers' fundamental position is that the child will do almost anything, even sacrifice his organismic valuing process, to satisfy the need for positive regard. For example, if a parent insists that a child behave like a "nice little boy" in order to receive love and affection, the child will begin to value experiences in terms of the parental image of "niceness" rather than in terms of his own organismic reaction to them. Instead of being free to discover how it would feel to say a "naughty" word, put a frog in his sister's bed, or steal a candy bar from the drugstore, he prejudges these experiences as "bad" and condemns them. Hence, the child's behavior comes to be regulated not by the degree to which experiences maintain or enhance his self-concept but instead by the likelihood of receiving positive regard. Rogers describes this state of incongruity between self and experience in the following way:

> This, as we see it, is the basic estrangement in man. He has not been true to himself, to his own natural organismic valuing of experience, but for the sake of preserving the positive regard of others has now come to falsify some of the values he experiences and to perceive them only in terms based upon their value to others. Yet this has not been a conscious choice, but a natural—and tragic—development in infancy. The path of development toward psychological maturity . . . is the undoing of this estrangement in man's functioning . . . the achievement of a self which is congruent with experience, and the restoration of a unified organismic valuing process as the regulator of behavior (Rogers, 1959, pp. 226–227).

According to Rogers, one needs positive regard not only from others but also from oneself. The need for *positive self-regard* is a learned need that develops out of the association of self-experiences with the satisfaction or frustration of the need for positive regard. Specifically, positive self-regard refers to one's satisfaction at approving and dissatisfaction at disapproving of oneself. From another perspective, it is as if the self had become its own "significant social other." The development of positive self-regard assures that the tendency toward becoming an independent person, which is part of the tendency toward self-actualization, will take the form of following behavior and development that is compatible with the self-concept. Consequently, one is unlikely to behave in ways which are inconsistent with one's self-concept because this would frustrate the need for positive self-regard.

Conditions of Worth   Given the fact that a child has a compelling need for positive regard, she becomes increasingly sensitive to, or influenced by, the attitudes and expectations toward her of the important people in her life. This is not surprising insofar as most adults in the child's life make their positive regard for her *conditional* (i.e., I will love, respect, and accept you *only if* you are the kind of person I expect you to be). Such *conditional positive regard*, or *conditions of worth*, characterizes the situation in which a child receives praise, attention, approval, and other forms of reward for behaving in accordance with others' expectations of what she ought to be.

For example, such is the case when a father tells his son that bringing home a straight "A" report card will not only earn him an increase in his weekly allowance but also excuse him from having to wash the family car and mow the grass. Conditional positive regard is also manifest in many other types of human relationships involving the giving or withholding of approval and support. Football coaches frequently award a gold star (pasted to the helmet for all spectators to see) to the player who gains the most yardage or makes the most tackles in a game. The college president awards or denies promotions to faculty members on the basis of their excellence in teaching or research activities. In each instance, the individual's view of his or her self-importance (self-esteem) is contingent upon fulfilling the demands or standards imposed by others.

Rogers states rather forcefully that conditions of worth imposed on a child are *detrimental* to his or her becoming a fully functioning person. This is because the child tries to attain standards set by others rather than to identify and attain what she or he really is or wants to be. Thus, he comes to evaluate himself and his worth as an individual (what is valuable and what is not valuable about himself) in terms of only those of his actions, thoughts, and feelings that received approval and support. She will feel that in some respects she is prized and in others not. This process results in a self-concept that is out of kilter with organismic experience and hence does not serve as a solid foundation for psychological health.

According to Rogers, conditions of worth act like blinders on a horse, cutting off a portion of available experience. Persons with conditions of worth must restrict their behavior and distort reality because even becoming aware of forbidden behaviors and thoughts can be as threatening as displaying them. As a result of this

defensiveness, such persons cannot interact fully and openly with their environment.

Unconditional Positive Regard   While it is obvious that no person is completely devoid of conditions of worth, Rogers feels that it is possible to give or
receive positive regard irrespective of the worth placed on specific aspects of a
person's behavior. This means that a person is accepted and respected for what he or
she is—without any ifs, ands, or buts. Such *unconditional positive regard* is strikingly evident in a mother's love for her child when—regardless of the child's actions,
thoughts, and feelings—he or she is genuinely loved and respected. She loves the
child because it is her child, not because the child has fulfilled any specific condition
or lived up to any specific expectation.

Rogers maintains that if the maturing individual experiences only unconditional positive regard

> then no conditions of worth would develop, self-regard would be unconditional, the
> needs for positive regard and self-regard would never be at variance with organismic
> evaluation, and the individual would continue to be psychologically adjusted, and
> would be fully functioning. This chain of events is hypothetically possible, and hence
> important theoretically, though it does not appear to occur in actuality (Rogers, 1959,
> p. 224).

Rogers feels that nothing in a child's behavior is so objectionable as to give a
parent a reason to say, "If you do this, or if you feel this way, then I can no longer
value and love you." Admittedly, for the average parent, this is a difficult principle
to remember while a 3-year-old is systematically kicking in the family's new color
TV screen. However, it is important to understand that unconditional positive
regard does not literally mean that significant others must condone or approve
everything the child does. For instance, if a young child tries to play with Daddy's
power saw, she must be restrained. Otherwise, she could saw the color TV, the
house, herself, or (for Freudians) even Mommy! But if her need to experience
positive regard is to be continued even though she is being restrained, it must be
perfectly clear from the parent's method of restraint that there is no loss of approval
and respect for her as a person. If the child is spanked or told she is a bad girl for
wanting to play with Daddy's tools, then she is not being positively regarded. If, on
the other hand, she is told in simple words appropriate to her age level that while it
may be fun to play with Dad's power saw, such an activity is unsafe, then she is still
being respected as a person.

It can be seen, then, that Rogers' emphasis on unconditional positive regard as
the ideal approach to child rearing does not imply an absence of discipline, social
constraints, or other forms of behavioral control. What it does mean is providing an
atmosphere in which a child is valued and loved for exactly what he or she is—a
precious human being. When children perceive themselves in such a way that no
self-experience is more or less worthy of positive regard than any other, they are
experiencing *unconditional positive self-regard*. For Rogers, the existence of
unconditional positive self-regard enables an individual to progress toward be-

coming a fully functioning person. In such an individual, the self is deep and broad, since it contains all the thoughts and feelings that the person is capable of experiencing.

Experience of Threat and the Process of Defense

Rogers has argued that most ways of behaving that an individual adopts are consistent with the structure of his or her self-concept. In other words, the individual seeks to maintain a state of consistency among self-perceptions and experience. It logically follows that experiences which are in accord with the individual's self-concept and its conditions of worth are permitted entry to awareness and are perceived accurately. Conversely, incoming experiences which conflict with the self and its conditions of worth constitute a threat to the self-concept; they are prevented from entering awareness and being accurately perceived. It should be noted here that the individual's conception of himself or herself is the criterion against which experiences are compared and either symbolized in awareness or denied symbolization.

Suppose a young woman has been taught by her parents to believe that it's a grave sin to engage in premarital intercourse. However, while attending college she is exposed to attitudes and values which give unqualified support to sexual relations, especially when one feels genuine love for another person. Although she continues to accept her earlier introjected values, the young woman is about to marry a man who feels that making love presents no moral dilemma since they are committed to each other. She complies and finds it rewarding. For Rogers, this experience is in direct violation of her self-image; she regards this behavior as immoral and definitely out of line with who she really is. Consequently, engaging in sexual behavior in these circumstances is threatening to her. It simply does not fit her self-concept.

In Rogers' theory, *threat* exists when a person recognizes an incongruity between his or her self-concept (and its incorporated conditions of worth) and actual experience. Experiences incongruent with the self-concept are perceived as threatening; they are kept from entering awareness because the individual's personality is no longer a unified whole. Thus, if an individual views himself as an honest person and he behaves dishonestly, he is in a state of threat. Or, as in the earlier example, the young woman who believes that premarital sex is wrong and yet experiences it is threatened. The individual's response to such a state of incongruence is one of tension and internal confusion.

Incongruity between self and experience need not be perceived at a conscious level. In fact, Rogers postulates that it is quite possible for an individual to feel threatened without being aware of it. Consequently, whenever incongruity between the self-concept and experience exists and the individual is unaware of it, he or she is potentially vulnerable to anxiety and personality disorganization. *Anxiety* is thus an emotional response to threat which signals that the organized self-structure is in danger of becoming disorganized if the discrepancy between it and the threatening experience reaches awareness. The anxiety-ridden individual is one who dimly perceives that the recognition or symbolization of certain experiences would force a drastic change in his or her current self-image. Thus, the awareness of deep feelings of aggression and hostility would demand a major reorganization in the self-concept of an individual who conceives of himself or herself exclusively as a loving person. This individual will experience anxiety whenever she or he feels and acknowledges anger and hostility.

For Rogers, as long as an individual is in no way threatened, he or she is open to experience and does not need to exhibit defensiveness. When, however, an experience is perceived or *subceived* (discriminated without awareness) to be incongruent or inconsistent with the self-concept, threat exists, which, in turn, is followed by a defensive response. Rogers (1959) defines the process of *defense* as the behavioral response of the organism to threat; the goal of defense is the maintenance of the current self-structure: "This goal is achieved by the perceptual distortion of the experience in awareness, in such a way as to reduce the incongruity between the experience and the structure of the self, or by the denial of any experience, thus denying any threat to the self" (Rogers, 1959, pp. 204–205). In essence, the organism erects defenses in order to preserve its self-consistency and to protect itself from the impending danger of threatening experiences.

The Defense Mechanisms

Rogers proposes only two basic mechanisms of defense: *perceptual distortion* and *denial.* Perceptual distortion is operative whenever an incongruent experience is allowed into awareness but only in a form that makes it consistent with the person's current self-image. For instance, suppose that a college student perceives herself as bright but receives an unexpected and yet fully justified grade of "F" on an examination. She can maintain her self-concept intact by distorting the symbolized conceptualization of this failure by saying "The professor has unfair grading practices" or "I just had bad luck." Rogers occasionally refers to such selective perceptions or distortions as *rationalizations.* In the case of denial, a far less common defensive response, the individual preserves the integrity of his self-structure by completely avoiding any conscious recognition of threatening experiences. That is, he ignores the existence of those experiences that are inconsistent with his self-concept. An example of denial familiar to many professors is that of a student who fails four of the required five examinations in a course and then appears on the morning of the fifth and final examination to ask what he or she needs on the final to pass the course. Because it is incompatible with his or her self-concept, the student has denied the mounting evidence that it would be mathematically impossible to pass. Obviously, when denial is carried to an extreme, it can have psychological consequences far graver than flunking a course.

Personality Disorganization and Psychopathology

Thus far in our presentation of Rogers' phenomenological theory of personality we have described events that apply to everyone to a greater or lesser degree. Even the most psychologically healthy individual is periodically threatened by an experience that threatens his or her self-concept and that forces him or her to distort or deny the experience. Anxiety is a conspicuous aspect of everyday life in modern society.

Correspondingly, most individuals possess adequate defenses for dealing with moderate levels of anxiety. When, however, experiences become more than moderately inconsistent with the self-structure or when incongruent experiences occur frequently, then the individual experiences a level of anxiety that is distinctly offensive and may seriously disrupt the daily routine. A person in such an incongruent state is typically labeled "neurotic" (although not by Rogers himself, since he avoids the use of such labels, maintaining that they cloud rather than clarify one's perception of the person involved). In such instances, a person's inner discomfort is such that she or he is likely to seek the help of a psychotherapist as a means of alleviating anxiety. Nonetheless, the neurotic's defenses are still partially effective in preventing threatening experiences from being accurately symbolized in awareness. The result is that the neurotic's self-structure is allowed to remain in a whole, if somewhat tenuous, state. Such a person may not, however, consciously appreciate the tenuousness of the position; he or she is really quite vulnerable in a psychological sense.

According to Rogers, if there is a significant degree of incongruence between one's self-concept and one's evaluation of experience, then one's defenses may become inoperable. In such a "defenseless" state, with the incongruent experience accurately symbolized in awareness, the self-concept becomes shattered. Thus, personality disorganization and psychopathology occur when the self is unable to defend against threatening experiences. Persons undergoing such disorganization are commonly tagged "psychotic." They manifest behaviors which are to an objective observer bizarre, irrational, or "crazy." Rogers posits that psychotic behavior is often congruent with the denied aspects of experience, rather than with the self-concept. For example, a person who has kept his sexual impulses under rigid control, denying that they were a part of his self-image, may make obvious sexual overtures toward those whom he encounters during his psychotic break with reality. Many irrational behaviors associated with psychosis are of this nature.

Rogers' *person-centered therapy* attempts to reestablish a more harmonious relationship between the self-concept and the total organism and to facilitate a greater degree of congruence between the self-concept and the phenomenal field of experience. The details of this therapeutic approach will be discussed in the "Application" section of this chapter.

ROGERS' VIEW OF THE GOOD LIFE: THE FULLY FUNCTIONING PERSON

Rogers, like most other therapy-oriented personologists, has advanced certain ideas as to what constitutes the "good life" in terms of concrete personality characteristics. Such views are largely based on his experiences with disturbed and troubled people who struggled to achieve that life.

The Rogerian view of the good life begins with an assessment of what it is not. Specifically, the good life is neither a fixed state of being (i.e., it is not a state of virtue, contentment, happiness) nor a condition in which the individual is adjusted, fulfilled, or actualized. Nor is it, to use psychological terms, a state of drive reduction, tension reduction, or homeostasis. The good life is not a destination but a direction. Rogers explains:

> It is a process of movement in a direction which the human organism selects when it is inwardly free to move in any direction. . . . the general qualities of this selected direction appear to have a certain universality. . . . the person who is psychologically free moves in the direction of becoming a more fully functioning person (1961, pp. 187–191).

"Fully functioning" is a term used by Rogers to designate individuals who are using their capacities and talents, realizing their potentials, and moving toward complete knowledge of themselves and their full range of experiences. Rogers specifies five major personality characteristics common to people who are fully functioning. They are enumerated and briefly discussed below.

1   The first and foremost characteristic of the fully functioning person is *openness to experience*. To be open to experience is the polar opposite of defensiveness. Individuals who are completely open to experience are able to listen to themselves, to experience what is going on within themselves without threat. They are acutely aware of their own feelings (but not self-consciously), they do not try to suppress them, they often act upon them, and even if they do not act upon them, they are able to admit them to awareness.

For example, the fully functioning person may suddenly, while sitting in a personality class, strongly experience the feeling that he would like to have sex immediately with the young woman seated in front of him. If he has any sense, he will not follow through with this impulse—it would disrupt the class and not, in the long run, facilitate his actualizing tendency. But the point is that he would not be threatened by the feeling itself—there are no internal barriers or inhibitions preventing conscious awareness of his feeling states. The fully functioning person is sufficiently rational to recognize his or her feelings and is able to make judgments about the prudence of acting on them at any given time. Feeling something does not automatically mean that one acts upon that feeling. Thus, the person in this instance would probably recognize and accept the sexual impulse for what it is, realize that it would be damaging to himself and others (particularly the young woman who is unknowingly its "object"), and thus put it aside and turn his attention to other matters (like the lecture being given at the time). For the fully functioning person, then, no internal experience or emotion is threatening in its own right—she or he is truly *open* to all.

2   The second characteristic of the optimally functioning person listed by Rogers involves what he terms *existential living*. This is the global quality of living fully in each and every moment of one's existence. By doing so, each moment of one's life is perceived as new—different from all that existed before. Thus, as Rogers (1961) describes it, what a person is or will be in the next moment grows out of that moment and cannot be predicted in advance by the person or others (the correspondence with existential philosophy is quite clear here). A related aspect of existential living is that the individual's self and personality emerge from experience, rather than experience being translated or twisted to fit some preconceived or rigid self-structure. Hence, people living the good life are flexible, adaptable, tolerant, and spontaneous. They discover the structure of their experiences in the process of living them.

3   Still another attribute of a fully functioning person is what Rogers calls *organismic trusting*. This dimension of the good life is best illustrated in the context of decision making. Specifically, in choosing the course of action to take in any situation, many people rely upon a code of social norms laid down by some group or institution (e.g., the church), upon the judgment of others (from spouse and friends to Ann Landers), or upon the ways they have behaved in other similar situations. In short, their decision-making capacities are strongly if not totally dominated by external sources of influence. Conversely, fully functioning persons attend to their organismic experiences as the valid sources of information for deciding what they should or should not do. Or, as Rogers says, "doing what 'feels right' proves to be a competent and trustworthy guide to behavior which is truly satisfying" (1961, p. 190). Organismic trusting thus signifies the ability to consult and abide by one's inner experiences as the major basis for reaching decisions.

4   The fourth characteristic of the fully functioning person noted by Rogers is *experiential freedom*. This facet of the good life involves the sense that one is free to live one's life in any way one chooses. It is subjective freedom, a *feeling* that of one's own volition one is able to play a responsible part in shaping one's world. At the same time, Rogers does not deny that a person's behavior is heavily influenced by his or her biological makeup, social forces, and past experiences, which, in fact, determine the choices that are made. Indeed, Rogers contends that there can be no freedom in accounting for human choice. Yet he also believes that fully functioning people operate as free choice agents, so that whatever happens to them depends on themselves exclusively. Experiential freedom thus refers to the inner feeling that "I am solely responsible for my own actions and their consequences." Because of this feeling of freedom and power, the fully functioning person sees a great many options in life and feels capable of doing practically anything he or she might want to do! (Rogers' overall position on the issue of freedom versus determinism will be discussed more fully in the ensuing section of this chapter.)

5   The final characteristic associated with optimal psychological maturity is *creativity*. For Rogers, the person who is involved in the good life would be the type from whom creative products (ideas, projects, actions) and creative living would emerge. Creative people also tend to live constructively in their culture while at the same time satisfying their own deepest needs. They would be able, creatively, to adjust to changing environmental conditions. However, Rogers adds that such people are not necessarily fully adjusted to their culture and are almost certainly not conformists. Their relation to the society around them might best be put this way— they are in and of the society of which they are members, but they are *not* its prisoners.

Rogers attempts to weld these qualities of the fully functioning person into a composite picture when he writes:

> the good life involves a wider range, a greater richness, than the constricted living in which most of us find ourselves. To be a part of this process means that one is involved in the frequently frightening and frequently satisfying experience of a more sensitive living, with greater range, greater variety, greater richness.
>
> I believe it will have become evident why, for me, adjectives such as happy, contented, blissful, enjoyable, do not seem quite appropriate to any general description of this process I have called the good life, even though the person in this process would experience each one of these feelings at appropriate times. But the adjectives which seem

more generally fitting are adjectives such as enriching, exciting, rewarding, challenging, meaningful. This process of the good life is not, I am convinced, a life for the faint-hearted. It involves the stretching and growing of becoming more and more of one's potentialities. It involves the courage to be. It means launching oneself into the stream of life (1961, pp. 195–196).

It is evident, then, that Rogers, like Maslow and to some extent Allport before him, wants the person to look up to what she or he *can be*. For Rogers, this means being fully alive, fully aware, fully involved in what it means to be a human being—in brief, "fully functioning." Upon further analysis, one cannot help but notice the basic communalities of Rogers' "fully functioning person," Maslow's "self-actualizer," and, to a degree, Allport's "mature personality." These three theorists (particularly Rogers and Maslow) are in general agreement about what humanity can be because they share certain basic convictions about what humanity is. It is to Carl Rogers' basic assumptions concerning human nature, then, that we now turn.

ROGERS' BASIC ASSUMPTIONS CONCERNING HUMAN NATURE

Throughout the 1970s, B. F. Skinner and Carl Rogers were considered to be among the most influential living American psychologists. Inasmuch as all psychologists have been exposed to the thinking of each, they have both attracted numerous followers. Symbolic figureheads of the deep split in contemporary American psychology between behaviorism and phenomenology, Skinner and Rogers differ from one another on many important issues, but *nowhere* do they differ more profoundly than in their images of humanity. And this difference is most apparent in the basic assumptions that each makes concerning the nature of human beings. Examination of Rogers' assumptions (depicted in Figure 11-1) makes this profound philosophic difference evident. In fact, on practically every assumption on which Skinner and Rogers can legitimately be compared, the reader will find that they are virtually polar *opposites*.

Freedom–Determinism In discussing his differences with behavioristic psychology in general and B. F. Skinner in particular, Rogers (1974) noted that his experience in therapy and in groups made it impossible for him to deny the reality and significance of human choice. For years, Rogers has observed all sorts of persons in both individual therapy and encounter group situations struggling to grow, facing difficult life decisions, and ultimately making those decisions. The choices that an individual makes, much as in existential philosophy, help to create in turn the kind of person he or she becomes. For Rogers, then, people are to some extent architects of themselves.

Freedom, in Rogers' theory, is an integral part of the actualizing tendency. The natural course of that tendency is away from control by external forces toward progressively greater internal and autonomous behavioral directions (Rogers, 1959). That is, the more the actualizing tendency can operate, (1) the more people can overcome the "conditions of worth" placed upon them in early life, (2) the more

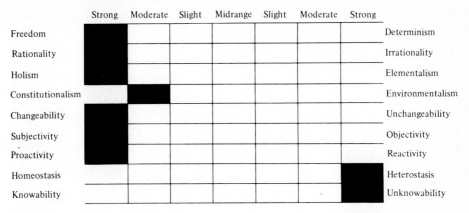

Figure 11-1   Rogers' position on the nine basic assumptions concerning human nature.

aware and open they are to experience, and (3) the more free they will be in creating themselves and charting the courses of their lives. The actualizing tendency is maximally operative in "fully functioning persons" who, as has already been noted, can be described in terms of experiential freedom, organismic trusting, and existential living. Here, human freedom reaches its peak; these individuals know they are free, look to themselves as the fountainhead of that freedom, and really "live" it every minute. Rogers's commitment to the freedom assumption is indeed strong.

Rationality–Irrationality   At the deepest level of being, the Rogerian person is rational. The irrationalities in human actions so apparent in everyday life—e.g., murder, rape, war, college administrative policies—result from humanity's being "out of tune" with its true inner nature. Again, as in the case of human freedom, humanity's true rationality rises highest when the actualizing tendency is operating maximally. When social conditions permit people to behave in accordance with their true nature, rationality will guide their conduct.

As Rogers clarifies in a published interview with Willard Frick (Frick, 1971), freedom, rationality, and the actualizing tendency are all inextricably interwoven in his basic image of humanity. When the operation of the actualizing tendency is facilitated, an individual becomes progressively more free and aware in directing his or her behavior. As one becomes more aware, one is correspondingly more able to select the course of one's self-actualization rationality. In the ideal situation, this beneficial spiral results in a fully functioning person whose behavior is exquisitely rational. Such a conception of human beings would not be possible without the rationality assumption firmly implanted at its base.

Holism–Elementalism   Rogers is very much committed to understanding and studying the person as a gestalt, or unified whole. As noted earlier, Rogers' holistic emphasis is evident throughout his theorizing. But it is perhaps most evident in his central theoretical construct of self. For a theorist to find it necessary to posit such a global, all-inclusive, and unitary construct to explain behavior requires as a precursor the holistic assumption.

Moreover, in Rogers' system, the self is always moving in the direction of greater wholeness (Rogers, 1963). This view is a salient feature of Rogers' account of human development, which begins with the infant's undifferentiated phenomenological field, continues as that field becomes differentiated into self and environment (as the self-concept emerges), and culminates in the organism's continuing efforts to achieve a unity of self and self-consistency. Developmentally speaking, then, a person, if he or she is healthy, is always moving towards progressively greater wholeness and unification. Holism is a basic assumption commonly found among humanistically oriented personologists; Rogers' theory epitomizes this principle.

Constitutionalism–Environmentalism   Rogers is moderately committed to constitutionalism in its very broadest sense. That is, in reading his theoretical writings, one is struck by the relative frequency of his use of such phrases as "human nature," "man's inner nature," "man's true self," "man's innate potential," all of which imply a biological base of human development and personality. This constitutional leaning is perhaps most evident in Rogers' concept of the actualizing tendency. It cannot be forgotten that life's master motive is inherent, rooted in the physiological processes of the body, and, in brief, a biological fact of life. To describe the unitary motive underlying all human activity in such terms reflects, quite simply, the constitutionalism assumption.

But that is not the whole story. As the self unfolds, it is significantly influenced by environmental variables. "Unconditional positive regard" from others who count in the environment facilitates healthy self-development; the imposition of "conditions of worth" impedes it. Thus, the person's emergent self-concept is laden with environmental influences. So Rogers' theory is by no means devoid of the environmentalism assumption.

Yet, to place Rogers' position on the constitutionalism–environmentalism assumption in proper perspective, one must see its relationship to his position on the freedom and rationality assumptions. As noted in Chapter 1, the nine basic assumptions are not entirely independent of one another; the same most certainly holds true for the position of any given theorist on them. In this instance, Rogers contends that human beings are the only animals who really can be aware of both their past and present life situations, thus making it possible for them to make choices about their futures (Frick, 1971). Thus, because people are rational and free, they are able (at least to some extent) to rise above the constitutional and particularly the environmental influences upon their development. In brief, Rogers' belief (like the existentialists') that human beings considerably shape their own destinies moderates the potency of his position on the constitutionalism–environmentalism question.

Changeability–Unchangeability   As noted in the first chapter, one clear indication of a personologist's commitment to changeability is a theoretical emphasis upon continuous personal growth. Rogers' theory reveals just such an emphasis in the concept of an actualizing tendency. For through the actualizing tendency, people are depicted as forever growing, unfolding their potentialities, and changing in the process. Viewed in this light, personality change is an integral part of what it means to be a human being in Rogers' system.

The possibilities for personality change become even more evident when we again consider the interaction of the actualizing tendency with freedom and rationality in phenomenological theory. According to Rogers, as a person grows, he or she becomes progressively freer and more rational in directing the course of that personal growth. Thus, to some extent, the individual can decide what kind of person he or she wishes to become in the future. All of this clearly suggests that people can change significantly in their lifetimes. Thus, Rogers' commitment to the changeability assumption is indeed strong.

Subjectivity–Objectivity   Subjectivity is the key assumption in Rogers' system. The entire structure of phenomenological theory is based squarely upon it. For Rogers, each person lives entirely in a rich, ever-changing, private, subjective world of experience of which he or she is the center. Each person perceives the world in subjective terms and responds to it accordingly. And at the very heart of one's perceptual system is one's perception of oneself—the self-concept. In Rogers' theory, then, human behavior is forever unintelligible without reference to the private world of experience. In direct opposition to B. F. Skinner and much of contemporary behaviorism, Rogers contends that we can never adequately understand human actions simply by examining objective, environmental conditions alone. Instead, we must *always look within the person* and attempt to see the world from his or her perspective in order to approach an understanding of behavior.

As an illustration of this phenomenological position, consider a so-called objective situation in which a group of people are involved—a college course in personality. The professor is the same, the students are the same, the room is the same, and the lectures are the same. What is *never* the same is the way that each person involved *subjectively experiences* and consequently responds to the entire course or any particular meeting of it. For example, Student A, who usually finds the course positive and enriching, has an intense headache one day and experiences the lecture as abstract, dull, and irrelevant. That she has been up virtually all night drinking and is functioning on two hours' sleep may have contributed to this experiential state. She finds herself dozing. Student B, who normally finds the course material irrelevant to his own concerns (he plans to be a hermit), experiences it as quite relevant and relates to it well. Usually mute, he asks a lot of questions. For some reason, the professor has decided to discuss the topic of "basic insecurity," and student B finds this simply fascinating. For her part, the professor, who normally loves teaching this personality course, arrives that day with many concerns: she has not prepared any lecture at all, she's worried that the pittance which the university gives her in the guise of a salary will not meet her rising family expenses, she is concerned about gaining tenure at the university, and is anxious about the results of a recent research project. So, on the spot, she decides to lecture on "basic insecurity" which, that day, she may really be more prepared to talk about than she thinks.

Nonetheless, she delivers the lecture in an uncharacteristically nervous voice accompanied by other signs of tension not typically exhibited.

Without elaborating further, the point is that in Rogers' system the behavior of these three persons (or anyone else in the class—or the world) cannot be explained by reference to objective external conditions alone. It can be adequately explained *only* in terms of each individual's private world of subjective experience —where he or she really *lives*. That's "where it's at" in Rogers' view: Subjectivity is the essence of the phenomenological position. Rogers' commitment to the subjectivity assumption could not be stronger.

Proactivity–Reactivity   The Rogerian person is purposive, forward-moving, and oriented toward the future. As a being who internally generates his or her own behavior, this person is eminently proactive. A person's proactivity, in Rogers' system, becomes apparent when one examines where all human behavior originates, viz., the actualizing tendency. Because of this master motive inherent in all life, humanity is forever moving forward, growing, in brief, "proacting."

While Rogers recognizes that a certain amount of external stimulation is probably necessary for self-actualization to progress (Frick, 1971), outer stimuli appear to be things that the innate actualizing tendency feeds upon rather than reacts to. The person psychologically *devours* external stimuli rather than simply reacting to them. A classroom learning situation is a good example of this distinction. In Rogers' view, one does not learn simply as a direct function of being "taught" (i.e., reacting to external stimuli). But people can profit from classroom learning; they have an innate tendency to grow and expand their horizons (the actualizing tendency) and the right classroom can facilitate this growth by prompting them to move in directions that they otherwise would not have. So, in Rogers' system, a person feeds upon external stimuli—they nourish his or her growth. But the sole moving force of human behavior is the actualizing tendency; one is not prodded into activity by external stimulation. This view reflects Rogers' strong commitment to the proactivity assumption.

Homeostasis–Heterostasis   Since this assumption deals with a motivational question, one need only turn again to Rogers' sole motivational construct to determine his position on it. Specifically, the actualizing tendency is a heterostatic concept.

As is by now clear, Rogers' actualizing tendency is always moving in the direction of growth, enhancement, and self-realization of the person. Drives that other theorists regard as homeostatic—e.g., hunger, sex, and competence—are subsumed by the heterostatic master motive in Rogers' system. And more—the actualizing tendency thrives on *tension increase, not tension reduction*. Humans naturally seek stimulation, challenge, and novel possibilities for personal growth. All this culminates in Rogers' view of the good life. Recall that it was described as a direction rather than a destination. Thus, Rogers' fully functioning person is always striving, always stretching, always seeking actualization of his or her potentialities. Rogers' commitment to the heterostatic assumption could not be stronger.

Knowability—Unknowability   Rogers' phenomenological position, when carried to its logical conclusion, implies that the human organism is unknowable in scientific terms. More specifically, as already noted, the subjectivity assumption is the philosophic essence of the phenomenological position. And subjectivity means that each individual lives in a private world of experience which he or she alone has the potential to comprehend. No one is fully able to understand anyone else and, hence, her or his nature. According to this view, neither can psychological science.

Rogers clearly addresses himself to this point in what is probably the most rigorous statement of his theory to date (Rogers, 1959). While he admits that there may be such a thing as "objective" truth or reality, no one is going to arrive at it because each of us lives in a private world of subjective experience. As Rogers puts it: "Thus there is no such thing as Scientific Knowlede, there are only individual perceptions of what appears to each person to be such knowledge (1959, p. 192)." If there's no such thing as scientific knowledge, it's a sure bet that human nature is never going to be understood by it.

So, from Rogers' perspective, what are we doing in psychology? Perhaps his answer here explains why he has been dubbed a "respected gadfly" of psychology by a scientific awards committee of the American Psychological Association and why he accepts this label so readily. Throughout his professional lifetime, Carl Rogers has consistently argued against the traditional strongholds of scientific psychology (e.g., the structure and inhumane nature of graduate education in the field), pioneered scientific research in areas pertaining to subjective experience (e.g., psychotherapy research), and, in general, has done everything that he can to broaden the scope of scientific concepts and methodology to incorporate *as much* human subjectivity as possible. Thus, by refocusing psychology on *human experience*, perhaps he hopes to catch a greater glimpse of what humanity is. While he has undoubtedly profited much from his scientific endeavors, however, one must conclude from reading him that he has learned far more about human nature from his many clients than he has from reading the literature of psychology or doing scientific research.

The following section reflects the research his theory has generated.

EMPIRICAL VALIDATION OF PHENOMENOLOGICAL THEORY CONCEPTS

Strictly speaking, Rogers' theory pertains not only to personality but also to psychotherapy and the process of change in human behavior. Practically all the empirical studies conducted by Rogers and his associates have been aimed at elucidating and understanding the nature of the therapeutic process, the conditions which facilitate personality growth, and the effectiveness of therapy in bringing about permanent behavioral change. The emphasis on psychotherapy research has indirectly produced considerable data concerning the self-concept and its governance of the individual's psychological adjustment. This is understandable insofar as the concept of self is pivotal in Rogers' theory. It is to Rogers' credit that he has opened up psychotherapy and the nature of self as meaningful areas of research. Largely through his efforts, personologists now recognize the self as a useful explanatory construct in accounting for human behavior. More importantly, Rogers' formulation of a phenomenological theory has made the self an object of respectable empirical investigation. No one in contemporary psychology has been more influential than Carl Rogers in providing an intellectual climate in which research on the self structure can flourish.

In this section we will consider three illustrative studies bearing upon the scientific validity of Rogerian concepts. First, however, it is necessary that the reader become acquainted with Rogers' view of psychological science and research, the method by which he measures the self-concept, and the research strategy he employs to study the changes in self-concept during the course of therapy.

Rogers' View of Science and Research

Rogers is strongly committed to phenomenology as a basis for developing a science of persons and as a method of examining the empirical validity of theoretical concepts. It will be recalled that phenomenology refers to a disciplined effort to understand the essence of a person's subjective experience—specifically, how people come to know and understand their world and themselves. The focus of the phenomenological method emphasizes the data, or phenomena, of consciousness with the ultimate goal of comprehending the essence of things appearing in consciousness (Misiak and Sexton, 1973). Rogers states that such effort is justified because

> it is satisfying to perceive the world as having order and because rewarding results often ensue when one understands the orderly relationships which appear to exist in nature. One of these rewarding results is that the ordering of one segment of experience in a theory immediately opens up new vistas of inquiry, research, and thought, thus leading one continually forward (1959, p. 188).

Relevant to the research enterprise, Rogers considers clinical observations, as obtained during psychotherapy, to be a valid source of phenomenological data. These clinical observations, usually based on selected excerpts from tape-recorded interviews in client-centered therapy, are then systematically analyzed (by means of content analysis) in order that refined hypotheses may be formulated and subjected to scientific scrutiny. In short, it is Rogers' belief that self-referent attitudes and values as expressed during therapy constitute valid and reliable sources of information concerning the self-structure and its pervasive influence on behavior. At the same time, he admits that observational data must be restated in terms of experimental operations if a theory is to be confirmed: "Science exists only in people. Each scientific project has its creative inception, its process, and its tentative conclusion in a person or persons. Knowledge—even scientific knowledge—is that which is subjectively acceptable" (1955, p. 274). Rogers applies similar logic to the utilization of science. He believes that since science itself is neutral, it will never depersonalize, manipulate, or control individuals. It is only people who can and will do that. Consequently, the way research findings in personology are utilized will depend on value choices made by human beings.

Rogers' notions of science are diametrically opposed to those espoused by B.

F. Skinner (Chapter 6). The views of these two eminent psychologists concerning the scientific control of human behavior were dramatized in a debate held before the 1956 convention of the American Psychological Association. In this debate, Rogers noted that he and Skinner are both committed to a science of human behavior. Moreover, both concurred that psychological science is making substantial progress in explaining behavior and developing the capacity to predict and control it. However, Rogers felt that Skinner has vastly underestimated the seriousness of the problems associated with behavioral control. Who will control whom? Who will control the controllers? By what means will behavioral control be exercised? And what forms of behavior will be deemed desirable in a Skinnerian-designed environment? The fact that values and subjective choice are implicitly involved in dealing with these kinds of questions is what makes Rogers hesitate to give unlimited power to the behavioral scientist. Ironically, Rogers has great faith in man in general, whereas he lacks Skinner's confidence in the scientist. Rogers proposes that science be used to create an open society (as opposed to Skinner's closed one) in which individuals are afforded the opportunity to develop the values of responsibility, happiness, security, productivity, and creativity. In short, Rogers believes personological research should ultimately be addressed to questions concerning the good life and how it may best be achieved.

Measuring the Self-Concept: The Q Sort

In the early 1950s William Stephenson (1953), then a colleague of Rogers' at the University of Chicago, developed a general methodology, called the *Q technique*, for investigating an individual's self-concept. Rogers and his associates quickly recognized the potential value of Stephenson's work for their own empirical studies on changes in the perceived self during the course of psychotherapy. Accordingly, they adopted the *Q sort*, a specific rating procedure devised by Stephenson, as one of their basic research tools in gathering data about therapeutic improvement.

What is the Q sort? Although it has myriad possibilities, essentially it is a method of studying systematically one's views about oneself and one's relationships with others. The procedure followed is quite simple. The subject is given a deck of cards, each containing a printed statement or adjective concerning some personality characteristic. The cards may contain such self-referent statements as "I am an aggressive person," "I like to be with other people," "I am emotionally mature." Or the items might be "methodical," "inventive," "sincere," "quick-witted." The subject's task is to sort the cards into a series of categories (usually seven in number), each corresponding to a point along a continuum ranging from those attributes which are *most* like to those which are *least* like him or her. The chief feature of the method is that the subject must sort the cards according to some prearranged or forced distribution. That is, he or she is required to place a specific number of cards in each of a specific number of categories. Although the number of categories varies from one study to another in accordance with the number of Q cards, the forced distribution is usually approximately normal. For example, in the Q-sort distribution illustrated in Figure 11-2, the subject is first required to select the two statements she believes to be most characteristic of the person she is rating and place

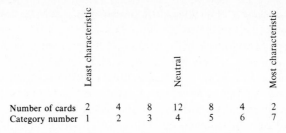

Number of cards	2	4	8	12	8	4	2
Category number	1	2	3	4	5	6	7

Figure 11-2 A forced Q-sort distribution for descriptive statements.

them in category seven. Then she chooses four statements that are more characteristic than the remaining thirty-six (and less descriptive than those in category seven) and place them in category six. The subject continues in this manner until she places the remaining two least descriptive statements in category one. As the example indicates, the number of cards to be placed under each category fan out symmetrically from the center pile (number four), resulting in a forced normal distribution.

Two additional facts regarding the Q sort should be noted. First, statements or adjectives may be culled from numerous sources—there is no fixed set of standardized Q-sort items. They may stem from a particular personality theory, from recorded therapeutic interviews, or from personality questionnaires. Second, the forced normal distribution allows for easy computation of statistical results since the mean and variance are held constant across subjects. The forced distribution also helps to control for response sets, since tendencies to give "average" or "extreme" ratings do exist. Conversely, the Q sort has been criticized for forcing subjects to sort statements in ways which may not accurately reflect their self-conceptions. For instance, a subject might feel that the majority of statements do not apply at all, yet he or she is forced by the directions to sort them into the prescribed categories. Another subject might feel that most of the statements are highly characteristic and do not belong in the middle category, yet he or she is also forced to abide by the instructions.

Research-oriented Rogerians generally have their subjects Q-sort the statements twice: once for *self-description* and once for *ideal self-description*. For the *self-sort,* subjects are instructed to sort the cards to describe themselves as they see themselves at the present time. This self-sort depicts the subject's experience of herself as she is. Following completion of the self-sort, the subject then is instructed to use the same cards to describe the kind of person she would most like to be—her ideal person. This second sort is called the *ideal-sort.*

Q-sort data can be analyzed in several ways. However, the product-moment correlation coefficient is the most commonly used statistic for indicating the degree to which an individual's self-concept and ideal self-concepts are congruent or divergent. Employing this method, each Q-sort statement is assigned two numbers, the first number representing the category number for the self-sort and the second the category number for the ideal-sort. It is these two numbers that are correlated. The magnitude of the correlation coefficient thus becomes an index of the degree of congruence or incongruence between the perceived self and the ideal self. A positive correlation reveals a state of congruence—whereas a negative correlation reveals incongruence—between the perceived self and the ideal self. Correlation coefficients not significantly different from zero indicate that there is no relationship (similarity) between the way a person sees herself and the way she would like to be.

The research strategy employed by Rogers and his coworkers for investigating psychotherapeutic personality change is quite simple. Clients repeatedly perform self and ideal Q sorts during therapy, at the end of therapy, and in some instances during posttherapy intervals. Each time, the correlation between the two sorts is calculated. It thus becomes possible to chart a progressive pattern of change in the relationship between the client's perceived self and ideal self over the course of psychotherapy by comparing the correlations between the two sorts. Rogers' studies also include a control group, to ensure that any detectable changes are due to therapy rather than the mere passage of time, familiarity with the Q sort, or other extraneous influences. Control subjects are matched with client subjects on such demographic variables as age, sex, education, and socioeconomic status. They complete self and ideal Q sorts at the same time intervals as the client group. The only difference between the two groups is that the client group is subjected to the independent treatment variable, client-centered (Rogerian) therapy, while the control group is not. This procedure has enabled Rogers to validate many of his theoretical notions concerning personality growth and change and the therapeutic conditions that bring them about (Carkhuff, 1969).

Self-Perception and Psychological Adjustment

As explained earlier, Rogers believes that psychological maladjustment results from incongruence between the self and experience. In other words, a psychologically disturbed person perceives himself and his relation to people and things in his environment in ways which fit some preconceived self-structure. He is therefore prone to deny or distort any experience which conflicts with his existing self-image because awareness of it would leave him vulnerable to anxiety, threat, and disorganization. In contrast, a psychologically healthy person is one who perceives himself and his interaction with others in a realistic manner (i.e., as outside observers would see them). Furthermore, the healthy person is open to experience (i.e., is nondefensive), accepts responsibility for his own behavior, and evaluates experience in terms of the evidence of his own senses.

A prime example of how these theoretical notions have been operationally defined and empirically tested is an early yet frequently cited study conducted by Chodorkoff (1954). This investigator tested three hypotheses regarding the functional relationships among self-perception, perceptual defense, and psychological adjustment:

    1 The greater the agreement between an individual's self-description and an objective description of him or her by others, the less perceptual defense he or she will exhibit.

    2 The greater the agreement between an individual's self-description and an objective appraisal of him or her by others, the more adequate will be his or her personal adjustment.

   3   The more adequate the personality adjustment of an individual, the less perceptual defense he or she will manifest.

   These theoretical predictions were tested by having thirty college students serve as subjects. The measure of self-description was obtained by having each subject Q-sort 125 self-referent statements into thirteen categories, from most characteristic to least characteristic. Another Q sort of the same items, made for each subject by four clinically trained judges, was employed as the "objective description" measure. The judges' Q sorting was based on clinical material about the subject gained from projective tests administered to each one, including Rorschach and TAT protocols, word association test data, and a biographical inventory.

   A measure of perceptual defense was secured in the following way. First, each subject responded to a word-association test consisting of 100 words, fifty emotional and fifty neutral. The subject's reaction time to each word was recorded by means of a voice-key type of reaction-time apparatus. Next, two groups of ten words each were selected for each subject to be presented as the stimuli for a perceptual defense test. One group consisted of the emotional words that had the longest reaction times; the other group consisted of the neutral words with the shortest reaction times. This procedure made it possible to select for each subject personally relevant threatening and neutral stimuli. These twenty stimulus words were then randomly presented by means of a tachistoscope, a device which visually displays material for controlled durations of time (e.g., 1/500 second). The exposure time for each word was increased until it was correctly recognized, with this time being used as the recognition threshold score for that word. The measure of perceptual defense was operationally defined by Chodorkoff as the difference between the mean recognition threshold for threatening stimuli (emotional words such as "raped," "Kotex," "penis," "whore") and the mean recognition threshold for neutral stimuli (such as "child," "apple," "stove," "tree"). The higher this difference, the greater the subject's perceptual defense tendencies were assumed to be.

   Personal adjustment, the third variable examined in Chodorkoff's study, was derived from two measures: (1) Rorschach scores and (2) ratings made by the clinically experienced judges along eleven adjustment scales.

   Each of the hypotheses was evaluated by computing the appropriate correlation coefficients. The first hypothesis stated that accuracy of self-description would be negatively correlated with perceptual defense. The correlation between these two variables was found to be highly significant ($r = -.53$). Thus, the more accurately the subject described herself, the less perceptual defense she showed. The second hypothesis compared the accuracy of self-description with the two measures of personal adjustment. A significant relationship was found between high scores on accuracy of self-description and judges' ratings of adjustment ($r = +.73$), but the relationship between accuracy of self-description and adjustment scores based on Rorschach scores failed to reach statistical significance ($r = +.34$). The third hypothesis was evaluated by comparing personal adjustment ratings with the measures of perceptual defense. A significant correlation was found between high scores on perceptual defense and low ratings of adjustment based on judges' ratings ($r = -.62$). However, the relationship between high perceptual defense scores and low adjustment scores based on Rorschach scores, while in the predicted direction, did not reach statistical significance ($r = -.29$).

General support for all three hypotheses led Chodorkoff to the following formulation:

> The better adjusted individual attempts to obtain mastery over threatening situations by getting to know, as quickly as possible, what it is that is threatening. He may be alerted to the possibility of threat and may be influenced by a set which leads him to try to differentiate and symbolize aspects of himself and his environment which are potentially threatening. The less adequately adjusted individual, in contrast, may be thought of as influenced by a set to keep threat inadequately differentiated and inadequately symbolized.
>
>   . . . If an individual cannot differentiate and symbolize aspects of himself and his environment, his behavior in turn will not be adequate. He will also be unable to resolve threatening situations when they confront him, for if he does not recognize threat, how can he be expected to deal with it effectively? (1954, p. 510).

Self-Concept and Accuracy of Recall

According to Rogers, experiential materials inconsistent with the self-structure are denied accurate symbolization in awareness. For example, if a young woman's self-concept has been built exclusively around her "femininity," experiences that might imply that she has some masculine qualities would threaten her severely. In all likelihood, she would erect defenses to avoid recognition of this disturbing thought. An attempt to validate this aspect of Rogerian theory was made by Suinn, Osborne, and Winfree (1962). These investigators hypothesized that memory material which is inconsistent with one's self-concept is more poorly remembered than memory material which is consistent with one's self-concept.

The procedure involved in testing this hypothesis consisted of having thirty college students in a classroom setting describe themselves on 100 socially desirable adjectives culled from the Gough Adjective Scale (Gough, 1955). Each subject rated each adjective on a scale ranging from 1 (most like me) to 6 (least like me). Directions were then given such that every subject believed that he or she had been rated on the same adjectives by two other students in the class. Five days later, each subject was presented a completed adjective rating scale said to represent the composite ratings of him or her made by the other students. This actually involved faked ratings designed to present each subject with a set of self-related items discrepant from his or her own self-concept. The faked adjective rating scale contained fifty adjective ratings that were zero degrees discrepant from the subject's own previous self-rating (group 0), twenty-five adjectives that were discrepant by one degree (group I), and twenty-five adjectives that were discrepant by two degrees (group II). Thus, group 0 adjective ratings were consistent with, while groups I and II ratings were to varying degrees inconsistent with, the subject's self-concept. The method of manipulating the discrepancy between self and other adjective ratings is best explained by illustration. If the subject described himself or herself on the adjective "considerate" with a rating of 6 (least like me), a zero discrepancy would be a composite rating also of 6, a one-degree discrepancy would be a rating of 5, and a two-degree discrepancy would be a rating of 4. The direction and magnitude of the self-other discrepancies were randomly chosen, as were the adjectives to form each group. Two days later, subjects again filled out the adjective rating scale, this time as they remembered the composite ratings to be.

Recall accuracy scores were computed for each subject for each of the three groups of adjectives in the following way. If the subject recalled the composite ratings correctly, he or she was given a score of 0 for that adjective; if he or she missed by one degree (e.g., by checking a rating of 3 where the composite rating was 2) a score of 1 was assigned, and so forth up to a maximum possible score of 3. High scores thus indicated low accuracy of recall. These scores were then summed across the subjects and divided by the sample size (thirty subjects) to provide a mean accuracy of recall score for each of the three groups of adjectives. As predicted, Suinn et al. found that accuracy of recall was best for adjectives used by others that were consistent with the self-concept and was poorest for adjectives used by others that were inconsistent with the self-concept. The mean accuracy scores for Groups 0, I, and II adjectives were 0.58, 0.68, and 1.09, respectively. All differences between means were statistically significant. These findings indicate that degree of accuracy of recall of self-related stimuli is a function of the degree to which the stimuli are consistent with the self-concept. This study also offers empirical support for a key aspect of Rogerian theory, namely, that material which is inconsistent with one's self-concept will be subject to psychological defense.

Self-Acceptance and Acceptance of Others

A final group of studies stemming from Rogers' theoretical position concerns the proposition that the more a person accepts himself or herself, the more likely he or she is to accept others. Such a theoretically proposed relationship between self-acceptance and acceptance of others is based on Rogers' observation that when clients enter therapy they typically have negative self-concepts; they are unable to accept themselves. However, once such clients become more accepting of themselves, they become more accepting of others. In other words, Rogers contends that if self-acceptance occurs (i.e., if the self-ideal discrepancy is small), then acceptance, respect, and valuing of others follows. Other theorists have also suggested that attitudes toward the self are reflected in attitudes toward others. Fromm (1956), for example, maintains that self-love and the love of others go hand in hand. He further notes that a failure to love the self is accompanied by a basic hostility toward others.

While numerous studies have supported the relationship between self-acceptance and acceptance of others, a majority of these have used as subjects college students or individuals receiving therapy (e.g., Berger, 1955; Phillips, 1951; Suinn, 1961). With regard to Rogerian theory specifically, however, accumulating evidence indicates that self-acceptance and acceptance of others characterizes parent-child relationships. A study performed by Medinnus and Curtis (1963) is one example. These researchers tested the hypothesis that there is a significant positive

Table 11-1   Correlations between Maternal Self-Acceptance and Child-Acceptance Measures

Measures	Bills self-acceptance	Semantic differential child-acceptance
Semantic differential self-acceptance	−.57†	.33*
Bills self-acceptance		−.48†

Source: Adapted from Medinnus & Curtis, 1963, p. 543.
* <.05
† <.01
NOTE: The negative correlations are due to the method of scoring the tests. On the Bills self-acceptance measure, the higher scores indicate greater self-acceptance while the semantic differential self-acceptance and child-acceptance scores are discrepancy scores with the higher scores denoting less favorable attitudes.

relation between self-acceptance and child acceptance in a group of mothers of young children.

Subjects were fifty-six mothers of children enrolled in a cooperative nursery school. Two measures of maternal self-acceptance were obtained. The first consisted of mothers' responses to the Bills Index of Adjustment and Values, a self-report questionnaire yielding a measure of the degree to which self and ideal are different. A semantic differential scale of twenty bipolar adjectives in which the distance between the mothers' ratings of "Me (as I am)" and "Me (as I would most like to be)" was defined operationally as the second measure of maternal self-acceptance. The measure of child acceptance was derived from the same set of bipolar adjectives. Specifically, the distance between the mothers' ratings of "My child (as he is)" and "My child (as I would most like him to be)" was defined as the extent of the mother's acceptance of her child.

The intercorrelations between the two maternal self-acceptance scores and the child acceptance measure are shown in Table 11-1.

As can be seen, each of the three correlation coefficients is statistically significant in the predicted direction. These results support the Rogerian notion that mothers who are self-accepting (i.e., who possess positive self-regard) are far more likely to accept their children as they are than are non-self-accepting mothers. Additionally, such findings suggest that the extent to which a child develops a positive self-image depends crucially upon the extent to which his or her parents are able to accept themselves.

APPLICATION: PERSON-CENTERED THERAPY

The variety of past and present types of psychotherapy offered to disturbed individuals is enough to boggle the imagination. Psychologists and psychiatrists have asked people to lie down on black leather couches and free-associate, tried to condition and countercondition them, had them enter "orgone boxes" to vibrate, encouraged them to go into empty rooms to let out primal screams, and told them to sit around nude in swimming pools and "encounter" one another. Yet, in spite of earlier evidence that various forms of traditional psychotherapy did not work (Eysenck, 1952, 1966), more recent and thorough evidence indicates that many types of therapy really are effective in helping people deal with their problems (Bergin, 1979; Meltzoff and Kornreich, 1970; Roback, Abramowitz, and Strassberg, 1979). How can so many diffuse therapeutic techniques all serve to help distressed people?

Rogers' essential answer to this question is that all true forms of psychotherapy have one element in common—a *relationship* between persons. Specifically, Rogers contends that the quality of the relationship between the therapist and the client is not only the single most important factor but also the only factor responsible for therapeutic personality change. Specific therapeutic techniques are secondary to the clinician-client relationship. This currently widespread approach to psychotherapy instituted by Carl Rogers is known as *person-centered therapy* (Rogers, 1977).

Evolution of Rogerian Therapy: From Techniques to Relationships

Rogers' approach to psychotherapy has undergone considerable evolution over the years. While his basic assumptions have remained stable, his means of implementing them, like the Rogerian person that he depicts, have continually developed. Specifically, Rogers' approach was first known as *nondirective therapy* (some still refer to it that way today). This term reflected Rogers' main concern at the time with techniques by which behavioral change might be achieved. Because the client was assumed to have the capacity for self-directed personality change, Rogers pioneered techniques which enabled the therapist to be much less directive in the relationship than was the case with other forms of therapy. For example, nondirective therapists of old never gave advice, answered questions, or probed by asking their own questions. Instead, they systematically attempted to reflect back to the client what he or she had said and to clarify his or her feelings in the process *(reflection* and *clarification).* In effect, the therapist acted as a kind of mirror exactly the opposite of the type found in amusement parks. Amusement-park mirrors distort one's image in various ways. Conversely, in nondirective therapy it is the client's self-image that is distorted so that the therapist's essential task, as a "mirror," was to reflect back to the client more accurately what he or she was really saying and feeling. These techniques, while still employed today, are somewhat limiting if they constitute the only function that the therapist provides in the relationship. To illustrate, if a client innocently asks "What time is it?" it is probably more productive for the therapist to respond "It's 10:45" than to say warmly and empathically "You feel you want to know what time it is."

With the publication in 1951 of his book *Client-Centered Therapy*, Rogers' approach progressed further and came to be known primarily by this label, as it still is today in some circles. While still retaining his nondirective techniques, Rogers at this time was emphasizing the importance of the clients' perceptions, of therapeutically entering the clients' world of subjective experience and focusing upon the clients' perceptions of themselves, their lives, and their problems. Hence the term "client-centered." Since that time, however, Rogers' approach has evolved to still another level. He has become more concerned with the issue of precisely what conditions must be met before the client can begin to resolve his or her problems. As stated earlier, he discovered that the relationship between therapist and client is the most important aspect underlying personality change; consequently, he funneled all his efforts on this in the late 1950s (Rogers, 1957b, 1958, 1959) and continues to do so today. Again, it should be stressed that Rogers' changes in thinking in this regard represent a progressive evolution to a more comprehensive and meaningful level rather than an abandonment of old, outmoded concepts. At present, the "label" which best captures the essence of the newer developments is "person-centered therapy" (Rogers, 1977). This newer term more accurately reflects the evolution of Rogers' thought—from techniques to relationships.

The Therapeutic Relationship Itself: What's Happening

Rogers (1957b) has spelled out *six conditions* as both necessary and sufficient if therapeutic personality change is to occur. These conditions, when taken together, provide an excellent framework for describing the theory of what actually happens in person-centered therapy.

1   *Two persons are in psychological contact.* Really more of a precondition than a condition, Rogers' first assertion simply means that some relationship or psychological contact between two people must exist. A therapist, no matter how good she or he is, cannot aid a client if that client does not even know her or him. Perhaps even more important, Rogers is postulating here that no significant positive personality change can occur outside a relationship.

2   *The first, whom we shall term the client, is in a state of incongruence, being vulnerable or anxious.* As described earlier, Rogers construes personality disorganization and psychopathology in terms of a significant discrepancy between the actual experience of a person and the person's self-concept with regard to that experience. To illustrate this concept, Rogers (1957b) uses an example of a college student who, at a total or organismic level, experiences a fear of the university and of examinations given on the third floor of a certain building, since these demonstrate a fundamental inadequacy in himself. He is dreadfully afraid of this inadequacy, and thus it is decidedly at odds with his self-conception. Consequently, he distorts the organismic experience in his awareness, consciously representing it instead as an unreasonable (phobic) fear of climbing stairs in this building (or any building) and an equally intense fear of crossing the open campus.

Thus, this student is out of touch with the wellsprings of his conscious experience, his total organismic experience; in this sense, he is a stranger within himself. Such an existential situation necessarily leaves him highly vulnerable since, at any unexpected moment, the world could thrust the truth upon him. Moreover, to the degree that he dimly perceives this deep incongruence within himself, he necessarily experiences tension or anxiety. His total position might be likened to the unfortunate existential condition of Chicken Little who, as the childhood tale would have it, was constantly awaiting and expecting the sky to fall. Given such an uncomfortable subjective state, it is easy to understand why the student seeks out the college counseling center for help. Undoubtedly, he will initially report to the psychologist that he intensely fears climbing stairs, walking across the campus, experiences anxiety, and does not know why.

3 *The second person, whom we shall term the therapist, is congruent or integrated in the relationship.* When the student arrives at the counseling center, Rogers' third condition specifies that he should meet a person who is congruent, integrated, and, in a word, genuine in the relationship. That is, in the particular therapeutic relationship itself, the therapist is accurately representing his or her organismic experience in awareness and genuinely being himself or herself without any knowing or unknowing facade. In brief, the therapist is whole and real (completely and fully himself or herself), and the client should have the distinct and accurate feeling that he is baring his soul to a genuine person in that relationship.

Rogers does not feel that the therapist needs to be open to all experiences in his life. Outside the therapeutic relationship, for example, the therapist may occasionally experience anxiety, depression, hostility, or any other mood state that might suggest that she or he may not be fully integrated in all aspects of life. But in that therapeutic relationship, for that one or two hours per week, it is imperative that he or she be congruent. This means that the therapist may occasionally experience feelings not traditionally considered ideal for psychotherapy, e.g., "Although I really like this client, I just don't feel like listening to him today—I wish I were playing golf." Of course, since the focus of therapy is upon the client's feelings rather than the therapist's, the therapist need not verbalize this feeling as long as she or he is consciously aware of it. Sometimes, however, the therapist's feelings become so intense that he or she may need to express them directly to the client or to a supervisor or colleague, e.g., "This client constantly expresses what I regard as racist attitudes, and I'm having great difficulty accepting him because of this."

4 *The therapist experiences unconditional positive regard for the client.* The phrase "unconditional positive regard" essentially means that the therapist warmly *accepts* the client, prizes him as a person in the process of becoming, and passes no judgments on his feelings or experiences. In short, the therapist imposes no "conditions of worth" upon the client, but rather fully accepts him as he is without approval or disapproval. So when the student begins to describe his fear of climbing stairs and walking across campus, the therapist unconditionally accepts these feelings as part of the student's world of subjective experience. He does not make judgments on the student's feelings, e.g., "Look, son, I was in the marines and the only way you're going to become a man is to forget these stupid feelings and get out there right now and climb those stairs and walk head held high across that open campus."

Person-centered therapy thus proceeds in a nonthreatening atmosphere in which the client feels understood and accepted as a whole person. Such a therapeutic climate permits the client to get back in touch with his or her organismic level of experiencing, allowing him or her to represent that experience in conscious awareness without feeling threatened, e.g., "If this therapist, who is genuine and truly likes me, can unflinchingly accept these feelings as a legitimate part of who I am, why can't I?" Thus, the therapeutic situation allows the client to delve ever more deeply into himself, express his true feelings without fear of reproach, and ultimately integrate these feelings with a necessarily changed self-concept. Unconditional positive regard, to the degree that it can be achieved in any therapeutic relationship, enables the client to examine those experiences which have been inconsistent with his self-concept and of which he was previously unaware because they were anxiety provoking.

   5 *The therapist experiences an empathic understanding of the client's internal frame of reference and endeavors to communicate this experience to the client.* The person-centered therapist has *empathy* for the client. As Rogers (1957b) describes it, empathy means that the therapist senses the client's private world of experience as if it were her or his own—but without ever losing that "as if" quality. In brief, the therapist *understands*. She or he is able to move about freely in the client's subjective word, perceiving as he perceives, feeling as he feels, experiencing as he experiences.

   Accurately understanding the client's feelings, the therapist constantly tries to communicate this experience to the client, e.g., he or she knows how the student really feels about climbing stairs and walking across campus. Thus, the therapist is really *with* the client, which enables him or her to accept, understand, and clarify the often conflicting and confused feelings of the client. According to Rogers (1957b), the client often experiences the therapist's empathy as akin to a sudden burst of sunlight through a dense tangle of foliage in a forest. As the client struggles with his confused and distorted representations of experience, the therapist, precisely because she or he has entered fully into the client's subjective world, is able to make empathic statements that shed considerable light upon it. The therapist accepts and understands the client and, in the psychotherapeutic relationship, both are led to progressively greater heights of acceptance and understanding.

   6 *The communication to the client of the therapist's empathic understanding and unconditional positive regard is to a minimal degree achieved.* Careful consideration of this condition should erase the stereotype of the now defunct nondirective therapist who did nothing but sit around, occasionally grunting warmly at the client and saying "Um-hum." Nor are contemporary person-centered therapists limited to simple restatement and/or clarification of what the client says (e.g., "I've just cut myself and if you don't give me that Band-aid, I'm going to bleed to death." "You feel you're bleeding to death."), which, when carried off improperly in the past, probably led many a client to want to ask, "Polly wants a cracker?"

   While examination of taped interviews of today's person-centered therapists indicates that they still engage in the use of warm responding—saying "Um-hum" or "I see," reflecting and clarifying feelings—they do this to make every effort to *communicate* their empathy and positive regard to the client: It is worthless for the therapist to experience these attitudes unless the client knows it. So the therapist must communicate these attitudes through his or her every word and action, and the client must perceive these as reflecting the therapist's acceptance and understanding of him. To the degree that the client does feel accepted, condition six is met and positive personality change can take place.

   Thus, Rogers insists that it is the client, not the therapist, who is responsible for personal growth. The therapist does, in fact, establish the conditions for change, but it is the client who is the real agent of change itself.

Psychotherapy and Gardening

To anyone schooled in Rogers' basic assumptions concerning human nature and his personality theory, his approach to psychotherapy makes perfect sense. Believing that individuals will naturally move toward growth, actualization, and health if the conditions are right, in person-centered therapy Rogers is simply creating the right conditions. The client's natural actualizing tendency can be relied upon to do the rest. In this sense, a Rogerian therapist sees himself or herself much more as a "facilitator of growth" than a "curer of ills" (as in psychoanalysis) or "modifier of behavior" (as in behavior therapy). Moreover, person-centered therapy has probably led to more empirical research than any other specific therapeutic approach and, in the opinion of at least one leading writer in the counseling field (Patterson, 1973), it is *supported* by more research than any other therapeutic approach.

So Rogers' person-centered therapy (supported by empirical research) reflects his image of human nature in general and the role of the therapist in particular. Upon reflection, one is tempted to draw an analogy between person-centered therapy and gardening. When one recalls Rogers' background in agriculture, the analogy becomes even more compelling. Concluding his acceptance speech for the 1973 APA Distinguished Professional Contribution Award, Rogers drew the analogy for us:

> And then I garden. Those mornings when I cannot find time to inspect my flowers, water the young shoots I am propagating, pull a few weeds, spray some destructive insects, and pour just the proper fertilizer on some budding plants, I feel cheated. My garden supplies the same intriguing question I have been trying to meet all my professional life: What are the effective conditions for growth? But in my garden, though the frustrations are just as immediate, the results, whether success or failure, are more quickly evident. And when, through patient, intelligent, and understanding care I have provided the conditions that result in the production of a rare or glorious bloom, I feel the same kind of satisfaction that I have felt in the facilitation of growth in a person or in a group of persons (Rogers, 1974, pp. 122–123).

SUMMARY

Reflecting a close affinity with humanistic psychology, Rogers holds that the innermost core of human nature is essentially benevolent, purposive, and trustworthy. These basic attributes of human nature will surface if the proper conditions encourage the fulfillment of the individual's innate potential. In Rogers' system, all human motives are subsumed under a single master motive—the actualizing tendency—the innate tendency of the individual to actualize, maintain, and enhance himself or herself.

Within the broad context of the humanistic movement, Rogers' particular theoretical position is phenomenological. He holds that the only reality, from the person's perceptual vantage point, is subjective reality—the person's private world of experience. And central to that subjective world is the concept of self, Rogers' most important personological construct. In his system, elements important in self-concept development are the need for positive regard, conditions of worth, and unconditional positive regard.

Rogers argues that most ways of behaving that an individual adopts are consistent with her self-concept. Threat exists when a person senses an incongruity between her self-concept and total organismic experience; she then attempts to defend herself by means of perceptual distortion and denial. When the incongruence between self-concept and actual experience becomes too great, personality disorganization and psychopathology result. In sharp contrast, persons who are open to their experience, fully trust it, and are freely moving in the direction of actualizing themselves are termed "fully functioning" in Rogers' system.

Rogers' basic assumptions concerning human nature are generally strong, explicit, and reflective of the fundamental cleavage between phenomenology and behaviorism in American psychology. Rogers' phenomenological theory reflects (1) a strong commitment to the assumptions of freedom, rationality, holism, changeability, subjectivity, proactivity, heterostasis, and unknowability and (2) a moderate commitment to the constitutionalism assumption.

Rogers' phenomenological theory, particularly its psychotherapeutic aspects, has stimulated an enormous amount of research. In this chapter, a primary method of studying the self-concept, the Q sort, was discussed along with illustrative research bearing upon aspects of the self-concept. Brief attention was also given to Rogers' view of science.

In the concluding chapter section, Rogers' unique and widely employed approach to psychotherapy, person-centered therapy, was described as it has evolved over the years. Emphasizing the critical importance of the relationship between therapist and client, Rogers' six conditions for positive personality change were listed and discussed.

BIBLIOGRAPHY

American Psychologist, 1973, **28,** 71–74.

Berger, E. Relationships among acceptance of self, acceptance of others and MMPI scores. *Journal of Counseling Psychology,* 1955, **2,** 279–284.

Bergin, A. The evaluation of therapeutic outcomes. In A. Bergin & S. Garfield (Eds.), *Handbook of Psychotherapy and Behavior Change* (2d ed.). New York: Wiley, 1979.

Carkhuff, R. *Helping and human relations.* Vols. I and II. New York: Holt, Rinehart and Winston, 1969.

Chodorkoff, B. Self-perception, perceptual defense, and adjustment. *Journal of Abnormal and Social Psychology,* 1954, **49,** 508–512.

Davis, C. Studies in the self-selection diet by young children. *American Journal of Diseases of Children,* 1933, **46,** 743–750.

Eysenck, H. The effects of psychotherapy: An evaluation. *Journal of Consulting Psychology,* 1952, **16,** 319–324.

Eysenck, H. *The Effects of psychotherapy.* New York: International Science Press, 1966.

Frick, W. *Humanistic psychology: Interviews with Maslow, Murphy, and Rogers.* Columbus, Ohio: Merrill, 1971.

Fromm, E. *The art of loving.* New York: Harper & Row, 1956.

Gough, H. *Adjective check list.* University of California: Institute for Personality Assessment Research, 1955.

Medinnus, G., & Curtis, F. The relation between maternal self-acceptance and child acceptance. *Journal of Counseling Psychology,* 1963, **27,** 542–544.

Meltzoff, J., & Kornreich, M. *Research in psychotherapy.* Chicago: Aldine-Atherton, 1970.

Misiak, H., & Sexton, V. *Phenomenological, existential, and humanistic psychologies: A historical survey.* New York: Grune & Stratton, 1973.

Patterson, C. *Theories of counseling and psychotherapy* (2d ed.). New York: Harper & Row, 1973.

Phillips, E. Attitudes toward self and others: A brief questionnaire report. *Journal of Consulting Psychology,* 1951, **15,** 79–81.

Roback, H., Abramowitz, S., & Strassberg, D. *Group psychotherapy research: Commentaries and readings.* New York: Krieger, 1979.

Rogers, C. *The clinical treatment of the problem child.* Boston: Houghton Mifflin, 1939.

Rogers, C. *Counseling and psychotherapy: New concepts in practice.* Boston: Houghton Mifflin, 1942.

Rogers, C. *Client-centered therapy: Its current practice, implications, and theory.* Boston: Houghton Mifflin, 1951.

Rogers, C. Persons or science? A philosophical question. *American Psychologist,* 1955, **10,** 267–278.

Rogers, C. Some issues concerning the control of human behavior (symposium with B. F. Skinner). *Science,* 1956, **124,** 1057–1066.

Rogers, C. A note on the nature of man. *Journal of Counseling Psychology,* 1957a, **4,** 199–203.

Rogers, C. The necessary and sufficient conditions of therapeutic personality change. *Journal of Consulting Psychology,* 1957b, **21,** 95–103.

Rogers, C. The characteristics of a helping relationship. *Personnel and Guidance Journal,* 1958, **37,** 6-16.

Rogers, C. A theory of therapy, personality, and interpersonal relationships, as developed in the client-centered framework. In S. Koch (Ed.), *Psychology: A study of a science.* Vol. 3. New York: McGraw-Hill, 1959, pp. 184–256.

Rogers, C. *On becoming a person: A therapist's view of psychotherapy.* Boston: Houghton Mifflin, 1961.

Rogers, C. The actualizing tendency in relation to "motives"; and to consciousness. In M. Jones (Ed.), *Nebraska symposium on motivation.* Vol. II. Lincoln, Neb.: University of Nebraska Press, 1963, pp. 1–24.

Rogers, C. Autobiography. In E. Boring & G. Lindzey (Eds.), *A history of psychology in autobiography.* Vol. 5. New York: Appleton-Century-Crofts, 1967, pp. 341–384.

Rogers, C. Graduate education in psychology: A passionate statement. In W. Bennis, E. Schein, & D. Berlew (Eds.), *Interpersonal dynamics* (2d ed.). Homewood, Ill: Dorsey Press, 1968.

Rogers, C. *Freedom to learn: A view of what education might become.* Columbus, Ohio: Merrill, 1969.

Rogers, C. *Carl Rogers on encounter groups.* New York: Harper & Row, 1970.

Rogers, C. *Becoming partners: Marriage and its alternatives.* New York: Delacorte, 1972.

Rogers, C. My philosophy of interpersonal relationships and how it grew. *Journal of Humanistic Psychology,* 1973, **13,** 3–15.

Rogers, C. In retrospect: Forty-six years. *American Psychologist,* 1974, **29,** 115–123.

Rogers, C. *Carl Rogers on personal power.* New York: Delacorte Press, 1977.

Rogers, C., & Dymond, R. (Eds.). *Psychotherapy and personality change.* Chicago: University of Chicago Press, 1954.

Stephenson, W. *The study of behavior: Q-technique and its methodology.* Chicago: University of Chicago Press, 1953.

Suinn, R. The relationship between self-acceptance and acceptance of others: A learning-theory analysis. *Journal of Abnormal and Social Psychology,* 1961, **63**, 37–42.

Suinn, R., Osborne, D., & Winfree, P. The self-concept and accuracy of recall of inconsistent self-related information. *Journal of Clinical Psychology,* 1962, **18**, 473–474.

SUGGESTED READINGS

Butler, J. Self-concept change in psychotherapy. In S. Brown & D. Brenner (Eds.), *Science, psychology, and communication: Essays honoring William Stephenson.* New York: Teachers College Press, 1972, pp. 141–171.

Pearson, P. A rational analysis of Rogers' concept of openness to experience. *Journal of Personality,* 1972, **40**, 349–365.

Richards, R., & Richards, A. *Homonovus: The new man.* Boulder, Colo.: Shields Publishing, 1973.

Rogers, C. *The therapeutic relationship and its impact: A study of psychotherapy with schizophrenics.* Madison, Wisc.: University of Wisconsin Press, 1967.

Rogers, C. Interpersonal relationships: USA 2000. *Journal of Applied Behavioral Science,* 1968, **4**, 265–280.

Rogers, C., & Stevens, B. *Person to person: The problem of being human.* New York: Simon & Schuster, 1971.

Wexler, D., & Rice, L. *Innovations in client-centered therapy.* New York: Wiley, 1974.

Wylie, R. *The self-concept* (rev. ed.). Lincoln, Neb.: University of Nebraska Press. Vol. 1, *A review of methodological considerations and measuring instruments,* 1974. Vol. 2, *Theory and research on selected topics,* 1978.

DISCUSSION QUESTIONS

1 How would you evaluate Rogers' concept of the actualizing tendency? More specifically, do you believe that all human motives can be subsumed under one master motive such as this one? Defend your position, pro or con.

2 How well does Rogers' phenomenological position fit your own experience? Specifically, do you feel that you live in a private world of experience of which you are the center—and does reference to this subjective experiential world within serve to explain your behavior better than any account of your actions based only on objective environmental factors outside yourself?

3 Compare Rogers' concept of the fully functioning person to your own idea of what constitutes mental health. Would you aspire to become a fully functioning person in your life? Why or why not?

4 Skinner and Rogers seem to differ sharply on virtually all major issues in personology. Which of the two positions do you prefer? Can you see any relationship between your preference and your own basic assumptions concerning human nature?

5 Do you believe that the six conditions for therapeutic personality change described in relation to person-centered therapy are applicable to other significant human relationships? That is, do these six conditions seem to apply to the positive personality growth

that takes place in love relationships, marriage, friendships, and child rearing? Try to give examples for each.

GLOSSARY

Actualizing Tendency In Rogerian theory, the primary motive in people's lives to maintain and enhance themselves—to become the best that their inherited natures will allow them to be.

Conditional Positive Regard The situation in which an individual receives praise, attention, and approval for behaving in accordance with others' expectations.

Congruence A state of harmony that occurs when there is no discrepancy between a person's experience and his or her self-concept.

Denial Defense mechanism with which we protect ourselves from unpleasant aspects of reality by refusing to perceive them.

Existential Living The quality of living in the "here and now" so that each moment of one's life is new and different from all that existed before.

Experiential Freedom The subjective feeling that one is free to live one's life in any way one chooses, e.g., "I am solely responsible for my own actions and their consequences."

Fully Functioning Person Term used by Rogers to designate individuals who are utilizing their potentials to the maximum.

Ideal Self The person an individual thinks he or she could and should be or become (includes aspirations, moral ideals, and values).

Incongruence State of disharmony that occurs when there is a discrepancy between a person's experience and his or her self-concept.

Need for Positive Regard Learned or innate tendency on the part of individuals to seek acceptance, respect, and love from significant people in their lives.

Need for Positive Self-Regard Learned need which develops out of the association of self-experiences with the satisfaction or frustration of the need for positive regard. It refers to the individual's satisfaction at approving and dissatisfaction at disapproving of himself or herself.

Openness to Experience The ability to experience what is going on within oneself without being threatened; the opposite of defensiveness.

Organismic Trusting The ability to consult and rely on one's inner experiences and feelings as the basis for making important decisions.

Organismic Valuing Process The Rogerian principle that experiences which are perceived as maintaining or enhancing oneself are sought after and valued positively, whereas experiences which are perceived as negating or opposing one's maintenance or enhancement are valued negatively and avoided.

Perceptual Distortion Type of defense mechanism used to transform threatening experiences into a form consistent with one's current self-image.

Person-Centered Therapy A form of psychotherapy developed by Rogers based on acceptance and unconditional regard for the client. Special emphasis is placed on the relationship between therapist and client as the vehicle for personality change.

Phenomenal Field The totality of an individual's experience (also designated *perceptual field*).

Phenomenology An approach to personology which emphasizes the importance of understanding the individual's subjective experiences, feelings, and private concepts as well as his or her personal views of the world and the self.

Q Sort   A self-report assessment procedure used to measure the degree to which an individual's actual and ideal self-concepts are congruent or divergent.

Self-Actualizing Tendency   The individual's tendency to develop in the direction of increased complexity, self-sufficiency, maturity, and competence.

Self-Concept   The overall pattern or configuration of self-perceptions as viewed by the individual himself or herself. Specifically, the individual's conception of the kind of person she or he is.

Unconditional Positive Regard   Rogers' term for respect and acceptance given to another whether or not that person behaves in accordance with the accepting person's expectations.

Unconditional Positive Self-Regard   Term used to designate a person who perceives himself or herself in such a way that no self-experience is more or less worthy of positive regard than any other. For Rogers, unconditional positive self-regard enables a person to progress toward becoming fully functioning.

Personality Psychology: New Directions in the Discipline

We have now reached the end of a long and sometimes arduous journey through ten major theoretical perspectives on human personality. The reader who has completed the journey will probably agree that the study of personality is at once the most exciting and yet most baffling and frustrating area in psychology. We hope that the subject matter has proved interesting and enlightening. The course we have traveled has revealed a wealth of unique concepts and formulations by which personologists attempt to explain the complexity of human behavior. Each theorist's position, while containing elements to admire or approve, does not overwhelm the others. Indeed, the reader may feel that it is imperative that new conceptual approaches be developed if our understanding of human affairs is to be advanced. If so, this book has succeeded in conveying a sense of the field as it presently exists—recognizing the value of past and present theories and yet aware that future progress depends on the ability to create more adequate theoretical perspectives for understanding the enormous complexities of human existence.

What remains to be done in this concluding chapter is to take stock of what we have studied and to identify some of the issues, trends, and problems likely to influence future developments in personological theory and research. It is important to have a sense of emerging trends and critical issues in order to know the directions in which personology is headed. Before proceeding, however, one word of caution: our perspective is not to be construed as the "final word" in the field; indeed, one of the few things that may be assumed with certainty is that new and challenging issues will continue to evolve as the field grows and changes. Accordingly, our effort to identify emerging trends and critical problems is intended only to offer a tentative look at what may lie ahead. We also need to consider the degree to which the ten perspectives discussed in this volume are likely to continue to exert an influence on present and future developments in personality theory. First, however, a few final thoughts are warranted on the approach taken in this text to the study and comparison of personality theories. It is our conviction that the examination of basic assumptions about human nature offers a compelling and useful framework for appreciating the broad range of viewpoints and theoretical orientations which exist in current personology. In fact, these basic assumptions can be considered to represent the conceptual pillars of personality psychology: they provide a framework for understanding how psychologists have sought to develop valid descriptions of human behavior.

BASIC ASSUMPTIONS IN PERSPECTIVE

The central, unifying theme of this text is that basic assumptions about the nature of the human organism constitute the bedrock from which theories of personality are formulated and, ultimately, tested. They also highlight the fundamental issues and problems about which personality theorists agree or disagree at the most basic philosophical level. (For an overview of our ten theorists' positions on the basic assumptions about human nature, see Figure 12-1.) In this concluding chapter, then, it is only fitting that we raise a few new questions and offer some tentative thoughts on the nature of these basic assumptions and their role in present and future theory construction in personality psychology.

The first question to consider is the origin of the assumptions, one which we have already addressed in Chapter 1. It is worth briefly reiterating here. Basically, we argue that basic assumptions about human nature reflect a theorist's *own personality structure*—they reveal what the theorist thinks of himself or herself and the world at large. To understand a theorist's basic assumptions (i.e., where he or she is "coming from"), it is to some extent necessary to understand *him or her* as a person. We hope that our biographical sketches in each chapter helped the reader approach this objective.

A second question pertains to the role of basic assumptions in theory construction. Precisely what effects do they have upon a personologist in the initial stages of theory construction? Whether they are consciously considered or not, *a*

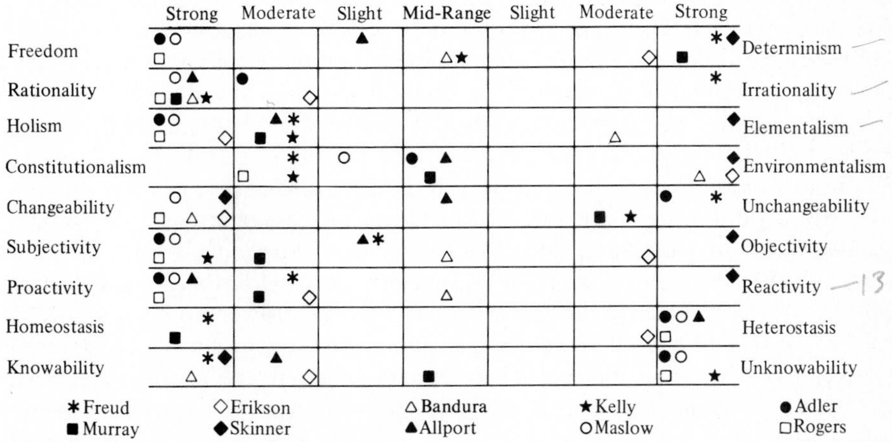

Figure 12-1 An overview of the ten theorists' positions on the nine basic assumptions concerning human nature.

theorist's basic assumptions about human nature simultaneously broaden and narrow her or his perspective on personality. The assumptions are mutually exclusive—belief in and acceptance of both poles on a continuum is impossible. As an illustration, consider the freedom–determinism assumption. Any theorist who assumes the free-will position will, by definition, examine and emphasize those aspects of human functioning that suggest that we are indeed free, e.g., our highly developed thinking capacities allow us to see alternatives and thus make choices. But this freedom assumption coupled with the sheer creativity of a personality theorist is apt to lead her or him farther afield—very probably in new directions and to undreamt-of-heights (in terms of previous personality theorizing)—as she or he searches for and finally manifests the freedom assumption in an ultimate theoretical account of personality.

Thus, one's perspective on personality has been significantly broadened by the assumption of freedom. The theorist has been prompted to explore in detail explicit areas of human functioning and to invent theoretical concepts to describe and explain them. Yet, simultaneously, one's perspective has also been narrowed. The theorist has not examined those areas of human behavior that are more readily explicable in deterministic terms (at least as closely as a deterministically oriented theorist would examine them), e.g., behaviors which appear to be physiologically determined, or those that are the products of one's conditioning history. Insofar as these are also aspects of human behavior, the theorist has ignored some considerations or at least downplayed their importance. The freedom assumption, then, has guided the personologist down certain theoretical paths, opening his or her eyes to some aspects of human behavior that might otherwise not have been seen, while, at the same time, producing theoretical "blind spots" about some areas of human psychological makeup.

Of course, this is also true of a theorist who begins by assuming a *deterministic* position. This assumption will take her or him down other theoretical pathways, emphasizing those aspects of behavior which appear to be deterministically based and ignoring or downplaying human actions that might reflect underlying freedom. The freedom–determinism assumption is only one of nine discussed in this book. It is our contention that the other eight basic assumptions function in precisely the same way in theory construction. While each may be more or less potent in a given theorist's thinking (e.g., subjectivity–objectivity is very important in the theories of Rogers and Skinner and not so significant in the positions of Allport and Erikson), all nine assumptions have the potential to influence a theory.

Still a third issue is whether or not these basic assumptions about human nature are the sole influences upon theory building. Bluntly put, *of course not.* A personologist's basic assumptions constantly interact with a host of other influences while a theory is constructed. Factors other than basic assumptions which obviously can influence one's thinking are the historical period in which one lives, one's society, what is known in psychology and other disciplines at the time, what one knows about psychology and other disciplines at the time, degree of academic training and other exposure to the world of ideas, thinking of one's professors, interaction with one's colleagues (and, in some instances, clients or patients), and, more generally, one's total, individual life experiences. In brief, it cannot be forgotten that personality theorists are human beings engaged in the task of theorizing about human beings. Like the rest of us, their thinking is influenced by many forces.

As an illustration of this *interactive effect,* again consider the freedom–determinism assumption. Both Freud and Skinner are staunch determinists; they agree completely that all human actions are utterly and totally determined, with no such possibility as free choice. But on the question of precisely what determines human behavior, these two theorists differ sharply, because the deterministic assumption is *interacting* with other sources of influence in each man's life. Freud, for example, was trained as a physician, was heavily influenced by European clinical medicine (discussed in Chapter 1), was living in a time and a society that repressed sexual expression, and treated patients for a living. Thus, he was led to look *within* man for behavioral determinants, to a biological kind of theoretical construct, to some locus of causality which his patients were unaware of in themselves, to that which was utterly bound up with the sexuality that his patients could not express in their daily lives and that troubled them so. The *id,* in all its biological, unconscious, and sexual power and glory, was the end result of Freud's search for the behavioral determinant.

In sharp contrast, B. F. Skinner, who showed a preference for "gadgets" even in his younger days (recall his biographical sketch), was academically nurtured on the brass instrumentation, rigor, animal interests, preoccupation with the learning process, and wholehearted environmentalism of American behaviorism (also discussed in Chapter 1 as a historical influence on personality theory). Skinner has earned his living as an academic psychologist in laboratories, working with animal and human subjects, inventing and building ingenious experimental devices, designing and carrying out experiments on the learning process, and, in general, manipulating environmental variables. Quite naturally, then, it is not surprising that Skinner would look *outside* the person for behavioral determinants. Obviously he has succeeded admirably in finding them in the environment in terms of his central and well-developed theoretical concept of *reinforcement.*

A similar case could be made for the positions of Maslow and Rogers on the freedom assumption. While both theorists basically agree that man is free, each presents a somewhat different picture of how that freedom manifests itself in human behavior (although the differences here are not nearly so dramatic as those between Freud and Skinner). Maslow viewed human freedom as an integral aspect of man's attempt to climb the motivational need ladder toward self-actualization; Rogers found it in a professional lifetime of therapy hours spent with his clients, observing and facilitating their ongoing struggle to grow as human beings. In sum, when one envisions the position of a given theorist on *all nine basic assumptions* as they continually interact with the theorist's individual life experiences, one begins to grasp what really goes into the construction of a personality theory. This view in no way diminishes the important role of basic assumptions about human nature in theory building; it merely places these assumptions in proper perspective.

One final question remains: what will be the role of these basic assumptions in the personality psychology of the future? Our somewhat cautious answer is that because they deal with the fundamental issue of *what humanity is,* their role will remain unchanged. Basic assumptions about the nature of human beings will remain the foundation of all future theories of personality, regardless of their specific content. What will change, though, are the theorists, the state of knowledge in psychology and other disciplines, and the world. New theorists will emerge, bringing their unique personalities and experiences to bear on these assumptions. Most certainly, they will glean new knowledge about human behavior from psychology and other relevant disciplines. And, as Heraclitus noted centuries ago, the world can be expected to continue to change. What directions the changes will take and precisely how they will affect the personality psychology of the future cannot be predicted here. (Psychologists, much like meteorologists, are infinitely better at explaining what has already happened than what will happen in the future.) It is a safe bet, however, that changed world conditions will have an impact on personality theory simply because they have done so in the past. The effect of World War I on Freud's theorizing about aggression is but one example. In brief, then, basic assumptions about human nature will have new minds, new knowledge, and a new world with which to interact. They will, nonetheless, continue to be the bedrock of future personality psychology.

Let us now examine our ten personality theories from yet another perspective.

EVALUATION OF PERSONALITY THEORIES: THE SCIENTIFIC BAROMETERS OF SUCCESS

In Chapter 1 we offered six major criteria for evaluating theories of personality, the "scientific barometers" of success in personological theory, if you will. Now that we have completed our study of the ten theories presented in this volume, it seems only fitting that we consider how each has fared with respect to these criteria. No attempt at exhaustive analysis will be made here. Instead, the focus will center upon a brief comparison of our theories on each criterion. In this way, the reader should be able to compare and contrast the current status of each theory previously studied (see Figure 12-2).

Verifiability

The criterion of verifiability requires that a theory contain concepts that are clearly and explicitly defined, logically related to one another, and amenable to empirical validation. The basic question here is: Are the theory's concepts capable of being empirically investigated? While personality theories generally do not fare very well in this regard, there are individual differences among them. For our purposes, any personality theory can be placed in one of three broad categories on this criterion (or any of the remaining five criteria): *high,* meaning that the theory generally meets the criterion well; *moderate,* meaning that the theory meets the criterion to some reasonable degree; and *low,* meaning that the theory generally fails to meet the criterion (see Figure 12-2).

Given this overall structure, the positions of Skinner, Bandura, and Rogers can be rated as high on verifiability. Skinner is particularly strong here, as his concepts and their relationships to one another are precisely defined and his position has

	Low	Moderate	High
Verifiability	Freud Maslow Adler Erikson Allport	Murray Kelly	Skinner Bandura Rogers
Heuristic value	Erikson Allport Kelly Maslow	Adler Murray	Freud Skinner Bandura Rogers
Internal consistency		Freud Allport	Adler Bandura Erikson Kelly Murray Maslow Skinner Rogers
Parsimony	Murray	Freud	Adler Allport Erikson Kelly Skinner Maslow Bandura Rogers
Comprehensiveness		Erikson Allport Murray Kelly Skinner Maslow Bandura Rogers	Freud Adler
Functional significance	Murray Allport Kelly	Adler Erikson Bandura	Freud Skinner Maslow Rogers

Figure 12-2 The positions of personality theorists on the six major criteria for evaluating theories of personality. (A designation of "high" indicates that the theory in question generally meets the criterion in question.)

generated a wealth of empirical data. While Bandura's theory has been criticized on the grounds of verifiability (e.g., Skinner, 1974), his concepts have nonetheless generated an impressive amount of empirical evidence to support them. And Rogers has formulated theoretical concepts designed to explain a complex set of phenomena (e.g., self, personality growth, how psychotherapy affects change in people), concepts which have clearly led to much empirical testing and support.

Satisfying the verifiability criterion to a moderate degree are the positions of Murray and Kelly. Murray's theoretical concepts have been sparsely tested, though the reasons for this are unclear. While some maintain that the fault lies within the theory itself (e.g., Hall and Lindzey, 1978), others argue convincingly that the intellectual climate within personological research militates against the kind of methods needed to test Murray's concepts (Epstein, 1979). A similar case could be made for Kelly; his theory is framed explicitly and hypotheses could easily be generated and tested from it. That they haven't been may reflect a shortcoming in the personality field as much as in the theory itself.

The positions of Freud, Adler, Erikson, Allport, and Maslow must be judged low on the verifiability criterion. Enlightening as these theorists may seem, each is composed of global constructs (e.g., Freud's death instincts, Adler's creative self, Erikson's epigenetic principle, Allport's proprium, Maslow's metaneeds) lacking operational specificity, so empirical testing is currently difficult if not impossible. In defense of these theorists, it should be recognized that they are attempting to grapple with an exceedingly complex phenomenon, i.e., the nature of the human being. Nonetheless, at this juncture, their basic concepts are such that we cannot empirically evaluate their overall merits.

Heuristic Value

The criterion of heuristic value refers to the degree to which a theory directly stimulates research. We do not, then, use this criterion in a global sense to address the question of how well a theory may stimulate people's thinking; rather, it is confined to the stimulation of new empirical research.

The theories of Freud, Skinner, Bandura, and Rogers fare quite well on the criterion of heuristic value. Although many studies relating to Freud's theory may not represent precise tests of his concepts (due to the low verifiability of the theory), there are nonetheless a large number of such studies within psychology as well as other disciplines (e.g., sociology, political science, anthropology). As noted earlier, Skinner's concepts are precisely defined and quite testable. And well they have been—there are entire psychological journals devoted to publishing empirical work related to Skinner's position. Likewise, Bandura's theory has stimulated a wealth of research in a variety of areas (e.g., sex-role development, helping behavior, social skills), employing subjects in widely different age groups. And Rogers' theory has also generated much research, especially in the realm of psychotherapy, with Rogers himself pioneering empirical work in this domain. His thinking has also led to considerable research on the self-concept.

The positions of Adler and Murray can be judged as moderate on this criterion. In both cases there has been little direct empirical testing of concepts, but selected aspects of each theory have led to a considerable body of research. In Adler's case, for example, there is the voluminous literature on birth order, while in Murray's it is nAchievement. In each instance, it is doubtful whether such a body of data would have come into existence without the related theoretical concepts serving as the initial impetus.

The theories of Erikson, Allport, Kelly, and Maslow fare poorly when measured by the yardstick of heuristic value. This is not to say that these theories do not stimulate people's thinking, for they most certainly do. To illustrate, it is difficult to read Erikson without thinking about the direction of one's own life (psychosocial stages), or Allport without thinking about how one describes others (traits), or Kelly without thinking about one's own thinking (constructs), or Maslow without thinking about one's fulfillment in life (self-actualization). Yet the fact remains that each of these positions has yet to inspire much empirical research. Regardless of their other considerable merits, then, these theories presently reflect low heuristic value.

Internal Consistency

Internal consistency means that a personality theory should not contradict itself—it should account for whatever phenomena it encompasses in an internally consistent fashion. As we noted in Chapter 1, theories of personality generally do well on this measure.

More specifically, the theories of Adler, Erikson, Murray, Skinner, Bandura,

Kelly, Maslow, and Rogers can be judged as high on this criterion. Each of these theorists' positions is based on a particular set of assumptions about human nature, leading to a network of theoretical concepts which account for human behavior in an internally consistent way. One may disagree with the explanation of behavior provided by any of these theories, while acknowledging that the explanation is nonetheless consistent with other concepts within the system.

Of the various theories presented in this book, Freud's and Allport's seem to fall a bit short on this criterion; their positions are best judged as moderate on internal consistency. In the case of Freud, it is widely recognized that the postdictive nature of the theory allows for essentially opposite behaviors to be accounted for by the same concept or the same behavior to be explained by different concepts, e.g., is always showing up on time for your analyst's appointment a sign of good motivation for therapeutic progress or an indication of compulsiveness rooted in the anal stage of development? Such explanatory problems suggest less than ideal internal consistency. In Allport's case, the emphasis on the idiographic approach suggests that a set of common traits to account for people's behavior has yet to be specified. This problem, coupled with the ambiguous relationship between traits and the proprium in the theory, renders it difficult to determine just how consistently human behavior can be accounted for from Allport's perspective. But neither of these theories could be said to be seriously deficient in this area, and indeed none of the positions presented in this text can be judged as low on internal consistency.

Parsimony

The criterion of parsimony highlights the notion that the preferred theoretical account of events is the one requiring the fewest number of concepts—the fewer the concepts, the more parsimonious the theory. The idea of parsimony also includes simplicity—the simpler the theoretical account, the more parsimonious the theory. A parsimonious theory, then, is lean in both the number and the unnecessary complexity of concepts required to account for relevant phenomena—in this case, personality. Given the nature and utter complexity of the phenomena with which our ten theorists are attempting to grapple, their theories come off rather well on this criterion.

More specifically, the positions of Adler, Erikson, Skinner, Bandura, Allport, Kelly, Maslow, and Rogers can be judged as high on the parsimony criterion. Adler's theory is extremely parsimonious in the sense that a limited number of core concepts support the entire theoretical system. Likewise with Erikson: personality is depicted in terms of psychosocial crises and eight major stages of development. Skinner too has a modest number of concepts, with a particular strength resulting from the fact that they all are anchored firmly to observable behavior. In Bandura's system, there are again comparatively few concepts, and these for the most part appear well-related to the social-learning phenomena that he is attempting to explain. And in Allport's theory, there are a relatively few, mostly straightforward, concepts which, with the possible exception of the proprium, do not seem unnecessarily complex for describing personality functioning. Kelly's theory too ranks high on parsimony, with his basic notion of constructs elegantly fitting the cognitive realm he addresses. Likewise with Maslow: his motivational hierarchy concepts, while few in number, seem to fit the complexities of human motivation without being too abstract. Finally, Rogers' theory seems almost too parsimonious, subsuming all motives under one master motive (the actualizing tendency) and all possible defensive strategies under two basic defenses (perceptual distortion and denial); nonetheless, his position satisfies the parsimony criterion.

Freud's theory ranks moderate on parsimony. There is little problem with the number of concepts he advances, with some indeed being especially parsimonious and potent for understanding personality dynamics, e.g., id-ego-superego interactions. Yet in the current psychological *Zeitgeist,* certain of Freud's concepts seem too complex and removed from the everyday behavior he attempts to explain, e.g., the concept of death instincts. Finally, Murray must be rated low on the parsimony criterion because of the sheer number of concepts and classifications he employs. While admittedly trying to account for very complex phenomena, Murray has generated a lengthy catalog of needs (twelve viscerogenic and twenty-eight psychogenic), an extensive system of classifying needs, and an exhaustive list of press. Whatever its other merits may be, such a personality theory falls short on parsimony.

Comprehensiveness

Comprehensiveness refers to the range and diversity of phenomena encompassed by a theory—the more comprehensive a personality theory, the more behavioral ground it covers. Of course, to be selected for inclusion in this book, a theory had to be at least reasonably comprehensive. So the dice are already loaded against theories too low on this criterion. And yet for the most part we do not presently have personality theories that squarely address all significant aspects of human functioning. One reason for this state of affairs is the basic modus operandi of the theorists: a theorist's basic assumptions about human nature partially lead him or her to focus on certain aspects of human behavior while downplaying or even neglecting others. The result is that most personality theories have a "focus of convenience" (Kelly's term), an area of human behavior which they account for very well. A related effect is that most theories lack comprehensiveness, since they do not adequately address areas of behavior removed from their focus of convenience.

Nonetheless, the positions of Freud and Adler can be rated high on the criterion of comprehensiveness. Freud's theory is indeed extraordinary in this respect, covering as it does an enormous range and diversity of behavioral phenomena, e.g., psychological disorders, dreams, humor, unconscious motivation, death, creativity, slips of the tongue and pen, forgetfulness, marriage, incest, myths and fairy tales, war, and social taboos. Adler's theory practically rivals Freud's in this respect, encompassing a broad range of phenomena such as psychological disorders, family relationships, mental health, and the numerous ways in which political, educational, and religious institutions affect personality development.

Ranking moderate on the comprehensiveness criterion are the remaining eight theorists. To illustrate, although Erikson's concepts have been applied to diverse phenomena, his focus on ego development necessarily limits the range of his theory. While Murray offers a comprehensive account of motivation, this is but one aspect (albeit an important one) of overall personality functioning. Skinner has deliberately emphasized the simple elements of behavior, and at first his position, grounded as it was in animal experimentation, was severely limited in scope. Over the years, however, Skinner's concepts have been developed and applied to wider areas of human behavior (e.g., behavior disorders, education, industry, prison systems); his position continues to grow in comprehensiveness. Bandura explains well the phenomena of observational learning and applies his concepts to a number of important areas (e.g., socialization, aggression), but surely there are realms of personality as yet unaddressed by his ideas. However, Bandura's is a theory that is still being developed, and we may reasonably expect increasing comprehensiveness in the future. Allport focuses on healthy functioning to the relative exclusion of psychopathology, and his descriptions of concepts are sometimes quite general (e.g., development of the proprium); his theory falls somewhat short on comprehensiveness in these respects. The thrust of Kelly's theory, in turn, is primarily cognitive, resulting in a rather intellectualized account of personality which highlights human rationality while bypassing other important behavioral areas, e.g., the developmental process. And Maslow's emphasis upon personal growth, while sorely needed in contemporary psychology, tends to steer his theory away from detailed accounts of behavior not clearly related to positive growth, e.g., types of abnormal behavior. Finally, Rogers' focus on the self-concept and the inner world of subjective experience leads him away from a consideration of objective factors in the external world and how these affect personality, e.g., a theory of learning.

Functional Significance

To people outside of psychology, there is probably no more relevant way to judge a personality theory than by how much it helps us to understand ourselves and others. The criterion of functional significance addresses exactly this issue, i.e., how useful a theory is in helping people (psychologists included) to understand everyday human behavior. And there seems to be a kind of circular relationship between functional significance and the "visibility" of a theory to laypersons. If a theory has functional significance, it tends to become known to laypersons; as it becomes more widely known (regardless of its other scientific strengths or weaknesses), its functional significance both within and outside psychology seems to increase in turn.

The positions of Freud, Skinner, Maslow, and Rogers rank high on the criterion of functional significance. Freud's theory is remarkable in this respect. Freudian concepts (e.g., repression, unconscious motivation, Oedipus conflict) have become part of the vocabulary of educated laypersons, countless individuals have been affected by some form of psychoanalytically based therapy, Freudian theory has been applied to human behavior in many different disciplines (e.g., anthropology, history, literature), and psychoanalysis has reshaped our image of human nature in the twentieth century. Likewise, Skinner's concepts have wide applicability, with the prospect of affecting all society (Skinner, 1971); presently the most obvious areas of application are psychopathology and education. Maslow's humanistic psychology is the theoretical root of the enormous interest in personal growth today; his views are widely employed in many contemporary counseling and business management programs. And like Maslow, Rogers has contributed more than his share to the personal growth movement (e.g., encounter groups); his ideas have been applied to such diverse areas as psychotherapy, education, administration, family relationships, and leadership (Rogers, 1977).

Ranking moderate on functional significance are the positions of Adler, Erikson, and Bandura. Adler constructed a very practical theory of personality— yet, especially when compared with Freud's position, his concepts have not had great impact outside the realms of psychotherapy and parent-child relationships. Erikson's ideas cut across many disciplines, but his theory of psychosocial stages has not enjoyed enormous practical influence, except within developmental psychology and education. Bandura's theory has made important inroads in the areas of psychotherapy and aggression, but his is a position which is still expanding and has yet to reach its full potential in terms of applied value.

The positions of Murray, Allport, and Kelly must be judged low on the criterion of functional significance. Outside of selected psychological tests (e.g., the TAT), Murray's concepts have had little clinical utility, and his theory is not presently well known or applied outside the context of personality psychology. While some of Allport's concepts seem enormously practical (e.g., traits), they have actually had little applied impact either within or outside psychology. Likewise with Kelly: intriguing and novel as his concepts are, they have had no widespread effects within clinical psychology or otherwise. One has the haunting feeling in the case of Kelly, however, that his ideas *could* have much more practical impact if only more people within psychology were made keenly aware of them.

Let us now consider where personality psychology is likely to go in the future.

COMING OF AGE IN PERSONOLOGY

The development of personology as a bona fide scientific discipline belongs to the twentieth century (the origins of the discipline are much older, of course). Consider Figure 12-3. With the exception of Freudian, Adlerian, and a few notable Freudian-derivative theories (e.g., Jungian and Frommian), all of which blossomed during the first third of this century, it is only within the last forty or so years that major personality theories have emerged. Also note that as of this writing four of the theorists considered in this book are still contributing to personality psychology and three of the remaining six died after 1965. It is obvious, then, that personology is a very young field of inquiry. But with age, it is hoped, comes wisdom. In but four decades, personality psychology has "come of age" by establishing itself as a respectable and fruitful area of study. No doubt the flourishing activity in personology points toward a growing realization that humanity's most vital problems are *within;* they concern the person and his or her relationships to others. Indeed, understanding the way in which human beings function has become a precondition for the survival of our species. Gardner Murphy eloquently expressed the real significance of the study of personality for our lives when he wrote:

> Lack of knowledge about human beings is not a trivial, but a major threat to life. Lack of knowledge about personality is perhaps the central core of the issue that is

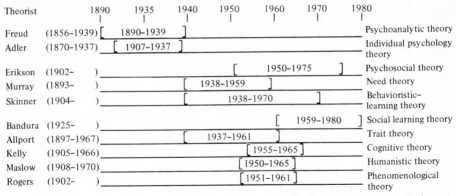

Figure 12-3 Historical period during which personality theory was constructed.

most relevant for us today; the issue of understanding what human beings can become under a new set of social arrangements (Norbeck, Price-Williams, and McCord, 1968, p. 38).

This statement, written more than a decade ago, seems more applicable than ever.

The Heart of the Matter

What, then, can be anticipated in the way of future developments in personality theory? What are the new and challenging frontiers for the personality theorist of tomorrow? Broadly speaking, whatever the formal shortcomings and deficiencies of the ten theories presented in this book, we believe that the ideas and insights embedded within them will have a decisive impact upon future conceptions of human behavior. In other words, *theoretical progress in the realm of personality will be based squarely on the contributions of past and present personologists.* This does not mean that future theories will be carbon copies of existing ones. On the contrary, as the short history of personology has disclosed, there is virtually no limit to the diversity of theoretical models of humanity that personologists can invent! There are as many possible conceptions of human nature as there are minds to conceive them. However, while personality theories, like fads, may come and go, the issues and problems with which our theorists have struggled will continue to attract serious attention.

The question that one is apt to ask next is, what are the critical and persisting issues in personality theory? Basically, they can be enumerated in terms of eight global questions: (1) How does the human personality *develop?* (2) What *motivates* human behavior? (3) How does a person come to *think* and *know* about the self and the environment? (4) What is the nature of human *social* life? (5) What makes each person *unique?* (6) What are the principal determinants of personality *disturbance?* (7) What are the defining characteristics of the psychologically *healthy* adult? (8) Why the direction of *competence* and *adaptation* for some people and *incompetence* and *disorder* for others? These are enormously broad and complex questions and their answers may never be known with certainty. Yet the necessity to know and understand more about each will be highly relevant to charting the future course of personality theorizing. This, then, returns us to our original premise, namely, that theorists of the future will be guided by the rich intellectual heritage of their predecessors. It is this belief that makes the study of Freud, Adler, Erikson, Murray, Skinner, Bandura, Allport, Kelly, Maslow, and Rogers worthwhile. Each in his own way has contributed something significant to the understanding of the experiences and events of our daily lives.

The Present in the Future

In this book we have presented illustrative studies bearing upon the empirical validity of various conceptions of personality. Our objective in doing so was to convince the reader that in the final analysis a theory's most important scientific function is to stimulate or generate new research. To perform this function successfully, a theory must not only be capable of aiding us in the comprehension of existing knowledge but must also be a fertile source of hypotheses that will lead to the discovery of new knowledge—in other words, the criterion of heuristic value discussed earlier. Thus, if personality theories are to be more than mere armchair speculations about human behavior, we must be able to convert them into testable form and study them empirically. This is what constitutes the essence of science, differentiating it from the simple assertion of opinions or beliefs. It is also what in our judgment will determine the *ultimate scientific significance* of current theories of personality. In short, critical scrutiny is not just a technical amenity—it is crucially important to establishing the validity of theoretical views of human behavior.

   This brings us to another point. Any theory of personality is merely a tentative statement that needs constant modification based on evidence gained from the testing of its offspring hypotheses. It must be so constructed that it can accommodate new empirical data. Accordingly, there may come a time in the life of any personality theory when it loses its elasticity and becomes obsolete. When our shoes no longer perform their function, we discard them for a new pair. Or if we gain weight, we buy a new belt. In the same way, a theory must be considered ultimately expendable, to be cast aside when it ceases to perform its function of incorporating new discoveries about human behavior. In sum, personality theories must be self-corrective in the light of new evidence.

   Despite the obvious importance of understanding existing theories, one can hope that personality psychology will eventually develop a set of theoretical constructs more adequate than the present ones—constructs which are more amenable to empirical test. Personology has come a long way since Freud, but no one can claim that human behavior is knowable or that all new lines of thought and research have been exhausted. The following section outlines some tentative notions on the creative impetus for emerging theories of human behavior.

NEW FRONTIERS IN PERSONALITY RESEARCH

What sorts of problems and issues are likely to capture the attention of future personological investigators? Without appearing too prophetic, we suggest that the agenda of future work will demand a high priority of serious inquiry into seven general problem areas. Each area, in our judgment, will require imaginative and critical study if our conceptions of personality are to be deepened and enriched.

1 Study of cognitive processes and their relationship to other aspects of psychological functioning With the exceptions of Kelly and Bandura, the personality theorists discussed in this text have almost totally disregarded the role of cognitive processes in understanding human functioning. Freud, for instance, viewed human nature primarily in terms of early childhood experiences and unconscious motivation. Skinner, on the other hand, treats personality as if it involves only the relationship between overt behavior and environmental reinforcement contingencies. Although the approaches of Adler, Erikson, Murray, Allport, Rogers, and Maslow all reveal an emphasis on internal variables, none has addressed himself to the cognitive aspects of personality. As psychology has developed, however, it has become apparent to students of personality that cognition represents an enormously important component of human functioning. Accordingly, recent years have seen extensive and significant developments in cognitive personality theory and research. In fact, it could be said that the study of how we think (cognitive processes or information processing) virtually dominates the field today—not just personology, but all psychology. In the words of one psychologist, the trend of the 1950s and 1960s has become something of a "revolution . . . in the sense that cognitive processes have become a very popular topic (Mahoney, 1977, p. 5)." This revolution is no less apparent in clinical psychology, where "cognitive therapies" are rapidly becoming among the most popular (Beck, 1976).

George Kelly has played a large part in the advancement of a cognitive perspective in contemporary psychology. He deserves special credit and gratitude from psychologists for directing them to the rational and intellectual aspects of psychological functioning. Granting the importance of Kelly's contributions, Albert Bandura's "cognitive social-learning theory" has proven itself to be an even more important catalyst for the emergence of a cognitive orientation in personology; as a result of his success in demonstrating that the key to observational learning is the human capacity to represent observed behavior symbolically, personologists are now beginning to think of human beings as seeking information, coding it, organizing it, retrieving it, and using it functionally.

Why this dramatic shift in the attention of psychologists of varied fields to the role of cognitive-symbolic processes in human affairs? Pervin (1978) suggests at least three reasons. First, it has become increasingly evident to psychologists that the stimulus-response reinforcement model of behavior can not adequately explain all the data flowing from research on the learning process. Specifically, it has been shown that organisms often learn in the absence of reinforcement as well as fail to learn in the presence of reinforcement. Moreover, the learning processes of an adult human are not identical to those of a rat, a rhesus monkey, or a child. Nor are they merely more complex processes. Pervin writes: "The ability to use symbols and think abstractly brings into play learning processes that are different in kind and not just in degree from those demonstrated by simpler organisms" (1978, p. 118).

A second reason for the emergence of a cognitive orientation in psychology is the influence of other thinkers in the field. Of particular importance has been the seminal work of the Swiss biologist-psychologist Jean Piaget (1970) with his emphasis on development of cognitive structure in the child. Piaget theorizes that the child's intellectual growth, competence, and ability to make moral judgments about behavior all follow a prescribed developmental sequence. At the same time, Piaget maintains that the child is constantly processing information from the environment, that is, assimilating input from the environment to fit its preexisting structures as well as changing these structures in accordance with new information from the environment.

Despite the significant influence of these factors, Pervin (1978) believes that they are of minor importance compared with the influence of a third factor—computers:

> The advent of computers presented psychologists with a new model of man—man the computer. Not a simple telephone switchboard but a system capable of processing many bits of information according to highly complex rules. Here we have the effect of a technological change upon thinking in the field of psychology. Information processing became a key concept. Computers suggested new kinds of thought processes that might be investigated and in turn were used for the study of these processes (Pervin, 1978, p. 119).

In sum, using a computer model to represent the human mind has made it commonplace in psychology to talk about input, central mediating processes, output, feedback, and the like.

At the present time, the focus of personality research in relation to cognitive processes has to do with the different ways in which individuals process information and the relationship between such processes and other aspects of psychological functioning. Of particular interest to personality researchers has been the concept of *cognitive styles.* A cognitive style is another way of conceptualizing the hierarchical organization of personality structure and dynamics. As such, it incorporates the individual's self-concept, personal belief system, world view, typical coping responses, and ideals. Stated differently, a cognitive style refers to an individual's mode and accuracy of perception, style of thinking, goal-directed behavior, and focus of attention. A cognitive style also organizes a person's emotional experience —what will arouse emotion, the kinds of emotions a person is likely to have, their intensity, and how he or she copes with them.

Much of the work on cognitive styles has been an outgrowth of the thinking of Kelly, who, as you will recall, formulated a theory of personality emphasizing how people construe or interpret the world around them. Here we will briefly consider one type of cognitive style so as to illustrate this trend in personology: *field independence* versus *field dependence.* While this is by no means the only cognitive style that has been identified and studied by personologists, it does serve as an example of the present emphasis accorded the role of cognition in understanding human behavior.

The study of field independence versus field dependence, an illustration of stylistic differences in cognitive functioning, is the product of many years of research by Herman Witkin and his associates (Witkin, Moore, Goodenough, and Cox, 1977). In its barest outline, this cognitive style has to do with individual differences in perceiving the upright in space and with the relation of perceptual orientation to the overall psychological organization of the individual. More directly, the construct "field independence versus field dependence," as formulated by Witkin, refers to differences in the ability to deal with a given field analytically or to perceive a part of the field independent of its surroundings. Let us illustrate.

Witkin systematically observed subjects' behavior in a perceptual task known as the *rod-and-frame test*. In this test, the subject sits in a completely darkened room and observes a luminous square frame surrounding a movable luminous rod. The experimenter tilts both the frame and rod to a variety of angles away from true vertical, and the subject's task is to adjust the movable rod to a position that he or she perceives to be upright. To bring the position of the rod back to true vertical, the subject must disregard the tilt of the field (frame) and rely on cues from his or her body position. This is an extremely difficult task to perform in the context in which it must be done: the only visual field cues available to the subject are the rod and frame; there are no other cues to help determine the true vertical position of the rod. Thus, there are only two ways of responding to this perceptual task. Either subjects rely on the visual cues supplied by the surrounding luminous frame or they perform the task independent of it (relying on body cues). Subjects whose perception of the vertical has been determined by the surrounding visual field (frame) are called *field dependent*. By contrast, subjects who can adjust the rod close to true vertical are capable of functioning independent of the surrounding field. They are able to concentrate on the rod and its relation to their own body position and are thus called *field independent*.

Witkin's research on how visual cues and bodily sensation cues influence perception of the upright has been linked to a variety of personality characteristics. The research literature on this topic—the relation of perception to other aspects of personality—is voluminous. Here we shall simply summarize some of the major personality differences between field-dependent and field-independent persons. First, persons with a field-dependent cognitive style tend to be anxious, to lack self-insight, to experience inferiority feelings, and to have a low evaluation of their body. Such persons are also prone to repress their feelings and impulses, particularly sexual and aggressive ones. Field-independent persons, by contrast, tend to express their feelings and impulses in a relatively controlled manner, have a lower level of anxiety, and a higher sense of self-esteem. Such persons also display greater tolerance for ambiguity, more willingness to take risks, and greater creativity. Second, field-dependent persons tend to be passive with respect to their environment. For example, they are unable to function independent of their environment, find it difficult to initiate tasks on their own, and are prone to change their views on social issues in the direction of the attitudes of authority figures. On the other hand, field-dependent persons tend to express an active coping in dealing with their environment. They are better able to initiate, organize, and direct activities on their own, and strive to achieve mastery and control over their environments. Third,

Witkin reports that women at all ages are more field-dependent than men, that is, they show more passive acceptance of the environment and are less responsive to bodily experience. This finding is not too surprising considering the fact that in our society women have been reinforced to be not only more dependent but also more conforming—to take the cues for their behavior from the environment rather than from themselves. Finally, although there is no difference in general learning ability or intelligence between field-dependent and field-independent persons, field-dependent persons tend to learn social material better than field-independent persons, while the reverse is true for nonsocial material. Furthermore, field-dependent persons prefer and do better in areas requiring social skills (e.g., counseling, social work, and teaching), whereas field-independent persons prefer and do better in areas that require analytical skills (e.g., engineering, mathematics, and science). Such differences have important implications for the type of career an individual may be suited for. On a broader scale, the body of research completed by Witkin and his associates points up the necessity of considering the role of cognitive as well as perceptual factors in human behavior. The research is of particular interest to personologists because of the attention it gives to the relationship between individual differences in cognitive style and mode of adjustment to the world.

As noted previously, the cognitive trend is the most significant development in contemporary personality theory and research. Indeed, one of the most striking aspects of the cognitive "revolution" has been its pervasiveness. Virtually no area of human behavior has escaped the speculation of possible cognitive influence. Cognitive processes have been implicated in such diverse areas as anxiety, depression, obesity, speech disorders, sexuality, art, and athletic performance. Nonetheless, a cognitive approach to personality is not without its drawbacks. Most significantly, there has yet been no systematic theoretical structure developed from this point of view. The development of a formalized theory is perhaps the most serious challenge facing today's cognitive "revolutionaries." A second major deficit at present involves what may be an inadequate terminology for scientific description. Mahoney, for example, asks: "What is a cognition? What differentiates a cognitive process from a noncognitive one? What is the difference between a process, a construct, and an event? (1977, p. 9)." Of course, fuzzy answers to these questions do not necessarily jeopardize the promise of a cognitive perspective. Behaviorists have yet to offer precise definitions of stimulus and response, but this has not appreciably slowed their efforts to study behavior. However, some consensus on terminology would certainly be useful to cognitive researchers.

Definitional problems do not exhaust the set of pitfalls which might impede the advancement of cognitive research. Mahoney, for instance, notes that at present there are inadequate tools for assessing cognitive phenomena. He also notes that not much is known about the impact of cognitive factors on other categories of experience (behaviors, emotions, etc). Still another task facing a cognitive perspective has to do with the identification of variables that influence the development, maintenance, and change of particular cognitive styles. It should be emphasized, however, that these concerns are raised in a constructive spirit, one which derives from a belief that our knowledge of the influence of cognition on other aspects of human behavior depends upon continued empirical inquiry. Mahoney states the matter this way: "If the cognitive-learning perspective continues to survive critical scrutiny, it may well mark the development of a new and challenging era in personality psychology (1977, p. 12)." In brief, then, the cognitive perspective seems to offer many lucrative assets. It combines an appreciation for both organismic (internal) and environmental factors and addresses the challenge of untangling their relationships. Moreover, it is a comprehensive approach that recognizes the awesome complexity of our subject matter.

2 *Study of especially productive, talented, and creative persons* For all practical purposes, the formal study of personality had its beginnings in Freud's concern with the causes and treatment of pathological behavior. The history of personological inquiry, therefore, reflects a strong emphasis on behavioral phenomena observed most readily in psychotherapeutic situations. Even today the study of personality remains closely tied to the investigation of psychologically disturbed persons. But times are changing, and so are the concerns and interests of personologists. In recent years, there has been a growing awareness that personology should not be exclusively preoccupied with pathological or defensive aspects of human functioning. Consequently, the emphasis previously accorded to pathology-centered problems has given way to the study of the characteristics of people who behave with unusual effectiveness. The "human potential movement" is clearly one factor that has drawn attention to the study of well-functioning persons, the objective of which is to identify and define the healthy personality. The emphasis is not so much on healing childhood-related conflicts and past emotional wounds as on releasing hidden reservoirs of talent, creativity, energy, and motivation. The focus is on what a person *can become,* not what she or he has been in the past or is now in the present.

The best example of this approach is the work of Maslow (Chapter 10), who based his humanistic theory of personality on the study of particularly well-functioning individuals. His focus on "self-actualizers" is centrally important because it established a vision of what humanity is and can be. In turn, this has prompted an increased volume of empirical work on creativity, competence motivation, empathy, positive affective states, values, self-esteem, self-realization, and a host of other psychological properties associated with exceptionally productive and integrative human activities (e.g., Helson and Crutchfield, 1970; MacKinnon, 1965; Tasman, 1976; Lewis, Beavers, Gossett, and Phillips, 1976). It seems reasonable to expect that the psychological study of unusually talented and gifted individuals will increase dramatically during the final decades of the twentieth century. This effort will lead to an inquiry into our basic nature and potentialities; our intellectual, emotional, and social competencies; our ways of coping with life stress and what happens when "things go wrong"; and the psychological resources available to us for personal growth and change.

In the years ahead, interest in growth psychology will by no means be confined to the study of well-functioning people. Of equal importance, too, will be the type of world we construct for ourselves. As Maslow has dramatically summarized the issue:

The equally Big Problem as urgent as the one I have already mentioned is to make the Good Society. There is a kind of feedback between the Good Society and the Good Person. They need each other, they are the sine qua non to each other. I wave aside the problem of which comes first. It is quite clear that they develop simultaneously and in tandem. It would in any case be impossible to achieve either one without the other (1969, p. 732).

Clearly, the chief message of Maslow's statement is that the quest for personal growth will greatly depend upon our ability to create a future society in which each individual has maximal opportunities for realizing her or his potentialities and living a meaningful and fulfilling life. Accordingly, it seems reasonable to predict that personologists will devote attention to the "sociology" of self-actualization, emphasizing the relationship between what constitutes healthy personality and the cultural context which may contribute to human fulfillment.

3 Study of the physiological and neurological determinants and bases of personality In all likelihood, the contemporary scientific era will be recorded as the age of biology—and as a period in which advances in behavior genetics, biochemistry, psychopharmacology, and neurophysiology produced remarkable and decisive changes in the constructs and methods that guide inquiry in psychology in general. Yet, with the exceptions of Freud and Murray (the only two theorists in this text who truly acknowledge and stress the biological bases of behavior), personologists have almost totally ignored the need to study the neurophysiological and biochemical components of human personality. The role of hereditary factors in determining personality has also been disregarded by most personologists. As Gottesman aptly noted more than a decade ago: "It is remarkable that, in this day and age, enlightened students of man's behavior should entertain doubts, if not outright disbelief, about the appreciable genetic contribution to variation in certain human traits (1968, p. 59)."

Research-oriented personologists of the future can ill afford to neglect the tremendous upsurge of biological knowledge. It is those studies that focus on the reciprocal interaction of behavior with its biological base (made possible by powerful electrophysiological and other techniques) that will highlight future developments in the field of personality. In particular, studies concerned with how biochemical and neurophysiological processes are related to psychological functioning (cognition, imagery, affect, sensation) will merit attention. Additionally, investigators will need to provide a coherent account of the meaning of psychobiological facts in terms of the development, behavior, and experience of the individual (Glass, 1968; Penfield, 1975; Wilson, 1975). Such accounts will inevitably lead to new dimensions in personality theorizing. Progress in personality research will thus be made on two fronts: (1) empirical study of the biochemical underpinnings of behavior and (2) development of conceptual schemes which will more adequately explain the individual's biological heritage and how it affects many of the different forms of behavior commonly associated with the domain of personality (e.g., aggression, intelligence, and mating patterns).

4 Study of personality development in middle and old age About one-quarter of our lives is spent growing up and three-quarters growing old. It is ironic, therefore, that psychologists have devoted so much of their efforts to the study of childhood and adolescence. Two major assumptions underlie and partially explain this one-sided emphasis on the study of child and adolescent development: (1) selected adult behavior patterns are firmly established at an early age and (2) parental treatment during the initial years of life is a significant determinant of personality formation. The historical impact of Freudian psychosexual theory is clearly evident in both these assumptions. There are a number of other person-ological theories which also emphasize that adult personality is formed during childhood based on the nature of parent-child interactions (e.g., Adler, Murray, and Rogers each endorse this view to some extent). It is further evident that chil-dren and adolescents are more readily available and cooperative subjects for study than are older individuals; for example, college sophomores are easier to round up and test than are 45-year-old business executives. Nevertheless, several influential personologists, most notably Erikson, Allport, and Maslow, have convincingly argued that children and adolescents are "unfinished" personalities. Erikson deserves special credit for making us aware of the fact that the hurdles of personality development continue in some ways until death completes the life cycle. His formulation of a series of interlocking developmental crises encom-passing the individual's entire life span has forced psychologists to reexamine tra-ditional beliefs concerning personality growth and change in adult life.

Despite such recognition by Erikson and others, our current knowledge about adult personality development remains at a primitive stage (Barrett, 1972; Lifton, 1976). In particular, there is a paucity of information on the developmental changes in intellectual, emotional, and social competencies which accompany the aging process. This situation will not endure. For one thing, life expectancy tables indicate that the life span itself has increased markedly during the last two generations, so that there are literally more adults to study. Approximately one of every ten Americans today is over 65, and the proportion is increasing every year. In fact, projections indicate that the number of Americans who are 65 and over will rise to nearly 32 million by the year 2000 (in a total population of 260 million) and to a possible 55 million by 2030, when people born in the post World War II baby boom are over 65 (Aiken, 1978). Society has also assumed a more sensitive posture in relation to the care of senior citizens (e.g., nursing homes, complexes for the elderly), which makes these people more accessible to the scientist. Finally, adults will command greater study for no other reason than to discover how the "story of human development ends." Thus, future basic research in personality will surely broaden its base of inquiry to include large-scale longitudinal study of individuals between the ages of 30 and senescence (Birren, 1970; Schaie and Labouvie-Vief, 1974; Levinson et al., 1978; Vaillant, 1977). It would also seem reasonable to expect that the formulation of ever more complex and comprehensive conceptions of human development (especially in relation to the middle and late years of life) will be a consuming task for future theorists (Goulet and Baltes, 1970). This effort, in our view, will undoubtedly culminate in a dramatic broadening of the field presently labeled *life span developmental psychology* (Baltes and Schaie, 1973). A comprehensive account of the theoretical and empirical contributions stemming from this burgeoning field may be found in Newman and Newman, *Development through Life: A Psychosocial Approach* (1975).

5 *Study of self-regulatory processes and plans* The ability of human beings to control their own personal world has intrigued not only philosophers and psychologists but most laypersons as well. This presumed ability has taken on added importance in the context of today's chaotic world in which increasing numbers of people feel unable to shape the direction of their lives (Seligman, 1975). Accordingly, future study in personology will need to systematically examine the extent to which humans are capable of regulating their own behavior through self-imposed goals and self-produced consequences. Some progress in this direction has already been achieved as a result of Bandura's theoretical and research contributions (see Chapter 7). His effort to delineate the ways in which we regulate our behavior by imposing goals or standards on ourselves and then reacting to our performances with self-praise or self-criticism promises to greatly enrich our understanding of self-control. Future study will especially need to consider the kinds of "priority rules" a person uses to select behavioral strategies that will lead to salient goals. That is, personality investigators will need to study the kinds of plans an individual makes to control the complicated sequences of steps leading to the attainment of a long-range goal, e.g., how do people plan and organize their behavior so as to become doctors, lawyers, teachers, or senators? Attention will also be focused on the psychological processes that enable people to construct for themselves outlines of intended sequences of activities. What we envision, then, are longitudinal studies aimed at elucidating the way in which self-regulation and long-range planning come about and how they may be facilitated in relation to individual development. The practical applications of this research are obvious, considering that self-control is essential in order to get along with others and to meet personal goals.

6 *Study of the interaction of situational factors and personality variables and their relative contribution to behavior* As the individual chapters on each theorist made clear, it is customary for most personologists (Skinner and Bandura excluded) to assume that personality variables (i.e., intrapsychic factors) are responsible for and can adequately explain a person's behavior as it varies from one situation to another. Freud's psychoanalytic theory and Allport's trait theory are by far the most thorough in their development of this *person-oriented* view. These two theorists have unequivocally assumed that personality is composed of broad and stable characteristics that operate regularly across a wide variety of situations, that is, traits underlie the observed consistencies in each person's behavior. This one-sided emphasis on person variables also characterizes much of the work of Adler, Maslow, and Rogers. Kelly's position too focuses almost exclusively on person variables, since he is most concerned with understanding how a person's unique construct system influences overt behavior. In brief, the assumption shared by all of these theorists is that situational factors play only a minor role in the acquisition, maintenance, and modification of behavior. At the same time, it is obvious that people change their behavior in response to changing environmental conditions throughout their lives. A person who marries changes in several ways as a result of the new status; so does a person who divorces. Entrance into an occupation and the playing of roles—for example, student, employee, and parent—also bring changes in behavior. We are changed by educational experiences, the death of loved ones, and advancements in technology and science. On a broader scale, it is obvious that at least some portion of our behavior is governed by the sociocultural context in which we live (e.g., living in a sparsely populated setting versus living in a crowded, crime-ridden ghetto). Murray's emphasis on sociocultural determinants as a major source of behavioral variability illustrates this position. Erikson's theory, too, is concerned with the interconnectedness of self and environment, but his primary focus is within the person. Of course, Skinner's position is exclusively environmental in emphasis, to the point of recognizing no organismic or intra-psychic variables with which situational factors can interact! Finally, Bandura's position, while considerably less extreme than that of Skinner, also acknowl-edges the impact of situational variables upon behavior.

Although the *situation-oriented* view just cited may seem reasonable, perhaps even compelling, most personologists have largely ignored the situational com-ponents of behavior (Mischel, 1973; Pervin and Lewis, 1978). That is, they acknowledge theoretically the importance of situational factors, but in practice most of their attention has been focused on person variables. Recent developments in personology suggest a changing perspective. Inspired by work in cultural anthropology and sociology, personologists are beginning to display greater aware-ness and concern about the social determinants of personality structure and development and the contemporary social environment. Specifically, a growing number of investigators are beginning to adopt an *interactionist* approach to the study of human behavior (Bowers, 1973; Endler and Magnusson, 1976). This approach, best exemplified in Bandura's theory and research endeavors, focuses on the contributions of both person and situation variables in understanding person-ality functioning.

Within an interactionist framework, personality is construed as a hypothetical construct that "refers to the distinctive patterns of behavior (including thoughts and emotions) that characterize each individual's adaptation to the situations of his or her life (Mischel, 1976, p. 2)." More precisely, person variables represent the totality of past experiences encoded in the central nervous system which help an individual to cope effectively with the demands of his or her current situation. Situational variables, on the other hand, represent the environmental conditions that confront an individual and affect her or him in some appreciable way. The ensuing reaction may range from a thought or affective response to an overt behavior of some kind. From an interactionist perspective, then, a person is an active, thinking organism with the capacity to reinterpret the flow of incoming stimuli in light of his or her past experiences. A person is seen as actively transacting with the environment, i.e., she or he is influenced by the environment, but also influences it.

An interactionist approach to the study of personality is seen by many as providing the best means for capitalizing upon the strengths of various theoretical positions while eliminating many of their weaknesses (Feshback, 1978). In particular, such an approach should prove useful in determining to what extent complex behavior is regulated by interactions that depend intimately on situational variables, as well as on dispositions. At the very least, an interactional model is a much needed corrective for an area of psychology that has heretofore focused on the individual as a unit, often ignoring the intimate links between a person and the constantly changing conditions of his or her social life. Furthermore, an interactionist approach should foster the development of theoretical constructs that will characterize a person's total ecological situation, so that it may be taken into account in the explanation and prediction of behavior (Insel and Moos, 1974). Recently, for instance, terms such as "role dispositions," "interpersonal reaction systems," "perceived social climate," "behavioral settings," and "social values" have crept into the personologist's vocabulary.

What we envision for the future, then, are psychological experiments that consider the relative contributions of both situations and individual differences in behavior. For example, not only will Mary Jones be studied as wife and mother, as she traditionally has been studied in the past, but also as chairperson of a conference, consumer of goods, vacationer, marine biologist, and churchgoer. Rather than being depicted as one person with a variety of occupational and social roles, she will be studied at home, at the office, at the camp grounds, at the supermarket, and in church. In short, the attempt to understand Mary Jones will reflect the recognition that many important aspects of her behavior not only fluctuate as her life situation changes but also depend crucially on the reciprocal relationship, or interaction, between her trait structure and the situation. To be sure, the question of how person variables and situational factors interact in producing behavior is a complex one requiring new research strategies. It is an urgent empirical issue that will in all likelihood receive substantial attention in the years ahead.

7 *Study of problems relevant to the practical world of human affairs*   As we have repeatedly noted, the history of personological inquiry is intimately bound up with the study of psychopathology and personal adjustment. Efforts aimed at improving the human condition were defined largely in terms of what could be done to diagnose and treat disturbed individuals so that they could regain their mental health and live more productive lives. This orientation especially characterizes the theories of Freud, Adler, Rogers, Kelly, and to some extent, Erikson. Individual effectiveness and proper psychological functioning are also emphasized in the theories of Allport and Maslow.

Change is an inevitable aspect of every field of intellectual and scientific endeavor, however, and events within recent years have produced an accelerating demand for the psychological study of *pressing social problems* (Miller, 1969; Sherif, 1970). The explosion of knowledge and creation of vast communication networks have combined to open our awareness to realities such as having a "neighbor" 10,000 miles away. War, medical advances, ecological violations, global energy crises, generation gaps, assassinations, expanding birthrates in impoverished countries, exploitation and imprisonment of minority groups, and explorations of unknown areas of land, sea, and space have caused us to reexamine our relationships to ourselves, each other, and our environment. Wherever we look, we see the world changing with incredible rapidity—and established customs, traditions, and values changing with it. Indeed, one of today's major problems is the continuing adjustment that individuals and groups must make to rapid social change (Coleman, 1979). Of necessity, then, growing numbers of psychological investigators have become concerned about the social relevance of their work and the contributions they might ultimately make toward solving the problems and challenges of the contemporary world. This trend toward a socially relevant psychology will undoubtedly have a profound effect upon the study of personality. Personality researchers of the future will need to broaden the scope of their activities considerably if they are to maintain a respectable and influential position in the behavioral sciences. Similarly, areas of application will need to become more diverse.

Contemplating this situation against the background of events in the world as a whole, it seems safe to predict that attention will be focused on the following areas: poverty, racial and sexual discrimination, population control, alienation, suicide, divorce, child abuse, drug addiction (including alcoholism), and crime. Clearly, the list could go on, and the problems span the length and breadth of human life itself. Psychology obviously has a crucial role to play in helping people to achieve meaningful and fulfilling lives. Bandura expressed the matter this way: "As a science concerned with the social consequences of its applications, psychology must promote understanding of psychological issues that bear on social policies to ensure that its findings are used in the service of human betterment" (1977, p. 213).

One consequence of this projected trend toward closer involvement with the concrete world of human affairs may be that personality concepts and theories will become considerably more complex and comprehensive than those we know today (Buss, 1975). Another likely outcome is that personologists will become more intimately involved with the work of social psychologists, sociologists, anthropologists, and ethologists. It follows that the field of personality will adopt a more *interdisciplinary* approach in dealing with research issues. In turn, greater emphasis will be placed on naturalistic modes of inquiry, i.e., observation and study of persons in real-life situations. Field research is, in principle, an ideal setting for investigating human functioning in the personality area: we do wish to understand behavior outside the psychology building! That personology will eventually pervade all sectors of the social world seems inevitable.

The scientific study of personality is very much like the assembly of a complex jigsaw puzzle. The ten theorists considered in this book have provided us with many possible pieces of the puzzle. Some pieces will probably be discarded as not fitting the puzzle at all, and many others remain to be discovered. One thing seems certain, however: when a more definitive picture emerges, many of the pieces offered by our ten theorists will be included.

SUMMARY

The central theme of this text is that basic assumptions about human nature constitute the bedrock from which personality theories are fashioned and tested.

Concerning their origin, it was noted that one's assumptions about human nature are acquired and developed in the same way as one's other basic beliefs about the nature of the world. Hence, a personologist's conception of humanity reflects to a large extent what he or she thinks of himself or herself and those in the world around.

Basic assumptions serve to both broaden and narrow a theorist's perspective on personality. For example, a theorist who adopts a free-will position will, by definition, attend to and emphasize those aspects of human functioning that bespeak the capacity to act as a free agent. At the same time, she or he will tend to ignore or downplay aspects of human behavior more readily explicable in deterministic terms.

Basic assumptions constantly interact with a host of other influences in shaping the personologist's theoretical account of behavior. Sources of influence other than basic assumptions which obviously affect a theorist's thinking are the historical period, the society, what is known in psychology and other disciplines at the time, academic training and exposure to the world of ideas, and life experiences.

The importance to personology of these basic assumptions will not diminish in the future, since they deal with the issue of what humanity *is*. Thus, basic assumptions about human nature will remain the foundation of all future personality theories. What will change, though, are the theorists, the state of knowledge in psychology and related disciplines, and the world.

In addition to basic assumptions, personality theories can legitimately be compared and contrasted according to other criteria. In this chapter, we evaluated our ten theories in terms of the six major criteria described in Chapter 1: verifiability, heuristic value, internal consistency, parsimony, comprehensiveness, and functional significance.

Personality psychology is a very young field of inquiry. With comparatively few exceptions, it is only during the past four decades that personality theories have emerged. Personology has nevertheless come of age by establishing itself as a viable area of study. The flourishing activity in personology is a function of the growing realization that people's most vital problems concern themselves and their relations to others.

Future theories will certainly not be carbon copies of existing ones, yet the ideas and insights embedded within the ten theories presented in this text cannot but have a decisive impact upon future conceptions of personality. This is because our ten theorists have struggled to resolve critical and enduring issues and because they have each contributed something to the understanding of the mystery of human nature. Accordingly, future theorists will be guided by the rich intellectual heritage of their predecessors.

The ultimate scientific significance of current personality theories will depend upon the extent to which they generate new research. Furthermore, theories of personality must be self-corrective in the light of new empirical evidence if they are to remain useful to the scientific enterprise.

In the concluding section of this final chapter we suggest that new frontiers in personality research will be explored in seven general areas: (1) study of cognitive processes and their relationship to other aspects of psychological functioning; (2) study of especially productive, talented, and creative persons; (3) study of the physiological and neurological determinants and bases of personality; (4) study of personality development in middle and old age; (5) study of self-regulatory processes and plans; (6) study of the interaction of situational factors and personality variables and their relative contribution to behavior; and (7) study of problems relevant to the practical world of human affairs. Imaginative and critical study in these areas promises to deepen and enrich our conceptions of personality.

BIBLIOGRAPHY

Aiken, L. *Later Life*. Philadelphia: Saunders, 1978.

Baltes, P., & Schaie, K. (Eds.). *Life span developmental psychology: Personality and socialization*. New York: Academic Press, 1973.

Barrett, J. *Gerontological psychology*. Springfield, Ill.: Thomas, 1972.

Beck, A. *Cognitive therapy and the emotional disorders*. New York: International Universities Press, 1976.

Birren, J. Toward an experimental psychology of aging. *American Psychologist,* 1970, **25,** 124–135.

Bowers, K. Situationism in psychology: An analysis and a critique. *Psychological Review,* 1973, **80,** 307–336.

Buss, A. Emerging field of the sociology of psychological knowledge. *American Psychologist,* 1975, **30,** 988–1002.

Coleman, J. *Contemporary psychology and effective behavior*. Glendale, Ill.: Scott, Foresman, 1979.

Endler, N., & Magnusson, D. Toward an interactional psychology of personality. *Psychological Bulletin,* 1976, **83,** 956–974.

Epstein, S. Explorations in personality today and tomorrow: A tribute to Henry A. Murray. *American Psychologist,* 1979, **34,** 649–653.

Feshback, S. The environment of personality. *American Psychologist,* 1978, **33,** 447–455.

Glass, D. (Ed.). *Biology and behavior: Genetics*. New York: Rockefeller University Press, 1968.

Gottesman, I. Beyond the fringe—personality and psychopathology. In D. Glass (Ed.), *Genetics*. New York: Russell Sage, 1968, pp. 59–68.

Goulet, L., & Baltes, P. (Eds.). *Life-span developmental psychology: Research and theory*. New York: Academic Press, 1970.

Hall, C., & Lindzey, G. *Theories of personality* (3d ed.). New York: Wiley, 1978.

Helson, R., & Crutchfield, R. Creative types in mathematics. *Journal of Personality,* 1970, **38,** 177–197.

Insel, P., & Moos, R. Psychological environments: Expanding the scope of human ecology. *American Psychologist,* 1974, **29,** 179–188.

Levinson, D., Darrow, C., Klein, E., Levinson, M., & McKee, B. *The seasons of a man's life*. New York: Knopf, 1978.

Lewis, J., Beavers, J., Gossett, J., & Phillips, V. *No single thread: Psychological health in family systems*. New York: Brunner/Mazel, 1976.

Lifton, R. *The life of the self: Toward a new psychology*. New York: Simon & Schuster, 1976.

MacKinnon, D. Personality and the realization of creative potential. *American Psychologist,* 1965, **20,** 273–281.

Mahoney, M. Reflections on the cognitive-learning trend in psychotherapy. *American Psychologist,* 1977, **32,** 5–13.

Mancuso, J. Current motivational models in the elaboration of personal construct theory. In J. Cole (Ed.), *Nebraska symposium on motivation.* Lincoln, Neb.: University of Nebraska Press, 1976, pp. 49–98.

Maslow, A. Toward a humanistic biology. *American Psychologist,* 1969, **24,** 724–735.

Miller, G. Psychology as a means of promoting human welfare. *American Psychologist,* 1969, **24,** 1063–1075.

Mischel, W. Toward a cognitive social-learning reconceptualization of personality. *Psychological Review,* 1973, **80,** 252–283.

Mischel, W. *Introduction to Personality,* 2d ed. New York: Holt, Rinehart and Winston, 1976.

Murphy, G. Psychological views of personality and contributions to its study. In E. Norbeck, D. Price-Williams, & W. McCord (Eds.), *The study of personality: An interdisciplinary appraisal.* New York: Holt, Rinehart and Winston, 1968, pp. 15–40.

Penfield, W. *The mystery of mind.* Princeton, N.J.: Princeton University Press, 1975.

Pervin, L., & Lewis, M. (Eds.). *Internal and external determinants of behavior.* New York: Plenum, 1978.

Piaget, J. Piaget's theory. In P. Mussen (Ed.), *Carmichael's manual of child psychology.* Vol. 1. New York: Wiley, 1970, pp. 703–732.

Rogers, C. *Carl Rogers on personal power.* New York: Delacorte, 1977.

Schaie, K., & Labouvie-Vief, G. Generational versus ontogenetic components of change in adult cognitive behavior: A fourteen-year cross-sequential study. *Developmental Psychology,* 1974, **10,** 305–320.

Seligman, M. *Helplessness: On depression, development, and death.* San Francisco: W. H. Freeman, 1975.

Sherif, M. On the relevance of social psychology. *American Psychologist,* 1970, **25,** 144–156.

Skinner, B. F. *Beyond freedom and dignity.* New York: Knopf, 1971.

Skinner, B. F. *About behaviorism.* New York: Knopf, 1974.

Tasman, A. Creativity, the creative process, and cognitive style and state. *Comprehensive Psychiatry,* 1976, **17,** 259–269.

Vaillant, G. *Adaptation to life.* New York: Little Brown, 1977.

Wilson, E. *Sociobiology.* Cambridge, Mass.: Harvard University Press, 1975.

Witkin, H., Moore, C., Goodenough, D., & Cox, P. Field-dependent and field-independent cognitive styles and their educational implications. *Review of Educational Research,* 1977, **47,** 1–64.

SUGGESTED READINGS

Carlson, R. Where is the person in personality research? *Psychological Bulletin,* 1971, **75,** 203–219.

Carson, R. *Interaction concepts of personality.* Chicago: Aldine, 1969.

Lidz, T. *The person: His and her development throughout the life cycle.* New York: Basic Books, 1976.

Pribram, K. Toward a neurophysiological theory of the person. In K. Pribram (Ed.), *Brain and behavior: I. Moods, states and mind.* Baltimore: Penguin Books, 1969.

Staub, E. (Ed.). *Personality: Basic aspects and current research*. New York: Prentice-Hall, 1980.
Wrightsman, L. *Assumption about human nature*. Monterey, Calif.: Brooks/Cole, 1974.

DISCUSSION QUESTIONS

1 What do you think of the idea that a theorist's basic assumptions about human nature reflect the theorist's own personality structure? If you agree, what do you believe each of our ten theorists thought of himself and those around him? Give some possible examples, speculative though they may be.
2 Of the six criteria for evaluating personality theories discussed in this chapter (and in Chapter 1), which one seems *most* important? Defend your answer.
3 In this chapter we asserted that one of the most critical and enduring questions in personality theory is "What are the defining characteristics of the psychologically *healthy* adult?" What do you think they are? Defend your answer.
4 Of the seven general problem areas discussed in the "New Frontiers in Personality Research" section of this chapter, which one do you believe holds the *most* promise for achieving a better understanding of the human personality? Explain your position.
5 In the "Discussion Questions" section of Chapter 1 you were asked to define personality and to specify your own basic assumptions about human nature. Now that you have read this book, has your earlier definition of personality changed? If so, how and why? Are you also now more aware of your own basic assumptions and how they affect your relationships with others? Think of some examples, if only for yourself.

GLOSSARY

Cognitive Process   The way in which an individual acquires, transforms, and stores information from the environment; that is, the higher mental processes we use to know the world.

Cognitive Style   A way of organizing perceptions, including one's self-concept, mode and accuracy of perception, style of thinking, and goal-directed behavior. Several cognitive styles have been identified and studied by personologists.

Field Dependence versus Field Independence   A set of terms coined by Witkin to represent individual differences in perception of the upright in space. The field-dependent person tends to rely on visual field cues whereas the field-independent person tends to rely on bodily sensation cues. Several personality characteristics are associated with differences in this cognitive style.

Interactionist Approach   An approach to the study and understanding of behavior which emphasizes the reciprocal interaction between internal (organismic) and environmental influences.

Interdisciplinary Approach   An approach to personology which emphasizes the importance of a multidisciplinary perspective, i.e., the contributions which sociologists, anthropologists, ethologists, and other behavioral scientists can make to the understanding of human nature.

Life Span Developmental Psychology   An emerging discipline in psychology which attempts to study personality development throughout the life cycle (i.e., from infancy to old age).

Person-Oriented View   A theoretical and empirical orientation in personology which assumes that the critical determinants of human behavior reside within the person (e.g., traits, feelings, motives, drives).

Situation-Oriented View   A theoretical and empirical orientation in personology which assumes that human behavior is almost exclusively determined by environmental or situational factors.

Acknowledgments

We wish to express our gratitude to the following authors and/or publishers who have granted us permission to use and reproduce material from their books and journals. Full citations are provided elsewhere in this text.

Academic Press, Inc.
>from Bonarius, J. Research in the personal construct theory of George A. Kelly: Role construct repertory test and basic theory. In B. Maher (Ed.), *Progress in experimental personality research;* from Kelly, G. A brief introduction to personal construct theory. In D. Bannister (Ed.),. *Perspectives in personal construct theory.*

Aldine Publishing Company
>from Kohut, H., and Seitz, P. Psychoanalytic theory of personality. Lundin, R. Personality theory in behavioristic psychology. Shlien, J. Phenomenology and personality. In J. Wepman and R. Heine (Eds.), *Concepts of personality.*

American Psychological Association
>from Allport, G. Traits revisited. *American Psychologist;* from Atthowe, J., and Krasner, L. Preliminary report on the application of contingent reinforcement procedures (token economy) on a "chronic" psychiatric ward. *Journal of Abnormal Psychology;* from Bandura, A. The self system in reciprocal determinism. *American Psychologist;* from Bronson, G. Identity diffusion in late adolescence. *Journal*

of Abnormal and Social Psychology; from Dignan, M. Ego identity and maternal identification. *Journal of Personality and Social Psychology;* from Epstein, S. Explorations in personality theory today and tomorrow. *American Psychologist;* from McClain, E. Further validation of the Personal Orientation Inventory: Assessment of self-actualization of school counselors. *Journal of Consulting and Clinical Psychology;* from Medinnus, G., and Curtis, F. The relation between maternal self-acceptance and child acceptance. *Journal of Consulting Psychology.* Copyright by the American Psychological Association. Reprinted by permission.

Basic Books, Inc.
from Ansbacher, H., and Ansbacher, R. The individual psychology of Alfred Adler: A systematic presentation in selections from his writings. © 1956.

British Journal of Social and Clinical Psychology
from Bannister, D., and Fransella, F. A grid test of schizophrenic thought disorder. *British Journal of Social and Clinical Psychology.*

Dialectia
from Murray, H. Some basic psychological assumptions and conceptions. *Dialectia.*

E. P. Dutton & Co., Inc.
from Evans, R. *B. F. Skinner: The man and his ideas.* Copyright © 1969 by Richard I. Evans. Reprinted by permission of the publishers, E. P. Dutton & Co., Inc.

Harcourt Brace Jovanovich, Inc.
from Allport, G. (Ed.), *Letters from Jenny;* from Murray, G. *Historical introduction to modern psychology.*

Harper & Row, Publishers, Incorporated
from Evans, R. *Dialogue with Erik Erikson;* from Maslow, A. *Motivation and personality* (2d ed.).

The Hogarth Press, Ltd., and W. W. Norton & Company, Inc.
from Freud, S. (J. Strachey, trans. and ed.), *The standard edition of the complete psychological works of Sigmund Freud,* Vols. 20 and 23.

Holt, Rinehart and Winston, Inc.
from Allport, G. *Pattern and growth in personality;* from Kelly, G. Man's construction of his alternatives. In G. Lindzey (Ed.), *Assessment of human motives.*

Houghton Mifflin Company
from Allport, G., Vernon, P., and Lindzey, G. *A Study of Values* (3d ed.); from Rogers, C. *Client-centered therapy: its current practice, implications, and theory.* Copyright © Houghton Mifflin Company, 1951. Used by permission of the publisher; from Rogers, C. *On becoming a person.* Copyright © Houghton Mifflin Company, 1961. Used by permission of the publisher.

The Journal of Humanistic Psychology
from Graham, W., and Balloun, J. An empirical test of Maslow's need hierarchy theory; Maslow, A. A theory of metamotivation: The biological rooting of the value-life; Rogers, C. My philosophy of interpersonal relationship and how it grew. *Journal of Humanistic Psychology.*

Gregory Kimble
from Kimble, G. Psychology as a science. *Scientific Monthly.*

Alfred A. Knopf, Inc.
from Kluckhohn, C., and Murray, H. Personality formation: The determinants. Murray, H., and Kluckhohn, C. Outline of a conception of personality. In C. Kluckhohn, H. Murray, and D. Schneider (Eds.), *Personality in nature, society, and culture* (2d ed.); from Skinner, B. F. *Beyond freedom and dignity.*

Little, Brown and Company
from Coles, R. *Erik H. Erikson: The growth of his work.*

Liveright Publishing Corporation
from Freud, S. *A general introduction to psychoanalysis.*

Macmillan Publishing Co., Inc.
from Allport, G. Personality: Contemporary viewpoints (I). In D. Sills (Ed.), *International encyclopedia of the social sciences*, Vol. 12; from Erikson, E. Life cycle. In D. Sills (Ed.), *International encyclopedia of the social sciences*, Vol. 9; from Skinner, B. F. *Science and human behavior.*

McGraw-Hill Book Company
from Rogers, C. A theory of therapy, personality, and interpersonal relationships, as developed in the client-centered framework. In S. Koch (Ed.), *Psychology: A study of a science*, Vol. 3.

W. W. Norton & Company, Inc.
from Erikson, E. *Childhood and society*, 2d ed., rev. By permission of W. W. Norton & Company, Inc. Copyright 1950, © 1963 by W. W. Norton & Company, Inc.; from Kelly, G. *The psychology of personal constructs.* By permission of W. W. Norton & Company, Inc. Copyright 1955 by George A. Kelly.

Oxford University Press, Inc.
from Murray, H. *Explorations in personality.* Copyright 1938 by Oxford University Press, Inc. Reprinted by permission.

Penguin Books, Inc.
from Bannister, D., and Fransella, F. *Inquiring man: The theory of personal constructs.* © D. Bannister and F. Fransella, 1971.

Prentice-Hall, Inc.
from Bandura, A. Social learning theory. © 1977; from Bandura, A. Aggression: A social learning analysis. © 1973; from Skinner, B. F., and Ferster, C. *Schedules of reinforcement.* © 1957. By permission of Prentice-Hall, Inc., Englewood Cliffs, New Jersey.

Psychology Today
from Evans, R. *Gordon Allport: A conversation.* April, 1971. Hall, M. *Conversation with Abraham H. Maslow*, July 1969. *Psychology Today* Magazine. Copyright © 1974 Ziff-Davis Publishing Company.

Random House, Inc.
from Maslow, A. Existential psychology—What's in it for us? In R. May (Ed.), *Existential psychology.*

B. F. Skinner
from Skinner, B. F. Critique of psychoanalytic concepts and theories. *Scientific Monthly.*

Society for the Experimental Analysis of Behavior
from Ayllon, T., and Azrin, N. The measurement and reinforcement of behavior of psychotics. *Journal of the Experimental Analysis of Behavior*. Copyright 1965 by the Society for the Experimental Analysis of Behavior, Inc.

Springer Publishing Co., Inc.
from Sarnoff, I. *Testing Freudian concepts: An experimental social approach.*

Yale University Press
from Allport, G. *Becoming: Basic considerations for a psychology of personality.*

Indexes

Name Index

Subject Index

C

M